# The BUMPER BOOK of QUESTIONS and ANSWERS

HAMLYN

# CONTENTS

# WORLD OF DISCOVERY

**THE year 1903 is not such a long time ago. Many people are alive now who were living then. But the changes that have occurred in these last 83 years are very great indeed.**

One of the biggest changes has been in the speed of aircraft. On these pages are shown some of the outstanding aircraft that were the fastest in the world in their time.

Strangely, the story ends in 1969 — but more of that later.

The beginning of it all was the biplane designed by the Wright brothers in America. It was capable of the then impressive speed of 48 km/h.

After the Wrights' initial triumph, much of the development of the aeroplane took place in Europe, particularly in France. This development was speeded up by World War I in which the aeroplane was used as a weapon for the first time.

After the war, Jacques Schneider, a French Engineer, started the sporting event 'The Schneider Trophy Races' for the speed and seaworthiness of sea planes. This event was mostly responsible for shaping the future of aircraft design. The event was for sea planes, and was won for the third time in succession by Britain in 1931, thus entitling Britain to retain the Trophy for all time.

The machine that won the 1931 race, the Supermarine S.6B, went on to set a new world speed record of 668 km/h.

But other countries were not out of the race for greater speed. Developed on similar lines to the S.6B, an Italian aircraft — the Macchi M.67 — raised the record to 708 km/h in 1934.

The Supermarine S.6 was designed by R. J. Mitchell. He used his experience to good effect when he ultimately designed the Spitfire, which was so well streamlined and efficient that, despite its wing span of 11 metres and a large powerful Rolls-Royce engine in front, its drag, or air resistance, was equivalent to that of a steel plate only 45 cm in diameter.

The next significant development of the aeroplane came with jet propulsion, which raised the speeds of aircraft by over 200 km/h. A jet aircraft — the de Havilland D. H. 108 — broke the 'sound barrier' (that is, it went faster than the speed of sound, 1,225 km/h) in 1948. But over the years jets got faster and faster.

The 'official' world airspeed record of 3,529.56 km/h is held by a jet, the American Lockheed company's SR-71A 'Blackbird' (see below, right). This record was set back in 1976 and has not been bettered since. Is Man slowing down in the race to go faster?

Not exactly. For a start, rockets do not qualify for the official airspeed record and all faster aircraft have been rocket-powered. In fact, the rocket-powered Bell XS-1 broke the sound barrier before the de Havilland D.H. 108, in October 1947.

While developing their space programme during the 1960s, the Americans produced an experimental rocket aircraft, the X15. This achieved a speed of 7,297 km/h in 1967.

But this sort of speed is of little value in normal day-to-day or even military aircraft — which is why aeroplane speeds have not increased since the SR-71A. How pointless these great speeds are is shown by what happened when the SR-71 (an earlier version of the SR-71A) broke the record for the quickest Atlantic crossing in September 1974, travelling at an *average* speed of 2,924 km/h. The cross-Atlantic flight, New York to London, took just 1 hour 56 minutes — but the plane was travelling so fast it could not land.

It had to overshoot not only the runway but *Britain!* It had travelled all the way to Amsterdam before it was going slow enough to turn round and come back to land.

So much greater speeds for aeroplanes are of no value. The X15 was developed for another reason — so that rockets could be made fast enough to break away from the Earth's gravity and travel out into space.

It is in space that Man has reached his greatest speed. On the way back from orbiting the Moon in 1969, Apollo 10 reached 39,897 km/h. To the Moon is the farthest and fastest that Man has gone.

But if Man voyages to distant planets, or even stars, even greater speeds will be needed so that he can travel across the vast distances.

Yet Man can't keep going faster and faster. Unlike the sound barrier, the 'light' barrier cannot be beaten. The speed of light — 299,792,500,000 km/s — is the ultimate, the fastest possible, speed in the Universe. When — and if — Man reaches it, he will have to be content. The story of going faster will have reached its end.

**The two insets in our main picture show two British warplanes that were the fastest in their time.**

**The S.E.5.A. (left) was one of several fighters developed to win the air battles over the trenches during World War I. It was tough, easy to handle and, for the time, very fast.**

**The Spitfire (above, right) will be remembered for its part in winning the Battle of Britain in World War II.**

# What is the Fastest possible Speed?

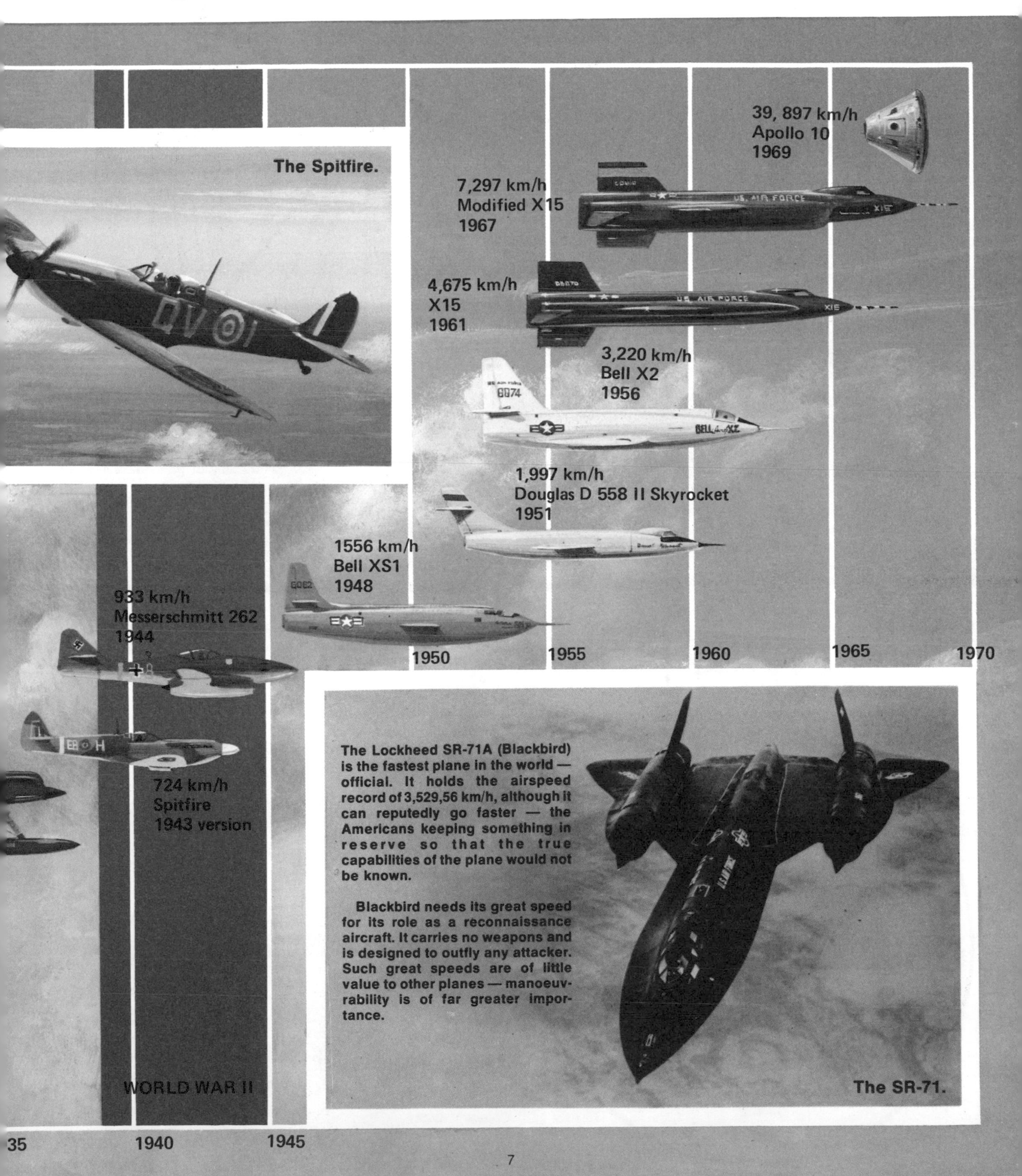


The Spitfire.

The Lockheed SR-71A (Blackbird) is the fastest plane in the world — official. It holds the airspeed record of 3,529,56 km/h, although it can reputedly go faster — the Americans keeping something in reserve so that the true capabilities of the plane would not be known.

Blackbird needs its great speed for its role as a reconnaissance aircraft. It carries no weapons and is designed to outfly any attacker. Such great speeds are of little value to other planes — manoeuvrability is of far greater importance.

The SR-71.

# How are Underground Tunnels constructed?

Structure of a typical Underground station

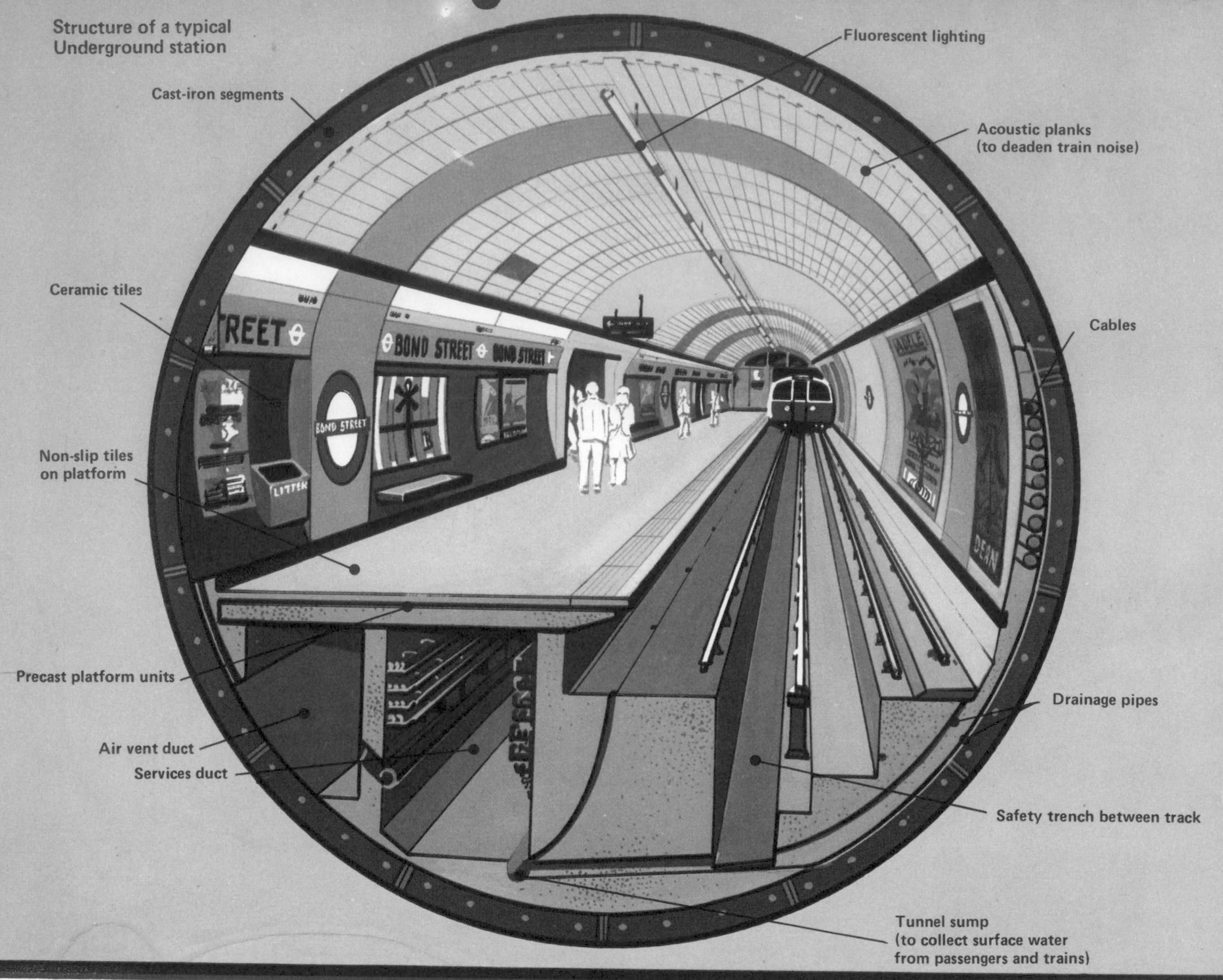


# The Don Valley project

**LIKE all built-up areas, the busy, bustling city of Sheffield has a continuing problem of waste disposal through its sewers. The existing system has become hopelessly overloaded so a big new project has been undertaken. This is called the Don Valley intercepting sewer and will consist of a tunnel through which sewage will flow from the city.**

**Sheffield is situated on uplands a few kilometres west of the River Don. The sands and gravels of this valley hold too much water to allow tunnelling so the tunnel is being con-**

**Left: Front view of a Dosco Roadheader tunnelling machine showing the cutter head with tungsten carbide teeth.**

**Right: The 'muck' excavated is passed back by conveyors to the small flameproof train which takes it to the exit shaft.**

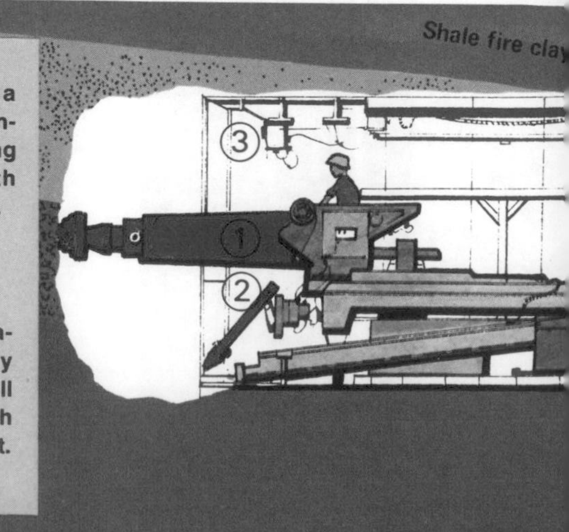

## If you live in a city the chances are that wherever you go you will be above a tunnel of some sort.

**UNDERGROUND, the great cities of the world — London, New York, Moscow, Paris — are like a rabbit warren. Tunnels criss-cross everywhere, carrying vast quantities of refuse material through sewers, transporting people in trains, housing vital power supplies and communications equipment.**

Tunnels are — like the veins and arteries in the body — the means of carrying the lifeblood of the city. And yet we often take these tunnels very much for granted.

Just think of the problems facing the engineers who designed the Jubilee Line, opened in 1979, as part of London's Underground network. Here they had to find a way of scooping out great lengths of clay and rock, of building a wide, safe tunnel to take high-speed modern trains and still not interfere with existing tunnellings or the foundations of buildings. One mistake in their calculations and perhaps Piccadilly Circus or the Royal Academy would have suffered the effects of settlement. A few centimetres could have proved disastrous.

Modern tunnelling is a highly complex procedure, using the skills of many different kinds of people. The engineers work out the boring and construction methods while geologists or earth scientists have to investigate the proposed bore area and estimate how it will stand up to the tunnelling. They advise the surveyors who plan the route down to the last few millimetres.

The easiest conditions for tunnelling are through clays and sandy soils that hold together fairly well. Very dry soils or very soft water-bearing ground present problems. When there is a lot of water to contend with the tunnel is sometimes treated chemically or even frozen to hold it back while linings are being put into place. Another approach is to sink the tunnel below the wet soils and carry on the bore instead through more solid rock. It takes longer but it's a lot safer.

### Shield

Some tunnelling is still done by hand but wherever possible large mechanical borers are preferred. These are often based on a type of machine invented by James Greathead in the middle of the last century. He devised a circular shield (the Greathead Shield) which was used to drive tunnels both under the Thames and the Hudson River in New York. Basically, the shield protects workers while they excavate the ground, while at the back it

## A SOFT GROUND TUNNELLING MACHINE

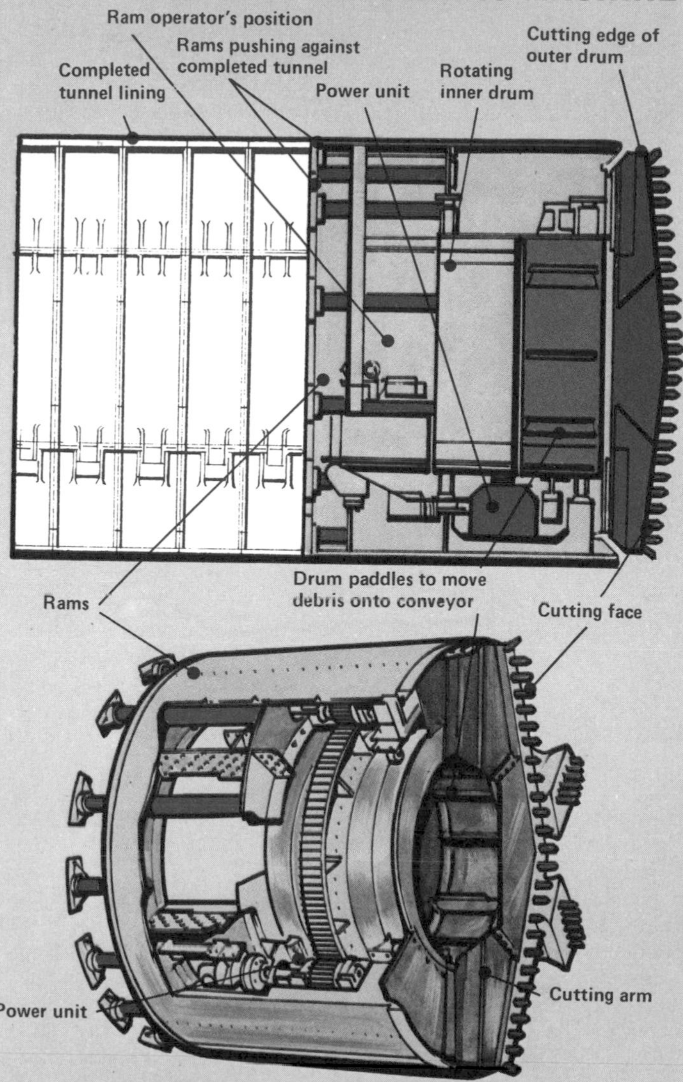


A mechanical excavator shield basically consisting of two drums. The rotating teeth cut the area of clay in front of the space between the inner and outer drums. The shield moves forward using hydraulic rams that push against the completed tunnel lining.

**structed through more solid coal-bearing rocks below the sands. It is being bored at an average depth of 20 m below the surface.**

**The tunnel will be 1.5 m in diameter at its start, under the city, but will gradually widen to take the inflow from all the connecting local sewers. At its final 'outfall' end it will be 5.24 m in diameter. Most of the tunnelling will be done by the type of machine shown here. The scheme should be completed in 1996.**

### THE DON VALLEY TUNNEL

1. Tunnelling machine
2. Mechanical 'rake'
3. Tunnel shield
4. Primary conveyor
5. Hydraulic power unit
6. Oil storage tank
7. Secondary conveyor
8. Butterfly chute
9. Skips
10. Flameproofed loco

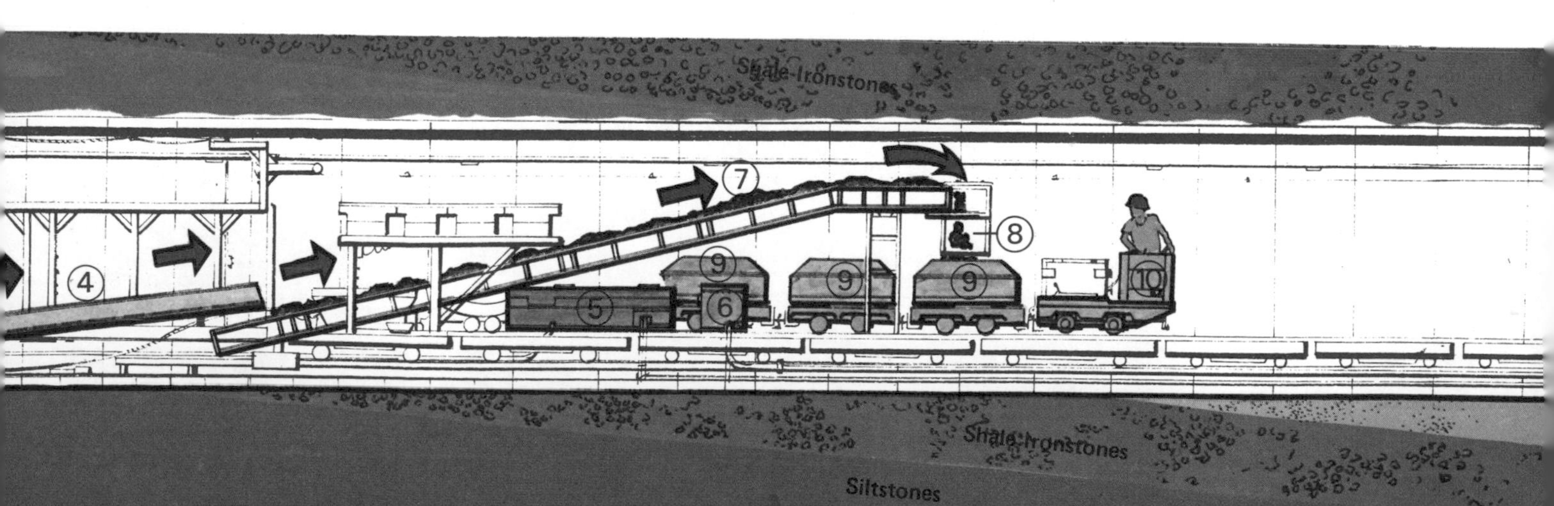

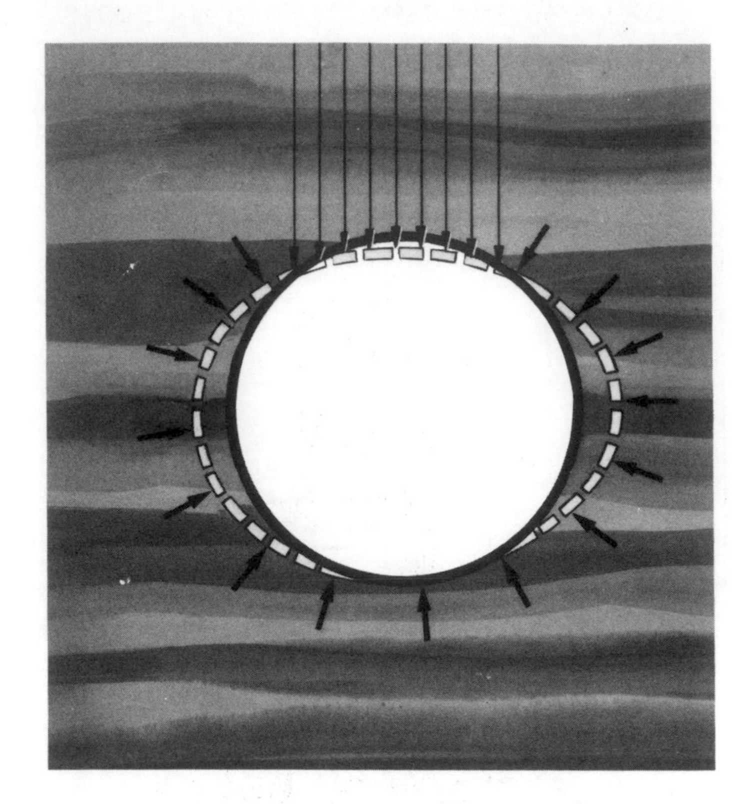

**Liner plates are designed and shaped so that assembly and bolting can be completed from inside the tunnel.**

Soil

Inside of tunnel

Surrounding soil or rock

Voids

Grout hole

Grout (usually liquid cement) is forced through the grout hole into the voids or gaps between the liner plates and surrounding ground.

Grout

Bolted plates

**Tunnels or shafts in soft ground need lining to control the ground during and after excavation. Plates of steel or special concrete are used, basically, to distribute the load on the tunnel to the surrounding ground. They are designed in such a way that they do not bulge out at the sides as the downward pressures are exerted. Sometimes because of the type of soil the pressures above are so great that it becomes necessary to protect the tunnel by reinforcing it with steel arches.**

extends to provide a safe area for erecting tunnel linings. Then the shield can be forced forward after a tunnel section is completed by levering it with jacks.

There are other boring methods, too. The thrust bore, as it's called, goes back many years and consists of a long corkscrew-like head thrusting out from the front of the machine, as opposed to the rotating cutting heads of the shield type system. Another way of shifting stubborn rock is by blasting it with explosives, a technique that calls for great skill and care if it is to be of any use.

Once the tunnel is dug the engineers' work is not ended. The tunnel has to be consolidated, that is lined and made waterproof — a difficult job — and then made pleasant to be in, which means providing access for heating, ventilation and lighting. And all the while that machines are boring their way through rock and men are digging alongside them, the motto has to be 'safety first'.

## Mini Tunnel

Not all tunnels need to be wide. Some sewers and power cable housings can be accommodated within bores one metre in diameter or slightly more. And this is where the newly developed Mini Tunnel comes into its own. The Mini Tunnel (built by a British firm) is strong yet economic to build. It combines the design of its concrete lining with a special method of installation — taking only one step to do two operations. An electro-hydraulic power source drives a rugged rotary cutting head which revolves within a shield. The position of the shield is accurately maintained by a special laser guidance instrument the Datum Laser — an advanced piece of electronic technology.

The waste or 'muck' is fed back through the borer's centre into skips or containers behind, and taken away for disposal. The borer can be used in various kinds of geological conditions, and the shield has a number of bolt-on attachments: a special hood at the front to keep back very loose crumbly ground; and a blast screen to protect the tunnel during drives through solid rock. There's even a machine to inject gravel during tunnelling to protect nearby houses and factories from settlement or other damage to their foundations.

The Mini Tunnel lining is made of unreinforced concrete cast under high frequency vibrations which causes the concrete to pack down tightly making it very strong. Each tunnel ring is 600 mm long and is formed of three segments, each 120 degrees to make up a 360 degree circle. Special stress-raising techniques are used to make these sections immensely strong. The three segment idea helps to make installation speedy and accurate.

In practice the Mini Tunnel has already proved its worth many times. When it was necessary to build a one metre diameter sewer in the historic town of King's Lynn the Mini Tunnel was ideal. It enabled the sewer — which cut through old timber piles and masonry dating from the Middle Ages — to run into the loose sandy soil near the River Ouse without disturbing the beautiful old Customs House built in 1683.

When a sewer had to be built at the popular seaside resort of Littlehampton the mini-tunnel method under a 750 metre stretch of a busy main road meant that disruptions were kept to a minimum. Traditional trench methods of laying the sewer would have meant a nine months closure of the road. And when the Post Office wanted to thread telephone cables under London's Oxford Street and avoid the main sewers in the process it was the

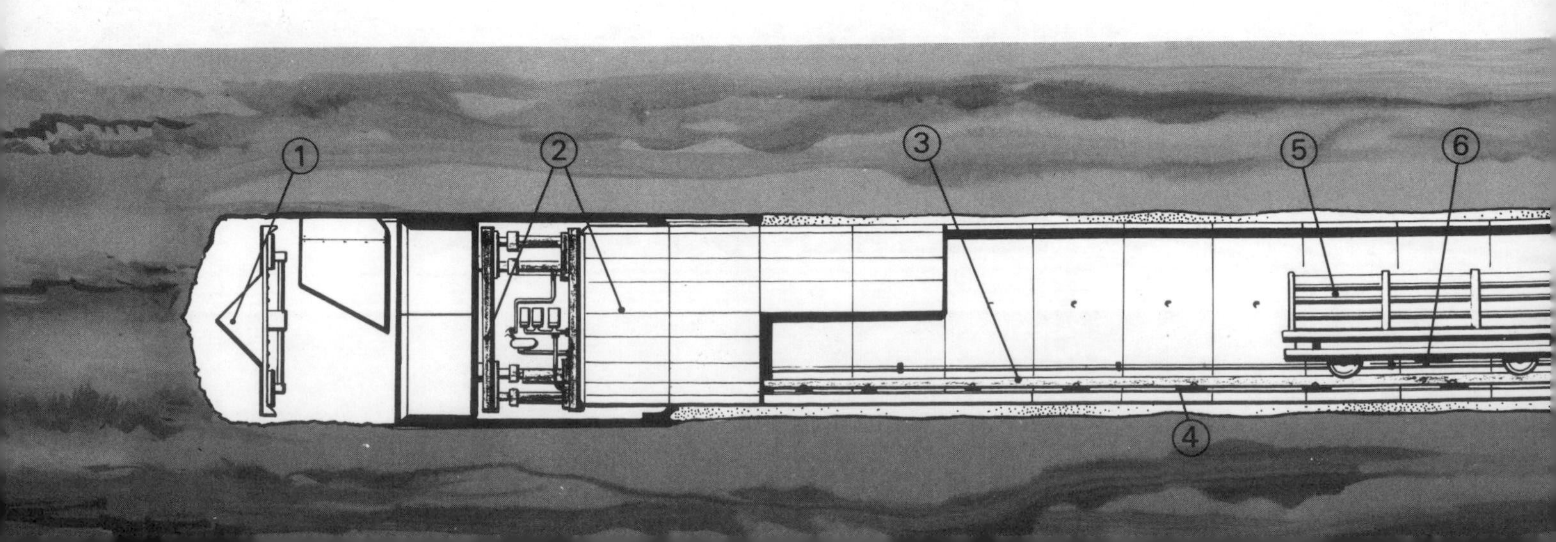

Boring through hard rock presents its own difficulties, especially if the tunnel has to be of relatively large diameter. But a new machine such as the Calweld Boring Machine can cut through substances as hard as granite and still provide a wide bore.

A recent project in Colorado has used the Calweld to excavate a tunnel four metres in diameter for a mining company. Hydraulic power drives the rotating cutter while hydraulic gripping devices fasten the machine to the tunnel sides to provide a solid base for the powerful thrust.

The Calweld machine is also providing tunnels for water, underground and sewerage systems in other parts of the world.

Mini Tunnel that again provided an answer to the problem of traffic and pedestrian disturbance.

The Mini Tunnel is being used for water distribution schemes like the twin tunnels (2.5 kilometres in total length) for bringing water from the River Tees to the British Steel plant at Redcar. It's being sunk under motorways and through soft difficult soils. Small wonder then that the Mini Tunnel design has won many prizes for its manufacturers, including the Queen's Award to Industry for "outstanding achievement in technological innovation".

The great advantage of the Mini Tunnel is that it removes the need for traditional trenching, known to the public as the 'hole in the road'. Since only a comparatively small exit tunnel is required for equipment and muck, this avoids prolonged road closure and traffic disruption. Tunnels can be installed at various depths.

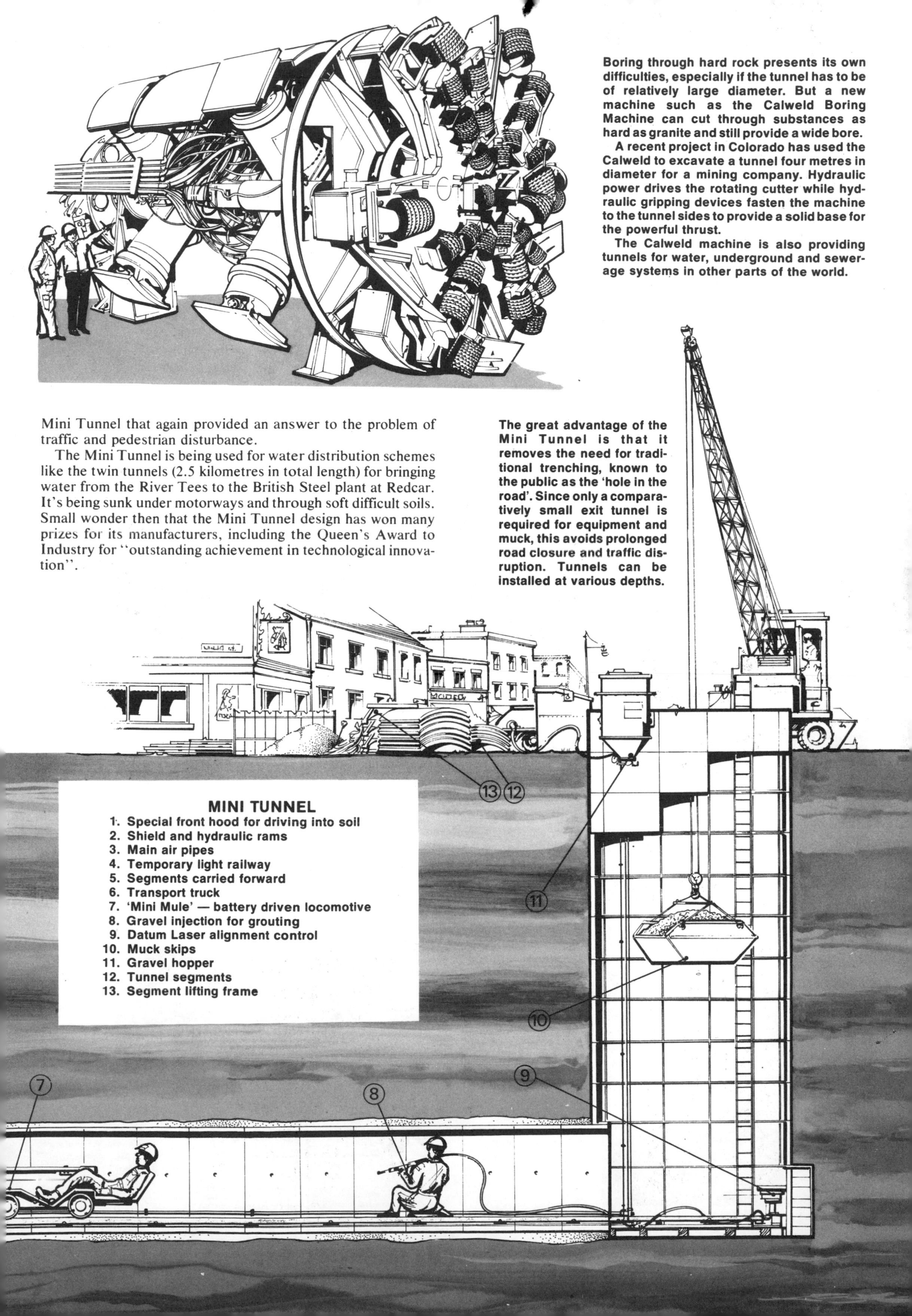

# Is the

## THE CONTROL CABIN

Pictured above is a view of the clean, uncluttered interior of the train's control cabin. On the right is the control desk where the operator sits when the train is running on automatic. The desk used for manual control is next to it (although it does not appear in our picture).

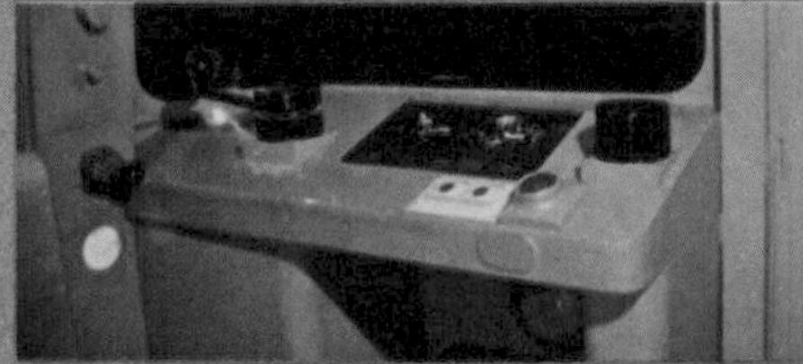

Left is the driver's seat. This is folded away into a panel in the wall when not in use.

Above is a close-up of the control desk showing the automatic control starting button. The handle on the left is the master controller.

The control panel at the back of the control cab showing the sliding door controls and the hand brake wheel used for 'parking' the train.

## AUTOMATIC SAFETY

The automatic train is controlled by equipment which is worked by electric currents carried in the track rails. These currents carry the signals forming the 'code' that works the automatic control equipment.

The system is special in that two different types of current are carried along the rails at the same time. These do not intefere with each other in any way and will only work on the correct part of the equipment.

The diagram below shows how the safety circuit works. There is a continuous signal to keep the train moving. If this is interrupted the safety box detects this and sends a signal to the trip valve which operates the brakes and the train is brought to a halt.

The command which controls the speed of the train works in a similar manner but the signals are picked up by a different set of receiving coils.

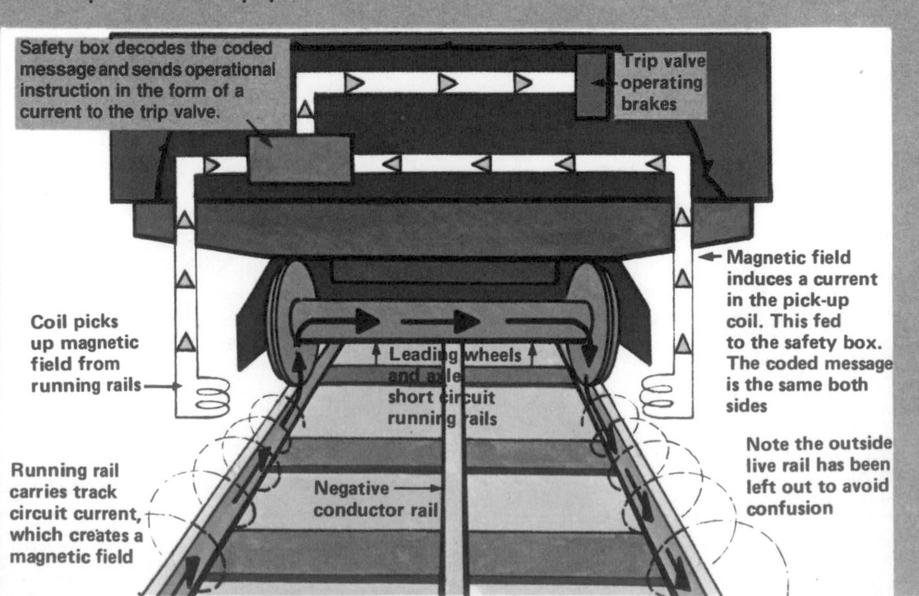

# Day of the Train Driver over?

**Over the years millions of youngsters have thought that they would like a job as a train driver. But the trains that run on the Victoria Line of the London Underground could change all that — because the trains have an automatic driving system. Perhaps the day of the driver is nearly over?**

**ON March 7, 1969, Her Majesty Queen Elizabeth II officially opened the Victoria Line, a new section of the London Underground rail network. After purchasing a ticket from an automatic machine — which refused her coins on the first two attempts — Her Majesty made a short speech on the platform at Green Park Station then stepped into the cab of a waiting tube-train. She pressed the 'start' buttons and the train moved off to Oxford Circus.**

**The Queen had not actually become a train driver for a day for as soon as she pressed the start controls the automatic driving equipment took over. The day of the self-driven train was becoming a reality.**

The earliest underground railway in the world had been built over 100 years before this. Opened in 1863, the first section of London's Metropolitan Railway was built underground to relieve traffic congestion in the streets. The first trains were steam-powered and their smoke created problems of ventilation in the tunnels. Electric trains avoided this and were adopted as soon as they became powerful enough to pull a useful load and were reasonably dependable.

The first deep-level tube line, the City and South London Railway, was opened in 1890 using electric locomotives working off a live rail in the track.

By the turn of the century an American, Frank Sprague, had invented a way of controlling a number of electric motors from one control mechanism. This made it possible to fit electric motors to several coaches in a train so that they could all be controlled by a driver in the cab of the leading coach.

This system had a number of advantages. It saved having a separate heavy locomotive, and it distributed the power along the length of the train which reduced the wear

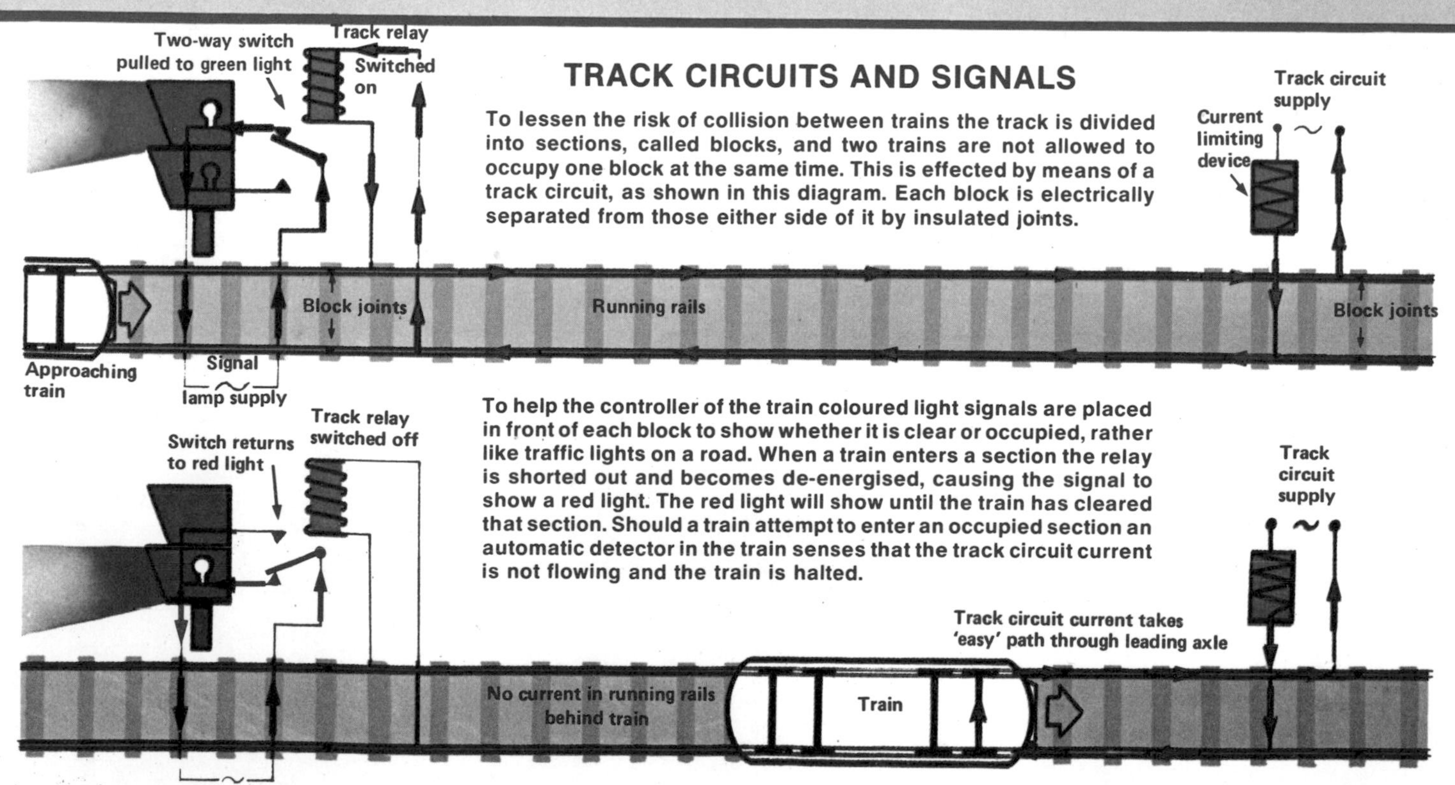

**A view of the London Underground that is familiar to many millions of people. On its journey along the Victoria Line a tube-train pulls into Oxford Circus station. It is perhaps surprising that there are so few people on the platform — the station is much busier during the rush-hours.**

and tear on the track and also reduced vibration.

The first 20 years of this century saw a great development in underground railways, and they appeared in France, Germany, Japan and the U.S.A. In London the Underground has grown in size so that it now has a total length of over 400 km, including the surface sections which serve the outskirts of the city.

The building of the Victoria Line, a stretch of track of approximately 20 kilometres running from Brixton to Walthamstow, was the first in-town London Underground development for more than 60 years. It was also an important development in automation because it was the first public line in Britain to be built, having trains fitted with automatic controls.

To the public there would appear to be no difference. There was still one man in the cabin at the front of the train, but his job had changed significantly. The train driver had now become the controller of the train. He was no longer doing the driving, but only pressing start buttons which set the automatic equipment working, just as the Queen did when she opened the line.

The automatic driving system has two separate parts; the safety system and the driving command system.

The safety system ensures that a train cannot run unless it receives a continuous series of electrically coded impulses through the rails. There are several codes which allow the train to run at different speeds. The equipment on the train responds to code frequencies, which are received by pick-up coils mounted in front of the first pair of wheels. If this series of coded messages stops for some reason, such as the train in front breaking down or a failure in the safety system, the train stops.

The driving command system is controlled by a different set of impulses in the rails. These are picked up by the train at specified sections of the track known as *command points*. This system acts as a check on the precise speed of the train when it passes the point. The train movements have been worked out so that a train must pass each command point at a specified speed for the safe operation of the timetable. If that speed is not maintained the command system brakes or speeds up the train depending upon what is necessary.

## Safety first

The safety sytem will over-ride commands given by the driving command system in an emergency.

When the train operator presses the start buttons the train accelerates under power until it reaches the point where the power should be shut off. On the track there is a command spot transmitting a frequency which the train equipment recognises as a command to turn off the power and coast along.

As a train approaches the next station the train goes through another series of command spots. At each point coded information is fed into the train telling it the speed that it should be travelling. The brakes are applied to gradually reduce the speed.

The train operator, as well as pressing the start buttons to activate automatic drive, operates the sliding doors of the carriages so that passengers can board and alight at stations.

However, in the event of an emergency and the failure of the automatic system the train operator can take over and drive manually using the controls normally used for shunting. These allow a maximum speed of only 16 km. This certainly is not fast, but at least it is enough to bring a stranded train into the next station and it shows that perhaps the day of the driver is not completely over.

**A view of the Underground that is not so well known. Removed from the hustle and bustle of the busy stations is the Control Room for the Victoria Line. The men are studying electric track diagrams which chart the movement of trains. The upper diagram shows by lighted strips the position of all trains on the line, while the lower one shows the track circuits.**

*The help of London Transport in the preparation of this article is gratefully acknowledged.*

**Just imagine if every town and village had a big heater in the sky which kept everybody down below warm and snug. Well, there is such a heater. It's everywhere and it's free.**

# How is Solar Energy collected?

EVERY day the Sun pours down on to the Earth enough energy to power every house, factory, car, ship and plane in the world for about 30 *years*. A tiny amount of this energy is used to evaporate the oceans to make clouds, to drive the winds, or by plants in photosynthesis. But all the rest is radiated back into Space, either by reflection from the clouds, or from the cooling Earth's surface during the night.

In these energy-short days the search is on to find ways to collect and make use of least some of this energy, rather than let it all radiate away and be lost.

There are many possible ways of collecting and using this 'solar energy' or energy from the Sun. The greenhouse, pride and joy of most keen gardeners, is one everyday example, and another, which has been in use since the earliest times, is the production of salt by allowing the Sun to evaporate sea water in shallow lagoons or ponds. Other simple ways are shown on these pages and overleaf.

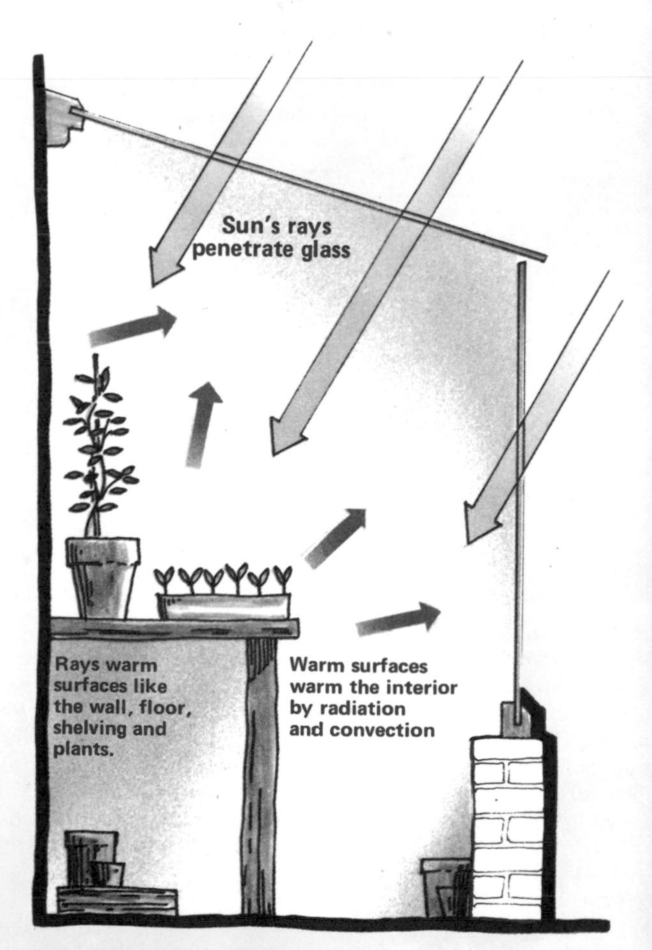


**One of the simplest ways of trapping the Sun's energy is the greenhouse. Although light will pass through glass, infrared radiation (see right) will not. So when the light heats up surfaces such as the floor or benches, the energy they radiate (infra-red) cannot escape.**

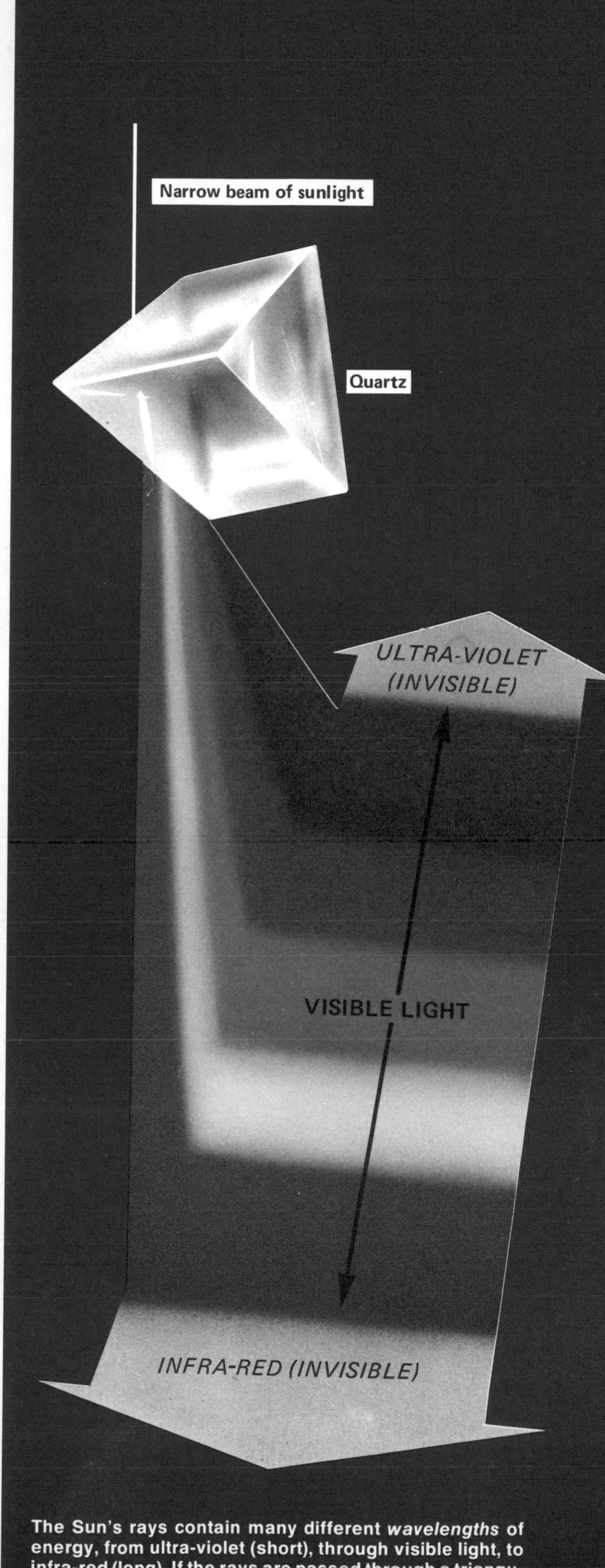


**The Sun's rays contain many different *wavelengths* of energy, from ultra-violet (short), through visible light, to infra-red (long). If the rays are passed through a triangular piece of quartz, they are split into parts — the visible light appearing as the colours of the rainbow.**

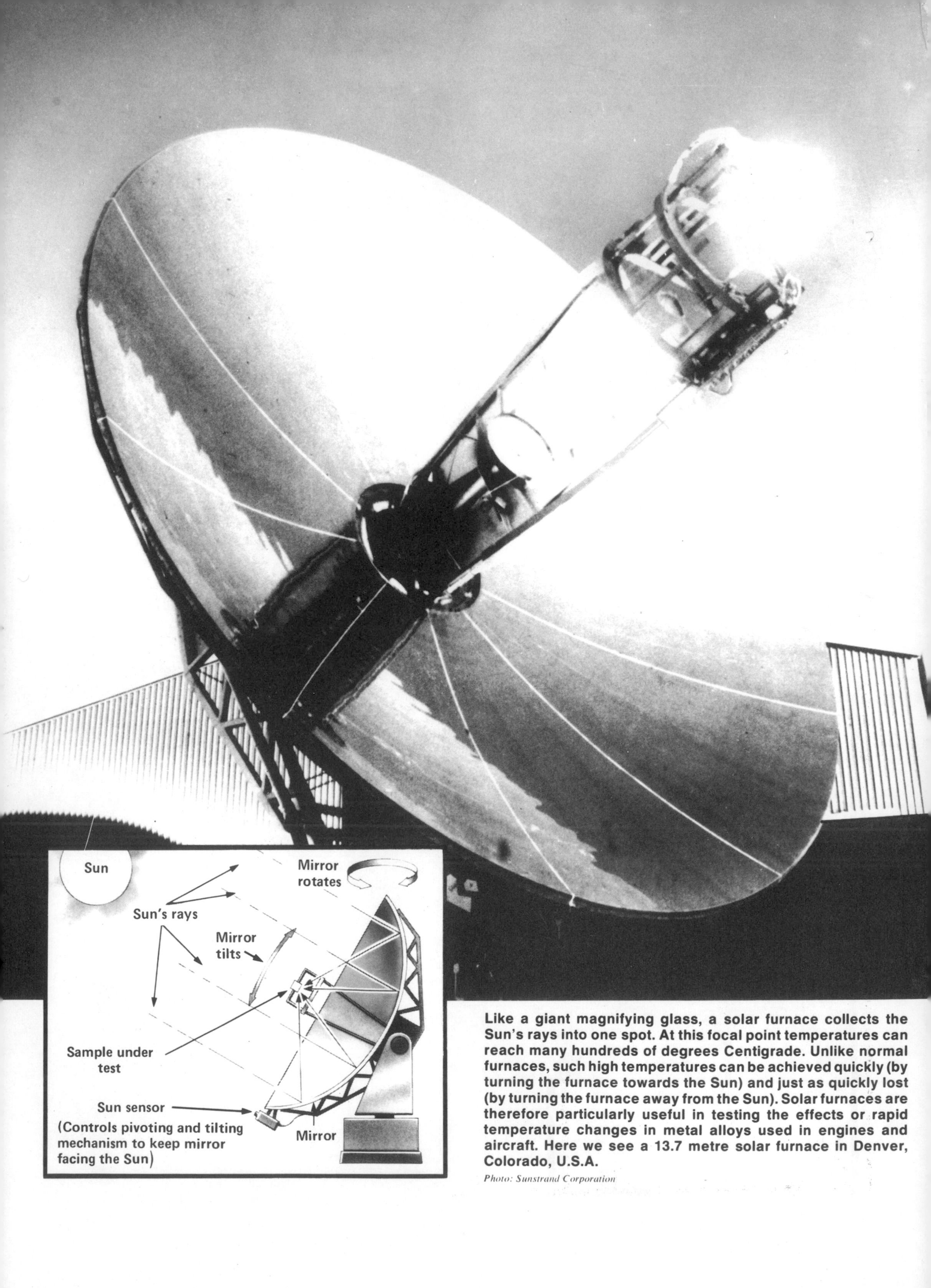


**Like a giant magnifying glass, a solar furnace collects the Sun's rays into one spot. At this focal point temperatures can reach many hundreds of degrees Centigrade. Unlike normal furnaces, such high temperatures can be achieved quickly (by turning the furnace towards the Sun) and just as quickly lost (by turning the furnace away from the Sun). Solar furnaces are therefore particularly useful in testing the effects or rapid temperature changes in metal alloys used in engines and aircraft. Here we see a 13.7 metre solar furnace in Denver, Colorado, U.S.A.**

*Photo: Sunstrand Corporation*

# Will the World be plugging into Sunbeams?

**THE idea is simple. Sunlight is energy; electricity is energy. All you need do is convert one form of energy to the other. If just a tiny amount of the Sun's enormous energy was turned into clean, easy-to-use electricity, the world's energy problems would be over.**

The idea is simple enough, but putting it into practice is anything but — at least not in the huge way necessary if it is to make a significant contribution to the world's energy needs.

It is fairly easy to convert sunlight into a small amount of electricity — one kind of photographic exposure meter, for example, does just that. The sunlight falls on a piece of silicon (silicon has the property of letting electricity pass through it in one direction only) and turns it into a tiny battery — a *solar cell.* Basically, the energy from the Sun drives the tiny electrical particles, called *electrons*, from their normal places in the atoms of the silicon. The flow of electrons *is* electricity. The more sunshine there is, the more electricity is produced.

The method works well for the tiny

*Continued on page 20*

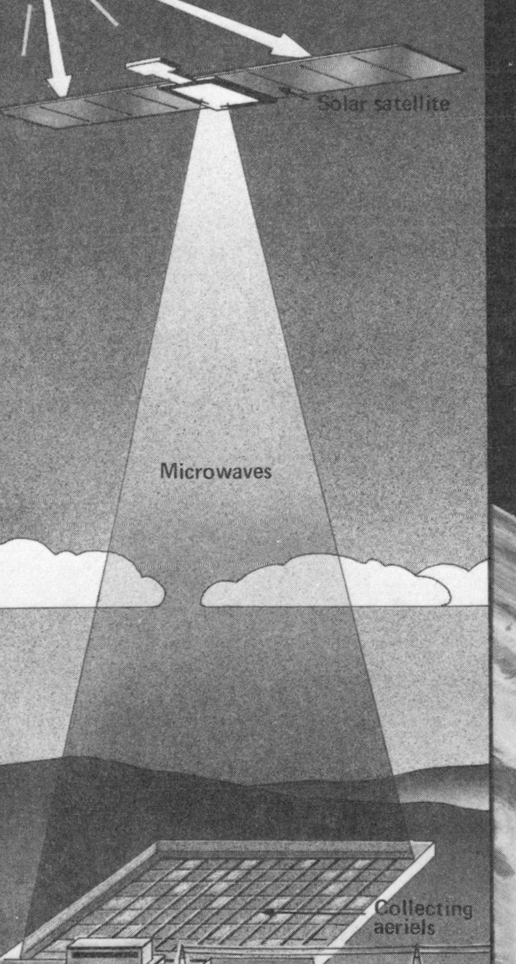

Science fiction? No, this huge satellite is being seriously considered by the United States government. Built in space by equipment and people brought up by the Space Shuttle — or a similar 'Space Tug' — it would contain millions of solar cells. The electricity produced would be beamed to Earth as microwaves — a form of radio waves — to a receiving station (see left).

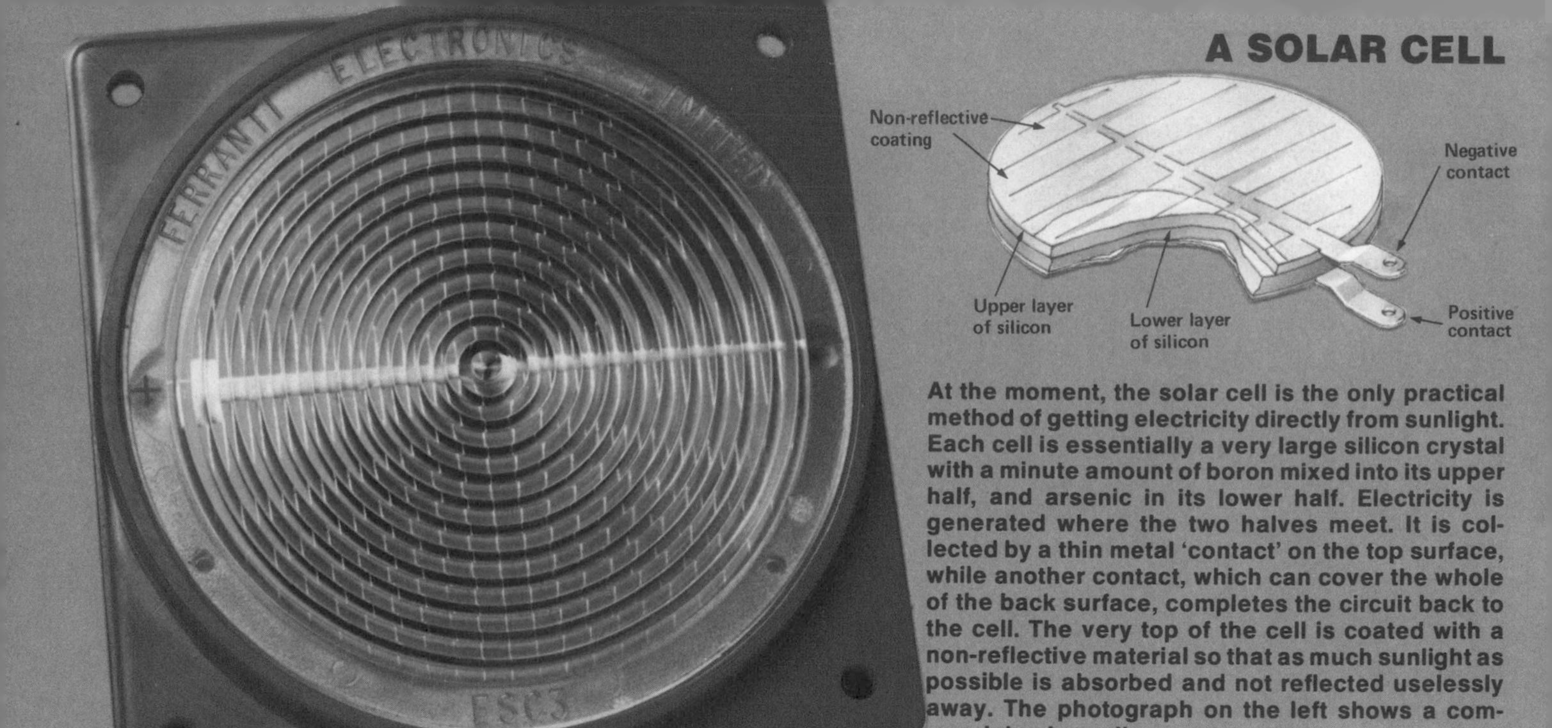


# A SOLAR CELL

At the moment, the solar cell is the only practical method of getting electricity directly from sunlight. Each cell is essentially a very large silicon crystal with a minute amount of boron mixed into its upper half, and arsenic in its lower half. Electricity is generated where the two halves meet. It is collected by a thin metal 'contact' on the top surface, while another contact, which can cover the whole of the back surface, completes the circuit back to the cell. The very top of the cell is coated with a non-reflective material so that as much sunlight as possible is absorbed and not reflected uselessly away. The photograph on the left shows a commercial solar cell.

# THE STIRLING HOT AIR ENGINE

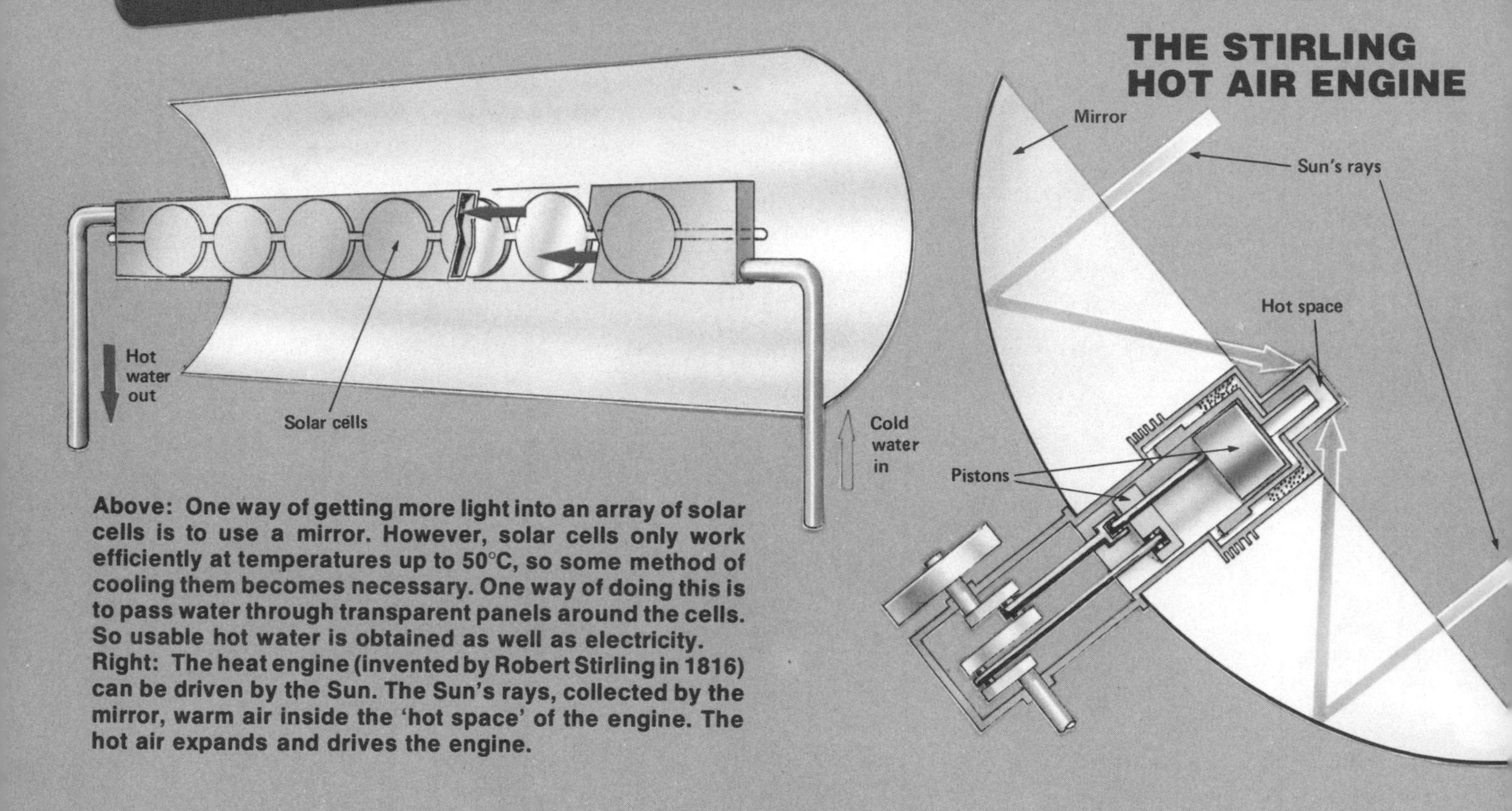


**Above:** One way of getting more light into an array of solar cells is to use a mirror. However, solar cells only work efficiently at temperatures up to 50°C, so some method of cooling them becomes necessary. One way of doing this is to pass water through transparent panels around the cells. So usable hot water is obtained as well as electricity.
**Right:** The heat engine (invented by Robert Stirling in 1816) can be driven by the Sun. The Sun's rays, collected by the mirror, warm air inside the 'hot space' of the engine. The hot air expands and drives the engine.

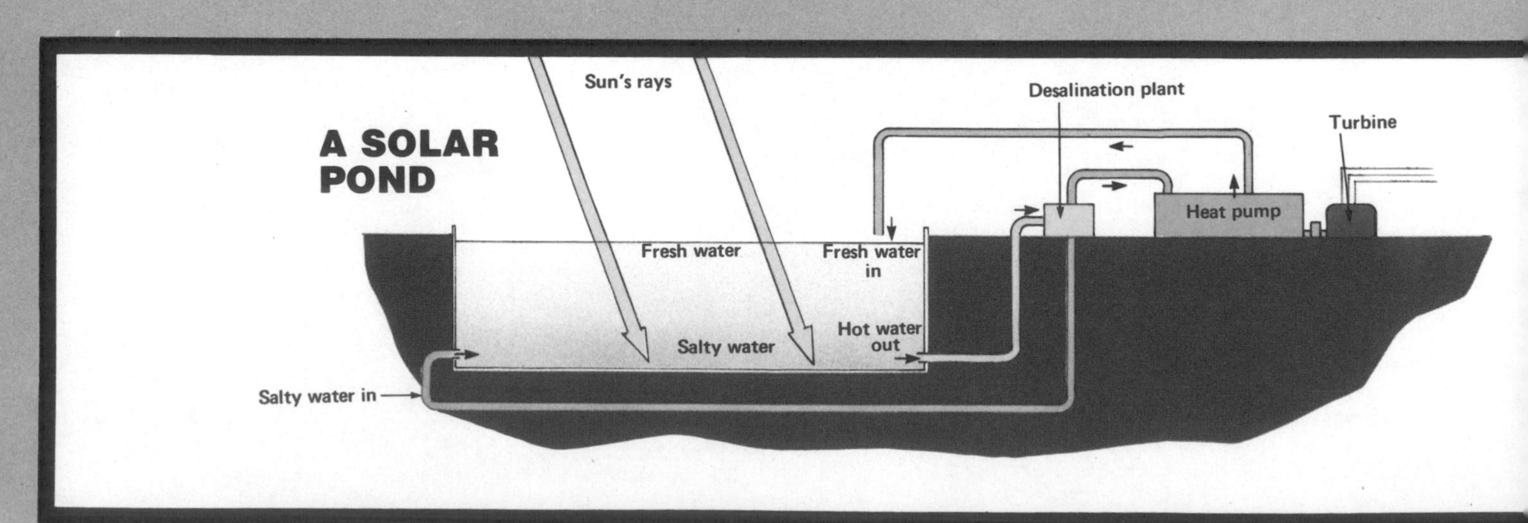

amount of electricity needed in an exposure meter, but there are problems in producing large amounts. Firstly, the method is very inefficient. Secondly, the silicon has to be very pure if it is to produce a reasonable amount of electricity. Very pure silicon is expensive, and because the total energy from the Sun in parts of the world that need electricity is only about 100 watts per square metre, solar cells have to cover a very large area to produce useful quantities of electricity. Large areas mean a lot of silicon and therefore enormous expense.

## Expensive

In fact, at present, solar cells are too expensive to be used except when the cost does not matter very much. The most obvious example of this is in space research. A satellite needs energy, and there is, of course, plenty of solar energy in Space. This is why *Skylab*, the space laboratory, was fitted with an array of solar cells — partly in the form of what looked like windmill blades on the top of the satellite. Nevertheless, although the windmill blades of *Skylab* are much more advanced than a simple exposure meter, the basic principle is the same.

But a cheaper, more down-to-earth method is needed where cost matters.

One approach is to use a different material. Pure silicon cells are very expensive partly because they must be made of an enormous number of very pure single crystals of silicon linked by delicate electrical connections. But some scientists have found that some other substances which are not crystals can be made to behave like silicon. There is hope that these substances could be made very cheaply. They could be the basis of a practical form of solar cell.

## Valuable fuel

Another possibility was being developed in Israel. Put very simply, the energy of the Sun is harnessed to split water into the two elements it is made of, hydrogen and oxygen. The hydrogen is a very valuable fuel — it can be used to drive motor cars or machinery.

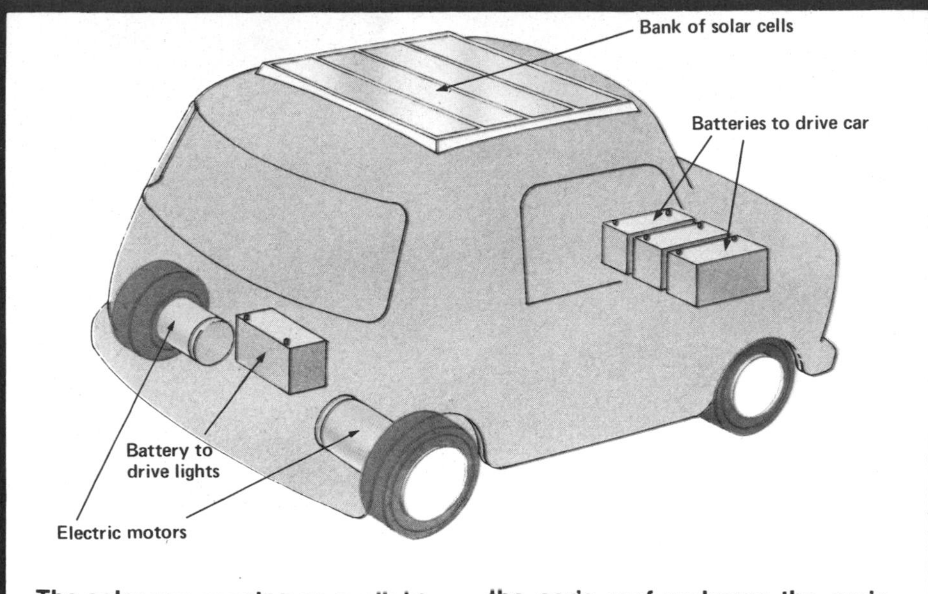


**The solar car, running on sunlight, has been a dream for years, although a commercial design has never been found. Solar cells on the car's roof recharge the car's batteries, which drive electric motors to power the car. A separate battery runs the car's lights.**

Once again the idea behind the invention is simple. The sun shines on a solar cell that is standing in water. The water has previously been treated with a chemical so that it conducts electricity, and the solar cell is connected by a wire to a piece of metal that also stands in the water. Because the sunlight turns the cell into a tiny battery, an electric current flows along the wire, and this current splits the water into hydrogen and oxygen.

Whether the idea proves to be practical commercially waits to be seen.

As well as their cost, another serious problem with solar cells is that they only produce energy when the sun is shining. However, a dramatic way of obtaining solar energy continuously is the 'solar space island'. This is a very exciting and imaginative idea that sounds at first like science fiction.

In reality, however, the idea is so sound that the United States government has invested a lot of money in developing it. Put simply, the idea is to place solar cells on an artificial satellite. The satellite would be put into an orbit 35,652 km above the Earth. At this distance, it would go round the Earth once a day, which means that provided it was travelling in the same direction as the Earth spins, it would seem to stand still, hovering above one place. Because it would be so high up, it would be almost constantly in sunshine. And at that height, there are no clouds or fogs, no weather at all in fact, to shut off the sunlight.

The electricity generated by the solar panels would be converted into microwaves — the sort of radiation used in microwave ovens. The microwaves would be beamed to earth, where they would be picked up by aerials. They would then be reconverted into electricity, and added to the mains supply.

## Exciting prospect

The planned satellite would be very large, about 24 km by 5 km. What is particularly exciting is that there is no need to construct this vast satellite on the ground and then try to build a rocket to take it into orbit. It can be built out in Space — astronauts already have the skills to do this. We still need an economical method of getting the materials up there, but this is not an insurmountable problem.

The Space Shuttle is being designed to take people up into Space cheaply, and a fairly crude 'Space Tug' could carry up the basic materials.

Building in Space has another advantage. At that altitude, the materials are nearly weightless. So the structure can be very flimsy and graceful — one that would not stand up on the Earth, where it would collapse under its own weight.

**One of the most promising ways of using the Sun to make electricity is the solar pond, working examples of which have been built in Israel. The water at the bottom of the pond is more salty than that at the top. The Sun's rays striking the floor of the pond heat up the bottom waters. In a normal pond this hot water would rise and mix with the cooler top water, but because salt water is heavier than fresh water, it does not rise in the solar pond and becomes increasingly hot. This hot water is pumped off and passed first through a *desalination plant* (which removes salt) and then through a *heat pump.* A heat pump works like a refrigerator in reverse and can be used to transfer the heat into a large amount of water to a smaller amount of water — which can become very hot indeed. In this way hot water from the pond is used to make steam to drive a turbine to make electricity. Very salty water from the desalination plant is pumped to the bottom of the pond, fresh water is returned to the top of the pond. So the top remains less salty than the bottom.**

## SOLAR COOKER

Here's one way of cooking the dinner!

Like a solar furnace, only much smaller, the curved mirror of the cooker reflects the Sun's rays into one spot. In hot countries, like India for example, enough heat is captured to boil water quite easily. The cook, however, must sit nearby and keep turning the mirror towards the Sun to keep the food cooking. She must also turn the mirror away from the Sun when she removes the pot to avoid being burnt.

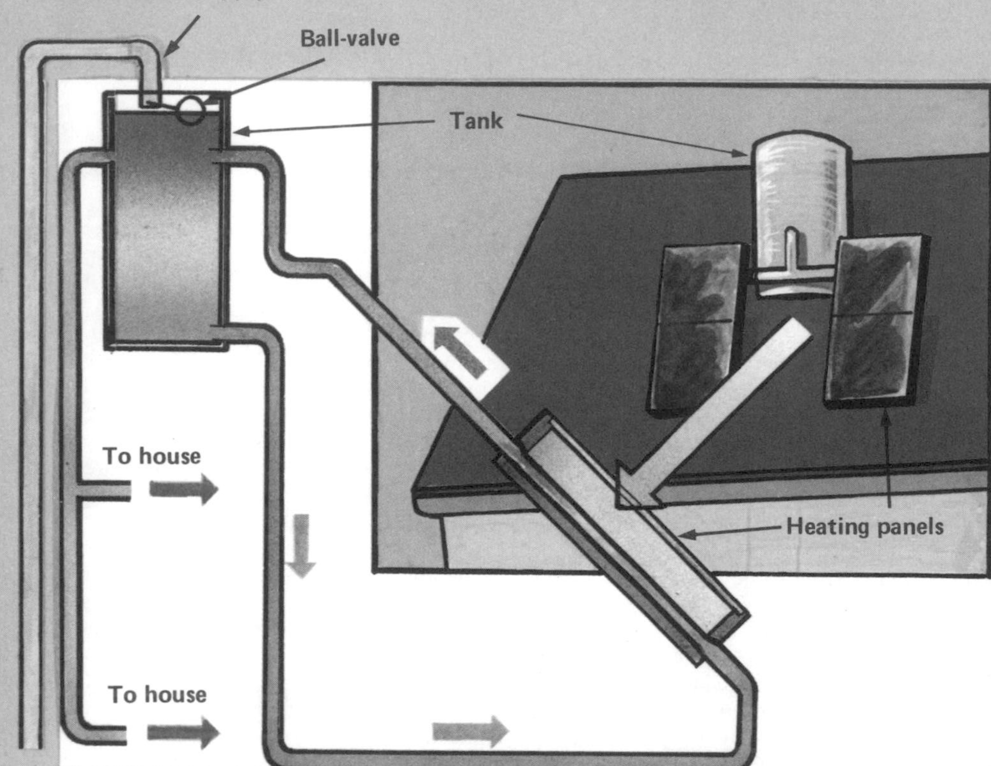


## SOLAR HOT-WATER SYSTEM

This sort of system is very often used in tropical and Mediterranean countries to provide hot water. A tank is placed on the roof of a house and connected to two or more glass box-like panels by pipes. Water in the panels is heated in the same way as inside a greenhouse. Because hot water is lighter than cold water, the hot water rises and flows into the tank, where it can be drawn off to be used in the house. The water used up in this way is replaced by cold water which enters the tank through a ball-valve — the sort of valve used in a lavatory cistern.

More complicated systems than this use pumps to move the water round, and have automatic controls, to stop the water getting too hot, or to turn the system off altogether in cold weather. In systems used in temperate countries, such as Britain, the hot water is not used directly because it rarely becomes hot enough. Instead it is pumped through a series of pipes (a heat exchanger) *inside* the normal hot-water tank. This warms the water in the tank which is then fully heated by gas or electricity.

# DO-IT-YOURSELF SOLAR STILL

Learn how to make this solar still — or water purifier — and the next time you are dying of thirst on a sunny beach, you'll be able to make fresh water to drink.

The still is simply a waterproof wooden box — lining the bottom and sides with plastic sheet will make even a roughly-built box waterproof — to which a little sea water is added. A container, such as a tall tumbler, is placed in the middle of the box. It must be taller than the sea water is deep so that no sea water enters it. (If necessary, put a stone in it so that it doesn't float.) A clear plastic sheet is now pinned across the top of the box and a stone placed on the sheet directly above the container.

The Sun's rays passing through the sheet evaporate the sea water, leaving the salt behind. The evaporated water then collects on the inside of the sheet, runs down to where the stone makes the sheet lowest, and then drips into the container.

Drink it — it is pure, clean water.

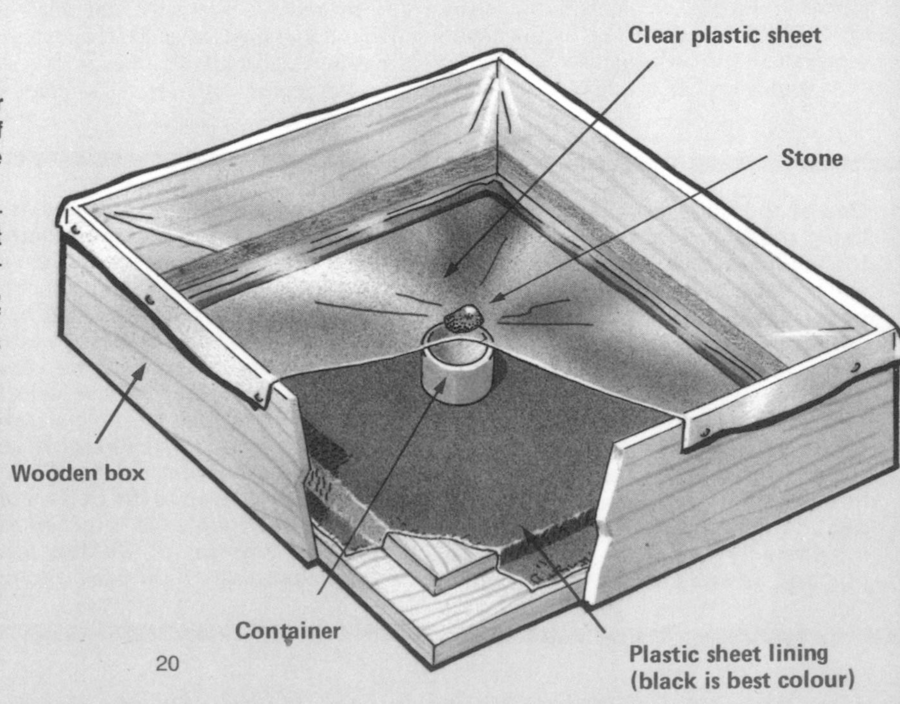

Oil, gas, coal — all will sooner or later run out. When this happens, many people advocate nuclear energy. But there are other ways.

# What Energy alternatives are open to us?

**OIL, gas and coal, which are the world's supply of fossil fuels, will sooner or later, run out. In preparation for this, considerable work is already being done to find alternative forms of energy.**

Nuclear power is just one of the considerations.

Another natural and perhaps most obvious source of energy, is the sun.

Here, we give thought to the many other alternative energy sources.

## Variations

Of course, many of the other sources are really variations of solar energy. They rely on rain, caused by the Sun evaporating the seas, on wind powered by the Sun's heat, and on waves powered by the winds. Even methane gas generators are solar collectors of a sort — they recycle the energy in waste which originally came from green plants photosynthesising in sunlight. Only geothermal power (power from the heat of the Earth's core) and tidal power do not tap the Sun's near-boundless energy.

All the alternative sources, however, do have one thing in common. They do not rely on fossil fuels and therefore there is no reason why they should not supply power for as long as Man can imagine.

Some of the projects described on these and the following pages are for large-scale schemes which would generate electricity suitable for adding to the *national grid* of power cables. But some energy is always lost when it is converted from one form to another and the real future for alternative energy sources is more probably many small, local 'power stations' rather than a few huge energy factories.

For centuries — before the invention of the steam engine — waterwheels and windmills supplied the power for grinding grain and for other simple tasks such as pumping water. It would be unrealistic to think that old-fashioned Don Quixote style sail windmills will again be built; nowadays they would be very expensive to construct indeed. Moreover a great number would be required to produce the amount of power used in modern society, many thousands of times more than that used in medieval times.

Nevertheless a 20-metre windmill can give quite useful amounts of power — say 75 kW — enough to supply a small village, although hardly enough to send halfway across the country on pylons.

The modern equivalent of the water-wheel — the turbine — is used extensively already to make power. Hydro-electric power stations are common wherever there is mountainous terrain and plentiful water.

## Biogas

In agricultural areas, particularly in rural countries like India, human and animal manure, along with vegetable waste, can also provide useful energy on a local scale. In *biogas* plants, bacteria are used to rot down the manure giving off the gas *methane,* which can be burnt to heat cookers, machinery or even cars.

But in a future new world, reliant upon alternative energy sources, cars would almost certainly be a thing of the past. They use far too much energy. Trains are more economical and are the best fast alternative. At sea, sailing ships are very cheap to run energy-wise! But perhaps the best alternative energy source as far as inland transport is concerned is leg power. You really can't better the bike!

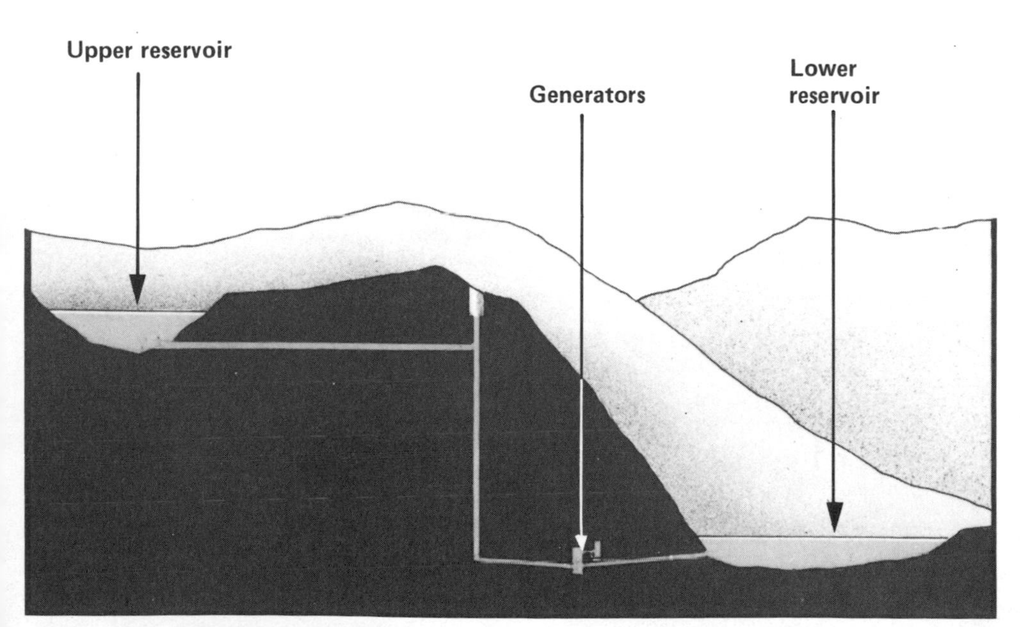


**HYDRO-ELECTRIC POWER**

**Rivers and streams have been used to drive mills since the earliest times. More recently, the power of flowing water has been used to drive electricity generators. Unfortunately, not all rivers are suitable to drive present-day generators. However, as it is certain that water power will continue to be an important source of energy for the future, a great deal of work is being put into finding ways of making the generating systems more efficient — able to use more slowly flowing water for example.**

## BIOGAS GENERATOR

Biogas plants like this are already in operation in many places. The gas is produced by bacteria as they break down manure and waste.

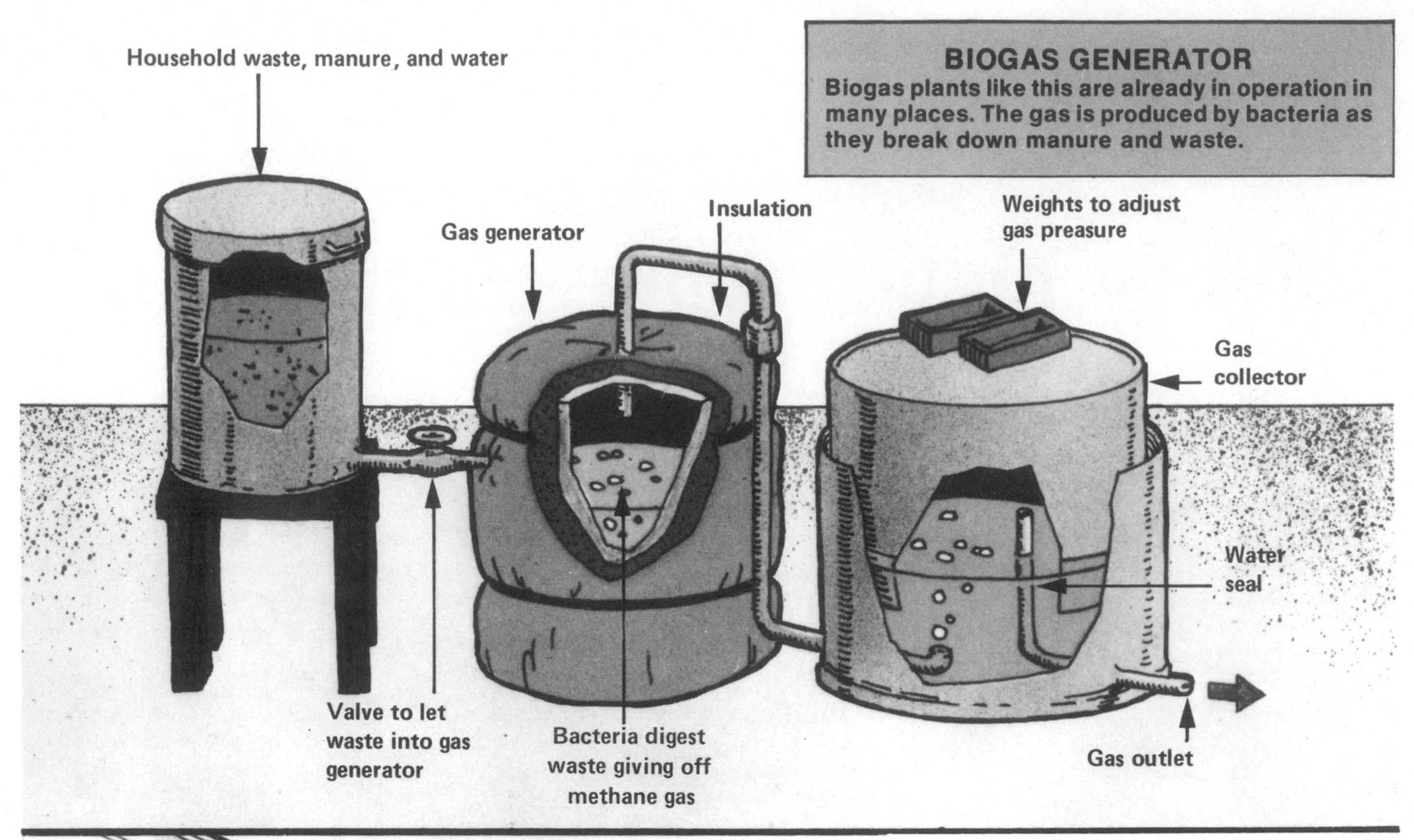


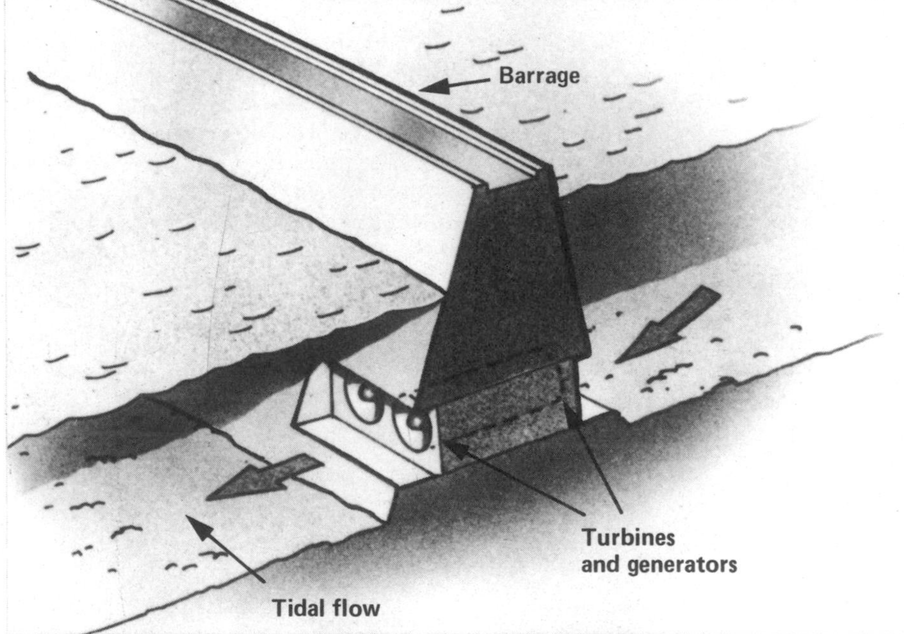


## TIDAL BARRAGES

A great deal of energy is available in the rise and fall of the tides. If a barrage, or dam, is built across a bay, it traps water behind it. As the tide runs out, this water is allowed to run out through turbines, which generate electricity as they spin. In some tidal barrages, the turbines can work in either direction, so generating electricity both as the tide rises and as it falls. A tidal barrage has been in operation for many years in France.

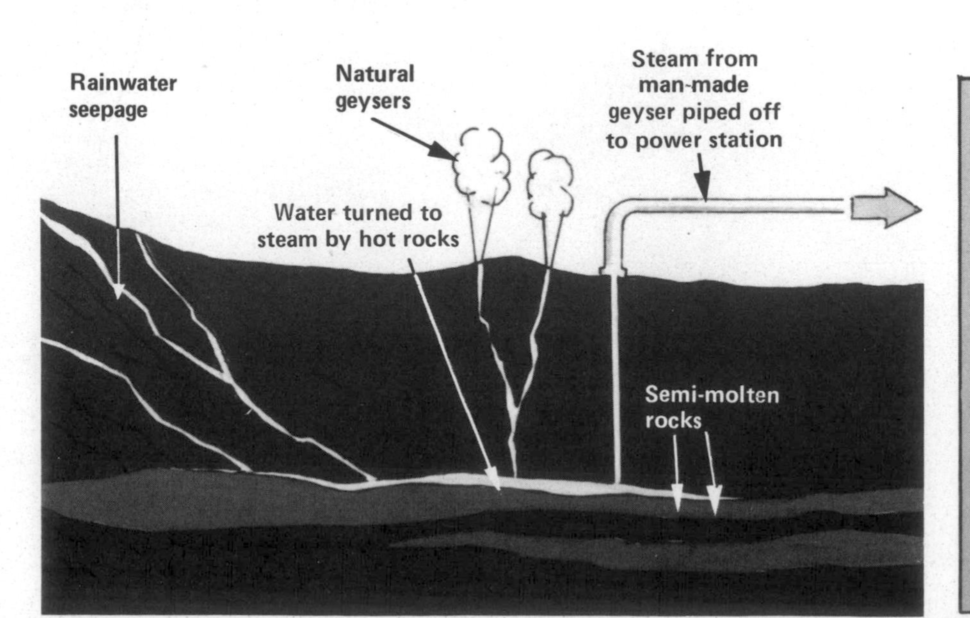


## GEOTHERMAL POWER

The centre of the Earth is hot enough to melt rock. This molten rock occasionally escapes as the lava spewn from volcanoes. When water seeps down into these hot rocks, it boils — escaping as *geysers*. In many countries, this naturally hot water is used to power electricity generators, and much work is going on to make more use of this power source, even in countries with no natural geysers. If a pipe is drilled down to hot rocks, it can make a man-made geyser just as useful as the natural thing.

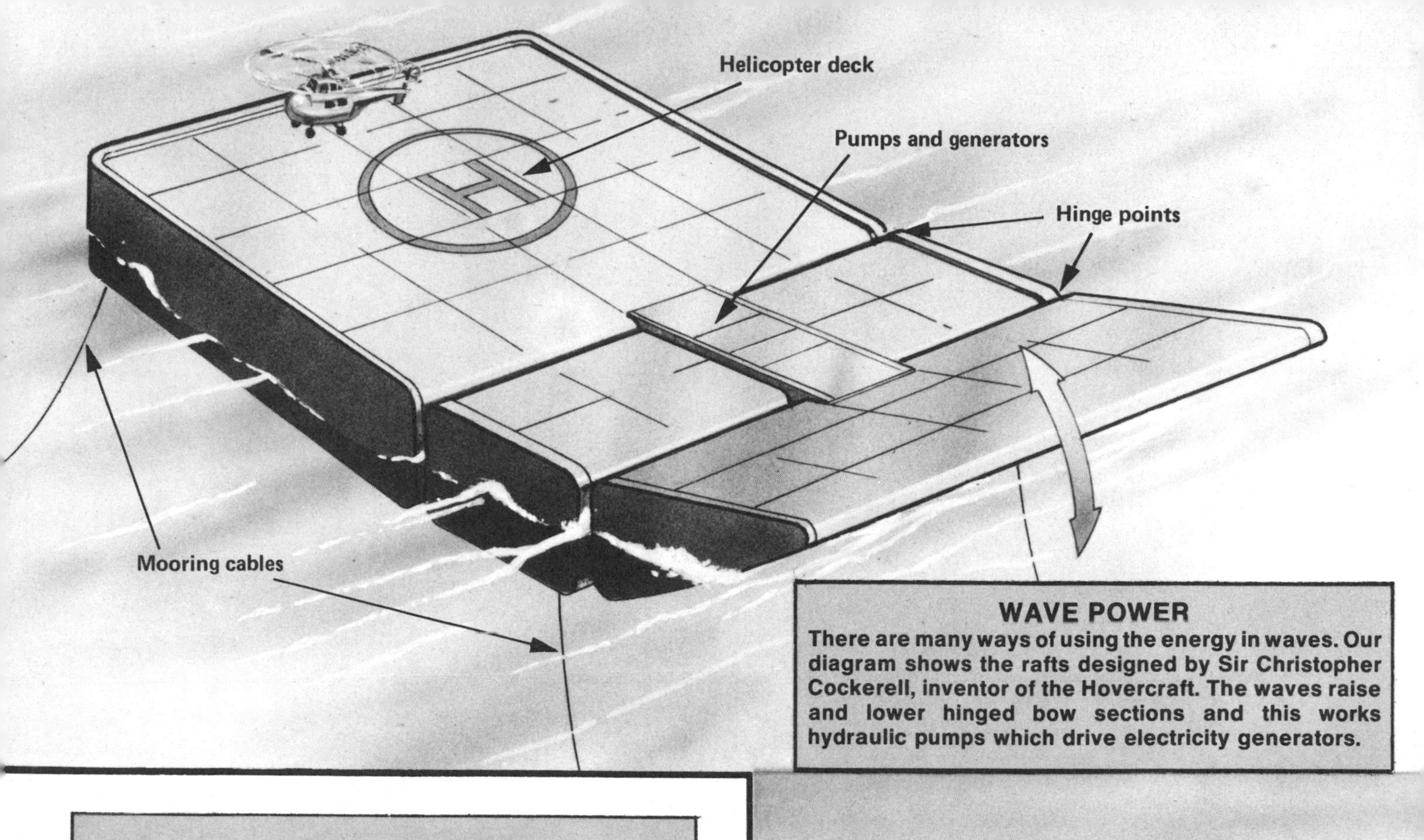


## WAVE POWER

There are many ways of using the energy in waves. Our diagram shows the rafts designed by Sir Christopher Cockerell, inventor of the Hovercraft. The waves raise and lower hinged bow sections and this works hydraulic pumps which drive electricity generators.

## WINDMILLS

There are many modern windmill designs. This one does not need to be turned to face into the wind, and, even in a gale, cannot go too fast because over-speeding makes the blades bend, thus reducing the wind pressure on them.

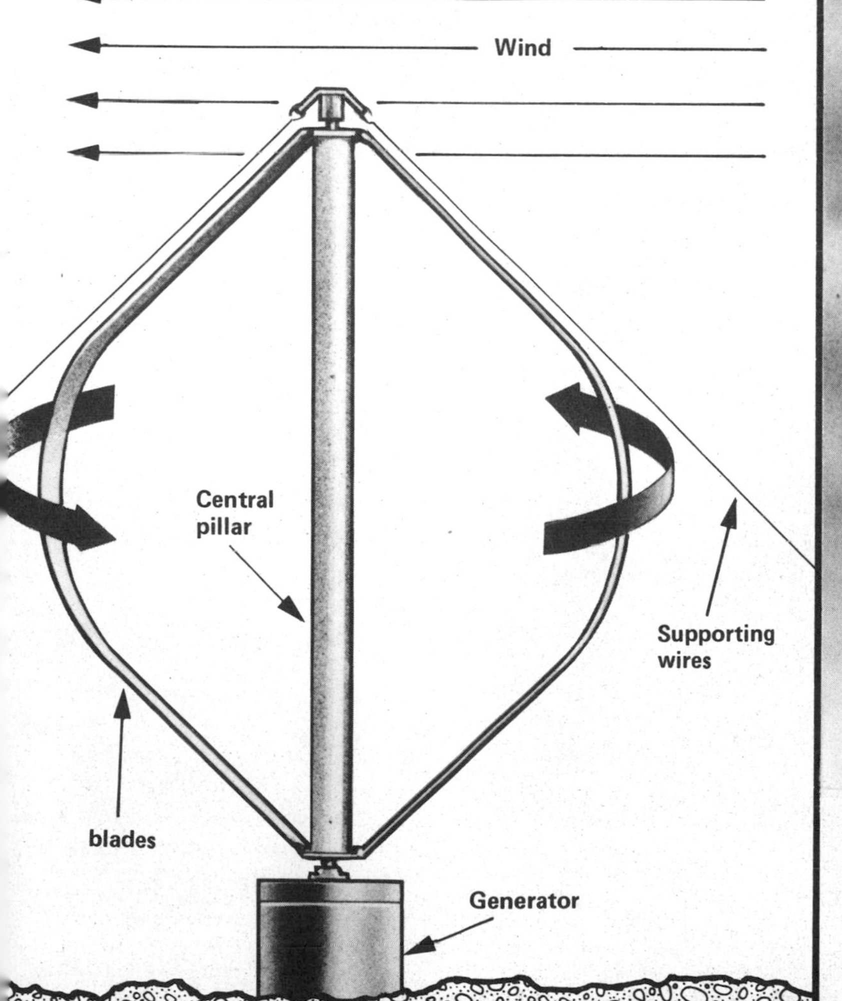


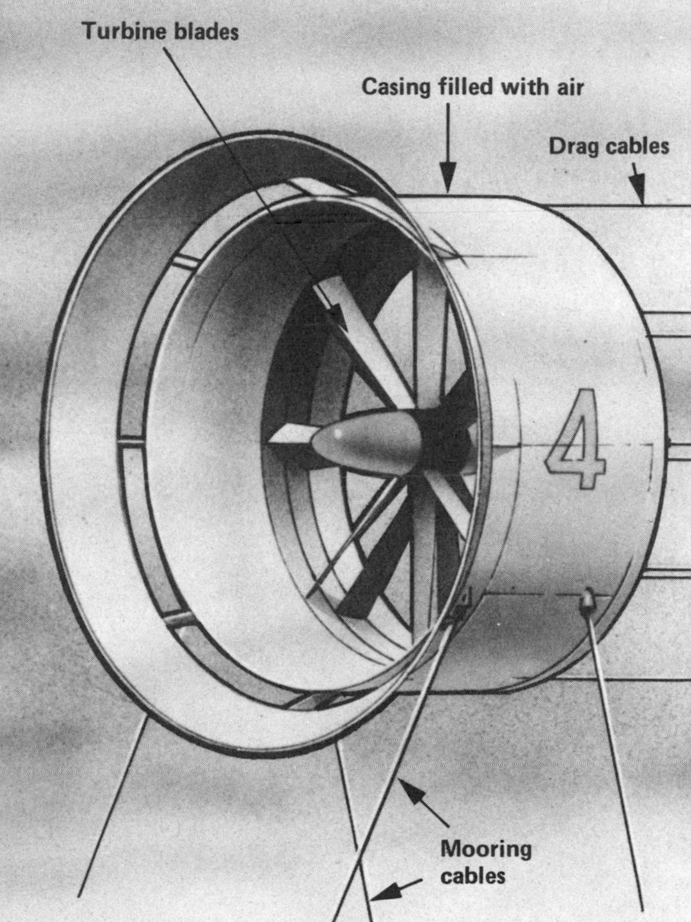


## OCEAN CURRENT GENERATOR

With turbine blades up to 20 metres long, turning at no more than one revolution per minute, machines like this could generate considerable amounts of electricity from great ocean currents like the Gulf Stream. They would be moored deep under water, well below the biggest ships and the effects of bad weather.

# Which Draper was a

1. Most scientists begin their careers after rigorous training and learning. But Antonius van Leeuwenhoek was an entirely self-taught amateur. Born in 1632, he spent most of his life in his native town of Delft in Holland, where he ran a drapery business. He lived a quiet life, respected by his fellow citizens, who appointed him Chief Chamberlain of Delft. But he had an enquiring mind, and a hobby which made him one of the foremost scientists of his time.

2. As a young man, Leeuwenhoek had been apprenticed to a cloth merchant in Amsterdam, and during that time he had also learnt how to grind glass lenses. Leeuwenhoek decided to use his lenses to study tiny things not visible to the naked eye. He perfected techniques to grind powerful lenses which he then made into simple microscopes consisting of a magnifying glass on a brass plate, with a second plate below to hold the object being viewed.

3. The amateur scientist was amazed at the new world revealed by enlarging everyday things. He studied pieces of skin, hair, teeth and plants. When he looked at muscle, he saw that it was made up of fibres. Looking at a drop of water, he noticed tiny 'animalcules' swimming about in it. Although he did not know it, these were single-celled animals called protozoa. In all his experiments, he made careful notes and drawings of what he had seen. In 1662, Charles the Second of England had granted a charter to the Royal Society, a scientific body of learned men. Leeuwenhoek wrote to them about some of his discoveries — describing enlargements of a bee's head, a fly's brain, and the lens of a bullock's eye. The Society was greatly impressed by Leeuwenhoek's work and asked him to send details of any other discoveries. In the end he sent them hundreds of letters over a period of 50 years.

# famous Scientist?

4. Leeuwenhoek continued to put more and more substances under his microscope to discover their structure. He soon realized that minute living things were to be found everywhere and grew from each other — the opposite of the then accepted theory of 'spontaneous generation', which said life could 'spontaneously' arise from non-living matter. In thinking this, Leeuwenhoek was 200 years ahead of his time. Louis Pasteur (top left) finally disproved the theory in 1894.

5. The list of Leeuwenhoek's findings is impressive. He discovered the red cells of blood, that yeast was made up of globular particles (the individual cells), and that aphids give birth to live young. He also produced the first drawing of bacteria (the living organisms which often cause disease). When Peter the Great of Russia visited Holland, he specifically asked to see Leeuwenhoek, who showed the Czar the magnified tail of a eel.

6. Despite his fame, Leeuwenhoek continued to live quietly, running his drapery business and sending his letters to London. When his wife died, his daughter Maria looked after him and wrote up his notes. Because he was so well trusted, the painter Jan Vermeer appointed him executor of his will. When Vermeer died, Leeuwenhoek had to sell the paintings to pay the artist's debts. It was not until the 20th century that Vermeer was acclaimed as a great Dutch master.

7. Leeuwenhoek continued to work right up to his death in 1723. Although the Royal Society had made him a Fellow in 1680, sending him his diploma in a silver box, the full importance of his work went unappreciated. Until Pasteur, no-one realized that Leeuwenhoek's microscopic creatures caused disease. In 1932, however, a celebration was held at Delft to mark the three-hundredth anniversary of the birth of this great amateur scientist.

# Who thought of the Railway

1. Andrew Carnegie, who became a dollar millionaire while still quite young, was born of poor parents in Dunfermline, Scotland, in 1835. His father was a weaver operating a hand loom and his mother added to the meagre family fortunes by making shoes. Young Andrew was bright even as a child and stood out at school as having a better grasp of detail and a greater understanding than the average pupil. But his difficulties as a child influenced his later life, making him aware of the needs of others.

2. In 1848, his father, fearing unemployment due to the growing numbers of power looms being installed in factories, decided to emigrate to America. So the whole family set sail and eventually arrived in Allegheny City, Pennsylvania (now a part of Pittsburg). There, Andrew started work as a bobbin-boy in a cotton factory, later moving to work as a telegraph operator and a messenger boy. When he was twenty, his father died and he was left with the responsibility of looking after his mother and brother.

3. But keen business sense saw him through. He invented the railway sleeping car, then bought a farm which provided enormous amounts of oil. He began the Keystone Bridge Company and acquired a large steel plant, building bridges of steel. He controlled a railway 684 kilometres long and ran a line of lake steamships. Money produced more money — and eventually he became very rich indeed. But already he wanted to use his wealth for the good of others, so he decided to return to Scotland.

4. From Scotland, Carnegie did indeed work to help others. The Carnegie Foundation still awards prizes for people who have benefited mankind. The Hero Funds of America and the United Kingdom recognise deeds of heroism. In fact, Carnegie's idea of the duties of the man of wealth is demonstrated in his own words. "To provide moderately for the wants of those dependent upon him; and after doing so, to consider all surplus revenues which come to him simply as trust funds . . ."

## Sleeping Car?

5. He was 66 when he set up a number of such trusts. In America, the Carnegie Trust helped the education of the Negroes and also provided pensions for all Carnegie's workers. In Scotland, he created a special Dunfermline Trust for his home town, and the United Kingdom Trust helped and founded welfare centres, libraries and museums. Two scientific institutes were established in Washington and Pittsburg, the latter today considered to be one of the most important in the world.

6. The cause of peace was dear to Andrew Carnegie's heart, so he built the Palace of Peace at The Hague in Holland. He also had a great deal to do with the building of the Music Hall in New York. This was renamed Carnegie Hall in 1898. When he died at Lennox, Massachusetts in 1919, it was estimated that his gifts during his lifetime amounted to around £70,000,000. His work is a memorial to a man who maintained that someone who dies with money he is free to distribute dies disgraced.

# He Remembered the Heroes

**THE Carnegie Trusts are still very much living organisations. Many operate in the United States of America, and others are in Britain, France, Norway, Switzerland, the Netherlands, Sweden, Denmark, Belgium and Italy.**

**One of the most interesting is the Carnegie Hero Fund Trust of Great Britain, established in 1908 and set up to recognize outstanding feats of heroism.**

The Trustees themselves decide if a person's act is worthy of recognition. It must involve the saving of life or the attempted saving of life and the risk of loss of life to the rescuer. The person must not be related to the man, woman or child involved, unless severe handicap is suffered or actual loss of life.

When an act has been accepted by the Trustees, the name of the hero or heroine is inscribed on the Roll of Honour and sometimes a Bronze Medallion is awarded. Varying amounts of financial assistance are given to people or the families of people who have acted heroically.

Here are some heroic deeds.

One was a 42-year old man who lost his life in 1977 while trying to rescue his two grandchildren. The house the children were in caught fire and no one could reach them. The man eventually managed to get into the house but was unable to save the children. All three were dead. The man's family receive a regular weekly allowance for his heroism.

Another was a 64-year old man who died from injuries he received in 1978 while trying to save a fellow workman from being drawn into a machine. He saved the man's life but was so badly injured himself that he died. Again, his family receive a regular allowance.

The Bronze Medallion and an award which brought electricity to the island was made to the people of Fair Isle in 1956 because of the heroism of 12 islanders who rescued a man badly injured while climbing there.

These are only a few of those who have benefited but as many as 170 families at one time have received awards from the Trust.

Andrew Carnegie would have been proud of them - so are we!

For 600 years the Old London Bridge straddled the River Thames until it was demolished in 1831. Begun in 1176 by King Henry II, five times it was swept by fire and each time rebuilt. The stone piers supporting the arches were designed to restrict the tidal flow and give a deeper anchorage to ships using the Port of London.

# How many kinds of Bridges are there?

**Getting to the other side — that has been the problem for men whenever they have been faced by a river or valley — and they have arrived at many different kinds of solutions.**

**THE Emperor of Rome stood with his Consuls looking over the River Tiber. In the distance, approaching the far bank, they could see the enemy; their horses, flags and armour bright in the sunshine. Only one thing could stop this huge army entering and destroying the city — the wooden Sublician Bridge over the Tiber must be cut down. But that would take time. How could they delay the enemy?**

Suddenly, Horatius Cocles and two other soldiers stepped forward. They offered to fight the enemy's champions to hold up the advance. Crossing to the other side of the bridge, they called out their challenge and began to fight while, unknown to the enemy, powerful arms swung heavy axes into the timbers supporting the bridge. Before long they began to crack and tumble into the deep waters of the Tiber.

Horatius's two companions fled back to safety but Horatius, still fighting, was left stranded, a gaping wound in his leg. Finally, the bridge gone, he too turned and plunged into the Tiber, swimming painfully to the safety of the other shore. Rome was saved.

In peace and war, bridges have always been important. When Man's remote ancestors wandered the forests and plains looking for food and shelter millions of years ago they might have come across a river that was uncrossable without some form of bridge. If they were lucky a fallen tree might have helped them. If not they needed to work out for themselves how to place trees to get them across.

Today at Beddgelert in North Wales a tree trunk bridge is still in use. The bridge-building technique was similar to that used by people in Neolithic times.

The same principle is used in the *girder* bridge — one of the three main kinds of bridge developed over the centuries to cross rivers, gorges and roads. Originally built of timber but nowadays of steel or concrete, the girder bridge

## WHY THE 'KEYSTONE' STONE ARCH DOES NOT FALL DOWN

Stone arch bridges are over 2,000 years old. The Etruscans, Romans and Goths all built bridges on this principle. They consisted of a number of blocks assembled in the form of a curved arch, the two limbs resting at the other ends on hard ground to resist the thrust. They were prevented from falling together at the centre by a wedge called a *keystone*.

All the Roman arches were semi-circular as in this picture. The central keystone was very accurately wedge-shaped and often elaborately decorated. Some weighed as much as six tonnes.

The Goths were not as great engineers as the Romans. Their semi-circular arches collapsed so they devised the wedge-shaped arch. The weight of any load was carried down to the abutments.

A later development was the elliptical arched bridge. This spanned a greater distance without rising as high as a semi-circular arch but required greater expertise in design and building.

consists of one or a number of horizontal structures or spans resting on foundations called 'abutments' at each end. Any load on the girder acts straight down on these foundations which must be solidly laid. When iron began to be used for building in the 19th century the great British engineers Stephenson and Fairbairn designed the Brittania Tubular Bridge across the Menai Straits to join Anglesey to the Welsh mainland. This allowed trains to run through two huge wrought iron tubes over four spans, two of 70 metres and two of 140 metres, and it set a pattern for thousands of similar girder bridges all over the world.

## Cantilever bridge

However, for very long spans a straight girder type bridge is not strong enough. The *cantilever* has to be used, a bridging method that dates back many centuries to ancient China. 'Cantilever' means 'bracket' and these support massively heavy structures such as the great Forth railway bridge in Scotland in the same way as they hold up bookshelves at home.

A simple cantilever bridge consists of two large wooden brackets jutting out into the stream from towers on either side. The towers are filled with stones and rubble that push down on to the outside ends of the cantilever, thus keeping them rigid enough for a simple beam to rest on and join up the two arms in the middle. In the Forth Bridge the cantilevers supporting the huge 521 metre spans are massive sweeping girders set on stone piers. Each sweep is really a double bracket supported in the middle by steel tubes four metres in diameter. Little wonder that no sooner have painters finished at one end of the bridge than they have to start all over again at the other!

By the way, it is not always easy to identify a cantilever bridge. London's Waterloo Bridge, built in 1942, looks like a series of five arches but is in fact made up of continuous cantilever spans, all in reinforced concrete, which is stronger than steel.

## Arches

Some of the very oldest bridges are built not with girders but with *arches*. The Romans in particular were very fond of this form of construction and some of their bridges, such as the Alcantara Bridge in Spain, are still standing after 2000 years. Other famous arch bridges include the Old London Bridge (demolished in 1831), on which were shops and houses, and the incomplete bridge at Avignon which inspired the folk song 'Sur le pont d'Avignon' known by every schoolchild in France.

Stone or concrete arch bridges, although they cannot be built with such wide spans as cantilevers, are immensely strong. The first to be built were 'corbelled' — constructed by laying stones so that each layer sticks out a

*Continued on next page*

## THE PRINCIPLE OF THE SUSPENSION BRIDGE

**A suspension bridge is a bridge hanging in mid-air and the basic simplicity behind its design is shown in the diagrams above. In its most primitive form, it consists of nothing more than a rope or creeper slung between two supports (top). But if you have ever tried to swing hand over hand along a rope you will know how tiring it can be!**

**The obvious improvement was to introduce two more creepers which would provide hand holds. Then the person crossing over could walk along the main rope and keep his balance by holding on to the handrails either side (centre).**

**A far easier way of crossing a gap like a river would be to use other ropes to hang planks from the main rope to walk across (bottom). And the next step, to allow boats to pass up and down the river, would be to raise the suspension ropes.**

**Even primitive peoples grasped the ease with which a simple suspension bridge could be built. Today natives in jungles and high mountains still construct these simple but very useful bridges.**

**In the modern suspension bridge the load pulls inwards along cables anchored to the banks and pushes down through the piers. Swaying in high winds can be a problem; this is overcome partly by stiffening the roadway and to a much greater extent, today, by aerodynamic design.**

## HOW THE CANTILEVER WORKS

**A cantilever is a kind of bracket. One cantilever on its own would tend to overturn unless specially supported, but if two are built out simultaneously from opposite sides they will counterbalance each other. Each man shown below represents a double cantilever. By linking these balanced units long spans can be formed, often set on stone piers.**

# CONCRETE

A mixture of water with cement, sand and either gravel or stone chips, concrete gives the bridge architect a great freedom of design when it is reinforced.

## REINFORCED CONCRETE

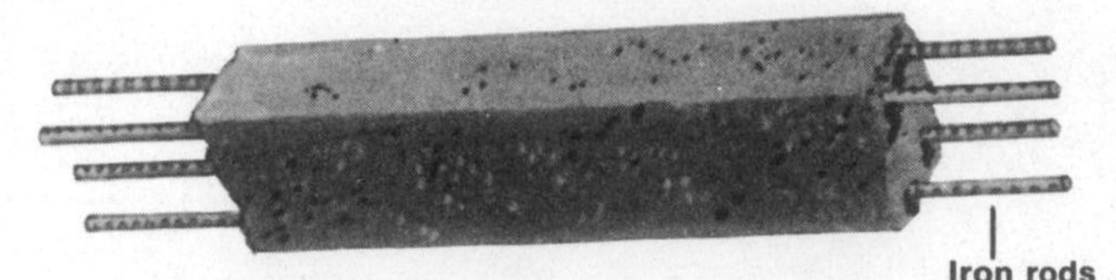


Ordinary reinforced concrete has steel rods or mesh embedded in it. The steelwork is shaped and the concrete poured around it and allowed to set.

## PRE-STRESSED CONCRETE

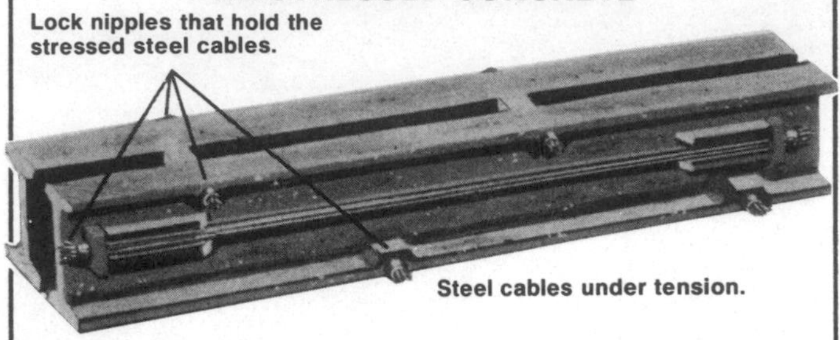


In this beam the steel cables are stretched and the concrete poured on. When tension is released the concrete is compressed and strengthened as the cables try to shorten.

## PRE-STRESSED CELLULAR CONSTRUCTION

The deck of the bridge on which a road surface will be laid.

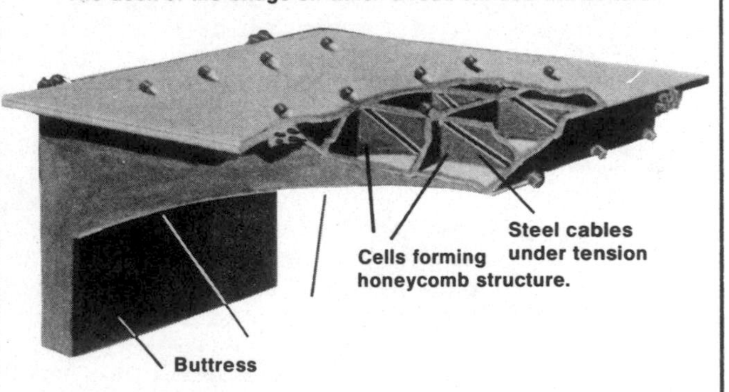


Part of a bridge road deck showing the cellular or 'honeycomb' structure together with stressing rods. This gives the deck great strength and durability.

little more than the layer below it until they finally meet at the top. Then this was improved on by forming a true arch from a semi-circle of stones, the middle one right at the top of the arch being wedge shaped. It was so important to get the shape of this stone correct that builders rightly called it the 'keystone'. Larger spans are possible using specially strengthened steel to form arches, one of the most spectacular examples of this type being the bridge over Sydney Harbour in Australia.

Some of the world's most beautiful and breathtaking bridges are *suspension* bridges. The famous Golden Gate Bridge at San Francisco, though not the longest despite its 1280 metre span, is perhaps the best known. Suspension bridges are so called because they literally hang from cables suspended between the anchorages at each end. But these cables are very special. They are not just slung across the river from one bank to another but 'spun' into place. Each cable consists of thousands of single steel wires carried over the span and spun round as they are being carried. The end result is a series of cables of immense strength.

## Brunel

The suspension system is used for spanning some very special river valleys. When the famous bridge builder Isambard Kingdom Brunel (1806–59) see page 32, was faced with the task of joining the two banks of the River Avon at Clifton just outside Bristol, he could not use a girder construction because the piers would be too high nor could he turn to an arch because the span was too great for techniques at that time. So he used suspension, hanging the road from vertical chains.

Bridges must be strong, firm and not too heavy, to avoid collapsing under the weight of traffic or their own weight. But they don't have to be completely fixed. One of the best-known bridges in the world is Tower Bridge in London, an example of the *bascule* bridge, designed so that its arms, which are on pivots and counterweighted, can be lifted up to allow taller boats to pass underneath. There are swing bridges where the arms are pivoted so that they swing horizontally. Then, there are vertical lift bridges in which the whole centre span section can be raised up vertically in one piece. Moveable bridges are quite numerous so look out for one.

In the Second World War the *Bailey bridge* came into its own because it was a type of bridge that could be assembled, taken down and driven away in a lorry very quickly. Perhaps a long way from Horatius . . . but then again, perhaps not so very different after all.

**Man's first bridges consisted of nothing more than tree trunks or large boulders thrown across rivers but the exact date in history is unknown. Arch construction was known to the Sumerians as early as 3200 B.C., and a reference exists to a bridge over the Nile from 2650 B.C. The oldest surviving dateable bridge in the world is the slab stone single arch bridge over the River Meles at Smyrna, Turkey. This dates from around 850 B.C.**

**In Britain the clapper bridges of Dartmoor date from prehistoric times and there are the remains of 2nd century A.D. Roman bridge in Northumberland.**

**The world's widest bridge is the Sydney Harbour Bridge in Australia which is 48m wide, it carries two electric overhead railway tracks, eight lanes of roadway and a cycle and footway.**

**The Quebec Bridge over the St. Lawrence River in Canada has the longest cantilever span in the world – 987m. Its building took 18 years and cost 87 lives.**

**The Tay Bridge, opened in June 1878 to carry a railway across the River Tay on the main Edinburgh-Dundee line was hailed as a masterpiece of Victorian engineering. But not for long. In December 1879, a gale swept away 13 spans of the bridge just as the Edinburgh mail train was going across. Of the 78 passengers and crew, not one survived.**

**The largest suspension bridge in the world is the Humber Estuary Bridge near Hull, England, which is 1410m long, and its towers are 36mm out of parallel to allow for the curvature of the Earth.**

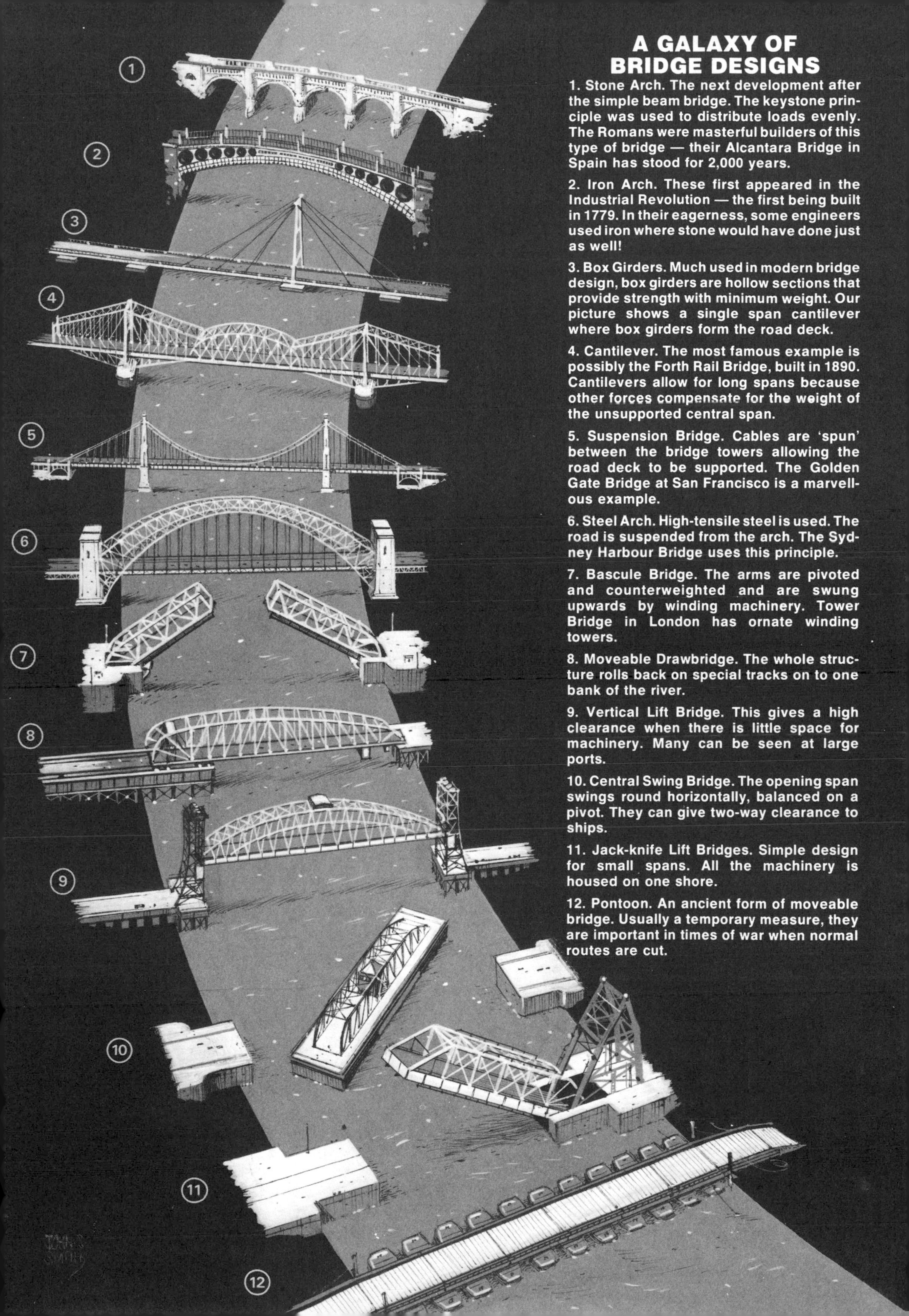


# A GALAXY OF BRIDGE DESIGNS

1. Stone Arch. The next development after the simple beam bridge. The keystone principle was used to distribute loads evenly. The Romans were masterful builders of this type of bridge — their Alcantara Bridge in Spain has stood for 2,000 years.

2. Iron Arch. These first appeared in the Industrial Revolution — the first being built in 1779. In their eagerness, some engineers used iron where stone would have done just as well!

3. Box Girders. Much used in modern bridge design, box girders are hollow sections that provide strength with minimum weight. Our picture shows a single span cantilever where box girders form the road deck.

4. Cantilever. The most famous example is possibly the Forth Rail Bridge, built in 1890. Cantilevers allow for long spans because other forces compensate for the weight of the unsupported central span.

5. Suspension Bridge. Cables are 'spun' between the bridge towers allowing the road deck to be supported. The Golden Gate Bridge at San Francisco is a marvellous example.

6. Steel Arch. High-tensile steel is used. The road is suspended from the arch. The Sydney Harbour Bridge uses this principle.

7. Bascule Bridge. The arms are pivoted and counterweighted and are swung upwards by winding machinery. Tower Bridge in London has ornate winding towers.

8. Moveable Drawbridge. The whole structure rolls back on special tracks on to one bank of the river.

9. Vertical Lift Bridge. This gives a high clearance when there is little space for machinery. Many can be seen at large ports.

10. Central Swing Bridge. The opening span swings round horizontally, balanced on a pivot. They can give two-way clearance to ships.

11. Jack-knife Lift Bridges. Simple design for small spans. All the machinery is housed on one shore.

12. Pontoon. An ancient form of moveable bridge. Usually a temporary measure, they are important in times of war when normal routes are cut.

# Who were

1. The Brunels, father and son, lived when Britain was becoming the world's main industrial power. The father, Marc, was born in France in 1769. His Royalist sympathies nearly cost him his life during the French Revolution but, in 1793, he was shipped to safety in America. There he became New York's chief engineer and later - in Britain - an inventor, being knighted in 1841 by Queen Victoria.

2. His most famous feat was the construction of the first tunnel under the Thames, begun in 1825 and finished in 1842. It was hampered by floods. Seven lives were lost and, undoubtedly, there would have been more but for Brunel's iron 'shield' which made tunnelling easier and safer. This was forced forwards by screw power, 36 men, in groups, working at the same time, and adaptions of this idea are used even today.

4. Brunel junior was also a superb designer of bridges. The Clifton Suspension Bridge was his work, although it was not completed until after his death. So was the Royal Albert Bridge over the River Tamar at Saltash (above), its strength coming from two wrought-iron arched booms. He is particularly remembered today though as an original designer of ships. A man who thought big, he built three famous vessels, each the largest of its day.

5. The first was *The Great Western* (1837). This was a wooden paddle steamer and the first to be used on a regular transatlantic service. The second was *The Great Britain* (1843). This again was a first. It was the first large iron-hulled screw steamship. And the third, *The Great Eastern* (1858) - shown in our picture above - was screw and paddle driven. This ship had a double iron hull. Almost certainly, it was Brunel's work on it that shortened his life.

# the Brunels?

3. Marc Brunel died in 1849 but his son, Isambard Kingdom (1806-59) was to become even more famous. He improved the Bristol docks then, when only 27, became engineer-in-chief of the Great Western Railway. One achievement, on the London to Bristol line, was the Box Tunnel (see above) which took five years to bore. He introduced, too, the broad gauge track (7ft.) later replaced by the standard gauge track (4ft. 8½ ins.)

6. Brunel did not live to see *The Great Eastern's* maiden voyage to New York in 1860. He was never able - or even willing - to delegate work to others. He was present when the engines were tried (and failed) on September 5, 1859 - and died ten days later, no doubt from strain. The great ship had taken nearly six years to build. For half a century it was the world's largest. Isambard Kingdom Brunel thought big to the very end.

The Brunels were unusual and very talented men. Both were highly original, versatile and imaginative. And Marc's great invention, the iron 'shield', saved the lives of many men involved in the dangerous work of tunnelling, particularly in those early days.

The principle on which it worked was to contain groups of men while they tunnelled, to provide an initial lining for the tunnel and to shield the men from any really heavy flooding which they could not have escaped.

Isambard Kingdom Brunel, on the other hand, was involved in two controversies — after his death.

One was concerning his masterpiece, the Great Western Railway — or, to be more exact, his introduction of the broad gauge — seven feet between the lines. There is no doubt at all that he believed it was more comfortable and safer than the narrower (later *standard*) one of George and Robert Stephenson. He also believed a higher speed was possible using it. Probably there were things to be said for both.

The main disadvantage, however, was that there *were* two different gauges at all. The Stephensons had already laid a significant amount of track at the four feet, eight and a half inches gauge when Brunel designed the Great Western. So, when the two systems met, there were irritating delays for both passengers and goods while they were transferred from one system to the other.

It was, however, some time after Brunel's death that the Great Western went standard, in keeping with the rest of Britain's railway systems.

## Great Eastern

The other controversy was to do with *The Great Eastern*. It was bold and imaginative in design but had two serious faults. The stern bearing of the screw shaft kept wearing away. This, of course, continued until it was replaced with a different type. Also, the lifeboats were hung from fixed davits over the ship's sides. Brunel wrongly thought that the Atlantic could not reach them. It could and did.

The vast ship would hold up to 4,000 passengers, almost twice as many as most big liners of the twentieth century but this was more than was really needed on the Atlantic run.

Finally, she was turned into a cable-laying ship, for which she was ideal and, in the end, she was broken up.

The Brunels provide a remarkable example in engineering history. No other engineering father and son have been so versatile, so widely ranged or so imaginative. So much of Isambard Kingdom Brunel's work can be seen around the nation that his fame is never likely to fade. Both were truly memorable men!

Astronomy has often been called the oldest of the sciences. Over 20,000 years ago early Man used the movements of the stars to tell him when to sow his crops. But the science did not really develop until some 400 years ago when the *telescope* was invented.

One of the mightiest telescopes now in use is the Hale telescope of the Mount Palomar Observatory in the United States, featured on these pages. This is a reflecting telescope of great proportions. The reflecting mirror is 5.1 metres in diameter and weighs 60 tonnes. The total weight of the telescope and its mountings is 500 tonnes.

The telescope took eight years to design and 13 more to build, being completed in 1948. It was the largest optical telescope in the world until the six metre reflector at Zelenchukskaya in Russia was completed in 1976.

Modern study of the heavens began with the invention of the telescope. It is considered that the first man to make a telescope was Dutch spectacles maker, Hans Lippershey, in 1608. A year later, the famous Italian scientist, Galileo Galilei, heard of the invention and constructed his own. By making steady improvements he produced a telescope that magnified 30 times, and he began to explore the Universe. He discovered previously unknown stars, and the moons of Jupiter.

Galileo's telescope was of simple construction. Because it used two *lenses*, it was known as a *refracting* telescope. The principle was that the front lens (the object lens) collected and focused light on to the second lens (the eye lens), which acted like a magnifying glass.

However, these early telescopes were hampered by the poor quality of their lenses. Images were blurred and the lenses broke the light up into a spectrum of colours.

## Reflecting telescopes

It was the famous English astronomer Sir Isaac Newton who provided a solution. In 1668, he built the first *reflecting* telescope, which used a mirror instead of a lens to collect light. The mirror reflected all parts of the spectrum equally so there was no colour trouble.

The idea proved popular and there were soon variations. Gregorian and Cassegranian reflectors (named after their inventors) used secondary curved mirrors to reflect the light back to an eyepiece in the side of the telescope tube. These telescopes were compact and portable.

But there were problems. The mirrors were made of polished metal which tarnished with time and reduced reflection. In 1757 it was found that by using two lenses, of slightly different composition, colour-fringe effects were removed. Refracting telescopes were back in favour.

In the late 19th century the art of lens-making was at its

*Continued on page 36*

**Actual interi photograph the 5.1 met Hale telesco on Mount Pal mar. Note size men in fo ground in co parison. T observation flo is 1,706 metr above sea-level**

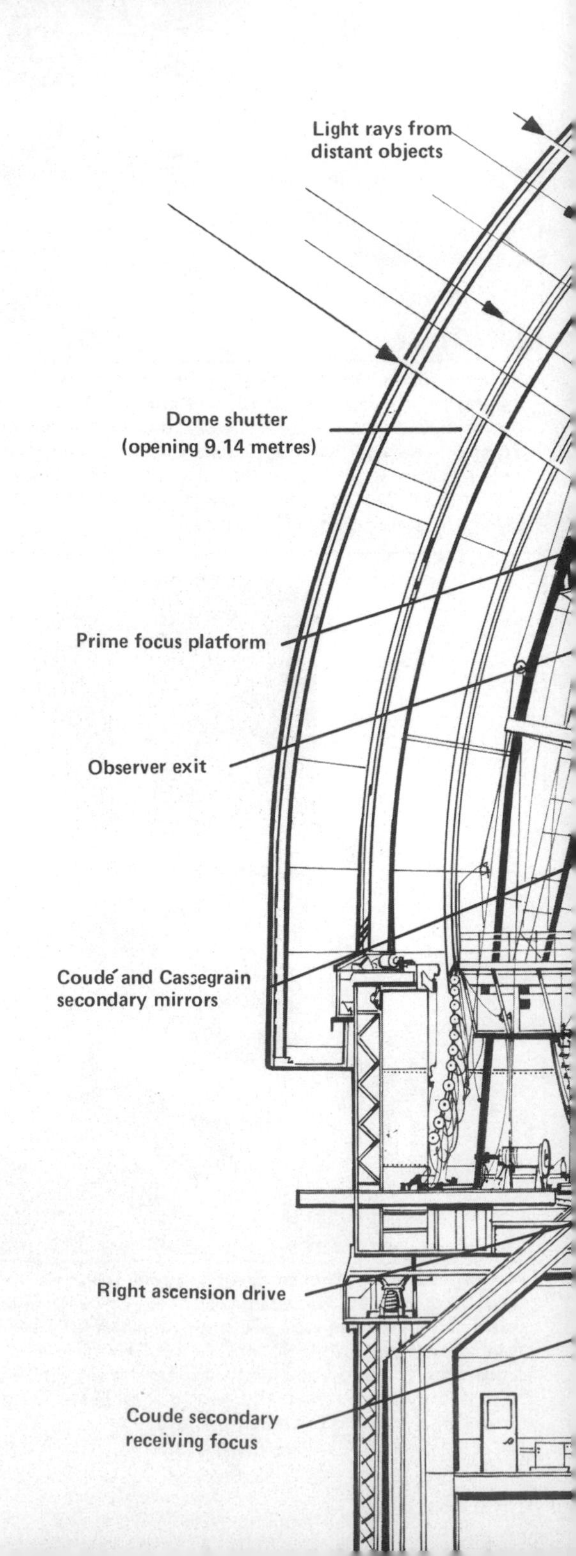

**It is important that large telescopes are sited in clear and steady air, to realise their potential. Most disturbance of light occurs in the lower levels of the atmosphere and this spoils definition. By siting in mountain areas, telescopes avoid the stray light scattered in the sky above cities, and are high above the disturbed air and ordinary fog-levels.**

# Where is the World's largest Telescope?

**Cavemen could only use their eyes to marvel at the sky. Today telescopes are helping us to understand our Earth, the stars and the Universe.**

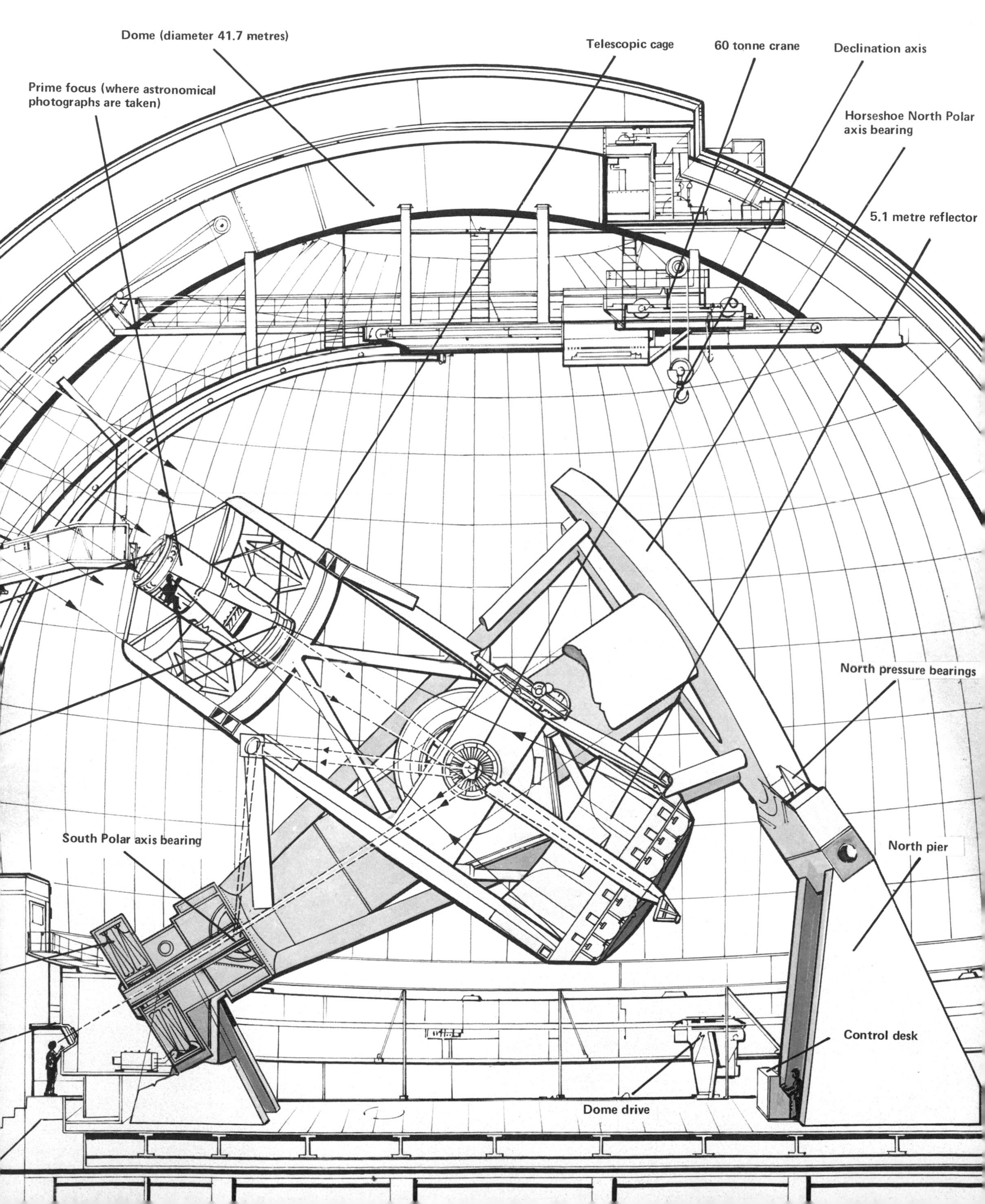

peak and the world's largest refracting telescope was built at Yerkes Observatory, Wisconsin, U.S.A. in 1897. The object lens had a diameter of 1 metre.

There was still a drawback, however. The lenses could obviously only be supported at their edges. The biggest lenses then had to be very thick to prevent sagging and distortion. But, in turn, this dimmed the view. Refracting telescopes could not get any bigger.

Scientists turned once more to mirrors. In a reflecting telescope, the mirror could be supported entirely at its base so mirrors could be made much larger than lenses. The reflective surface too had been improved, first by using *silver* on glass and later *aluminium*, which is cheaper.

The telescopes at Mount Palomar and at Zelenchukskaya were then built.

It is unlikely that a bigger telescope will now be built on Earth. By having telescopes on satellites in space the blurring effects of the Earth's atmosphere are removed. But the object will remain the same — to tell us more about the Universe of which we are such a very, very tiny part.

The Cone Nebula. A region where new stars and galaxies are forming out of dark clouds of gas and dust. (Mt. Palomar 5.1 metre reflector).

A spiral nebula of the constellation Eridanus, some 60 billion, billion kilometres from Earth. Its brightest stars are 80,000 times as bright as our Sun. (Mt. Palomar 5.1 metre reflector).

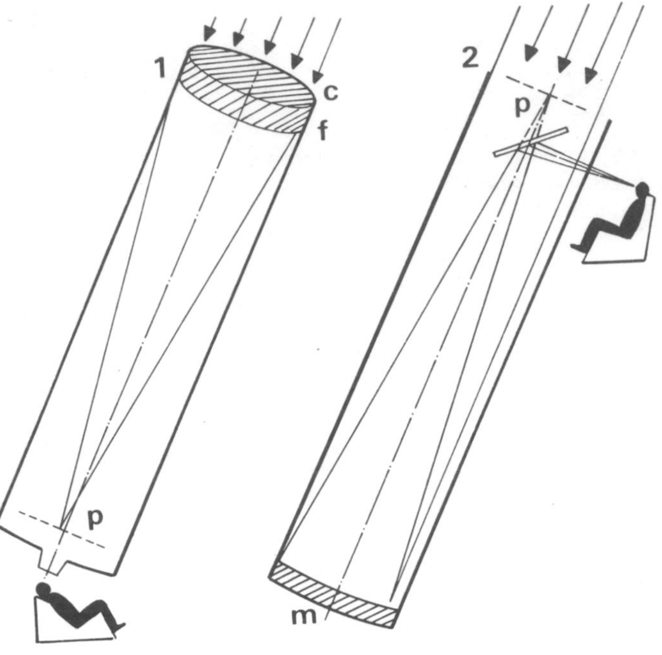


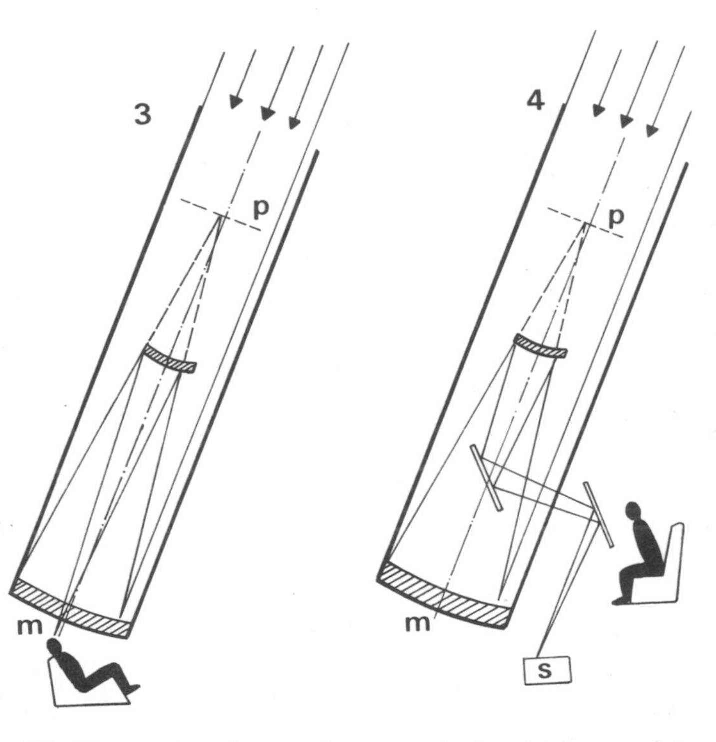


**(1) The refracting telescope (refractor) consists essentially of an object glass made up of two lenses, one convex (c), the other concave (f). The image of the star is formed in the focal plane (p).**

**There are three principal types of reflecting telescopes (reflectors):**

**(2) Newtonian reflector. The light rays collected by the curved mirror (m) and reflected to the focal plane (p) at which the image is formed. It is viewed in a small flat mirror.**

**(3) Cassegranian reflector. The light collected by the curved mirror (m) is reflected to the observer by a convex mirror.**

**(4) Spectroscopic reflecting telescope. The light from the mirror (m) is reflected from two flat mirrors to the spectrograph (electromagnetic radiation detector) at (s).**

# How correct is an Atomic Clock?

**TIME has fascinated and mystified men for centuries. To measure and record the passing of the hours, minutes and seconds is to be part of the great pageant of the Universe, to step into another dimension — Time.**

The great dream has been to build a clock that will be so accurate that it never runs fast or slow, making us certain of our time and place in the Universe. That is why attempts to measure time over hundreds of years have been important not only to people in their daily lives but to philosophers and thinkers. Is time never ending? Can we go back in time as the earth goes back around the sun in an eternal cycle?

The first and most perfect clock that Man has ever known is the Sun. Primitive man realised that during the various seasons, by shining on a particular object, the Sun creates a shadow that moves regularly with the passing of the hours.

Ancient peoples used this phenomenon to construct sundials, probably first made by the Sumerians over 5,000 years ago. Pictured above is a type found in Ancient Egypt. Below (centre) is the Meridiana of the Babylonians from about 900 B.C.

The Ancient Egyptians also originated the Clepsydra (above right). This worked on the hour-glass principle, water or sand dripping from the vessel at a constant rate. The Greeks and Romans used it at meetings to measure the time allowed to speakers. They also improved on the sundial, giving it a familiar classical appearance (left). Sundials of similar design are still seen in many gardens today. It was the Romans who took the water principle to construct ingenious water-clocks like the one on the right, made in about 50 B.C. As the level of the water went down, so the little figure descended, indicating the time on the cylinder.

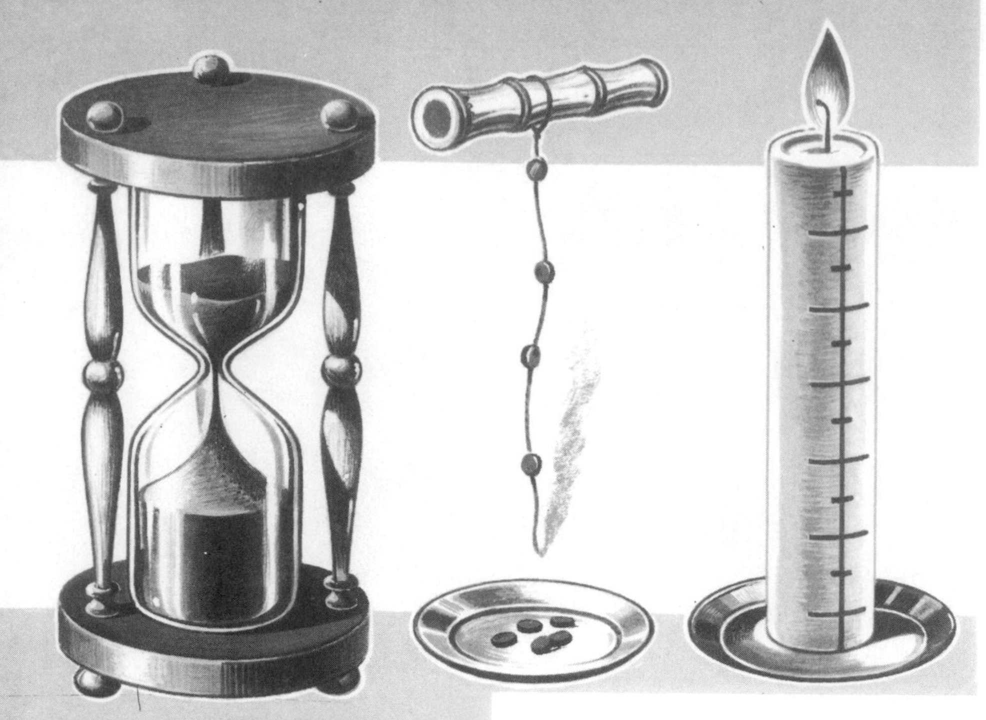

Later methods of measuring time. From left to right: a sand hour-glass; Chinese slow-burning taper clock with dropping weights; a marked candle clock. These were very inaccurate, possibly by as much as a quarter-hour in an hour. However, they were still used until about 1800.

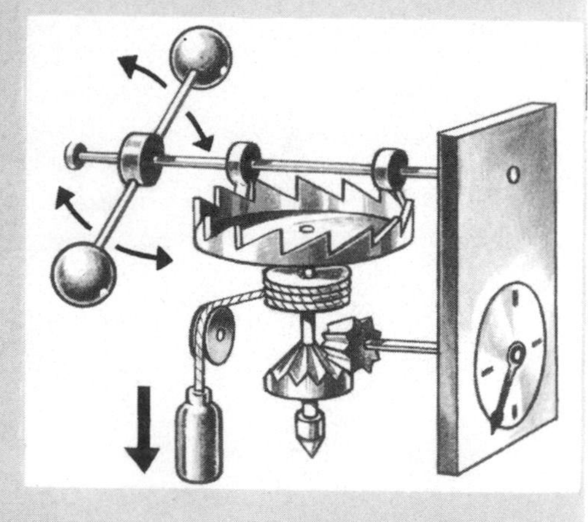

In Europe, the Foliot system of 1300 used falling weights (above) while Dondi's clock (below) had an elaborate mechanism of flywheels and counterweights.

It was in the great Italian cathedral at Pisa that the development of man-made clocks took a big step forward. Sitting, perhaps inattentively, during a service over 400 years ago, the young Galileo suddenly noticed something curious.

Great incense lamps were swinging to and fro, in regular time. Galileo realised that this regularity, whatever the range of swing, was so precise that it could be used to mark the pace of something. Trained as a doctor, he applied this idea to the measurement of pulse rates – indicating the pumping rhythms of the heart. But later on he began to apply it to building more accurate clocks. the *pendulum* clock was devised.

A heavy weight makes the pendulum swing by turning a drum to which a wheel is attached. This wheel turns another wheel using a cog mechanism and is attached to the pendulum. But at the top of the pendulum arm is a sort of lever called an 'escapement'. This takes the swing motion and converts it into a regular turning motion, moving the hands of the clock around the face.

But although Galileo invented this escapement device he was by no means the first to build an accurate clock.

## Ancient Clocks

The story of timekeeping goes back to very ancient civilisations who worked out methods for regulating their activities using the tools at their disposal. A stick thrust upright into the ground forms a crude sundial, the hours being shown by shadows formed by the Sun as it moves round in the sky. We know that the Egyptians living about 900 B.C. used sundials. Later the Israelites, Babylonians and Greeks also built them, all based on the shadow cast by a central projection or *gnomon*.

In the 16th century 'nocturnals' or moon dials were also made during the reign of Henry VIII. These told the time at night by observing fixed stars such as the Pole Star instead of the Sun.

Another ancient form of clock is the *clepsydra* or water clock which again dates back long before the birth of Christ. It consisted of a water vessel marked with rings or notches with an outlet from which the water flowed at an even rate. In many water clocks this outlet was a hole bored through a pearl because it was thought that this would not wear away. Sand or hour-glasses were used too, though like the water clock no one knows who invented them.

Interestingly we use this ancient technology today. Egg-timers are one example but so too is the famous two-minute hour glass in the House of Commons that marks the time the division bells ring to call members to vote.

Among other ancient time-measuring methods was the use of fire. An example is the Chinese slow burning taper clock. This was arranged underneath spaced and weighted strings. As the flame burnt through the strings the weight fell noisily into a brass tray underneath – a tiny clatter on every hour.

In Saxon Britain, it is said that Alfred the Great invented perhaps the simplest of all timepieces, a candle scored with lines at equal distances. The melting of the wax told the passing of the minutes.

## Wheels and Weights

Moving shadows, burning candles and falling water levels were useful within limits. But it was with the use of wheels, springs, weights and regulators that accuracy began to improve enormously. No one know for sure who made the first real clock, that is a mechanical devise powered by weights. What we do know is that they did not become numerous until the 13th century. Then a famous clock was built at Westminster on the proceeds of a fine imposed on a corrupt Chief Justice, Ralph de Hengham showing that crime does not pay – unless you are a clockmaker!

The clockmaker or horologist (a word formed from the Latin 'hora' meaning 'hour') became a sought-after member of society. When Dondi the Italian built his weight-driven clock for the Prince of Cararra, he and his descendants were given a title.

Clocks became smaller and smaller until, in the 15th century the pocket watch came on the scene. But by this time the weight supplying the driving power had been replaced by a device that is still with us today, the coiled spring. Coil up a

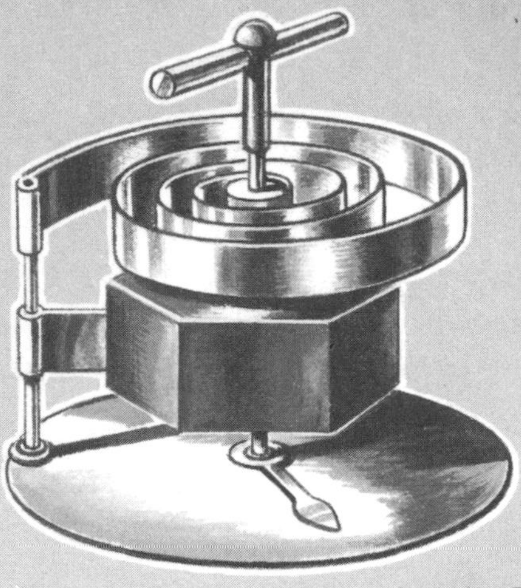

**Left: Galileo's 'escapement' clock. The escapement lever at the top of the pendulum turned the wheels and so the clock hands.**
**Above: This clock, from about 1500, used a wound-up mainspring whose tension was gradually released to drive the mechanism.**

**Above left: Huygen's balance spring clock of 1675. This was the first timepiece with accurate minute and second hands. This spring replaced the pendulum so the clock could be kept constantly moving.**
**Above: A fob watch with winding key. Invented about 1510, these were very popular until the wristwatch was invented.**

**Left: The grandfather pendulum clock; still popular after nearly 500 years.**
**Centre: A quartz crystal clock, developed in 1942, and regulated by a quartz crystal vibrating at constant frequency. Now available in smaller wristwatch form.**
**Right: The atomic clock — last word in accuracy. The steady frequency of vibrating atoms gives them an accuracy of one second in 3,000 years.**

spring and let it go. It releases energy which can be harnessed to power a watch. As it unwinds it turns a balance wheel which moves (like a pendulum) at a steady speed. The balance wheel moves the escapement which in turn moves the hands.

Thomas Tompion, the son of a Bedfordshire blacksmith, pioneered the first flat watches. He built clocks that ran for a year without winding — and this was more than 250 years ago.

Another great craftsman was John Harrison. In the early part of the 18th century he set out to win a prize offered by the Government for anyone who could make a watch so accurate that it could be used to ascertain the longitude of a ship at sea. This meant having a watch that would not vary by more than two minutes in six weeks, which at the time seemed to verge on the miraculous. But Harrison won the prize with his watch or *chronometer* ('time measurer') which turned out to have only varied by five seconds.

## Fashion

Not all new inventions were well received though. When the wristwatch was first introduced many people scorned it, preferring large fob or pocket watches. But the fashion caught on. Soon wristwatches were commonplace, with variations such as waterproof casing and self-winding mechanisms.

These were quickly seized on by willing customers. The mechanical watch was here to stay, and with it everyone had a convenient and accurate form of time measurement literally at the flick of the wrist. Clocks too underwent changes, with electric motors being used for powering their movements. Again no winding was necessary.

## Digital Quartz

Although even a cheap mechanical watch enables anyone to measure time with a precision undreamed of by the early clockmakers, modern technology has improved even on this. The digital quartz watch has no mechanical moving parts. It works by the vibrating effect of a quartz crystal driven by a tiny battery on a special light display and is accurate to within a few seconds a month.

But even this is nothing compared to the accuracy of atomic clocks used by scientists in experimental work. These require precision far beyond that we could possibly need in our everyday lives. The atomic clock, which works by monitoring the activity of atomic particles in special substances is the clock of the future, correct to within a tiny fraction of one second per year. It is the ultimate timepiece.

# What is the biggest Shovel in the World?

**Man has been digging and moving the earth for centuries, but where once he had only picks and shovels, now he uses engineering marvels like huge excavators.**

**THERE are many reasons for digging holes and moving earth. Apart from the familiar 'hole in the road', made to detect a leaking gas main or broken waterpipe, trenches are dug for laying services (drains, electric cables and so on) while holes are dug for the foundations of buildings. Earth is moved to fill in existing holes, for reclaiming land, for levelling the routes of roads and railways and for smoothing areas for use as airfields, playing fields or preparing a site ready to build an estate. The machines used to dig these holes are as varied in shape as they are in size.**

Men have dug up the earth and changed the profile of the landscape since earliest times. Their first efforts were simple holes with straight sides making a trap for animals to fall into. They probably also built small dams across streams to create water holes for washing and watering their herds.

The next development came when tribes recognised that some land formations were easier to defend than others. For instance high ground and gulleys helped the defenders. Communities learned to construct earth fortresses consisting of large mounds of earth surrounded by ditches which were difficult for an enemy to cross, with defendable trenches at the top of the mound. Remains of such forts can still be found in many places as you can see if you look at an Ordnance Survey Map of Great Britain. Long ditches were dug in some districts and these were probably boundaries of kingdoms.

Once early civilisations had developed, some impressive pieces of engineering were undertaken. The Romans built roads across Europe and the Middle East which entailed moving vast quantities of quarried paving stones and broken rock for foundations. Even before this, the Egyptians had dug a canal to link the River Nile with the Red Sea.

At first the barbarians who destroyed the Roman Empire were not interested in building, but after a few hundred years they evolved their own form of defence. This was a small man-made hillock, called a mote. On the top was constructed a

*Continued on page 42*

## CONTRAST IN STYLES

**The Victorian 'navvy' was probably the most efficient human earth mover in history. A typical recorded performance was that a fit navvy could lift 20 tonnes of muck from the ground into a truck in a day — and this meant throwing each shovel load up over the side of the truck which was considerably higher than his head.**

**To achieve this performance they ate well: their demands were 1 kg of steak and 4 litres of beer a day plus bread and vegetables or whatever else they fancied!**

**They were independent and well aware of their worth to any contractor. If they did not like a job they gathered their tools and tramped off to find another. They supplied their own basic tools, so on the march they carried all their tools and worldly goods: pick and shovel, wheelbarrow, lantern (for mining), blanket, flask (full of rum, beer, or water) and usually a sword or knife, because neither the camps nor the countryside were very safe in those days.**

**The *Queen* works one of the largest opencast mines in the world! *Queen,* a Type 5960 Marion Self-Propelled Electric Shovel, is the largest type of shovel in the world. Its weight in working order is over 8,000,000 kg! Its boom is 65m long, and the bucket scoops 95 cubic metres at a time.**

**It is working on the River Queen Surface Mine, Western Kentucky, U.S.A., and in one year it shifted nearly 200,000,000 cubic metres of earth to uncover 10,000,000 tonnes of coal. When it moves any considerable distance the boom is swung backwards. Its mobility was demonstrated in 1978 when it travelled nearly 12 km to a new coalfield under its own power.**

5960
RIVER QUEE
PEABODY
COAL CO.
5960

stockade called a bailey, which later was replaced with a castle.

Earthworks of this kind required the effort of a large number of local people and they needed to be organised. In the early empires this was not difficult. They used slaves and naturally the slaves had no alternative but to do as they were told, urged on with whips and threats of an unpleasant death.

The barbarians also had slaves, but not as many and not so well organised as the early empires, so their numbers had to be supplemented with freemen. No one is quite sure how this was done. 'Volunteers' were probably made to help under the threat of being thrown out of their village or losing the protection of their chieftain.

The methods these people used were simple but effective. They used picks and shovels of wood to break up the soil, fire to split rocks and baskets to carry the refuse from one place to another.

A modern example of how people in the ancient world may have used their manpower was demonstrated in China recently. There, although machinery is still expensive and in short supply, people are plentiful. A dam was needed across a large river to create a reservoir for an irrigation scheme. An appeal was made to the local population. They came in their thousands; men, women and children. They were told where to dig the soil, where to carry it and deposit it. The weaker members carried a little and made one journey each day; the fit carried large baskets of soil and made several journeys. Within a few weeks the dam was completed! Even with modern technology it would probably have taken a couple of hundred men with massive machinery several years.

## Industrial Revolution

Eventually the need for large castles disappeared and there was little need to move large amounts of earth until the Industrial Revolution occurred. Then the development of industry, particularly heavy industry, made it necessary to carry goods between factories and their suppliers and markets.

The roads at that time were in a very bad state. On many, wagons could not be used and goods had to be carried by pack horses. Wherever possible rivers were used for transport and some were made navigable. Then came the breakthrough — the introduction of canals.

The first major canal in Britain was the Bridgewater canal in Lancashire. It was built in 1761 for the transport of coal by barge from the pits at Worsley to the River Irwell where it could be transferred to larger ships.

A large number of towns and factories, encouraged by the success of this canal, began to build their own and this led to a period of 'canal mania'.

To build all the canals, or *navigations* as they were called, required huge armies of men, who were soon nicknamed 'navvies'.

The navvies of the 18th and 19th centuries were among the greatest earthmovers of all time. With the introduction of the railways, the demand for the navvies' services switched from canals. When they had finished building all the main railways in Britain they crossed the Channel and built many of the lines on the Continent.

With the harnessing of steam power it was inevitable that, before long, a steam-powered mechanical digger would be invented. The first steam shovels appeared in the 1840s.

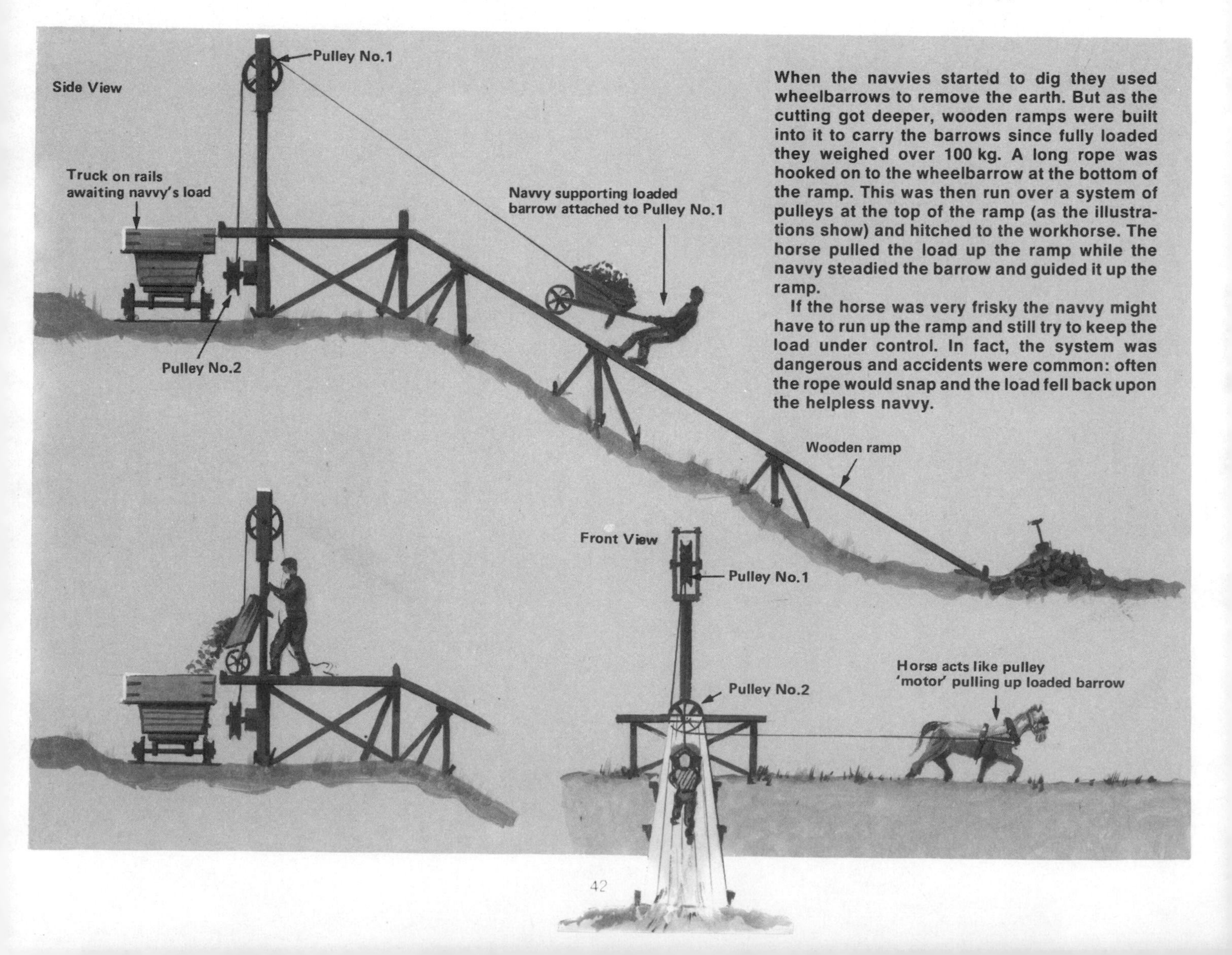


When the navvies started to dig they used wheelbarrows to remove the earth. But as the cutting got deeper, wooden ramps were built into it to carry the barrows since fully loaded they weighed over 100 kg. A long rope was hooked on to the wheelbarrow at the bottom of the ramp. This was then run over a system of pulleys at the top of the ramp (as the illustrations show) and hitched to the workhorse. The horse pulled the load up the ramp while the navvy steadied the barrow and guided it up the ramp.

If the horse was very frisky the navvy might have to run up the ramp and still try to keep the load under control. In fact, the system was dangerous and accidents were common: often the rope would snap and the load fell back upon the helpless navvy.

**Firms which undertake big construction jobs are known as contractors. They are usually equipped to undertake a variety of heavy work with machines which can be adapted to undertake a wide range of jobs. The vehicle shown below is typical. It weighs about 20 tonnes and the mobile boom to which different fitments can be attached is 7-8 metres long. The boom and the attachments are moved hydraulically by the driver. He controls the movements by means of a group of short levers. The hydraulic system receives its power from the pumps driven by the diesel engine. On the right are sketches of the main attachments which can be fitted and what work they carry out.**

Although the contractors were slow to accept this mechanised form of digging, eventually the machines took over from the navvies and a new age of mechanical excavators and earthmoving equipment had arrived.

The machines fall into three main categories: those that scoop, such as steam shovels, draglines and scrapers; those that drill, and (not counting the tools that make holes for piles) these are seldom seen because they usually work in tunnels; and those that push — the bulldozers. Some vehicles can do the work of several earth movers at once. A number of machines have a bulldozer at one end and a jib at the other, which can carry a number of different tools depending upon the job being done. They are an indispensible part of the construction industry.

**1. The back hoe (which is the attachment shown on the drawing below). It has a raking action drawing the earth towards the vehicle and is suitable for most earth-moving jobs including digging moderate trenches.**

**2. The clamshell — a tried and tested tool. It has a pincer action which enables it to bite into earth that is not too hard. It lifts about half a scoopful at each bite. The boom is used as a crane to lower the clamshell into position and for this reason it can dig deeper than the back hoe.**

**3. The ditch cleaning tool is a variation of the back hoe but has a more efficient design.**

**4. The face shovel scoops away from the vehicle; an action which has been found more suitable for quarry work and opencast mining.**

**5. Boring tools are lowered into position in a similar way to the clamshell. They only drill holes, usually for piles in foundations.**

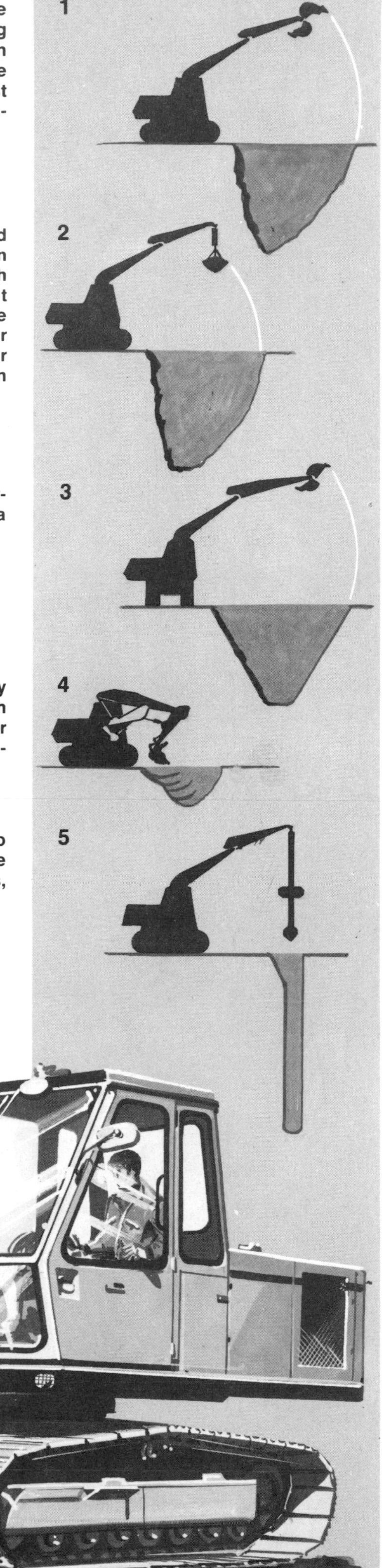

# Who Split the Mighty Atom?

1. Although remembered as having one of the most brilliant minds ever, Albert Einstein seemed academically slow as a child and still spoke poorly at nine years. Born into a Jewish family in Ulm, Germany on March 14, 1879, he disappointed at school, but when he was 10 years old developed a passionate interest in modern science and mathematics which was balanced by a deep love of music. In 1894, following several business failures, the Einsteins settled in Switzerland and two years later Albert entered the famous Zurich Polytechnic.

2. He was a gifted student and graduated in 1900 with a high-standard degree in mathematics and physics. He hoped to embark on a teaching career but no one could offer him a suitable post. In 1901 he took out Swiss citizenship and a year later found a job as a patents officer in Berne. It was interesting work but not difficult, and left him time for other studies. In 1905 he published some of the most famous papers in the history of physics, successfully challenging previous scientific laws. The scientific world now took notice of the previously obscure theorist.

3. In the years following, Einstein developed and perfected his ideas and various academic positions came his way. In 1912 he became a professor at the Zurich Polytechnic and then director of the prestigious Kaiser Wilhelm Institute in Berlin. 1919 saw the publishing of his brilliant 'Theory of General Relativity'. When its predictions were confirmed by observation of an eclipse of the Sun, Einstein became world renowned and an eagerly sought-after personality.

4. His life was transformed. In 1921 he was awarded the Nobel prize for Physics. He took visiting professorships in England and America explaining his theories and making speeches. The First World War had disturbed him greatly and his constant message was that nations should co-operate intellectually and scientifically for their mutual benefit. But the dark clouds of Fascism were gathering over Europe and Nazi Germany was no place for a Jew, not even the famous Einstein.

5. In 1933, while lecturing in America, Einstein learned that the Nazis had confiscated his property. He could not return to Germany. Instead he took a post at the Institute of Advanced Study in Princeton, New Jersey, U.S.A. When world war broke out in 1939 Einstein had to make a critical decision. His theories made possible the construction of an atomic bomb of huge destructive power. The idea of such a weapon in Nazi hands was appalling, so Einstein wrote his famous letter to President Roosevelt. As a result the 'Manhattan Project' was born ensuring that America produced the bomb first.

6. Although a pacifist, Einstein knew he had to reveal the secrets of the atomic bomb. But he was now so famous that it was very difficult for him to maintain his scientific output. Much of the war he spent helping refugees from Europe. His health was failing and he wanted peace and quiet, playing the violin and sailing his boat. Even so, he always remained humble and approachable — a shambling, good-natured genius. This century's greatest man of science died in Princeton on April 18, 1955.

**THE Theory of Relativity destroys conventional 'logical' thinking on many subjects, but perhaps one of the most bizarre things it shows is that time itself varies. This is as difficult for us to grasp today as it was for medieval people to realize that the Earth went round the Sun.**

**The top diagram shows a man sitting in a moving train. If he switches on a light on the floor (1), the light is then reflected by a mirror (2) back down to the floor again. We cannot see light moving, but if we could, the man would see the light go up to the ceiling and straight back down (3).**

**Now look at the bottom diagram. This shows what a man standing outside the train would see as it passed him by. In the time it takes for the light to go up to the ceiling and back down again the train has moved a small distance to the right, that is from 1 to 5.**

**So the man outside the train sees the light go from 1 to 3 to 5. And as the diagram shows, the light's path (2 and 4) that he sees is longer than its path (3) as seen from inside the train. In the 'same time', the man outside has seen the light go farther than the man inside.**

**However, it is a fundamental law of physics that light always travels at the same speed — 2,998km per second — so how can this be?**

**There is only one answer. Time itself must vary and be relative to the two men. Because he saw the light travel farther, the man outside the train *must* have been there for a longer time than the man inside the train.**

**Of course, with trains on Earth the difference between the times inside and outside is so infinitesimal that there would be no measurable difference between the two men's watches. In our everyday lives, time never varies.**

**But imagine if a spaceman set off round the Universe at a speed approaching that of light. His time is far shorter than time back on Earth. So it is possible that if he left his twin brother behind when he set off, when he got home his brother could be 20 or 30 years older than he was.**

# How does an Ejection

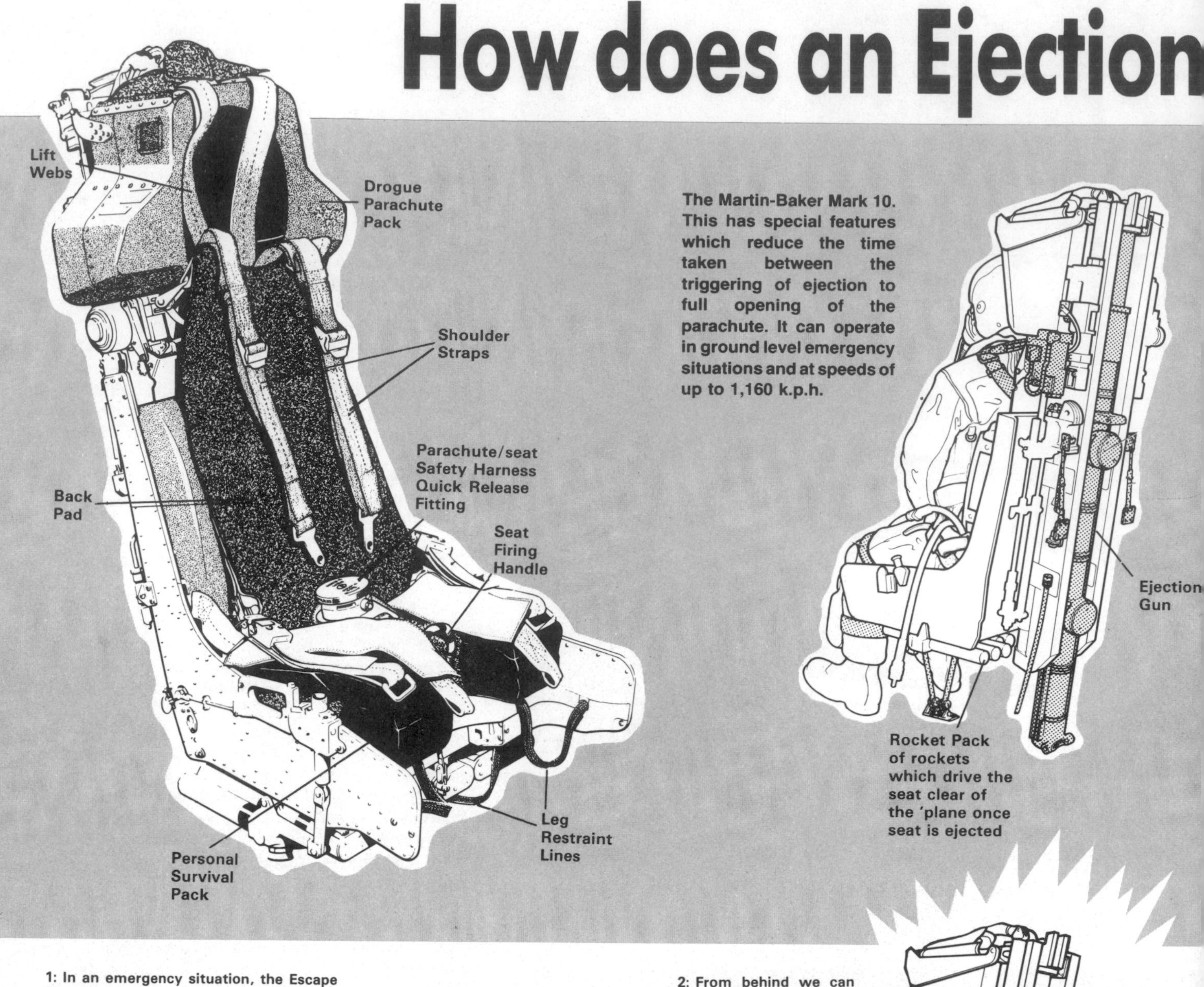


The Martin-Baker Mark 10. This has special features which reduce the time taken between the triggering of ejection to full opening of the parachute. It can operate in ground level emergency situations and at speeds of up to 1,160 k.p.h.

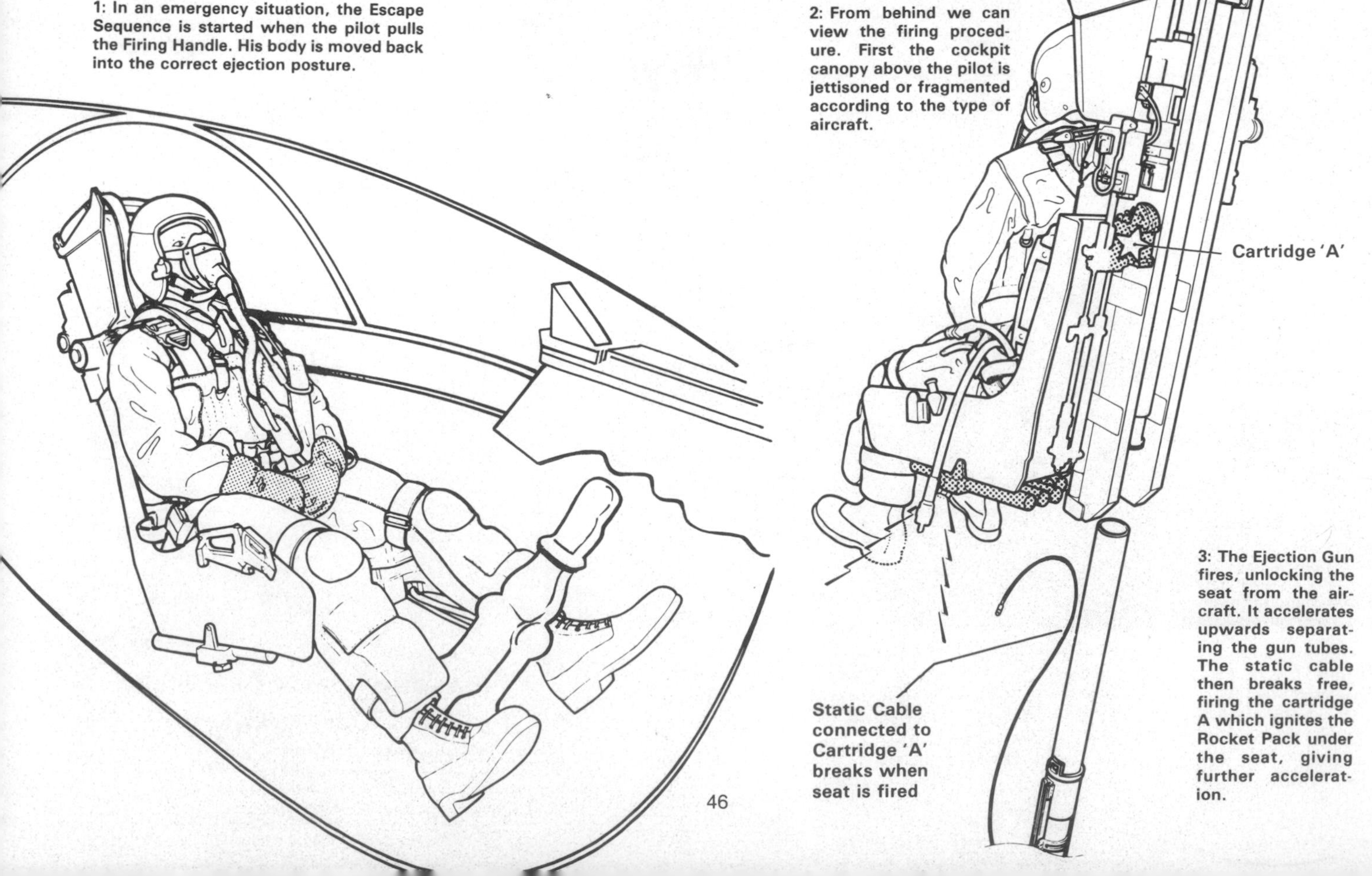


1: In an emergency situation, the Escape Sequence is started when the pilot pulls the Firing Handle. His body is moved back into the correct ejection posture.

2: From behind we can view the firing procedure. First the cockpit canopy above the pilot is jettisoned or fragmented according to the type of aircraft.

3: The Ejection Gun fires, unlocking the seat from the aircraft. It accelerates upwards separating the gun tubes. The static cable then breaks free, firing the cartridge A which ignites the Rocket Pack under the seat, giving further acceleration.

# Seat operate?

**Hundreds of pilots are alive today thanks to an engineering marvel the ejection seat — which in an emergency can hurl a man to safety with the speed and accuracy of a bullet. And much of the credit for this proud record must go to a man named James Martin, his design team and human 'guinea pigs', for it is their dedicated work which has helped to perfect this life-saving device.**

*See story on next page*

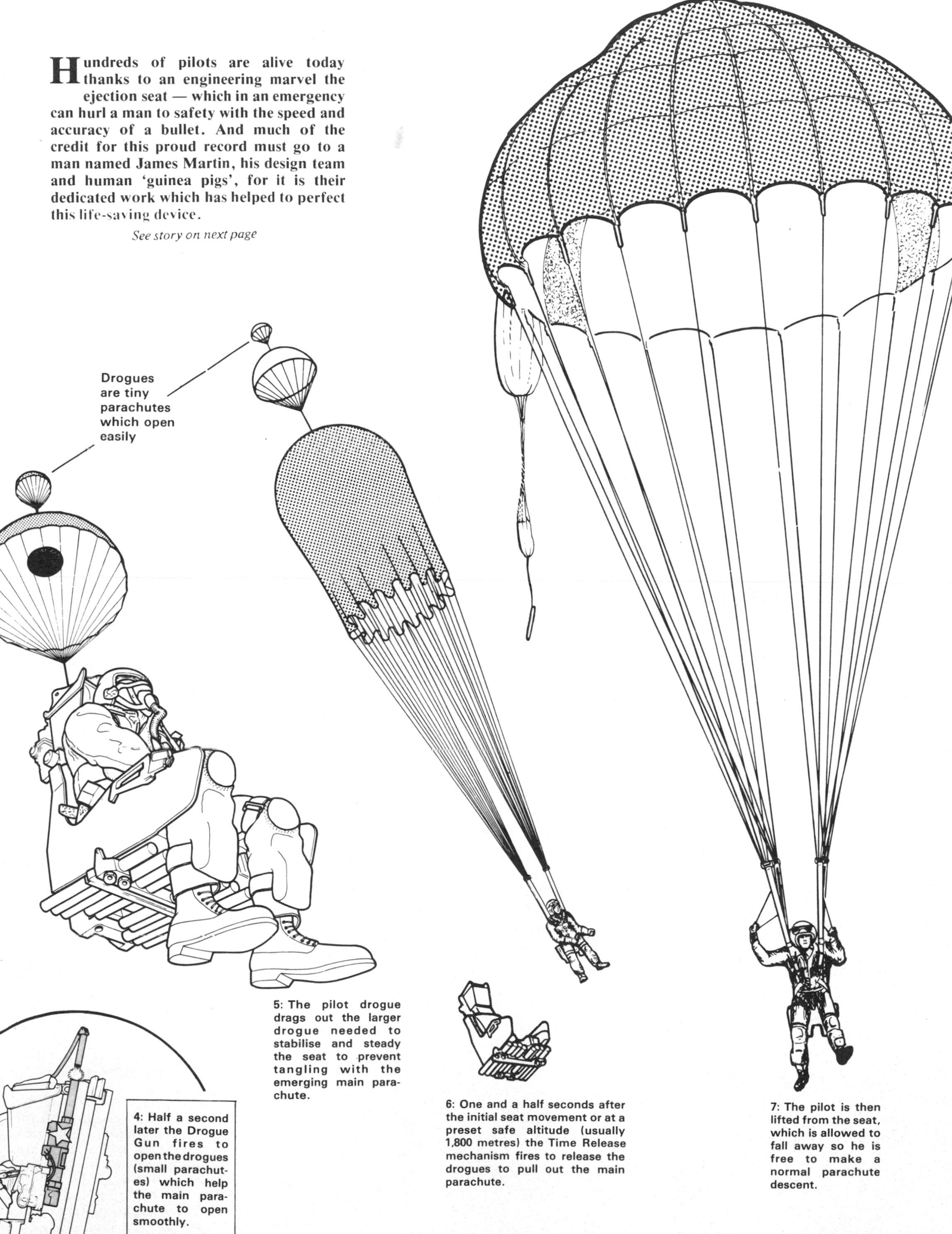




The help of the Martin-Baker Aircraft Company Limited in the preparation of this article is gratefully acknowledged.

# Up, up, and away from death!

Towards the end of World War 2 emergency parachute jumps from military aircraft were becoming increasingly difficult. The introduction of jet-powered aircraft with their vastly increased speed virtually eliminated the possibility of a successful 'over the side' bale-out.

The first ejection seat, installed in a German Heinkel He82 jet fighter, was operated by compressed air, and saved the life of the pilot, Major Schenk, in January 1942. However, serious research did not begin until 1944 when Mr James Martin (later Sir James Martin), of the Martin-Baker Aircraft Company, was invited by the Ministry of Aircraft Production in London to investigate practical methods of assisted escape for pilots in an emergency.

After investigating alternative schemes it became apparent that this could best be achieved by forced ejection of the pilot's seat using an explosive charge. Once out, the pilot would release himself from his seat and continue his descent on a conventional parachute.

To investigate the effects of this thrust on the human body an experimental fitter with the firm, Mr. Bernard Lynch, made nearly 200 test 'shots' in an experimental seat fired on a five metre ramp. Finally, on July 24, 1946, Mr. Lynch ejected from an aircraft flying at 2,400 metres. He suffered no ill effects and the seat went into production.

Research has continued ever since and seats have become increasingly sophisticated. Considerable experimentation finally produced automatic seats which could save the life of an injured man who became unconcious during ejection. Some seats are fitted with rocket motors as well as the ejection gun to increase the height attained by the seat. This means that the seats can be operated even in ground level emergencies as the seat is propelled to a height of 300 feet (91 metres), which is high enough for a parachute to open fully. The most up-to-date systems can be programmed to eject four crewmen in succession on the single pressure of a button, and some ejection seats work under water, first ejecting the pilot and then inflating a buoyancy device automatically.

Martin-Baker ejection seats are in use with air forces all over the world. Many thousands of lives have been saved, a tribute indeed to the progress that has been made since 1944 and the research that continues to keep pace with the development of modern aircraft.

**This extraordinary photo-sequence shows an ejection seat operating in an emergency situation. As the F8 Crusader jet fighter touched the aircraft carrier's flight deck a landing wheel buckled, starting a fire in the undercarriage. The blazing jet had nearly reached the end of the deck (picture 1) when the pilot decided to eject. The cockpit canopy was blown off (inset picture) and the pilot in his seat was shot 55 metres into the air (2). As his plane plunged into the sea the pilot's seat fell away and the smaller drogue parachutes emerged to pull out the main chute (3) which opened a moment before he landed in the water. One soaking the pilot didn't worry about!**

# What is an Electron Microscope?

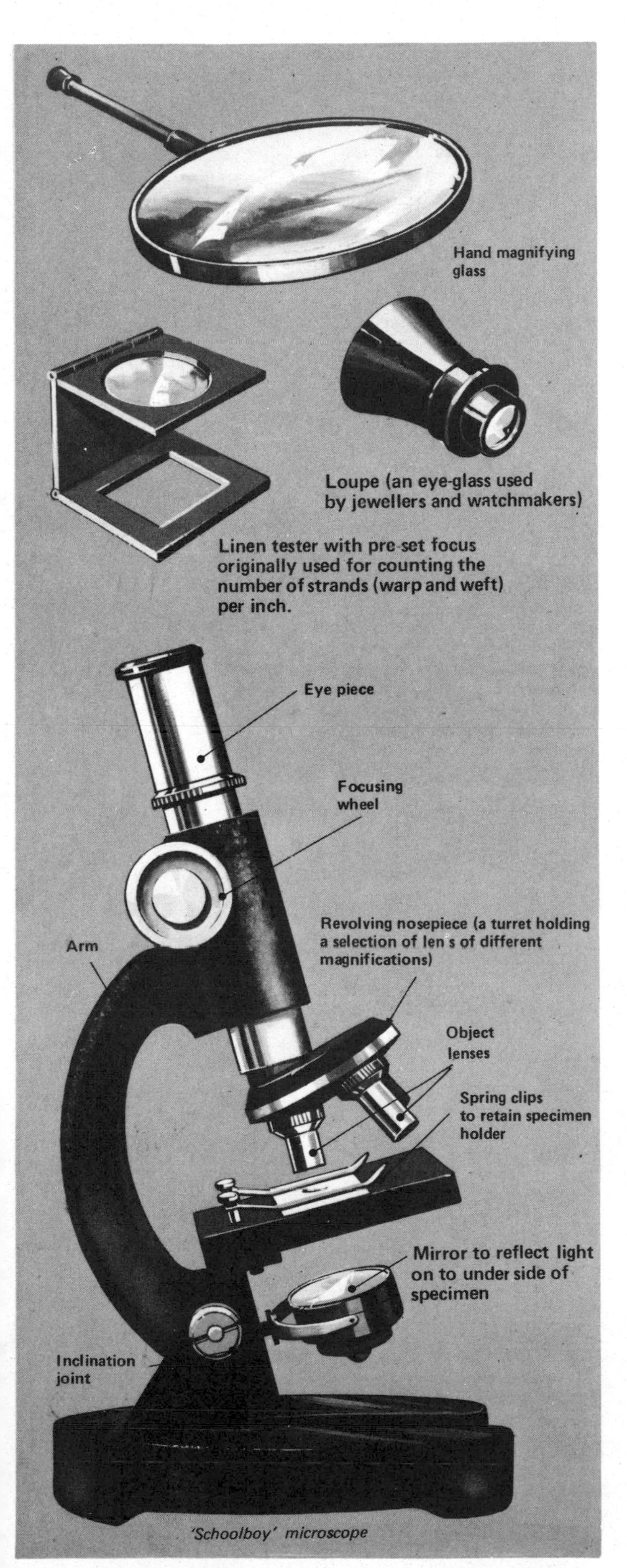

*'Schoolboy' microscope*

**MICROSCOPES, which enable us to examine objects much too small to be seen clearly, or even at all, with the naked eye, are one of the most important instruments in scientific research.**

The most elementary form of microscope uses one lens and is known as a *simple* microscope. Among the most common examples are the pocket magnifier and the hand reading glass. These

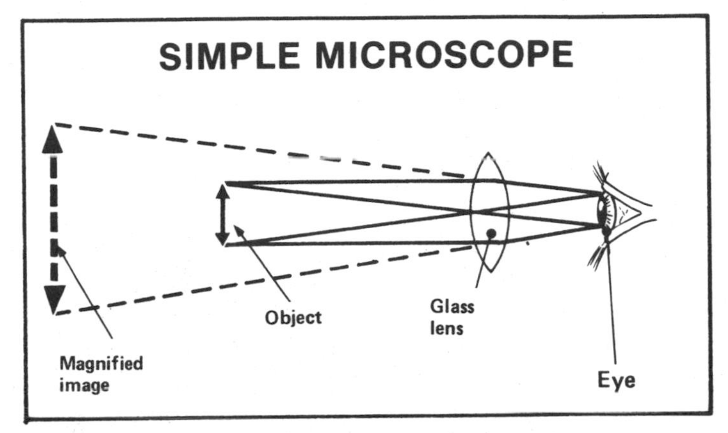


consist of a single lens and they work by bending the light waves from the object being viewed so that you see it as if it were much larger than it really is.

But a single-lens microscope's range of enlargement is only about three times the size of the original object. After that, distortions appear, particularly towards the edges, because the lens cannot be ground fine enough.

This difficulty can be largely overcome by using a combination of lenses in what is called a *compound* microscope. Such a microscope has two lenses, the second lens magnifying the image already magnified by the first lens. The first such instrument was invented as long ago as 1590 by Zacharias Janssen.

## New world

The limit of magnification of a compound light microscope is around two thousand times. But even half this strength of magnification is sufficient to reveal a whole new world of knowledge. Many germs can be seen clearly, red blood cells are nearly five millimetres across, the make-up of the tissues of the body and of plants can be identified and examined.

But it was only with the invention of the *electron* microscope in the first half of this century that it became possible to view even tinier objects.

The reason that an electron microscope can give greater magnification than a light microscope is the nature of light itself.

Light is made up of waves, and the distances between the individual troughs and peaks of these waves is about half a micron. (One micron is one millionth of a metre).

With most objects — which are much bigger than the wavelength of light — the light waves are reflected by the object, and it is these reflected waves that are seen by the eye. But problems occur with tiny objects less than about half the wavelength of light. Such objects cannôt reflect light properly and hence, however good the microscope, it is impossible to see objects this small.

The electron microscope solves this problem. Instead of light, it uses a beam of *electrons* — the minute negatively charged particles that orbit the central core of atoms. (Atoms are the tiny particles that make up all matter).

The electrons are generated by an *electron gun,* like the one in the tube of a television set. The beam of electrons produced by

*continued on next page*

## COMPOUND MICROSCOPE

**Upside down, but much bigger — that's the effect looking through a microscope has on the object being viewed. The first lens — the object lens — produces an enlarged 'real' image (that is the image could be thrown on to a screen if one were placed there), and it is this image that you see when you look through the eyepiece lens. This lens bends the light entering your eye making it *look* as if it came from a bigger object — the second image. This second image is unreal (scientists call it a *virtual* image); it cannot be thrown on to a screen and is the same sort of image as that produced by a simple magnifying lens or simple microscope.**

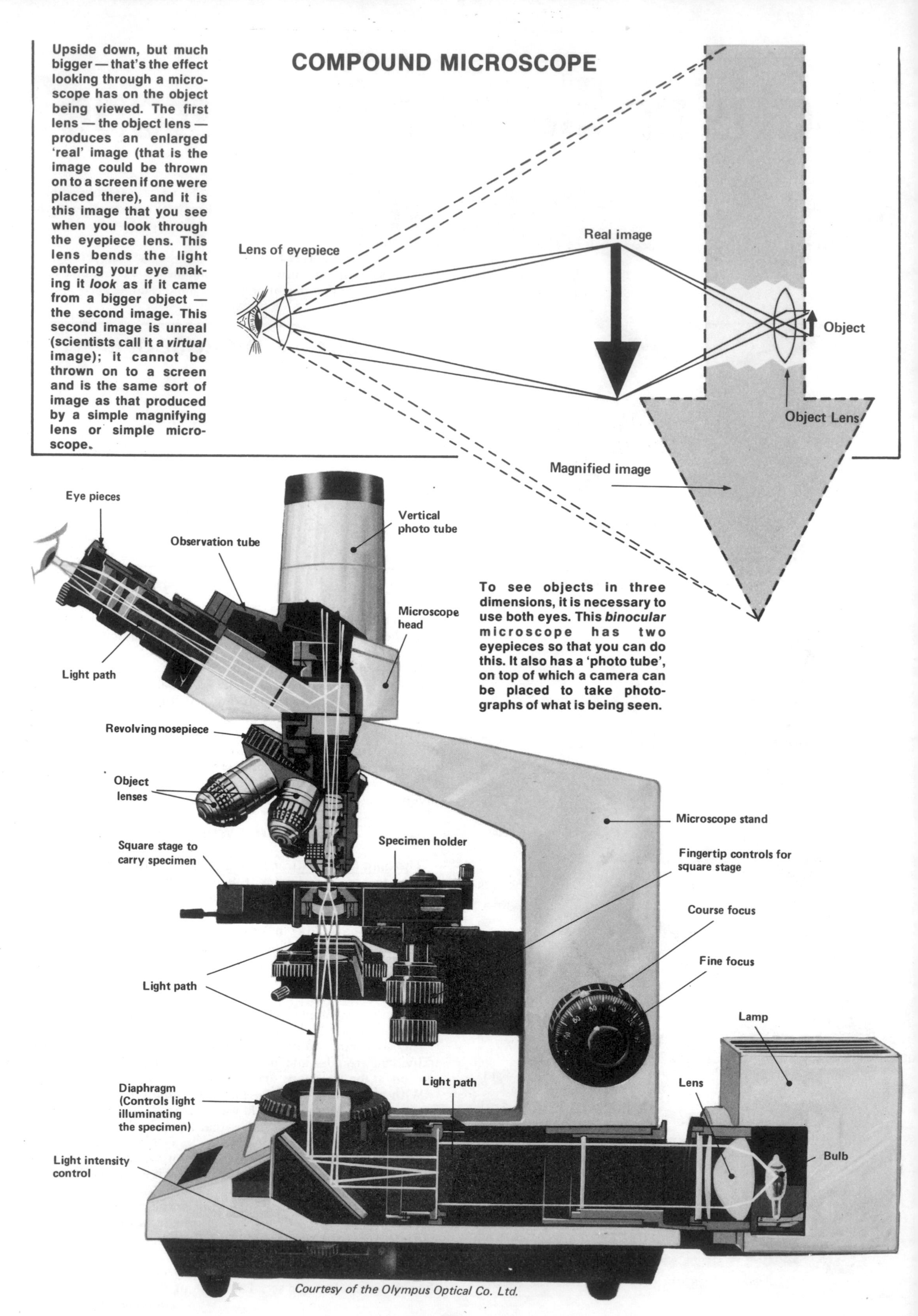


**To see objects in three dimensions, it is necessary to use both eyes. This *binocular* microscope has two eyepieces so that you can do this. It also has a 'photo tube', on top of which a camera can be placed to take photographs of what is being seen.**

*Courtesy of the Olympus Optical Co. Ltd.*

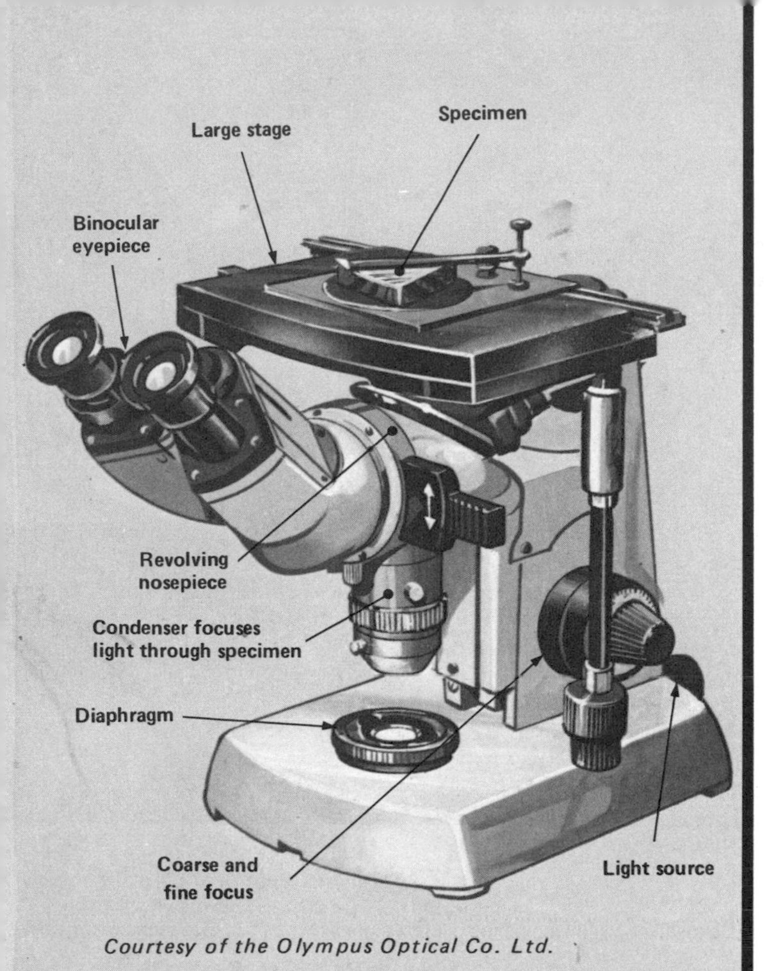


*Courtesy of the Olympus Optical Co. Ltd.*

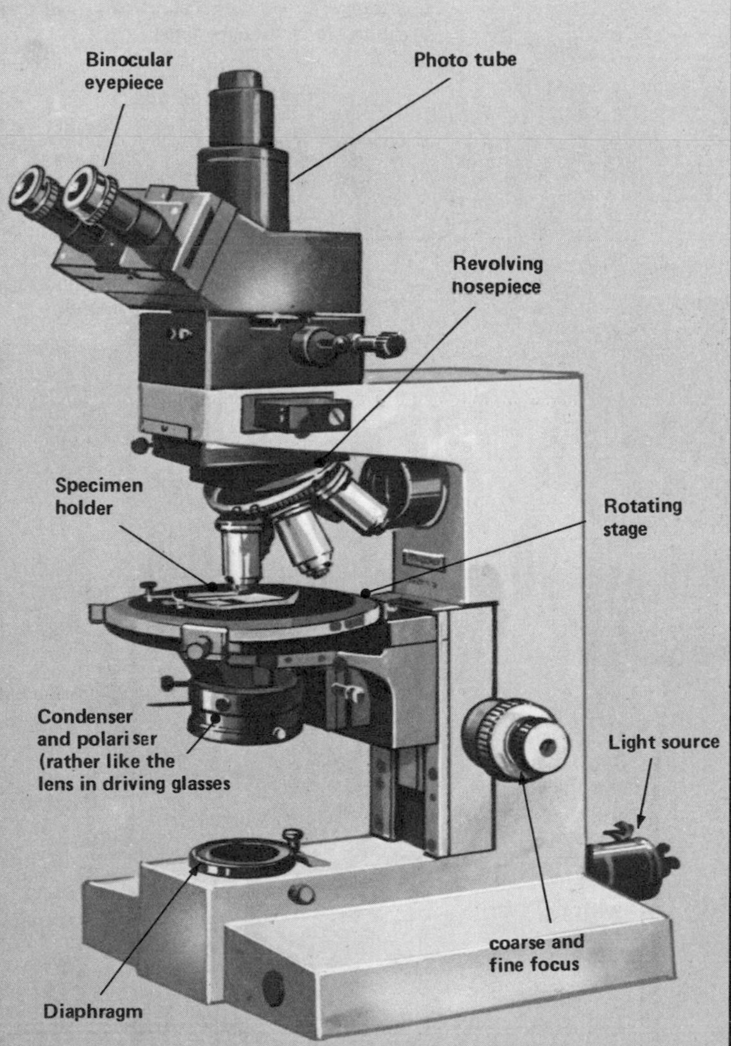


**Specialist microscopes are used for specialist tasks. These two are used by geologists for studying rocks. The 'inverted' microscope (top) is used for viewing whole samples rather than thin slices of them. The light is reflected from the surface of the rock. The 'polarising' microscope (above) uses polarised light (light in which all the waves are vibrating in the same direction as in Polaroid sunglasses) to give a clearer image.**

the gun can be bent by electromagnetics or by electrostatic forces (as produced by a capacitor) in much the same way as a beam of light can be bent by a lens. So a microscope can be made using a beam of electrons passing through one or more electromagnets or electrostatic fields instead of a beam of light passing through one or more lenses.

There would be no point in doing this, of course, if it were not for the fact that an electron microscope can 'see' objects much smaller than those visible with a light microscope. This is because the wavelength of the beam of electrons is more than 100,000 times shorter than the wavelength of light. This means that an electron microscope can 'see' things as small as 0.0002 microns.

With the electron microscope it is possible to see distinctly rust crystals, although there are more than 150 million of them in a square one centimetre across; it is also possible to see viruses, and the genes that are the units of heredity.

Of course, the electron beam cannot be 'seen' in the same way as light can be. But it can be focused on to a screen similar to a television screen. The final image produced on the screen may have been magnified by up to 800,000 times. This screen can then be photographed and even greater magnification obtained by enlarging the photograph.

Looking at such photographs, we can 'see' with our own eyes things far too small to be properly seen at all.

**Below: Part of the new world of the electron microscope. This is 'fur' inside a kettle magnified about 1300 times.**

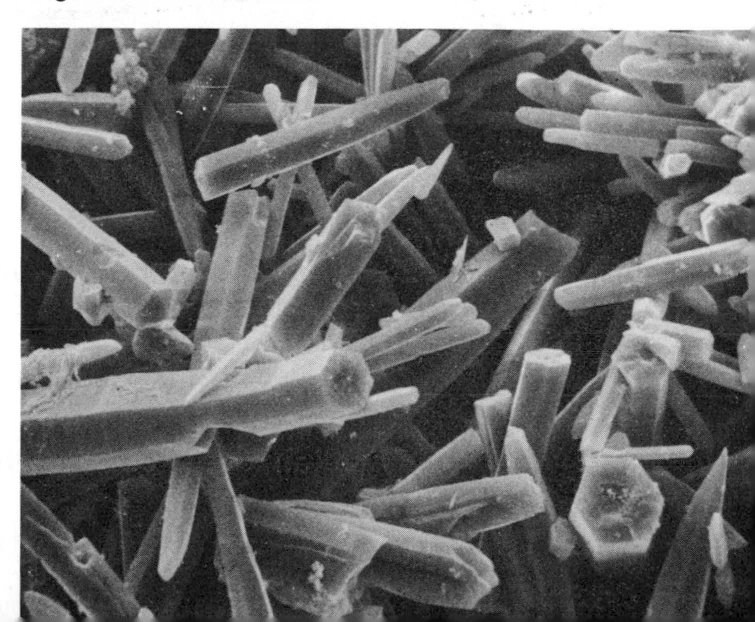

## THE ELECTRON MICROSCOPE

**Because it works by means of a beam of electrons rather than a beam of light, the electron microscope allows us to see things as small as 0.0002 microns (one fifty-thousandth of a millionth of a metre). These pictures show the Philips EM400T electron microscope which uses condensors (capacitors) as lenses to bend the beam of electrons. The microscope can be combined with auxiliary equipment such as an X-ray analyser (for studying crystal structure using a beam of X-rays) and a computer to give even more detailed analysis of the specimen.**

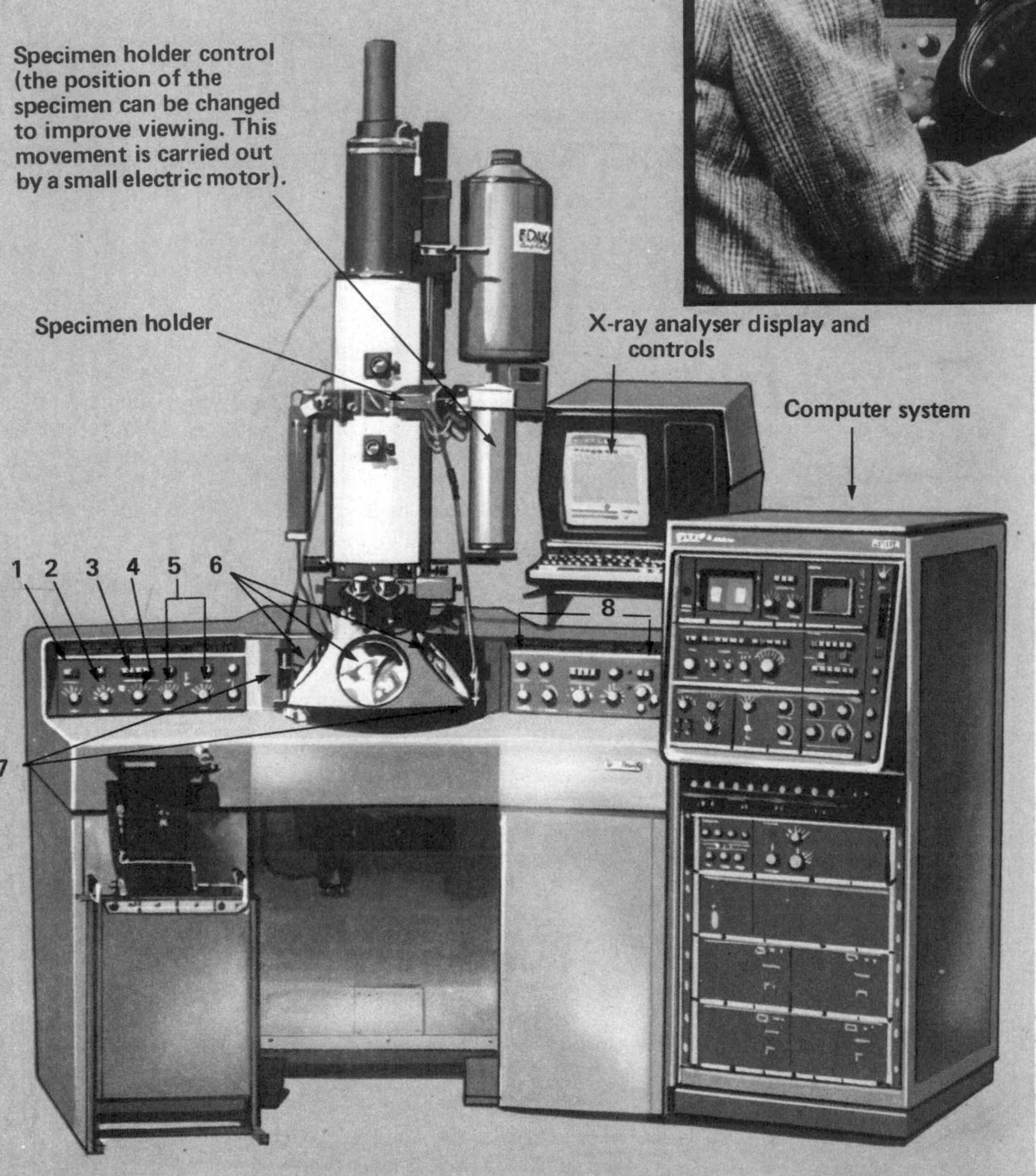


**A**

Electron gun alignment coils (like the barrel of a gun, these make sure the electrons start off in the right direction).

**B**

Condensers focus the electrons – like an ordinary lens focuses light

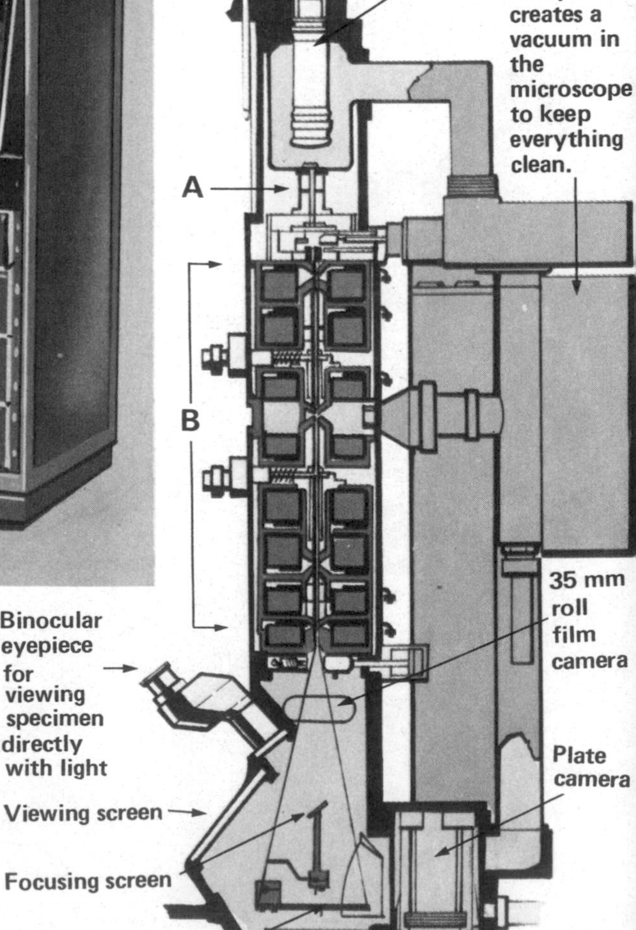


## THE ELECTRON MICROSCOPE

1. **Mains electricity supply switch**
2. **Electricity controls**
3. **Camera selector (plate camera or roll film camera)**
4. **Exposure time control**
5. **Camera controls**
6. **Viewing screens**
7. **Focusing control for viewing screens**
8. **Vacuum, magnification and specimen-holder controls**

# Who invented the first Lift?

**IF the lift had never been invented the skylines of the world's big cities would look very different today. Just think how impossible it would be to live and work in a skyscraper without one.**

For example, it would probably take several hours to reach the top of the Empire State Building, New York's famous skyscraper, and that's assuming you had enough energy to climb all the stairs! People working in London's tower block, the National Westminster Building, would find that by the time they walked up to their offices it would almost be time to start off down again! Lifts transport people up those stairs in minutes.

But although skyscrapers are a modern development, lifts are not. In 236 B.C. Archimedes, the Greek scientist and inventor, had used a lift. This would have been a windlass lift, raised or lowered on a rope that unwound from a spool. It would have been hand operated.

## The 'flying chair'

A similar type of lift was used in medieval times by the monks at Meteora in Greece. They built their monasteries high on the top of natural rock pinnacles, safe from bands of robbers. The only entrance was hundreds of metres up a sheer rock face, and to reach it the monks used a windlass lift fitted with a net.

During the 17th century a passenger lift, known as the 'flying chair', was invented by a Parisian builder named Villayer. This was nothing more than a chair attached to a rope which passed over a

Continued on page 55

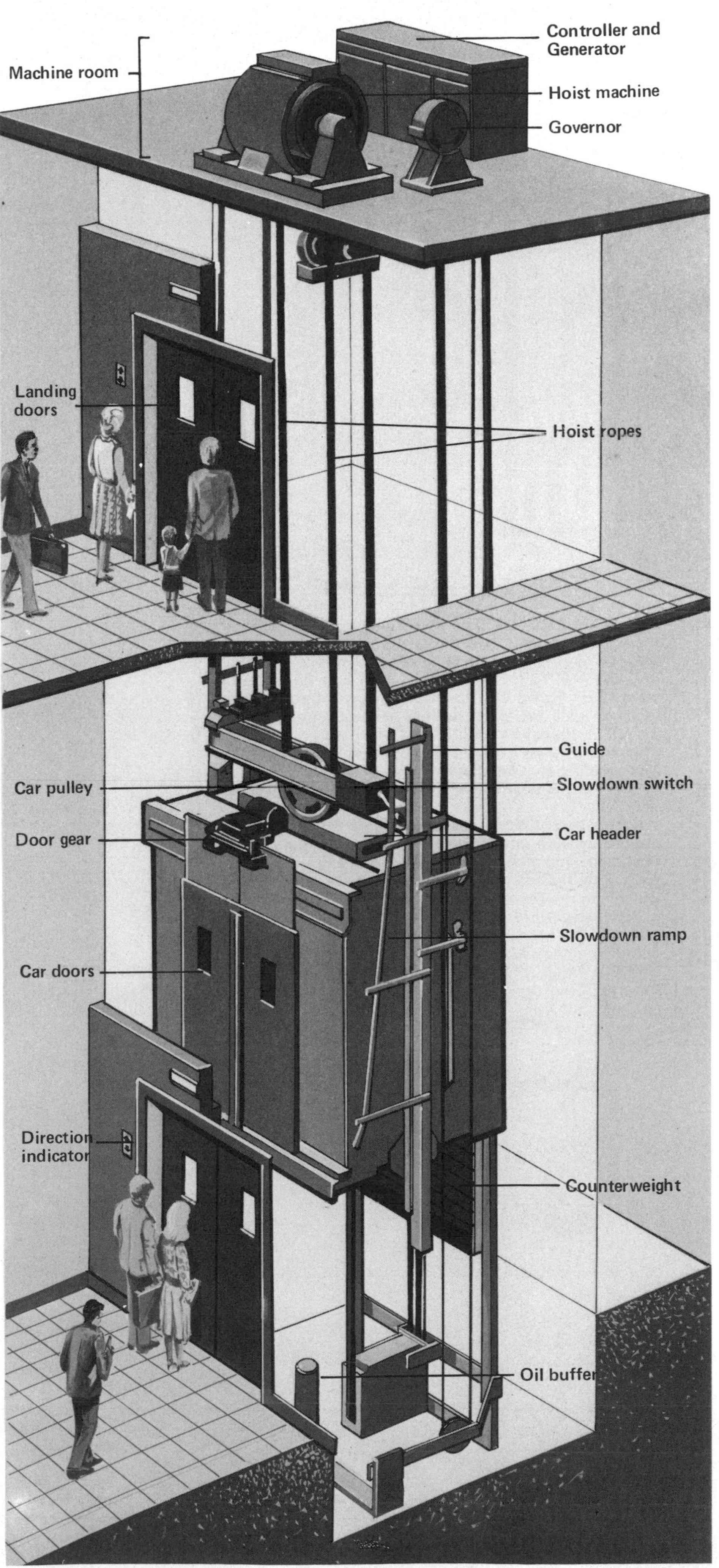


**The electric-powered lift shown on the right is typical of modern design. Though it is only depicted as serving two floors it might very well serve many more.**

**The diagram shows how the hoisting ropes — which, despite their name, are steel cables — are attached to the top of the car of the lift and run up to the hoisting mechanism. From there the hoisting ropes are led to the side of the lift shaft and attached to counterweights.**

**For clarity the diagram shows only one hoisting rope but in practice there are always six or eight cables, each of which is capable of holding the car.**

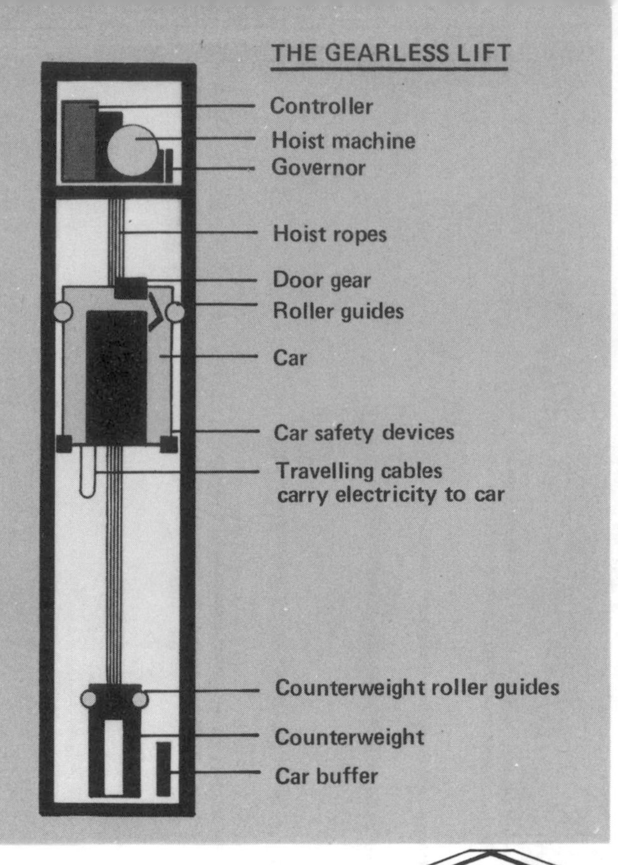


The GEARLESS LIFT (see above) is so called because the electric motor drives directly onto the hoist sheave. This is a roller that in turn drives the hoisting ropes which are attached to the car on one side and the counter weights on the other. This arrangement means that the motor is only lifting the weight in the lift and not the weight of the car as well.

Geared lifts work on a similar principle but have gears interposed between the motor and the sheave. This makes for a slower lift but permits a heavier load to be handled.

HYDRAULIC LIFTS (see below) were popular at one time. They were raised and lowered by means of a 'ram', or plunger. The plunger was a piston working in a cylinder (or a series of pistons working in a series of cylinders) which was driven upwards by water being forced into the cylinder under pressure. To lower the lift the water was let out of the cylinder under careful control. At that time many big cities had hydraulic companies which ran pipes carrying water at high pressure under the streets to be used to power services such as lifts, hoists and cranes.

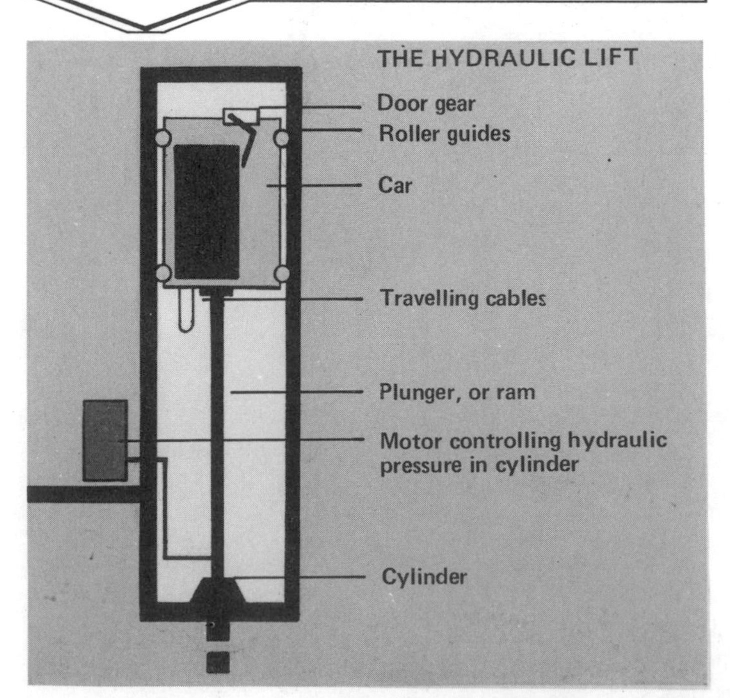

The 23-storey Hyatt Regency Hotel in Atlanta uses capsule-like elevators for hotel passenger service. Can these lifts outside a building be the pattern for the future?

pulley to a lead counterweight, and enclosed in a shaft. However, it caught the imagination of the wealthy and is said to have been installed at Windsor Castle for Queen Anne. But Villayer disappeared shortly after Louis XVI's daughter was involved in a serious accident while using one of the chairs at Versailles.

When power was substituted for muscle with the coming of steam, great strides were made in the design of lifts. At the beginning of the 1880's a German is recorded as having invented a mechanical mine hoist, and there are also records to show that a power driven lift was operating in an English factory in 1835.

By the middle of the 19th century many factories had installed lifts to carry components from one floor to another. One type consisted of a simple wooden platform supported by a steel ram surrounded by a cylinder. Water was pumped into this cylinder so causing the ram to rise, taking the platform with it. Another type was supported by a huge iron screw, which ran through the middle of the lift car down the whole length of the lift shaft. A steam engine in the basement of the building turned the screw and so propelled the lift up and down.

## Safety first

The early faster-moving rope-suspended lifts were very unsafe for, if the rope snapped, the car simply crashed down to the ground, having no other means of support to keep it up. Then, in 1854, an American, Elisha Otis, demonstrated a safety device at the World's Fair in the Crystal Palace Exhibition, New York. This device consisted of a large waggon or coach spring which, if the rope broke, immediately locked into ratchets and held the car firmly in position.

During the demonstration Otis was enthusiastically applauded by an admiring crowd when the rope of the car was cut through and he, and the car, remained safely suspended in the lift-shaft.

At first the Otis company was selling lifts purely for freight purposes. Then, on March 23, 1857, Otis installed the world's first passenger elevator in the store of E. V. Haughwout and Company, situated in New York. The building was five storeys high, which was considered quite tall for its day. Power for the lift came through a series of shafts and belts driven from a central steam power source. It was capable of lifting 450 kg at the rate of 12 metres per minute.

Although Otis died in 1861 his sons carried on the work of the Otis company.

In 1878 a new development came into operation — the hydraulic lift, (see diagram on previous page) and in 1889 the first successful electric lifts were installed.

## Higher and better

Along with the electric lift came a system of electric motor-control, called the Ward-Leonard system, which gives the smooth operation of lifts that we have today. The new system provided a simple means of electric control of the generator that supplied electric power to the lift hoisting machine.

From then on lifts were really going up. Between the years of 1929 and 1931 four of the world's tallest skyscrapers were built in New York. Topping the lot was The Empire State Building with 102 floors.

More recently the Sunshine 60 building in Ikebukuro, Tokyo set a new speed record for the fastest domestic passenger lift which operates at 36.56 km/h.

So what will be next in the development of the lift? Can today's high-speed electrically controlled lifts with their sophisticated design and built-in safety systems be bettered?

One possibility is for lifts to go outside the building. The Hyatt Regency Hotel operates such a system (see picture on previous page). These outdoor glass-walled lifts not only save space inside the building, but they also give passengers a thrilling 'bird's eye view' of the surrounding city.

MICROLIFT ELECTRIC POWERED SERVICE LIFT
(can serve up to 12 floors)

A. Electric motor
B. Wall mounting brackets
C. Winding unit
D. Electronic totally enclosed control panel
E. Shutter frame (upper)
F. Lift support frame
G. Rise and fall shutter (top)
H. Lift indicators.
J. Fully automatic pushbutton control
K. Rise & fall shutter (lower)
L. Counter weight
M. Main wall mounted supports.
N. Shutter Frame (lower)
P. Cage
Q. Adjustable shelf

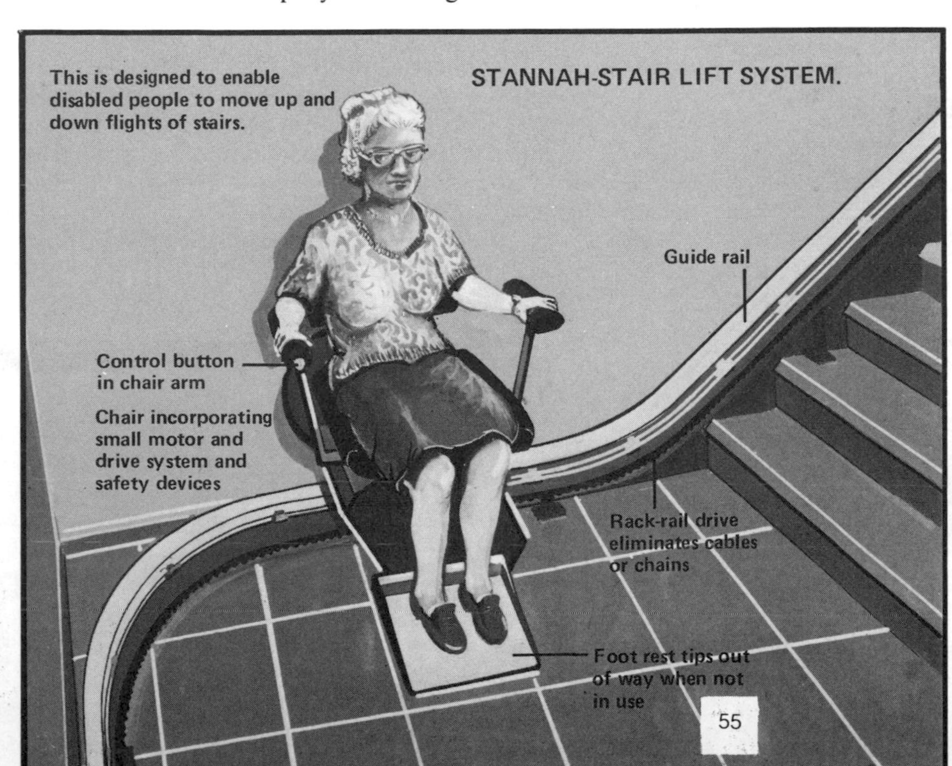

Modern techniques are helping the weathermen

# How is the Weather forecast?

Information from balloons, ships, satellites, planes and ground stations is all used by the weather forecaster. Computers help to analyse the figures.

**IF you've ever been out walking with just a map as guide, then you've probably learnt the golden rule: 'If you want to know where you are going, you've got to know where you are'.**

What holds good for maps also applies to the weather. Depressions, anticyclones and fronts are always moving and the winds carry the cloud patterns along at speeds varying from less than 18 km/h (10 knots) up to occasionally 110 km/h (60 knots).

The first requirement of the weather forecaster, therefore, is to collect observations of the weather from several places. The most important observations are temperature, pressure, humidity, visibility, clouds, precipitation (rain, fog and snow), and wind.

Apart from clouds, whose type, amount and height are usually estimated by the observer, these things can all be measured accurately.

Temperature is measured by a thermometer located inside a *Stevenson screen*. This is simply a white painted box with louvres, allowing free passage of air past the thermometer, but which keeps out direct sunlight.

Humidity is measured by covering a thermometer bulb with a piece of wet cloth. The drier the air, the more moisture evaporates from the cloth so cooling the thermometer. (You know how cool it feels on coming out of the sea on to a beach, and this is because your body is supplying heat to evaporate the sea water into the air.) By comparing the difference in temperature shown by the 'wet-bulb' thermometer and an ordinary 'dry-bulb' thermometer, it is possible to work out how wet the air is.

A *barometer* is used to measure atmospheric pressure. An *anemometer* is used to measure windspeed.

Weather observations are simple to make, but they cannot be made in a haphazard way. They must be systematic. There are three important considerations.

Firstly, all the observations must be made at — or as near as possible at — the same time, that is within about 15 minutes of each other. This is because the forecaster needs to be able to analyse his collection of observations as if they were taken at the same time, bearing in mind that the weather is changing all the time.

Secondly, the area over which the observations are made is important and depends on how far ahead the forecaster wishes to predict. In general, the further ahead he has to forecast, the larger the area from which he has to have observations.

For example, forecasting for somewhere in central England up to two to three hours ahead requires observations from all over the British Isles and perhaps the nearby coastal areas of the Continent, including observations from ships at sea. Forecasting for periods up to three to four days ahead needs observations from all over the northern hemisphere. And if the forecaster is interested beyond five days ahead, he almost certainly needs observations from the southern hemisphere as well.

Thirdly, how often should the observations be made? Basically, the more precise the forecast required, the more often they should be made. Usually, however, they are made every hour on land and every three or six hours at sea.

There are over 5,000 observation stations on land and sea around the world making the type of observations described above. However, it is also essential to know somethings about the temperature, wind, humidity and pressure in the atmosphere above the ground up to a height of about 13 km. For this balloons are used.

Hydrogen-filled balloons carrying instruments (*radio sondes*) are released into the atmosphere from ground sites and from ships at fixed times each day. By following them with radar and listening to signals transmitted from the instruments by radio, it is possible to receive details of the pressure, temperature, humidity and wind at various levels in the atmosphere.

Because radio sondes are expensive to make and use, far fewer observations are obtained from them than from ground stations even though their information is just as important. However, aircraft help fill in any gaps by recording the wind, temperature and weather along their flight routes.

A further major advance in observing the weather has come during the last decade. Satellites travel around the world taking frequent pictures of cloud systems. Precise knowledge of the distribution of cloud is invaluable to the forecaster because there are many areas of the world where no other weather observations are made. The satellites also help to determine the distribution of temperature, wind and humidity in the atmosphere and they may eventually provide most of the data now being supplied by radio sondes.

Making frequent, reliable and detailed observations

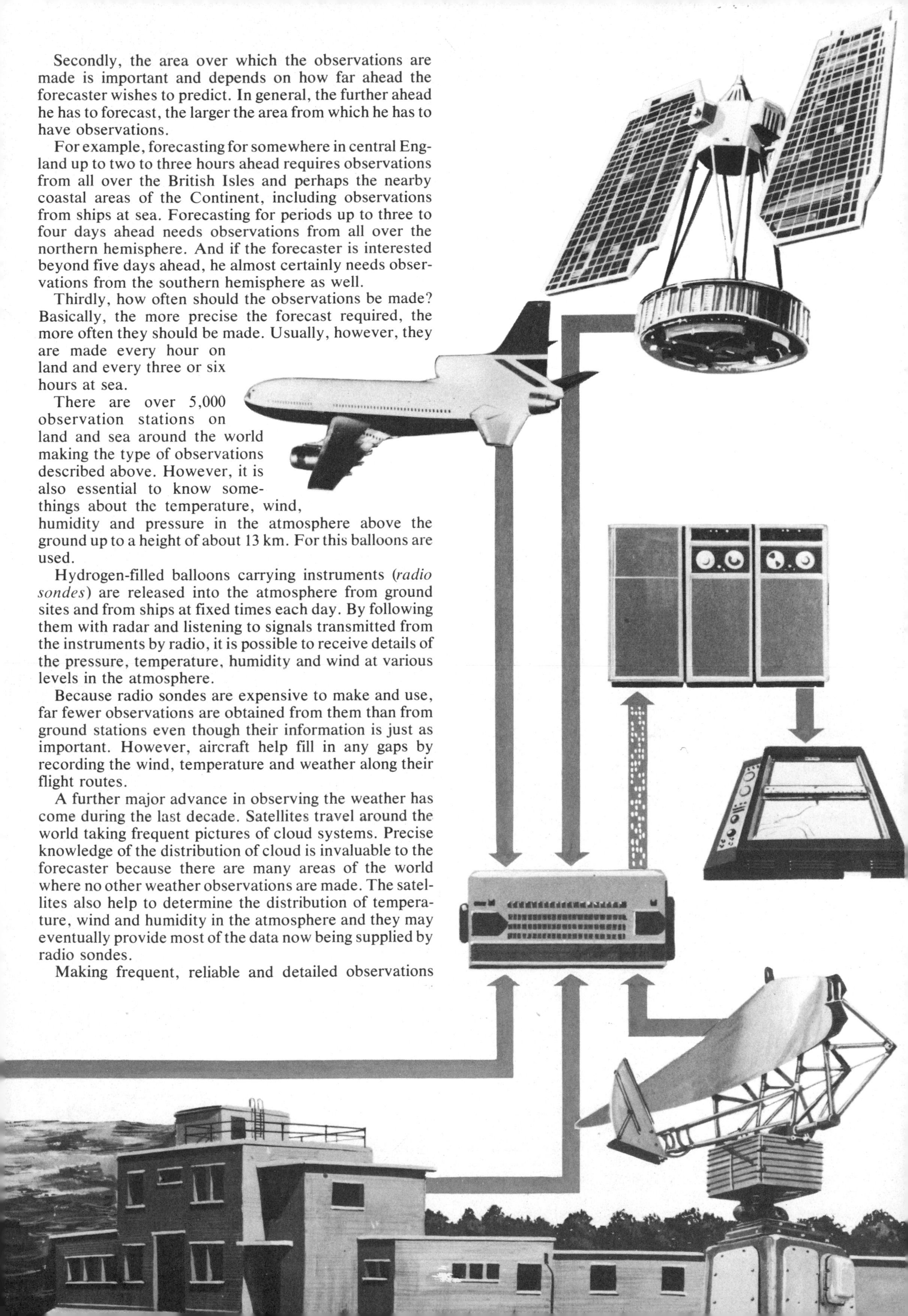

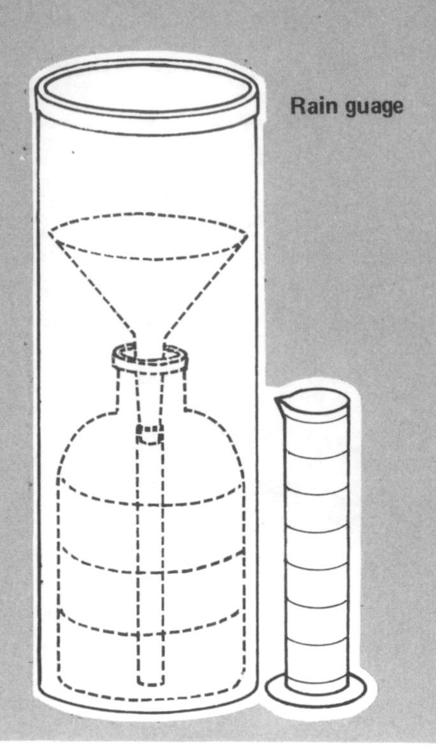


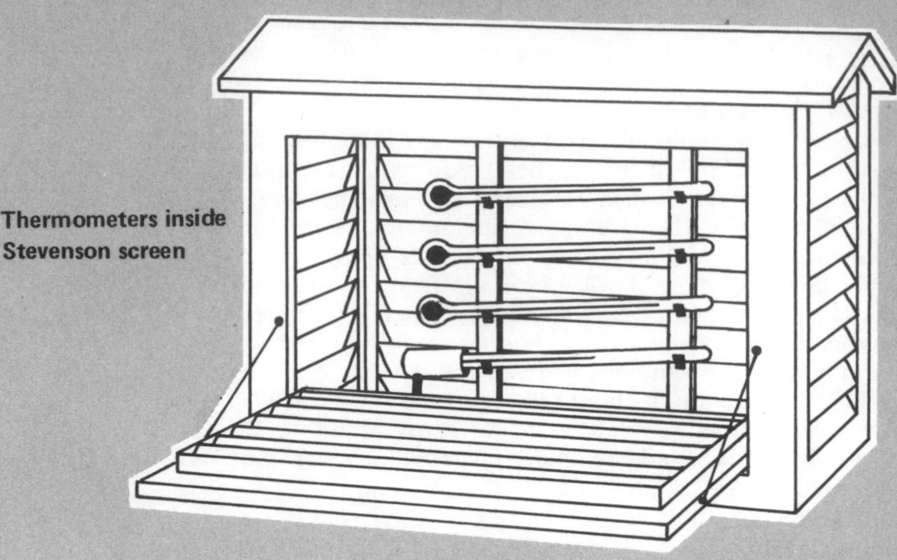


may be the essential first requirement of the forecaster, but it is all a waste of time unless the observations can be collected in a very short period of time. The British forecaster needs observations from the British Isles within half an hour in order to make good use of them. Even observations from China need to be received within three to six hours to be of value.

All this means that high speed communications are essential. The major weather centres around the world are all linked together by electronic circuits which can transmit massive amounts of data extremely quickly. Weather moves freely from country to country and there is maximum co-operation between the nations of the world in passing on their weather information.

Having been collected, the observations are quickly plotted on to charts using an international code which can be easily understood through the world.

The plotted chart containing all the ground (and sea) level observations is called the 'surface' chart. Charts are also plotted for special levels in the lower atmosphere and contain the information acquired from radio sondes, satellites and aircraft reports.

The forecaster analyses the surface chart by drawing *isobars* (lines of equal pressure) and perhaps also *isotherms* lines of equal temperature). He also tries to locate fronts by comparing the observations from place to place to distinquish between air masses of different origin. Observations of cloud and precipitation are extremely important in helping to locate the fronts. Satellite pictures can be even more useful, because they reveal precisely the extent of cloud.

Surface charts are analysed as frequently as every hour in areas of local interest (e.g. British Isles), but upper air charts are analysed every six or twelve hours. This is mainly because there is less information available at less frequent intervals at these levels, but is also because the movement of wind and temperature systems is much smoother at higher levels. Since pressure, wind, temperature, humidity and upward and downward motion of the air are all related, the forecaster can deduce the distribution of these elements by very careful analysis of all the information he has acquired.

If weather systems were not continually changing, forecasting would be a relatively simple task of calculating the speed at which a depression, an anticyclone or a front is

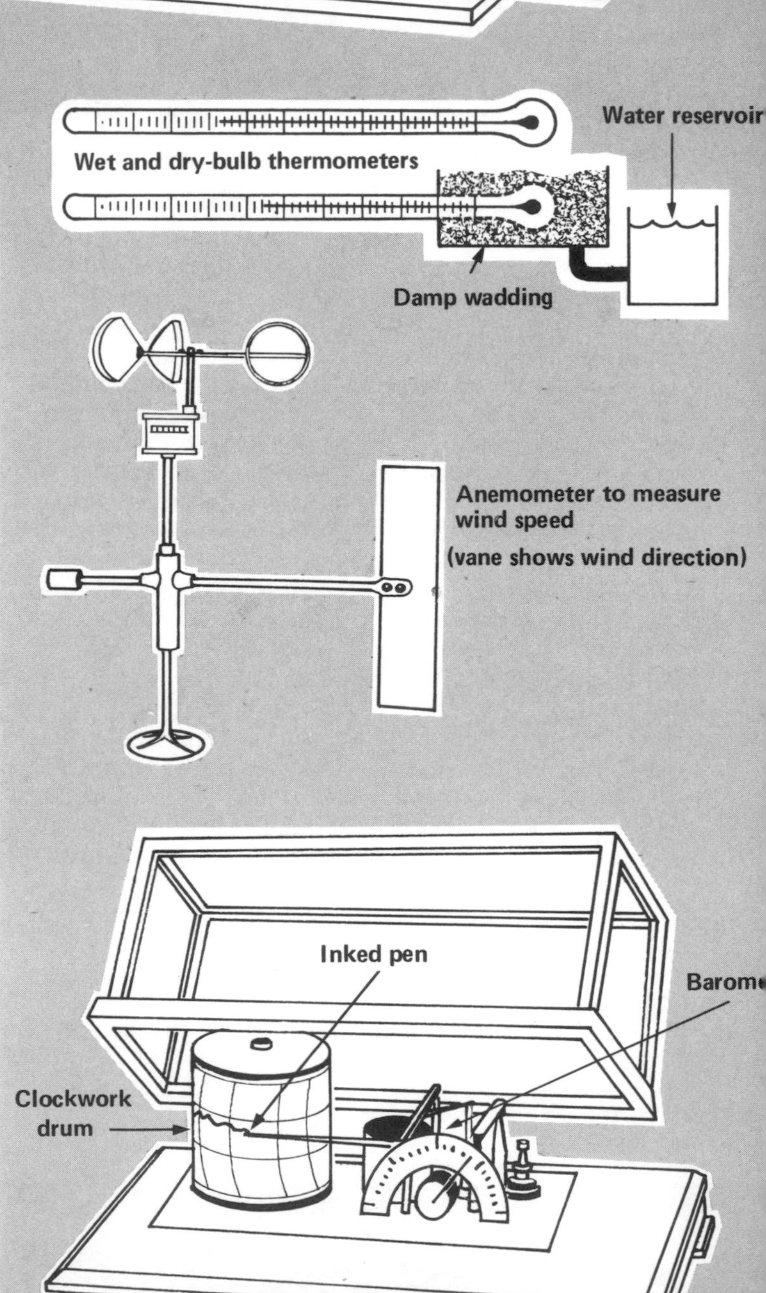


Barograph records pressure changes

**Some of the instruments used to monitor the weather. Thermometers are kept in a *Stevenson screen* — a white-painted louvred box which allows free circulation of air but stops direct sunlight. Thus, temperatures are always quoted as 'in the shade'.**

moving and predicting where the system will be at some future time. But even this can create problems, because unless speeds are calculated to within an accuracy of about 9 km/h (5 knots) timing errors can make all the difference between a sunny or wet afternoon tomorrow. Indeed, many apparent errors in weather forecasts are due to timing difficulties – the weather simply fails to reach the forecast position at the specified time but arrives some hours later.

In general, weather systems are always changing as they move, and forcasters have to anticipate the developments by studying the jetstreams and the frontal zones and using complex mathematical equations to predict what is going to happen. The equations give predictions of pressure, wind, temperature, humidity and rainfall, and nowadays computers are used to work them out.

## Local problems

But weather forecasting is not only about globally moving depressions and fronts. Every day there are local problems to solve as well.

For example, fog will form at night only under certain conditions. There must be little or no wind and the temperature must fall to a level at which the air cannot hold its moisture, and all this in turn depends upon the amount of cloud present to allow cooling of the air. (Clouds absorb and reflect back heat which would otherwise be radiated into Space from the ground at night, hence cloudy nights are usually warmer than clear nights.)

Forecasting the development of showers is another daily problem, particularly in summer. The forecaster has to predict the maximum temperature in order to assess the amount of convection and hence deduce the likelihood of showers. He will also have to take into account the temperature of the atmosphere in the layers above.

Quite simply, forecasting the weather isn't easy, but the constant use of the weather satellites that have been launched, enables the weathermen to predict more accurately than ever before what sort of weather we may expect.

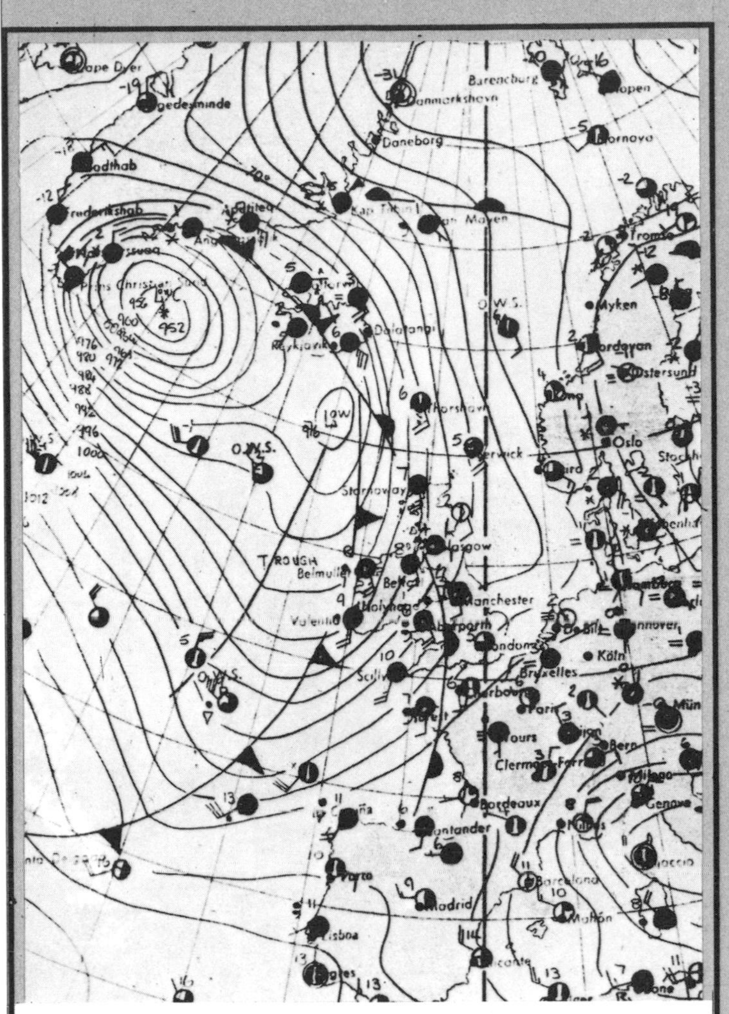


**This is a weather map of the type used by weather forecastors. It shows the weather depicted by satellite photograph. The lines are *isobars* (lines of equal pressure). Just like contour lines on an O.S. map, the closer together they are, the steeper the gradient – only instead of the climb being steeper, the result is that the winds blow more strongly.**

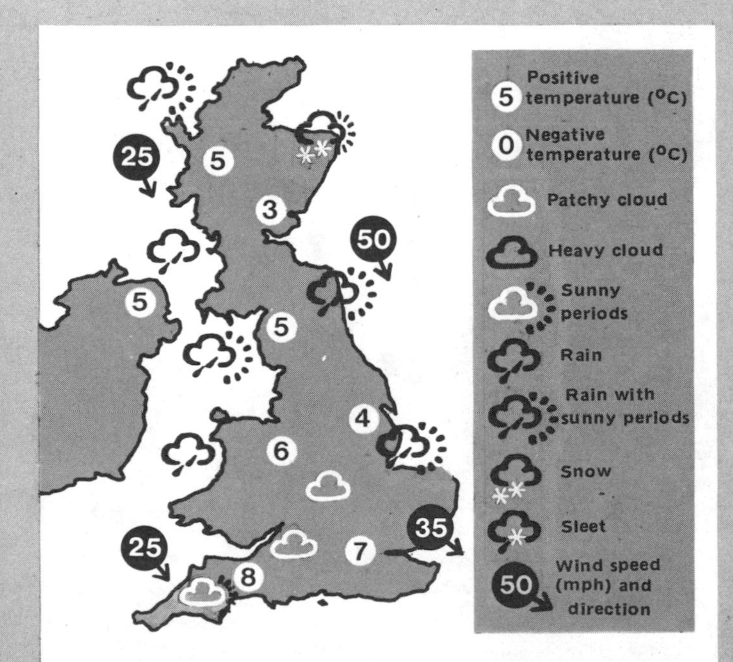


**The weather symbols given on B.B.C. TV weather maps pictorially describe all common weather conditions. Winds are given in miles per hour with their direction shown. Temperatures are given in degrees centrigrade, in a yellow circle for above-freezing temperatures, in a blue circle for below-freezing temperatures.**

**Amount of cloud**

- Clear sky
- 1/8 sky covered
- 1/4 sky covered
- 3/8 sky covered
- 1/2 sky covered
- 5/8 sky covered
- 3/4 sky covered
- 7/8 sky covered
- Complete cloud
- Sky obscured (fog)

**Wind (arrow gives direction)**

- Calm
- 1–2 knots
- 3–7 knots
- 8–12 knots
- 13–17 knots
- half 'feather' added for each further 5 knots until 48-52 knots, then further half feathers added as before

- Mist
- Fog
- Drizzle
- Rain
- Snow
- Shower
- Hail
- Thunder
- Sleet
- Snow shower

- Cold front
- Warm front
- Occluded front (warm front above cold)

# Who discovered

**1.** Dr. Alexander Fleming worked in St. Mary's Hospital, London, studying germs which caused illnesses. Before his annual holiday in 1928, the 47-year-old researcher filled several little dishes with a special jelly in which he placed specimens of the germs he was studying. He wanted the germs to feed on the jelly and multiply so that he would have plenty for experiments. Unnoticed, a speck of mould blew in through a window and settled on one of his dishes.

**2.** When Fleming returned from holiday, the mould had grown and had killed all the germs near it. Fleming examined it under a microscope and found that it had made a substance that destroyed germs. This substance he called 'penicillin'. Doctors knew other germ-killers, such as antiseptics and Fleming himself had discovered 'lysozyme' in 1921, effective against weaker bacteria. Now he knew that penicillin killed germs, but would it kill people too?

**3.** Fleming tested it on some mice and it had no ill effect on them. It seemed that his germ-killer was safe. But Fleming's discovery did not impress the medical world. And, because penicillin did not keep, it was not used in hospitals and it was almost forgotten for nine years. Then a Professor Chain, at Oxford, came upon Fleming's notes on penicillin and set out to make it in quantity. This sparked off a revival of interest in penicillin.

**4.** Working with a team of scientists and doctors, Professor Chain made penicillin, using milk bottles, churns and a dog bath. The suffering caused by the infected, gangrenous wounds of the soldiers in the First World War had started Fleming's search for a germ-killer. By 1940, penicillin was needed for use in the Second World War and, having learned how to mass-produce it, Dr. Florey, one of the Oxford team, went to ask for American help.

# Penicillin?

5. British factories were producing armaments but Dr. Florey persuaded American firms to manufacture penicillin. By the end of the war, great quantities of penicillin were being made. In the 1940s, though, it was still a very expensive substance to produce. If another type of mould could be found which increased the amount of penicillin being made, the cost perhaps could be reduced. One was needed that could be grown in tanks rather than bottles.

6. American servicemen all over the world were told to send back samples of earth which scientists examined for suitable mould and eventually a cheaper type *was* found. Today, it costs less than its glass bottle. So Alexander Fleming, the sport-loving son of an Ayrshire farmer, made a major contribution to medical science. Penicillin cures many illnesses and its discovery led to the search for more antibiotics.

**Strange though it may seem, the fame which Alexander Fleming achieved was due to his love of sport as much as to his undoubted intelligence. Born in Ayr in 1881 and raised on his father's farm, Fleming loved swimming and playing football with his brothers. When they left home to seek work in London, Alec, as they called him, joined them and found a job as a shipping clerk. But for a legacy left by an uncle, he would probably have remained there quite happily. His brother Tom, however, suggested that Alec should go to medical school.**

**After sitting the entrance examination - he passed top of all the candidates in the United Kingdom in 1901 - Alec chose to study at St. Mary's Hospital, Paddington, because he had played water polo against them. Once there, he was invited to work in the laboratory of Almroth Wright, the famous bacteriologist, mainly to influence him to join the St. Mary's Rifle Club.**

**These chance occurrences put Fleming on the road which led to his great discoveries. In 1944, he was knighted and a year later, he, together with Chain and Florey, was awarded the Nobel Prize for Medicine. He died in 1955.**

**Penicillin was the first drug known as an antibiotic. That is a substance which attacks disease-giving bacteria and destroys them without harming the body being treated. It is obtained from the natural mould *Penicillium notatum* and is perhaps the most commonly used of all antibiotics.**

**The reason it is so valuable is that it will destroy many different types of bacteria. Also, although it is sometimes necessary to give it in large doses, it is usually safe to do so.**

**Bacteria against which it is effective are those which cause types of pneumonia, those which cause types of meningitis, those which cause erysipelas, a disease characterised by widespread skin inflammation, those found in the pus discharged from boils, and many, many others.**

**Penicillin is now available in a number of different forms. They are given often by injections into muscles or sometimes can be taken through the mouth. In a few cases, though, this latter method is not possible as acids present in the stomach destroy them.**

Arms of Henry VIII and Jane Seymour, Nonsuch Palace

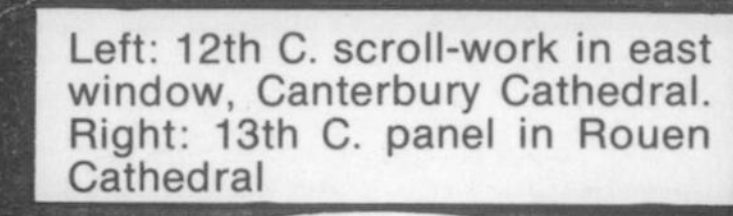

Left: 12th C. scroll-work in east window, Canterbury Cathedral. Right: 13th C. panel in Rouen Cathedral

Royal Arms (15th C.) in a Westminster Abbey window

## The Glory of Stained Glass

**Stained glass windows were originally intended to be instructive as well as beautiful. They illustrated scenes from the Bible for those who could not read. But, gradually, the designing of these windows became an art in its own right. Chartres Cathedral in France and York Minster in England contain some of the most outstanding examples. The coloured pieces of glass are produced by adding various chemicals to the molten glass mixture. The pieces are cut to shape using a diamond and fitted into the design rather like assembling a jigsaw puzzle. Strips of lead hold the pieces together. Details such as faces and drapery are painted on with a special enamel which is then fused into the glass itself. The whole process has been described as 'painting in light' and glass has seldom been put to more impressive use.**

60th London Division Memorial, St. George's Cathedral, Jerusalem

Northumberland Fusiliers' Memorial in Newcastle Cathedral

The Annunciation (14th C.) in Church of St. Ouen, Rouen

Figure of St. Stephen (14th C.) from York Minster

Angel in apse of Chartres Cathedral, France (13th C.)

Two prophets in Fairford Church, Gloucestershire (15th C.)

# Is Glass a liquid?

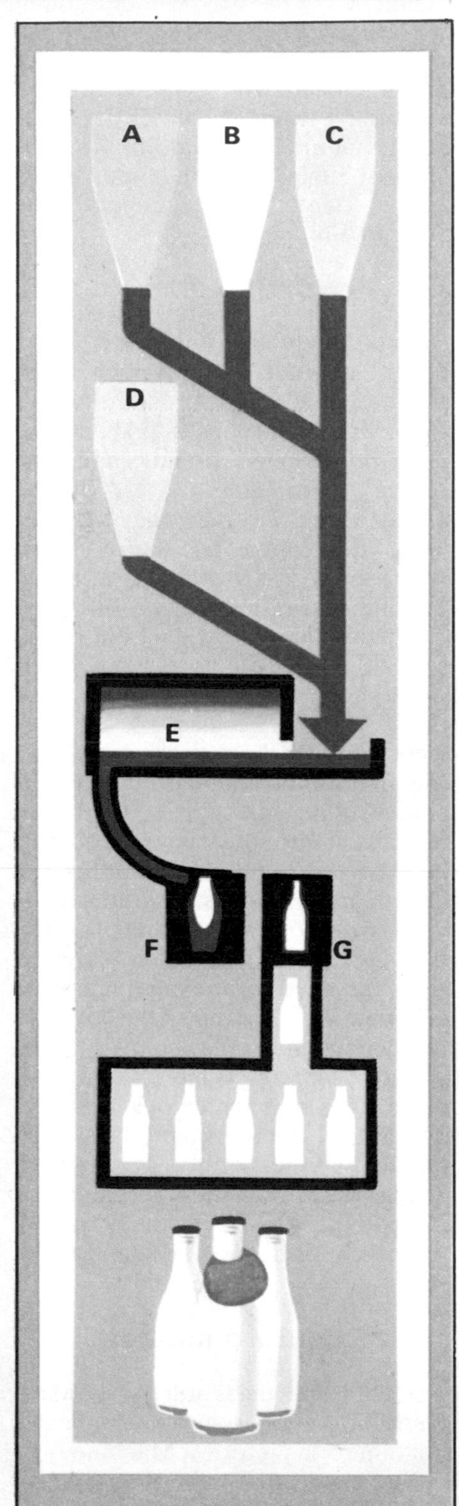


Above, left: Glass-blowers at work, rolling and shaping a blob of molten glass on the end of a metal tube.
Above: To make milk bottles, sand (A), soda ash (B), limestone (C) and broken glass (D) are mixed and melted in a furnace (E) then blown into moulds (F) before being *annealed*, or slowly cooled, (G) to reduce internal stresses in the glass.

**One of the oldest, most versatile materials known to man, glass is very much part of our everyday lives.**

**YOU don't have to belong to the Magic Circle to master a seemingly-impossible 'trick'. Most of us do it each day without realising just how amazing it is, for it takes only seconds to perform. You pour a quantity of one liquid into another liquid and carry them around in your hand, without using any other container — and without spilling a single drop.**

All you need is some water and a glass container, such as a milk bottle. Pour the water into the bottle and carry the bottle around in your hand. Hey presto! You have done the trick.

For glass, you see, is really a liquid. It looks like a solid and behaves like but one but it is, in fact, a molten liquid of sand which has been cooled.

Sand, which is a mixture of tiny silica or quartz crystals, melts at 1700° Centigrade and when it is cooled from this very high temperature to the everyday temperatures in which we live, it thickens and becomes viscous (stiff), like toffee setting.

Unfortunately, sand on its own does not make good glass. Apart from requiring a great deal of heat, it produces a glass which tends to crystallize and the crystals affect the glass's clearness. So, some things have to be added to the 'melt' to help overcome these difficulties. These are chiefly *soda* (sodium carbonate) and *limestone* (calcium carbonate) and what they help to produce is called 'soda glass' the most common form of glass in production. Light bulbs, bottles, window panes and tableware are made of it. If better quality glass is required, other chemicals are added in controlled quantities.

But who first discovered glass? Some claim it was discovered in the deserts of the Middle East where the heat produced by lightning melted the sand; others say that early pottery makers were the discoverers as they could put glazes on their products long before glass was known; and yet another theory is that shipwrecked Phoenicians, those seagoing merchants of the ancient world, discovered particles of glass

*Continued on next page*

in their camp-fires after resting their cooking pots on lumps of soda which, when heated, fused with the sand nearby.

Whichever theory is right, it is likely that glass was discovered by accident. Syria was without doubt foremost in the production of glass in the ancient world and the skills of her glass-makers were passed to the Egyptians around 2000 B.C. After Rome conquered Egypt, the Romans spread their newly-learned glass-making techniques throughout the Roman Empire.

## Syrian skill

The Egyptians employed fairly crude methods to produce their decorative glassware. Hot slabs of glass would be rolled into shape and perhaps wrapped around sandstone 'plugs' to form glass vessels. But for almost three centuries, they lacked a skill, developed by the Syrians, which was to revolutionise glass-making — the skill of glass-blowing.

This method of shaping hot glass, probably devised in a moment of inspiration, is now used for only the finest work. The glass-blower collects some molten glass on a long, thin metal tube and, with the help of skilful rolling and spinning, he blows the glass into the shape required. Apart from requiring skill, this job also demands very strong lungs!

Nowadays, traditional glass-blowing methods are too slow to meet the needs of the mass markets. Automation is the rule of the day. But in ancient times, glass-blowing provided better vessels more simply and more quickly than previous methods. The glass 'gob' was either free blown, giving a strong spherical shape, or blown into a mould, a method used by the Romans to give precise, repeatable shapes with patterns on them if necessary.

## Standard method

Mould-blowing is still the standard method for mass-producing glass containers in factories. Machines can churn them out by the thousand all round the clock and to set standards. An important part of the process is the cooling stage, known as *annealing*. Shaped glass needs to be cooled very carefully to remove stresses in it. Glassware in factories is passed while still hot along the *annealing lehr,* a long tunnel in which the temperature is strictly controlled.

The cooling rate is especially important in the manufacture of optical glass as it determines its *refractive index* — the light bending power of the glass. And in this field, the name Ravenscroft looms large. To understand why, we have to go back in time again.

When the Roman Empire collapsed, glass-making went into decline until the Venetians revived interest in it, relearning all the old skills and adding some of their own. They made beautiful coloured glass and learned how to make mirrors.

## Ravenscroft

But in 17th Century England, the Worshipful Company of Glass Sellers, dissatisfied with the quality of the glass from Venice, encouraged George Ravenscroft to experiment in the medium. In 1675, he rewarded them with an invention which ushered in a new style of glass-making and set England on the road to becoming the world's leading glass producer.

His invention was *flint glass,* a brilliantly-clear glass which was fairly heavy but not durable. This fault was rectified by introducing lead oxide to the mixture to produce *lead crystal*. Today, crystal is used to make lenses and prisms as well as decorative tableware. Imitation jewellery often contains a heavy lead glass called *paste* as a substitute for precious stones.

Jewellery, bottles, lenses, bulbs, cups and saucers, ovenware and ornaments — all of them can be made from glass but the list is far from comprehensive, such is the versatility of this remarkable material.

**Above: A skilled craftsman demonstrates the versatility of glass by cutting a design on a vase, using a special grindstone.**

*Photo: Glass Manufacturers' Federation.*

**Right: Beautiful examples of lead crystal, a brilliantly clear glass which sparkles after it has been polished.**

# How is Flat Glass made?

**LOOK out of your window and what do you see? The house on the opposite side of the street, a car driving past and perhaps a wind-blown shopper struggling home with an armful of groceries? What you probably don't notice is the 'invisible barrier' which separates you from the outside world — the window pane.**

Apart from patterned and stained glass, we regard window panes as things to look *through* rather than to look *at*. They let light in and they keep bad weather out. But two thousand years ago, only the latter was true. Ancient glass was not transparent because of the imperfect mixture of ingredients and the rough texture of the finished article.

So, when the Romans introduced the fashion of having glass window panes, they did not have the luxury of being able to see through them with ease. Each window pane was made by hand, a sheet of hot glass being rolled to make it thinner. Inevitably, the glass was not perfectly flat and its surface was marked, problems which were to trouble glass-makers for centuries.

Another method of making window panes — and one that has stood the test of time — is the crown process. Developed from a principle used by the ancient Syrians, it involves blowing a blob of molten glass on the end of an iron blowpipe then transferring the resultant globe to a *punty* or solid iron rod. The globe is then reheated and rotated at great speed until the centrifugal force opens the glass out into a large, flat disc. This is then cut to shape to form a window pane.

## 'Bull's-eye' mark

Small crown glass panes, sometimes bearing the mark of the punty in the centre or 'bull's-eye', are still fashionable in modern windows, although they are most often seen in very old buildings.

From the 14th century until nearly the middle of the 19th century, most of Europe's windows were of crown glass. Normandy in France became particularly associated with the industry, which is why crown glass is often referred to as *Normandy glass*.

Of course, until fairly recent times, glass was an expensive material and few people could afford to have window panes.

In Britain, the introduction of a Window Tax in 1690 to finance King William III's wars restricted the numbers of windows even in the largest houses. Some of them had windows bricked up to reduce their liability to taxation.

The Window Tax existed on and off until it was repealed in 1845 during Queen Victoria's reign. There followed such a demand for glass that manufacturers could not satisfy it. Glass prices tumbled as firms vied fiercely for business. New methods of mass-production were sought desperately.

It was in this period that the name Pilkington came to the fore in British glassmaking. Started in Lancashire in 1826 as the St. Helens Crown Glass Company, a small family business, the firm of Pilkington Brothers has grown to become one of the world's leading glassmakers.

Pilkington was an innovator in the mechanical production of *plate glass,* first made in France in the 17th century in individual sheets. In the Pilkington process, molten glass from a furnace was rolled into a continuous ribbon before being cooled then ground and polished to optical perfection. But this led to a lot of wastage.

The *blown glass process* involved swinging a molten globe of glass to produce a cylinder which was cooled, split and flattened to make a sheet of glass.

The production of *sheet glass* followed in the early years of this century. By the French *Fourcault* process (1904) and the American *Pittsburgh* process (1926), a ribbon of glass was drawn vertically from a furnace by means of powered rollers. Brilliant though the surface of this glass was, distortions within it meant it could not replace plate glass. But it was cheaper to produce and was suitable for domestic or horticultural glazing.

What was needed was a combination of the best features of plate and sheet glass. In 1959, Pilkington supplied it.

Realising that rollers marked molten glass — indeed, special patterned rollers are used to produce the glass

*Continued on next page*

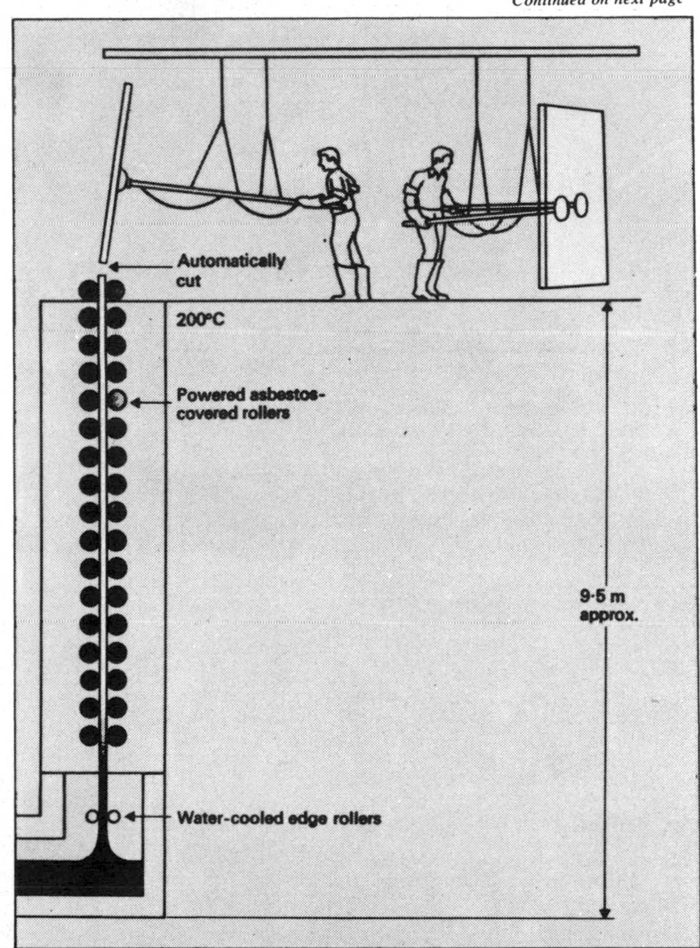


**Sheet glass production uses 'drawing towers'. A metal frame — a 'bait' — is lowered into molten glass. Glass attached is then teased out and held by water-cooled rollers and the ribbon is fed up through powered asbestos-covered rollers. At the top, the 'bait' is removed and the glass cut.**

Above: A continuous ribbon of glass, 3.3 m wide, is carried from the annealing lehr (or cooling area) on rollers, having been cooled down in controlled stages on its way to the automatic warehouse. It has been made by the float glass process (shown below).

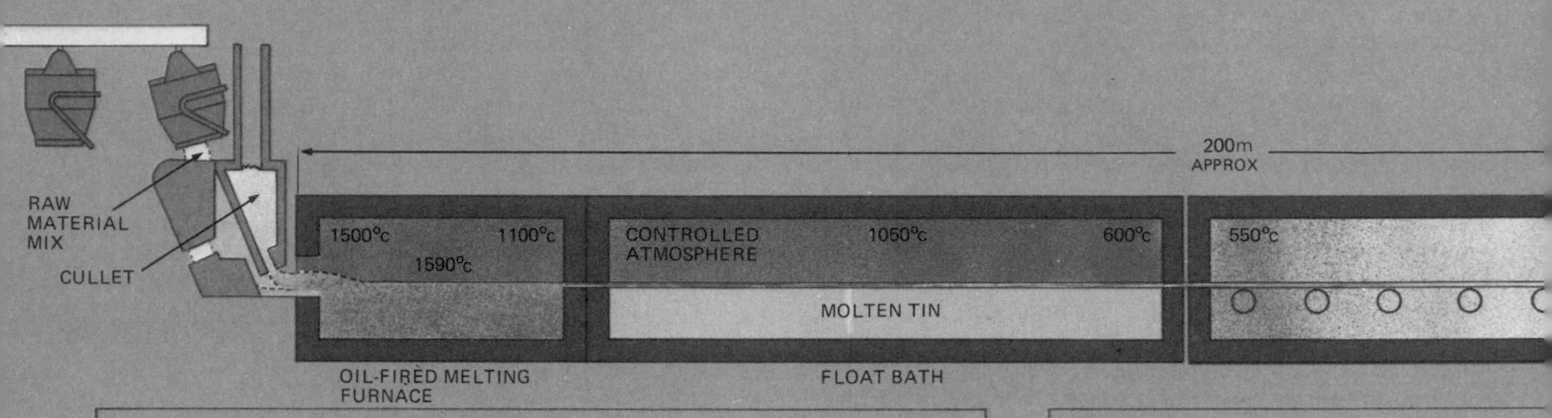


## Patterned Glass and Wired Glass

First made in 1890, patterned glass allows light to pass through it while retaining privacy. It is used for partitions, windows and doors. In the production process, the glass leaves the furnace and passes between powered rollers. One of these (the green one in our diagram) has a surface pattern which is transferred to the glass before it passes to the annealing lehr.

Wired glass, which has the advantage of holding together when broken by impact or heat, was first made in 1895. Today it is manufactured by feeding a layer of wire mesh on to a ribbon of glass, half the required thickness, just after it has left the furnace. Another ribbon of glass is then fed on top to form a sandwich with the wire in the middle. This fuses together in the heat. Clear wired glass is made by grinding and polishing the surfaces of the finished product.

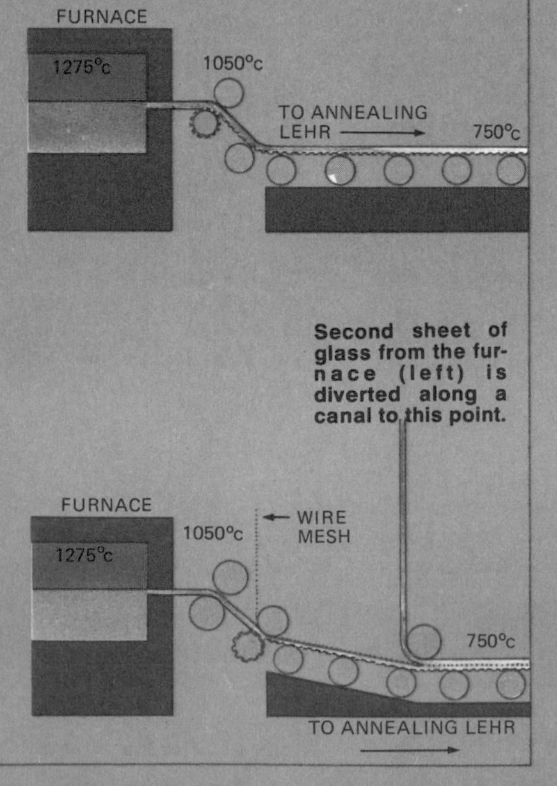


Second sheet of glass from the furnace (left) is diverted along a canal to this point.

## Preparation of Motor Industry Glass

Computers are programmed to produce float glass of the required sizes.

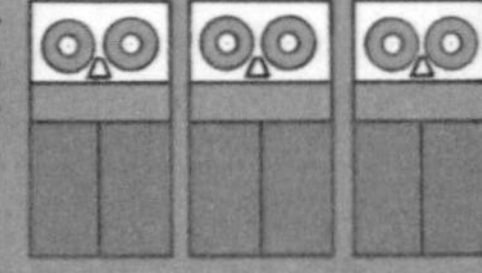

The float glass rectangles are delivered to the Safety Glass factory on pallets.

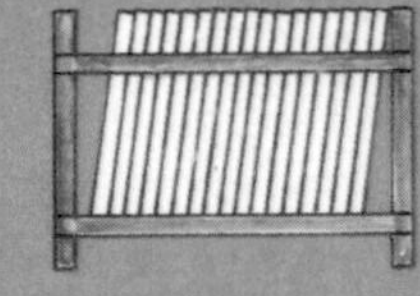

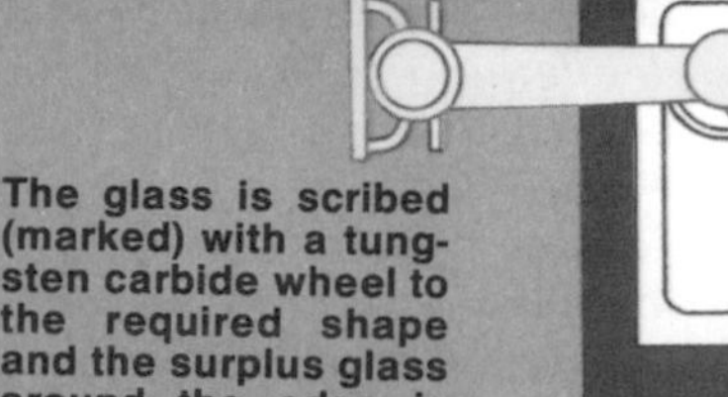

The glass is scribed (marked) with a tungsten carbide wheel to the required shape and the surplus glass around the edge is removed.

The edges of the glass are ground and angled, or 'round polished' using diamond-impregnated wheels.

which most of us have in our bathroom windows — Pilkington invented a completely new process which required no rollers at all.

The *float process*, introduced by Pilkington in 1959, employs a bed of molten tin which carries the glass from the furnace to the annealing (slow cooling) area. The tin provides a temperature high enough to melt out the irregularities in the glass and a surface which makes the glass perfectly flat.

Most of the world's flat glass is now made by the float process which is being developed still further by its creators. Pilkington announced the development of the *Electrofloat* process in 1967. It employs the use of electrodes to make glass with a bronze tint. And in 1975 the *Pulsed Electrofloat* process arrived, making a glass with the coloured pattern actually within the body of the glass.

These new glasses can be seen in modern office blocks which, because of the amount of glass used in their construction, have become vast sun-traps in the summer. It is hardly surprising that solar control glass has become big business. So, too, has safety glass and the two are often combined as in the manufacture of tinted car windscreens.

Safety glass is either *toughened* or *laminated*. If it is toughened, it has been heated in a special furnace and then cooled quickly by being blasted with cold air. This makes the glass much stronger.

Laminated glass is a sandwich composed of a layer of plastic between two sheets of glass. The plastic is welded to the glass by being heated in a vacuum. If extra-strong glass is needed, more layers are added to the sandwich. Bullet-resistant glass 19 millimetres thick will, for example, stop a pistol bullet fired even at close range.

Today, the range of sheet glasses available is quite remarkable and yet largely unnoticed by most of us. Daily we glance through panes of this amazing liquid without giving it a thought — unless, that is, it has been coated with metallic silver and called a *mirror*. But that's a different story.

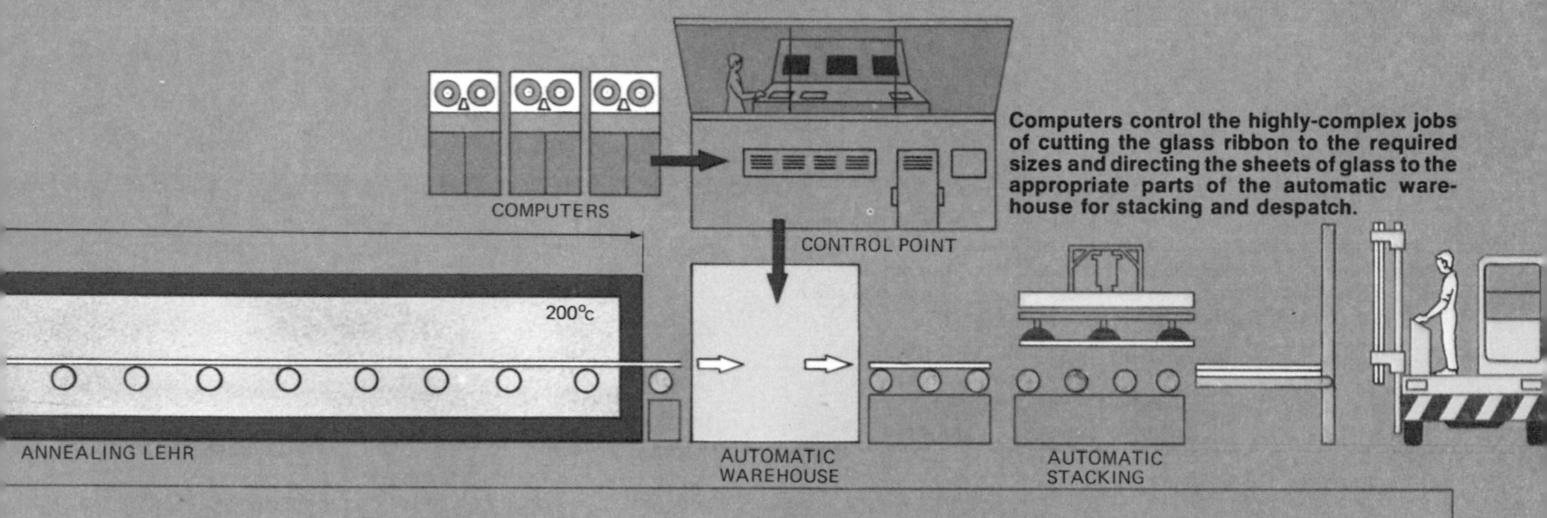


**Computers control the highly-complex jobs of cutting the glass ribbon to the required sizes and directing the sheets of glass to the appropriate parts of the automatic warehouse for stacking and despatch.**

## Toughened Car Windscreens

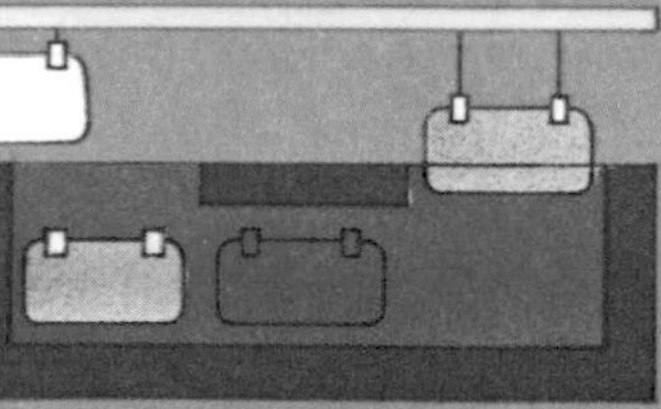

**Glass 'blanks' heated to 650°C.**

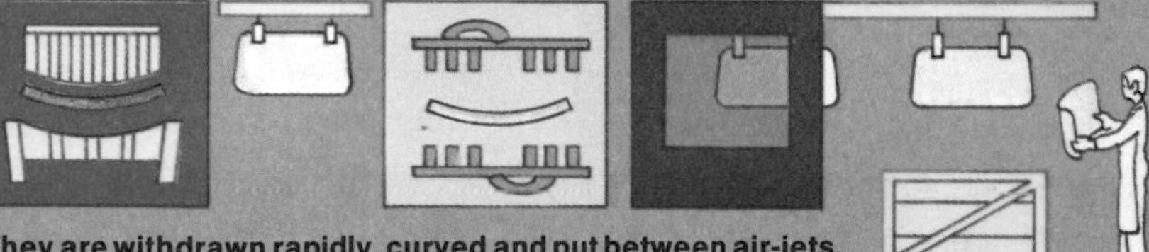

**They are withdrawn rapidly, curved and put between air-jets. The surfaces, cooling first, are compressed, so increasing resistance to impact.**

**Toughened windscreens are about four times stronger than ordinary glass but may break when hit by sharp road flints. This sort of glass is so treated that when it shatters, a driver can still see enough through it to pull up safely.**

## Toughened Car Door Glasses

**'Blanks' on a continuous bed are curved, and toughened by being cooled rapidly.**

**Side glasses are toughened but where windows open on hinges, holes are made before toughening. Rear windows often include printed circuit demisting.**

## Laminated Windscreens

**recut pairs of glass are heated nd curved.**

**They are cooled slowly, sandwiched with polyvinyl butyral and heated under a vacuum.**

**Now inseparable, they are checked for delivery.**

**A laminated screen, when hit, usually forms a star crack. The inner layer is undamaged and a driver can still see clearly. He is safer, too, in the event of a front collision.**

# What was the World's first Passenger Railway?

The *Rocket* won the Rainhill Trials quite simply because it was the best locomotive present. Its very efficient boiler and exhaust-pipe design meant it could pull a 14 tonnes train at a top speed of 48km/h, nearly double that of its rivals. This replica was made for the 150th anniversary celebrations.

The *Northumbrian* was the last of the *Rocket*-type locomotives, with the cylinders at the rear. With George Stephenson aboard it led the way at the opening celebrations.

The *Planet* was the first of the second generation of locos, and showed several improvements over the *Rocket*-types. The cylinders were at the front (inside) and the design had the basic principles followed by nearly all mainline locomotives until the end of steam. *Planet*-types were operating soon after the L&M opened.

**TO be able to go to a railway station, buy a ticket and travel on a train is something we all take for granted nowadays. But not so 150 years ago when the poor passenger was of little importance to the few railway companies operating. In fact, they were often ranked lower than coal, minerals or even sheep!**

Then, in 1830, a line was nearing completion that was to change all that; where people would receive at least the same consideration as goods. It was to link the cities of Liverpool and Manchester. Not a great distance, but a very significant one. For this was the very *first* time a railway had been authorised by Parliament to carry passengers as well as goods, using steam locomotion.

The Stockton & Darlington Railway, the world's first public railway which opened in 1825, also used steam locomotives, but not for passengers. In a sense though, the Stockton & Darlington and the Liverpool & Manchester were connected, in the shape of one man — George Stephenson. With his son Robert, and Edward Pease, Stephenson founded the locomotive building firm of Robert Stephenson at Newcastle. This built the locomotives for the Stockton line which was a great success, and Stephenson was appointed consultant engineer for the building of the Liverpool & Manchester.

## Rainhill Trials

Strangely, steam power was not an automatic choice for the new line. There was an 'anti-steam' group pressing for horse or cable traction throughout, so in 1829 the world-famous 'Rainhill Trials' were arranged to test whether a steam design was suitable for the railway. The competitors had to complete a series of runs in quick succession to qualify for the £500 prize. The trials took place on a completed section of the line at Rainhill, and from the four entrants it was the renowned *Rocket,* designed by Robert Stephenson, that emerged triumphant.

The building of the Liverpool & Manchester Railway proved no easy task, and many significant achievements

The British Rail Advanced Passenger Train, or APT-T which holds the British railway speed record, is still being used as a mobile test-bed to gain knowledge which will be used in the next generation of high-speed trains.

in civil engineering were made during its construction.

Work had commenced at the Liverpool end of the line towards the end of 1826. The first terminus, called Crown Street, was connected by tunnel to the first major station and junction on the line, Edge Hill. Here, another track branched off to the Wapping Docks on the River Mersey. Over this point was constructed the elaborate 'Moorish Arch', designed by John Forster, as an impressive entrance to the Liverpool railway complex. Here, too, the anti-steam group had a little revenge as the branch to Wapping was thought too steep for locomotives, which were cable-worked up to the station at Edge Hill.

The next major engineering work was the excavation of a 3.2 km long cutting through the sandstone rock at Olive Mount. In places this reached depths of over 30 m. Both this cutting and the 260 m. long Liverpool tunnel are even more impressive when one considers that there were no huge mechanical diggers or excavators available like today. There was some blasting but much of the work was carried out with simple picks and shovels and only candles for lighting.

The line climbed for much of the 10 km from Crown Street to Rainhill, then continued along fairly level ground for 14 km until reaching the Sankey Brook and canal. Here was constructed the impressive nine-arched Sankey Viaduct. Engineered by William Allcard, it was the most expensive individual item on the line, costing £45,200 — a huge sum in those days. It carried the L & M line some 20 m. above the river and canal.

But if anyone had thought the Liverpool Road Station under construction at the other end of the line, in Manchester, was then within easy reach, they were very much mistaken! For in the way was the supposedly impassable Chat Moss — a vast, soggy peat bog, 30 sq.km. in area and 8 km west of Manchester.

Stephenson was undoubtedly advised that it was madness to cross the Moss directly and the line would have to go around the morass. But no problem like this had been tackled before and Stephenson was determined that the line should be direct. For three years from 1827, gangs of navvies toiled across Chat Moss, laying drains and filling in the proposed route with vast quantities of heather, brushwood and earth to act like a 'raft' for the line. On January 1, 1830, the *Rocket* successfully crossed the 6 km section and Chat Moss had been conquered. That the same foundations are crossed today by much heavier traffic is a tribute to Stephenson's techniques.

The remaining 7 km into Manchester were constructed on level ground ending at the purpose-built passenger station at Liverpool Road. All was ready for the official opening!

The ceremonies were performed at Edge Hill Station, Liverpool, on September 15, 1830, by no less a person than the Duke of Wellington. But the day was marred by tragedy. At Parkside Station, the trains taking part stopped to take on water. As William Huskisson M.P., a great supporter of the railway, stepped off one train to stretch his legs, he was struck by the *Rocket* moving up to take on water. The unfortunate man died that evening — it was the world's first fatal railway accident.

## Standard gauge

But the line was finished and operating. It was almost 50 km long and consisted of a double line of rails of the 'fish-belly' type (since they were much shorter than any used today, only about a metre long, and the bottom of the rails swelled at the centre to make them stronger). These were laid on stone or timber sleepers. The distance between the inside edges of the rails, known as the gauge, was 4 feet 8½ inches (1.42 m), and became the most widely adopted gauge in the world.

Passenger trains started at Crown Street Station in Liverpool and were moved by gravity (if leaving) or by cable and stationary engine (if entering) through the descending tunnel. The locomotives took over in the Wapping Cutting and then hauled the carriages to Manchester.

As outlined in the Act of Parliament, for the construction of the line, the L & M was authorised to carry passengers in what was seen as its principal role. Passenger accommodation on the line was well provided and divided

*Continued on next page*

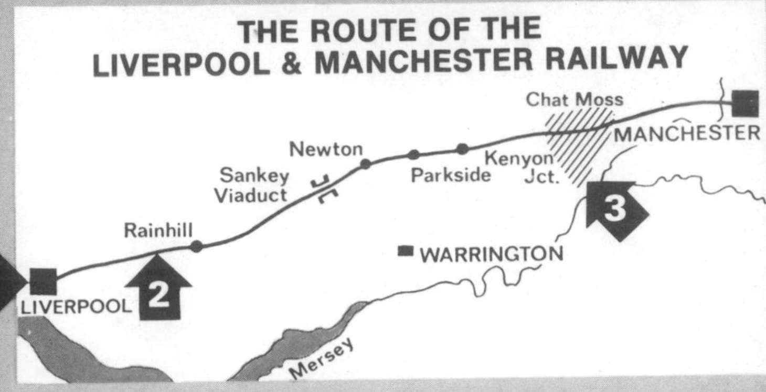


(1) The entrance of the Liverpool & Manchester Railway at Edge Hill, Liverpool, in 1829. The chimneys of the two winding engine towers can be seen. There were two main tunnels; one connecting with the Crown Street terminus, the other with the Wapping Docks in Liverpool.

(2) An engraving of the Olive Mount cutting as it was orginally built — only 6m wide. The cutting was over 3km long and over 20m deep. Its construction is even more impressive if one considers that it was constructed with only pickaxes and shovels as the major tools and candles for lighting.

(3) This engraving gives an impression of how bleak Chat Moss was. A vast peat bog, it was a formidable barrier between Liverpool and Manchester. Many observers thought Stephenson was mad to try and cross it directly, but he succeeded in building a firm base for the line — a remarkable engineering triumph.

(4) The *Rocket*-type locomotive *North Star* (which took part in the opening ceremony) hauling three second class and three third class carriages. In the early days of the railway first class passengers travelled on separate trains with covered carriages. Locos of this type were soon obsolete.

into 1st, 2nd and 3rd classes. Each class had a different carriage design ranging from the luxurious 1st class to the primitive open wagons provided for 3rd class passengers.

The 1st class design was based on the old stagecoach-type body arranged in groups of three on a four-wheeled chassis. As with road coaches, luggage was carried on the carriage roofs but, unlike the road types, passengers did not have to sit there too!

At the other extreme were the open wagons for 3rd class passengers — and open to all types of weather — sometimes fitted with wooden benches. A hole in the floor let out rainwater!

The line carried a very considerable livestock traffic, and special vehicles of generous proportions were provided. In fact, the comfort provided by some of the so-called sheep and cattle trucks was possibly better than that of the 3rd class passenger wagons. As you might expect, goods and passengers were moved in separate trains. But a curious feature, at least in the early days, was that there were even separate trains for 1st and 3rd class passengers.

And the fare in those days? For the journey from Man-

**An engraving of the scene in Wapping Cutting near Liverpool on September 15, 1830 — the official opening day of the railway. On the left can be seen the director's special train with the Duke of Wellington's ornate carriage. The eight locomotives taking part set off promptly at 10 a.m. with *Northumbrian*, driven by William Huskisson M.P.**

chester to Liverpool it was 5 shillings (25p) in the covered wagons, and 3 shillings 6d (17½p) in those exposed to the elements. Nowadays it might not seem much to have paid the extra 7½p to make sure you stayed dry, but remember the value of £1 today does not correspond with its value 150 years ago, In fact, the difference today would have been about £6!

## Double triumph

The opening and successful operation of the Liverpool & Manchester Railway was a double triumph for George Stephenson and all the other determined engineers who had helped in its construction. Their confidence had been justified not only in the steam locomotive but also in railways themselves. Journey times between Liverpool and Manchester had been cut from 5 hours by road and 36 hours by water to just 2 hours, and at less cost for both passengers and goods.

The Railway was a marvellous achievement. Of its 50 km length only about 3 km were dead level. Long tunnels and cuttings had been dug, over 60 bridges and viaducts built and, of course, the Chat Moss bog defeated. All at a cost of over £¾ million, an astronomical figure at the time.

But it was undoubtedly worth every penny. The Liverpool & Manchester Railway gave a massive boost to the development of railways in Great Britain. By 1845, when the L & M's independent existence came to an end and it became part of the Grand Junction Railway, there were connecting lines with several major Northern cities as well as Birmingham (1837) and London (1838). It was the age of 'Railway Mania', opening up the country and helping it to develop into the world's most powerful nation as head of the British Empire.

Could George Stephenson ever have imagined that from this first passenger line, with locomotives travelling no faster than 30 km.h., would develop the vast network that is British Rail today? In 1983 alone, B.R. carried 695 million passengers and 145 million tonnes of goods traffic, and at speeds of up to 225 km.p.h.

As long as railways exist, the name of the Liverpool & Manchester Railway will always be remembered.

# Is the Oil running out?

**I MAGINE four baths full to the top with thick, black oil. That's how much *every* man, woman and child in the world uses on average each year.**

If you live in a rich country, in Britain for example, you use twice that amount — eight bath-fulls. If you live in the richest country, the U.S.A., you are responsible for using up something like 20 baths of black gold every year — or nearly half a bath-full a week.

So what do you do with it all — all three-quarters of a tonne of it (or four tonnes if you're an American)?

You use very little just as oil of course — unless you own a car — but oil's other uses are legion.

There is obviously fuel for industry, transport and agriculture and to provide heat, light and warmth for millions. But oil is also the basis of man-made fibres like nylon, terylene, acrilan and orlon, used in shirts, dresses, carpets and curtains.

It provides the plastic for a whole range of household and garden necessities such as washing-up bowls and watering cans; it is used to make detergents, washing-up liquids, fly-killer sprays, anti-freeze solutions for car radiators, synthetic rubber and foam rubber to fill chair and settee cushions.

**The answer has got to be yes — sooner or later. But how quickly depends on many factors: how much we can save, how much we can find, and whether other energy sources are fully exploited. And, increasingly, 'black gold' is becoming a major political weapon in the delicate relations between the countries of the world.**

Candles and polishes contain petroleum wax. Scents, cosmetics and even a substance which will keep cheese fresh are made out of oil. Products as diverse as fertilisers, medicines, high explosives, chewing gum and paints may contain petroleum products. Propane and butane gas, often used for lighting and cooking, are bottled petroleum gases which have been liquified by cooling and compressing them.

Techniques are also being developed, particularly in Japan, in which micro-organisms, such as bacterias and yeast, are fed on the paraffin contained in petroleum. The protein produced is then extracted from their cells with the initial aim of producing animal fodder. However, some of the basic ingredients of the human diet consist almost entirely of protein, so one day we could well be eating food made from oil.

World production of crude oil has increased steadily throughout this century. It was 45 million tonnes in 1910; 95 million tonnes in 1920; 205 million tonnes in 1930; 300 million tonnes in 1940; and 540 million tonnes in 1950. Current oil production is about 2167 million tonnes a year.

Yet demand has kept pace with supply, although two crises in the last few years have underlined the dangers inherent in industrial economies heavily dependent on oil.

In the mid-1970s the big oil-producing countries of the Middle East raised the price of oil dramatically. This had disastrous consequences for the Western world (Western Europe, the U.S.A. and Canada, Australia, New Zealand and Japan), already struggling with inflation — prices going up, or the value of money going down — resulting from the mismanagement of their affairs.

## The Oil Refinery

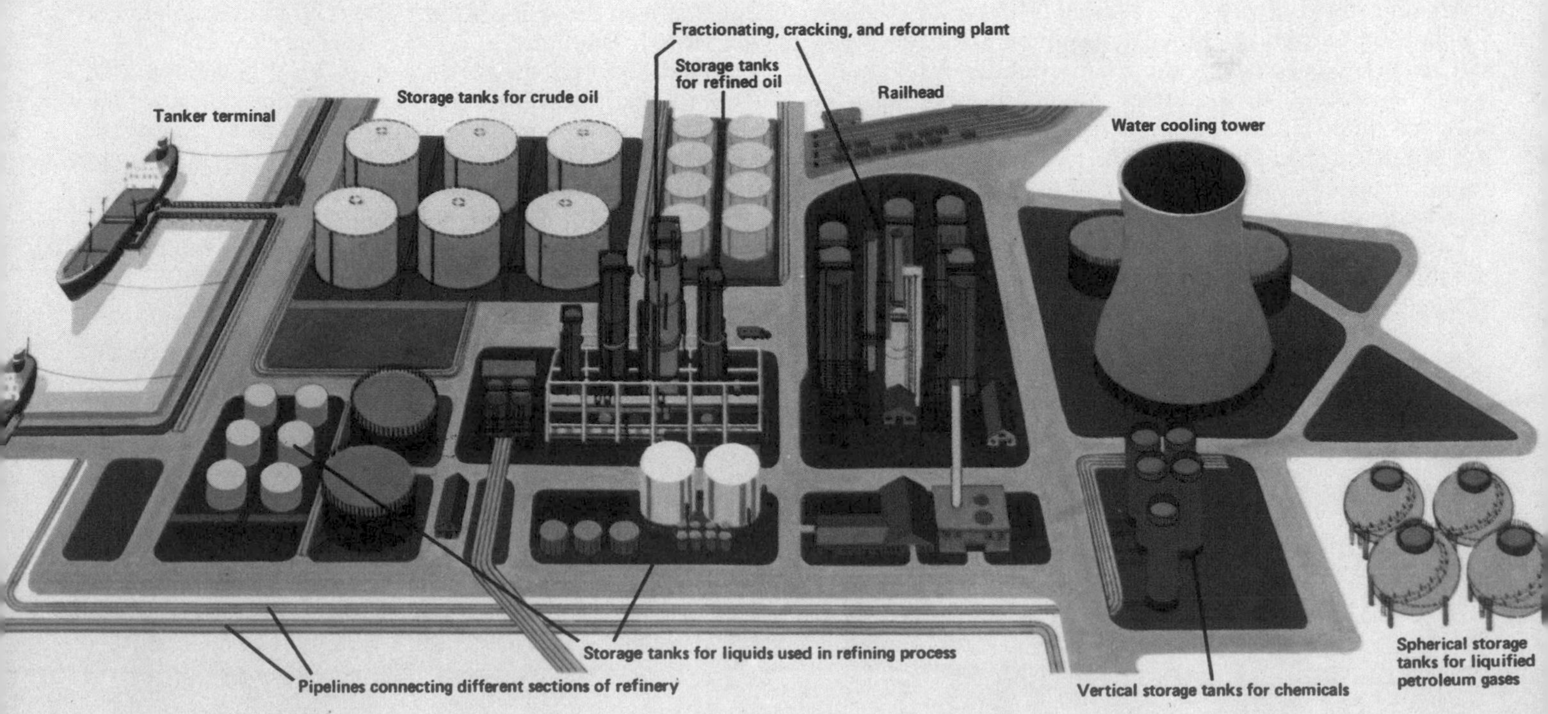

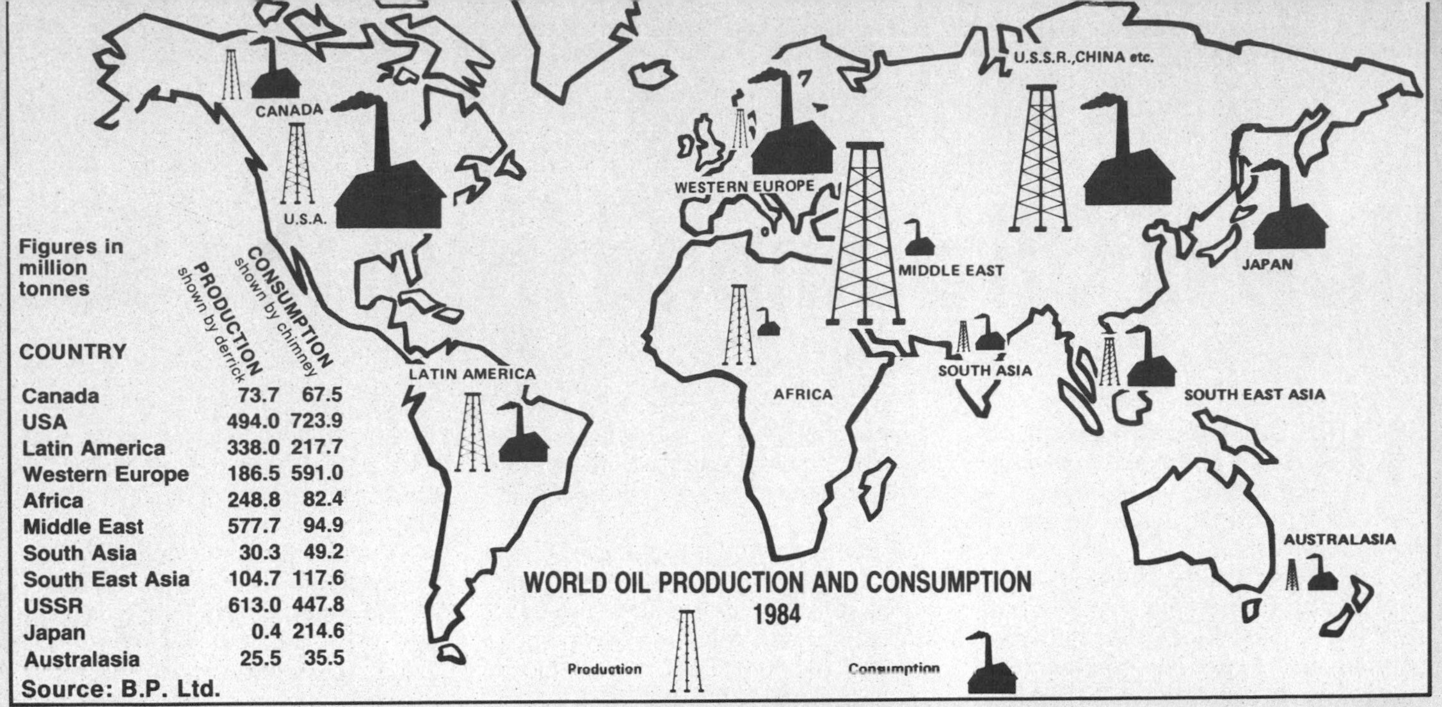


| COUNTRY | Production | Consumption |
|---|---|---|
| Canada | 73.7 | 67.5 |
| USA | 494.0 | 723.9 |
| Latin America | 338.0 | 217.7 |
| Western Europe | 186.5 | 591.0 |
| Africa | 248.8 | 82.4 |
| Middle East | 577.7 | 94.9 |
| South Asia | 30.3 | 49.2 |
| South East Asia | 104.7 | 117.6 |
| USSR | 613.0 | 447.8 |
| Japan | 0.4 | 214.6 |
| Australasia | 25.5 | 35.5 |

Source: B.P. Ltd.

**A look at the map above shows how the world relies on the Middle East. The huge Arab oilfields supply the oil-hungry countries of America, Europe and Japan.**

Then, in 1979, a political upheaval cut off the Iranian supply of 284 million tonnes a year. While Saudi Arabia, which boasts the biggest oil field in the world (the Ghawar, 240 km by 35 km), made good some of the shortfall, the outcome was an international shortage of petrol. Garages introduced unofficial rationing schemes and governments speed limits to reduce petrol consumption.

The outcome of these crises has been a new awareness of the wasteful way we have been using oil and its products (big, uneconomic cars, for example) and the urgent need to find an alternative fuel.

Ulf Lantz, executive director of the International Energy Agency, has predicted a world oil shortage of 200 million tonnes a year in 1985, 500 million by 1990, and 1,400 million by the end of the century. This estimate takes into account the known supplies yet to come on stream.

The biggest unexploited source at the moment is in Mexico. Pemex, the Mexican State Oil Company lists 6,125 million tonnes in proven reserves (more than the United States of America), and almost 18,000 million tonnes in potential reserves — second only to the Saudi Arabian reserves of 23,000 million tonnes.

But these vast Mexican reserves are still a long way from being tapped, and even when they are tapped it is debatable to what extent they will benefit the rest of the world. There is a strong feeling in the country, so long the poor, looked-down-upon neighbour of the United States, that it should resist firmly any attempt at foreign exploitation and that the greater part of this new-found wealth should be preserved for Mexico's own use.

The United States, despite being one of the world's leading oil producers, is also an importer of oil. This is because of lack of refineries in the right places rather than inability to produce domestic oil in sufficient quantities. Nevertheless, the world-wide oil crisis has caused the U.S. Bureau of Mines to take a closer look at ways of making oil production more efficient.

Only about a third of the oil in any particular reservoir is normally recovered. The Bureau of Mines estimates that, when all U.S. oil wells have officially run dry, they will still contain sufficient oil to meet U.S. needs for nearly half a century. The Bureau believes that 95 per cent of this oil could be tapped by drilling a system of vertical and horizontal mine shafts and then pumping in hot water to make the heavier oils flow more freely.

Long-term concern about oil supplies, allied to soaring demand and soaring price, has also led to increasing emphasis on trying to recover oil from the source where it was first formed — under the sea.

Fractionating column
Crude oil
Gas
Gas and light oils
Gasoline
Kerosene
Reforming plant
Medium oils
Diesel
Heavy oils
Hydrodesulphurization plant
Gasoline
Vacuum distillation plant
Cracking tower
Chemicals
Dewaxing unit
Wax
Solvent extraction plant
Fuel oil
Viscosity breaker
Bitumen
Bitumen blower
Fuel oil
Bottled gas
Chemicals
Petrol for vehicles, industry and some light aircraft
Paraffin for industrial and domestic use
Diesel fuel
Plastics
Detergents
Synthetic rubbers
Man-made fibres
Fertilizers
Insecticides and herbicides
Glycerine
Solvents
Lubrication oils
Chemicals
Ointments
Polishes
Candles
Fuel oils for ships, factories and central heating
Asphalt and similar road surfaces. Water-proofing compounds. Roofing. Sealants
NATURAL GAS

**Left: An oil refinery has been described as the nearest thing to perpetual motion. It is one huge area of interrelated plant, tanks and pipes. And out of it come the raw products for a very large proportion of the things we use every day.**

# How is Oil pumped from the Sea?

**DRILLING for oil beneath the sea is no different in principle from drilling on dry land. It's just more difficult, more dangerous and more costly.**

The first offshore drilling platform was set up in the Gulf of Mexico in the late 1940s. Since then offshore drilling has expanded continuously until nowadays more than 20 per cent of all the world's oil comes from beneath the oceans.

Britain, once entirely dependent on imported supplies, has reaped a rich harvest from the extensive oil fields she shares with Norway in the North Sea. As a result she is now exporting something like 35 million tonnes of oil more than she imports. There are also indications that additional supplies, to be shared with France, may lie south-west of Cornwall beneath the waters of the Atlantic.

But offshore oil is expensive. Drilling rigs have to be constructed, each at a cost of several million pounds, and towed into position. Then, when the drilling rig strikes oil — or, more often, fails to strike any oil at all — the rig has to be moved to another location to start again.

Finally, if oil has been discovered and the find looks good, a production and storage platform, also costing millions of pounds, must be built and towed into position.

The world's largest fixed-leg drilling rigs are the four used by British Petroleum in their North Sea Forties Field. Each weighs 58,000 tonnes. The overall height from below the mudline to the top of the drilling rig is 209 metres, and their foundation piles, the deepest in the world, penetrate 100 metres into the sea-bed.

The concrete production and storage platform built for the Ninian Field, also in the North Sea is even bigger. It has an overall height of 250 metres and a ballasted weight of 600,000 tonnes.

The largest single-piece steel structure designed and constructed for the North Sea is the new platform in the Magnus field off Norway. This giant oil-drilling platform weighs 77,400 tonnes compared with the average of 50,000 tonnes. The platforms

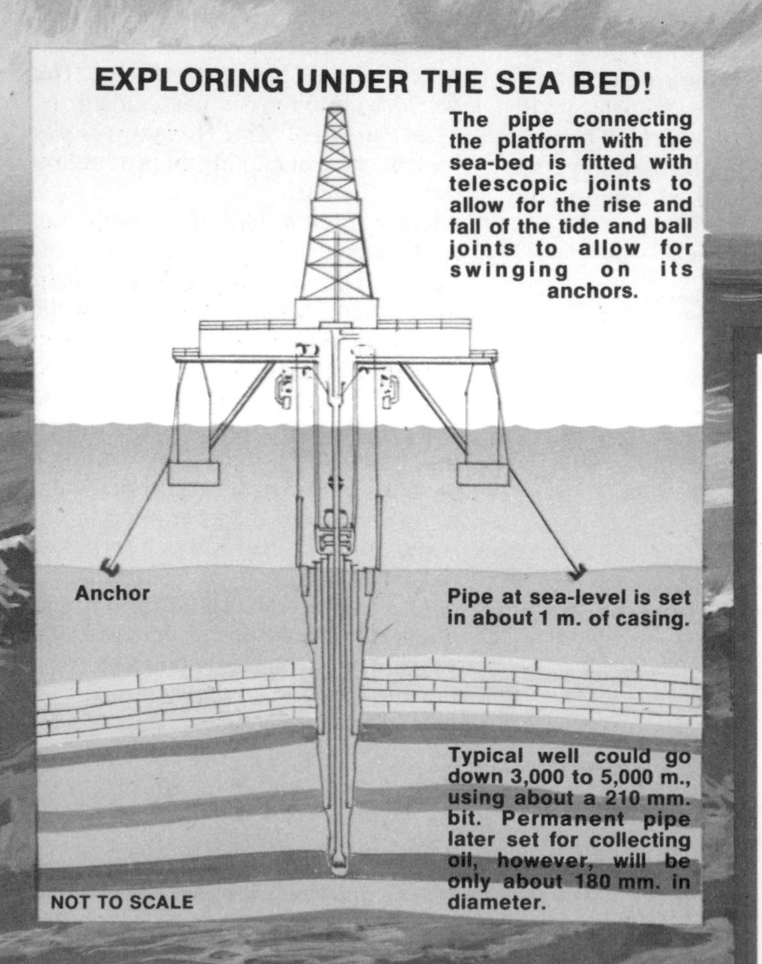

## SEA DRILLING RIGS

**THERE isn't really much difference between a land rig and a North Sea drilling rig – except that the North Sea rig floats on huge air-filled legs and is anchored to the sea by cables.**

**Although more expensive than a fixed rig in shallow water, floating rigs are cheaper in deeper waters such as those of the North Sea. The diagram on the left shows an exploratory drilling rig in fairly shallow water, while our main picture shows a fixed production platform — the well that actually produces oil — that stands on the sea-bed. In the future, however, huge floating production platforms are planned for use at deeper North Sea sites.**

**From the base of the production platform, wells are drilled in all directions to reach as much of the precious oil as possible. In the Forties Field in the North Sea, for example, 27 such wells lead from each platform so that one platform taps over an area of 2,400 hectares. The deepest wells may sink to 3,400 metres below the sea-bed, but the average depth is about 2,100 metres. The platform itself stands over 120 metres above the sea-bed.**

Drilling platform tapping wide area of sea bed.

## WHY FLARES? WASTEFUL? NO!

**At first sight, the bright, dancing flame that always seems to be burning above an oil rig seems to be a terrible waste. The flame is burning gas. Surely precious fuel should not be wasted in this way?**

**In fact there are three good reasons for these flares. Firstly, often after all the useful gas has been extracted, a small amount is left which is uneconomic to process. Secondly, highly poisonous gases — such as hydrogen sulphide, the gas that produces the 'rotten egg' smell of stink bombs — must be burnt. Thirdly, sometimes the pressure of gas in a well builds up so rapidly that the only safe way to dispose of the gas in an emergency is to burn it immediately.**

**In addition, some of the gas that would have been burnt off is used to heat and power the oil rig.**

**Below: Different drill bits have been developed to deal with different rocks. Mud is pumped down to lubricate the bit and to carry away rock particles.**

**Above: Floormen manhandle a pipe on an offshore drilling rig in the Arabian Gulf. The large circular 'table' at the bottom turns the drill pipe and hence the bit.**

**Left. The most common drill bit has tungsten (a very hard metal) teeth set on rollers.**

**Right: Mud is pumped down the drill pipe and out through the bit to lubricate it.**

**Left: This bit is studded with industrial diamonds and is used for cutting very hard rocks.**

are built to withstand waves up to 30 metres high.

Each production platform is sited where it can tap a large area of oil-bearing rock. To achieve this, bore holes are drilled out at an angle from the platform. There may be as many as 40 or 50 of these holes, each bringing in its harvest of hard-won oil. The incoming oil is controlled by what oilmen call 'a Christmas tree', a complicated arrangement of pipes, taps and valves.

Crude oil is sometimes pumped ashore through a pipeline which lies in a specially cut trench on the sea-bed. But some oilfields are far too far from land, or do not have enough oil, to make the laying of an expensive pipeline worthwhile. Then tankers are normally used.

## Problems

But large tankers are difficult to manoeuvre, and cannot be brought alongside a production platform. So a mooring buoy is anchored to the sea-bed about two kilometres from the platform. The tanker can swing at the buoy while the crude oil is pumped aboard. In some cases the buoys are attached to huge storage tanks on the sea-bed into which the oil is pumped to await the tanker's arrival.

As well as the high costs of drilling and production platforms, plus the high failure rate of test bores, the price of labour adds to the expense of seeking offshore oil. Life on board an oil rig is hard and uncomfortable. The men work 12 hours a day, often on cold, wet, oily decks. Accidents are not uncommon. There is always the danger that storms will wreck a rig and place everybody's life in jeopardy. Men have to be compensated for the hardship, the loneliness and the danger by being paid high wages.

In addition, there is the cost of actually getting them to the rig. The crew may number a hundred men, committed to a fortnight on, a fortnight off. At the start of their two-week spell of duty it is quite likely that they will have to be flown from Scotland to Norway, then ferried out to the rigs by ship, while the men they are replacing make the journey in the opposite direction.

But as our need for oil grows, men will search for it in deeper and deeper waters. Bigger and bigger platforms will be built, and, before long, oilmen may be working in special chambers on the sea-bed, searching out, processing and pumping to the surface the 'black gold' on which — at the moment, at least — our civilisation depends to such a formidable extent.

# How do the tides produce energy?

**THEY are unstoppable. Each day throughout the world they flood on to the land and then retreat back into the oceans. They are driven by the colossal forces of the spinning Moon and Sun. They are the tides. Can Man harness their power?**

Hundreds of years ago one answer was the *tide mill*. This was just like the more common water mill, but instead of using the flow of river water down to the sea it used the tides. As the tide rose, sluice gates let in the waters to fill a large pool. When the tide began to fall these gates swung shut, holding in the newly collected water. This dammed-up water was then allowed to escape through a water wheel which turned in the normal way.

The power released in this way depended on the difference in water levels between high (in the pool) and low (in the sea below). This is called the *head* of water.

Unfortunately, the tides are not constant. They vary in size from month to month. Moreover, they also come at different times each day

It was the period following high tide that gave the mill most power, but this period did not always occur at a time convenient to those who used the mills. What's more, it was difficult to find men willing to work such irregular hours!

## Ancient principle — Modern plant

Yet this principle of using the tide to produce a head of water in a reservoir is still being used in one of the most spectacular energy producing plants in the world — the tidal barrage on the River Rance in Northern France.

Every year the Rance Tidal Power Station produces 500 million kilowatt-hours of electricity: that is enough to keep a million one-bar electric fires burning for 500 hours non-stop.

Rance was chosen because along the north coast of Brittany there is a large difference between the levels of high and low tide. In the Rance estuary the waters rise on average by 11.4 metres while the biggest tides rise 13.5 metres. The wide estuary collects water at the rate of 18,000 cubic metres every second during the rise (or flood) and fall (or ebb tide), and because the Rance itself is such a small river there is no great build up of silt to hinder this accumulation of water.

The water is collected by a huge barrage 15 metres above sea level which encloses a reservoir with a capacity of 184 million cubic metres of water. Every day there is an assured flow, whatever the state of flooding or drought in the region. Every day the tides can be relied on.

However, the Rance Station is not just a simple tidal mill which takes its power from the flow of water in one direction only. Far from it. The construction of the barrage is such that energy is produced both when the tide rises and when it ebbs.

A typical energy producing cycle would be:

**Stage 1:** The tide rises and enters the reservoir. As it does so it passes through 24 turbines or 'power bulbs' — each with blades nine metres in diameter — set in concrete under the barrage. The flow of water generates electricity for the French 'national grid' of power cables.

**Stage 2:** Near the top of the tide, when the head of water is insufficient to drive them, the turbines are put into a neutral position or 'feathered'. Then six huge sluice gates are opened so that the filling of the reservoir is completed.

**Stage 3:** As the tide turns, the sluice gates are closed and water from the reservoir is allowed to run out to sea. As it passes through the power bulbs it once more generates electricity.

## Variations

However there are many variations on the way the barrage can be used. Indeed there are so many that a computer is used to work out the best sequence according to the circumstances.

For example, sometimes it is worthwhile running the turbines as pumps to pump extra water into the reservoir. One occasion when this is done is during a period when little electricity is being used — for example early on a summer morning. Surplus energy in the national grid can then be used to pump water into the reservoir — to be let out to generate electricity during a time of peak demand.

The power produced by the barrage varies with the tide. Outflowing water produces more than a rising tide because of the way the power bulbs are designed and because the outgoing water is more controllable than the incoming tide.

But the really crucial issue is: how big a head of water is there? A head of 11 metres gives 10 megawatts per power bulb. But a mere 3 metres gives only 3.2 megawatts when the flow is from estuary to sea and 2 megawatts when the flow is from sea to estuary.

So tides may be reliable but not so reliable as to produce all the energy Man would like.

One obvious problem with tidal barrages is that by blocking off an estuary the passage of ships is prevented. So an important feature of the Rance Barrage is that it dams the water but still allows ships to pass. At the western end of the barrage is a lock through which ships can pass.

Despite the problems, however, tidal power stations, provided that convenient sites can be found, are clearly of value if the experience of the French is anything to judge by. There are plans in the U.S.S.R. to site a huge tidal station on the White Sea which would produce 10,000 megawatts — the equivalent of a quarter of the electricity used in England and Wales in mid winter. In the more distant future outputs could exceed even this.

This is what the Rance Power Station would look like if it were cut vertically down through the roadway. It shows the ship lock and the 'power bulbs', or turbines, which generate the electricity. To let ships through, the roadway lifts (above).

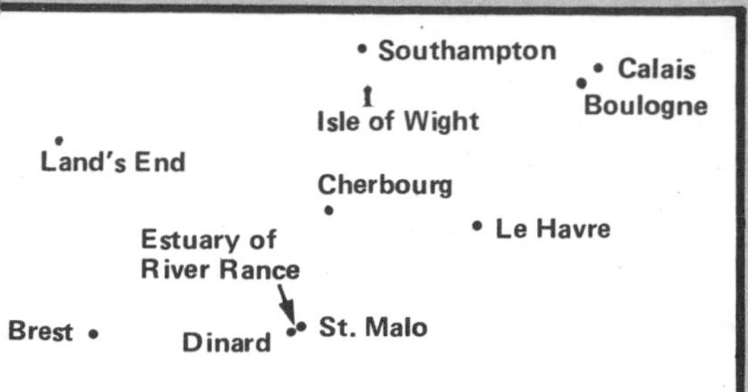


Large tides are common on the Brittany coast of northern France. The Rance Power Station not only puts those tides to work, it also provides a direct road between St. Malo and Dinard.

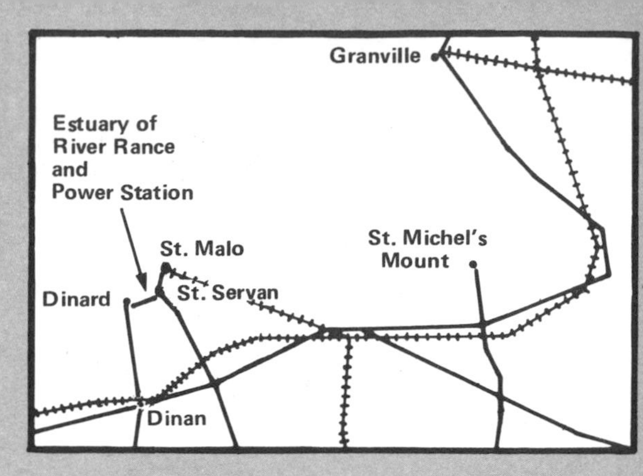


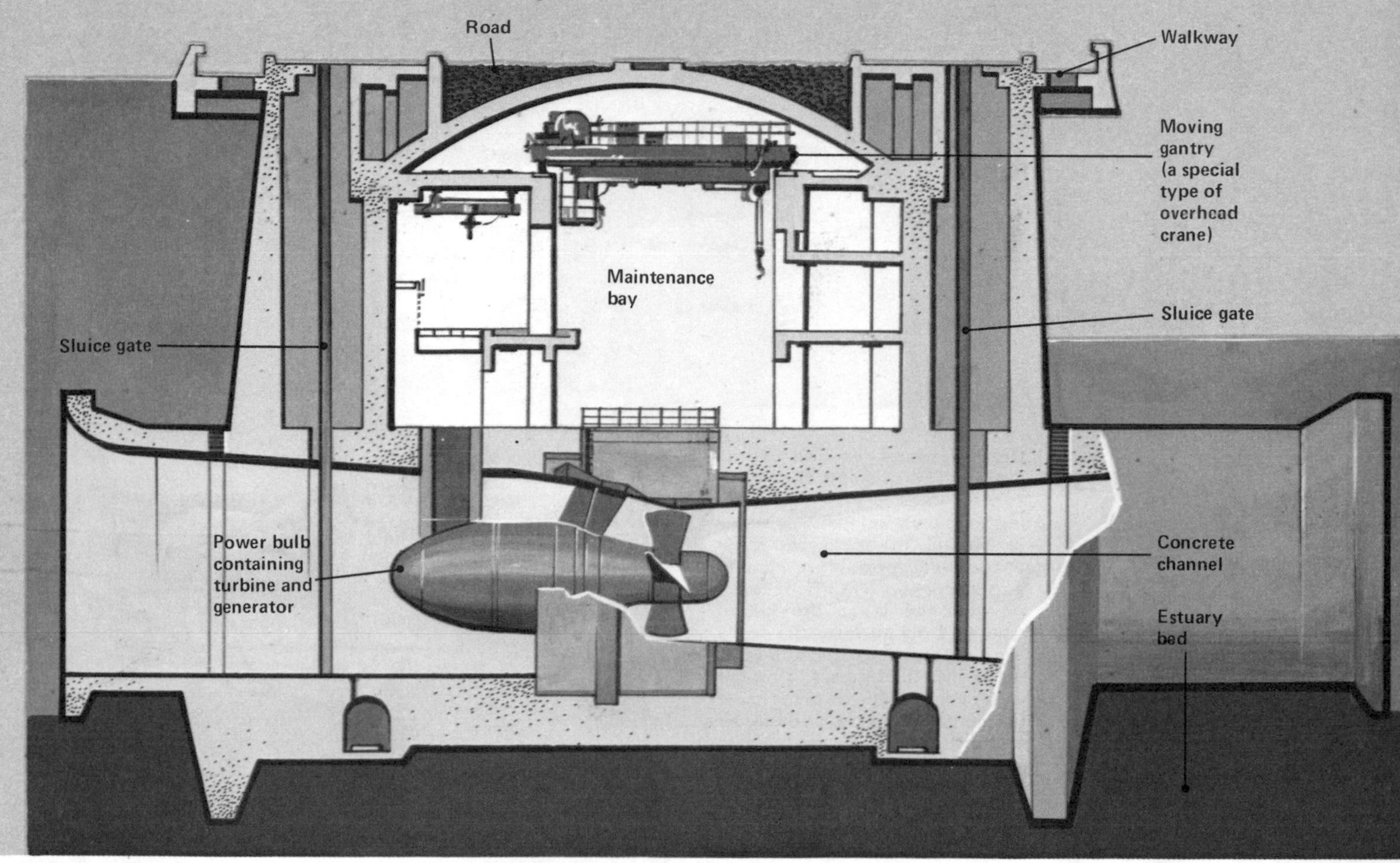


Above: This cross-section through the barrage shows how the power bulbs are set in channels through which the water passes. Stairs lead down to the bulbs from a maintenance bay set inside the barrage itself.

# How does a Submarine submerge?

ON 7th May, 1915, the luxury liner *Lusitania* was heading towards Southampton on its return voyage from New York. Suddenly, at 2.09 p.m. without any prior warning, a German torpedo struck her square amidships. Within twenty minutes, the *Lusitania* and 1,200 of her passengers went to the bottom.

The reaction to the barbarous act was immediate. From every quarter of the world, outraged protests flooded into Germany. The lethal power of the submarine could not have been given a more telling demonstration.

The rapid development of the submarine during the last half of the 19th century was one of trial and error, in which the engineers of many nations participated.

After the Confederates had lost the American Civil War in 1866, and their fleet of "submarines" had either been scuttled or sunk, it was temporarily left to France to continue work on the idea of a fully submersible boat. Germany was close on her heels.

One man does deserve to be singled out for his contribution to the development of the submarine. J.P. Holland was an American without any capital, or the ability to find backers for his schemes — yet somehow he managed to build a submarine which could be depended on to perform with a fair degree of efficiency.

Holland's vessels could convey five men for 80 kilometres underwater at an average speed of five knots. One major design breakthrough was the electric battery which drove the submarine underwater — it did not need oxygen. The only problem was that the batteries were quickly exhausted, leaving the sub no

**On the surface, the main ballast tanks are full of air (1). For diving, special holes in the bottom called free flood holes, allow water to rise into the tanks and force the air out through the open vents on top (2). Fully submerged, the tanks are full of water (3). To surface, the vents are shut and high pressure air is blown into the tanks, forcing the water out through the holes in the bottom (4). Near the surface, air is drawn in through the conning tower (5) and compressed to help "blow out" the tanks (6). Underwater, movements are controlled by *hydroplanes* (moveable side fins) at the front and rear (7, 8 & 9).**

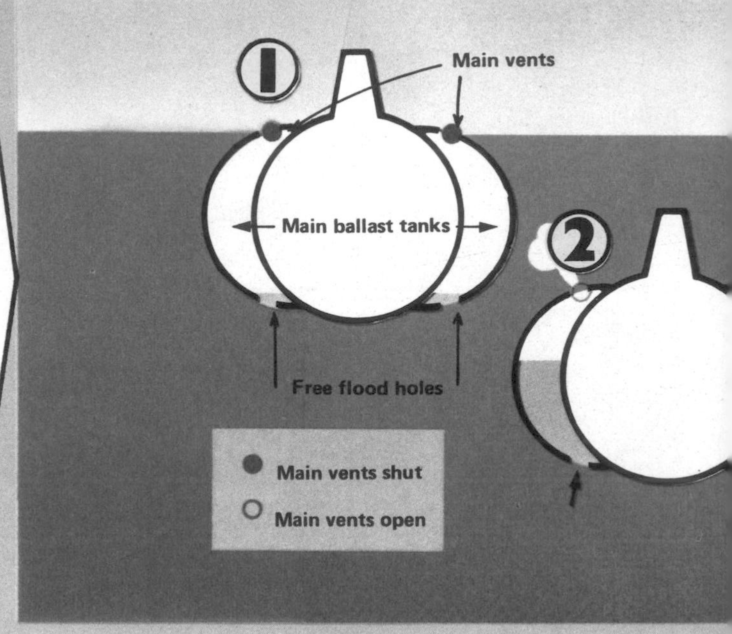


130m

52m

Double-decker bus

**Left: To give some idea of the size of a modern nuclear-powered Polaris submarine (130 m long), we have compared it with Nelson's Column (52 m high) and a conventional double-decker bus.**

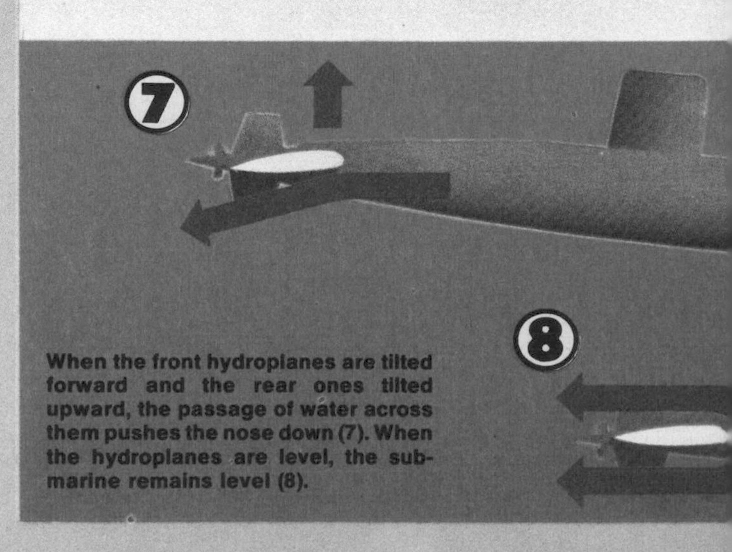


**When the front hydroplanes are tilted forward and the rear ones tilted upward, the passage of water across them pushes the nose down (7). When the hydroplanes are level, the submarine remains level (8).**

option but to return to the surface.

Holland's submarines could submerge in a matter of minutes, fire a self-propelled torpedo and return to the surface on command. In 1901, the British Navy reluctantly ordered five Holland submarines, despite the widespread conviction that they were "unfair, underhand and damned un-English".

But in Germany, submarines were treated with more respect. When the First World War broke out in 1914, they were well-equipped to take on the finest navy in the world — the British Navy. They could only bring Britain to her knees by cutting her vital trade routes.

Submarines held a key role in this strategy. Throughout the war, Germany concentrated on increasing her U-Boat fleet. Any ship, regardless of nationality, was fair game for the underwater attackers in Europe's crowded sea lanes.

This policy almost won the First World War for Germany. One of the darkest moments for the British came in 1915. During the month of April, over 500 ships were sunk by German U-Boats. One ship out of four never returned. In all, more than 5,500 Allied ships were sunk during the course of the war.

No longer was there any question of the strategic value of submarines. They had boldly taken their place in national armoured forces.

But as the military importance of the submarine increased, so did the measures to render them ineffective. During the 1920s, a new invention called ASDIC enabled surface warships to detect enemy submarines. ASDIC (the initials stood for Allied Submarine Detection Investigation Committee) was a method of

*Continued on next page*

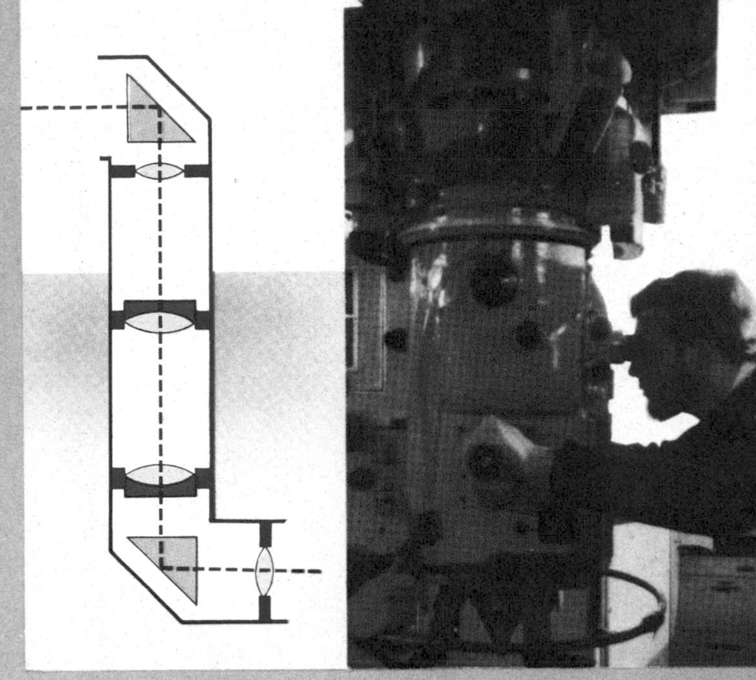

**The modern periscope is a complex instrument, employing a series of prisms and lenses to carry the image from the objective piece (above water) to the eyepiece (below water). Today, submarines have two periscopes — a large *binocular* search periscope, visible to radar and lookouts, and a smaller *monocular* attack periscope, less efficient but harder to detect.**

## How a Submarine Dives

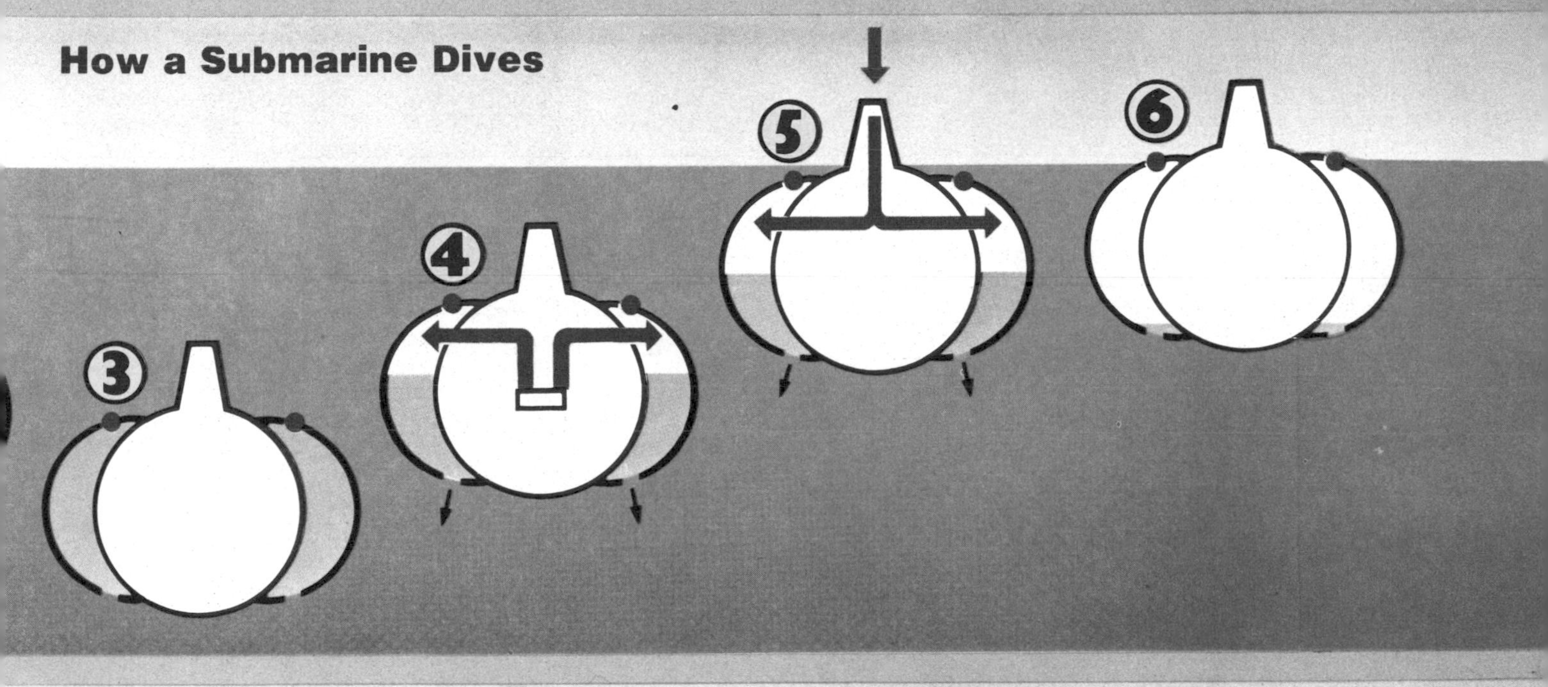


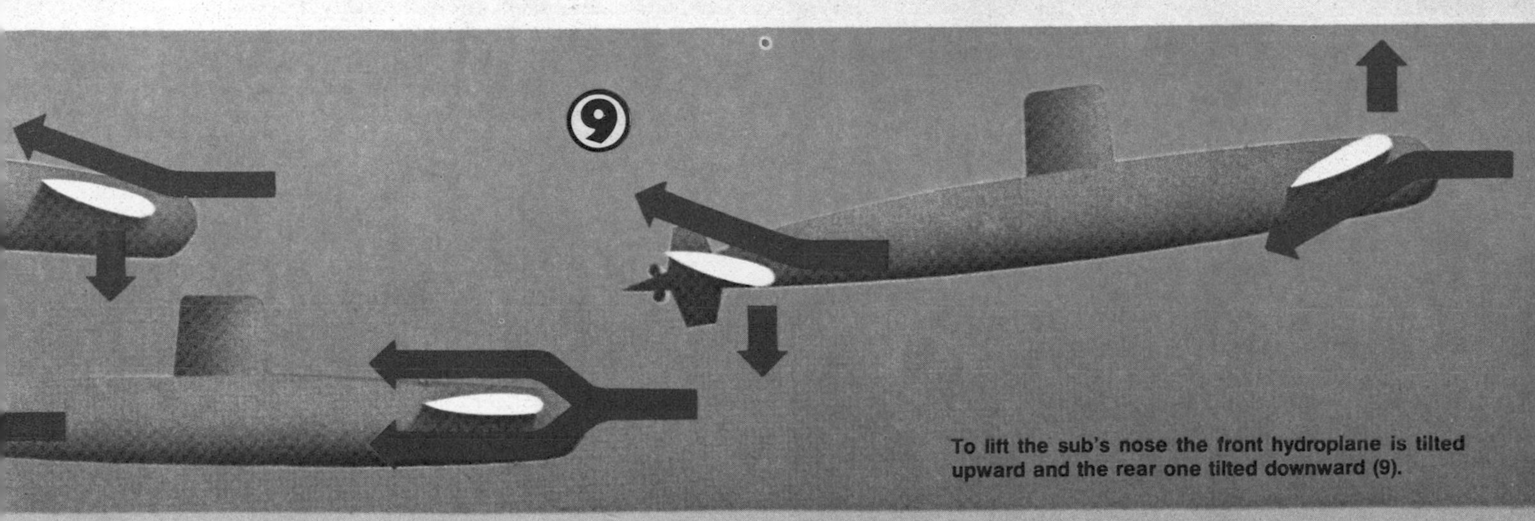


To lift the sub's nose the front hydroplane is tilted upward and the rear one tilted downward (9).

The world's first nuclear-powered submarine was the US Navy's *Nautilus*, launched in 1954. Nearly 100 m long, it had a maximum speed of 20 knots and carried a crew of 96. Two years after its first sea trial, it was refuelled for the first time, having covered a distance of 111,000 km.

pinpointing nearby vessels using sound waves. These were sent out by a scanner fitted on the bottom of a destroyer, and would bounce back to the destroyer if they met any objects in their path. In this way, the destroyer could get a "fix" on a submarine's position — and hopefully destroy it with powerful underwater explosives.

It was not long, however, before submarines were equipped with the new device — and the deadly game of cat and mouse under the waves only became more complicated.

When the Second World War opened, the concept of submarine warfare was still the same: attack and destroy enemy commerce. Submarine campaigns were waged world-wide by the navies of Britain, Germany, the United States, Italy and Japan.

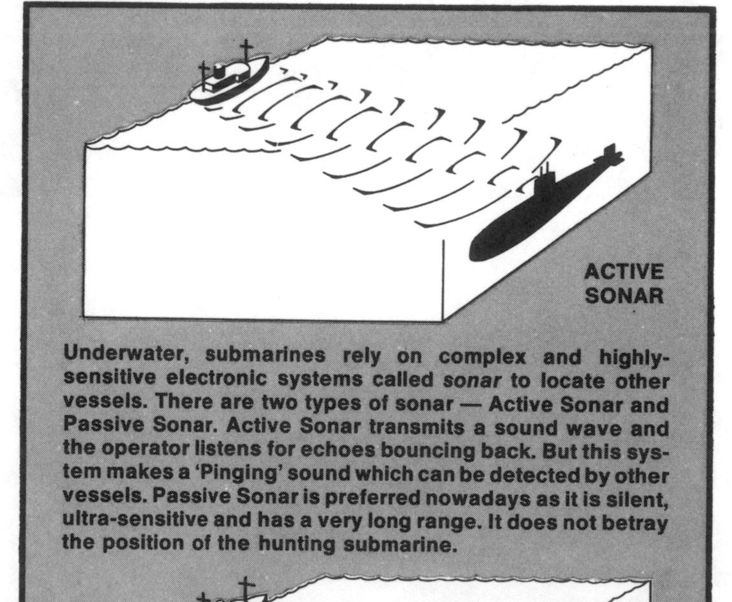

Underwater, submarines rely on complex and highly-sensitive electronic systems called *sonar* to locate other vessels. There are two types of sonar — Active Sonar and Passive Sonar. Active Sonar transmits a sound wave and the operator listens for echoes bouncing back. But this system makes a 'Pinging' sound which can be detected by other vessels. Passive Sonar is preferred nowadays as it is silent, ultra-sensitive and has a very long range. It does not betray the position of the hunting submarine.

Yet it was the process involved in building the bomb which ended the Second World War that produced the most significant advance in the submarine's development.

Scientists had discovered nuclear fission, a process in which enormous amounts of energy could be created in a very small space. At first, naval technicians wanted to use this energy to drive submarines.

The advantages were obvious. Nuclear fission does not need oxygen to produce energy — a major problem with any vehicle which has to be propelled underwater. If a nuclear engine could be installed in a submarine, it would be able to cruise indefinitely under the surface without needing to come up for air.

Work on this project was halted in favour of the Atom Bomb — but after the war, it was resumed in the United States. Success finally came on 17th January, 1955 when the USS *Nautilus* sent the triumphant signal, "Underway under nuclear power". Five years later, the USS *Triton* sailed completely round the world submerged.

## Missiles

The next chapter — and perhaps the most frightening one in the submarine's history came in the 1950s with the development of the intercontinental ballistic missile —ICBMs for short.

These were rockets capable of carrying a nuclear warhead to any target within a 1,600 km radius. Later this was extended to a 3,200 and then a 4,800 km radius.

But when the ICBM was paired with the nuclear submarine, man had created a weapon of war that was deadlier than anything before. Nuclear submarines armed with nuclear missiles could spend months underwater, ready to unleash global destruction at a moment's notice.

Both the Americans and the Russians have large numbers of nuclear submarines patrolling the oceans of the world on a round-the-clock basis. Submarines have now become the most important strategic weapon in any World War, for their "deterrent" role.

The argument runs that should a major power wish to win a war by launching an all-out nuclear attack, it will be prevented from doing so by the knowledge that the enemy has submarines capable of retaliating with nuclear missiles.

It is a curious fact that these once-shakey craft have developed into the most powerful weapons the world has ever known.

# What is the Workhorse of the Sea?

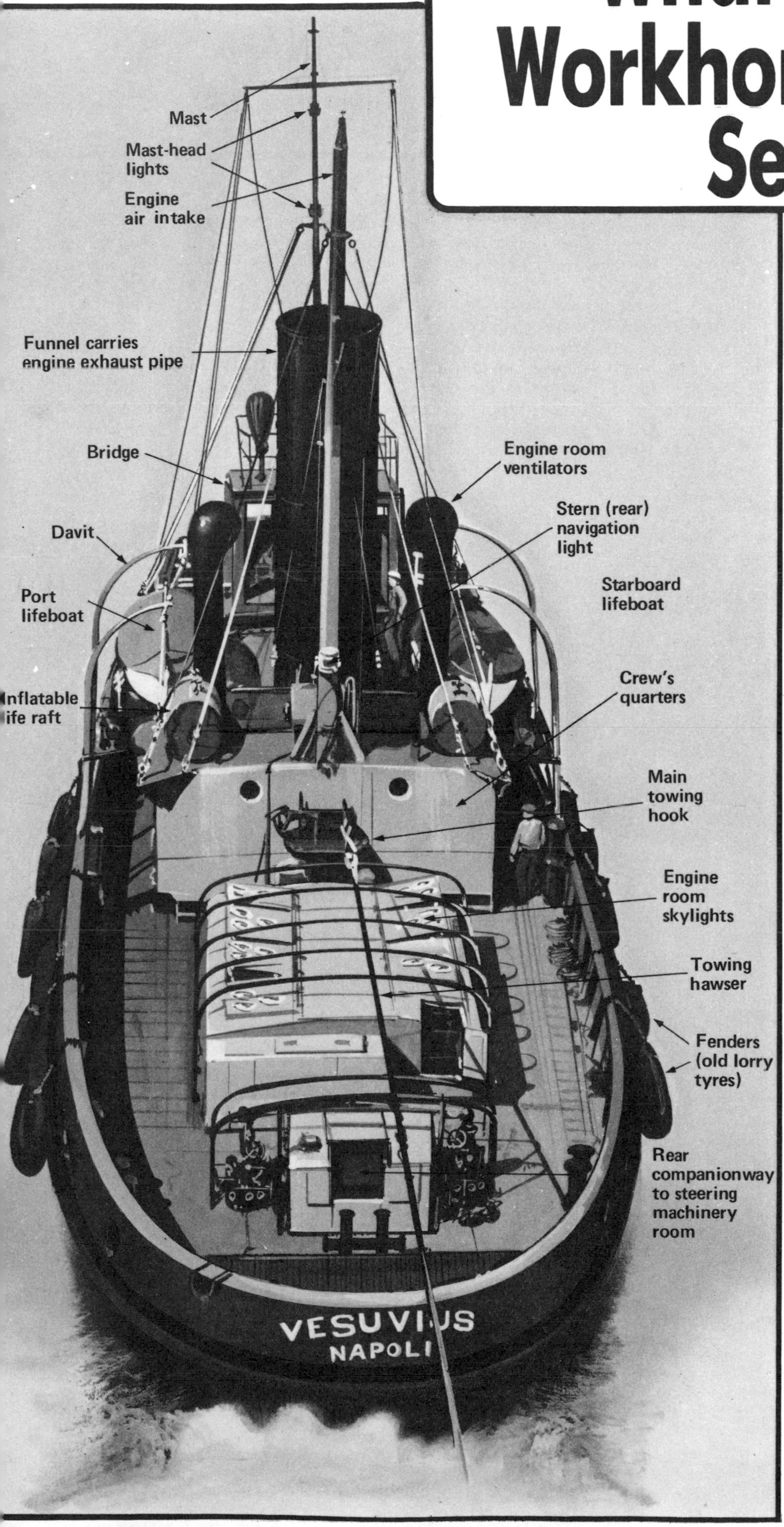

**THROUGH the darkness and the ferocious storm the captain of the huge cargo ship could just make out the small fleet of tugs approaching to bring help. He breathed a deep sigh of relief, knowing that these little workhorses of the seas would be able to drag his vessel, which had been damaged by fire in the engine room, back to the safety of the harbour. The tugboats would save his ship — and the lives of all those on board.**

In other places tugs are helping to manoeuvre passenger liners into port, towing or pushing barges alongside the wharves for unloading, and helping to keep the steady stream of floating traffic going in the busy ports of the world. Without tugs there would be river-based traffic jams and valuable cargoes would stand idle in the holds.

Tugs are very versatile craft. They can be large, sea-going vessels or tiny — though powerful — river craft weaving in and out of many obstacles. The practice of using one boat for towing another goes back to the beginning of the 19th century when steamships such as the *Charlotte Dundas* were pulling barges along the Forth and Clyde Canals in Scotland. How useful it was in the days of ocean-going sailing ships that tugboats from London, the Mersey and the Clyde could venture out to the waters off the south-west coast of Ireland and help them into harbour!

Today a modern tug may, with the aid of a 300m long towrope, help pull a floating dock thousands of kilometres to its destination or bring an obsolete warship across the Atlan-

*Continued on page 85.*

On the Mississippi River, as in New York Harbour, tugs do not tow but push. Now some remarkable 'pusher trains' are seen. Tugs are around 60m long with diesel powered engines. These push trains of up to 15 barges carrying tonnes of coal and steel. The whole train can be over 300m in length. At the bow of the tug is a strong 'head log' on which are mounted four large 'knees'. These act by transmitting the thrust of the boat to the fleet of barges. The picture below is of the bow arrangement of the Mississippi tugboat *Richard Moyle*. The bottom of the boat often has a sloped design to allow a good flow of water to the propellors giving more pushing power. The Mississippi pushboat began when it was realised that the early river steamships, with their rear paddle wheels, were unsuitable for towing because there was nowhere astern on the boat where a towline could be attached.



## Tugs and barges around the World

The busy waterways of Northern Europe are picturesque. But they are also quite distinctive in the types of vessels they use to move cargoes. Sails are a common sight in the windmill-dotted Netherlands where the men who navigate the *tjalks, schuyts* and *hoogasts*, all traditional types of small Dutch canal barges, shut off their engines at every opportunity. These long canals connect busy ports like Hamburg, Rotterdam and Antwerp to the farthest corners of Europe.

In contrast, barges over 60m long are loaded at the ports with huge amounts of grain from North America or the Argentine which is carried to the inland cities. The barges are usually painted black with white cabins and have strong towing bitts to take the strain on the ropes. Some tugs have screw-driven engines while others have distinctive paddle wheels and glide down the River Rhine at a leisurely 12 to 14km/h. Often the crew have comfortable quarters on board the barges. The barges can be towed in twos (as in this picture) or in threes or fours.

# BARGIN-

# BARGING AMERICAN STYLE

tic for demolition. The tug is also called into service to put in place a massive offshore oil drilling platform — a steel island-home for scientists and oil men trying to tap valuable fuel resources under the sea.

So tugs have to be powerful. A typical seagoing vessel today will be about 60m long, and 10m wide, driven by two diesel engines giving powerful thrust.

Most large tugs are equipped with fire-fighting gear and powerful pumps to help leaking ships in danger of sinking. Most important is the towing gear. The 'rope' is not ordinary rope at all but a steel or nylon cable made up of many thin strands. It is attached to the tug by means of a winch driven by a big engine. The winch is set to take a certain strain. If this is exceeded — say by a ship being towed lurching suddenly — more cable is instantly paid out. When the strain is released, the cable is automatically winched back in.

From the large tugs we move right down in size according to the job in hand. In fact some smaller tugs have been fitted with a special propellor to give them increased manoeuvrability. This is called the *Voith-Schneider* propeller after its inventors. Fitted to the underside of the ship, rather than the stern, it is like a large turntable with five blades hanging down into the water. Since each blade can turn on its own axis, water can be forced through the blades and the tug's direction changed — all under the control of the pilot's joystick. This means the tug can turn in a very confined space. But large or small, a tug is an indispensable part of the world of navigation and can certainly be called the workhorse of the sea.

**Right: The *United States* is one of the most modern Mississippi tugboats. With four powerful diesel engines and very modern navigation equipment, this boat can push a fleet of 40 barges weighing 40,000 tonnes and over 500m in length. There are 10 rudders for steering accuracy.**

**The decks serve as accommodation for car drivers when the boat is pushing barges ferrying hundreds of cars.**

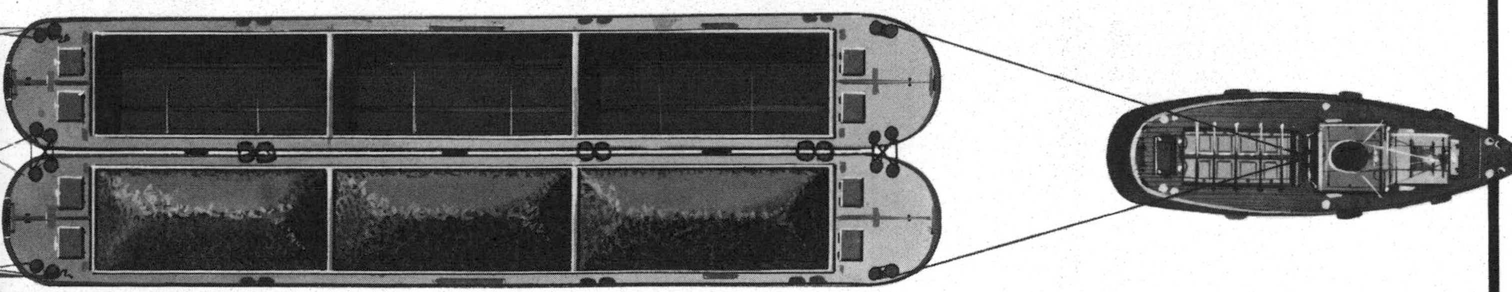

# EUROPEAN STYLE

# Who invented the Glider?

Otto Lilienthal (1848-1896) and his brother Gustave (1849-1933) began their research into gliders in 1871. They studied bird flight, laying the foundations for the modern science of aerodynamics. In 1891, Otto built his first monoplane (single wing) design and by 1894 was experimenting with a biplane design (as above). He crashed in a test flight on August 9, 1896 and died the next day.

## Otto Lilienthal's 'Flying Machine'

**This design was patented on August 20, 1895. The wing was curved as the bottom side view shows. The pilot's weight was carried by the bar arrangement at the centre of the wing.**

**Above: Lilienthal's gliders were light in construction but long in the wingspan. To transport them to gliding sites, the wing could be folded in this arrangement.**

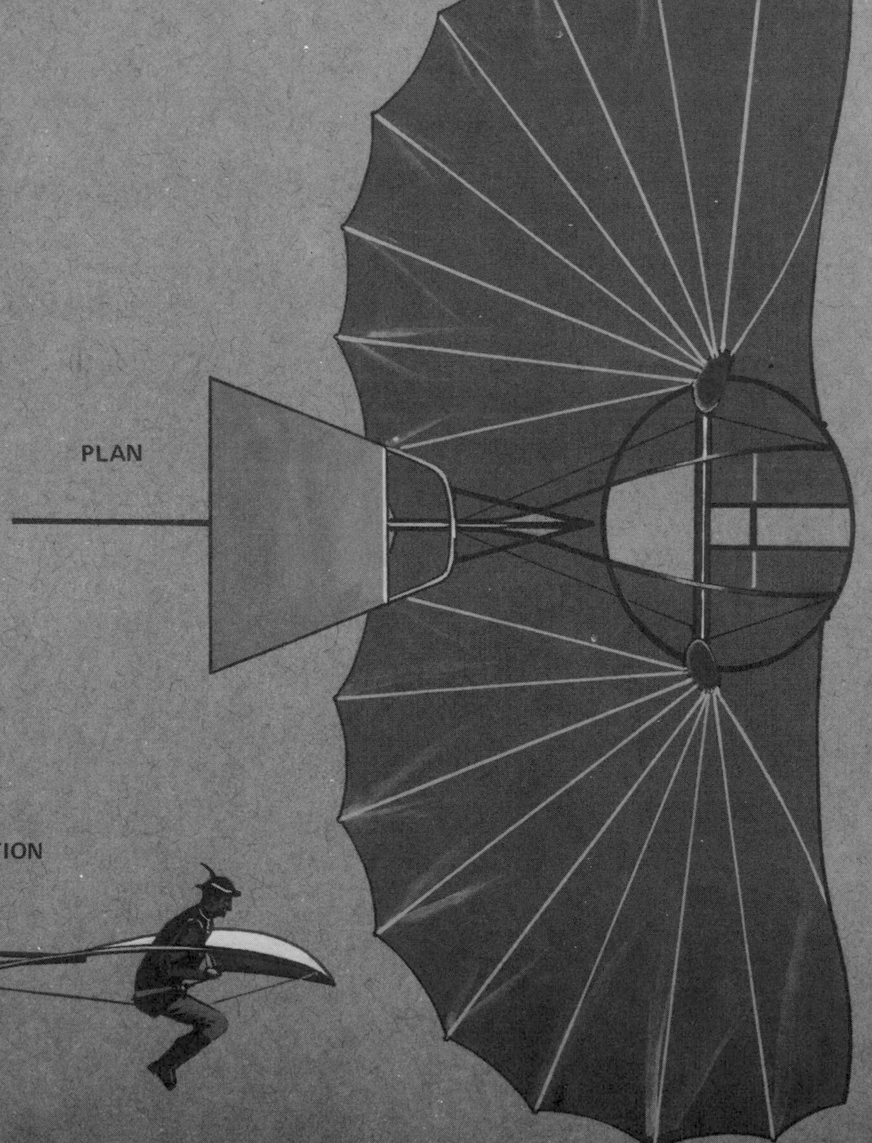

**THINK of hang-gliding and chances are you will think of tanned, T-shirted young Californians leaping off the hilltops around San Francisco Bay; or enthusiasts launching themselves off the cliffs at Brighton; or dare-devils swooping down from mountain peaks in France.**

Instead, cast your mind back to the year 1891. The place is not San Francisco or Brighton but Stöllen in Germany, where two dedicated young men — Otto and Gustave Lilienthal — are preparing for yet another test flight with their frail-looking, unpowered flying machine.

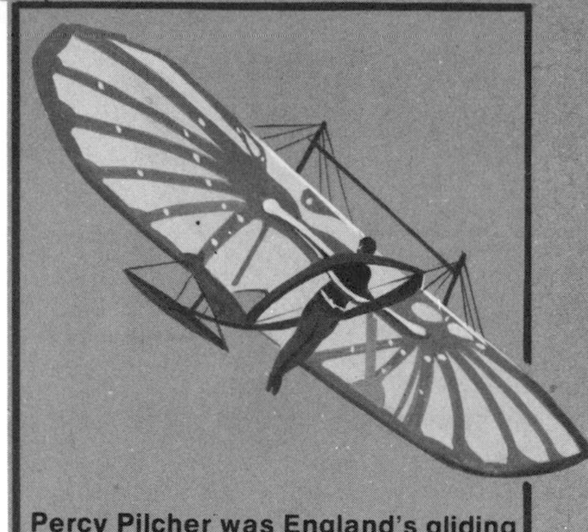

Percy Pilcher was England's gliding pioneer and designed several successful monoplane gliders. He was killed in a test flight in 1899 aged 33.

Octave Chanute (1832-1910) was another important gliding pioneer. His biplane design (shown here) was very successful and first flew in 1896. The pilot sat in an open cage beneath the wings. It was very stable and made over 1,000 flights, some nearly 50 m long. Chanute's work greatly influenced the Wright brothers.

They have carried this strange device to the top of a hill by dead of night to avoid being ridiculed by their friends. After the test has been made, the brothers will return to their workshop to record every detail of the flight for future reference. Their ultimate aim is to achieve the seemingly impossible goal of fully-controlled, powered flight.

Even as schoolboys, Otto and Gustave Lilienthal had experimented with model gliders. At the age of only 13, Otto even went so far as to equip himself with artificial wings of his own design and attempt to fly by furiously flapping his arms — alas to no avail!

Otto's enthusiasm remained undiminished and the brothers began to adopt a more serious approach. They studied the flying characteristics of birds with great intensity, and were the first researchers to carefully note the exact angles of the birds' wings as they reacted to crosswinds and air currents.

In 1889, after many years of careful study, came, the publication of Otto's book, *Bird Flight as the Basis of Aviation,* which was subsequently read with great interest by the handful of inventors then engaged in aeronautical experiments on both sides of the Atlantic.

Otto Lilienthal's first glider was built in 1891 and was a monoplane (single wing) design formed by a willow frame covered with waxed cotton. It had a wingspan of seven metres and was controlled by Lilienthal shifting his body weight forwards or backwards, or from side to side, from his position at the centre of the wing. From there, with his legs dangling down, he was able to launch the craft by running down the side of a slope, though earlier test flights were made from an improvised springboard in his back garden!

## Disaster

Lilienthal's subsequent designs were of similar construction to his first glider, though he soon added a long tail for improved stability and later experimented with biplane (double wing) gliders. He often leapt from a 'hill' he constructed on flat ground in order to avoid freak air currents from the surrounding countryside.

Lilienthal's work produced increasingly impressive results, but disaster struck on August 9, 1896 when, whilst making a test flight in one of his monoplane gliders, he lost control of his craft and plunged 15 metres to the ground. He broke his spine in the accident and died the following day. Up until the time of his death, Otto Lilienthal had made over 2,000 test flights. His dying words were 'Sacrifices must be made'.

The quest for controlled flight claimed another life just three years later when, on September 30, 1899, the British aviator Percy Pilcher crashed as a result of one of his glider's rudder cables breaking during a public demonstration. He died three days later, aged only 33. Pilcher had earlier visited Otto Lilienthal in Germany to discuss gliding and was close to achieving powered flight at the time of his death.

The machine with which he had hoped to achieve this goal, *The Hawk,* was already built and lacked only a suitable engine. This was in fact being constructed in the months leading up to his accident.

# The modern sport of hang gliding

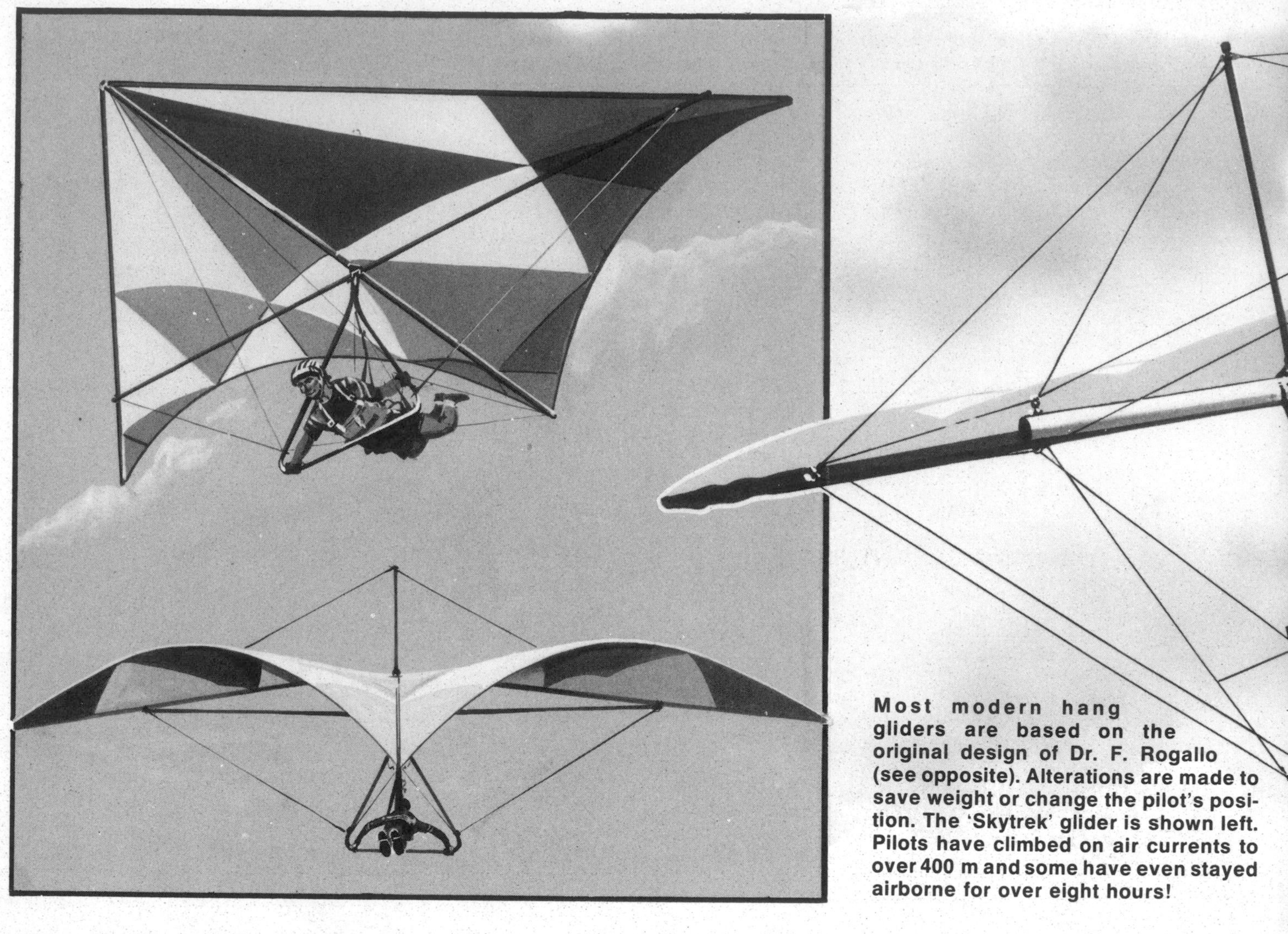

Most modern hang gliders are based on the original design of Dr. F. Rogallo (see opposite). Alterations are made to save weight or change the pilot's position. The 'Skytrek' glider is shown left. Pilots have climbed on air currents to over 400 m and some have even stayed airborne for over eight hours!

The pilot in the prone-flying position, and in the standing position (usually for running take-off).

Meanwhile, other people were hard at work in the U.S.A. Foremost amongst these was Octave Chanute. He had already made a great name for himself by laying down some of the most important railway lines in the United States. He is credited also with inventing the technique of preserving wooden railway sleepers by coating them with creosote.

Some of Chanute's glider designs were multi-wing devices, others were of a more conventional construction but featured moveable control surfaces on the wings, operated from the pilot's 'cockpit'. This was because Chanute, felt that it was unwise for the pilot to have to sway around from side to side to control his aircraft. He decided that some kind of precision control was needed.

Perhaps Chanute's most important contribution to aviation was his willingness to pass on his vast knowledge of practical aeronautics to others. This factor played a significant part in the subsequent success of the famous Wright brothers, with whom Chanute was in constant contact for some 10 years.

But it is only in the last decade that this very basic method of flying came back into its own — this time as a sport. In the early 1970's, groups of young Californians took to the air in frail kite-like craft constructed of aluminium tubing and covered with plastic sheets.

This 'new' craze soon took hold and spread all over the world. Much work on the design of the craft had been carried out by a space research scientist, Dr. F. M. Rogallo, whose surname was rapidly adopted for these strange-looking flying machines. Just like Otto Lilienthal and the other pioneers, these modern birdmen control their Rogallos by shifting their body weight from one place to another.

With an increasing number of followers, this exhilarating new sport looks like staying with us for many years to come.

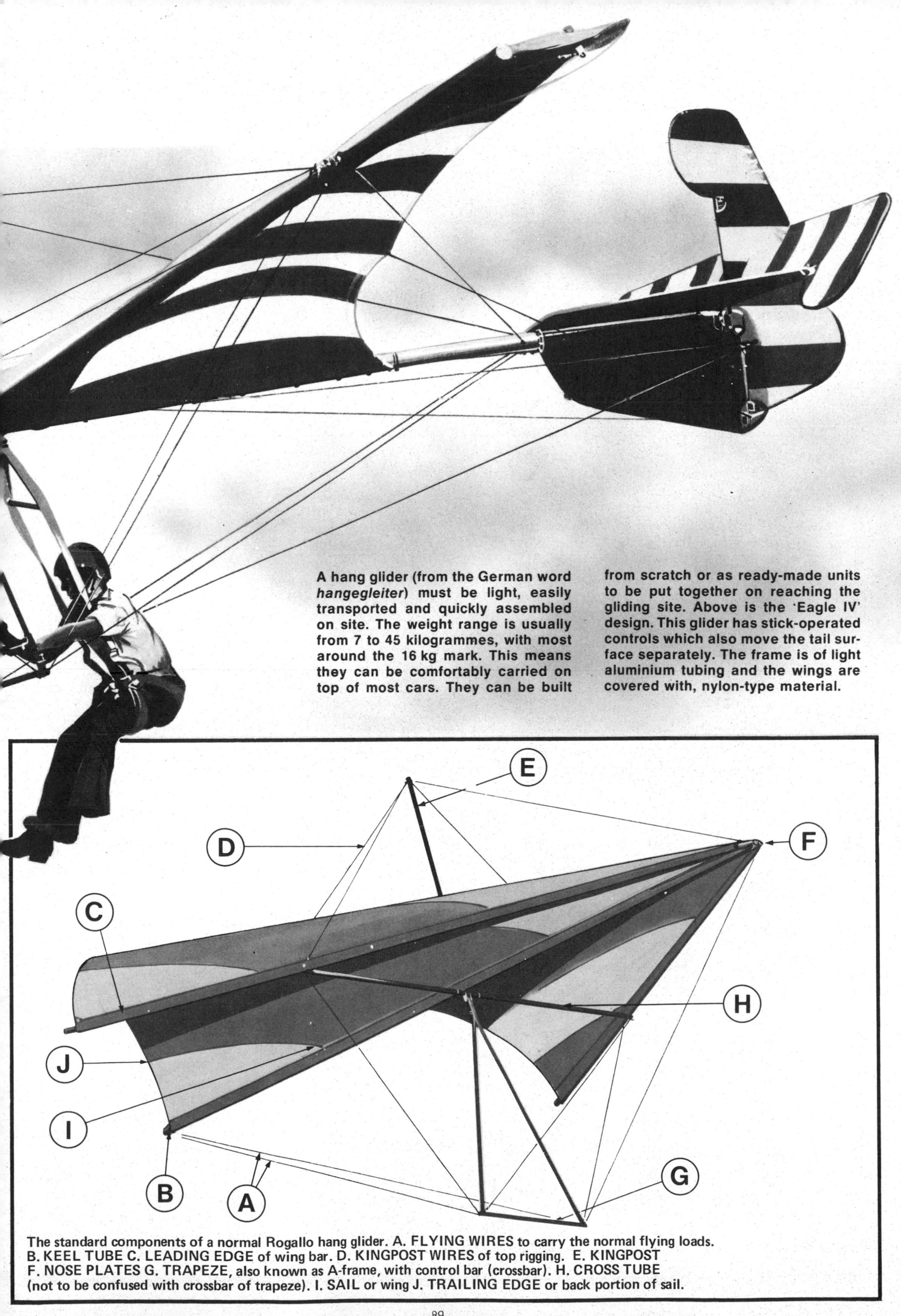


A hang glider (from the German word *hangegleiter*) must be light, easily transported and quickly assembled on site. The weight range is usually from 7 to 45 kilogrammes, with most around the 16 kg mark. This means they can be comfortably carried on top of most cars. They can be built from scratch or as ready-made units to be put together on reaching the gliding site. Above is the 'Eagle IV' design. This glider has stick-operated controls which also move the tail surface separately. The frame is of light aluminium tubing and the wings are covered with, nylon-type material.

The standard components of a normal Rogallo hang glider. A. FLYING WIRES to carry the normal flying loads. B. KEEL TUBE C. LEADING EDGE of wing bar. D. KINGPOST WIRES of top rigging. E. KINGPOST F. NOSE PLATES G. TRAPEZE, also known as A-frame, with control bar (crossbar). H. CROSS TUBE (not to be confused with crossbar of trapeze). I. SAIL or wing J. TRAILING EDGE or back portion of sail.

# When were Anaesthetics first used?

Below: A horrifying depiction of 'the Knife' at wor in the 18th century. Nowadays it is hard to imagin such barbaric practices taking place.

**LESS than 150 years ago, people were terrified of what was called 'the Knife'. It was considered the worst torture that anyone could face, and many preferred to die rather than endure it. The 'Knife' was, in fact, the surgeon's knife used in medical operations, and the terror it inspired came from the fact that it was used without the aid of *anaesthetics* — the painkillers so important to medicine today.**

Patients needing a leg or arm amputated (cut off), or another surgical operation, were simply held or strapped down to keep them as still as possible. The only thing surgeons could do to help them was to work as quickly as possible, so that their agony would not be prolonged more than was necessary.

Even so, very few patients survived: about nine out of 10 died after surgery, from infection, shock or loss of blood.

There was a constant search for some substance that would reduce or control this appalling suffering. But it was not until 1842 that the first surgical anaesthetic was successfully used; and together with the vital development of *antiseptics* (bacteria-destroying chemicals) by the British surgeon Joseph Lister in 1865, surgery was finally made painless and much safer from infection than before.

The development of anaesthetics was made possible by the work of the English scientist Joseph Priestley. He discovered the gases nitrous oxide (in 1772) and oxygen (in 1774). Nitrous oxide has anaesthetic properties, and in 1799 another English scientist, Sir Humphrey Davy, suggested its use in surgical operations.

Other substances were also under investigation. One was the drug ether, and this was inhaled by the famous scientist Michael Faraday (working in the same laboratory as Davy) so that he could report on its effects.

Below: The old laboratory of Humphrey Davy and Michael Faraday at the Royal Scientific Institution in London. Both men played a part in establishing which substances could be used as anaesthetics.

## Breakthrough

The practical breakthrough occurred some time later in the United States. A Doctor Crawford Long was giving ether demonstrations which were more like magic shows than anything else. But in the small town of Jefferson, Georgia, he allowed some youngsters to sniff some ether fumes. This made them very drowsy and Long realised that a stronger dose of ether could produce anaesthesia (absence of sensation). On March 30, 1842, he used ether to operate on a student named James Venable, and successfully removed a growth from Venable's neck.

Unfortunately for Dr. Long he had to stop performing these operations when the older, more superstitious citizens of Jefferson threatened to lynch him! It seems they suspected Dr. Long of sorcery.

However, this did not stop the advance of anaesthetics. On December 11, 1844, Dr. Horace Wells had a tooth pulled in a public demonstration after he had been given an anaesthetic combination of nitrous oxide and oxygen. He felt nothing and nor did a patient named Gilbert Abbott who had a growth removed from his jaw in the first major operation with ether at Massachusetts on October 16, 1846.

The next big step came in 1847 when a servant, James Churchill, had his leg amputated at University College Hospital, London — without feeling any pain. This time the anaesthetic was the gas *chloroform* whose use had been proposed by the Edinburgh surgeon Sir James Simpson. Six years later, Queen Victoria took chloroform during the birth of her son, Prince Leopold, and paved the way for the acceptance of anaesthetics.

Although chloroform was easy to use, it was much more powerful than ether and an overdose could kill a patient. The dangers involved in using anaesthetics were already well known; in 1844 a patient had nearly died when too little oxygen was mixed with the nitrous oxide given to him. Eventually it became the practice to use chloroform in short operations and ether for longer, more complicated surgery.

Since then many different anaesthetics have been used to try and discover the safest and most efficient. One of them, trichloroethylene, proved less poisonous than chloroform but did not make the patient relax completely. Others included gases mixed with oxygen but these mixtures were often explosive and so had obvious drawbacks!

## Risks

Much more satisfactory was *halothane*, first used in the 1950 s. This was not explosive and could be mixed with any amount of oxygen. Even so, halothane contributed to the deaths of some patients who were too sensitive to it. The truth is that no anaesthetic can be absolutely safe under all circumstances and on all the patients on whom it may be used. Fortunately the risks become smaller as medical research develops better methods of surgery and anaesthesia.

Today reseach has given us a wide range of anaesthetics — *local* anaesthetics to deaden the pain in a specific area and *general* anaesthetics to abolish sensation in the whole body. But their blessings go far beyond relieving patients of the pain operations once involved. Anaesthetics allow much more delicate surgery and doctors can now operate inside the body on internal organs. Prolonged anaesthesia is vital in such complicated operations as open-heart surgery which can take many hours.

Plastic surgery, the repair of burned and otherwise damaged skin tissues, is another complex technique which cannot be performed to any great extent if the patient is conscious. In some operations, like eye operations, the patient must remain conscious, but here the surgeons make use of local anaesthetics to deaden the area being operated upon.

The development of anaesthetics has unquestionably proved one of the most marvellous breakthroughs in modern medicine and science. Pain has been defeated and millions of lives saved which, in former times, would certainly have been lost.

Above: Joseph, Lord Lister (1827-1912). His use of antiseptics to keep operations free of infection was the next step after anaesthetics to make surgery safer.

Left: Sir James Simpson (1811-70). His use of chloroform made anaesthetics acceptable but when he first experimented on himself and became unconscious, his servant thought he had been attacked by thieves (below).

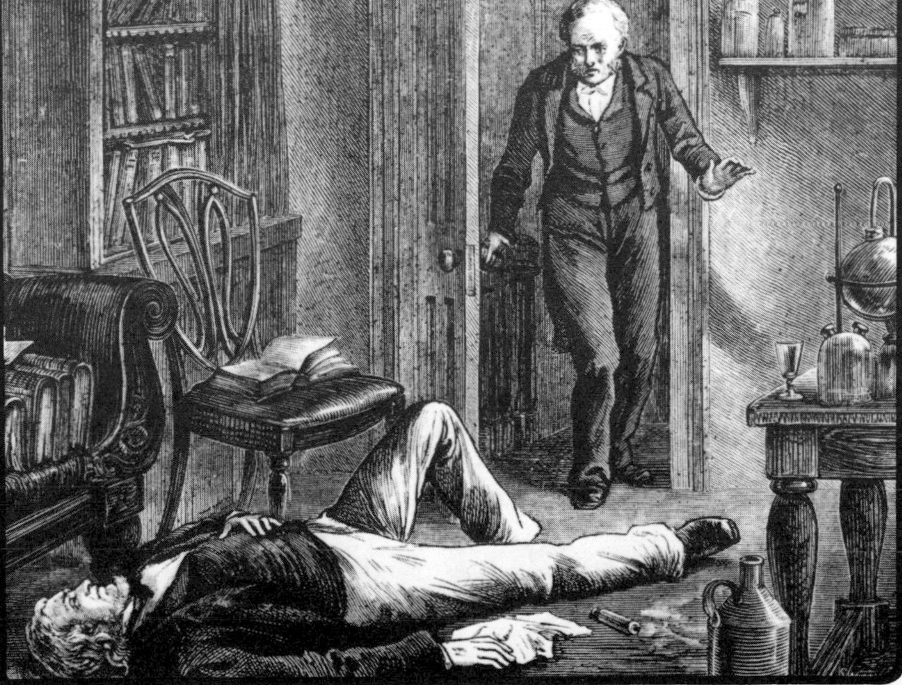

# How is Electricity created?

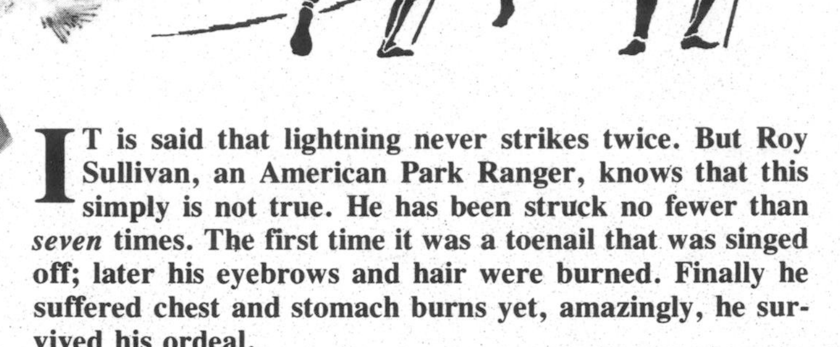

The Greeks believed that bolts of lightning were hurled down by angry gods.

Benjamin Franklin, the great American statesman, was interested in science throughout his life. Using the ingenious method of flying a kite in storms he proved that lightning is a form of electricity and showed that it could be safely conducted by metal.

**IT is said that lightning never strikes twice. But Roy Sullivan, an American Park Ranger, knows that this simply is not true. He has been struck no fewer than *seven* times. The first time it was a toenail that was singed off; later his eyebrows and hair were burned. Finally he suffered chest and stomach burns yet, amazingly, he survived his ordeal.**

He was lucky. Others have been killed or had their homes wrecked by terrifying bursts of lightning that last only a millionth of a second but which contain vast amounts of energy. It is not surprising that the ancient Greeks and Romans considered the flash of lightning and the crash of thunder that accompanies it as the actions of angry gods, venting their spite on erring mortals.

Only in the past 200 years or so has lightning been understood for what it is — one of Nature's most spectacular electrical phenomena. The great American statesman and scientist Benjamin Franklin was the first to realise that lightning was basically a huge electrical spark jumping long distances and with power a million times as great as that used to light your home.

He used a kite to demonstrate the movement of lightning along the wet string towards the earth. In 1752 he made practical use of this knowledge by constructing a *lightning conductor* to protect his house in Philadelphia. A pointed iron rod on the roof collected the electrical charge from the lightning and this was conducted down a copper strip fixed to the outside wall and so to a metal plate in the earth. In 1780 Saint Paul's Cathedral in London was also fitted with a conductor thus helping to preserve one of the world's most treasured monuments.

But where does lightning come from and how are such large amounts of natural electricity produced? To understand this we need to understand a little about the inside of the atom. Whirling around the nucleus of the atom is the *electron* — a tiny particle with a negative electrical charge. Inside the nucleus are other particles carrying a positive charge and normally the positive and the negative forces

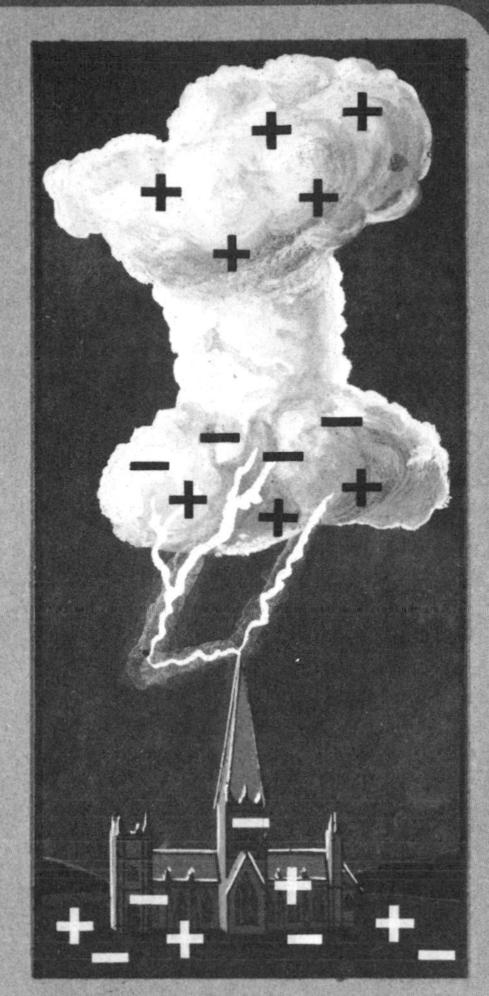

**Lightning flashes are caused by the build-up of electricity in storm clouds within which there is a temperature difference. Electrons (negative charges) move down and positive charges move up within the cloud, causing positive charges to gather on the ground below. At first the lightning jumps from negative to positive in the cloud but when there are enough electrons the air breaks down and a stream of electrons shoots down to the positive earth.**

are perfectly equal and balanced.

However, this balance can be upset. In a storm cloud the positive and negative charges carried by water in the air become separated by temperature changes. Electrons (negative) move down towards the bottom of the cloud leaving the positive ions near the top. There is then a further build-up of positive ions in the ground beneath the cloud. The process goes on and the electrons increase until a breakdown point is reached. Suddenly there is a discharge of electricity as a stream of electrons whizzes towards the earth to be met by another stream of upward-moving positive ions. The charges are then said to be neutralised.

Lightning takes many forms. Indeed the discharge itself may not necessarily occur between cloud and ground but can take place between one cloud and another or even within the cloud itself. The first stroke called the *leader stroke* reaches the ground at speeds of up to 1,600 kilometres per second while the return stroke from the ground can be as fast as 140,000 km/s which is half the speed of light. During this return stroke the temperature of the surrounding air may increase to as high as 30,000° Centigrade — five times that of the Sun's surface!

The commonest form of lightning we see is streak lightning. Sometimes this may split into two or more paths and

**DANGER! Never shelter under a tree in a storm. If struck by lightning, the sap in the tree is instantly superheated,, expands rapidly and the tree can explode violently. Crouch down on the ground if there is no reasonable shelter.**

form forked lightning. Sheet lightning is thought to be forked lightning obscured by other clouds — we see only the reflection of the discharge. Less common types are beaded, chain, and zig-zag lightning. But the most mysterious is ball lightning. Does it even exist at all? Some people think it does, including the observer who saw a ball of lightning pass through his house and out again without damaging anything in its path. Weather experts, however, are divided. Some think it is all imagination. Others believe that these spherical or pear-shaped forms, usually about 200 mm in diameter, can indeed be seen either stationary or moving erratically along conductors or metal window frames.

Ball lightning is thought to be potentially very damaging. It floats slowly doing no harm then suddenly — on meeting a solid object — it shatters it like a shell from a cannon. While scientists have been able to produce artificial fork or sheet lightning in the laboratory so far they have been unable to produce ball lightning — a mysterious and controversial object.

Everyone knows that lightning can be harmful but few people realise in how many ways. It can cause any moisture in a container to expand suddenly, shattering the vessel or even brickwork of a building. It can melt and fuse sand to form small particles of rock called fulgarites or even cause metal to fuse. A cricket umpire once found himself made immobile when lightning struck his artificial leg and seized up the joint!

Lightning can start fires, both in crop fields and in tankers carrying tonnes of oil. It can compress or squeeze air then quickly decompress it producing a blast that is so strong as to knock people over. And of course it can strike directly or through materials that conduct electricity.

Is there any way you can protect yourself against these powerful flashes? Sometimes people receive a violent shock through a television set during an electric storm because the power supply line has carried down the charge — so always pull out the plug. There's still a risk that the aerial will carry a charge down, but that's really very small, especially if your house or flat is one of many in the neighbourhood. The solitary high-rise building is more at risk.

If you are out in a storm, and caught in the open in the middle of a field, crouch down low with your feet together. By standing upright with feet apart, or walking with long strides, you greatly increase the force of a possible shock. Remember that high landmarks — such as church steeples and trees — are more vulnerable than flat, unobtrusive countryside.

Many would consider that of all places a metal motor car is one of the most dangerous places to be when there is lightning about. In fact the opposite is true — it is one of the safest. This was shown in an experiment carried out by two motor companies, who asked volunteers to sit in cars while they were bombarded with artificial lightning set at *two million* volts. The volunteers were completely unharmed because the flash ran over the outside surface of the cars and was discharged through the tyres. These contain materials other than rubber to make them conduct electricity, especially on wet roads.

Perhaps the most bizarre lightning of all — thankfully uncommon — is that which strikes out of a clear sky when there is no storm at all. Such a flash occurred in Australia a few years ago and did the sort of damage you might expect from a laser beam. Nobody knows how it occurred.

But lightning is not altogether destructive. When it flashes it combines with nitrogen in the air and brings down to earth quantities of this gas dissolved in raindrops. Nitrogen is essential to plant life, so every year plants receive a bonus of one hundred million tonnes of valuable chemical fertiliser. Lightning is yet another natural phenomenon well worth our respect.

**Left: A striking photograph of forked lightning set against telegraph poles and telephone wires. The lightning can be clearly seen leaving the base of the storm cloud. Lightning may cause telephone stations and transformers to blow out. Below: Flying in an aircraft in lightning looks dangerous but is really quite safe. Because there is no link to the earth little damage is caused even if the lightning actually strikes.**

# Who helped the Blind to see?

**HAVE you ever thought what it would mean to be blind? Apart from the difficulty of simply finding your way around, how would you keep yourself informed about what was going on in the world? TV is to be watched, books and newspapers are to be read. Nearly all methods of teaching people assume they have the use of their eyes . . . and it is here that blind people are forgotten. Or used to be until a young Frenchman named Louis Braille invented an alphabet that the blind could 'read'.**

For Louis Braille was blind himself — and only a blind man can know what is best for others like him. He was born in 1809, in the small French village of Coupvray, where his father was a saddler. He and his brother and two sisters were brought up in a little cottage, and although their parents were poor, they were a happy and united family.

Young Louis was fair-haired and blue-eyed; he was a child with a sense of fun, and very intelligent. He was very fond of watching his father at work in his saddlery. Monsieur Braille, hoping that Louis might follow in his footsteps, encouraged his son by allowing him to go into the workshop — but only when he was present.

One day, soon after his third birthday, Louis disobeyed his father. Finding the workshop door open, with nobody inside, he rushed to the bench, picked up a knife and a piece of leather, and tried to cut out a thong as he had watched his father do. But the leather was too tough for his small hand. The knife slipped and sprang, point first, into his eye.

His father heard his screams of pain and hastily removed the knife. Then he sent for an old hermit woman who claimed to have miraculous healing powers. But her treatment, far from curing him, only made the wound more serious. Soon Louis's second eye was affected too. Within six months, he was totally blind.

When Louis was 10, his father took him to Paris, to a special school for blind children. There he got on very fast, quickly mastering music and maths. It was reading that held him up.

He found himself bogged down by the effort of reading the large clumsy letters which were raised up from the surface of the page. This system was known as the Huay alphabet and it featured letters of an enormous size.

But then a strange stroke of destiny occurred. A French artillery officer called Captain Charles Barbier visited the school. He had just invented a method of 'night writing' with which soldiers could transmit messages to each other in the dark using patterns of 12 dots raised up on paper. It was a method of communication during 'blackout' — and it bought instant illumination to Louis Braille.

From then on he was obsessed with dots. Gradually he reduced Captain Barbier's 12 dot system to six. Then he reduced the dots in size, so that any combination of dots could be quickly deciphered by the tip of the finger.

At 16, he had the basis of his system — each letter of the alphabet and important punctuation marks were represented by a particular pattern of the six dots. All forms of writing and literature could be produced in a form which could be understood by the blind.

Now Louis Braille faced the struggle of getting his system adopted by the authorities. But while Louis's fellow blind pupils preferred his system once they had mastered it, the authorities did not approve. They felt that the blind must be treated in the same way as people who could see, and refused to adopt the Braille method.

## Little success

Louis soldiered on — but without success. Then at 30 he caught tuberculosis, a second difficulty to combat. But he continued to work for the blind — as a teacher at the school where he had been taught as a child.

But it was not until some years after his death in 1852 that the school — the Institute for the Young Blind in Paris — was fully won over to Braille's system.

In Britain, too, people were slow to fully appreciate the advantages of Braille. But then from his London home, a blind English doctor called Thomas Rhodes Armitage set about producing books in Braille.

Today the Royal National Institute for the Blind, founded by Armitage in 1868, is a leader in Braille production. Its presses churn out hundreds of books, magazines and journals, and its library contains over a million books in Braille. Braille books are sent all over the world, and the system has been adopted to dozens of languages, including Chinese and African dialects.

Louise Braille is dead, but the system he invented goes marching on to help the blind overcome their handicap, and to enable them to compete with those people lucky enough to have the gift of sight. The world is still closely in touch with Louise Braille.

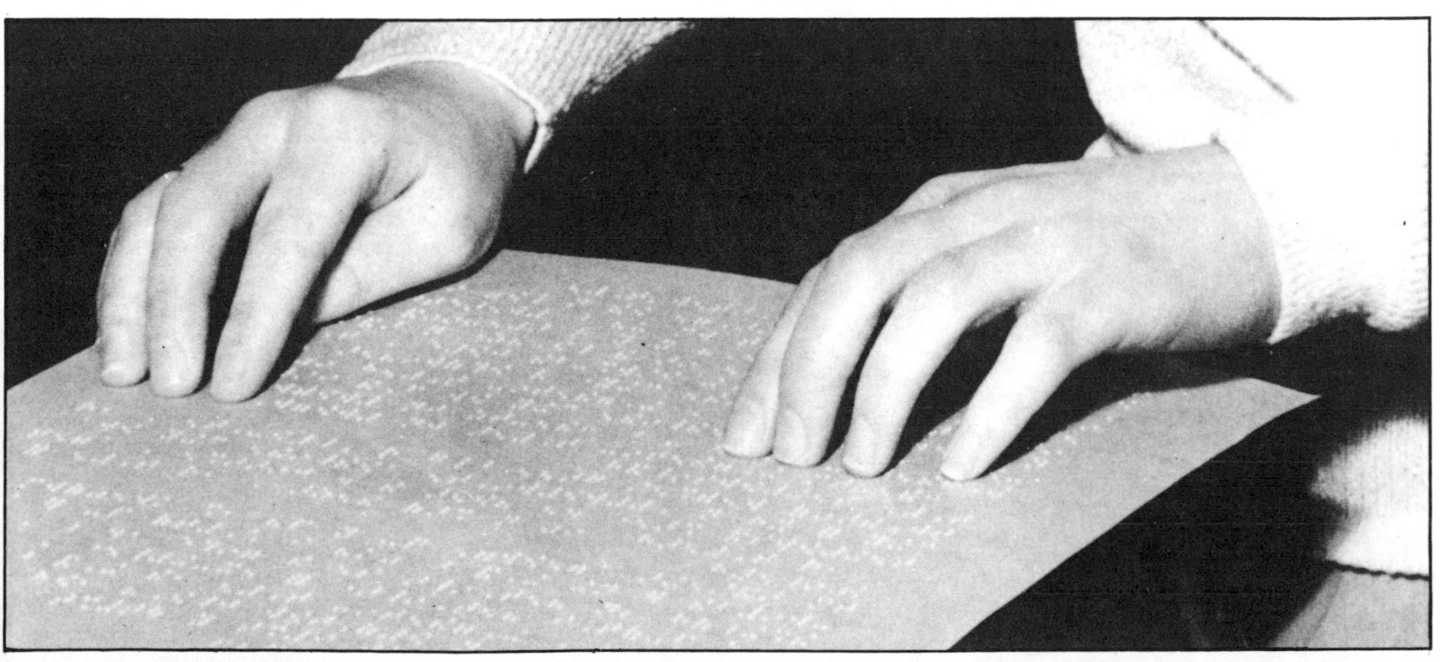

# How is Rubber made?

The tree is tapped for latex early in the morning when it flows more easily. A very thin channel is cut in the bark with the jebong. Each tree is tapped along a half-spiral as below.

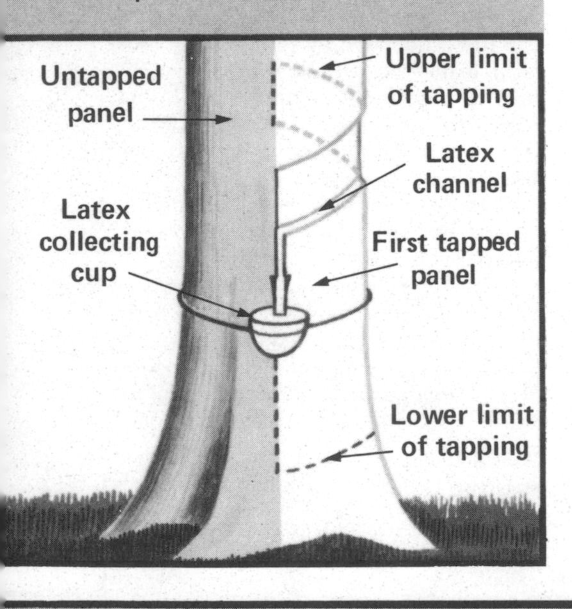


**WHEN Christopher Columbus and his crew returned from their tremendous voyages to the New World they brought with them many stories of the wonders they had seen. One gave an account of a game played by American Indians using an amazing ball. The small sphere, it seemed, was alive. It would hit the ground and bounce back up into the hands of the delighted player. No material in Europe was known that would produce this effect.**

The material of course was *rubber*, one of the substances on which our society is built. It is rubber that is used to produce hundreds of millions of tyres for cars and trucks; to act as insulation in a thousand and one electrical devices; to provide waterproof seals and draughtproof flaps; to make sheeting, clothing and footwear for special purposes. The list goes on and on.

And yet, to begin with, rubber was little more than a curiosity, useful for making bouncy balls and rubbing out pencil marks from paper — from which it gets its name. Not until the nineteenth century, hundreds of years after rubber was first known of in Europe, did it become obvious that here was a versatile, strong and unusual material with unlimited uses for a society becoming more and more industrialised.

Rubber is really the end-product of a process that begins with a huge tree *Hevea brasiliensis* that is specially grown in plantations in tropical countries. Originally it was found only in South American jungles but when its value was realised it spread elsewhere, particularly the Far East where seeds were transported to begin new forests.

The rubber tree produces a juice called latex in which natural rubber is present as tiny droplets. The milky-white latex is removed from the tree in the mornings when the air is still cool and the latex will flow freely. To do this a technique called 'tapping' is used. To tap a tree the plantation worker first strips away a shaving of bark with a sharp knife — a jebong — cutting a downward pointing 'V' shape and making sure that the cut goes into the latex tubes under the top surface. This allows the latex to run freely down into a collecting pot — about 2 kilos of rubber per annum is the yield from an average tree.

The next step is to extract the useful rubber from the latex. The latex is first put in a centrifuge — a high-speed rotating machine that separates off water (which makes up about 60 per cent of the solution) from the rubber.

The purified latex is poured into a large tiled bath to which is added acetic acid (which is like household vinegar) which turns the solution into a sticky, sponge-like substance. This is then 'cured' or smoked to dry it out

1. The seeds of the rubber tree are about the size of large acorns and grow three to each pod. 2. The seeds are sown singly in polythene pots in a 'basket nursery' where they are carefully tended for up to nine weeks. 3. The seedlings are then transplanted in pairs to prepared fields on the plantation. 4. When the seedlings are nine months old they are ready for *bud-grafting*: a strip of bud wood taken from a tree of good latex yield is grafted on to the young plant by

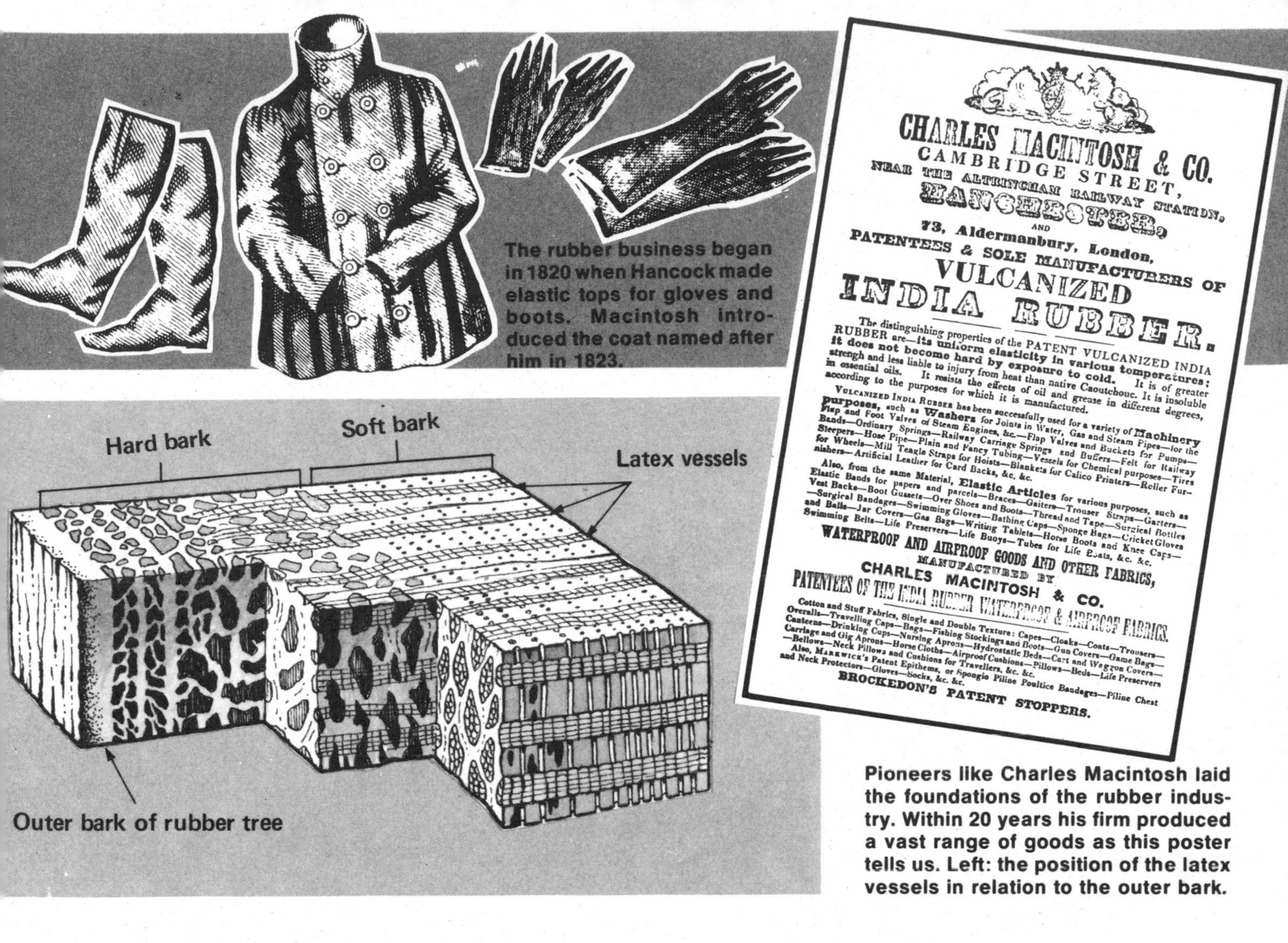


The rubber business began in 1820 when Hancock made elastic tops for gloves and boots. Macintosh introduced the coat named after him in 1823.

Pioneers like Charles Macintosh laid the foundations of the rubber industry. Within 20 years his firm produced a vast range of goods as this poster tells us. Left: the position of the latex vessels in relation to the outer bark.

into a tough, durable material. It may also be passed through rollers and then dried by air to make it lighter in colour.

Sometimes the liquid latex is not treated locally near the plantation but is transported in tanks by ship and rail. Ammonia gas is used to keep it fresh before processing.

The next step depends on what the rubber is to be used for. One problem with rubber which you may have noticed yourself is that it is not a stable material. In very cold conditions it can — if untreated — go hard and crack while in hot weather it is soft and pliable. Now this instability meant that rubber-made goods were of doubtful quality until the American Charles Goodyear — the founder of the famous tyre-making empire — discovered how to prevent it by heating it with sulphur.

Then, in 1843, the other great rubber pioneer Thomas Hancock took out a patent for this type of stabilising process that used sulphur and the application of heat. He called the process *vulcanisation* and it transformed the industry. Now it was possible to use rubber not only to waterproof clothing but also to make such important items as steam hoses that remained flexible and strong even when carrying high pressure steam.

The rubber industry in Britain grew steadily throughout the end of the nineteenth century but then came an invention that dramatically increased its use to astonishing levels — the pneumatic or air-filled tyre.

The first bicycles had literally been 'bone shakers', running on solid rubber tyres, until a Scottish vet named John Boyd Dunlop became annoyed at the jolting his small son was given every time he rode his tiny tricycle.

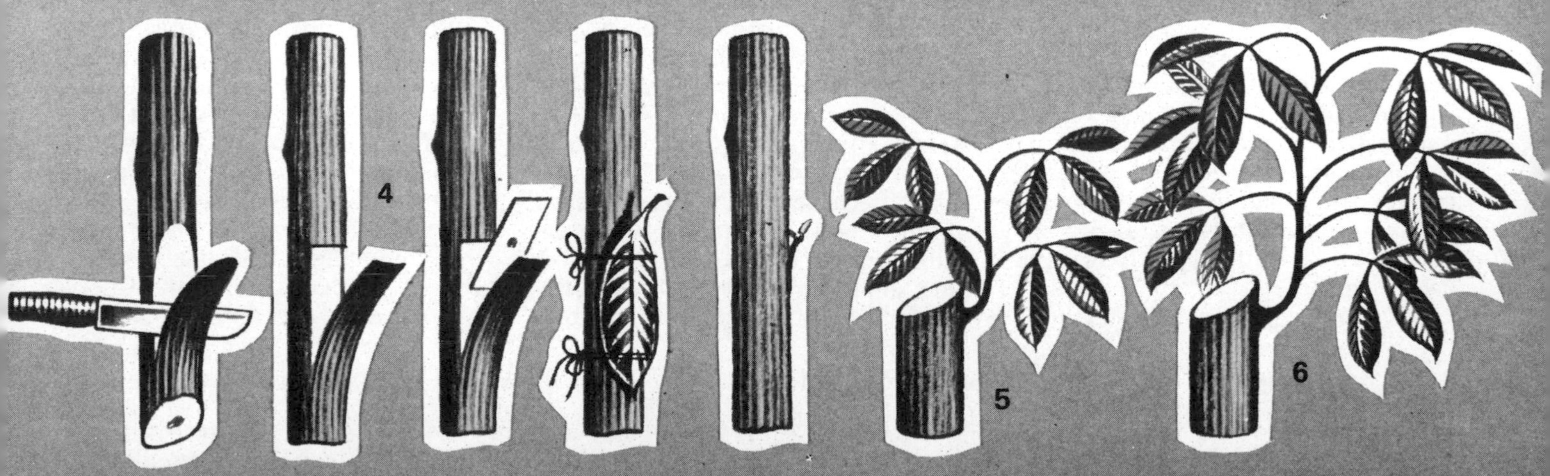


cutting a flap on its bark, inserting the graft, and then binding the flap and protecting it with a cover of leaves. 5. After about three weeks a young shoot appears on the graft and the stem of the original plant is cut off just above it in order to help the new shoot grow more strongly. 6. The new shoots grow into young trees and the less promising of each pair is cut down. Trees are ready for tapping after about five years.

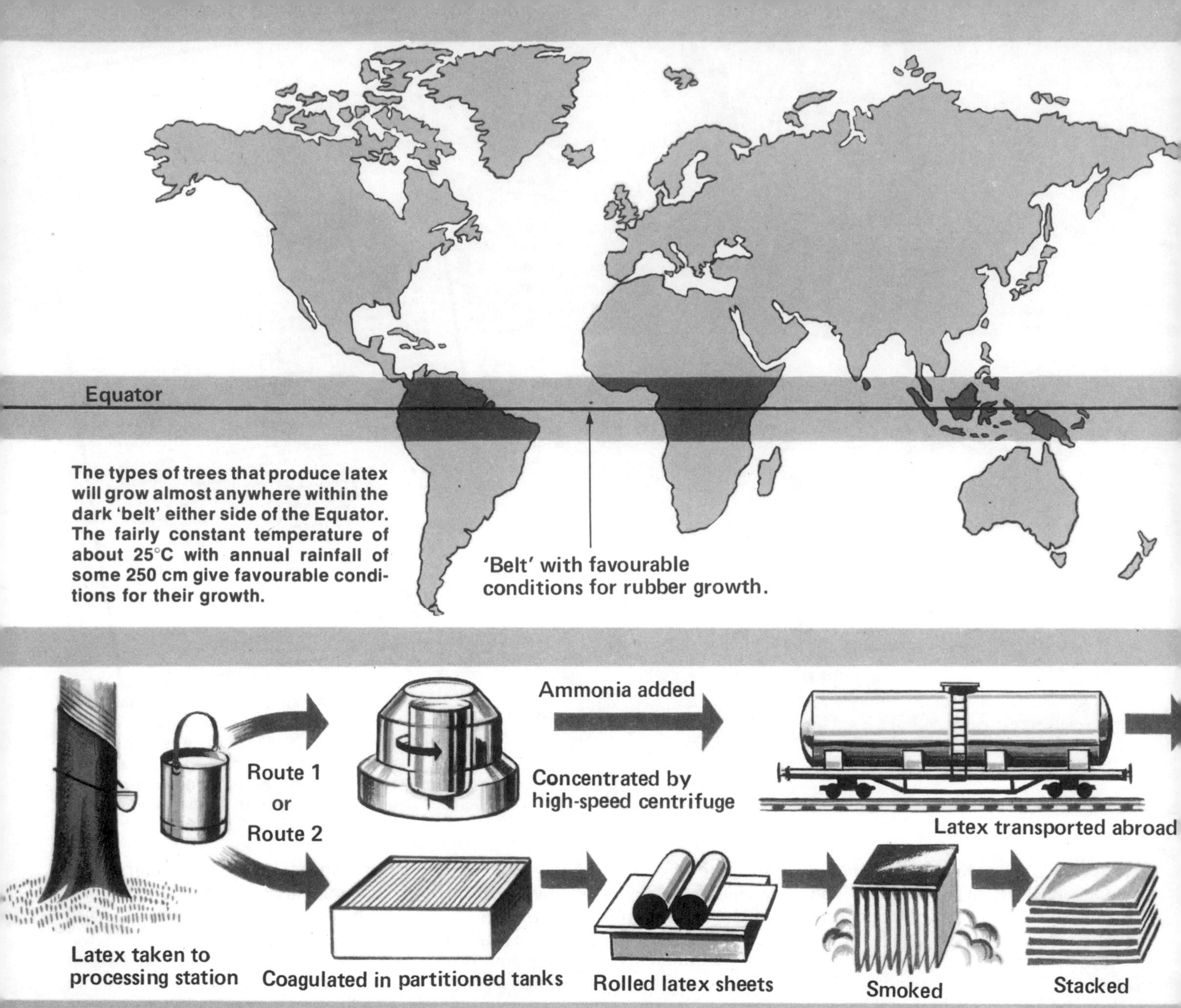


**When the latex has been collected it is taken to a central processing plant. It may take Route 1 where it is centrifuged to remove water; ammonia is then added to keep the latex fresh while it is transported abroad. In Route 2 the latex is partitioned and formed into sheets which are smoked and stacked for export.**

Dunlop experimented with an air-filled rubber tube fitted round a wooden wheel and covered with a protective canvas. It worked, and before long air-filled tubes protected by canvas became the rage. A smoother ride on a bicycle and in a car meant that the rubber industry reached a new peak of activity.

Today the industry uses four main methods of manufacturing rubber goods. Sometimes all four are combined to produce one product such as a car tyre.

*Extruding* is squeezing rubber out like toothpaste. It passes through a specially shaped nozzle and comes out in strips or rods.

*Calendering* means passing sheets of rubber through heavy rollers and stamping out articles from them. This is rather like cutting pastry with a pastry cutter.

*Moulding* works like a plaster cast. The roughly-shaped rubber article is put into an exact mould. The rubber is then compressed and either heated or vulcanised to form the exact shape of the mould.

*Foaming* uses liquid latex into which millions of small air bubbles are whisked like an egg-beater. The resulting liquid can then be poured into a mould and vulcanised to form foam rubber. This is the material that is made into cushions and feels so soft to sit on.

Rubber is seldom used in a 'pure' form. Because it is used for so many different jobs, a variety of different substances are added to the rubber and sulphur mixture: oils for better workability of the solution; paraffin for better resistance to light; carbon black for resistance to wearing down and so on. Vulcanisation too varies according to the rubber needed. Sometimes it is rapid, taking only a few minutes, while on other occasions it may take a number of hours, depending on such factors as the size of the article being manufactured.

Soft rubbers; hard rubbers; rubbers that withstand great heat or great impact; rubbers that can be colourfully styled for clothing or proof against the most harsh climates; even rubbers used to save lives: all these are the gifts of a giant tree from the Amazon jungle and the discovery that the Indians of North America liked to play with a bouncy ball.

**The help of the Education Section of DUNLOP LIMITED in the preparation of this article is gratefully acknowledged.**

# Who discovered Radium?

**1** Marie Skłodowska was born in Warsaw, Poland, on 7 November, 1867, the daughter of a professor and a teacher at the university. Her early training and great interest in science came from her father, as did her dislike of the then political situation. But the young revolutionaries were betrayed and Marie had to leave the country, going first to Cracow (at that time occupied by the Austrians), and then to Paris.

**2** There she got a job, washing chemical apparatus in a laboratory at the Sorbonne. But soon her potential was realised and she obtained her degree. It was there, too, she met Pierre Curie, another young scientist, whom she later married. The two became interested in the discovery of Henri Becquerel in 1896 that the metal, uranium, gave out rays that affected a photographic plate through paper.

**3** In fact, they passed through materials not transparent to ordinary light. Becquerel called the property 'radio-activity'. The Curies decided to research it further. After a great deal of work and the use of residue from the separation of uranium from pitchblende, they further separated two other elements. One, Marie Curie called polonium, after her birthplace, and the other, radium.

**4** The Curies found that the radioactivity of pure radium bromide was much greater than that of uranium of equal weight, about 2 million times as great. In 1903, they were recognised for their services to science by the sharing with Henri Becquerel of the Nobel Prize for Physics. The £8,000 divided between them proved of great help in their later work.

## The woman who risked her life for science

**5** Radium, however, is a highly dangerous substance, and Pierre suffered very badly from radium burns, and he warned that exposure to a large amount of the new element could cause death. In 1906, Pierre was killed while crossing a Paris street, and although heart-broken, Marie continued with the work they had shared. In 1911 she received the Nobel Prize for Chemistry.

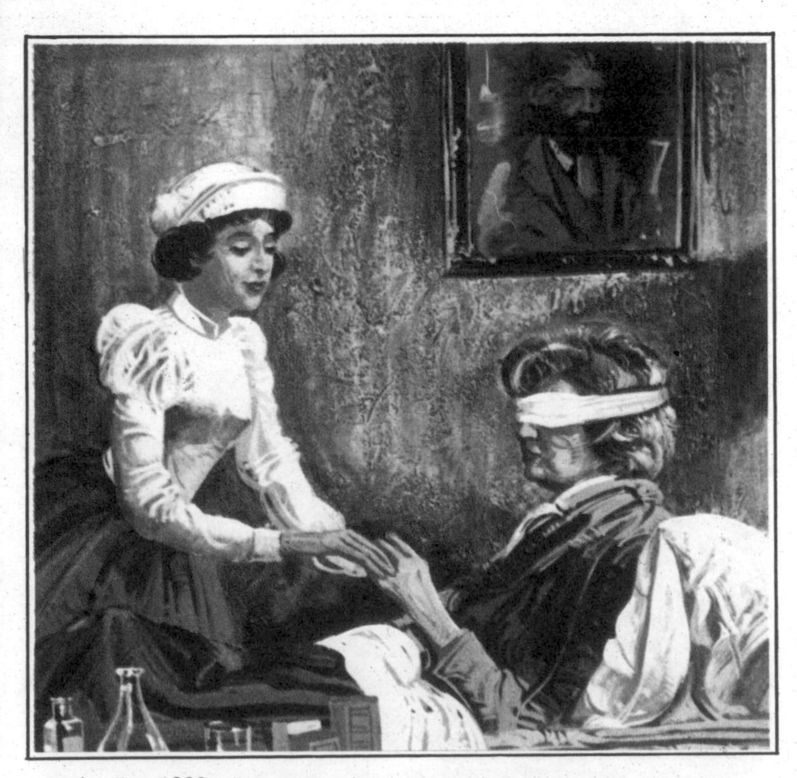

**6** In the 1920s, however, she had great trouble with her eyes. Operations brought some relief, although she had to wear thick glasses until the end of her life. She died of leukaemia, probably caused by radiation, in 1934, leaving two daughters. Leukaemia is a form of cancer, and some forms of cancer can be cured by deep-ray treatment involving Marie's great discovery — radium.

# Can you recognise Radio Activity?

This experiment shows how radioactive chemicals discharge static electricity and one of the two original ways of recognising radioactivity.

First of all, we make an electroscope, which is an instrument to detect static electricity. Find a small bottle with a fairly wide neck. Get a cork which fits it tightly and bore a hole in the cork about 9 mm. wide. Then fill the hole with melted candle wax and let it harden. Make a small hole in the wax with a thin piece of wire. Bend the bottom of the wire into a hook and hang on to it a folded piece of thin silver foil.

(The reason for the cork and the wax is to prevent leakage of electricity from the bottle. Drying out the parts by putting them in a fairly warm place will also help.)

When you have put all the parts together, you will have an electroscope. Now rub a plastic comb on your sleeve to produce a static electrical charge and hold the comb near the top of the wire of your electroscope. The pieces of foil will receive a like electrical charge and since like electrical charges repel, the foil will open out. Removal of the comb, and so the charge makes the pieces of foil come together again. If the wire is *touched* by the comb, however, giving a stronger electrical charge and the comb is *then* removed, the foil will remain open for quite some time.

The charge, however, escapes at once if you put a luminous clock or watch near the electroscope's wire. The radioactivity from the paint causes a change in the air's nature and the foil comes together.

## A simple electroscope which you can make

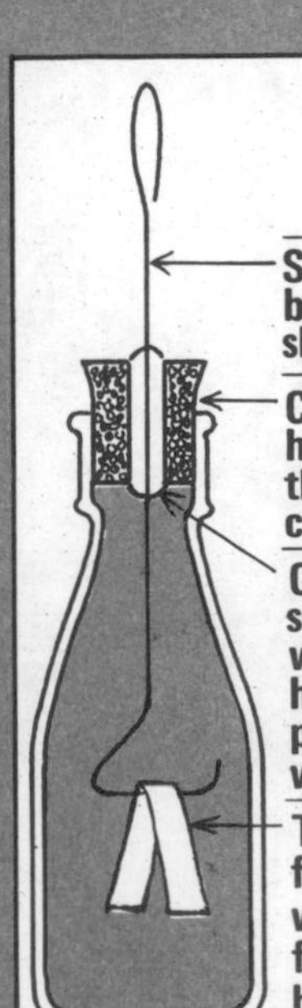

# What is Plastic?

**IN the crowded operating theatre the surgeon carefully implants a replacement part for his patient's heart valve, thereby saving his life. In an orbiting space ship thc astronaut prepares to descend on to the Moon's surface, comfortable in his ultra-strong lightweight spacesuit with its complex life support system. In the kitchen of a large hotel the chef and his staff prepare and serve food for 200 guests.**

**Plastic need not mean cheap and nasty. This beautiful model of a vintage Bentley is an Airfix plastic kit.**

What do all these occupations have in common? They, like thousands more, rely on the use of modern plastics — materials that are so familiar to us that we all take them for granted.

Yet the use of plastics is very recent. Difficult though it is to imagine life without plastics, they have only come on the scene in any number in the past few decades — even though the first to be made dates back 100 years.

Basically plastics belong to the group of compounds called *polymers*. That is, they are made by a chemical process that adds together many small chemical molecules into long chains of molecules.

How the molecules are linked together to form polymers varies. Hard, rigid plastics such as those used for picnic cups have tightly linked molecules, knitted together in a mat. But plastics with rubber-like properties (such as polythene sheeting for example) are joined in long thread-like chains with few links between individual chains. By altering the degree of linkage between these two extremes, industrial chemists can make plastics with virtually any properties they like.

Let's look now more closely at how plastics are actually made. They start life in a variety of forms. Plastics can be made from raw materials such as wood, coal, petroleum, plants and vegetable juices. These original materials are broken down into the chemicals that make them up and then mixed with various other chemicals to give stability, flexibility or even colouring to the finished product.

The ingredients are either reduced to powder form and mixed up in huge drums or — if the material is more flexible — kneaded like dough or mixed between rollers. The end product can take a number of forms: sheets, pellets, blocks or 'bristles' according to how it is used. It can also leave the manufacturer in liquid form.

The next step is to shape the plastic for use. And here the type of plastic is all important.

*Thermosetting plastics* set hard on heating and cannot be softened up by

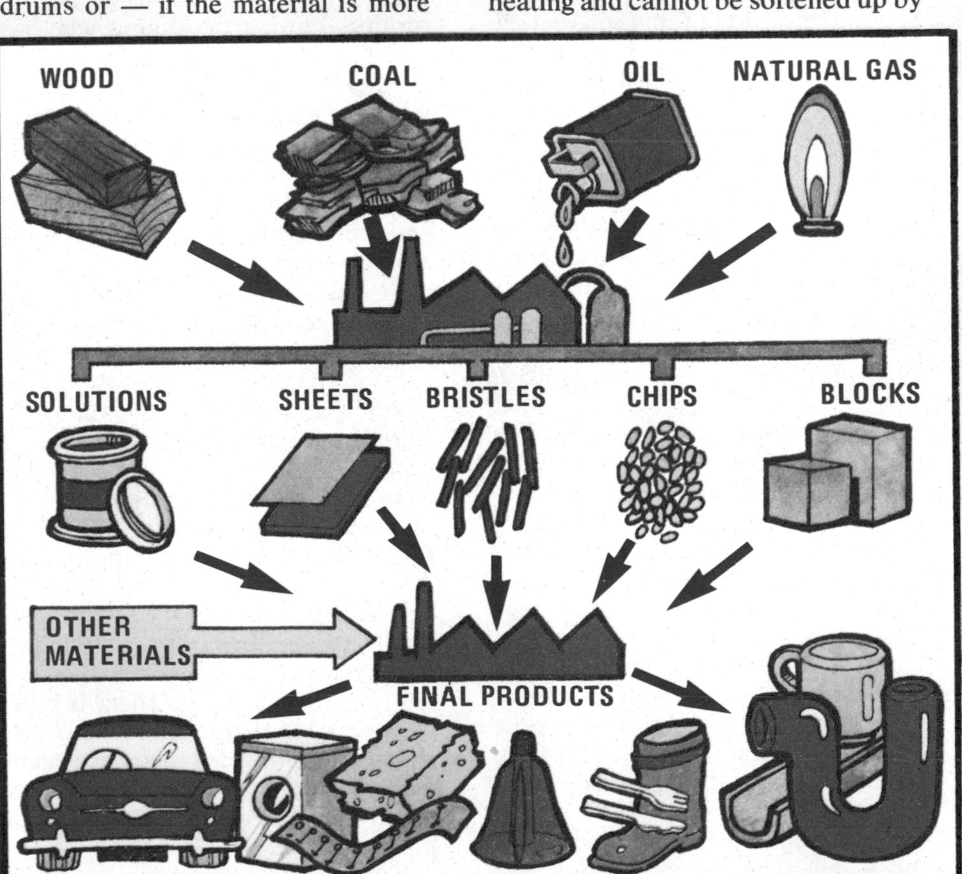


**Plastics are made from wood, coal, gas and oil. After manufacture, they come in the form of solutions, sheets, 'bristles', 'chips' or blocks. These are then turned into the thousand-and-one plastic and part-plastic articles we use today.**

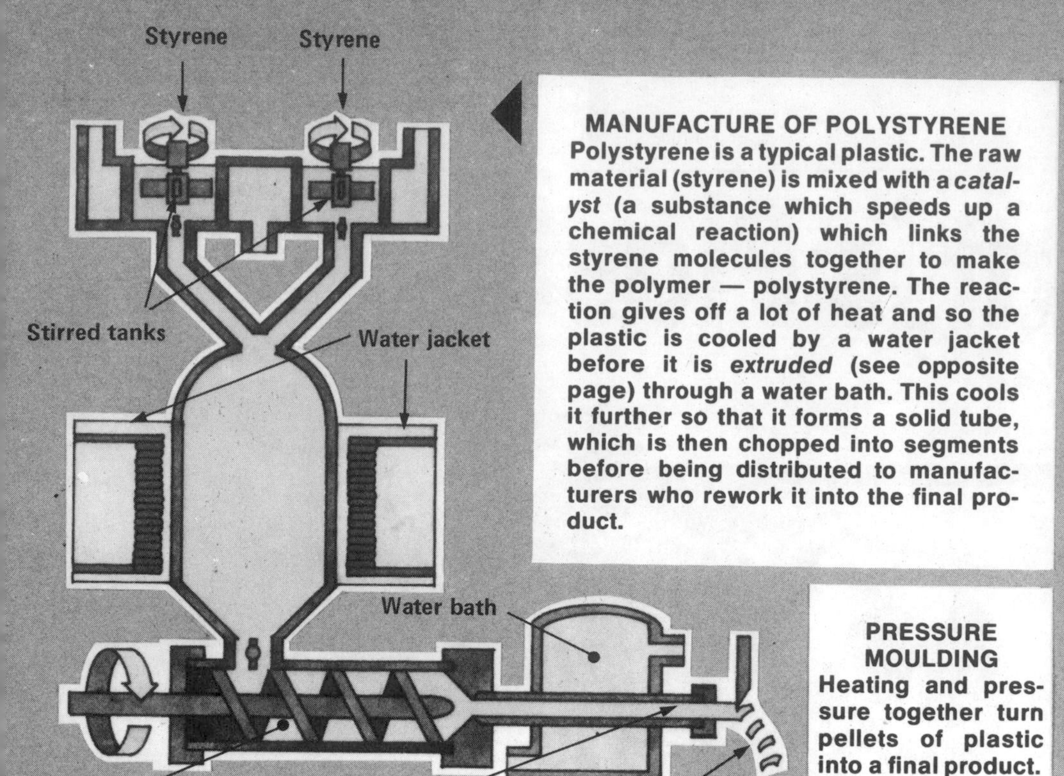


**MANUFACTURE OF POLYSTYRENE**
Polystyrene is a typical plastic. The raw material (styrene) is mixed with a *catalyst* (a substance which speeds up a chemical reaction) which links the styrene molecules together to make the polymer — polystyrene. The reaction gives off a lot of heat and so the plastic is cooled by a water jacket before it is *extruded* (see opposite page) through a water bath. This cools it further so that it forms a solid tube, which is then chopped into segments before being distributed to manufacturers who rework it into the final product.

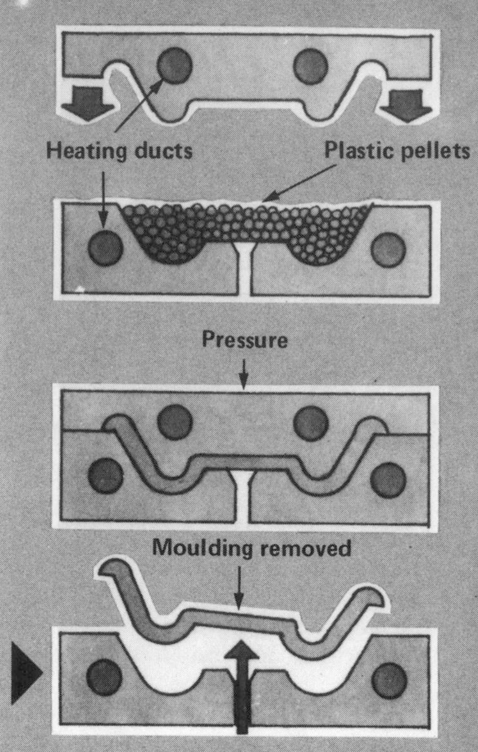


**PRESSURE MOULDING**
Heating and pressure together turn pellets of plastic into a final product.

melting without being damaged. A good example of a thermosetting plastic is *melamine* used for unbreakable crockery and decorative surfaces on kitchen furniture, chopping boards and trays. Another familiar thermosetting plastic is epoxy resin glue. This is mixed with another chemical from a different tube which acts as a 'hardener' by turning the resin to a polymer. So a firm joint is made.

*Thermoplastics* are so-called because they do become soft and pliable (or 'plastic') when heated. This type of compound is used for *polyester* (nylon and similar) fabrics; PVC (poly vinyl chloride) clothing and some non-stick coatings for pots and pans.

Both thermosetting and thermoplastics can be *moulded*, the simplest method of shaping. The plastic, often in pellet form, is squeezed or compressed until it begins to flow freely and so moulded into the correct shape.

Thermoplastics are usually moulded using pressure and heat, often by the *injection moulding* or *extrusion* method. Here granules of plastic are fed through a funnel or hopper into a cylinder where they are heated until they become pliable — rather like bread dough.

Then a moving piston literally pushes the plastic through a nozzle — like toothpaste from a tube. At the other side of the nozzle is the mould into which the soft plastic flows and hardens.

A variation on this ram method is the screw type extruder which can force material through any shaped hole or die, emerging more or less in the correct shape.

As well as being moulded, plastics are also shaped by machines that use material, in the form of film, sheets, rods or tubes. This is especially useful where the final shape is a particularly complicated one or where only a small number of the finished items are required.

After moulding, thermosetting plastics can only be finally shaped by turning, cutting or drilling whereas thermoplastics — being more flexible — can be shaped by heating and joined to other sections by welding. Shapes such as 'U' sections can be achieved by 'drawing', that is by lightly gripping the plastic, heating it and then shaping it into the appropriate curve (see diagram).

Modern production methods in the plastics industry are ingenious. Vacuum moulding for example is a clever way of shaping materials. In this a heated plastic sheet is laid over a hollow (or 'female') mould and air is sucked out from holes in the mould. This leaves a vacuum in the cavity which the plastic settles in to fill, thus following exactly the lines of the mould.

A variation is when the mould is on the inside and the plastic is stretched round *outside* it. Such a mould is called 'male'. The plastic sheet is both heated and prestretched in the rough shape of the mould. Then, once again a vacuum is formed to suck the sheeting around the mould, thus giving a perfect shape.

For forming large sheets, a *sheeting calender* is used — a machine consisting of a number of cylindrical rollers which can be heated. As the plastic sheet passes between the rollers it is stretched and becomes thinner — like rolling dough under a rolling pin.

The last in the series of rollers gives the sheet a final smoothing out, but if an embossed or textured design is wanted then this last roller has on it a pattern in relief which it stamps into the plastic. After the calendering process the sheet passes through cooling rollers and last of all is wound on a drum or roll.

Plastics are used in a variety of specialised ways, such as for coating paper or metals for strengthening or insulating. They are also good for stopping chemicals eating away or corroding other materials. Two methods are used for applying this layer of protective plastic: 'coating' in which the plastic in the form of a solution is spread on by a special coating knife or 'doctor knife' as it is sometimes called; and laminating in which the layer is in the form of a thin film. A good example of this is laminated floor tiles where clear plastic is laid on cork.

So when you pick up a beautifully moulded plastic telephone, or play a favourite disc, or screw new plastic studs into soccer or hockey boots remember that behind these familiar products is an ever-growing technology. It is impossible to say just how important plastics are to us. What we can say though is that they are assured of a very long and interesting future.

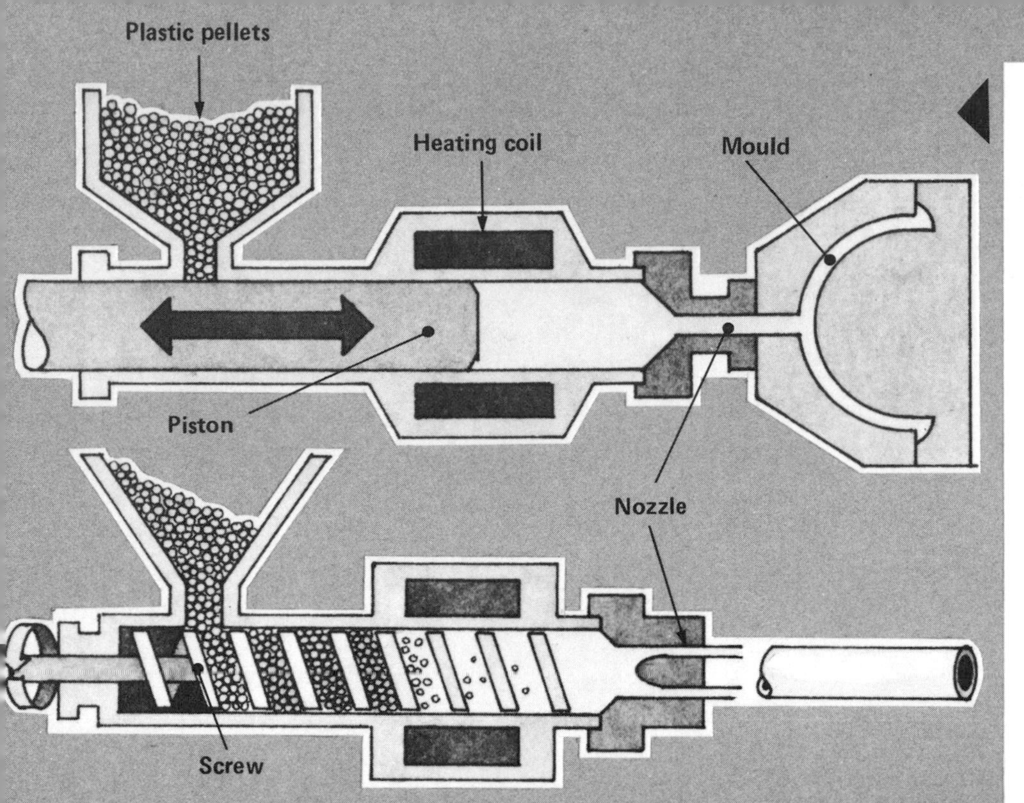


## EXTRUSION

The most common method of moulding *thermoplastics* — those which become pliable when heated — is by extrusion. In this process, near-molten plastic is squeezed out of a container through a small nozzle. Either the nozzle itself can produce the required product — as in the case of the pipe produced by a circular opening (below) — or the plastic can be squeezed into a mould which produces the required shape (top). The plastic is fed into the extruder in the form of plastic granules, and is heated inside the extruder to make it pliable. It is then rather like bread dough. The pressure which then forces this near-molten plastic through the nozzle can come either from a moving piston (top) or from a screw thread (bottom).

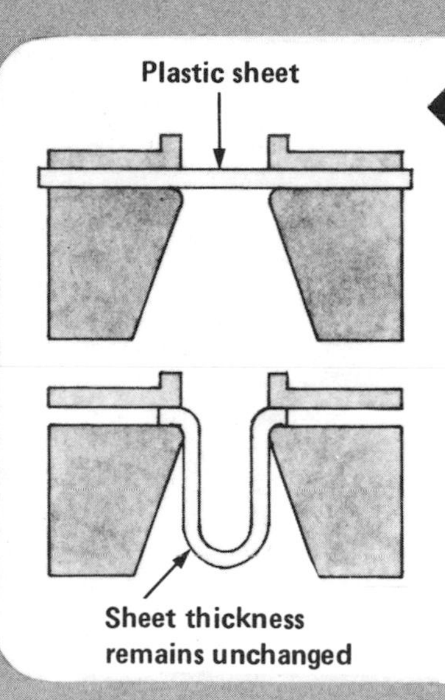


## DRAWING

In this process a sheet of plastic is heated and then lightly gripped at its edges. It can then be formed, using a metal bar for example, into the required shape.

## VACUUM MOULDING

Plastic can be shaped round a mould using a vacuum. It can be either sucked down into shape (top) or first stretched across the mould and then sucked into its final position (bottom).

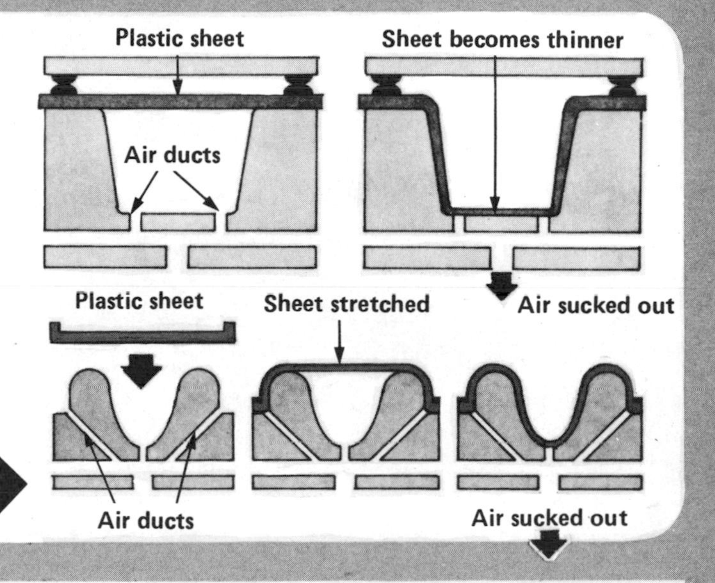


## CALENDERING

A rough sheet of plastic can be finished off using a process called calendering. The sheet is passed between revolving heated cylinders which smooth and thin the sheet rather like a rolling pin rolling out pastry. If required, a raised pattern can also be *embossed* on the plastic using a final roller with a raised surface.

## COATING

Plastics are often used to coat other materials such as textiles. The plastic is spread on to a moving sheet of the material to be coated and then distributed evenly by a 'doctor knife'.

## Birth of a Genius

The story has it that James Watt was fascinated by steam from his earliest days. A delicate boy, he was kept at home much of the time to study.

He was scolded for drawing geometrical problems on the kitchen flagstones, but more to the point, as far as Watt's future career was concerned, he was constantly preoccupied with watching the way a kettle lid rose and fell, as the water boiled.

Why, James asked himself, time and time again, did the kettle lid rise under the pressure of steam? The questions about steam which little James put to the family kettle were finally answered for all time by Dr. Joseph Black, whose work on the latent power of steam, disclosed a new world of power in the vapour rising from a half a litre of boiling water.

Fortunately, for the world, Black made this discovery just about the time that Watt began to question the value of Newcomen's steam engine.

# Who invented the Steam Engine?

**MEN had realised the potential power of steam for many years and even written stories about it. The fact that steam expands to an extent where it needs 1600 times the space occupied by the original amount of water, provided the steam is contained, suggested a great source of power.**

Yet nobody could fathom how this power might be harnessed and made to work until a breakthrough came in 1698 when an Englishman named Thomas Savery built a steam engine that operated on the principle that 'nature abhors a vacuum'.

Savery needed to pump water out of some mines which were flooding. In his day the normal way of doing this was by hand pumps like those used on ships but these needed a team of men working in relays and even then very little water could be raised.

## Savery's plan

Savery's plan was to draw water up into a tank without pumping it. To achieve this a big copper tank was filled with steam which was allowed to cool and change back to water, thus converting most of the tank into a vacuum. Into this vacuum, through a pipe, the water from below was drawn up in much the same way the vacuum in a straw placed in a glass of lemonade causes the drink to rise once the air has been sucked from the straw.

It can be said Savery's invention was a steam engine that worked backwards and nearly a hundred years passed before James Watt found the way to reverse the process.

But first Thomas Newcomen, who had worked with Savery, took another step in the harnessing of steam power. After fifteen years of experiments to find a machine that would drain Cornish mines that were for ever flooding, in 1712 he built a new type of engine.

This consisted of an upright cylinder with a piston inside able to move up and down and this cylinder was supplied with steam from a giant boiler below. Above the piston was attached to a great beam which rocked on a high bearing while the other end of this beam was connected to a water pump. When steam entered the bottom of the cylinder it was cooled quickly by the introduction of cold water. The resultant condensation created a partial vacuum in the cylinder allowing the atmospheric pressure built up to force the piston down. Constantly repeated this forced the beam to move slowly up and down and operate the pump. But the method was slow and costly in fuel.

James Watt, a sickly boy who was to suffer poor health all his life, was the son of a master carpenter who ran a ship-chandler's store and became a mathematical instrument maker. Asked by the University of Glasgow to repair a model of Newcomen's engine Watt became convinced he could make a better machine to do the work.

## Watt's advance

After pondering for some two years the problems Newcomen's Atmospheric Engine posed Watt became convinced he had the answer to its shortcomings. The greatest weakness was that the cold water condensing the steam also cooled the whole cylinder so that the next charge of steam came into a cold cylinder thereby losing much of its effect. Watt planned that the steam should be condensed in some vessel separate from the cylinder.

In a few days Watt had made a model that proved his ideas were fundamentally correct and in so doing made the greatest single advance in the early history of steam.

But for a while there were problems. Watt could find no men in all Glasgow skilled enough to make a full scale working machine and the inadequate machine tools of his day were no help, either. Salvation came when Watt formed a partnership with Matthew Boulton, an enterprising Birmingham toy manufacturer, who was prepared to finance the new invention. This partnership lasted for twenty five years and but for Boulton's constant support Watt might have been tempted to give up.

The Industrial Revolution was now truly under way and the old hand operated machines in workshops had given way to factories still called 'mills' because originally so many of them were operated by huge watermills. Now with so many mills operating all over England the lack of a constant source of power was an acute problem.

A machine that could turn a wheel rather than just pump it up and down was

**An exhibition reconstruction of James Watt's workshop displaying machines and equipment used by the inventor. On the bench are busts of Watt and his business associates.**

needed particularly as the crank had recently been patented, a device which could convert backward and forward movement into circular motion.

Watt was able to convert his engine to a rotative principle and built two enormous rotative engines for the Albion Flour Mill, near Blackfriars Bridge in London in 1786. The output thus achieved was considered so remarkable that crowds flocked from far and wide to see the great machines at work. Sadly the mill was destroyed by fire only five years later.

Despite his fame and success Watt was not a man to rest content and went on perfecting and improving his steam engine, though absorbed by other inventions right up to his death in 1819.

## Limitations

Remarkable as it was Watt's engine was not without its limitations. Not least that it was a low pressure engine working at about 10lbs lbs per square inch. As early as 1812 another mine-machinery engineer, Richard Trevithick, had built and used a high pressure engine which operated at 40 lbs per square inch. Watt had roundly condemned this as irresponsible and risking a boiler explosion, an accusation not without truth.

Today electrically driven engines have almost entirely replaced those driven by steam but for all that James Watt is assured of a permanent place in history for the miracles he wrought with steam, so vital to the manufacturing industries and economy of nineteenth century Britain.

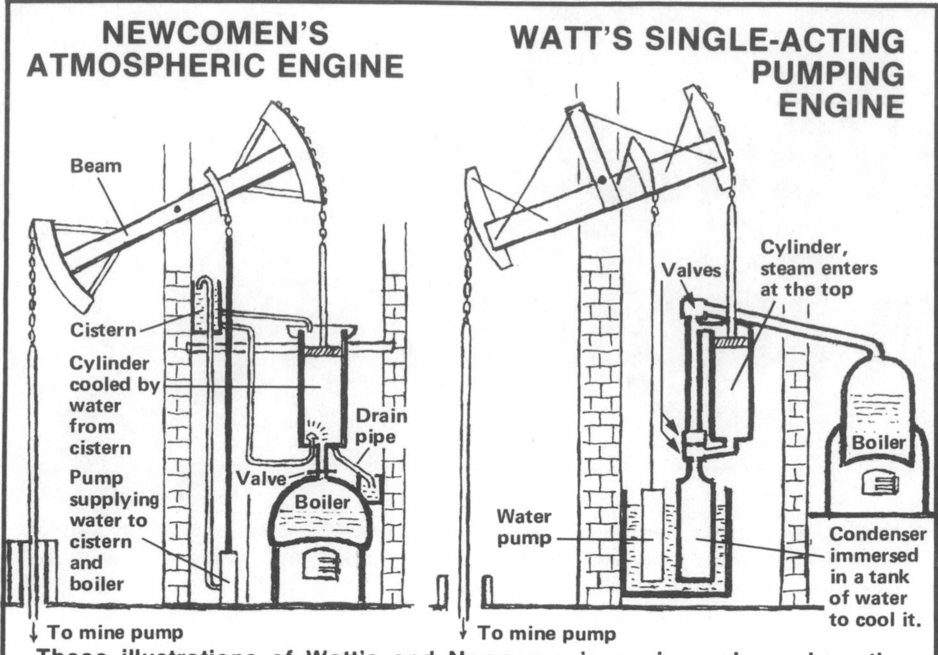


**These illustrations of Watt's and Newcomen's engines shows how the former improved upon the latter. Steam travelled from the boiler of Newcomen's engine into the cylinder when the valve was opened. Then, as the valve was closed, the water was poured on to the top of the piston and sprayed into the cylinder. As the piston descended the water escaped through a drainpipe. Watt's engine, however, had a condenser which eliminated the need for water to be sprayed into the cylinder to cool it. Steam was admitted to the top of the cylinder and when the piston reached the bottom, one valve was closed while another opened so the escaping steam was driven into the condenser. Both engines are known as 'reciprocating', that is, they are incapable of rotating a wheel.**

### WATT'S ROTATIVE STEAM ENGINE

**The Piston (A) which moves up and down in the Cylinder (B) is connected with the Beam and the Crank (C). Watt eventually used the Crank to transform a simple pumping action into a rotative action. The Condenser (D) functioned inside a cistern of cold water.**

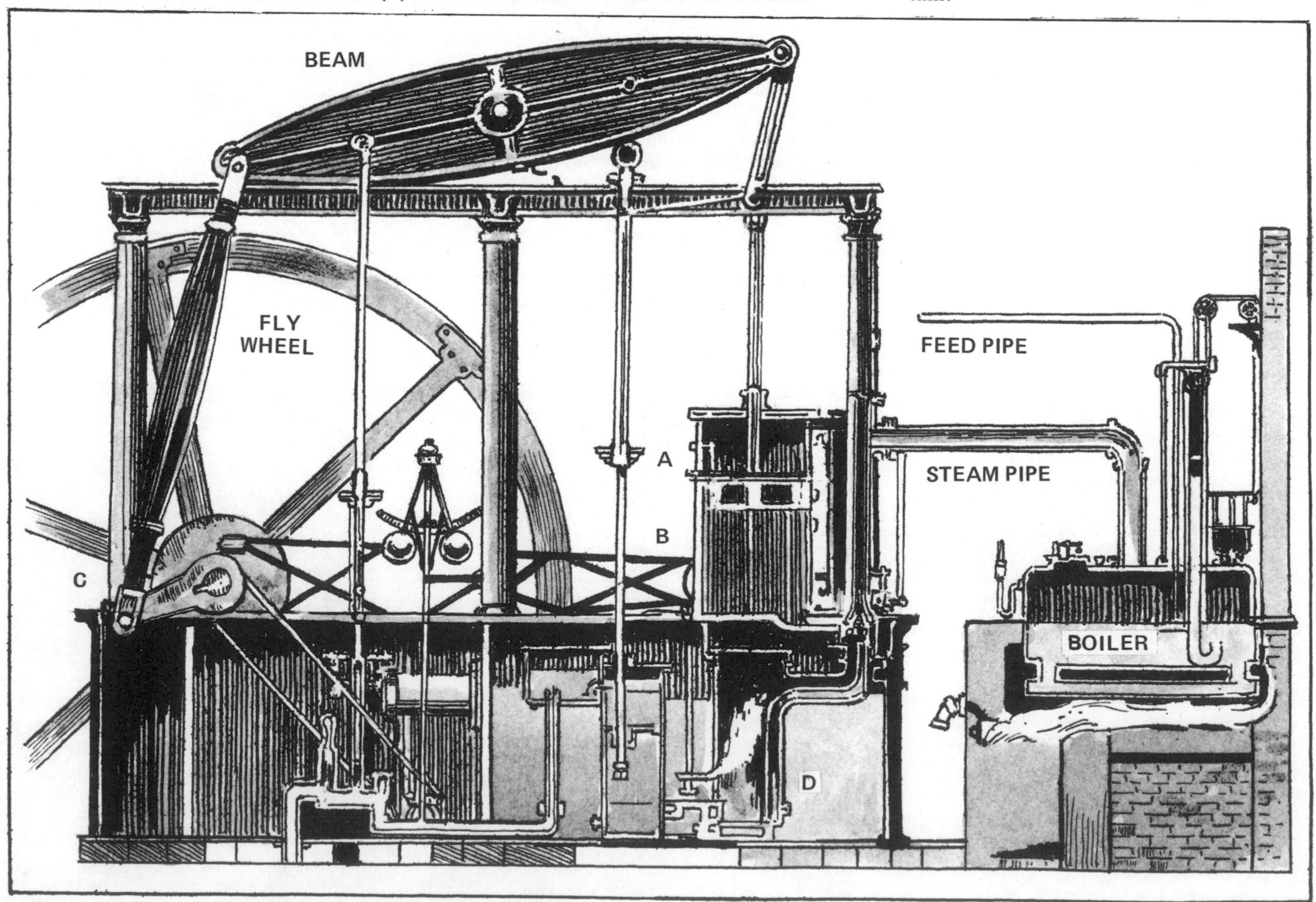

# What is Black Gold?

**OIL is such a precious commodity that it has been called 'black gold'. We depend upon it for products ranging from fuel to fertilisers. Demand is currently so high and increasing so rapidly that some experts predict world oil supplies will dry up within 40 years. If that happens we shall have managed, in little more than a century and a half, to exhaust a gift which took Nature several million years to create.**

Oil is formed from the dead plant and animal life of ancient seas. The remains decayed on the sea-bed into fatty and oily substances, which gradually became buried under mud. As the centuries went by, the mud was squeezed into a layer of rock and, under the pressure from the rock, the remains of the tiny plants and creatures of the deep were transformed into oil.

The process did not end there. As a result of upheavals in the Earth's crust, what had once been seas became dry land with the oil trapped in giant lakes thousands of metres below the surface. There most — but not all — of the deposits remained undiscovered until recent times.

Some of the oil travelled, often many kilometres, through tiny holes in the rocks and eventually reached the surface. Thus, while our great modern oil industry is little more than a century old, many of the properties of oil have been known for thousands of years.

Six centuries before Christ, the King of Babylonia, Nebuchadnezzar, used bitumen — the substance left when oil evaporates — for paving and cementing. In the fourth century B.C., Alexander the Great, King of Macedonia and conqueror of the Persian Empire, was welcomed to a Persian town by a giant 'bonfire' created by spreading oil across a street and setting fire to it. From Sicily, the Romans obtained asphalt, another by-product of oil, and used it to build roads. In some countries, including Italy, Germany, North America and Burma, crude oil was also long thought to have medicinal properties.

The first modern development came in 1850 when the Scottish scientist James Young invented a method of obtaining kerosene (paraffin) from shale, a kind of clayey stone resembling slate but much softer. This was followed in 1859 by the drilling of the first oil well by Edwin L. Drake, an American, at Titusville, Pennsylvania. He struck oil at 21 metres.

Oil's chief value at this time was as an alternative to the rapeseed oil burned in lamps to provide light for

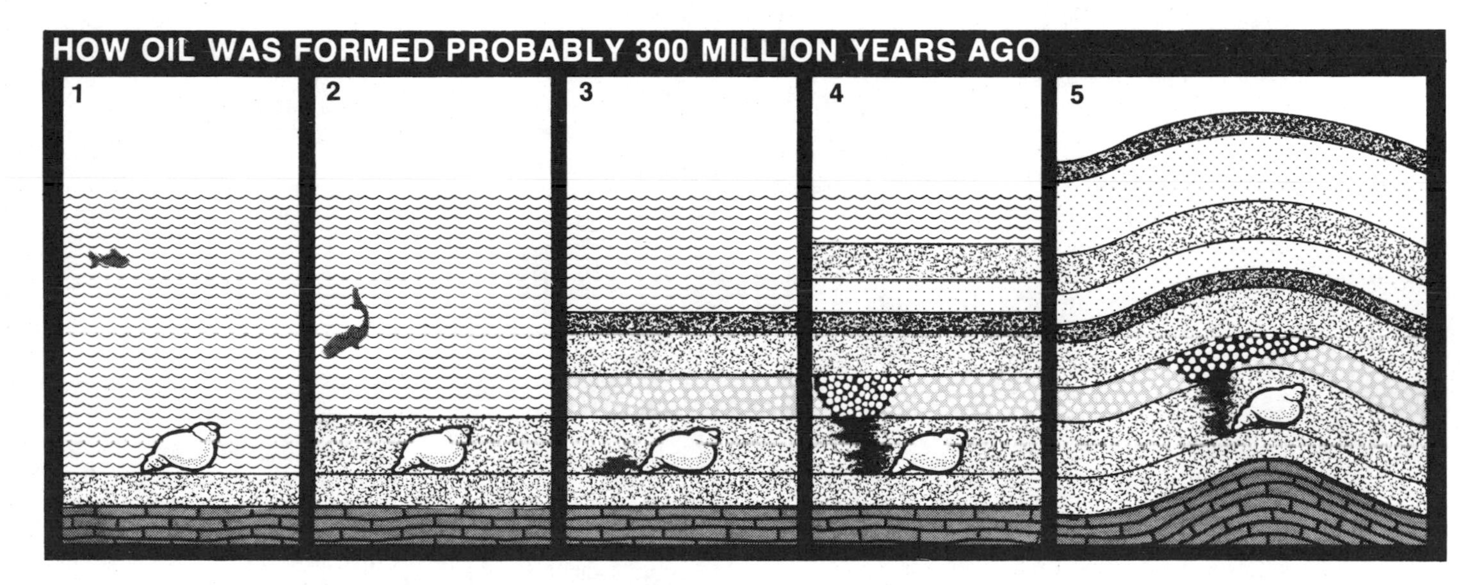


1. Millions of years ago shallow seas covered many areas that are now land. When the animals and plants in these seas died they fell to the bottom and became several metres thick.

2. The dead remains — we have used just one large shellfish to represent billions — were now buried beneath mud and sand which were carried down to the sea by rivers.

3. As more and more mud and sand were brought down, the remains were buried deeper and deeper.

4. The weight of all the mud and water turned them into oil and the mud at the bottom into a rock called shale.

5. Later the rocks were lifted up. Trapped in the shale is the oil squeezed out of those billions of tiny creatures many millions of years ago.

**USING 'EARTHQUAKES' TO FIND OIL →**

Scientists make their own 'earthquakes' to determine where oil is likely. They drill a hole up to 30 metres deep and then explode high explosives in it. The shockwaves are reflected by the different layers of rock and are measured by sensitive instruments on the surface.

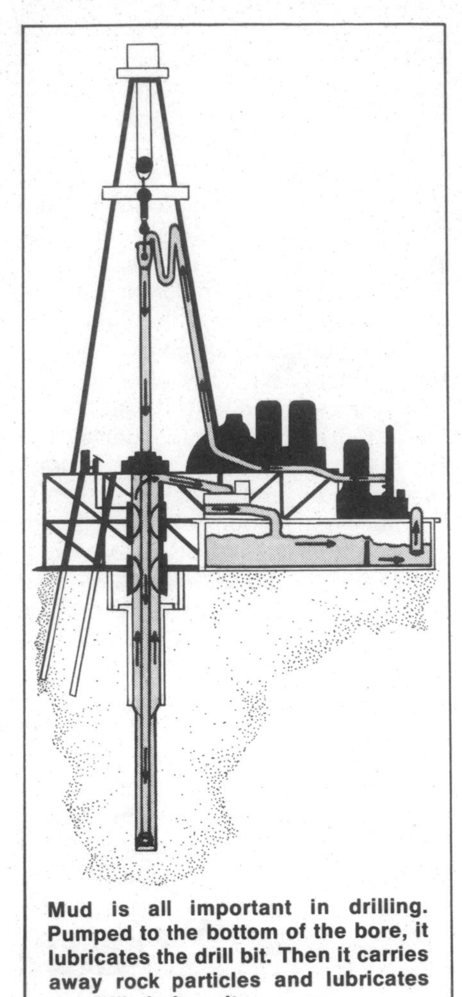

**Mud is all important in drilling. Pumped to the bottom of the bore, it lubricates the drill bit. Then it carries away rock particles and lubricates the drill shaft on its way up.**

homes, offices and factories. Only after the invention of the internal combustion engine — the engine used in cars — by another Scot, Sir Dugald Clerk, at the end of the 19th century, was our modern oil industry born.

The escalating demand for oil — and for petrol in particular — has resulted in an endless quest for new sources of 'black gold'.

In the end, the only real measure of whether oil is likely to be present on a site is a *test bore*. This can mean drilling more than 6,000 metres beneath the Earth's crust at a cost which, in remote areas, may run as high as £600 for every metre drilled.

With this kind of money involved, companies carry out preliminary tests before beginning to drill.

If a test bore is considered worth while, it operates rather like a drill boring through wood. Just as a drill throws back wood shavings, the test bore provides rock samples which support or deny the long-range predictions of the scientists. Results are frequently disappointing. The deepest bore carried out in Texas went to a depth of 7,600 metres, cost nearly £1.5 million, and did not produce a single drop of oil.

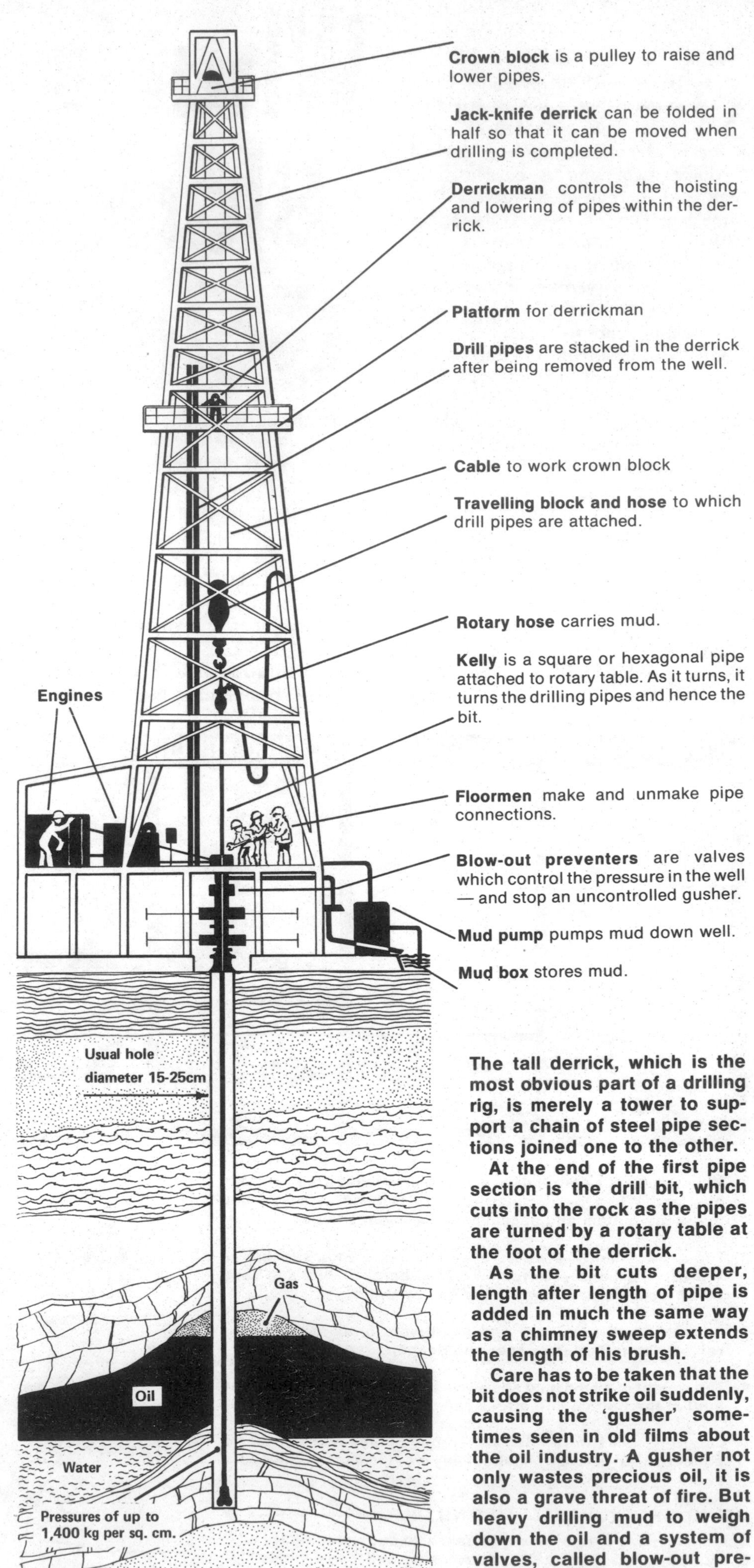


**The tall derrick, which is the most obvious part of a drilling rig, is merely a tower to support a chain of steel pipe sections joined one to the other.**

**At the end of the first pipe section is the drill bit, which cuts into the rock as the pipes are turned by a rotary table at the foot of the derrick.**

**As the bit cuts deeper, length after length of pipe is added in much the same way as a chimney sweep extends the length of his brush.**

**Care has to be taken that the bit does not strike oil suddenly, causing the 'gusher' sometimes seen in old films about the oil industry. A gusher not only wastes precious oil, it is also a grave threat of fire. But heavy drilling mud to weigh down the oil and a system of valves, called blow-out preventers, allow the pressure to be released safely.**

When an oil strike is made, the site is usually a long way from the refinery where the oil will be separated into its various products. The cheapest way of moving the thick, dark fluid is to pump it through pipelines. The longest crude oil pipeline in the world is currently in the United States. It runs from Edmonton, Alberta, to Buffalo, New York, a distance of 2,856 km. However, it will eventually be surpassed by the 3,732 km Trans-Siberian Pipeline in the Soviet Union which has already been under construction for more than 20 years.

Alternatively, crude oil is transported to refineries in giant tankers, from which it is pumped into massive storage tanks. From this starting point, it moves to a distillation unit where it is broken down into what are called 'fractions'. These fractions boil and become gas — just as water boils and becomes steam — at different temperatures. This is the basis of the separation process.

Crude oil is heated and pumped as a mixture of liquid and vapour into a steel tower called a fractionating column. The liquid, which flows out at the bottom, becomes heavy products such as fuel oil and bitumen. The vapours rise within the tower, cooling as they ascend.

Heavier oils, like diesel, liquify first and are collected in trays at different levels. Petrol vapour is the last to leave, right at the top of the tower, and is condensed to liquid. 'Cracking' is a high-temperature treatment which breaks heavy fractions into lighter ones, thus increasing the amount of petrol.

In the United States, refining techniques are much more sophisticated than they are in eastern countries. As a result, a barrel of oil — 159 litres — may yield 64 litres of petrol in America compared with half that amount in less advanced countries.

'Reforming' is another advanced technique in which both high pressure and high temperature are used to convert heavier oils into petrol.

But, even if we tend to think of fuel when we think of oil, fuel is only a part — if a highly important part — of the oil story.

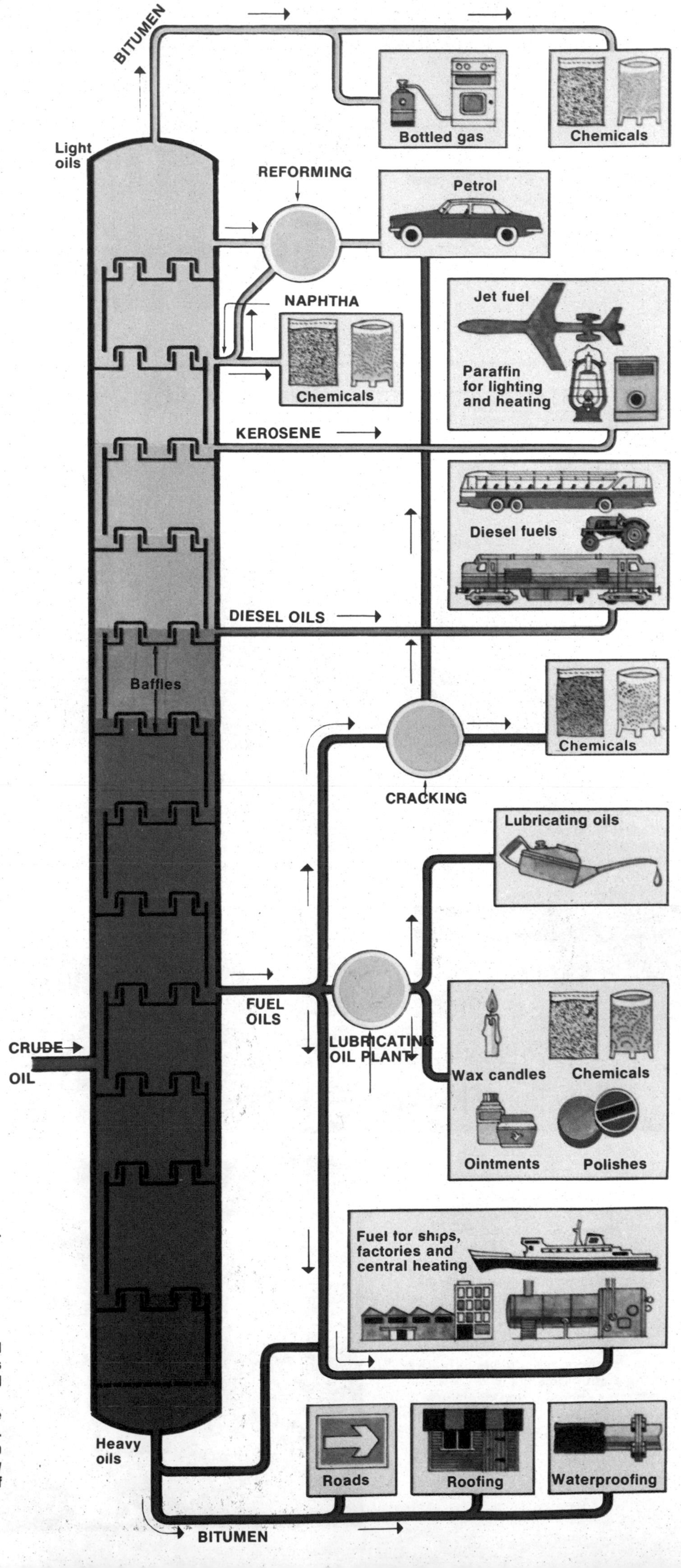


**Right: In the first stage of turning crude oil into the many products made from it, it is heated and then pumped through a tall steel tower called a *fractionating column.* Heavy oils pass out at the bottom of the column, lighter oils and gas out at the top. Some heavier oils are then put through one of two further processes — *cracking* and *reforming* — to increase the amount of the most valuable product — petrol.**

# Who was the Father of Radio?

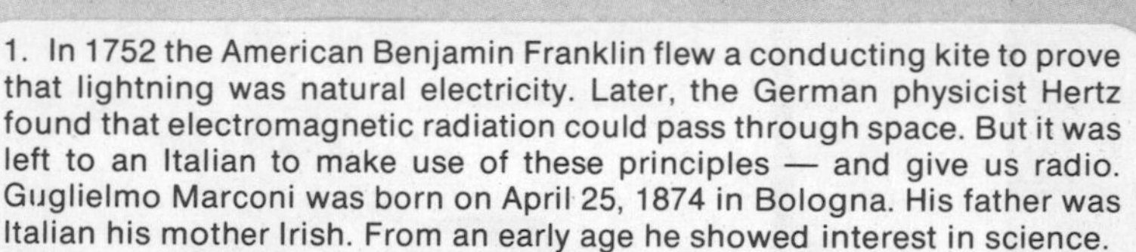

1. In 1752 the American Benjamin Franklin flew a conducting kite to prove that lightning was natural electricity. Later, the German physicist Hertz found that electromagnetic radiation could pass through space. But it was left to an Italian to make use of these principles — and give us radio. Guglielmo Marconi was born on April 25, 1874 in Bologna. His father was Italian his mother Irish. From an early age he showed interest in science.

2. One idea he had was to send the Morse Code through the air instead of through telegraph wires. To do this he made an oscillator which could break up his signals into long and short pauses. One night he woke his mother and rushed her to his workshop. There he pressed a morse key — the inventor had sent signals through the air!

3. Nobody in Italy seemed interested in his work, so in 1896 Marconi went to England to continue his experiments and try to get some backing. Soon William Preece, chief engineer at the Post Office, offered to help him demonstrate his invention. He set up his apparatus at the General Post Office in London watched by several eminent men, who were convinced it was a waste of time. Marconi astounded them by sending a morse telegram to a station a kilometre away.

4. Soon afterwards he formed the Wireless Telegraph and Signal Company and in 1897 installed wireless on the Royal Yacht travelling off the Isle of Wight. From the boat messages were sent to Queen Victoria who was on the island. Marconi continued with his work and in 1901 sailed to Newfoundland to prove that radio messages could defeat the Atlantic. Few people believed this possible but Marconi set up his primitive receiving station on a hill with the aerial attached to a kite. And on December 12, 1901 he first heard the morse symbol for the letter 'S' which had been tapped out more than 3,000km away at Poldhu in Cornwall. Wireless had crossed the Atlantic!

5. Throughout this historic occasion Marconi remained completely calm — he was utterly confident that transmission would be achieved. Over the next few years the use of radio grew, especially on ships, and in 1910 radio messages between ship and land led to the historic arrest of Dr. Crippen the notorious murderer. The captain of the Atlantic liner became suspicious of one man on board and sent a radio message to the police. When the liner reached Canada the police were waiting and Dr. Crippen was unmasked! It was the first time radio had helped to make such an arrest. In 1909 Marconi had shared the Nobel prize for Physics and was made a member of the Italian senate. His fame became world-wide and by 1912 moves were being made to make radio compulsory in shipping. It was soon shown why this was necessary.

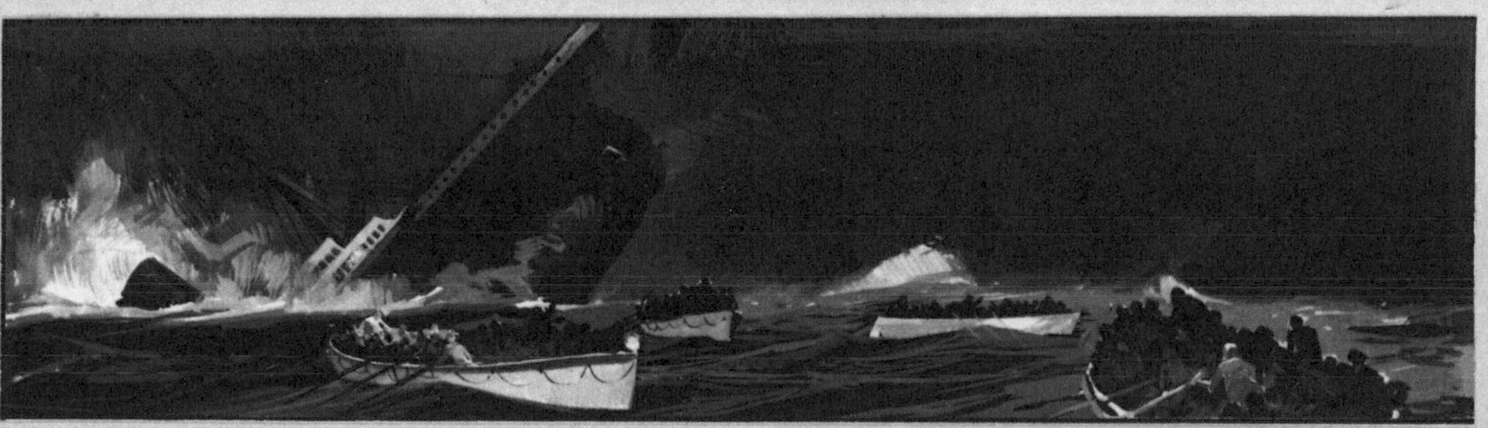

6. In April 1912 the *Titanic,* then the largest ship in the world, struck an iceberg in the north Atlantic. Many of her 1,000 crew and nearly 1,400 passengers perished but a large number were saved due to the two Marconi operators whose S.O.S. calls brought other ships to pick up survivors. A few years later Marconi made another important discovery — short wave transmissions. Working with long radio wavelengths he and his associates found that these could not be detected over very great distances. By using a short range Marconi found that radio waves could carry from Europe across the world to Australia. A world-wide network could now be set up.

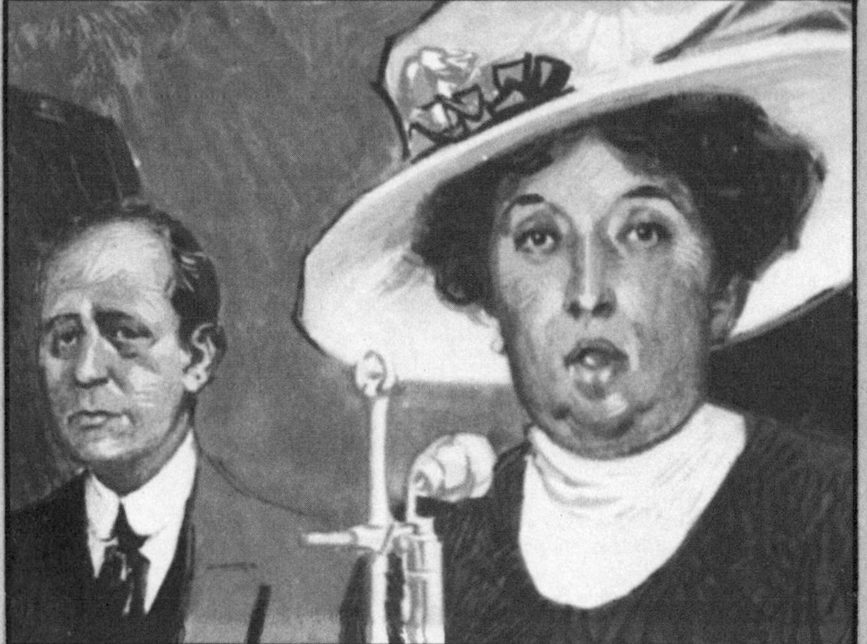

7. Besides science Marconi had always been interested in the sea. In 1920 he combined these interests when he bought a yacht which became a floating home and workshop. Also in that year the British scientist Ambrose Fleming invented the thermionic valve making it possible to transmit speech clearly. Radio could now be a source of entertainment.

8. The first public broadcast was made in June 1920, when the world-famous singer Dame Nellie Melba sang into a microphone at the Marconi works at Chelmsford, Essex and was heard by an enthralled audience at the Royal Albert Hall in London. In November 1922 the first broadcasting station was opened in London and soon the whole world was linked by radio stations. Marconi never took all the credit for the invention of wireless but before he died in 1937 he knew that he had made it possible for each home to have a link with all parts of the world.

# Who was the Pioneer of Aviation?

**EVER since human beings first watched the birds soaring and wheeling and hovering in the sky, they have felt rather envious and have sought some means which would enable them to do the same. The human body was never built to fly, so flight could be achieved only in a powered machine.**

It was through the work of Sir George Cayley that Man came to understand the requirements that were necessary to enable a machine to travel through the air. He laid the foundations of the science of aerodynamics — the study of motion and control of solid bodies in air.

Born in Yorkshire in 1773, Sir George Cayley became 'flightstruck' while he was still a young boy. When he was ten years old, the first men to take to the air travelled in the hot air balloon constructed by the Montgolfier Brothers in France. Balloons, however, could not be directed very easily, and they were subject to the moods of the weather. This was not good enough for Cayley. He realised that controlled flight could be achieved only by a heavier-than-air-machine with fixed wings. Balloons, of course, were lighter than air and had no wings.

Cayley set about designing a machine. By 1799, he had already worked out the basic 'fat sausage' shape that is associated with our modern aircraft. Cayley's design had fixed wings, a fuselage and a tail unit which combined two features for controlling the aircraft — a rudder and an elevator. The only impractical thing about this design was Cayley's method of propulsion: he had known about airscrew propellers since 1796, but because no engine was available he gave his aircraft flappers which were worked by the pilot sitting in his gondola-shaped seat.

## Birdmen

The flappers, which could never have made the aircraft fly, showed the influence of the 'birdmen' or 'ornithologist' who advocated bird-like flight with artificial wings. Cayley knew the 'birdmen' were working along the wrong lines: the only thing that could happen when they jumped off cliffs or high buildings, flapping their wings, was that they would drop straight downwards, crash, and probably kill themselves. Their arms were simply not strong enough to get them off the ground.

Cayley studied birds more closely than most of the ornithologists. He observed how they flew and how they managed to remain in the air even when their wings were not moving. For hours, he watched them glide with outstretched wings, and saw how they moved their tails so that they remained stable in the air.

Many of these observations found their way into Cayley's designs, which included the cambered, or slightly arched wind surface of birds: this aided 'lift' when they were attached to the body at the proper angle. Cayley also copied the birds' streamlined body for the gondola shape of his craft believing this helped them to fly. A third feature was the manoeuvrable tailplane, which like a bird's tail helped to keep an aircraft stable.

Cayley tested his ideas about flight in several gliders which looked very much like kites. The first was a model, about 1.5 metres (5 ft) long, which Cayley made in 1804. As a model, this aircraft proved that its shape and configuration were the correct ones for flight, but there was a big drawback: Cayley had no engine that could drive the plane through the air. He experimented with engines for many years, but without success. Steam engines, the 'wonder powerplants' of his time were powerful, but were too heavy.

Cayley produced an engine fired by gunpowder in about 1807, but it failed to work. So did his 'hot-air' or calorific engine.

For the next thirty years or so, Cayley's interest in aviation took second place to other activities. For instance he spent much time on another great invention: the caterpillar tractor. Meanwhile, many others became interested in aviation and began to produce designs for aircraft. One of them was William Henson who, in 1843, produced a design for his Aerial Steam Carriage. The Carriage never flew, but it renewed Cayley's own interest in aviation, and led him to produce the first biplane (two wing) design in 1843: this had four helicopter rotors and two pusher airscrews to carry the aircraft forward.

**An artist's impression of the craft designed by Cayley in 1843. Although Cayley never built this machine he produced plans of the first two-winged aircraft — a biplane.**

Cayley also did further work on his earlier gliders, and in 1849 built 'Old Flier' a triplane (three wing) glider with a wheeled under-carriage. With a ten-year-old boy on board, 'Old Flier' was towed in kite-flying fashion down a hill near Cayley's home in Scarborough and flew for several metres. Four years later, in 1853, Cayley built another triplane: the 'New Flier'. This time the passenger was his coachman, who had to be ordered to fly in it. The terrified coachman glided safely across a small valley, and after he landed and clambered out, shaking all over, the first thing he did was tell Cayley that he was leaving his employ.

## Glider

Cayley, who died in 1857, built the Old and New Fliers with multi-wings because he realised that more than one wing provided increased lift and that with the materials which he had available could be built with the necessary strength and minimum weight. However, Cayley also looked forward to the monoplane — the aircraft with one wing which characterises aircraft today — in his glider design of 1852.

Over a century later, in 1973, this design was discovered and an aircraft built from it. It was successfully flown, with a tow, so proving how much the far-sighted Cayley deserved his title, 'Father of Aviation'.

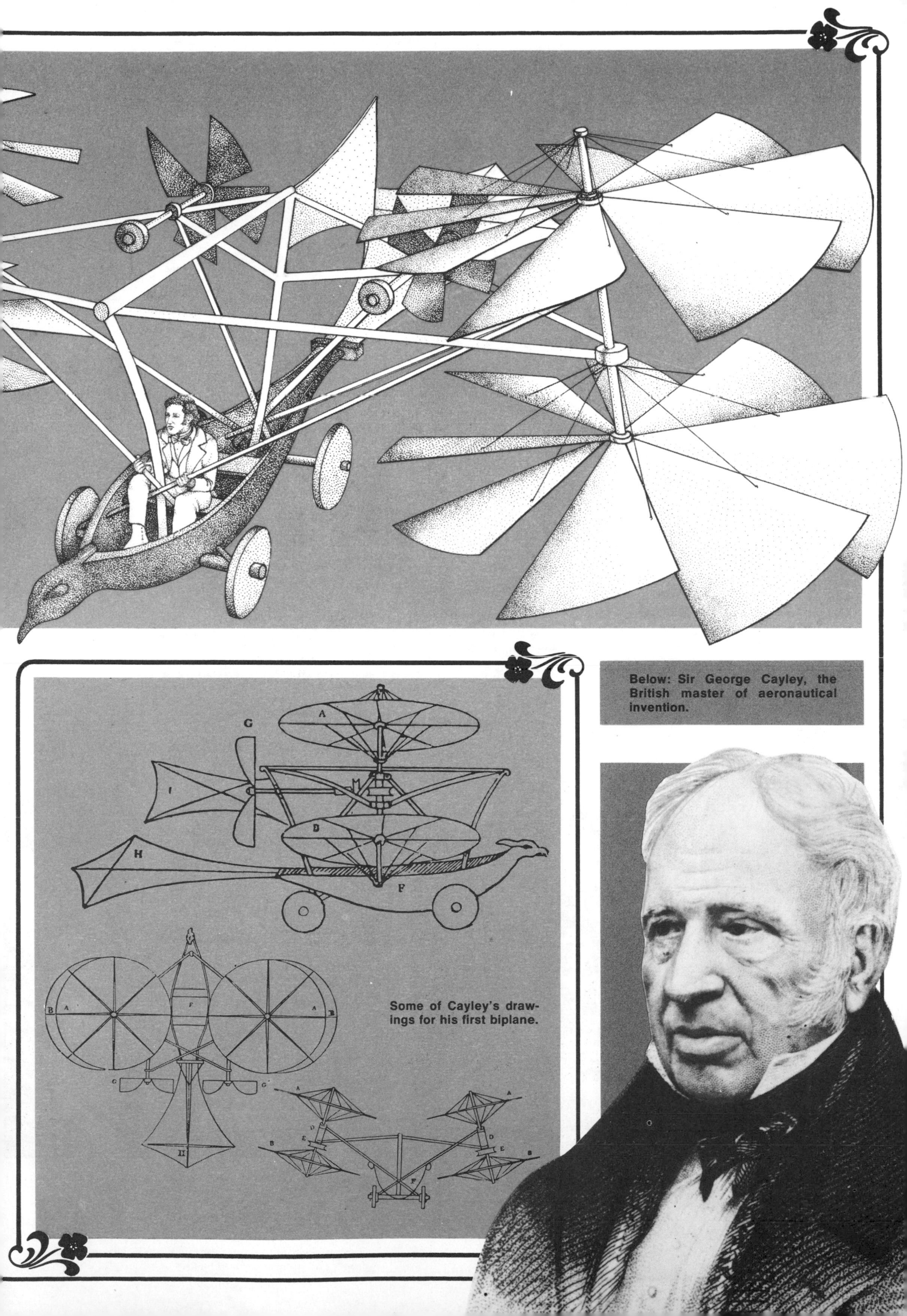


Below: Sir George Cayley, the British master of aeronautical invention.

Some of Cayley's drawings for his first biplane.

# Who had 1033 Inventions

1 Born in Milan, Ohio in 1847, Thomas Alva Edison, one of the greatest inventors of all time, attended school for only three months. Declared backward by the headmaster, Thomas was withdrawn from school for ever by his indignant mother, who taught him at home. At 12, he earned money selling newspapers on a train and was soon printing and selling his own newspaper from the baggage wagon. There, he experimented with chemicals until an accident with phosphorus caused a fire.

2 The railway guard threw away all his chemicals but young Edison kept his job and continued to produce his newspaper, gathering news items from telegraph offices along the track. In those days before television and radio or even the telephone, this teenage boy's newspaper often carried important news before the major newspapers could print it. When 15 years old, Edison became a telegraph operator himself.

3 He often neglected his duties to study and experiment with electrical science. Before he was 21, he had invented an automatic repeater which could transfer a message from one wire to another without requiring an operator. In 1869, he came to New York where he invented the first 'ticker tape' machine to print out in words the messages which it received over the telegraph wire. This earned him a 40,000 dollar fortune from grateful businessmen.

4 Within a few weeks, he had spent the money on a small laboratory and factory in Newark, New Jersey, where a staff of mechanics worked with him, trying out his ideas and inventions. There he produced his carbon telephone transmitter and established a reputation as an inventor of some genius. Of his success, he once said that genius was "one per cent inspiration and ninety-nine per cent perspiration", and no one worked harder or longer than he.

# to his name?

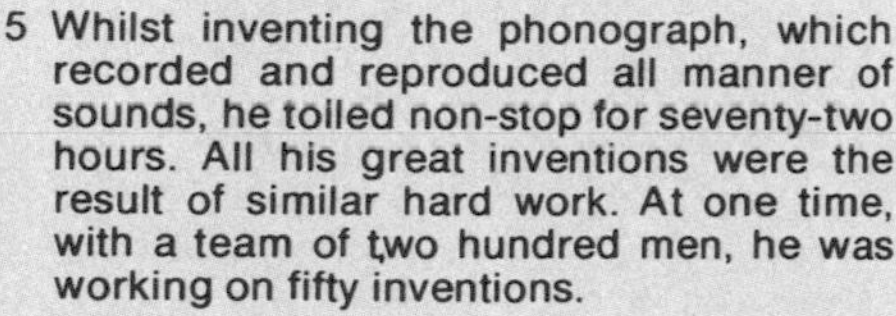
5 Whilst inventing the phonograph, which recorded and reproduced all manner of sounds, he toiled non-stop for seventy-two hours. All his great inventions were the result of similar hard work. At one time, with a team of two hundred men, he was working on fifty inventions.

6 The electric light bulb caused Edison problems. Bulbs had been made which would glow for a few moments but the problem was to find a substance which shone brilliantly when electricity passed through it, but did not melt. Edison spent 40,000 dollars and tried 3,000 ideas before he discovered that charred cotton (carbon) would serve the purpose.

7 Edison made the first cine camera practicable. It was he who suggested equidistant holes along the sides of cine film to regulate its flow through the camera. The first movie pictures, including the first Western starring Buffalo Bill, were made in his film studio. Before he died in 1931, Edison had registered 1,033 inventions at the United States Patent Office. His life was not one long success story as he lost a lot of money on a machine for crushing iron ore which failed. But failure only made Edison try harder to solve a problem and produce an invention which would benefit mankind.

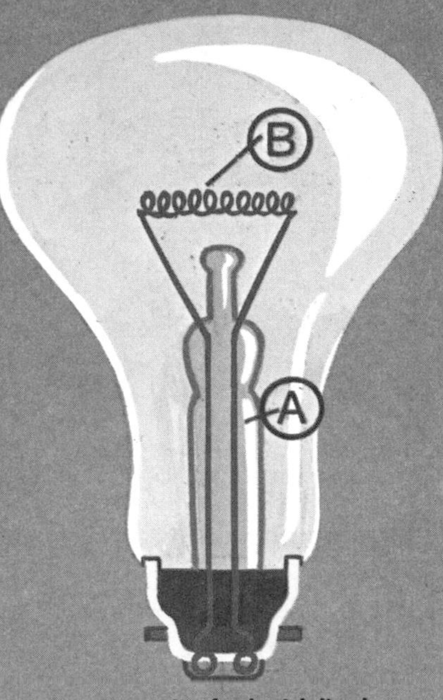


**When a current of electricity is passed through wire (A), it reaches the filament (B) which is a coil of material with a higher degree of resistance to electricity than the main wire. The electricity forces its way through the coil giving off energy in the form of heat and light. Edison used a filament of carbon but, nowadays, tungsten is used in filaments which, when coiled, are about 3cm. (1¼ inches) long. However, if uncoiled, they would stretch to about 45cm. (18 inches).**

**A version of an early light bulb with a platinum filament coil.**

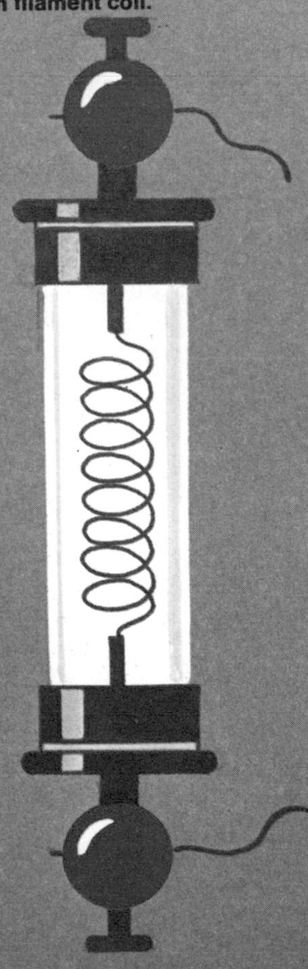

**The first light bulbs had all the air removed to prevent the hot filament combining with oxygen in the air and so burning up. Today's light bulbs contain an inert gas which helps to prolong the life of the tungsten filament.**

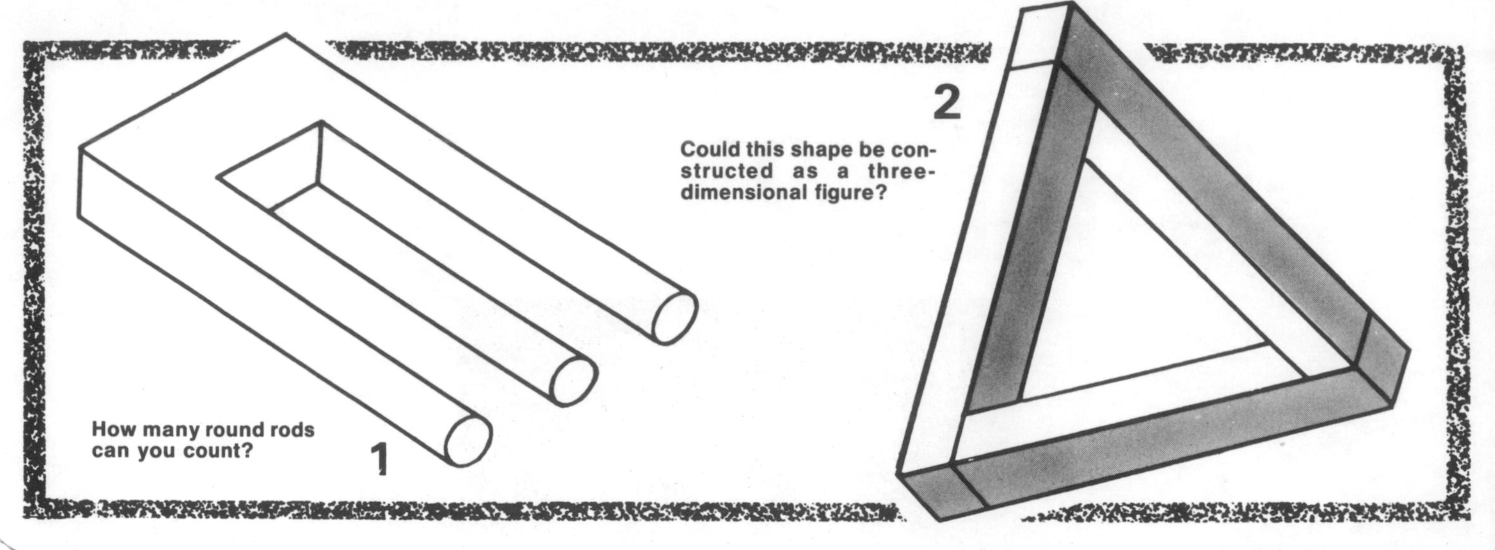


How many round rods can you count?

Could this shape be constructed as a three-dimensional figure?

# Can your Eye...

3

The day of the giants? Or are these two figures the same size?

PULLING the door open, the detective burst into the room. He gasped at the sight before him. *He could hardly believe his eyes!*

The saying is used often enough, not just in thriller stories — and usually implies that the scene is so unexpected that the beholder questions whether or not his eyes are 'playing tricks'. But can you always believe your eyes, or do they sometimes deceive you?

## Illusions

Look at figures 1 and 2. At first sight nothing appears to be wrong with them, but try counting the rods in figure 1 or trying to analyse how figure 2 could be constructed as a three-dimensional figure. You will soon discover that the drawings could not be made into real, solid objects.

They are no more than optical illusions. The eye merely records the scenes before it and its images are interpreted by the brain. In trick pictures like these, it is the brain that is fooled, but because vision plays an important part in the deception, they are known as optical illusions.

In figure 3, which man is the taller? Probably, you will say figure B, but measure the two figures and you will see that they are both the same size. The railway lines and telephone lines follow the rules of perspective drawing, whereas the figures do not, although the eye still records the fig-

4

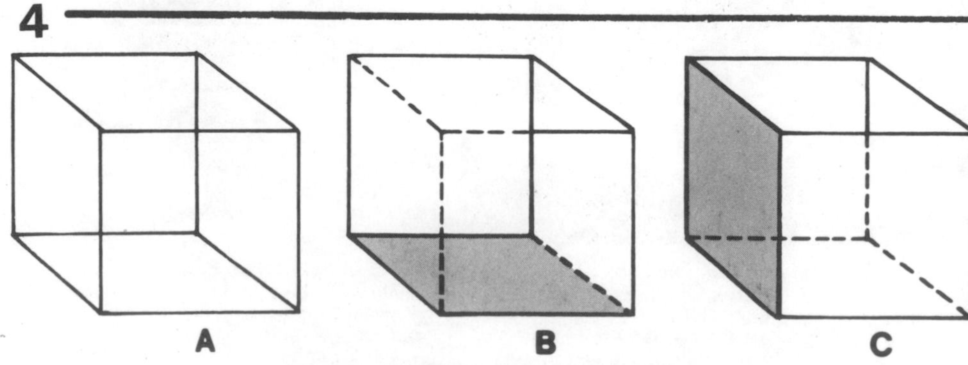


Stare at box A and make up your mind whether it resembles box B or box C.

As the eye looks down into the water it has no problems in seeing any object, such as a fish. The problem is the fish is not where it appears to be!

This is because a ray of light travelling obliquely from one medium to another (in our case water to air) is bent or REFRACTED at the surface between the two media. The diverted line shows where the fish actually is and how light travels between it and the eye. The straight line of vision illustrates where the fish appears to be.

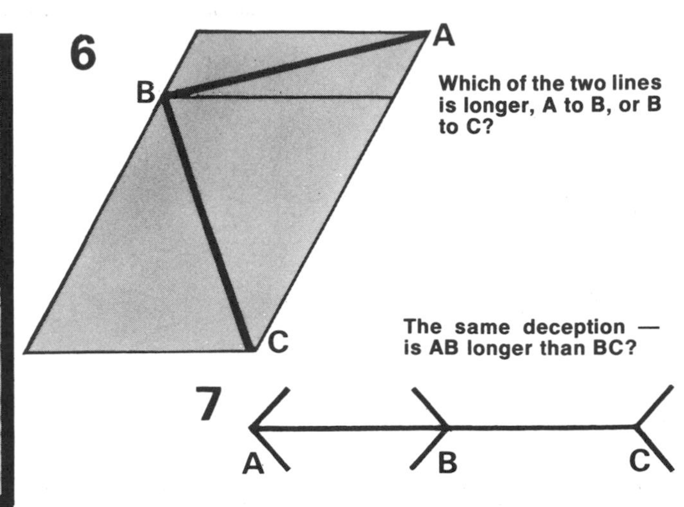


Which of the two lines is longer, A to B, or B to C?

The same deception — is AB longer than BC?

# deceive you?

ures along with their surroundings.

Some optical illusions even make 'solid' objects appear to change shape. Look at box A in figure 4. Are you looking from below the right-hand corner as in box B? Or down onto the top left-hand corner as in box C? In fact, if you stare at box A you will find that every few seconds it 'switches' in and out, alternately resembling boxes B and C.

The brain is presumably fooled by the perspective and just cannot determine which box is depicted.

In figures 6 and 7, which line is the longer — A to B, or B to C? Perhaps you have the answer — both lines are exactly the same.

## Are they straight?

Now for some illusions about the shape of lines. Look at the two thick lines in figure 8. Are they straight or are they bowed outwards at the centre? They certainly look bowed, but a ruler placed along them will prove them to be perfectly straight and parallel to each other. In figure 9, the white squares may appear to be of different sizes, but measure them and see!

Illustrations 5 and 10 both show instances when the information that the eye relates to the brain leads to deception, but in both cases it is the nature of the movement of light that results in the illusion.

Once again, the brain has been fooled by the information presented to it by the eyes.

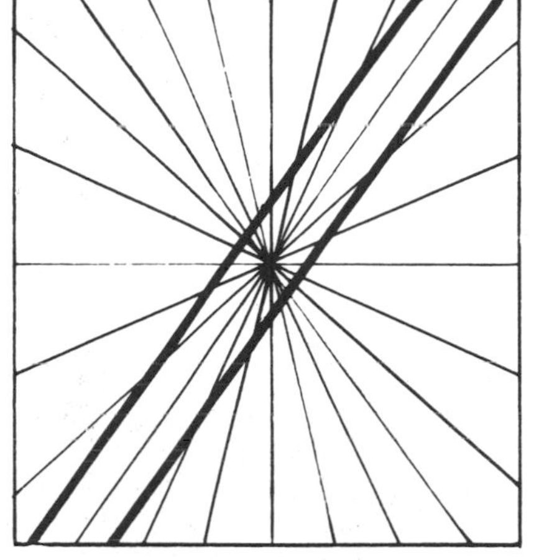


Look at the two thick lines. Are they straight or bowed outwards at the centre?

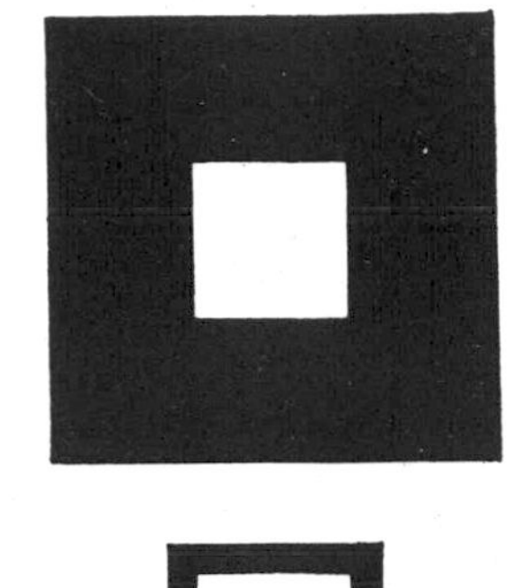


Which of the white squares is the bigger?

Weary travellers in the desert sometimes 'see' an oasis, when in fact there is no such thing there. This is a mirage, an optical illusion caused by atmospheric conditions.

# Who made the Study of Microbes his life work?

1. Louis Pasteur was born in December, 1822, the son of a sergeant-major who had served in the French army. As a boy, Louis went to Arbois College in the Jura. He was dreamy and slow to learn, but he would spend hours after school studying his various subjects, and he soon outstripped his fellow students. It was decided that Louis should continue to study in Paris, and with his parents and most of the village waving him farewell the young student set off.

Homesick, but determined to make good, Pasteur set to work and slowly absorbed all that was taught him. When he finally graduated he decided to concentrate on the study of physical science. His first major research was with tartaric acid, the results of which earned him the Cross of the Legion of Honour. He then went on to study fermentation — a chemical reaction produced by tiny living organisms, usually producing alcohol.

2. Fermentation was thought to be caused by tiny creatures which grew out of the substance in which they appeared. Pasteur, after five long years of research work, found that the cause of fermentation was due to the action of tiny living micro-organisms found in the air. If wine or milk are heated rapidly, the microbes which would turn them sour are killed. Today, our milk is treated this way and it is known as 'pasteurization' after Louis Pasteur who discovered the process.

It was the French scientist who was the first man to convince the scientific world that micro-organisms cannot be spontaneously generated from non-living matter. In short, all life comes from life. But many people scoffed at Pasteur's ideas. Although we accept his ideas today it must be remembered that they would be completely revolutionary and strange in Pasteur's time.

3. The study of microbes was to become Pasteur's life-work. By painstaking effort he was able to prove that his discoveries were based on sound facts. In 1873, one of Pasteur's daughters died of typhoid fever. He determined to try and discover the cause of typhoid and other diseases which killed so many people. Hospitals in those days were dreaded places, for nearly 50 per cent of patients died after the most simple of operations because of germs and lack of cleanliness.

4. Although the doctors and staff of the hospital where Pasteur started work were not convinced about his idea of germs, they agreed to carry out some of the changes that he wanted. Pasteur instituted a regime of strict hygiene and the use of strong disinfectants in the operating theatres and wards. Within six months time the wards controlled by Pasteur had a death rate of only five per cent — totally justifying Pasteur's theories.

5. Pasteur's next research was into anthrax, a deadly disease which annually killed thousands of pigs and sheep. He prepared a vaccine of dead anthrax germs and injected them into healthy sheep, and the vaccinated animals lived (left). He also produced a vaccine to prevent humans catching rabies. Its first trial on a boy bitten by a mad dog proved successful (above).

6. Thanks largely to a French banker who left a fortune to build a special institute for the study of diseases, Pasteur was able to see the building of the Pasteur Institute, founded in 1888, seven years before his death. In the grounds is a statue of a boy struggling with the mad dog that bit him, a symbol for all time of the scientist who devoted his life to the service of mankind.

# WORLD OF NATURE

# Why do Beavers build Dams?

IT IS perhaps fitting that one nation, Canada, should have recognized the elegance, industry and charm of the beaver by selecting it as its national animal.

Regrettably, this acknowledgement is quite recent since historical records clearly state that beavers were once more numerous and widespread than they are today.

The European Beaver *(Castor fiber)* was common in Britain until the Middle Ages when determined hunting largely eliminated the population, a story that was repeated in the rest of Europe.

The North American Beaver *(Castor canadenis)* was initially hunted by the Red Indians, who wisely selected mature individuals and so minimized the effect of trapping on the beaver population.

Unfortunately the white hunters were not as discriminating. At the height of the fur trading the Hudson's Bay Company, for instance, marketed 120,000 pelts per year with the predictable result that throughout much of the United States, as in Great Britain and most parts of Europe, the beaver was exterminated.

Today the beaver lives in Scandinavia, Russia, France, Canada and the adjacent states of the U.S.A. In all areas it is a protected animal.

Beavers are large rodents, males weighing up to 27 kilograms (55lbs) and measuring up to a little over a metre (3½ feet) in length.

They live in lodges or burrows in streams and ponds and the young beavers remain for two years with their parents. Since a litter of two to four young are born every spring, then at any time a family consists of

**The large, flat scaly tail is often as much as one third of the beaver's total length. It is used in an up-and-down motion in swimming and for slapping the surface of the water as a warning signal.**

**Nose and ears can be closed with the aid of special flaps of skin when swimming.**

**Only the hind legs have webbed feet.**

**Beavers are expert swimmers and they spend much of their time cruising just below the surface when often all that is visible are their nostrils and the V-shaped wake. Most of the power is provided by their webbed hind feet but the tail also helps at low speeds.**

the parents, the young of the previous year and the current infants. When a two year old beaver leaves home it finds a mate and the pair, which remain together throughout their lives, may settle in the parental pond or one nearby.

Beavers do not depend on natural ponds but can create their own by building dams and it is this ability for which they are famous.

## Dam builders

Sitting up and balancing on their tails, they use their incisor teeth to gnaw through the bases of aspen saplings and young trees and can then manipulate the trunks and branches into position at a dam site using their hands.

If the tree is a long way from the site the beaver may float the log into position or they may dig flotation ditches to ease the movement of saplings.

The trees and branches are stuck together with mud and the dam is then kept in a state of good repair. Once a pond has been filled with water the beaver may dig a hole in the bank using the claws of its forelimbs or it may construct a lodge. In either case the entrances to this home are under water with a tunnel running upwards to a living area which is located above the water level.

The lodges are made from successive horizontal layers of branches stuck together with mud, and finally covered by a roof of branches about three feet above the surface of the water. Inside there is the living platform and in the roof there is a chimney which provides for circulation of air.

In any one pond there may be several families but they all live independently, cutting their own trees and mending their own lodges. Even the dams are maintained by all the beavers separately and they do not co-operate together at all.

However, in a large pond with several dams a certain minimum number of beaver families is necessary to keep the dam in good condition and so maintain the pond water level. If this water level drops below the entrance to the lodges predators can enter and the beavers lose their security.

## Expert swimmers

Beavers are good swimmers, well adapted to life in the bitterly cold waters of the northern latitudes, Their thick, furry, waterproof coats keep them warm even in the winters when the pond surface is covered with ice. Their webbed hind feet push them through the water powerfully and their ears and noses can be closed to keep the water out.

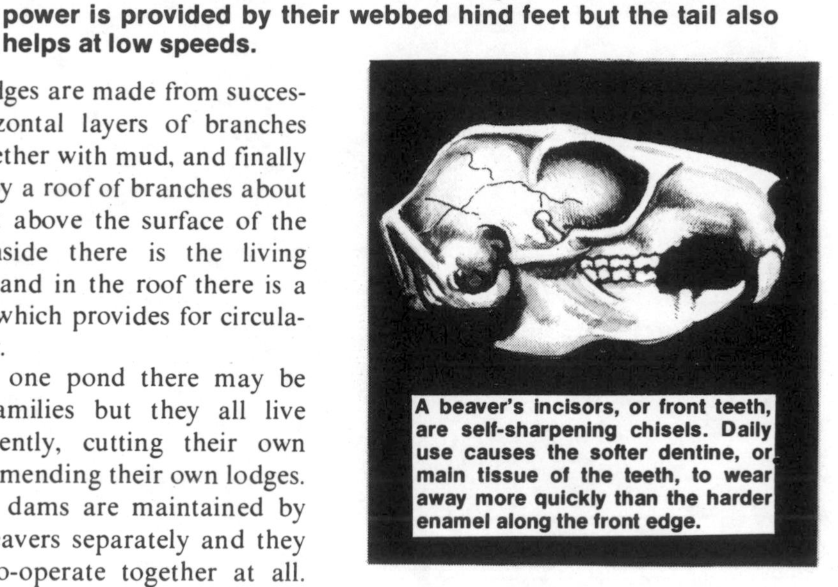

**A beaver's incisors, or front teeth, are self-sharpening chisels. Daily use causes the softer dentine, or main tissue of the teeth, to wear away more quickly than the harder enamel along the front edge.**

**The dam is constructed of branches, cemented with grass and mud.**

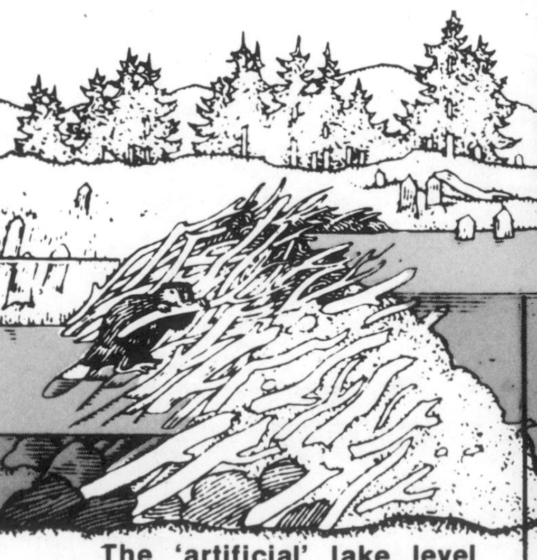

**The 'artificial' lake level may be raised several feet above the outlet stream.**

The tail of the beaver plays a special role; it is large and scaly, broad and flattened and functions in several ways.

In summer, when the beaver is in danger of overheating because of its thick fur, the tail provides an area from which heat can be lost. A beaver also uses its tail as an oar in swimming and if danger threatens a swimming beaver, it can warn the colony by slapping the tail against the surface of the water as it dives to safety.

Beavers feed on berries, leaves, roots and the bark of trees. Having felled a tree, a beaver may strip the bark from its surface with its incisors. The fronts of these teeth are covered by a thick layer of orange enamel and this wears away slowly while the backs of the teeth wear away more rapidly, thus ensuring a constant sharp cutting edge. This is, in fact, a feature common to all rodents.

## Food store

In the autumn the beavers store quantities of twigs and branches beneath the surface of the water near the lodge. They do not hibernate in the true sense of the word but remain in the lodge during the winter, using these stores of food to sustain themselves.

Beavers have a considerable effect on their environment. The damming of the streams increases the amount of water available, by slowing the flow of mountain snow meltwater and provides the perfect habitat for a variety of ducks, geese and other water birds which feed on the increased number of plants and invertebrates.

Fish flourish in beaver rivers including the valuable trout and salmon. Predators, such as wolves, coyotes, bears, and cougars also increase in number. These animals prey not only upon the beaver but also on the moose and elk which feed especially in the areas where the beaver ponds have silted up to form valuable meadows.

It is this effect that the beaver has upon its environment which makes it so useful. Consequently, its conservation and reintroduction to areas where it is extinct, become all the more important.

*Beaver on top of his lodge. Note the size of the log in the foreground.*

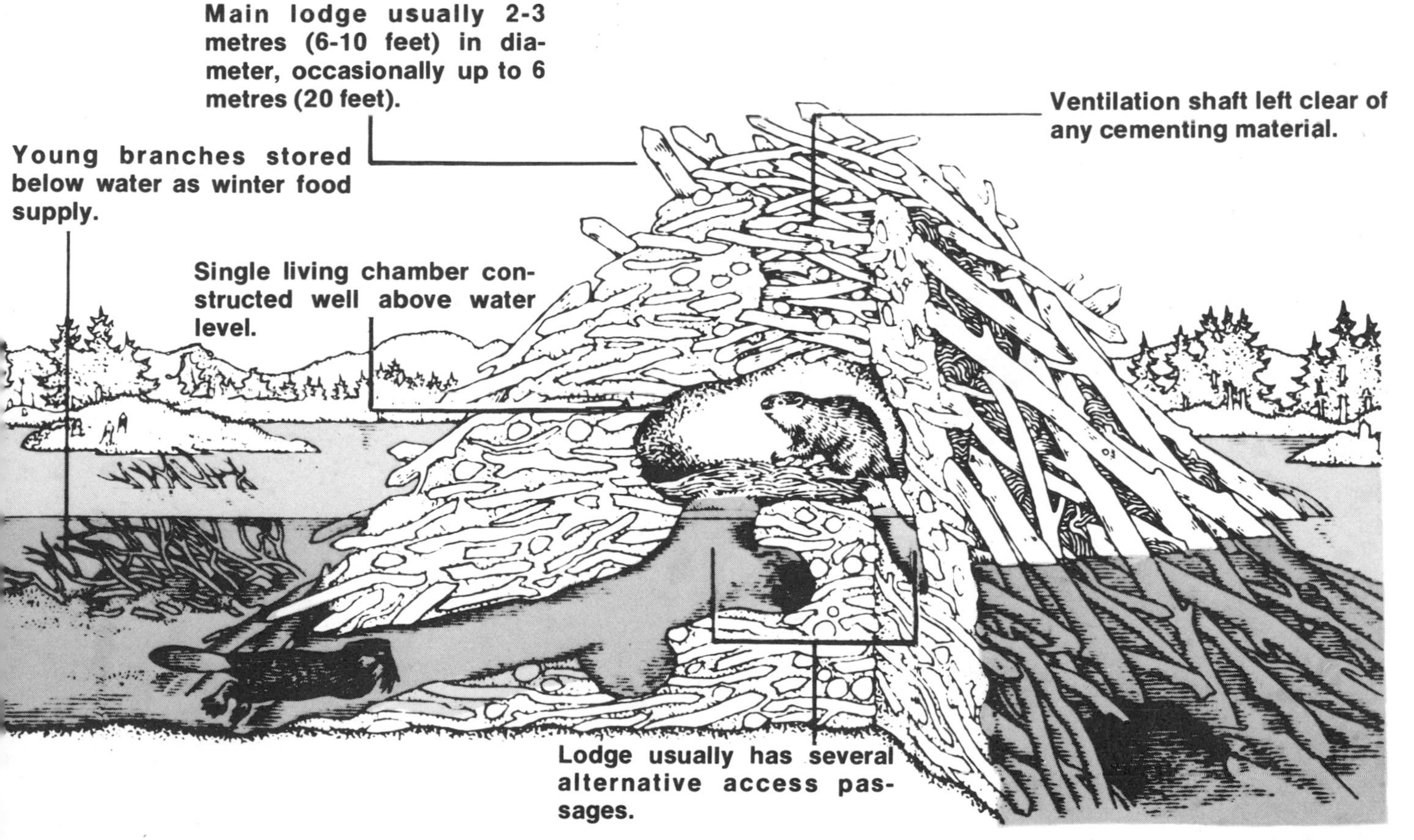

# Which Snakes can kill?

**They're not slippery or slimy. They don't seek out people to attack them. In fact, they're shy creatures and hide from Man if they can. But the snake in the grass *is* a killer — more deadly than all other animals except insects.**

POISON GLAND

**Below, left: Snake venom is only dangerous after it has been injected beneath the skin. The most ingenious method of achieving this occurs in the vipers. These snakes — which include the adder (the only poisonous British snake) and the American rattlesnake — have teeth which normally lie flat along the roof of the mouth. But when the snake opens its mouth, they swing forward. The teeth are also hollow, like a hypodermic syringe. When they pierce the prey's skin, the poison is squeezed from a gland above the roof of the mouth down through the teeth and deep into the victim's flesh. For most small animals — snakes' normal prey — this means almost instant death.**

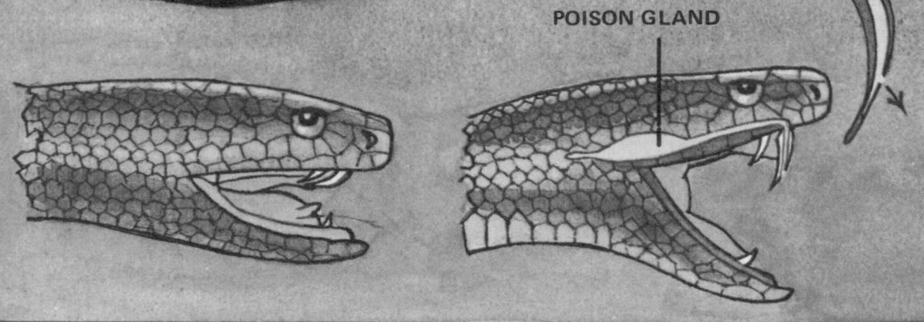

**Below: The world's three biggest snakes are pretty large by any standards. They don't normally attack Man, but we don't advise hanging on to the end of one!**

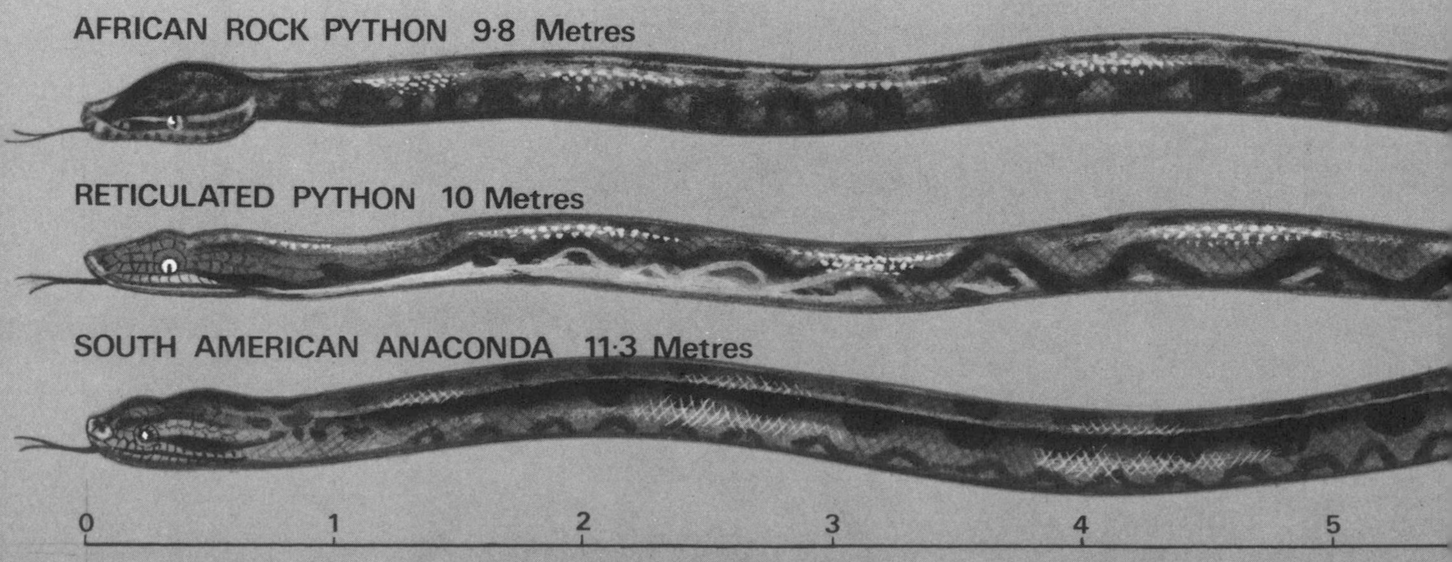

AFRICAN ROCK PYTHON 9·8 Metres

RETICULATED PYTHON 10 Metres

SOUTH AMERICAN ANACONDA 11·3 Metres

0 1 2 3 4 5

**ALTHOUGH many animals are potentially dangerous to Man, most have been greatly exaggerated as killers by sensational fiction. Tales of man-eating tigers, voracious sharks and blood-thirsty wolves abound, but most are pure invention. A pet dog suffering from rabies is a far greater threat than any of these animals.**

The most dangerous creatures — to Man — are undoubtedly insects. There are something like three-quarters of a million types of insect, and they exist in uncountable numbers. They are a threat because many species carry disease. For example, thirty diseases, including cholera, typhoid, plague and leprosy, are transmitted by the house-fly.

## Irrational fear

Far fewer people die because of the next most dangerous group of animals — snakes. Nevertheless, an irrational fear of snakes haunts people even in countries where snakes are rare.

There are no reliable estimates of the number of people who die every year from snakebite. Some experts put the figure as high as 30-40,000. But most deaths occur in remote parts of undeveloped countries where it is difficult to collect accurate information.

For example, about half the total deaths are said to occur in India. It seems highly unlikely that an incredible 20,000 people die from snakebite in India every year. What is more likely is that in remote areas a large number of unexplained deaths are blamed on snakebite. As there are few, if any, medical facilities nearby the numbers go unchecked.

But whatever the true statistics, it can be fairly stated that snakes cause more human deaths per year than all the other land and water animals combined, with the exception of insects.

There are two types of snakes — the *venomous* (those that are poisonous) and the *non-venomous*. Of the non-venomous, the most fascinating are the constrictors.

It is commonly thought that constrictors crush their prey to death. This is not so. They coil themselves round their victim and, by applying slow but steady pressure, suffocate it. Each time the victim breathes out the constrictor increases the pressure until the unfortunate animal can breathe in so little air that oxygen is prevented from reaching the brain. At this point, the prey becomes unconscious and can be swallowed by the snake, insensible but alive. Some constrictors, however, continue to apply pressure until the heart stops.

There is no doubt that the largest constrictors *could* kill and even swallow a human. The constrictors are the world's largest snakes and six species (out of about sixty) are true monsters:

- the boa constrictor of Central and South America can grow to a maximum length of 5.8 m
- the Indian python can reach 6.1 m
- the amethystine python, found in Australia and the Philippine Islands, may grow to 7.6 m
- the African rock python reaches 9.8 m
- the reticulated python of Asia may reach 10 m
- the monster of them all, the anaconda of South America, may grow to a massive 11.3 m.

These enormous snakes can take large animals as food. For example, a 4.8 metre African rock python is known to have killed and swallowed an impala (a kind of antelope) weighing 59 kg. So it is possible that a large constrictor could kill and eat an average 70 kg man, although small women and children would be the more likely victims.

But *do* these snakes ever attack and eat humans? Stories abound to say they do. In 1978 there was a report from the Far East stating that a dead human had been found intact inside the body of a large constrictor, and over the years several similar cases have been cited. In 1927 a 14-year-old boy was said to have been eaten by a 4.3 metre reticulated python in the East Indies, and in the same year an Indian newspaper ran a news item about a Burmese salesman — Maung Chit Chine — who had been swallowed, feet first, by a python. In 1975, the *Pretoria News* in South Africa reported that a gardener was attacked by a 2.1 metre python and managed to escape its clutches only after a fierce struggle.

But such cases are news just *because* they are rare. A large constrictor *is* capable of killing and eating a human, but for it to do so is highly unlikely.

## Snakebite

Far more people die from snakebite.

There are some 2,700 species of snake, and about 400 of these can give a fatal bite. But being bitten by a venomous snake does not mean instant death. If it did, the death rate would be far higher than it is.

So much depends on the condition of the victim and the type and position of the bite. A strong, healthy man has a better chance of surviving than a frail, elderly woman or a very young child; a bite near a vital organ

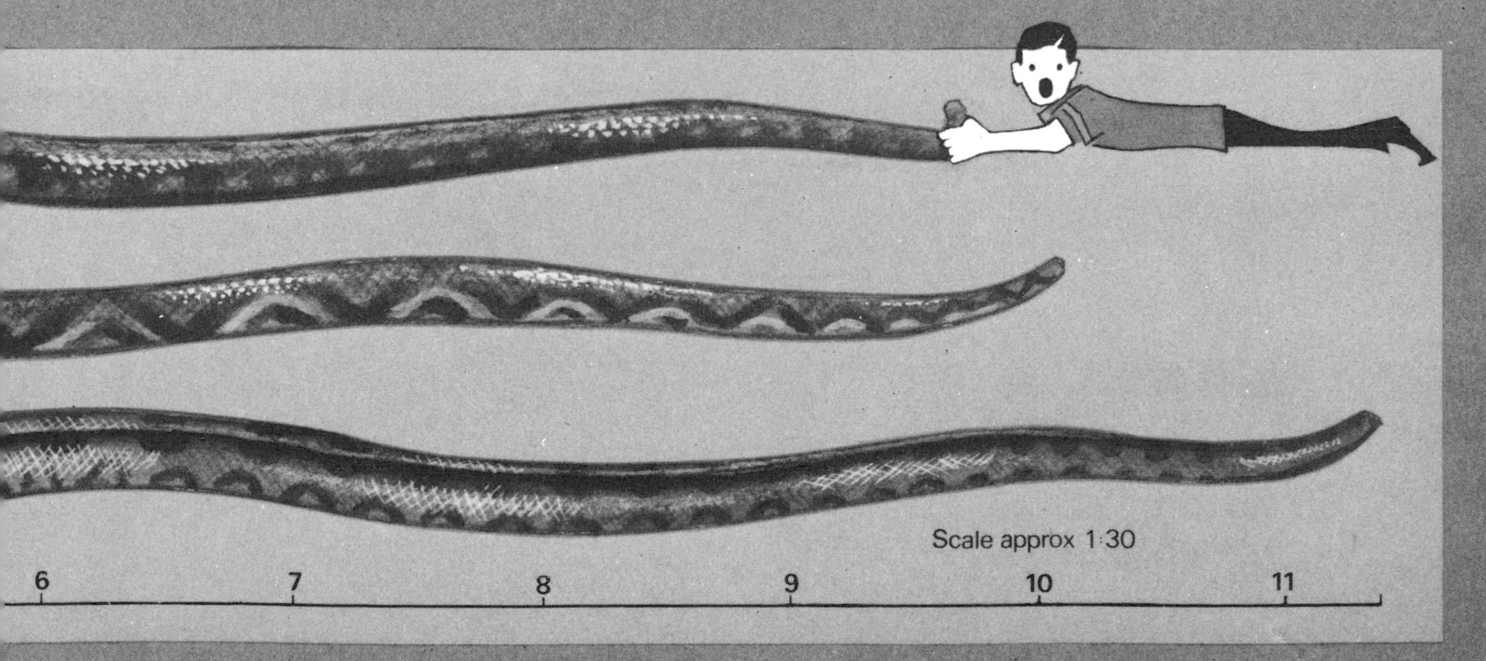

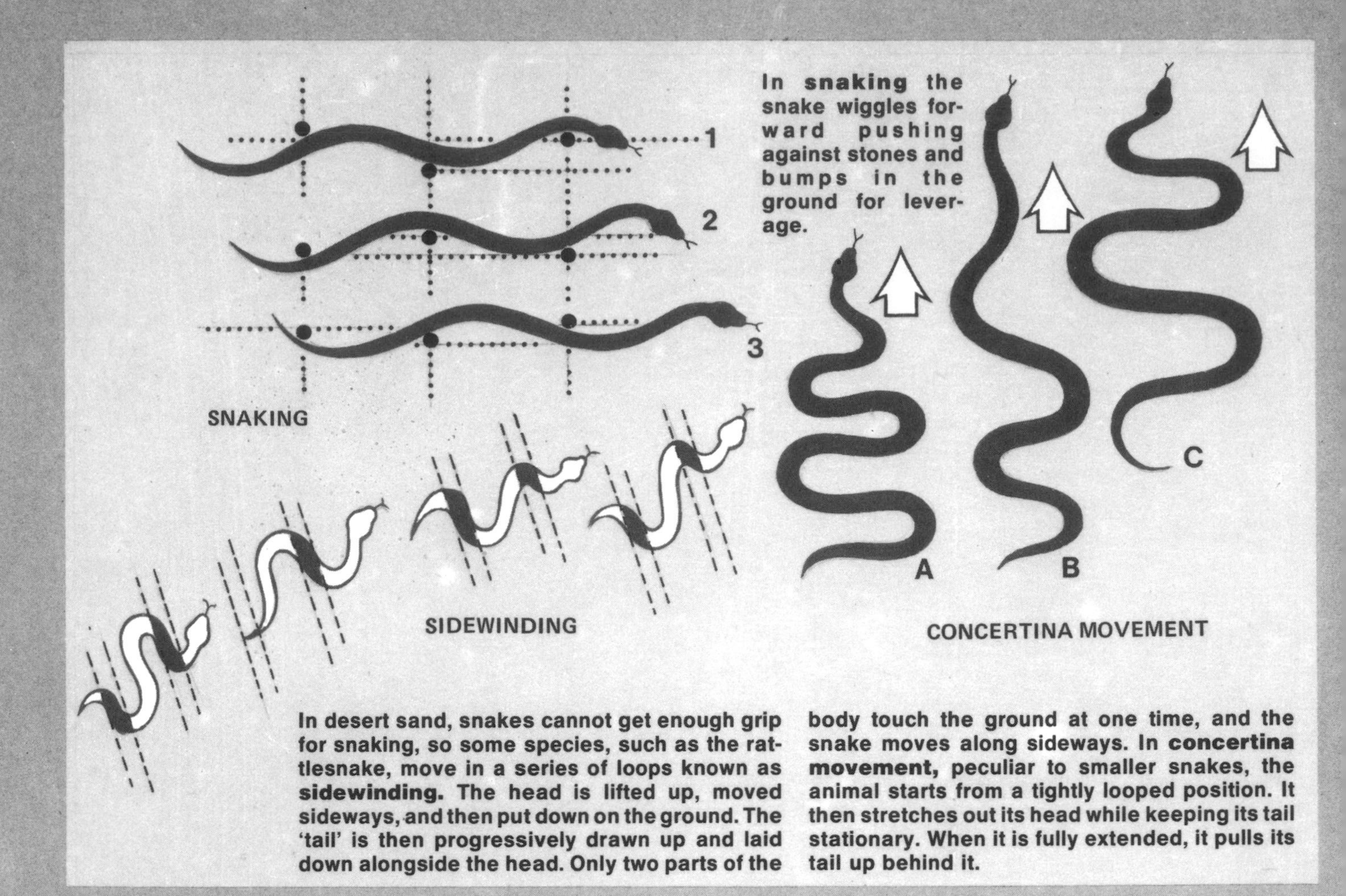


In **snaking** the snake wiggles forward pushing against stones and bumps in the ground for leverage.

In desert sand, snakes cannot get enough grip for snaking, so some species, such as the rattlesnake, move in a series of loops known as **sidewinding.** The head is lifted up, moved sideways, and then put down on the ground. The 'tail' is then progressively drawn up and laid down alongside the head. Only two parts of the body touch the ground at one time, and the snake moves along sideways. In **concertina movement,** peculiar to smaller snakes, the animal starts from a tightly looped position. It then stretches out its head while keeping its tail stationary. When it is fully extended, it pulls its tail up behind it.

is more dangerous than one to the hands or feet because the venom is carried to where it can do most damage more quickly; and obviously if the fangs are fully sunk into the flesh the bite is more dangerous than a glancing scratch.

There are two types of venom — nerve poisons which paralyse the victim, and body poisons that attack the body tissue, destroy cells and interfere with the clotting of the blood. Some venoms combine both effects.

The snake with the most poisonous venom is the southern Australian tiger snake — a mere 0.6 milligrams (three-fifths of a thousandth of a gram) of its venom will kill a 70 kg man.

## Most dangerous

Of course this doesn't make the tiger snake the most dangerous snake in the world. This dubious honour is most often awarded to the king cobra, because of its size — it can grow to 4.5 m, making it the world's longest venomous snake — its cunning, and its aggressiveness.

Most venoms (cobra venom is an exception) can be swallowed without ill-effect. They are only poisonous if injected beneath the skin. To get their venom beneath the skin, snakes have evolved highly efficient fangs.

Most commonly, the fangs are fixed at the front of the snake's mouth. There are grooves along the front edge of the fangs that conduct the venom into the puncture made by the fangs. The poison is held in glands placed behind the eyes; as soon as the victim's skin is holed, muscles squeeze the gland and force the venom down the grooves into the wound.

Other species of snake have fangs at the back of the mouth rather than at the front. These snakes cannot puncture the skin and inject poison into the body in the same operation; they must chew the venom into the wound. Accordingly, most snakes of this type are harmless to Man, although the African boomslang is an exception.

The most sophisticated fangs of all are found in vipers, including rattlesnakes, bushmasters, pit vipers and others. These fangs are 'swivelled' — they fold back into the roof of the mouth when not in use, but when the animal opens its mouth to strike they spring forward. This allows the snake to have unusually long fangs that can sink deep into the victim.

Viper's fangs also have an ingenious injection system — just like the hypodermic needle familiar to anyone who has been inoculated — through which the venom is introduced. The fangs are hollow and form a tube down which the poison passes and is forced into the wound.

Such features make venomous snakes very efficient killers. But it should be remembered that fangs and poison are primarily for disabling and/or killing small, fast-moving mammals, birds and amphibians so they can be eaten. Their use as a defence is secondary. Snakes do not seek out humans to attack them. That would be pointless. No venomous snake is large enough to eat even the smallest child, and generally, snakes strike at humans (or at any larger animals like horses or cattle) only if they have been disturbed and cannot escape.

## Undeserved reputation

Most human deaths occur because someone has trodden on a snake (and most people who do this are usually barefoot and far from medical help), attempted to handle it, or inadvertently cornered it. Venomous snakes *are* dangerous, some are deadly if the victim is not quickly given *antivenin* (the serum that neutralises snake venom), but despite this, the fear they cause (and which leads to the slaughter of any snake, venomous or not) is undeserved.

# How is the Black Bear different from the Grizzly?

When American bears are mentioned, one thinks at once of the mighty Grizzly Bear. But another type of bear lives in America and this is the Black Bear which is not as big as the Grizzly. The Grizzly Bear does not climb trees but the Black Bear is often to be seen resting on a high bough. The Grizzly eats the flesh of animals it kills. The Black Bear is a vegetable-eater and likes roots, herbs, the leaves and twigs of certain trees, mushrooms and all sorts of berries. Best of all, it likes honey and is also extremely fond of ants. ("Ugh!" say you).

Like other bears, the Black Bear goes to sleep during winter-time. Having fed itself fat in autumn, it chooses a snug den under a rock or in a hollow tree and sleeps the winter through. It is during this period that Mother Bear has her cubs.

# Which is the most important group of Plants?

**PLANTS are the source of all life. They are the only things capable of catching the energy of the sun and turning it into living tissue. Without plants there would be no animals and no people.**

There are millions of species of plants — from the giant oaks and redwoods, through beautiful orchids to humble grasses. But globally one group of plants is far more important than all the other types put together. These are the *algae* — singular alga — simple plants which usually live in water. Seventy per cent of the world's surface is sea, and nearly all sea plants are algae.

Most people think of seaweeds when they think of algae, but the majority of algae are tiny single-celled plants which float in water. Chlamydomonas which grows in fresh water is a good example of this sort of alga. It is only one fiftieth of a millimetre long, but it is able to perform all the functions necessary to a living plant inside its one small cell.

Much of Chlamydomonas is made up of a structure called a *chloroplast*. This is green because it contains the pigment chlorophyll, which is able to absorb the energy of sunlight so that the plant can turn it into starch, which the plant then lives on. (This process is called *photosynthesis*.) It is chlorophyll which makes the leaves of all plants green.

As well as the chloroplast, Chlamydomonas contains a starch store, a *nucleus* containing genetic information, a

*Continued on page 132*

Below: This simple plant is the fresh water alga Chlamydomonas. Our artist has added colours to show the plant's structure clearly, but in fact it is colourless except for the green chloroplast that traps sunlight and turns it into living tissue.

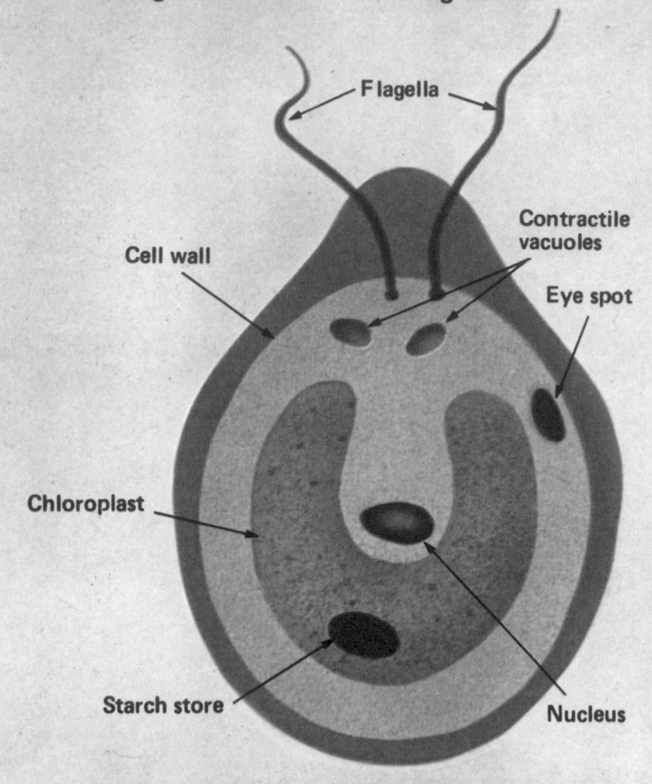

Right and below: A long 'necklace' of green cells make up Spirogyra —an alga often found in ponds. The chloroplast spirals round the edge of each cell, and the cytoplasm stretches in thin strands from the cell edge to the central nucleus, but most of the plant is water.

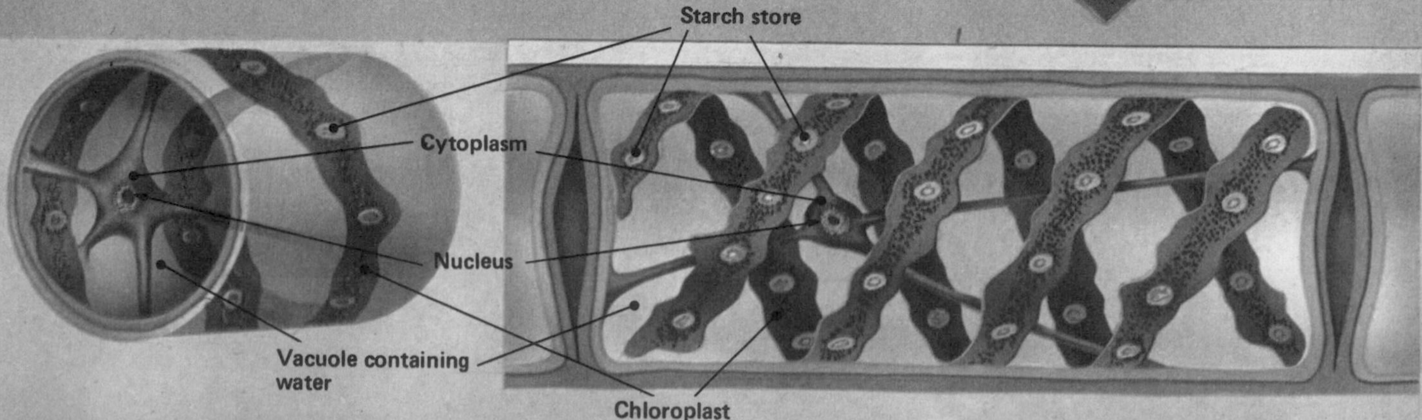

**Below: Bladder wrack, a brown seashore seaweed. The bladders full of air keep the plant floating in the water.**

**Above: Seaweeds have no roots. But they do have 'holdfasts' like these which anchor them to rocks.**

**Below: If you hold up a glass of water, you have no difficulty in looking straight through it. Nevertheless, water does absorb light, although it does not do so at the same rate for all the different colours that make up white light. It absorbs red light first, blue last. This means that different types of algae live at different depths. Green algae can only live on red light, so they are only found in shallow water. Red algae can live on blue light and are therefore able to grow at greater depth. Brown algae can use greenish light and can live in water of medium depth.**

red *eye spot* which is sensitive to light, and two whip-like flagella to move the plant about. (Many — although not all — simple algae have the ability to move about.)

The rest of the plant is made up of the *cytoplasm*, in which the plant's body functions are carried out, and *contractile vacuoles* which store and excrete water which enters from outside. Around the plant, holding it together, is the cell wall.

Although all algae contain chlorophyll, not all are green. This is because they contain other pigments that mask the green colour. In particular, there are brown algae, containing the pigment fucoxanthin, and red algae, containing phycobilins.

There is a special reason why algae contain these other pigments while land plants do not. Water absorbs sunlight; so that even in clear tropical seas it is pitch black at depths greater than about 100 metres.

However, the different colours of light which make up sunlight are not all absorbed at the same rate. Red light is absorbed most, green and blue least. So at depth there is more green and blue light than there is red.

Chlorophyll absorbs red light — which is why it *looks* green, because the green light is reflected — phycobilins absorb green and blue light, which is why they *look* red. So red algae, containing phycobilins, can live at greater depths where there is only green and blue light. Green algae must live in shallow water where there is red light.

Brown algae usually live at medium depths between the green and red algae. Many, however, are seaweeds that live on the seashore.

Seaweeds are algae which have developed into a many-celled form. Some grow as large as the biggest land plants — up to 60 metres long — but most are about one metre. The major differences between them and land plants is that they have no real roots, stems or leaves.

Seaweeds have got to be tough to survive on the seashore. Clinging to the rocks, they are constantly bombarded by the waves and dried and rewetted as the tides rise and fall. To survive these conditions, they have developed thick rubbery 'skins'

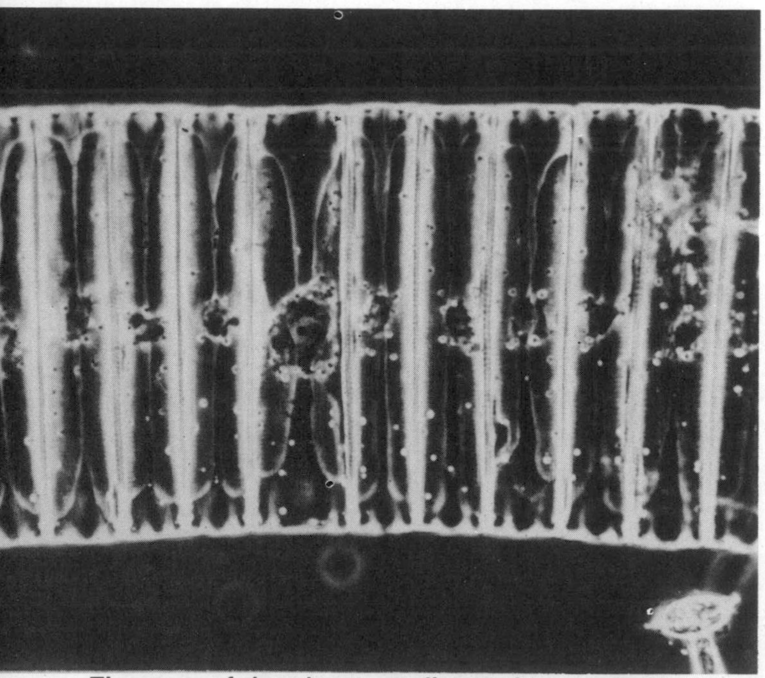

**Above: Feather of the sea. Many red algae — like this one — have beautiful, finely divided bodies.**

Algae are not only the food source for all the fish in the oceans, brown seaweeds are also collected throughout the world to make alginates — chemicals used to make cosmetics, polishes, paints, car tyres and even ice cream!

But, perhaps most importantly, algae are responsible for producing the very air we breathe. Oxygen is given off as a by-product during photosynthesis, and by far the largest source of oxygen in the world is the billions of minute algae in the sea.

**The group of algae known as diatoms have a 'shell' made up of silica (the chief component of sand). Because of this they are often preserved as fossils. This one (right — magnified about 2,000 times) is many millions of years old. Above is a living colonial (made up of many individual plants joined together) diatom about 700 times life size.**

# Are we related to the Ape?

**1.** (Above) Although Charles Darwin was an unpromising schoolboy and student, his family decided he should be a doctor. But he was far too squeamish for the blood and horrors of 19th century medicine, and so after a miserable time studying medicine at Edinburgh, his father sent him to Cambridge to study theology (religion). This didn't interest him much either, but while there he attended the lectures in botany given by the botany professor, J. S. Henslowe.

In 1831, his big chance came. The little HMS *Beagle* was going on a five-year cruise to chart the coast and islands of South America, the Pacific, New Zealand and Australia. It was decided that it would be useful to take along a naturalist to study any interesting plants and animals that were found. Henslowe put forward Darwin's name, and the 22-year-old landlubber found himself aboard the tiny 24-tonne ship.

The voyage was to be a turning point in Darwin's life. The observations made on the trip were to help formulate a theory that would anger the world.

**2.** (Above) The young naturalist enjoyed 'geologizing', as he called it, and would leap ashore at every opportunity and scramble among the thickets and over boulders to collect samples. His careful study of rocks convinced him of the truth of the assertion made by the geologist Charles Lyell in his book *Principles of Geology* that the Earth was far older than 4004 B.C. — the age of creation as calculated from a factual reading of the Bible. Darwin also discovered the fossilised remains of some prehistoric creatures in a cave in Patagonia, South America. Why had the Creator made such wonderful creatures if only to let them die out in a great catastrophe like the Great Flood in the Bible?

**3.** (Left) Many months were spent along the bleak, cheerless coast of Tierra del Fuego, the large island off the southernmost tip of South America. But even here Darwin made good use of his time, collecting specimens of plants and pressing them as shown by Professor Henslowe.

**4.** (Right) As the *Beagle* travelled round South America and on into the Pacific, Darwin collected rocks and shells, bones and fossils, as well as plants. He began to notice how the same kind of creature, a chaffinch for example, would vary slightly from region to region. He noticed this especially on the Galapagos Islands in mid-Pacific, and made a close study of the giant tortoises there. Why was each type of tortoise a little bit different on each island?

**5.** (Below) The naturalist of the *Beagle* was beginning to formulate a theory about these different variations or *species*, although he had little time to work out his ideas. The expedition was busy — and dangerous too at times. Once Darwin witnessed the effects of an earthquake that wrecked the city of Concepcion.

**6.** (Below, left) In all, the voyage lasted for five years, ending in 1836. But 23 years passed before Darwin published his famous book *The Origin of Species*, based largely on his observations during his world cruise. In *The Origin* he explained his belief that all the living things in the world today have developed gradually through millions of years from strange and extinct ancestors. Even man, somewhere in the mists of time, shares a common ancestor with the modern ape.

**7.** (Below) Darwin's book made many people angry because they thought his ideas were against the teaching of the Bible. There were many furious arguments between learned men who supported Darwin and those who did not. Darwin suffered ill-health (probably a disease he contracted while in South America) for most of his life and he did not join in the disputes. He lived quietly in the country at Downe, in Kent with his wife and children. When the arguments died down, few people still doubted that life in all its forms had evolved slowly as Darwin had stated. The study of biology — and of Man as one of the animals — was revolutionised.

# Which Creatures are active at Night?

WHILE you sleep, part of the animal kingdom is very busy. Most animals feel much safer during the hours of darkness — and Nature has ensured that they will be.

Why should so many animals be active at night? The answer lies in the story of their development from the earliest and most primitive stages.

Members of the lemur family, BUSH BABIES live in trees and sleep by day, usually in a hollow tree or in the middle of thick foliage. They vary in size, but the largest is not much bigger than a domestic cat. Bush babies have an unusual cry which has earned them their name of 'babies'.

BATS belong to an enormous and varied family and are found in all parts of the world except polar regions. Although they are generally disliked by people, there seems to be no good reason, for they are not fierce. The only mammals with real wings, they also have a natural 'radar' system which aids them with direction finding in their nocturnal life.

Those early animals felt much safer if they kept hidden while the light was bright enough for them to be seen by their hunters.

Gradually, those creatures which spent more and more time in the dimmer light, developed very sensitive eyes which enabled them to find their food without having to venture out in the daylight.

In turn, the hunters too, developed the kind of senses that would allow them to stalk and catch their prey at night.

Creatures who had less reason to fear being attacked, such as birds, continued to be active during daylight.

Almost all birds feed and fly by day because they have always been able to protect themselves by sheltering in trees and other safe places.

The owl is one of the few nocturnal birds and the reason is that mice and small rodents — its food — are also nocturnal creatures.

In order to hunt and survive in the darkness, animals have developed many marvellous ways of seeing and sensing their environment.

Small and lithe, GENETS are found in parts of Europe, Africa and Asia. They are solitary creatures and come out to hunt at night. Although they do not live in trees, they are all very good climbers and kill their prey (birds, insects and rodents) by pouncing on them and biting them in the neck.

If Lewis Carroll had not made the DORMOUSE popular in "Alice in Wonderland", it is doubtful if many people would know about it. It hibernates during the winter for up to six months and, even during the waking season, ventures out only at night. Probably, the 'dor' in its name comes from the French verb, *dormir* — to sleep.

Spaniards gave this unusual-looking creature its name when they first found it in the New World. They called it the ARMADILLO — 'the little armoured thing'. Its armour would seem to fit it for fighting. But it rarely does so. Timid and only too happy to spend most of its active life under cover of darkness, it feeds on roots, worms, insects and the like.

In our own eyes, the retina absorbs only a fraction of the light reaching it through the pupil. Many nocturnal animals have a membrane behind their retina which reflects light back into it, just like a mirror. It enables these animals to see in light that would be much too dim to allow the human eye to function effectively.

This reflecting quality in the eyes of animals is demonstrated when one of them is caught in the glare of a car headlight. Their eyes shine, because the light is too strong for the membrane to process, and the light not being absorbed is being reflected out again.

Another characteristic of night-time eyes is that the pupils react much more quickly to changes in the intensity of light. For instance, an owl's pupils dilate twice as quickly as our own.

This protects the eye from long-term damage and prevents temporary dazzlement which could prove fatal, especially for the hunted.

Acute hearing also enables animals to maintain activity in darkness.

The bat-eared fox and the aardwolf eat termites which they catch by *listening* for their movements in their burrows.

Most animals can pick up a sound at a much higher pitch than is audible to man, but it is important not only to hear, but to know exactly where the sound is coming from.

To pin-point the position of a sound, animals have a well-developed ability to analyse and compare the different volume of sound reaching each of their separate ears. The difference in sound level picked up by one ear compared to the other assists the animal in establishing the direction of the sound.

# The wide-eyed hunter

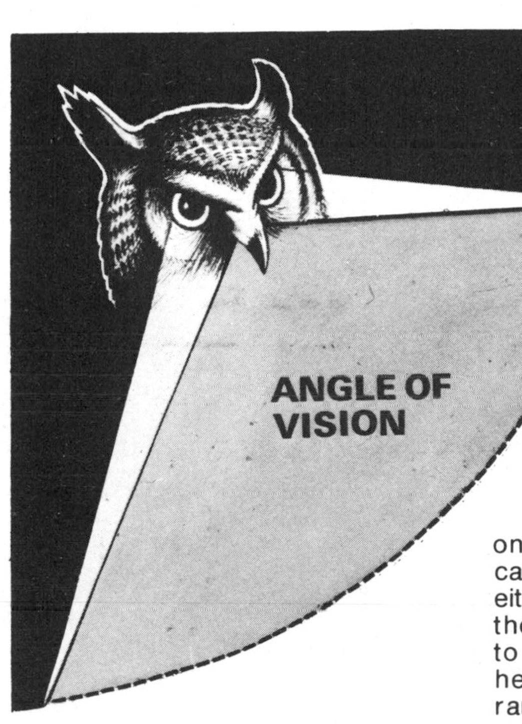


**On the left is an owl's angle of vision when its head is pointing straight ahead. Its judgement of distance is most accurate over the dark grey portion of the area. Very few birds have eyes that focus together in this way. Most see in different directions at the same time. Human eyes focus together but their clarity of vision is not so great as owls, because human eyes have much less sensitivity.**

THE bird most usually thought of as 'of the night' is the owl. It has features common to other creatures of darkness and some peculiarly its own.

Found in most areas of the world, there are over 130 species, varying considerably in size. For example, the Little Elf Owl is no more than 14cm. (5½ins.) long and the Snowy Owl is over 60cm. (2ft.) long.

All owls, however, are birds of prey. That is, they are meat eaters, feeding on mice, rats, shrews, worms and the like, which they hunt and kill usually at night. Some, though, venture out quite happily during the day. The Snowy Owl, in fact, **has** to do so, as it lives within the Arctic Circle where, for part of the year, the Sun never sets.

An owl's eyes are enormous in relation to its size. The eyeball of the large Snowy Owl is not much smaller than that of an adult man. The retina (sensitive sight membrane) of an owl is particularly receptive to light, thus enabling the bird to see in semi-darkness. Its eyes focus together, giving it three-dimensional vision, unlike most other birds, whose eyes are situated on either side of their heads. An owl can turn its head in a half circle in either direction, so that in spite of the eyeballs themselves being able to turn only a little way within its head, it has a completely spherical range of vision.

It is wrong, though, to think that an owl can see in complete darkness. No creature can do that. Nor is it blind in sunlight. Its eyes have what amount to extra eyelids which shield them from bright light.

An owl's hearing, too, is very acute. Some locate their prey more by sound than by sight. Their ears are large and the openings differ in size from each other, so helping in judging the position of the prey.

The plumage of an owl is particularly soft, making its flight noiseless. Again, this aids its hearing, at the same time increasing the element of surprise in its hunting.

The distinctive flat face of an owl, too, is thought to pick up sound waves, acting as a sort of 'noise reflector'.

We tend to think of the owl as a 'wise old bird', but the description is really a myth, based solely on the fact that the bird was held sacred by Athena, the Greek goddess of wisdom. Owls deserve more praise for their hunting skills than their wisdom.

**The eyes of the owl are among the most effective light-gatherers in all Nature, providing them with great clarity of vision. Above are two drawings of a rat, the one on the left as an owl might see it from the top of a tree, and the one on the right as a man might see it from the same height.**

# Which Animals live on the Tundra?

**EXPLORERS and fur trappers have described it as the last great wilderness on Earth. It stretches for 13 million flat, featureless square kilometres from the snow and ice of the North Pole to the great northern forests. It is a cold, hard place in which to eke out a living, but large numbers of animals and plants do just that in this frozen desolation that is called the *tundra*.**

Our picture shows the vast marshy plain of the North American tundra just before the big winter freeze. For nine long, empty, chilling months temperatures can drop below −60°C, and remorseless icy winds, carrying ice needles and snow blizzards, scour the frozen wastes, blanketing the vegetation with snow.

## Brief summer

Summer, however, is brief and busy. During its three short months, the tundra becomes a dense green carpet of summertime grasses and small flowering plants, packed together with spongy lichens and mosses, and dotted with isolated strands of willow and dwarf birch among countless small lakes and rivers. Every grey slab of rock, pushed up out of the ground, split and shattered by constant freezing and thawing, is brightened by patches of orange, red and yellow lichen. The dr er land is covered by the greyish-green and bushy reindeer moss, which is not a moss at all, but also a lichen.

During the Arctic's brief summer it is almost always daytime. For the tundra in summer is the land of the midnight sun.

Among the lichens there is an explosion of colour as soon as spring arrives. Flax, white saxifrage, Arctic roses, dwarf dandelions, white stars of stitchwort, yellow patches of cinquefoil, red and golden poppies, purple saxifrage and bluebells all burst into flower. And among the flowers, there are thickets of crowberry and blueberry.

All the plants are dwarfed, lying close to the ground to avoid the ravages of the fierce Arctic winds and the abrasive action of ice and snow.

The greater part of a tundra plant is below the surface, but the root is long and shallow, prevented from pushing downwards by the frozen soil. Thirty centimetres or so below the surface of the soil is permanently frozen throughout the year. After the annual summer thaw, this subterranean ice-block prevents the surface water from draining away and the tundra becomes a trackless marsh covered by acre upon acre of bog moss.

Insects are the most abundant tundra animals. Mosquitoes and blackflies, having overwintered as eggs and rapidly changed from larvae to pupae, emerge in unimaginable numbers from the tundra swamps.

But Man is not the mosquitoes' main victim. Great herds of caribou or reindeer (1) trek ceaselessly from pasture to spongy pasture, feeding particularly on reindeer moss. If they stopped in one place, they would quickly overgraze the moss which grows at the extraordinarily slow rate of 1.6 mm a year. So to survive they must keep moving.

Ptarmigan (2) often follow the shifting herds. During the winter the caribou paw the ground to expose the lichens and the ptarmigan take advantage of any food unearthed by the scraping hooves.

Ptarmigan and caribou are favourite prey for the legendary predator of the North — the wolf (3). A wolf can sprint at 40 km/h and trot for hours on end at 8 km/h. Built for endurance, wolves usually hunt in packs with a highly developed

social system. After a chase, they will raise their muzzles into the air and howl, the sound bringing together a widely separated pack. As each wolf returns, it wags its tail and whimpers, showing that it is friendly.

In deepest winter, when caribou are scarce, having moved further south, a wolf pack may chance an attack against a herd of animals that might have walked straight out of the Ice Age.

Bull-like with long shaggy coats, they are musk-oxen (4). They are not true oxen at all, being more related to the chamois goat of Central Europe. When attacked by wolves, the adult bulls form a defensive square with calves and females on the inside. They lower their heads and rub their forelegs, producing a powerful odour which can be detected several hundred metres away. This seems to snap the herd out of its normal quiet state, ready to face the enemy with lowered heads and vicious horns.

Another animal that stays in the Arctic all winter long is the Arctic hare (5). In the worst winter weather, it crouches in rocky crevices, venturing out only to nibble at some frozen plant leaves. As the autumn frosts strike so quickly, the fully ripe plants are quick-frozen, remaining green all year round. The Arctic hare has long pincer-like incisors for tweezering out these green stems and nipping off buds deep in the snow.

But the hare can never rest safely. Its two main enemies — the snowy owl (6) and the Arctic fox (7) — prowl for prey throughout the day and night.

Nevertheless the hare is probably not the most hunted creature. This unfortunate title probably goes to the vole-like lemming (8). These little mammals live in a labyrinth of shallow tunnels. In winter, foxes can often be seen digging in the snow with their noses to find them.

Lemmings are remarkable in the way their numbers rise and fall dramatically.

*Continued on next page*

They breed twice a year, and rapidly build up their numbers until the tunnels become overcrowded and they just cannot find enough lichens, fungi, moss and carrion on which they feed.

When this happens, suddenly, at some invisible sign, they come out of their burrows in their thousands, and great armies of them march off across the tundra in search of new pastures. The predators have a gluttonous field-day. But the feast is short-lived. As the numbers of lemmings drops so does the number of predators.

### Summer visitors

Throughout the long Arctic winter these few animal species scratch a living as best they can. Then, one long empty night, the silence is shattered by the yodelling whistle of the long-tailed duck or 'old squaw' (9). Through the early spring, it migrates north by night in loose flocks and descends on the tundra lakes to breed. Its arrival marks the start of spring, when the summer visitors come. They come in their millions.

The red-breasted merganser (10) announces its arrival with a series of low short quacks. It is joined by the magnificent black-throated diver or Arctic loon (11), with its loud, barking call.

The loon quickly seeks out the best nest sites close to the water's edge, for its legs are far back along its body, ideal for swimming but not for walking. So the bird inelegantly drags from nest to water and back with its belly scraping along the ground.

The unobtrusive little black-and-white snow bunting (12) betrays its presence with a piping 'tihee', as it flits from rock to rock, pausing for long periods and gripping the surface with tiny claws, braced against the buffeting of the wind.

### Skua

In winter the long-tailed skua lives out at sea, but in the summer it flies north to nest. It is particularly dependent on the lemming. Somehow it seems to be able to sense how many lemmings there are going to be and lays its eggs accordingly. In a bad lemming year it may not nest at all; in a good year it lays more eggs, *before* the lemming swarms have actually emerged.

Canada geese (14) always return to the area where they first hatched from the egg year after year. Their honkings and cacklings fill the air. They mate for life, and each pair seeks out flat meadow-like land, nesting as far from the next pair as possible. But even so, there may be as many as 40 nests per square kilometre.

Nowadays one animal that used to be rare in the tundra can be seen in increasing numbers. This is Man. Recent discoveries of oil and other minerals have meant more people, bringing with them their paraphernalia of civilisation. If we are not careful the last great wilderness on Earth may be permanently scarred by misuse.

# Who are Nature's Healers?

**IT is generally believed that Nature is ruthless. If any wild creature is sick or injured it is always left to die or is actually killed by its companions rather than become a liability to**

**them. This is not strictly true. Many creatures act as their own doctors in an attempt to cure themselves.**

It is known that a cat or dog will eat grass if its stomach is upset, but other animals also eat various leaves and grasses for their medicinal value. They always pick special plants and avoid all others. This seems to suggest that the animals have acquired a knowledge of the value of herbal treatment.

Some years ago a man who caught a gibbon noticed it had a curious swelling on its side over which ran a long scar. Curious to see what was wrong the man had the animal operated upon. The swelling proved to be a large ball of masticated leaves from a plant known for its medicinal value. The ape had obviously been wounded and had gathered the leaves, chewed them into a ball and stuffed them into its open wound. This appeared to have done the trick and helped heal the injury.

### Splint

A moorhen was once found with its leg bound with a kind of plaster cast at the knee joint. The bone had been broken but had grown together again and was fully healed, but the cast of dried clay must have been put there by the bird itself. Woodcock birds are alleged to have been seen doing the same thing, applying a splint of stiff grasses and clay to an injured limb. First-aid of another kind is seen in the ant world, where a worker with a broken leg will have it amputated by its fellows. Ants also isolate and tend sick members of their communities in

special chambers in the nest.

Black bears and other creatures coming out of hibernation in the spring are known to search for and eat certain berries and fruits which have a laxative effect. This is presumably to tone up their body systems after their long sleep.

Deer prefer lime-filled water when growing new antlers so that these will grow quickly, while pregnant mule deer will eat only certain kinds of food until their young are born. Many other creatures will search for certain leaves and roots when they are ailing.

Animals with bleeding wounds have been known to place spiders' webs on them. These have *styptic* properties which constrict the blood vessels and reduce bleeding. And the tiny, and to us 'unpleasant', maggots which crawl in their hundreds inside the naked wound of some animals are never disturbed by the creature itself. Laid by mayflies, these maggots actually destroy dangerous bacteria in the wound and assist natural healing. Perhaps a case of animals knowing better than Man, for we would be unlikely to let maggots get near any of our wounds!

But not only are there animals who act as their own doctors on occasion; some also perform as dentists. Apes sometimes act as skilled dentists on their own and each other's teeth.

An orang-utang performed such a feat of self-treatment. Kept in semi-captivity it was noticed one day dejectedly holding its cheek. In fact, it had actually applied a lump of damp clay as a cold poultice to its face to soothe a gumboil in its mouth. A few days later it pulled out a rotten tooth which it showed to its master with obvious pleasure.

Chimpanzees in particular practise more skilled dentistry — inspecting, cleaning and even extracting teeth. American scientists have observed many bouts of dental grooming among a group of older chimps kept in a large outdoor enclosure, four of them using what can only be described as primitive dental implements.

## Clean

In one instance, an eight-year-old female opened the mouth of a younger male, who co-operated fully by gaping his jaws. She removed food particles using her two forefingers like forceps. Then she picked up a short twig with which to clean the 'patient's' teeth further. Usually the patient's head was steadied with one hand and dental work performed with the other. Often the sticks were peeled of leaves, trimmed or had their ends chewed off before use.

On another occasion, a chimpanzee carefully extracted a fellow ape's loose tooth using a pine twig. The patient lay flat on the ground and the ape 'dentist' sat close alongside his head, carefully performing the extraction in about 90 seconds. The only difference from a human dentist was that the considerate chimps did regularly hold the twig implements in the mouth like a cigarette, using them and their bare fingers alternately!

Only by such scientific research, involving groups of animals in a reasonably wild state, will we gain a further insight into this fascinating and valuable aspect of animal behaviour. Perhaps then we will fully understand that in Nature it is not always a case of 'survival of the fittest'. For it seems that — within certain groups of animals at least — there is still a chance for the lame and infirm.

# What is Soil?

Nowadays Man has a greater ability to modify the soil than ever before. Tractors, for instance, are more powerful than even the biggest horses.

**THERE is a thin fragile layer lying on a small part of the surface of the Earth. Few people think much of it or understand it. Yet this layer — *the soil* — is perhaps the greatest gift of Nature to Man. It is a complex living thing without which there is nothing but desert.**

The soil beneath your feet keeps you and supports you. It is soil that enables plants to grow; and it is plants that ultimately feed you.

But why is soil essential to plants? What is it about the dust upon the ground that makes crops flourish — or die?

The short answer is that soil is *not* essential to plants. They can grow quite happily without it. In fact, in one form of horticulture — *hydroponics* — soil is not used at all. Instead of growing plants in soil, the horticulturalist himself supplies a careful balance of water, air and nutrients to the plants' roots.

But hydroponics is an exceptional way of growing crops. To achieve the right balance of air, nutrients and water requires a great deal of care — and expense — from the horticulturalist.

A good soil will naturally provide this balance.

Moreover, soil gives plants something in which they can anchor themselves. Without this anchorage, all but the smallest plants would simply blow away in the wind.

Soil provides a balanced medium in which living plants can grow because it is itself a balanced living thing. It is made from the complex interaction of rock, water, air, plants, animals, fungi and bacteria. The soil is usually only about 25 centimetres thick, but it is a complete living world.

The beginning of any soil is rock. The action of water and air breaks the rock down into fine particles. These fine particles are the basis of the soil.

Coarse particles — between 0.5 and 2 mm in diameter — are called *sand*. Fine particles — less than 0.002 mm in diameter — are called *clay*. In-between-sized particles are called *silt*. It is the different amounts of sand, clay and silt that largely determine the characteristics of a soil.

Soils with a lot of clay tend to become easily waterlogged and difficult and 'heavy' to work. Plant roots need air

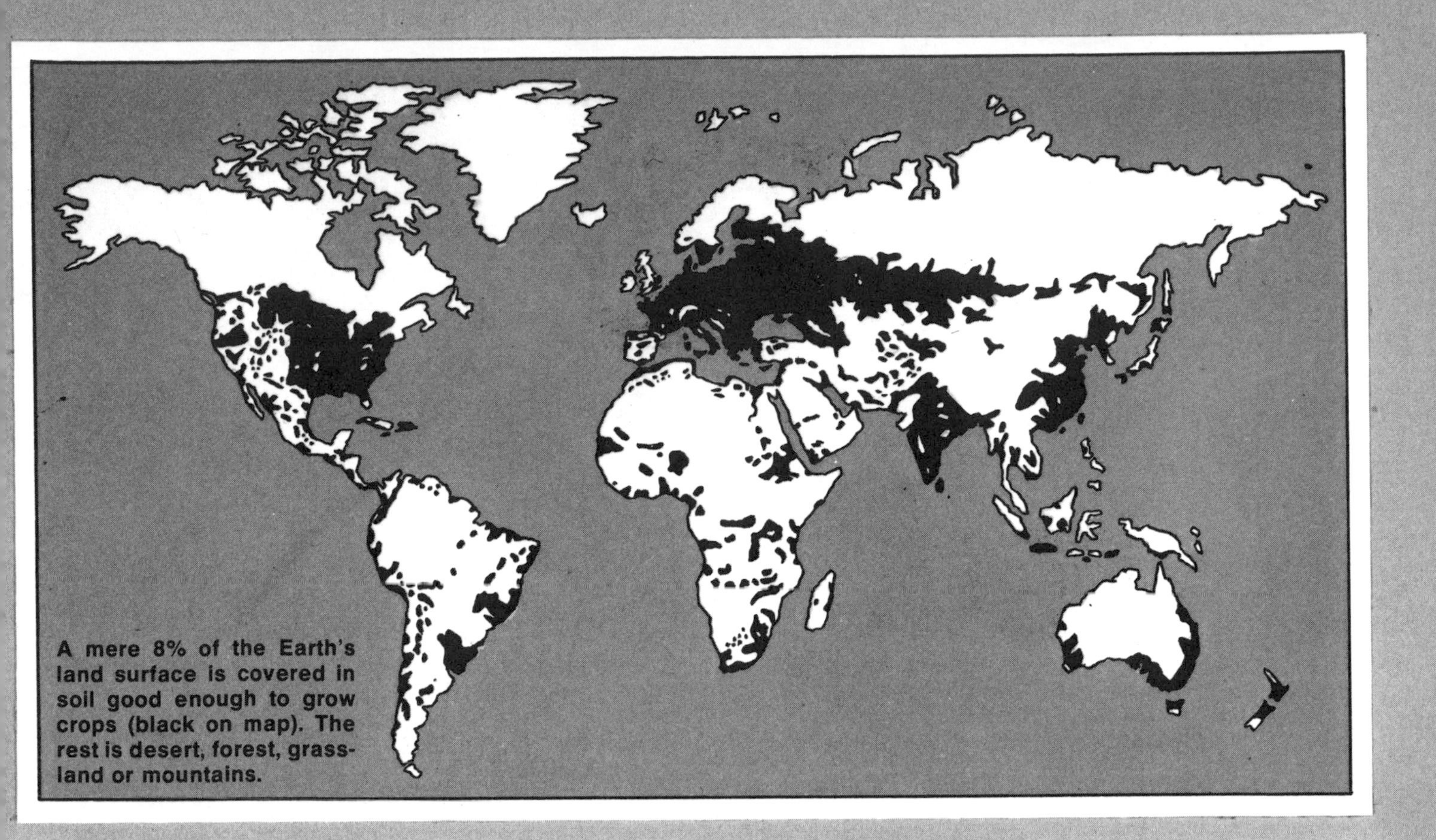
A mere 8% of the Earth's land surface is covered in soil good enough to grow crops (black on map). The rest is desert, forest, grassland or mountains.

to grow just like people do, and can drown in a soil if there is no air in it. In addition, clay particles often stick together into big lumps or 'clods' into which neither air nor plant roots can penetrate.

Soils with a lot of sand tend to be well-drained and easy to work. The relatively big spaces between the sand particles mean that there is a lot of air in the soil and it is difficult to waterlog it — although there may be too little water in a dry summer. But sand is infertile, because it is made up almost entirely of the inert material *silica* — the main constituent of rock. Silica does not contain the mineral nutrients plants need. Clay, however, does contain other minerals as well as silica and so clay soils are usually more fertile than sandy soils.

A first-class soil contains between 10 and 20 per cent clay and is called a *loam*. It is well-drained, easy to work, and fertile.

But there is more to soil than rock particles. There is also a *biological* part. This is the part made up of living — or once-living — things: plants, animals, fungi and bacteria.

The once-living part is called *humus*. If some soil is mixed with water and shaken in a flask, and then allowed to settle again, the coarse sand settles first, then the silt, and finally the clay. Left floating on the water surface is a black, sticky substance. This is humus. It is composed of the dead remains of plants and animals.

Whether a soil is poor because it is too clayey, or too sandy, whether it lacks important plant nutrients, or is too well-drained or poorly drained, humus makes it better.

The sticky black substance attaches itself to the surface of the soil particles. It sticks together clay particles which are too small to make good soil, thereby making bigger particles. It attracts water and chemical nutrients making too-dry sandy soils moist, thus preventing nutrients being washed away by rain. It also slowly and continually breaks down itself, partly chemically and partly by the action of fungi and bacteria, releasing nutrients into the soil.

So one of the best ways of improving a soil — and so growing more crops — is to add humus. But you can't buy humus in the shops. Humus is part of the soil and the only way you can obtain it is from soil. It's not very often a farmer sells his soil!

However, you can increase the amount of humus by adding *manure* or *garden compost*. Both of these are basically rotted plant and animal remains. If they are added to the soil, fungi and bacteria turn them into humus.

There are other ways of improving the soil, too. One of the most important is *ploughing*. This is particularly important on clay soils. What the farmer does is dig large chunks of soil up from under the surface and leave them lying on the top. During the winter, the frost and rain break these lumps up into smaller pieces more suitable for plant growth.

A farmer can also add lime if a soil is too acid to grow healthy plants — as it often is on sandy soils. And, of course, he can add chemical fertilizers to increase a soil's fertility — although, unlike adding manure, this does not improve the soil's physical structure.

It is important that a farmer does look after his soil by doing some or all of these things. Every time a crop is harvested, the nutrients that make up that crop are removed from the soil for good. (On uncropped land, such as the Amazon jungle, plants die and rot where they stand, and so their nutrients are returned to the soil). If a soil is to keep producing crops, thereby continuing to support Man, nutrients must be given back to replace those that are harvested.

If they are not, the fertility of the soil is slowly, and inevitably reduced. In the end, fertile soil can become barren dust.

Just eight per cent of the Earth's surface is capable of growing crops. This eight per cent is the main support of the 4,470 million people on the Earth — which means there is about one fifth of a hectare each. Spread thinly over this fifth of a hectare is some 700 tonnes of soil. That 700 tonnes isn't just dirt. It is each person's life-support layer.

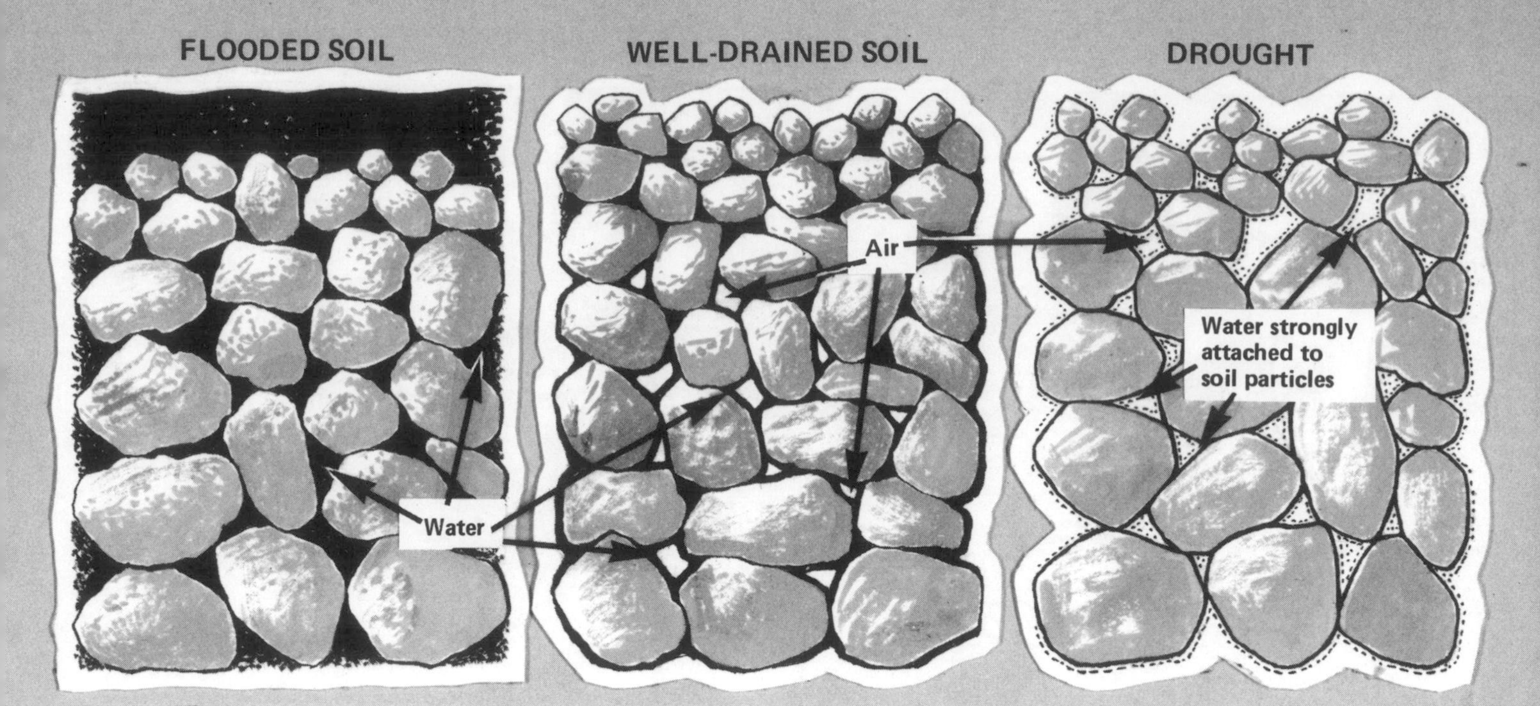


**Above:** Plants only flourish in soil containing both air and water trapped in the spaces between soil particles. In flooded soil, all the spaces are full of water, and without air, the roots 'drown'. In a drought, there is still some water in the soil, but it is so strongly attached to the soil particles that roots are unable to absorb it. Plants die of lack of water.

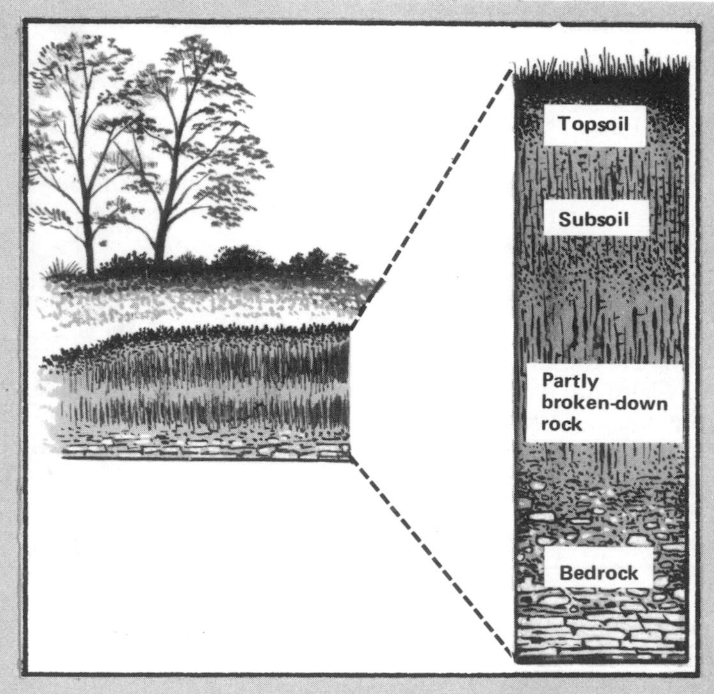

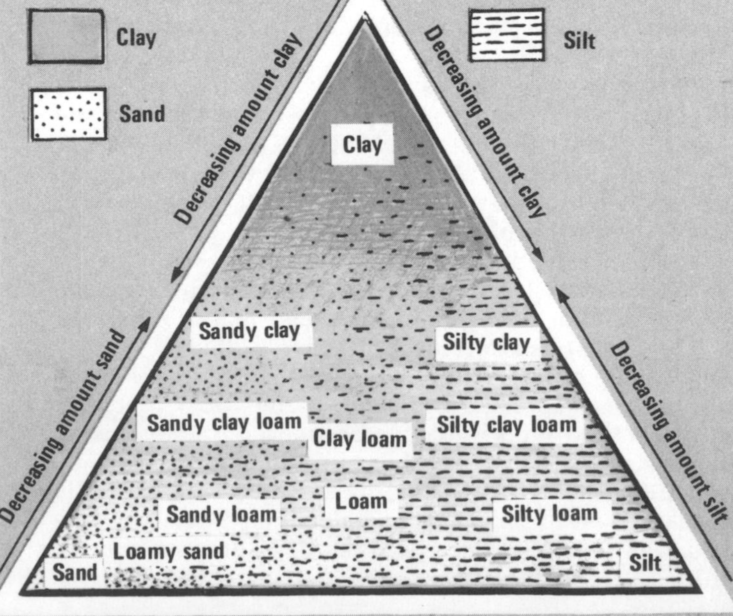


**Above:** If you could cut into the soil like a cake, you would see several different layers. The top layer is the fertile *topsoil.* Beneath this is the *subsoil,* which contains less plant and animal material; and beneath that is partly broken-down rock and then bedrock. **Above, right:** Compared with the size of soil particles, roots are huge. But to be effective at obtaining water and nutrients, they must grow into the spaces between the particles. Accordingly, they are covered in tiny 'hairs' which mingle among the grains of soil. **Right:** Soil is made up of three types of particle — sand, silt and clay. Different names are given to soils depending on how much of each type they contain. The best soils contain little clay and are called *loams.* In the triangle, each corner represents 100% of either clay, silt or sand. The amount steadily decreases as you move towards the opposite side.

# Which are Flightless Birds?

Among the 12 to 14 thousand species of birds found all over the world, only a very few are unable to fly. Most flightless birds are fairly large, indeed the biggest of the bird family is the ostrich whose undeveloped wings are useless for lifting its great weight off the ground. A large male ostrich can weigh as much as 300lb, but in spite of its inability to fly it can move over the ground swifter than a galloping horse! At full speed, one stride can carry it 25 feet, and it is said to have a kick more powerful than a mule.

1. Ostriches and zebras are great friends and are often seen together.

2. This odd-looking fellow is a takahe of New Zealand

3. The kiwi is also a native of New Zealand.

4. The cassowaiy lives in Australia and in New Guinea.

5. The emu is found in Australia and Tasmania

# Why do some Animals lay millions of Eggs?

Sturgeon: This fish is found in the Northern Hemisphere and lives in both salt and fresh water. The Atlantic sturgeon is found in the Eastern Atlantic and the Mediterranean and Black Seas. It spawns in rivers but is now very rare because of pollution and overfishing. The larger beluga, which grows to 5m, lives in the Caspian and Black Seas. The sturgeon can lay about 5 *million* eggs, and humans enjoy these as expensive caviar.

Lizards: Most of these orders of reptiles live on insects. Some lay eggs while others have the young hatching inside the parent's body. Lizards can shed their tails in an emergency and many have special characteristics. The chameleon changes colour for camouflage, and the Gila monster has a venomous bite when severely provoked.

Penguins: There are some 15 species of this flightless bird, found only in the cold Antarctic waters. They breed in colonies and each bird usually lays two eggs which are incubated by huddling between the feet and belly. They feed by diving for fish.

**AN egg breaks open to reveal the way to a bright new world. Fluffy, feathery, scaly and horny creatures of all kinds burst into life from eggs in the warm sand, swaying tree tops or even deep in the sea.**

Of these the oldest is the turtle. Its ancestors crawled among the giant animals which roamed the Earth in prehistoric times. Danger lurks from the moment turtles hatch underground in warm countries. As the babies with their soft armour crawl to the sea, hungry birds pounce upon them. Once in the sea, big fish are waiting with eager mouths. Only the luckiest survive.

Speed is the ostrich's answer to danger — not a head buried in the sand. It skims at 60 kilometres per hour over the African sandy grasslands with 5 metre strides. At mating time, the male takes several wives who lay 1.4 kilogram eggs in a sandy cavity. Hatched in six weeks, the chicks soon travel in coveys with the adults.

Snakes: These reptiles do not have legs or ear membranes while their eyes are permanently protected by transparent eyelids. Eggs are laid in warm places in clutches of 20 to 100 or incubated inside the body until ready to hatch.

Ants: With over 6,000 species and over 10 million inhabitants in a single colony, there are far more ants in the world than people. Most colonies have just one fertile female — the queen, and she is really just an egg-laying machine. The eggs are tended by worker ants which are infertile females. They also gather food and protect the nest from attack. Males develop from unfertilised eggs. All they do is fly away from the nest to find a queen with which to mate.

Turtles, Tortoises: The oldest order of living reptiles in the world. As a general rule tortoises are land creatures while turtles are found in marine and fresh water. Turtles lay their eggs well up on the shore and the hatchlings must survive a very hazardous journey to reach the safety of the water. In tropical countries the tortoise lays its eggs in mud to incubate in the Sun. Both groups vary in length from about 10cm to 2m.

Ostrich: The world's biggest living bird although it cannot fly. Nearly 3m tall, weighing 160kg, it is found only in Africa. It lives on dry, open plains and escapes danger by running. Ostriches lay the biggest eggs in the world (about 17cm long) and these are often laid in one nest by several females. The hot sunshine is sufficient to incubate them.

The lizard is swift, too. One desert lizard in North Africa dashes from bush to bush — not only to find food or escape its enemies, but to keep out of the scorching Sun. Unable to sweat to cool its body, it would die in the blazing desert sun in about 10 minutes.

Hog-nosed snakes of eastern North America meet danger with bluff. Pretending to be bold they swell up, strike and hiss. But when attacked, they lie on the ground playing dead. Although these snakes are egg layers, some kinds give birth to live young.

Penguins cannot fly, but they are birds. In the sea, they swim in a kind of underwater flight around the bleak Antarctic coasts. Most of the incubating is done by the male on eggs in a nest of stones.

Ants, on the other hand, can fly — but not for long. Young winged males and females fly from their birth-nests to make a new colony. After the flight the males die. Before laying their eggs in a crevice or under bark, the queens remove their wings.

For records in egg laying it would be hard to beat the Sturgeon, a fish which can produce as many as five million eggs each time. Pickled, these are an expensive delicacy — called caviare. Humans enjoy this, and a small type of sea anemone eats sturgeons' eggs too by burrowing inside the soft shells.

The feature of multiple egg laying has a logical explanation. The number of eggs produced by an animal depends on the risks to which they, and the young that hatch from them, are exposed. So while some animals lay only one egg at a time, those like the turtle and sturgeon lay thousands or even millions to ensure that at least a lucky few will survive the attacks of predators or other dangers.

**Crocodiles: These large aquatic reptiles are the closest living relatives of the dinosaur. Quite sluggish on land they can move at alarming speed in the water. Food is ground up by stones in the stomach which the crocodiles have swallowed. Their small white eggs are laid in warm sand to incubate. As our photo shows, the young are alert from the moment of hatching!**

**Duck-billed platypus: One of the monotremes – primitive mammals that lay eggs – it is found in eastern Australia and Tasmania only, which isolated it from an evolutionary point of view. About 45cm long with a flattened 15cm tail, it searches out food with its bill. Eggs hatch after about 10 days and the young suck milk that oozes from the skin of the mother's belly.**

**Spiny ant-eaters: There are five species. Also monotremes, they live in tropical rain forests in New Guinea, Australia and Tasmania. Two eggs are laid with a rubbery shell. After laying, the mother uses her beak to transfer the eggs to a kangaroo-like pouch on her belly where they will develop. The animal is also known as the echidna.**

# How do Animals survive on the barren peaks of the Rockies?

**Beautiful, majestic, rich with the power from mighty rivers and valuable minerals, the higher reaches of the Rockies offer a refuge to some of the rarest animals of the region.**

**LIKE a giant back bone, the towering range of the Rocky Mountains, stretches for 5,000 kilometres from New Mexico in the south to the Yukon in the north of the American continent.**

As the winter snows settle on its slopes, sometimes for as long as six months, the local residents (who make a small and select club) busy themselves with the task of survival: the small, plump, rabbit-like pika, the hoary marmot, the shy and only rarely glimpsed mountain goat and the grizzly bear, for whom the marmot and pika would make a welcome meal.

Man has, of course, made his inroads into this gigantic chain which is over 500 kilometres wide in Utah, and towers to nearly 6,000 metres on the Canadian-Alaskan border.

The rivers of The Great Divide, which flow down to the Pacific on its western slopes and to the Arctic and Atlantic on the eastern side, have been tapped for hydro-electric power, and the vast coniferous forests have been harvested for their timber. Great tunnels have been driven through the rocks to allow the railroads to unite the continent.

## Young mountains

Geologially speaking, the Rocky Mountains are relatively young; indeed this accounts for their splendour for if they were older they would have been worn down by ages of wind, frost and river action.

They have been formed over the last 120 million years as a result of the buckling of sediments laid down in the sea some 600 million years previously. Massive earth movements have produced a very complicated mountain chain which geologists are still trying to understand. But, for most of us, the jagged peaks, the snow-filled valleys and the relentless march of the glaciers provide satisfaction enough.

The Rockies have a profound effect on the climate of North America and, in turn, on the vegetation and the animals. In the northern United States, for instance, to the western side of the mountains, lie lush rain forests, while to the east are vast, relatively dry prairies.

The mountain areas themselves are quite different again, with a unique complement of plants and animals. To see this best we must climb to some 3,000 metres, beyond the tree line and among the mountain meadows. Here, as one climbs, the trees become progressively stunted and give way to scree slopes and broken rock and eventually to the crags and crevices of the peaks themselves.

The pika, sometimes called the rock rabbit, is often seen scampering among the rocks of the scree slopes, pausing only occasionally to bask in the sun. It is a close relative of the rabbit and hare, although the ears are very short and the tail is almost non-existent. Pikas are very individual creatures. They mark out and defend their own territories and constantly whistle to announce 'this is my patch'.

In Russia the pika is called the 'haystacker', an apt name since this is precisely what it does in late summer. Each animal makes its own stack of grasses which it dries in the sun. Later, it moves the hay into a 'larder' beneath a rock. This store keeps it going throughout the winter when it spends most of its time scurrying along tunnels in the snow, occasionally coming to the surface to sunbathe in the winter sunshine. The fur coat thickens up for winter and it

*Continued on next page*

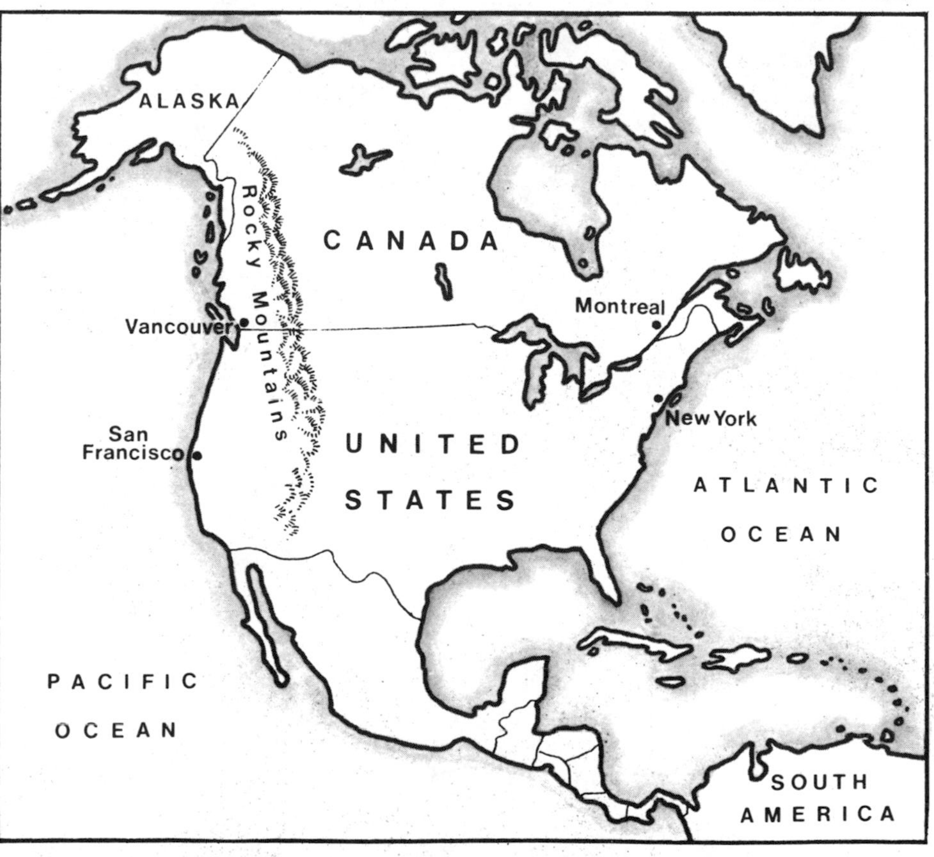

Grizzly bear

even has hair on the soles of its feet. These 'fur boots' help keep the feet warm.

The hoary marmot is quite a different inhabitant of the high mountains. This large rodent, which can weigh 7 kg, prefers succulent plants which are, of course, unavailable in the winter and which cannot be stored like the pika's hay. So the marmot goes into a deep hibernation for up to eight months of the year.

During this time the body temperature drops dramatically to just a few degrees above freezing and the breathing and heartbeat become barely perceptible. Deep within its grass-lined nest beneath the ground the marmot chooses to shun the rigours of winter.

While the pika and the marmot scamper at the base of the scree slopes, the mountain goat looks down from the crags of the dizzy heights above, briefly descending to graze in the meadows. This is a truly remarkable animal but one rarely seen. It moves slowly and deliberately to reach the most inaccessible rock ledges for safety. It generally shuns fights with its enemies, Man and the grizzly bear, but if cornered the stiletto-sharp horns can inflict a fatal wound.

But the mountain goat also has its comic moments, because while it is quite willing to climb upwards, it prefers to slide down scree slopes on its bottom. In fact, the hide becomes notably thicker on the rump.

Winter is passed largely sheltering in caves and beneath overhangs while it searches for those few clumps of grass peeking through the snow cover. Curiously, the mountain goat cannot withstand a soaking. The white winter coat is very thick but if it should get thoroughly wet the animal is in grave danger of catching pneumonia.

Regrettably this odd, almost prehistoric-looking animal is in danger of becoming all too rare. Only about 1200 exist in the United States and there are only a few thousand left in Canada. It would be sad indeed to lose this most adept cliff walker.

Another rocky mountain dweller that is dwindling in numbers is the grizzly bear. These animals wander over the mountains searching for bulbs and berries in the spring and summer, and in the autumn they hunt for pikas, marmots and other small animals. Grizzlies have even been known to chase mice. This must present a ridiculous sight, a 450 kg bear trying to catch its tiny, scampering 100 g prey.

Grizzlies spend the winters high up on the rocky slopes in caves and it is here, in midwinter, that the blind, helpless babies are born. Mother and cubs drowse through the long cold months in a sort of semi-hibernation and emerge in the spring to begin their search for food. The cubs spend their second winter with mother before setting off on their own.

The Rockies are undeniably beautiful and they provide a last refuge for some of the rarest and most persecuted animals of the North American continent. However, their increased use for recreations such as skiing and camping have threatened this refuge and some of these magnificent animals may become extinct if wild natural areas are not set aside for their use. The importance of the national parks that have been established cannot be over emphasized.

Hoary marmot

Pika

**WINTER is all too long in the Rocky Mountains. On the high peaks, snowfalls are heavy and the winds fierce. Added to this is the ever-present threat that the relentless action of the frost will send tons of rock tumbling downwards in an avalanche.**

**The animals that live in this harsh environment have to be highly adapted to withstand the rigours of the climate. They also need to be able to protect themselves from other animals that prey on them.**

Rocky Mountain sheep, for instance, face danger from avalanches and from the cougar, wolverine and eagle. When not in immediate danger, they graze on the warmer, south-facing slopes where they feed on grasses and other 'alpine' plants nourished by snow melting in the sun. But when threatened, they retreat to virtually inaccessible cliff ledges. There they are usually safe, but, as a last resort, they can defend themselves with their horns.

Both sexes have horns, although the male's are larger. The males use them against each other during breeding rites, when they argue over which male should mate with the females.

One of the sheep's fiercest enemies is the wolverine, the largest member of the weasel family. A full-grown male measures about a metre and its feet are equipped with formidable claws. Many stories are told about its legendary strength, endurance and cunning. It is not only a hunter but also a scavenger, and will claim a meal whenever and wherever it can. It will readily rob bait from a hunter's trap, break into a cabin and rifle cupboards, or hunt grouse, chipmunks and mice.

Normally a wolverine would not be large enough to tackle a 100 kg mountain sheep, but it is perfectly capable of killing and eating such an animal trapped in a snowdrift.

The prowess of a wolverine on snow adds greatly to its fame. Wolverine tracks have been found where the animals have obviously moved with ease over deep snow where other animals, such as wolves, would find it difficult to tread. The wolverine has hairy soles on its feet that insulate them and prevent frostbite.

A solitary animal, the wolverine hunts by night. On its prowls it can travel great distances using its keen sense of smell to detect food or danger. It seems to have an uncanny knack of avoiding traps.

## Bird life

Some Rocky Mountain birds escape the hardships of the mountain winter by spending only the summers there, but others, like the blue grouse, live all their lives in the mountains. In fact, in summer the blue grouse nests on the lower slopes where food is plentiful, retreating to the higher peaks, where it is safer, only in the winter. However, even there it may still fall prey to predators such as cougars, wolves and, of course, Man.

Golden eagles are not troubled by predators. These huge, beautiful birds, soar among the higher peaks, taking advantage of every swirling upcurrent of air. Each pair mates for life, and they make several nests of sticks and greenery on ledges, perhaps using one for several years before moving on to another.

Mountain sheep

If they do use the same nest again, it is rebuilt a little higher on the foundations of the last year's. With time, it may become so high that it nearly touches overhanging rock and the birds have difficulty in entering it. They then build another nearby, letting the old nest fall to pieces. Before it is completely destroyed, however, they may move back. By re-using old nests in this way, they need to find less new building materials — an important fact since the materials may have to be gathered from a long distance away.

The breeding season lasts six months, and two eggs are laid. But usually only one youngster is raised, normally the first to hatch. This first hatchling appears several days before its brother and is consequently stronger and more competitive right from the start. The other chick, losing the battle for food, usually perishes. Both parents hunt for food, but the mother always prepares the meal, tearing up the food for the chick.

Golden eagles hunt at dawn. They launch themselves on their two-metre wings, circling and scanning the ground for quarry. Once prey is detected, they then fold their wings back and plunge at over 145 kph towards the ground. They then rise with a rabbit, pika or mouse clutched in their talons.

Eagles will also scavenge if they find a large carcass. On such occasions, they may share the carrion with another large bird, the raven, the largest member of the crow family. Like eagles, ravens nest on cliffs, but they do not kill large prey, preferring seeds, insect grubs as well as carrion.

The raven is the acrobat of the Rockies. In the spring, pairs tumble and roll together in the air and some have even been seen to fly upside down — no mean feat for a bird. Nobody knows the reason for these antics; it may just be joy that the long Rocky Mountain winter is over.

A look at a map of North America suggests that the enormous expanse of the Rocky Mountains would be adequate sanctuary for its birds and mammals. But they have not escaped interference from Man. Eagles were once persecuted for killing livestock, but even though they are now recognised as posing no threat — at least by scientists if not by ranchers — the destruction of their hunting territories by logging forests or damming rivers for hydroelectric schemes is much more serious in the long run. Hopefully, at least the American and Canadian National Parks will provide somewhere where these animals can live in relative peace, pursued only by the occasional over-eager camper or tourist.

Wolverine

Grouse

# What is mysteri

Top: A white-handed gibbon. The gibbon's long fingers make it easier for it to grasp branches as it swings through the trees.
Above: A further adaption to tree-life is the gibbon's long arms. Relatively, they are nearly twice as long as a Man's.

**GIBBONS remain the most mysterious as well as the most beautiful of the apes. Also known as the lesser apes, in contrast to the orang-utans, chimpanzees and gorillas which together constitute the great apes, they live in the remote tropical forests of southern Asia and the East Indies.**

It is most likely the very inaccessibility of their chosen domain, added to an apparent innate shyness, that has resulted in our lack of knowledge of the gibbon. Our knowledge of the great apes is, by contrast, much more extensive.

Gibbons are famous for two characteristics: they produce a great variety of calls and other vocalizations and they are able to swing easily and powerfully through the trees.

They live in family groups consisting of two adults and their young. Either the adult male or female may be the dominant animal in contrast to some of the other apes where the male is always dominant. This situation is probably associated with the similarity in size and appearance of males and females.

Scientists recognise seven species of gibbon, the two largest of which are sometimes known as siamangs. These grow to 1 metre in height and can weigh up to 16kg. The true gibbons are much smaller, averaging 90 cm. and weighing approximately 7kg.

True gibbons are covered in beautiful thick fur which, as in other primates, is thickest on the head and chest. The gibbons have by far the thickest fur of the apes with about 1700 hairs per cm. of skin on the chest as opposed to an equivalent of 100 in chimpanzees.

Some experts have posed the question as to why these animals have such thick fur coats when they live in the tropics and the problem of how they prevent overheating has yet to be solved. However, they do not have a layer of fat between their bones and skin as do humans, so presumably this solves part of the problem.

The day of a gibbon begins at about 6.30 each morning, when it awakes in the top of a tree. Trees used are always the most inaccessible ones in the gibbons' territory and so the animals are as safe from predators as they can be. They sleep singly, making use of the axils, where the branches meet the trunk. A mother and infant will sleep together.

At dawn the adults indulge in a dawn chorus which rings throughout the whole forest. This burst of sound informs other gibbons that territorial boundaries are still in operation and have to be observed. The gibbons call both while at the nest site and while beginning the day's trek and they will call throughout the day to reinforce the territorial limits.

## Feeding habits

During the day they spend about 60 per cent of their time feeding on leaves, flowers, fruits, insects or their eggs. One of the characteristics of their feeding behaviour is the way they use their ability to swing hand over hand to remain suspended beneath slender branches while

gathering food. This brings the tender young terminal shoots easily within their reach whereas if they were sitting on the branch their own weight would bend those terminal shoots away from them and make feeding much more difficult and hazardous.

The gibbon's ability to swing hand over hand or 'brachiate' as it is termed is justifiably renowned.

During slow movement the body is held vertically and the legs are flexed except at the base of the swing when they hang directly downwards. As the speed of movement increases, the body becomes more horizontal.

Gibbons are also expert leapers and can jump 8-10 metres between trees either from a standing start or as part of a movement pattern already in action. Some people have suggested that gibbons change direction during 'flight' but this is an illusion caused by deflection off stray branches. However, they do show considerable mid-air manoeuvrability since they have been known to snatch flying birds.

These breath-taking acrobatics, which demand stereoscopic vision, do sometimes result in mistakes. There is ample evidence from the healed bones of dead animals that falls and subsequent bone breakage are common. Fortunately, apes and monkeys seem to have the ability to repair such injuries easily and naturally.

Since monkeys also live in trees they face the same hazards but their methods of locomotion differ. Many monkeys are quadrupedal in stance, that is they travel on all fours on the upper surfaces of the branch. In contrast to this way of life, the great apes spend much time on the ground.

Although chimpanzees can swing through trees the orang-utans and gorillas are too heavy ever to do so. However, many experts believe that these apes are descended from tree swinging ancestors, since they show certain anatomical features associated with life in the trees.

The hands of gibbons are elongated and they are hook-like in shape thus

| | Insects Grubs etc. | Fruit Nuts Seeds | Leaves Roots Grasses | Main Food Sources |
|---|---|---|---|---|
| Gorilla | | | ■ | ■ |
| Orang-Utan | | ■ | ■ | ■ |
| Chimpanzee | ■ | ■ | ■ | ■ |
| Siamang | ■ | ■ | ■ | ■ |
| Baboon | ■ | ■ | ■ | ■ |
| Langir | | | ■ | ■ |
| Hasler | | | ■ | ■ |
| Macque | ■ | ■ | ■ | ■ |
| Gibbon | ■ | ■ | ■ | ■ |
| Spider Monkey | | ■ | | ■ |
| Capuchin | ■ | ■ | | ■ |
| Lemur | | ■ | ■ | ■ |
| Potto | ■ | ■ | ■ | ■ |
| Galago | ■ | | | ■ |
| Squirrel Monkey | ■ | ■ | | ■ |
| Loris | ■ | | | ■ |
| Marmoset | ■ | ■ | ■ | ■ |
| Tarsier | ■ | | | ■ |

**Primates eat a wide variety of foods, and gibbons are particularly unspecialised in their choice. They live on fruit, leaves, insects, small birds and their eggs.**

enabling the animals to grasp the branches very firmly. The hands of the great apes and the quadrupedal monkeys are similar in many respects although they are generally broader and are less hook-like.

The bodies of gibbons are well-adapted to their swinging way of life. Not surprisingly, it is the gibbon's arms and shoulders which nature has particularly designed for the task of moving through the trees. The humerus or upper arm bone is very long and slender. In the quadrupedal monkeys the humerus is much shorter and thicker. The gibbon has lower arm bones which are longer than its upper arm bones and its arms are long in relation to its body size.

These elongated arms are, of course, just what the gibbon needs as he stretches out from branch to branch. But he also possesses another invaluable 'modification' that allows him to indulge in his acrobatic feats. The structure of his shoulder joints is such that he, in common with the great apes, can rotate his arms through a full 180°. But the gibbon goes one better even than the great apes in being able to draw his arms backward further.

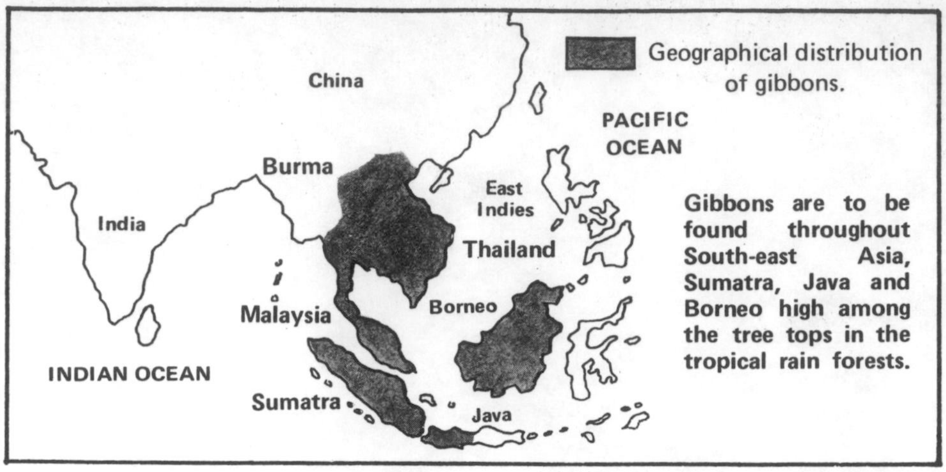

This adaptation imparts a high degree of manoeuvrability to the arms in swinging or reaching for food. One of the dangers faced by an animal swinging between trees is that of dislocation of bones while swinging or landing. In the gibbon, the muscles of the shoulder region and of the elbow joint are positioned in such a way as to absorb the shocks of swinging through trees and to prevent the dislocation of the joints.

Finally, we must admit that the situation is rather more complicated than it first appears for not all monkeys are quadrupedal. Some of the South American ones, for instance the Spider monkeys, swing through the trees in a similar manner to gibbons; however in addition to using the normal limbs as do the apes, these monkeys also use their prehensile tails for clasping branches while swinging. It is likely that this ability evolved independently in apes and in the New World monkeys as the primitive mammals from which they arose do not appear to have had this ability.

Geographical distribution of gibbons.

China
PACIFIC OCEAN
Burma
East Indies
India
Thailand
Malaysia
Borneo
INDIAN OCEAN
Sumatra
Java

**Gibbons are to be found throughout South-east Asia, Sumatra, Java and Borneo high among the tree tops in the tropical rain forests.**

**GIBBONS: Are noisy, agile and sociable.**
**There are seven species:**
**Siamang (largest).**
**Dwarf siamang**
**Lar, or white-handed.**
**Hoolock.**
**Kloss's Gibbon.**
**Black, or concolour.**
**Wau wau, or capped.**

**They live on fruit, leaves, insects, small birds and their eggs.**
**Gibbons are well known for their remarkable "whooping" calls, rising to a screaming howl and then dying away as they call back and forth across the tree-tops at sunrise.**

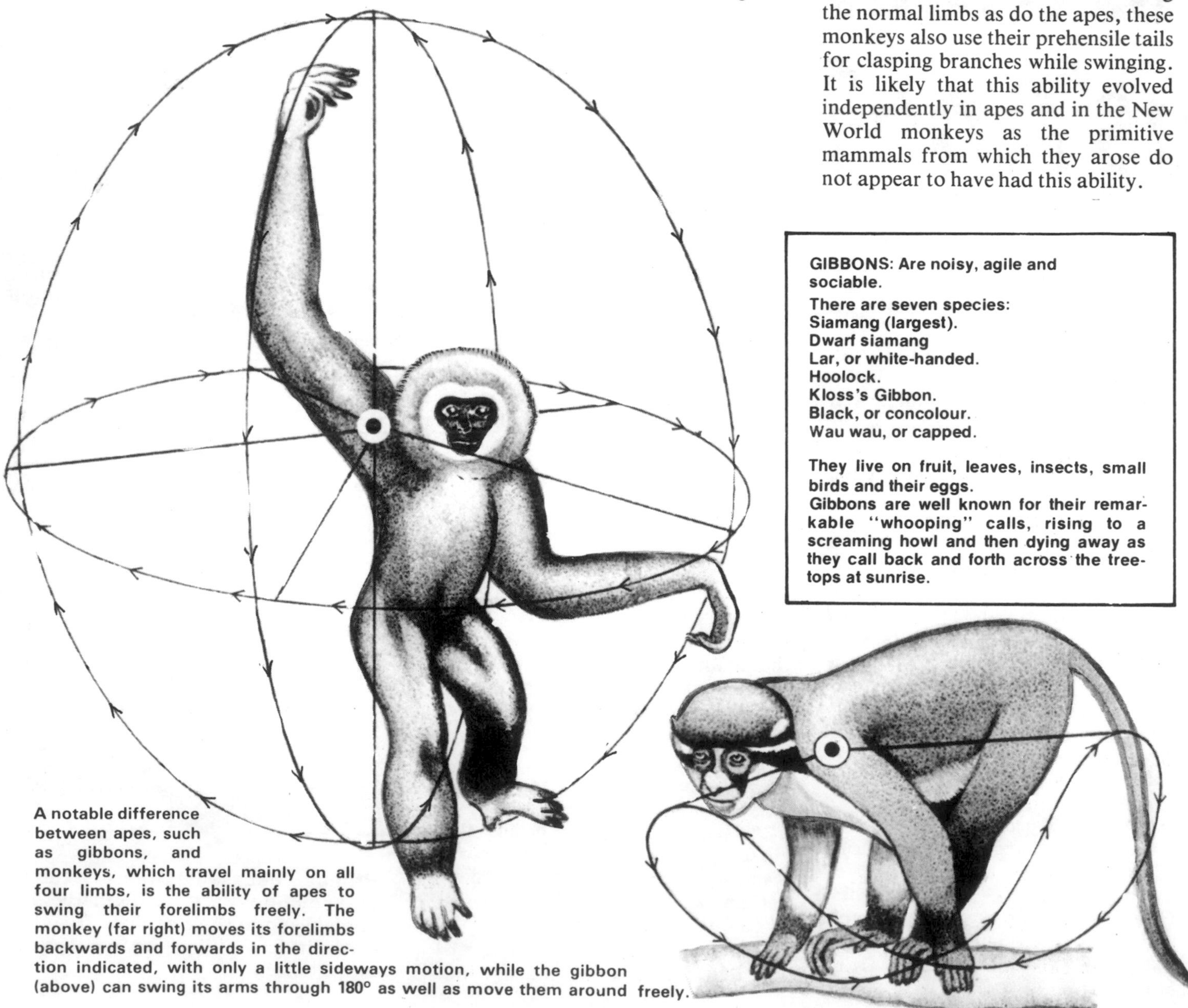

**A notable difference between apes, such as gibbons, and monkeys, which travel mainly on all four limbs, is the ability of apes to swing their forelimbs freely. The monkey (far right) moves its forelimbs backwards and forwards in the direction indicated, with only a little sideways motion, while the gibbon (above) can swing its arms through 180° as well as move them around freely.**

# What is Cork?

**JUST as human beings and animals are covered with skin, one of the main functions of which is to keep out diseases, so for the same purpose young trees are covered by 'tree skin', a compact layer of cells. As the tree grows and increases in girth, this skin is often replaced by another layer, formed from a row of dead cells beneath the surface. This is *cork*, one of Nature's most wonderful materials. Man has made use of it for many purposes for at least 2,300 years.**

Water cannot pass through cork, so all the cells outside it die off to form the rough outer layer of a tree we call bark. However, some water and air must pass through from the atmosphere if the inner cores of wood are to remain alive, so small gaps of very loosely-packed cells, called *lenticels,* are developed at different places in the corky layer. Air and water can pass freely through these.

Lenticels can clearly be seen as the dark streaks on an ordinary bottle cork. Each year a new layer of cork is formed just beneath the old. In this way cork oak trees can go on producing fine cork for cutting for at least 100 years.

Beneath the ever-thickening layers of dead bark, the work of cork formation goes on. This explains why when initials are cut in the outer bark of a tree, they begin to close up as each year passes. For such a wound is, in a sense, 'healed' by successive layers of cork around it.

Cork, in fact, is a seven-fold natural wonder, and no completely satisfactory artificial substitute has yet been produced by scientists. It has seven unique properties:

(1) Each individual cork cell has a geometric pattern of 14 faces. This divides all the inner space effectively, without gaps, so cork will not let air, water, or water vapour through.

(2) Each cork cell is more than half-filled with air, which explains why it is one of the lightest solid substances known.

(3) This 'dead' air is separated by the finely-divided honeycomb pattern of cork cells and after a vacuum, is the best insulator of heat or cold known.

(4) For the same reason, it is also a near-perfect insulator against the vibrations that cause sounds.

(5) The light yet tough walls of the cork cell holding in this air form a safe, chemically unreactive material that will last almost indefinitely. Only tunnelling insects can normally destroy cork, not age or decay.

(6) Cork cell walls are tougher and more resilient than rubber, even when enormously compressed.

(7) If a section of raw cork is sliced cleanly with a sharp blade, myriads of the hexagonal open cells are exposed on every square centimetre, each one acting as a tiny vacuum cup. This gives cork tremendous shock-absorbing, non-slip and also polishing properties to add to its 1,000 or so recorded uses.

The cork oak of southern Europe and North Africa is the most important source for cork used in industry. Spain and Portugal are the world's

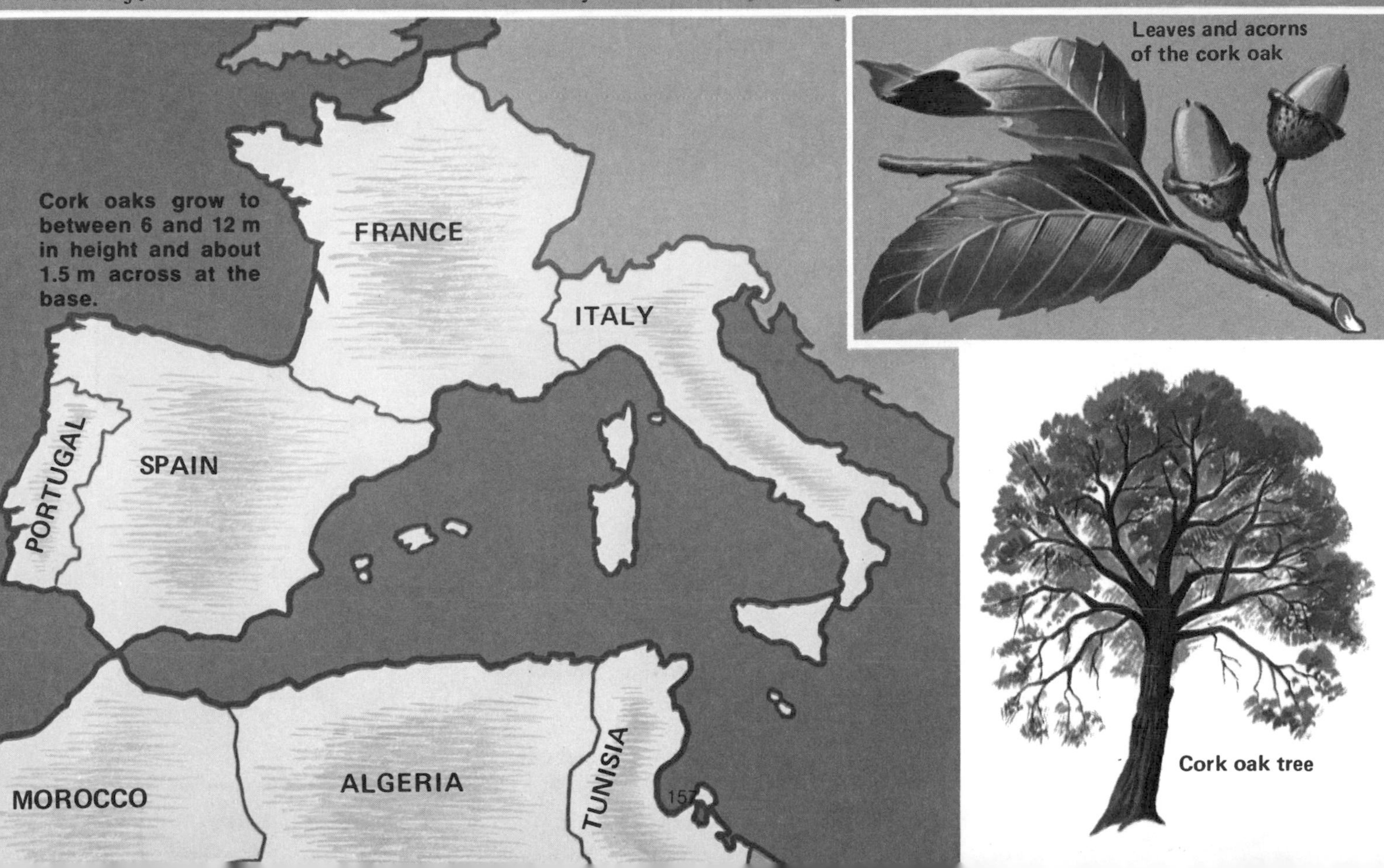


Cork oaks grow to between 6 and 12 m in height and about 1.5 m across at the base.

Leaves and acorns of the cork oak

Cork oak tree

leading producers and between them produce about two-thirds of the world's supply. Other important producers are France, Italy, Algeria, Tunisia and Morocco. The cork oak is an evergreen (never sheds its leaves) and grows best in mountainous areas.

Harvesting cork is an expert job. It requires great knowledge of each tree's development and capabilities of further production, plus the fine skill of a tree surgeon.

No tree is cut until it reaches the age of about 20 years, and this is usually carried out in July or August. Careful cuts are made just above the roots, and these are linked with long vertical cuts that follow the bark's deepest natural cracks. The outer bark is prised off, and a reasonable layer of cork removed without injury to the tree's living inner core, especially the *phellogen* layer, which actually produces the cells from which cork is composed.

## Improving with age

These first crops of cork are low-grade material, often used only to make granulated cork for packing or sound-proofing purposes. It is another nine or 10 years before the same tree is harvested again, but this time the new growth of cork is fine-grained and much more valuable. In fact, the quality improves until the cork oak is about 40 years old, after which it will produce steadily increasing amounts until it dies, some time before its 150th birthday.

The curved slabs of cork are boiled in large vats. This softens the roughly-creviced outer layer so that it can be removed, and also enables the layers to be flattened before grading and trimming.

The corks we pull from bottles come from the best quality product; but they represent only a tiny fraction of its many uses in industry, science, medicine, building and manufacture. For example, modern cars may use cork or cork composition in as many as 50 different places.

Nature's special protection for some of its trees seems likely to continue as a major blessing to mankind, for in the absence of any better man-made substitute, world demand for cork continues to increase every year. As a veteran cork-cutter recently said: "Cork will always be better than plastic. Plastic stoppers are no use to the chemical trade, nor for stopping fine wines and spirits. Cork is Nature's gift to the world."

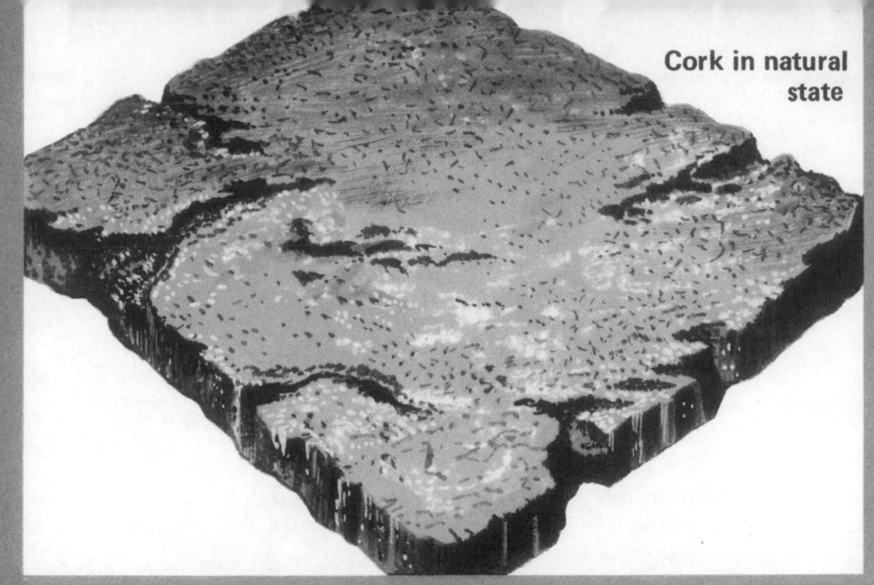


**Above: A sheet of natural cork. After it has been stripped in this form, the cork is taken to a nearby boiling station. First it is stacked and left to season for a number of weeks, just like fresh timber, before being boiled to soften the cork and remove unwanted chemicals. The cork is now a flat sheet several centimetres thick and ready to be sent to cork factories all over the world.**

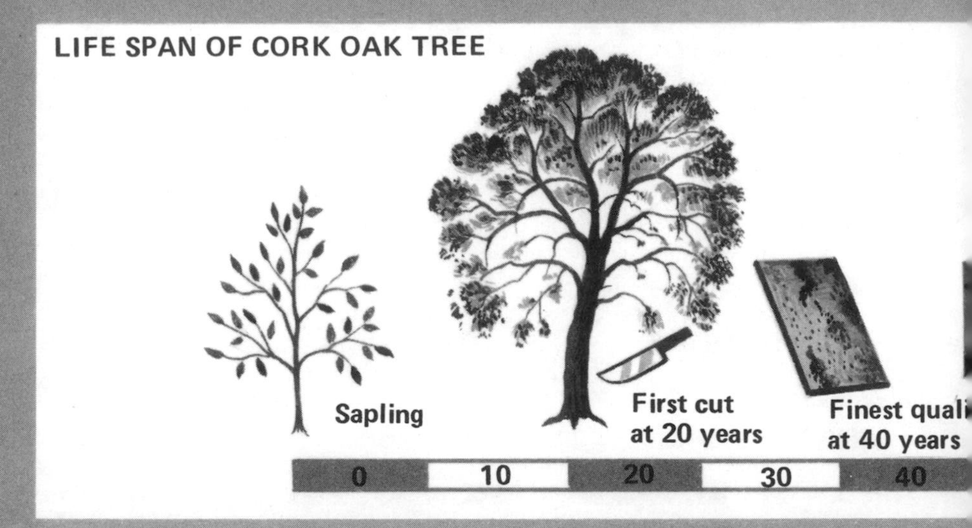


**Above: A cork oak may live for up to 150 years. No cuttings are made until the tree is 20 years old. This first crop of cork is of poor quality though some is used as packing material. Another crop is not taken for another ten years by which time the cork is of much higher quality reaching a peak at 40 years. More crops are taken at roughly 10-year intervals.**

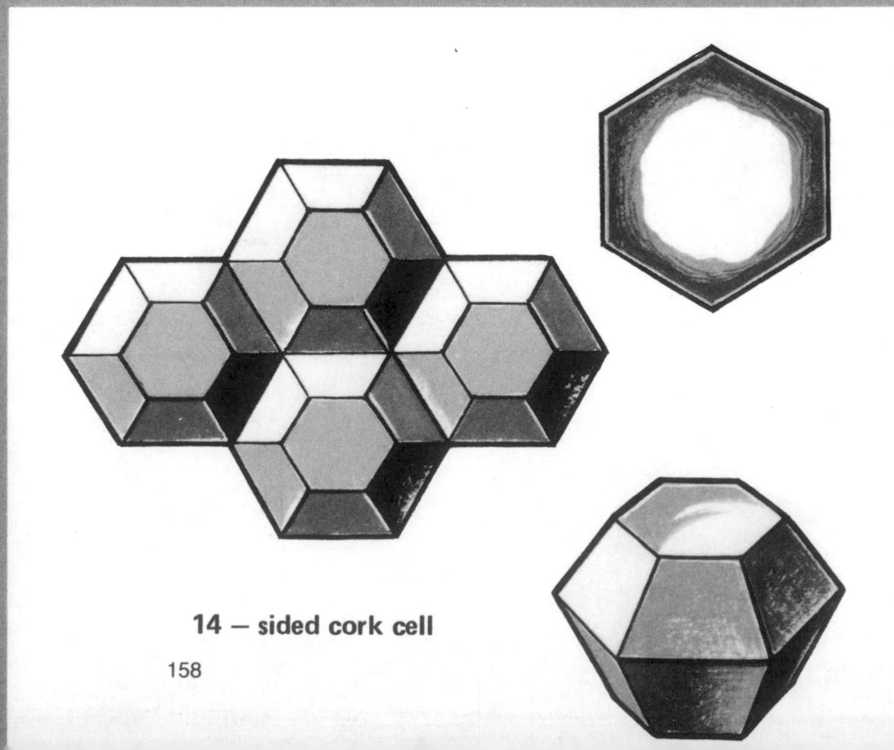

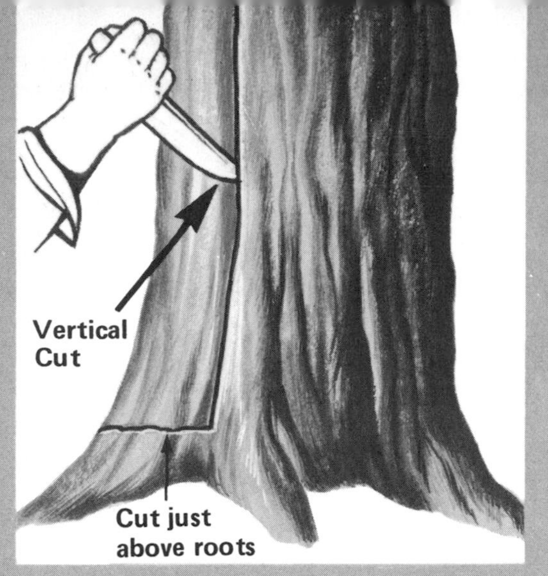


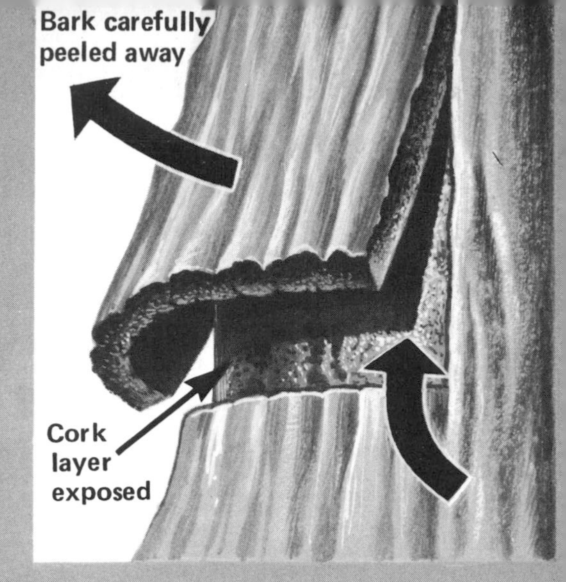


Left: The position of the cork layer in the trunk of the tree. Especially in hot countries, the cork reaches great thicknesses to protect the living inner wood from summer droughts.

Stripping cork is a careful and precise operation (centre). A horizontal cut is made just above the roots using a razor-sharp knife followed by vertical cuts down the trunk. The bark is prised away and the cork can then be stripped carefully so as not to injure the living wood (right). Stripping is usually carried out in July or August and an average cork oak may produce over 20 kg of cork. Cork may also be stripped from the branches.

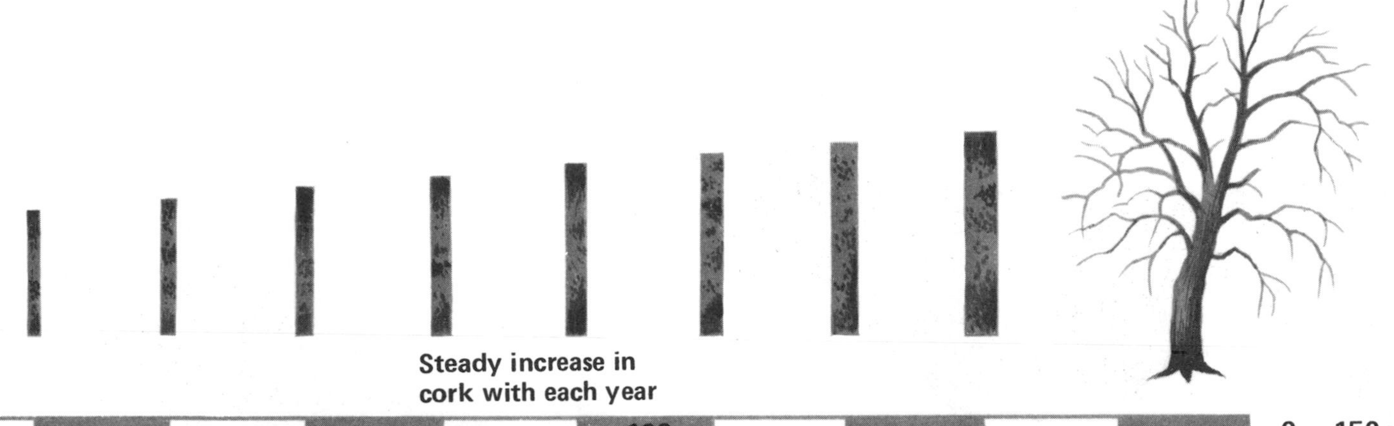


Below: Each cork cell has a precise, symmetrical shape with 14 faces and is strongly linked to the surrounding cells. Since there are no gaps, no air or water can pass through helping to explain the insulation and buoyancy properties of cork. A cell that has been cut open acts like a tiny 'suction cup' making it useful as a non-slip material.

Some of the major uses of cork. It does not conduct heat very well so makes a very effective insulating material in houses. Cork also absorbs sound vibrations very well. Cork is a very tough and resilient material. Even when compressed by a great weight it can recover its original shape and so is used as a shock-absorber.

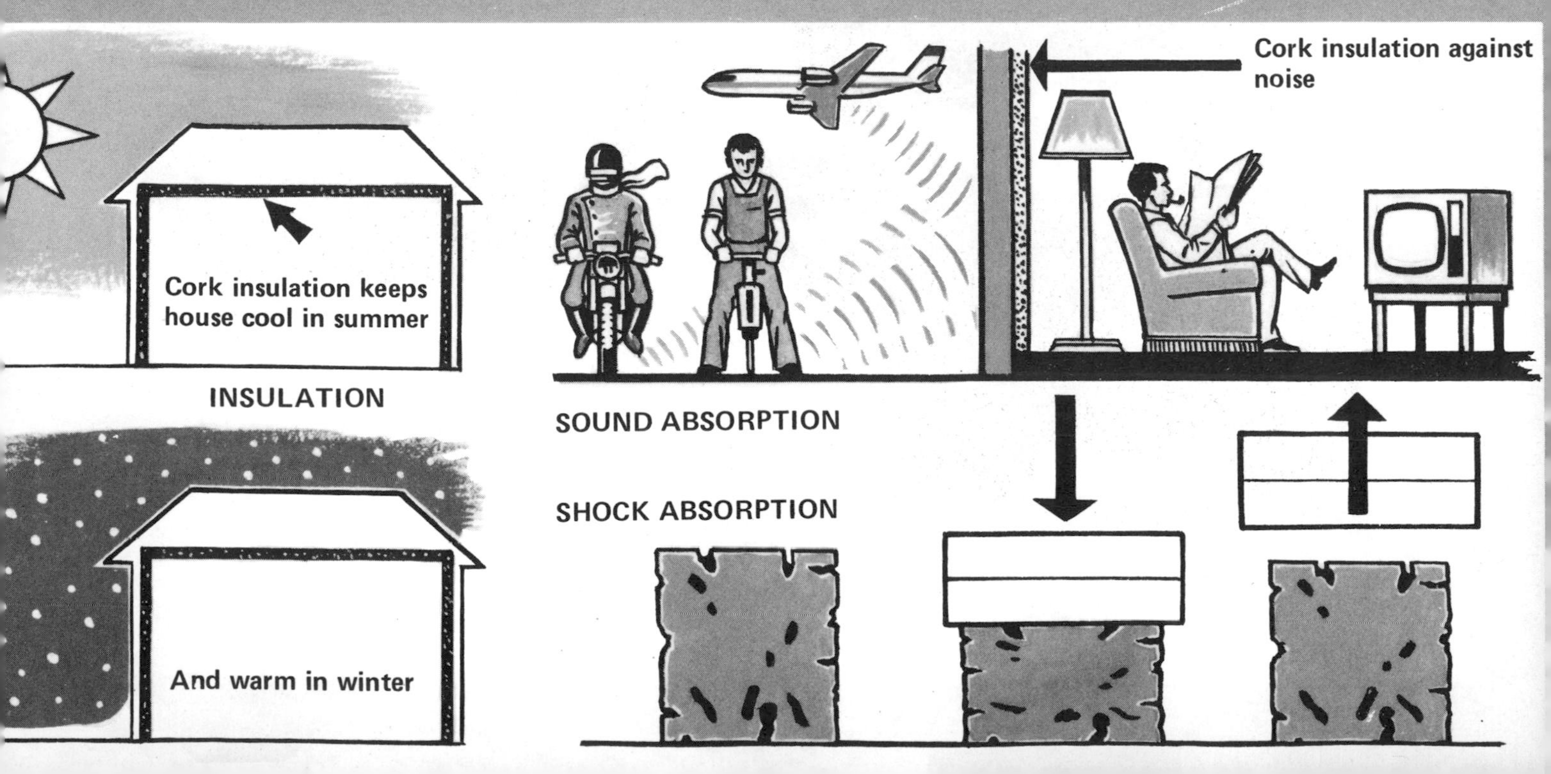

# Do cows have pedigrees?

**The cow you see in a field may be as highly bred as any Supreme winner of the Crufts Dog Show.**

**FEW animals serve Man as faithfully as cows. They provide us with meat, with milk, with butter, cheese, yoghurt and a host of other products. In many poorer countries of the world they are used to pull ploughs and carts.**

This is particularly the case in India, where there are more cattle — over 200 million of them — than in any other country in the world. One of the reasons there are so many is that Hindus consider the cow as a sacred animal that cannot be killed.

In most developed countries, however, cattle are reared mainly for their meat and milk. Since the 18th century they have been selectively bred so that both the quality of the meat and the amount of milk produced by each cow have risen dramatically.

The result of this selective breeding has been the formation of *pedigree* breeds of cows, just as there are pedigree breeds of dogs. Some of the breeds are shown on these pages.

Traditionally, cattle breeds have been split into those designed for milk production (dairy breeds) and those designed for beef production (beef breeds). But nowadays this distinction has become a little blurred.

In Europe by far the most common breed is the Friesian. (In America, Friesian-type cows are called 'Holsteins'.) Although this breed was originally bred for milk production, it was found that the male calves — which would previously have been killed for veal — could be fattened to produce a good lean carcass for the butcher in about eighteen months — faster than most beef breeds. So the Friesian became popular as a beef cow and a dairy cow.

Nevertheless Friesians are not as hardy as Herefords or Shorthorns, which are widely reared on ranches in America. Nor do they produce such high quality meat as the Aberdeen Angus.

They do however produce more milk than other cows. In the year April 1983 to March 1984 the average British cow produced 4,940 litres of milk a year as against 3,980 litres in the year April 1973 to March 1974. The changes from poorer breeds to Friesians was responsible for a large part of this increase.

Other important dairy breeds are the Jersey and the Guernsey. Although these breeds produce less milk than Friesians, their milk contains more cream and is therefore more valuable.

But no breed of cow is static in the way that a pedigree dog breed must be to conform to an unchanging written standard. Instead, farmers are continuously trying to improve their herds.

FRIESIAN (Dairy and beef)

JERSEY (Dairy)

SUSSEX (Beef)

HIGHLAND (Beef)

BEEF SHORTHORN (Beef)

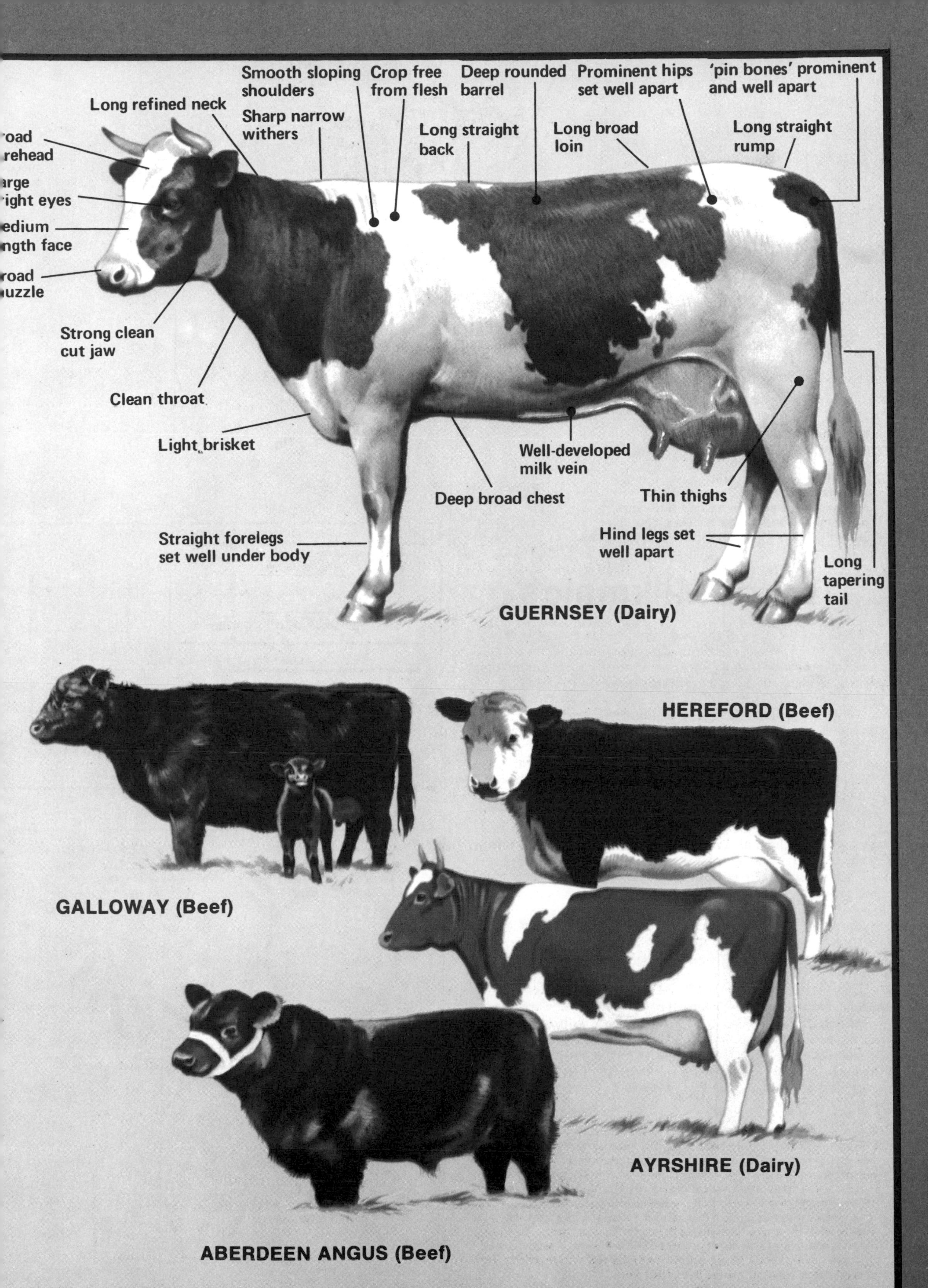
Smooth sloping shoulders
Crop free from flesh
Deep rounded barrel
Prominent hips set well apart
'pin bones' prominent and well apart
Long refined neck
Sharp narrow withers
Long straight back
Long broad loin
Long straight rump
oad
rehead
arge
ight eyes
edium
ngth face
road
uzzle
Strong clean cut jaw
Clean throat
Light brisket
Well-developed milk vein
Deep broad chest
Thin thighs
Straight forelegs set well under body
Hind legs set well apart
Long tapering tail
GUERNSEY (Dairy)
HEREFORD (Beef)
GALLOWAY (Beef)
AYRSHIRE (Dairy)
ABERDEEN ANGUS (Beef)

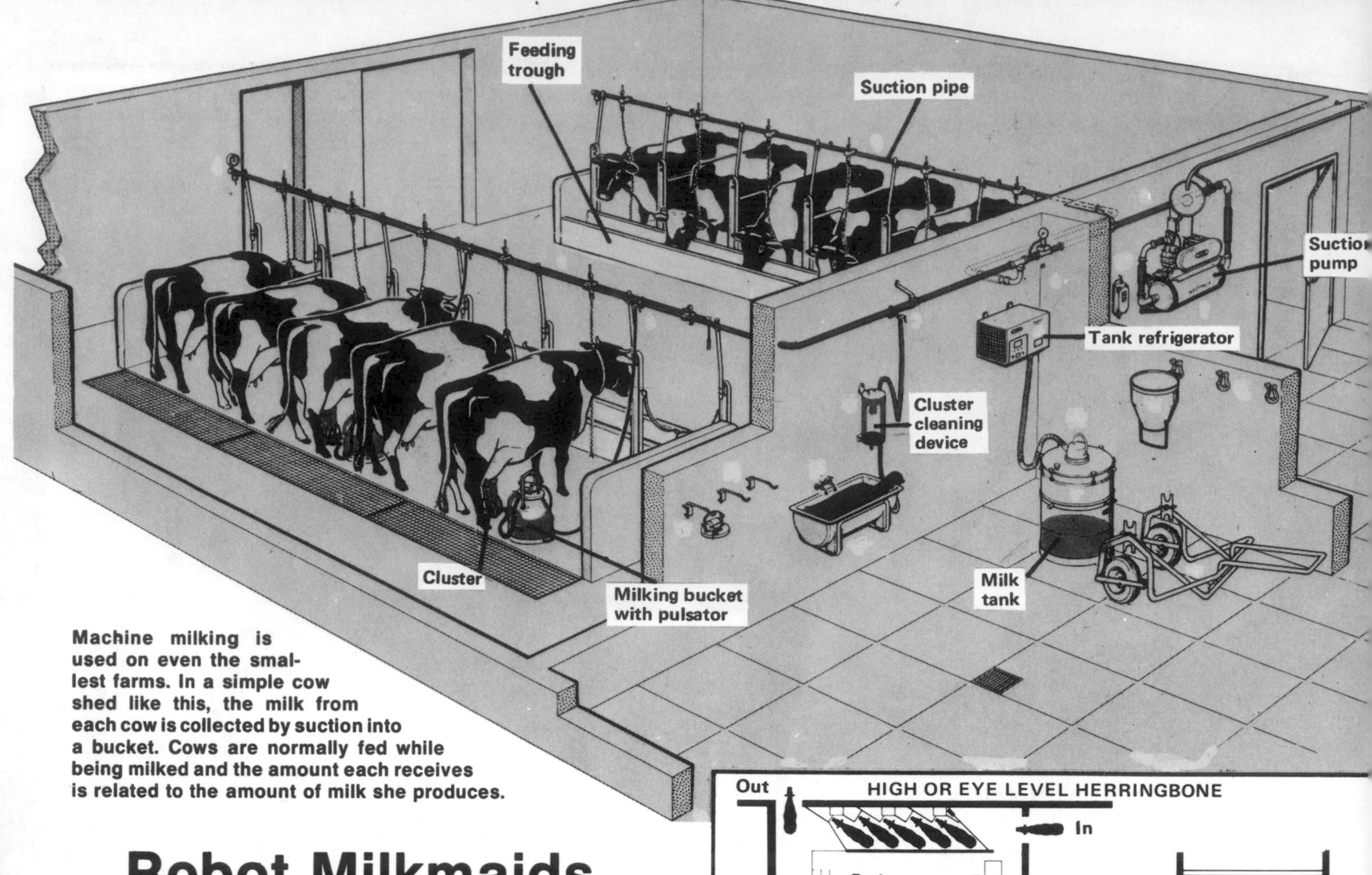


**Machine milking is used on even the smallest farms. In a simple cow shed like this, the milk from each cow is collected by suction into a bucket. Cows are normally fed while being milked and the amount each receives is related to the amount of milk she produces.**

# Robot Milkmaids

Gone are the days of the milkmaid and her two pails of milk slung from a yoke over her shoulders. Gone are the three-legged stool and the hand-aching, unhygienic business of hand-milking. Nowadays it is all done by machine down on the farm.

When a calf suckles at a cow, it stimulates a process called 'let down'. During let down, the sac-like cells (*alveoli*) in which the milk is formed contract and squeeze the milk into a resevoir called the 'milk cistern'. But the milk can't come out because it is held by a muscle (the *sphincter*) which closes the end of the canal which leads from the cistern to the udder.

In hand-milking, the milk is forced out through the sphincter by squeezing the milk canal. But machines work in an entirely different method. They use a pump that creates suction in a rubber and metal cup which is placed round the teat. This sucks the milk out through the sphincter.

However, it is uncomfortable for the cow if the suction is constant. So while the cow is being milked the suction is continuously varied using a device called a 'pulsator'.

Cows are sensitive animals. As there is no calf, let down is usually stimulated by washing the cow's udder in warm water, although all the sounds and sights associated with milking, such as the whine of the suction pump, also help. But if the cow is disturbed, she won't give her milk. And if a cow is not milked, she quickly stops producing any milk at all — just as she would have done in nature once her calves had stopped suckling.

**Right: On bigger farms, buckets are not used to collect the milk. Instead, it flows by pipe to a tank, the amount produced by each cow being recorded on the way. The most normal plan of a *milking parlour* — where the cows are milked — is a 'herringbone' pattern, in which the cows are housed in two rows of diagonally-arranged stalls. Usually the central path between the two rows is at a lower level making it easier for the farmer to attach the milk cups or 'clusters' to the cows' udders. In the most modern farms, however, rotary parlours are sometimes used. These slowly revolve while the cows are being milked, unmilked cows walking in at one end, milked cows walking out at the other end.**

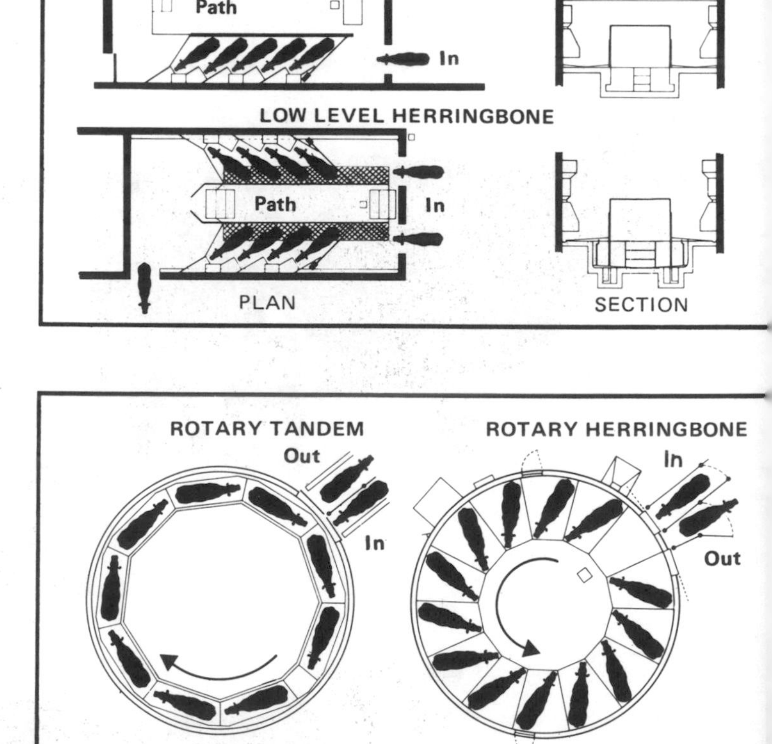

# For what is John Audubon famous?

1. John James Audubon was born in 1785 in the West Indies on the island of Hispaniola or, as we now call it, Haiti. His father was a French sea captain and his mother was of Spanish descent. However, he was soon taken to the United States and, from there, to France. As a child he collected birds' eggs. Later, on his father's farm in Philadelphia, he began to develop an interest in drawing birds — as many different kinds as he could find.

2. At first he experimented by sketching birds he had shot, but, not surprisingly, he found the finished sketches had a lifeless look about them, which was not the effect he wanted. He tried suspending them on wires, but achieved only moderate success. Eventually he used wires to arrange the dead bodies in life-like positions. In 1808 he married and, with a partner named Ferdinand Rozier, opened a store in Louisville, Kentucky.

3. Rozier usually did the counter work for, more often than not, Audubon was off sketching birds. Eventually they went down river to Henderson, a town in western Kentucky, hoping to improve their profits. There they settled into the same way of life, Rozier looking after the store and Audubon doing his painting. During that period Audubon often went out hunting — and on more than one occasion he narrowly escaped death at the hands of Indians.

In 1810 the three of them moved onwards again, this time to Ste. Genevieve. Rozier decided to settle there, but Audubon and his wife returned to Henderson where, with no Rozier behind the counter, trade went from bad to even worse. Before long he went bankrupt and (with two sons this time as well as a wife) he set up as a taxidermist in Cincinnati.

This was not a success, either, and now he decided to give his life to art. He left Lucy working as a teacher and became a wanderer.

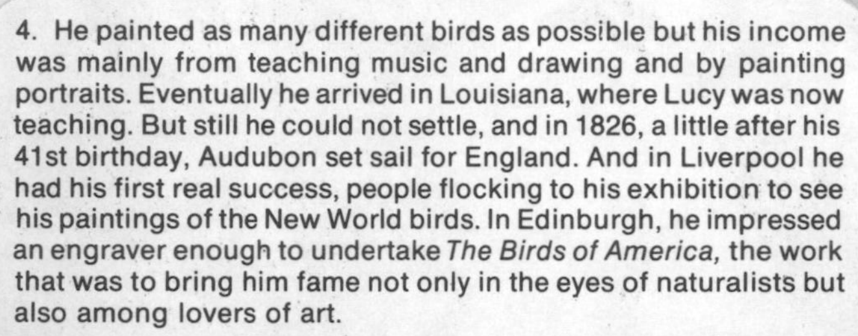

4. He painted as many different birds as possible but his income was mainly from teaching music and drawing and by painting portraits. Eventually he arrived in Louisiana, where Lucy was now teaching. But still he could not settle, and in 1826, a little after his 41st birthday, Audubon set sail for England. And in Liverpool he had his first real success, people flocking to his exhibition to see his paintings of the New World birds. In Edinburgh, he impressed an engraver enough to undertake *The Birds of America,* the work that was to bring him fame not only in the eyes of naturalists but also among lovers of art.

5. It was an enormous task, for the work consisted of 435 hand-coloured plates. But the magnificent pictures and his vivid writing made the work an instant best-seller, bringing as it did a completely new dimension to the depiction of Nature. Subscriptions were gathered for the various instalments of the work and cost 1000 dollars — in those days an enormous sum.

6. Later, when he and his wife had settled in New York, he published a revised, smaller edition of *The Birds of America.* He was working on a similar book on four-legged animals when, in January, 1851, he died. The work was finished by his sons and a friend. Audubon's work still lives on and even today prints of his superb bird paintings can find a ready sale. The National Audubon Society, founded in 1886, associates Audubon's name with the protection of birds, although this is somewhat misleading for Audubon killed birds all his life. He did not protect them — but he did preserve them for all the world to see.

# A Bird in Hand

**BIRD watching, for many years, has been an extremely popular hobby. People of all ages will happily go out into the countryside, down by the rivers, along the sea shores, into the parks and even into their own gardens. They will settle down and will wait quietly and patiently hour after hour, just for the joy of seeing a bird return to its nest, feed its young, collect or catch its food or do any one of the many fascinating things that make up a bird's life.**

For some of them, this is enough. Others, requiring a permanent memory of their enjoyment, will take photographs of the birds.

**Above: the great grey owl.**

*(Both pictures – New York Historical Society).*

Photography is a harmless way of capturing and recording memories. The resulting pictures often give a real feeling of life and movement. Texture and colour can be recreated without any necessity to kill the birds.

In Audubon's lifetime, however, this was not true. The only way to observe a bird's shape and colours at leisure was to kill it. Even then, not surprisingly, there was little 'life' in the resulting carcass.

Artists often before had tried to draw and paint birds and they had succeeded — up to a point. But the paintings had been — in Audubon's opinion, at least — 'strictly ornithological'.

Audubon determined to change all that. He wanted paintings that had a life-like quality, birds that looked as though they were living and breathing.

That he did so artistically, colourfully and superbly is the measure of his achievement. And it is great indeed.

He spent a lot of time and trouble — most of his life, in fact — on the study of birds.

## Pioneer work

He is supposed to have been the first man in America ever to have banded birds for the purpose of checking their return the following spring. He did this with phoebes (American flycatchers). All his observations and investigations were equally detailed and original.

On this page we show two reproductions of Audubon's pictures. Both belong to the New York Historical Society. Their detail is remarkable and their 'life' indisputable. It is interesting to note that nowadays an original Audubon print in good condition can fetch many hundreds (if not thousands) of pounds.

A photograph may reproduce a living bird accurately and pleasantly but, many people think, for beauty and emotion there is nothing to compare with a work of art by a skilled and caring human being — although perhaps that is a matter of opinion!

**Below: two female gyrfalcons from Audubon's *The Birds of America*.**

# Do some animals carry their young on their backs?

Do your mummy and daddy ever carry you on their backs? Well, here are some parents of the wild who do just that.

For instance, there is the long-nosed Tamandua from South America. How tightly little baby clings to mummy. The cheeky little baboon from Africa sits perkily on its mother's tail. The Australian possum takes a firm hold of a branch while its young one struggles to hang on. Mother Koala and her little son, also from Australia, search for eucalyptus leaves – and the Rhesus monkey from India trots along with her shy little daughter on her back. The Great Glider, yet another Australian animal, protects her baby – see him peeping over her shoulder? From Europe comes the handsome Great Crested Grebe with her two chicks.

# How many different Trees are there in Britain?

**CAN you imagine a treeless Britain? No great spreading oaks to sit under in summer, no chestnut trees shedding conkers in autumn, no sycamore seeds whirling like mini-helicopters to the ground, no vast, swaying, heavily-scented pine forests. The landscape would be unrecognisable — and yet there was a time when Britain did lose all its trees.**

Ten thousand years ago, during an Ice Age, our islands' trees died off. It took several thousand years for any of them to return, their seeds borne by the wind or birds. These early species have come to be regarded as our native trees. Among them are oak, ash, willow, Scots pine, yew and birch.

Over the centuries new species were introduced. The Romans brought sweet chestnut and walnut trees; sycamore arrived during the Middle Ages; and the legions of empire-builders who visited all parts of the globe brought back with them many other kinds of trees. Such has been the influx that today, of the 1300 different kinds that can be found in Britain, only 35 are native species.

Britain's oldest trees are yews which have lived for almost 2,000 years and our tallest trees are firs at 57 metres. None of these sets a world record. The world's oldest living tree, a pine, can be found in

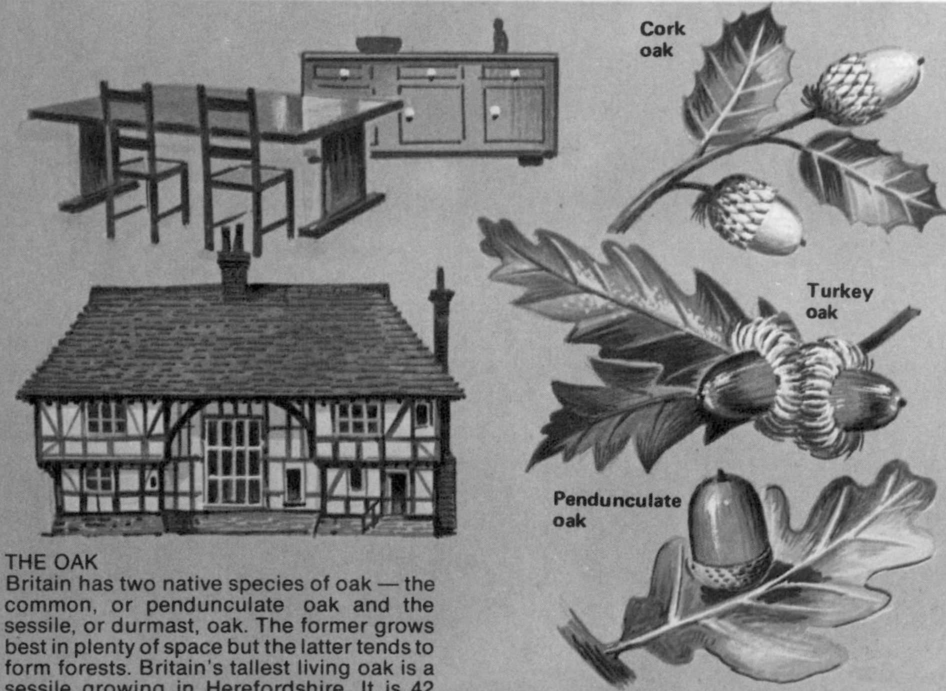


THE OAK
Britain has two native species of oak — the common, or pendunculate oak and the sessile, or durmast, oak. The former grows best in plenty of space but the latter tends to form forests. Britain's tallest living oak is a sessile growing in Herefordshire. It is 42 metres tall. The common oak is quite easily distinguishable from its rival by its stalked acorns and short-stalked leaves. The sessile oak bears stalkless acorns and has long-stalked leaves.

Three species of foreign oaks have been introduced to Britain — the Turkey oak which grows straighter and spreads less than our common oak; the Mediterranean holm oak, an evergreen, which looks like a large holly tree; and the American red oak, which is grown for decoration.

Oak wood, close-grained and brown in colour, is used in furniture making and in the past for ship-building and housebuilding.

Note: The cork oak, shown above, is a non-native oak. Cultivated in India, around the Mediterranean, and the U.S.A., the inner bark provides the commercial cork.

THE CHESTNUT
Of the two species of chestnut found in Britain, one, the horse chestnut, came from the Eastern Mediterranean in the 16th C. and the other, the sweet chestnut, was probably introduced by the Romans who made a nutritious flour from its nuts. The nuts of the horse chestnut are too bitter to be edible to us. These trees can live for 500 years but their wood is seldom used for commercial purposes as it tends to crack, but sometimes it is used to make charcoal. Some chestnut wood is grown as coppice — the trunks are cut back causing clusters of stems to shoot up. These can be cut and used in fencing. Squirrels are often instrumental in spreading the tree's range, carrying off the nuts, burying them for later use and then forgetting where they have put them. The lost chestnuts then sprout as young trees.

California. It has been judged to be 4,600 years old! And the tallest tree found to date was a eucalyptus measuring over 114 metres, growing in Australia. So British trees have some way to go to catch up with the real giants.

Regardless of records, however, one species stands out as being the most traditional of English trees — the oak. Ancient druids used to worship in oak groves, medieval peasants used to feed their pigs on acorns in the forests, and the pride of England's sailing ships were built of strong, durable oak. Nelson's flagship, *The Victory*, is said to contain the wood of 3,500 oaks, which in itself sounds astonishing. But the full significance of such a

*Continued on next page*

THE ASH
The ash is another tree native to Britain. It prefers a moist cool location but will grow almost anywhere. Easily recognised by its grey/olive bark and black velvety buds, it usually sheds its leaves in October, rather earlier than most trees. Its timber is at its best when the tree is 50 years old and is very strong and able to be manipulated into a variety of shapes. This shaping is usually done by steaming the wood, which is then used for such things as hockey sticks, carts, tool handles, barrels, oars and ladders. Often, an ash is cut back or 'pollarded', encouraging it to throw up straight boughs which are often cut to make oars.

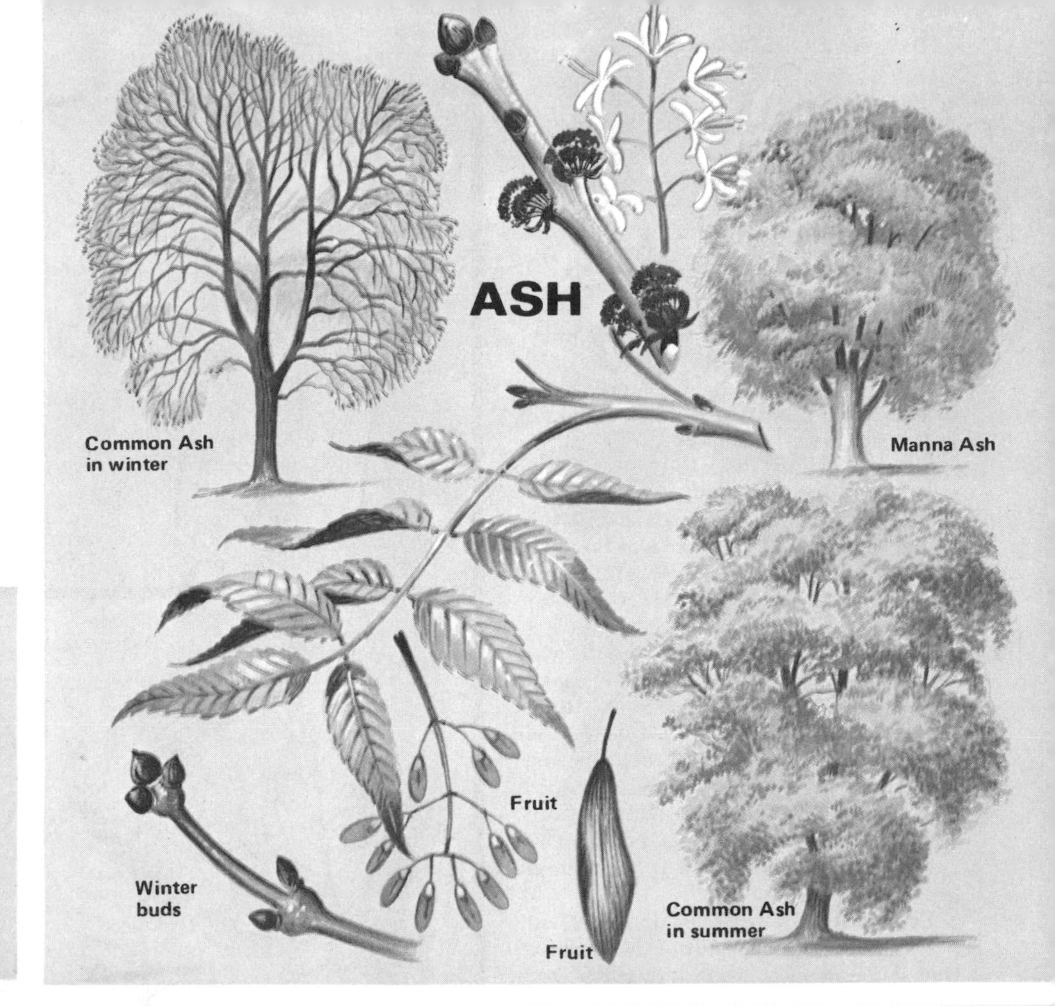


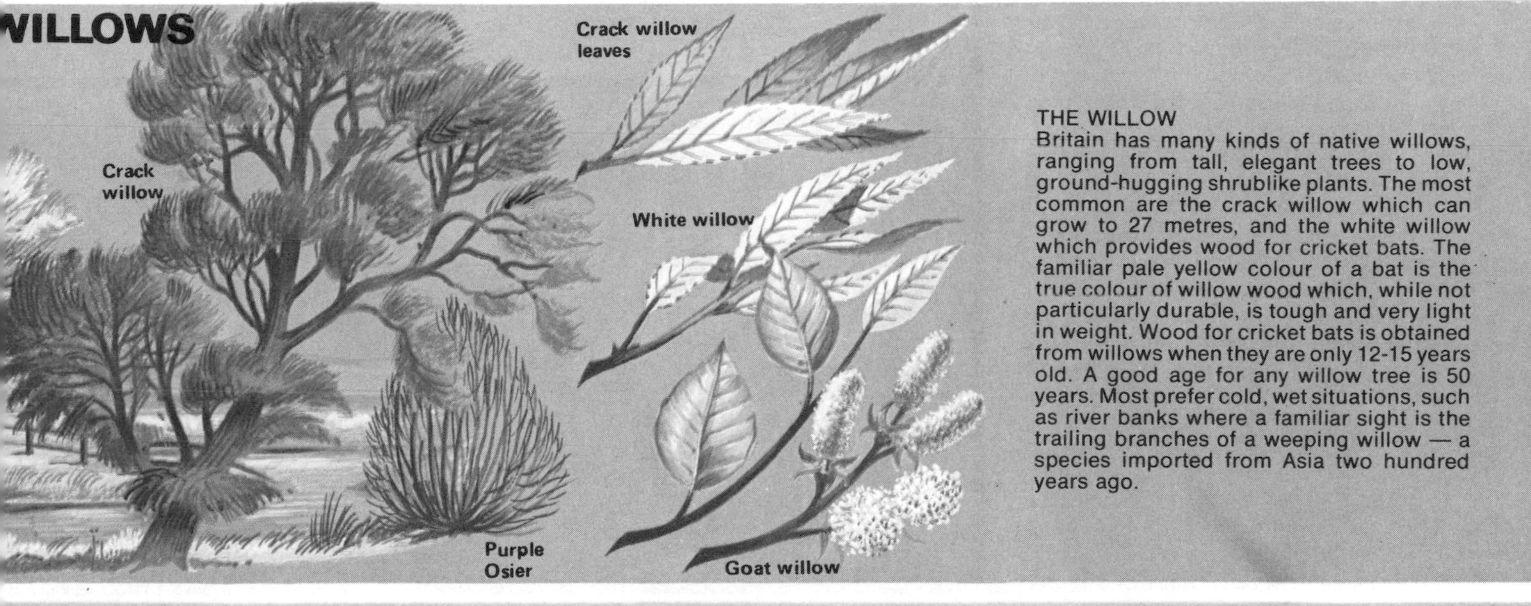


THE WILLOW
Britain has many kinds of native willows, ranging from tall, elegant trees to low, ground-hugging shrublike plants. The most common are the crack willow which can grow to 27 metres, and the white willow which provides wood for cricket bats. The familiar pale yellow colour of a bat is the true colour of willow wood which, while not particularly durable, is tough and very light in weight. Wood for cricket bats is obtained from willows when they are only 12-15 years old. A good age for any willow tree is 50 years. Most prefer cold, wet situations, such as river banks where a familiar sight is the trailing branches of a weeping willow — a species imported from Asia two hundred years ago.

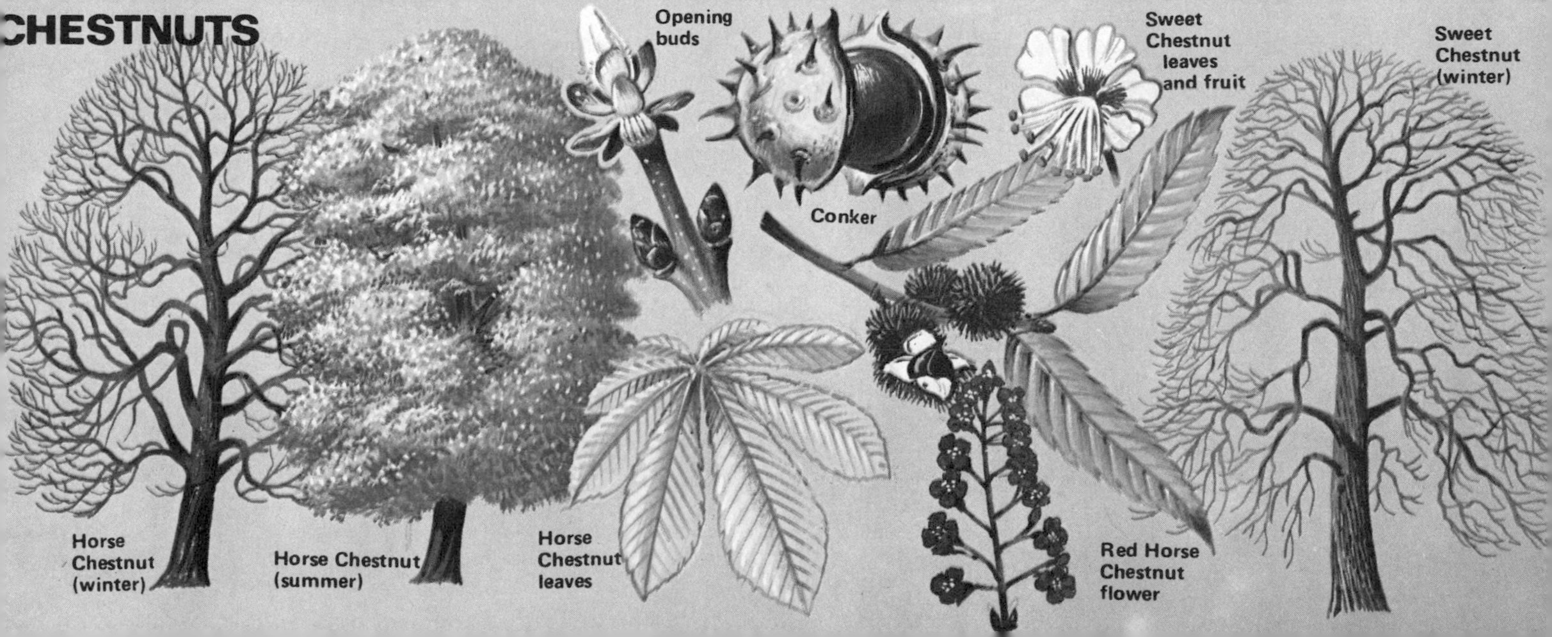

massacre does not sink in until you realise how slowly an oak grows. Its timber is unsuitable for most purposes until it has grown for two hundred years! Yet, despite the terrific demand for this prized wood over the years, the oak is still the most numerous of England's trees.

Of the non-native species, the horse chestnut is one of the most common. Adorning city parks with its brilliant display of white, candle-like flowers in May, it litters the ground with nuts or 'conkers' in the autumn.

One of the most distinctive features of the chestnut tree is its leaf, unmistakeable with its finger-like spread of five or seven leaflets clustered on a stalk. This is called a *compound* leaf as it has several parts. The leaves of most trees are less complex and are called *simple* leaves.

In describing the leaves of different trees, attention is paid to their shapes and to the nature of their edges. Some of the descriptive terms used are shown on the right. Whether a leaf is fat and tapering (heart-shaped) with fine sawlike edges (serrate) or round (oval) with smooth edges (entire), an *arborist*, or person who studies trees, can record it with great accuracy in words.

Leaves, of course, play an important part in determining the outline of an entire tree. Some leaves, even in summer, are so thinly spread that the branches can be seen through them. Others, such as the quarter of a million or so on a large oak, form a solid barrier, concealing most of the branches. When these trees shed their leaves, they assume startlingly new outlines, their branches revealed for the first time in months. Below, we show several trees in their winter guise. The pine, cypress and spruce are, of course, evergreens so their outlines remain virtually the same throughout the year.

As the winter comes to an end, each tree prepares to grow its next season's leaves. As the twigs and buds slowly burst into life, they, too, provide clues to the identity of each tree species. Each has its own type of bud with its own special shape.

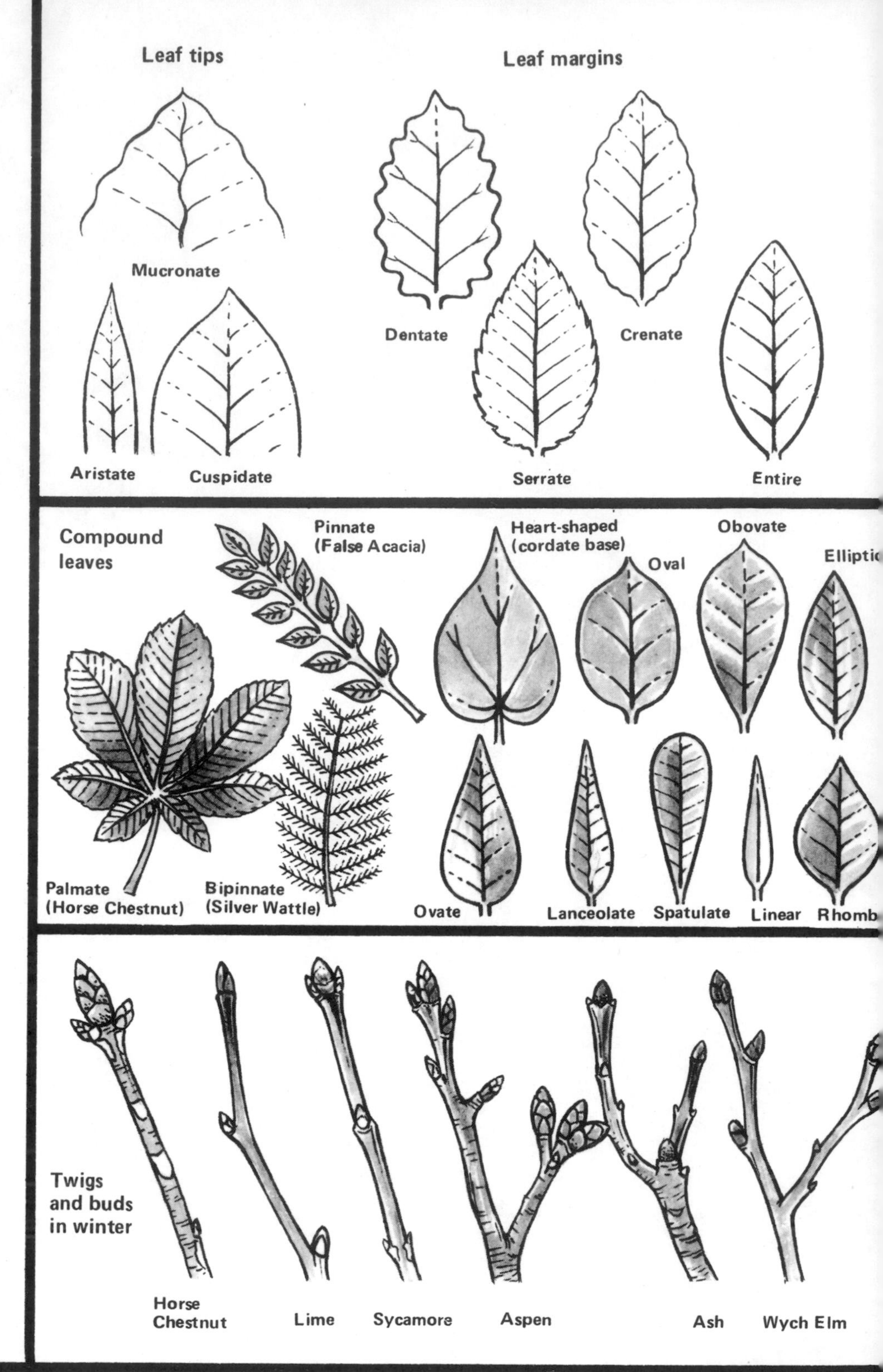


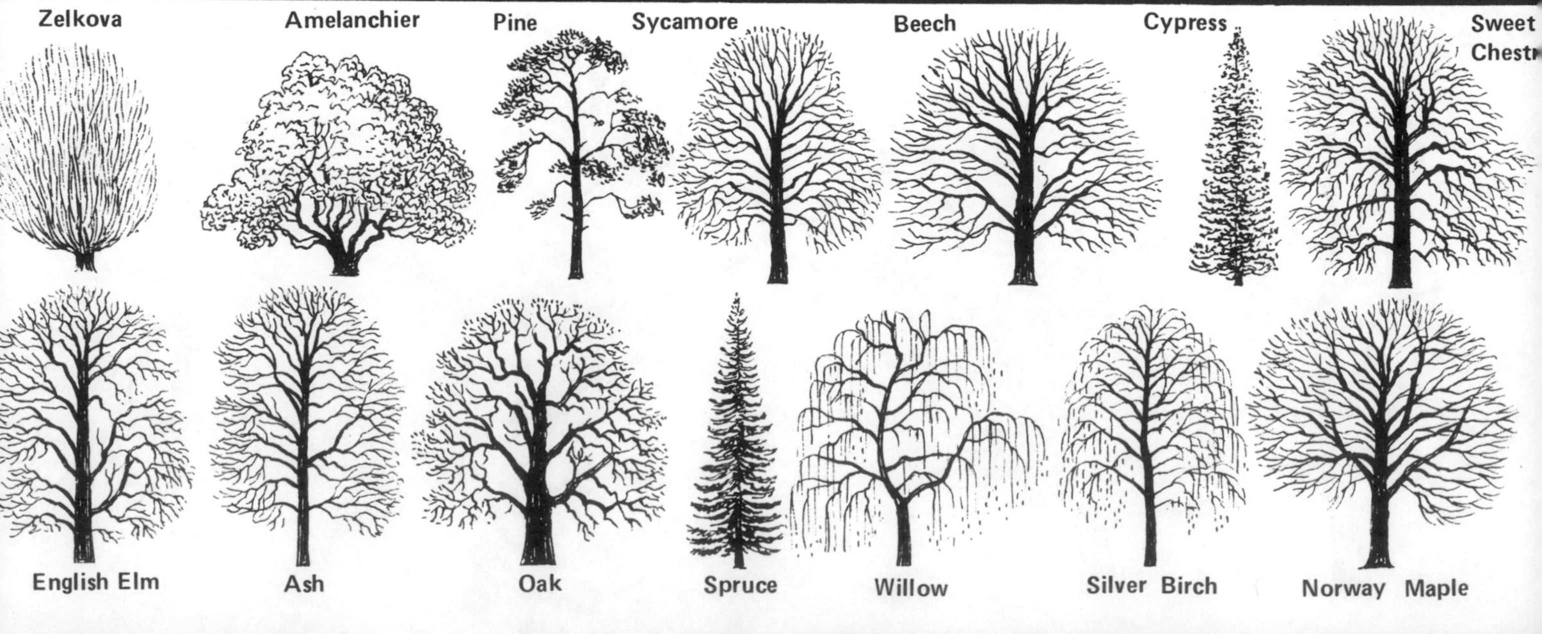

# What are the many uses of Wood?

## SCOTS PINE

SCOTS PINE
One of the hundred species of the pine family, the Scots pine is native to Britain. Grown mainly for timber production, its wood is referred to as *redwood*. Rich in resin and very strong, it is used in housebuilding (where it is called *deal*), fencing and for wood pulp.

## TEAK

TEAK
A large, deciduous tree, native to India, Burma and Thailand. Its wood is very hard and is used mainly for shipbuilding. The recent popularity of teak furniture has threatened to devastate Asia's vast natural teak forests as the trees are slow to reproduce.

**MOST houses contain some items of wooden furniture. That it is made of wood is taken for granted. But what kind of wood? Is that kitchen chair beech or oak? Is the hall stand mahogany or walnut? The answers will probably depend on when they were made and upon how rich you are — for wood is no longer a cheap material.**

Like any other material, wood has suffered over the centuries from the fickleness of fashion. But fashion is often dictated to by cost. Few of us are likely to own a genuine walnut dresser or a rosewood piano. The 'in' wood of today is pine — plentiful, highly functional, relatively inexpensive and pleasing to the modern eye. Yet 200 years ago, the sight of a pine dining table would have raised howls of derision. For in those days, walnut was king.

From being made chiefly of oak in Elizabethan times, Furniture makers have now experimented with the full range of woods at their disposal. Each wood — walnut, mahogany, sycamore, cherry, beech, elm and yew, to name just a few — has enjoyed a spell of popularity. Some have become too costly to use in making solid furniture so they are used to veneer cheaper items of furniture. But although fashions may change, wooden furniture in whatever guise is here to stay.

## MAHOGANY

MAHOGANY
First discovered in the West Indies, these elegant trees provide a very durable wood, red in colour and capable of taking a very high polish. True mahogany trees flourish in wet tropical forests and can be found today in the Americas, especially British Honduras. But, as with teak, the popularity of mahogany for furniture making has meant a scarcity of the wood. 'Mahogany' has, therefore, come to describe woods from other species such as Spanish and Australian cedars.

## ROSEWOOD

ROSEWOOD
The term 'rosewood' is used to describe several different kinds of ornamental timber. In Britain, however, it applies mainly to Brazilian rosewood which, because of its reddish-brown colour and its ability to take a high polish, is much in demand by cabinet makers and piano manufacturers. The rosewood tree, a large, deciduous plant, seldom provides great slabs of timber as the heartwood is usually decayed before the tree reaches maturity.

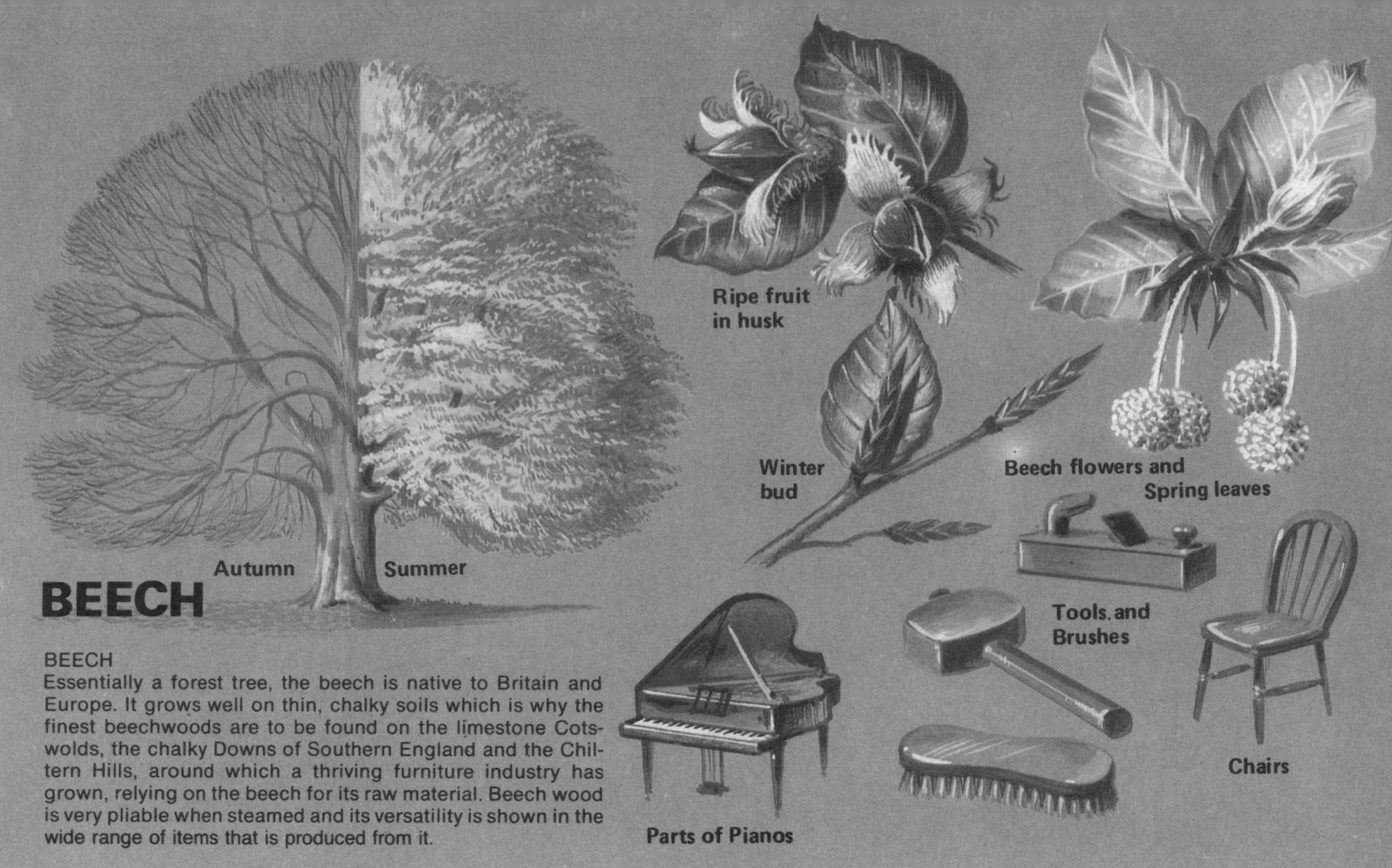


BEECH
Essentially a forest tree, the beech is native to Britain and Europe. It grows well on thin, chalky soils which is why the finest beechwoods are to be found on the limestone Cotswolds, the chalky Downs of Southern England and the Chiltern Hills, around which a thriving furniture industry has grown, relying on the beech for its raw material. Beech wood is very pliable when steamed and its versatility is shown in the wide range of items that is produced from it.

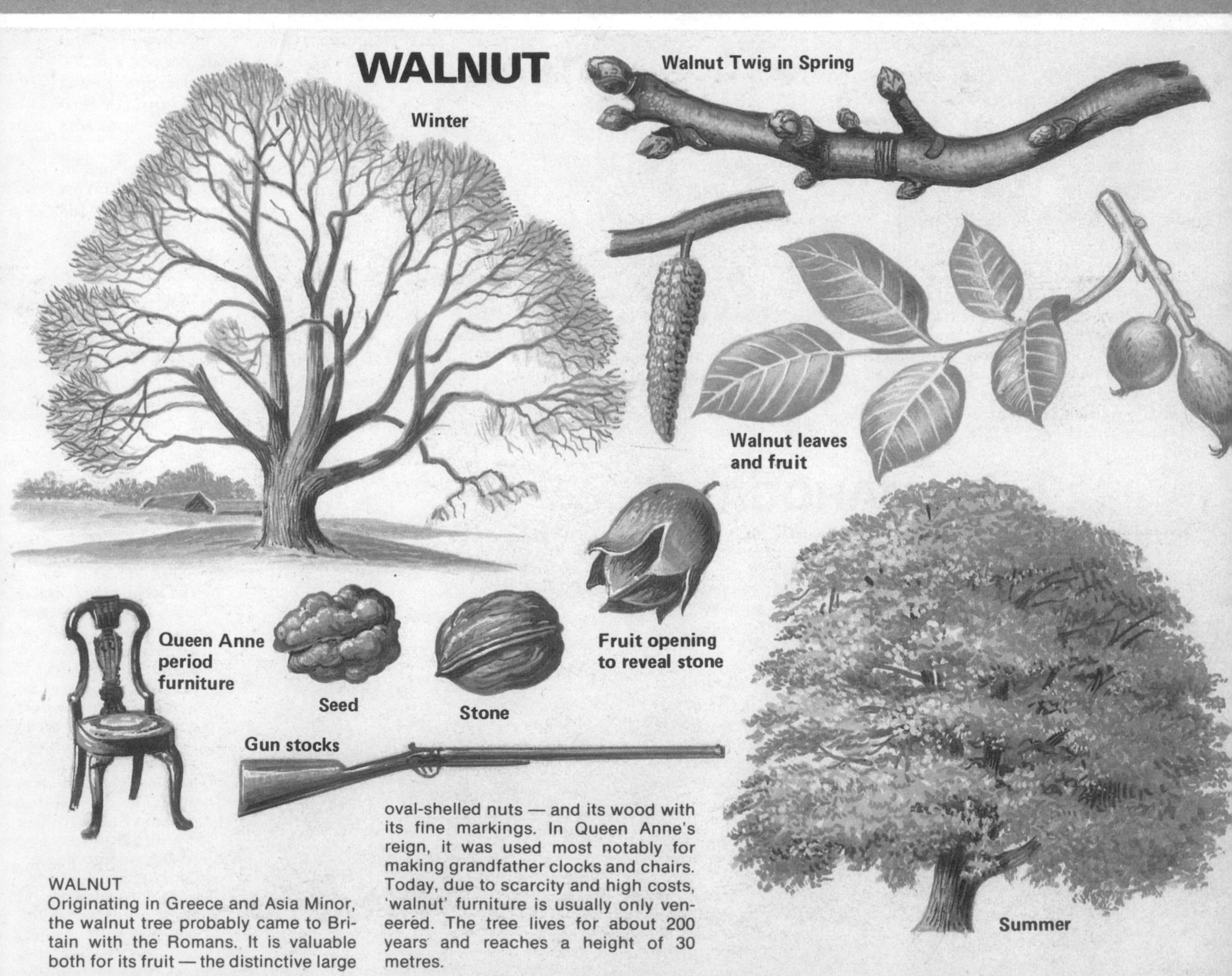


WALNUT
Originating in Greece and Asia Minor, the walnut tree probably came to Britain with the Romans. It is valuable both for its fruit — the distinctive large oval-shelled nuts — and its wood with its fine markings. In Queen Anne's reign, it was used most notably for making grandfather clocks and chairs. Today, due to scarcity and high costs, 'walnut' furniture is usually only veneered. The tree lives for about 200 years and reaches a height of 30 metres.

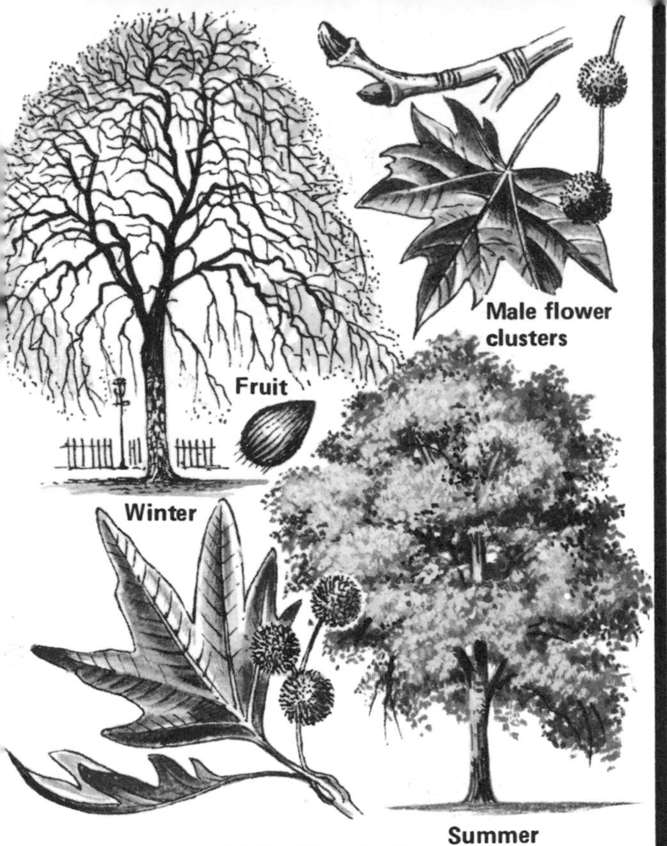


# PLANE

PLANE
In Britain, the London plane is the most commonly grown member of this tree family. Fast-growing and capable of reaching a height of 35 metres, it thrives in cities because of its resistance to pollution. What helps it to sift vital oxygen from our fume-filled city air is its method of shedding bark. The tree sheds its dead bark in irregular patches and this gives its trunk and branches their characteristic yellow, olive and green blotchy appearance. The bark itself is smooth and thin.

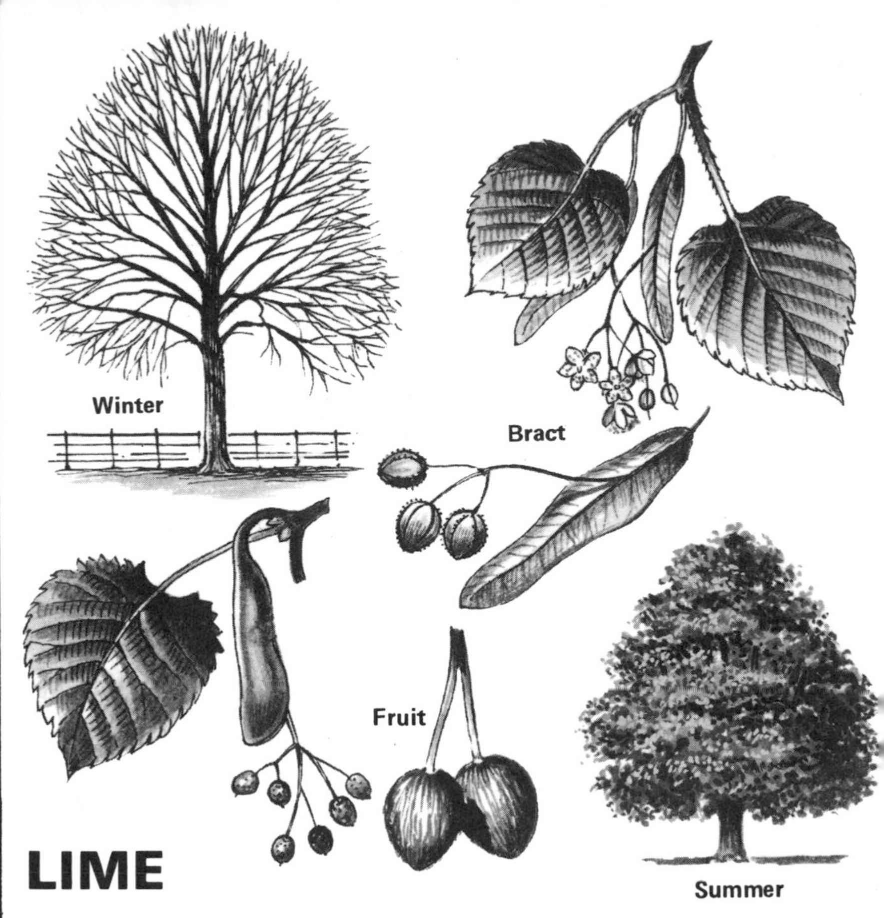


# LIME

LIME
There are 300-400 species in the lime family, most of them found in warm, tropical zones. Those limes which are found growing in cooler Northern regions are not citrus fruit bearers — the type which provide us with the lime juice to drink. Instead, our lime trees bear small nutlike fruits. Stately, imposing trees, sometimes over 40 metres tall, they are often seen growing along the verges of our streets or in large estates. Britain has two rare native limes — the broad-leaved lime and the small-leaved lime. The creamy-white wood is ideal for carving. Grinling Gibbons (1648-1720), the famous English wood carver and sculptor, used it a lot. It is also used for making piano keys, although much of it goes to making wood pulp for the paper industry.

# YEW

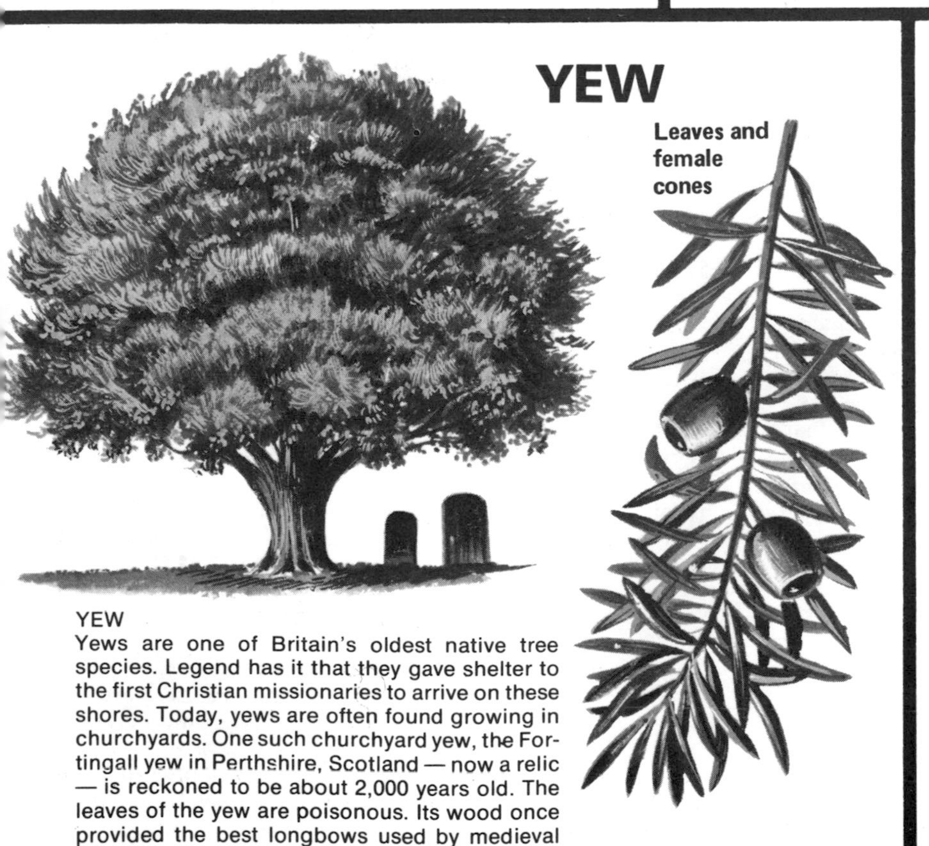


YEW
Yews are one of Britain's oldest native tree species. Legend has it that they gave shelter to the first Christian missionaries to arrive on these shores. Today, yews are often found growing in churchyards. One such churchyard yew, the Fortingall yew in Perthshire, Scotland — now a relic — is reckoned to be about 2,000 years old. The leaves of the yew are poisonous. Its wood once provided the best longbows used by medieval archers.

# HOLLY

HOLLY
One of our few native evergreens, the holly tree brightens up the forest in winter with its scarlet berries, so attractive to birds such as wood pigeons and starlings seeking food. Usually small and bush-like, it can reach a height of 15 metres, although it grows very slowly. Partly because of its religious associations, it has long been popular as an indoor decoration — its blood-red berries and spiky leaves being linked by legend with Christ's Crucifixion.

# What Animals live in the Arctic Ocean?

**THE Arctic Ocean is a vast and forbidding ice-sea surrounding the North Pole. Unlike the Antarctic, it is all ice, perpetual ice. In deepest winter fingers of solid pack ice reach south to the Arctic Circle. Within its boundary night is continuous.**

That is until spring, when light and warmth from the sun break up the frozen waste into ice-floes and icebergs, revealing dark patches of islands, and the cliffs and beaches of the northernmost parts of Canada, Alaska, Scandinavia, and Siberia.

With the spring comes life. There are no penguins in the Arctic, but their place in Nature is taken by members of the auk family, a group of birds that 'fly' equally well in the air or under the water. The colourful, red, yellow and blue-striped triangular beak is easily recognised in the comical puffin or sea parrot (2 and 10).

During late March and April, when these little birds flock to the cliff tops, this multi-purpose bill may be used for excavating nest burrows in the soft sea-cliffs, brandished as a weapon in the inevitable territorial squabbles that break out in the overcrowded colonies, displayed as an enticement to attract a mate, and used as a fish catcher during frequent dives below the waves. The chicks, fluffy black-and-white balls of down, have an insatiable appetite. Instead of swallowing the fish and regurgitating them at the nest, parent puffins are able to keep 20 or so fish dangling in their beaks, yet still dive and catch more, without dropping the rest. How they do it is a mystery.

Often joining the puffins on the inaccessible sea-cliffs, safe from marauding predators, are the fulmar petrels (1). Looking like miniature albatrosses in flight, they soar, with long, narrow wings on updraughts of air, occasionally swooping down to the sea surface to scoop up squid, sand eels and young herring. Their summer nests are precariously perched on ledges and crevices on the vertical cliff-faces which they approach with tails fanned out to act as stabilising rudders in order to land safely. The fulmar gets its name from 'foul-bird', for its defence against intruders is to spit a foul-smelling, sticky, warm oil. The more vulnerable chicks can spit further and with greater accuracy than can the parent birds. The oil, which has the aroma of very strong cod-liver oil, is secreted from the lining of the stomach, and is more usually used in preening and waterproofing the bird's delicate plumage.

To reach the Arctic breeding grounds some birds will have travelled thousands of kilometres across the world. The champion migrant is the Arctic tern (11), which may have flown 18,000 km non-stop from the Antarctic in the south to the Arctic in the north. Even more amazing than the distance it flies is that it is able to accurately locate the same breeding site every year; an incredible feat of navigation. In a way, Arctic terns enjoy two summers, and are probably the only birds that see nearly continuous sunlight throughout the year.

One of the resident birds hunting overhead, both day and night, is the snowy owl (3). It will be on the look out for prey on the ground or out on the flat expanse of ice. A herd of musk ox (5), large woolly mammals related more closely to goats than cattle, have little to fear. But a small group of lemmings (8), caught out in the open while trying to swim across a patch of open water during migration, might have to quickly seek protection on a small ice floe.

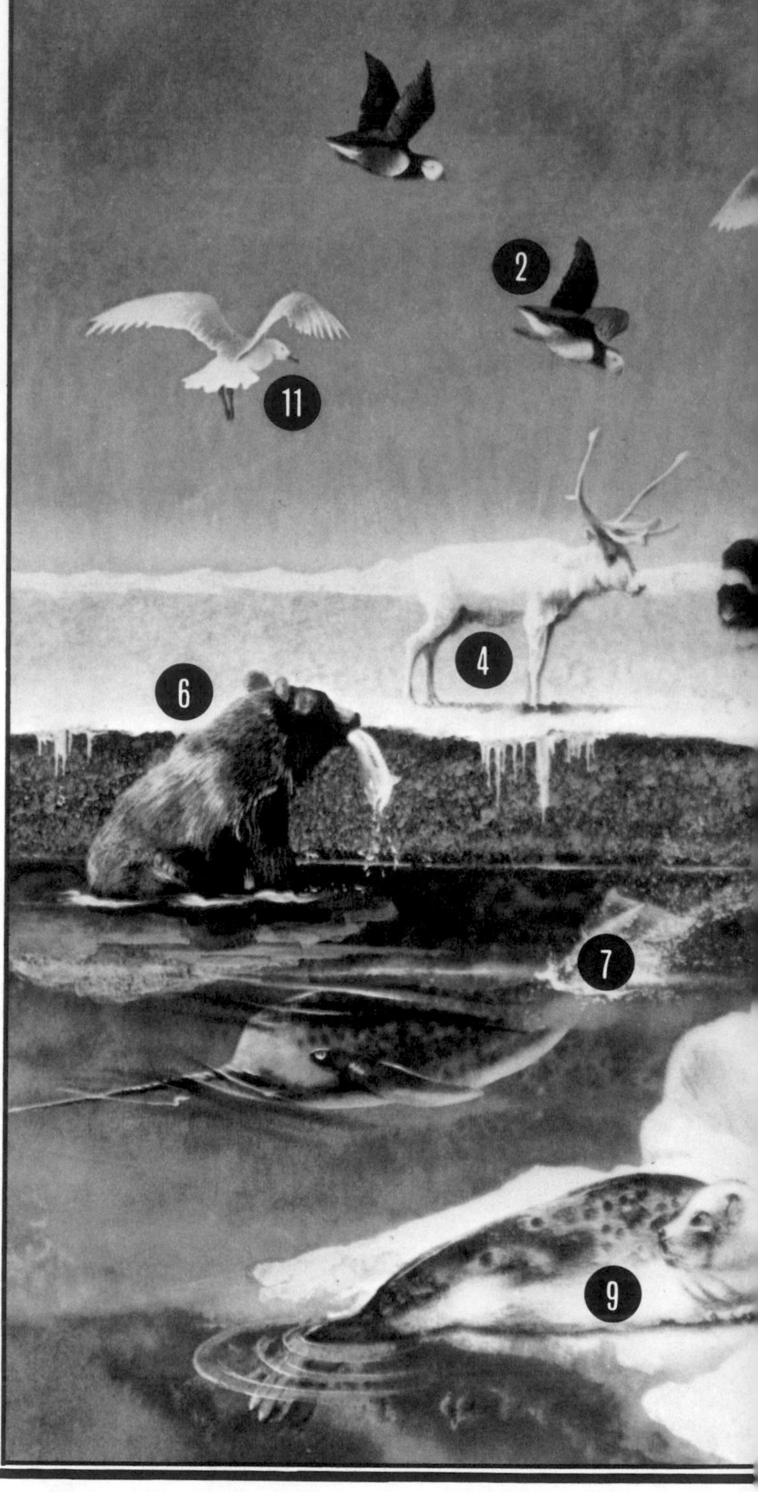


Many of the Arctic animals, both large and small, are good swimmers. The great herds of migrating caribou (4) often cross icy rivers. Their broad hooves, adapted primarily for walking across soft snow, are also helpful in swimming. Herds, consisting of thousands of individuals, trek northwards across the tundra, following well-worn paths and trails, and covering 30 kilometres a day.

## One tonne of bear

Often found immersed in rivers and coastal waters, swimming and fishing, are the brown bears (6). One type, the Alaskan Kodiak bear, can weigh up to a tonne, and stand 3.6 metres above the ground. It is the largest terrestrial carnivore living on Earth, and although primarily a land-lubber it will enter the water when hunting fish. One swipe from its claws may hook a tasty, wriggling salmon.

But the most common bear in the Arctic is the polar bear (12); truly a marine mammal. More streamlined than the brown bear, and better insulated with 8 centimetres of fat and huge fur-covered feet that can double as paddles and clubs, it is equally at home hunting across ice or under the water. Surprise is the polar bear's secret weapon, not speed. A sleeping seal is approached with caution, the bear swimming just below the surface, raising its head occasionally to breathe and check the distance. On reaching the victim, it silently leaves the water and crushes the seal's head with one mighty blow from its massive forepaw.

Common or harbour seals (9) form the bulk of the polar bear's diet. They tend to spend more time in shallow water, or lolling about on beaches or icebergs. Although slow and vulnerable on land, they are more than a match for predators below the surface. They swim fast, dive deep, and are capable of amazing agility in the pursuit of fast swimming fish.

The largest fin-footed mammal from the Arctic Ocean is the walrus (13). Enormous groups of walrus congregate together, following the ice south in winter and back north again in summer. Both sexes have tusks, but the males' grow larger, sometimes one metre long. The tusks, which are oversized canine teeth, are thought to have a multitude of functions. Using them as a pick, a walrus can stir up the sea-bed to whittle out the burrowing molluscs that it likes to eat. Tusks can also be used for defence, to make holes in the ice, and as an aid to hauling one tonne of quivering blubber out of the water and onto a rocky beach. The unforgettable walrus face also has a well-developed, prickly moustache of sensitive whiskers, important when digging about on the sea bottom.

## Unicorn whales

Another bizarre Arctic creature is the narwhal or unicorn whale (7). Its three metre-long, single horn is, in fact, an elongated and twisted, left canine tooth. It is found only in the male and is thought to be associated with courtship battles between rival males during the breeding season. Recent studies suggest that narwhals fight with their horns like duelling fencers.

The single horn gave rise to stories that the narwhal was connected in some way with the mythical horse, the unicorn, and in medieval times it was worth considerable amounts of money. It was attributed with all manners of powers including the ability to cure all ills, and to neutralise poisons. Fortunately for the narwhal, people now know better, and the creature is more or less left in peace.

# What Animals live at the Pole of Cold?

**AT the 'Pole of Cold', a high and desolate plateau in the Eastern Antarctic, the temperature can plummet to −80°C and savage, biting winds can reach speeds of over 300 km/h. Without doubt, the Antarctic is the coldest and windiest place on Earth.**

Unlike the Arctic far to the north, the Antarctic is formed on solid rock, and with an average height of nearly 2,000 m it is the world's highest continent. Concentrations of cold, dense air forming high in the mountains accelerate down the steep coastal slopes, whipping up razor-sharp ice crystals that sting painfully on exposed skin. Covering the rock is a centuries-old blanket of ice, sometimes as much as five kilometres deep.

Some 90 per cent of the world's snow and ice lies in Antarctica, equivalent to all the rain and snow that has fallen all over the world during the last 50 years. If it melted, the global sea-level would rise by more than 50 m and most of New York, London and the Netherlands would disappear below the waves!

Throughout the year, Antarctica has sub-zero temperatures but during the short summer months the ice melts in places to reveal 'nunataks' or isolated mountain-tops protruding through the ice, and patches of rocks and gravel along beaches on the coast. Little lives permanently in the Antarctic. There are no trees or ferns, only two flowering plants — a sea pink and a grass — and some mosses and lichens. The largest permanently resident land animal is a simple midge, less than one centimetre long.

In the sea it is a different story. The rich life of the Antarctic is to be found leaping and diving in the vast Southern Ocean or flying and swooping over the wave tops, scooping food from the surface waters.

The largest of all sea birds, the Wandering Albatross (number 1 on our large colour picture), with its long, narrow, pointed wings (over 3 metres across) soars on rising currents of air. Their wanderings are linked to the movement and distribution of plankton, the microscopic plant and animal life that floats in the upper layers of the sea and on which all the larger creatures depend for food.

Once every two years they abandon their solitary life, arriving at beaches on the Antarctic islands for breeding. With their webbed feet dangling below as air brakes, they land clumsily, often overshooting their target, and crashing in a heap of flying feathers!

With wings outstretched and head thrown back the male then courts the female. In the nest, a small mound scraped together with the bill, a single large egg is laid. Young albatrosses hatch after two months incubation and are fed by the parents for a further three months until they grow larger and fatter than the adult birds themselves. Then they are left alone for another three months, living on their reserves of fat, until they are ready to fly away. The young birds will not return to the breeding sites for six years.

Only 17 species of birds actually nest

Key on following page

on the Antarctic mainland. The rest seek out the many surrounding islands with their slightly milder climates.

The Gentoo Penguin (8), with a conspicuous white patch on the top of the head, and the yellow-crested Rockhopper Penguin spend most of their life at sea, chasing and feeding on small fish. Their wings, perfectly adapted as flippers for underwater movement, propel these little penguins through the water at 25 km/h on long journeys and twice that on short bursts. To breathe, they leap periodically out of the water like porpoises.

During the southern spring the Gentoos and Rockhoppers come ashore. They hop, waddle or toboggan on their bellies inland to their breeding sites where several thousand birds may gather. Their noise and the stench of their droppings is incredible.

Two eggs are usually deposited in a makeshift mound of pebbles that serves as a nest. Both males and females incubate the eggs and also both rear the fluffy-down chicks. Breeding is completed in three months in order to beat the oncoming winter.

The larger King Penguins (5), on the other hand, have their breeding period in deepest winter and it takes six months to complete. The female lays a single egg which is quickly transferred to the male. He begins incubating it under a flap of abdominal skin where it is out of harm's way from the bitter, scouring winds. Each of the pair then take it in turn either to feed-up at sea or rear the chick.

The larger chicks, having outgrown their snug parental hidey-hole, huddle together in nurseries protected from the winter blizzards by a ring of adults. In spring the adults, followed by the chicks, return to the sea. But there danger lurks.

Waiting for the young penguins to make their first sortie is a three metre-long, mottled-grey Leopard Seal (6), the only seal that regularly eats warm-blooded animals. Together with the Killer Whale, it is the main predator in the Southern Ocean. An unfortunate penguin caught in the water is brought to the surface, shaken violently to death, and gulped down headfirst.

The other seals of the Antarctic waters are a little more docile, feeding on fish, crabs and squid. Several species of southern Fur Seals (3) are to be found breeding along the rocky shores and shingle beaches of the islands. Harems of breeding cows (females) are grouped together under the charge of a dominant bull (male). Calves born this year are the result of last year's mating.

Fur Seals get their name from the two layers of hair that cover the body, a short, velvet-like undercoat and a longer, coarser outer layer. The males have a thick bushy mane around their neck and the combination of blubber-fat and bubbles trapped in the fur acts as insulation against the near-freezing sea water.

The Elephant Seals (7), though, are nearly all blubber. They may weigh as much as two tonnes and are the largest members of the seal family, with bulls reaching six metres in length. Elephant Seals, too, come to the beaches to breed. The bulls arrive first, announcing their right to a particular stretch of the foreshore by snorting loudly.

Other bulls challenge the territory and vicious chest-to-chest battles ensue. Eventually one backs down with the victor becoming supreme beachmaster. The beachmaster gathers about him a harem of smaller female seals and spends the entire summer tending to their needs, defending the borders of his territory, fighting off rival young pretenders to his title and mating with the cows; and all this without food.

The calves, however, grow fast. They put on 9 kg every 24 hours. Elephant Seal milk is said to be the richest of any animal food, being 80% fat. When breeding is finished, the adults head for the sea first, only to return a few weeks later in order to moult. Then the group splits up, each individual slipping away, not to be seen again until breeding time next year. Where they all go nobody knows.

Both Elephant Seals and the Fur Seals were exploited for their blubber and fur. The prospect of two barrels of oil from a mature bull Elephant Seal and the first-class pelt of a Fur Seal once meant near extinction for these helpless creatures. Unsuspecting seals were battered or shot by the mid-nineteenth century seal hunters. Some cubs were clubbed and stripped of their fur even while still alive.

Today we are equally ruthless, but the victim is the last animal in our picture — the whale. Swimming effortlessly in the Southern Ocean, feeding on krill (shrimp-like creatures) and small fish which it sieves out of the water through rows of balleen plates which line the mouth, is the Fin Whale or Common Rorqual (2). It is the largest whale after the Giant Blue Whale, and shares with it the attributes of being the gentlest and least offensive of all the large animals.

Yet, hunting has reduced the Fin Whale to a quarter of its estimated original population. Each whale is hit by an explosive harpoon and the water foams red. The whale turns over and, after half-an-hour, it dies. Whales are still being hunted today despite increasing world pressure for this to stop, as it surely must if we are to save these wonderful creatures.

At present, Antarctica is protected by an international treaty, in an attempt to keep the continent intact. But the discovery of potential mineral wealth, the prospect of oil and coal on the mainland, and the realisation that the krill of the Southern Ocean may be a valuable food source, now threatens the Antarctic's existence as the last really wild place on Earth.

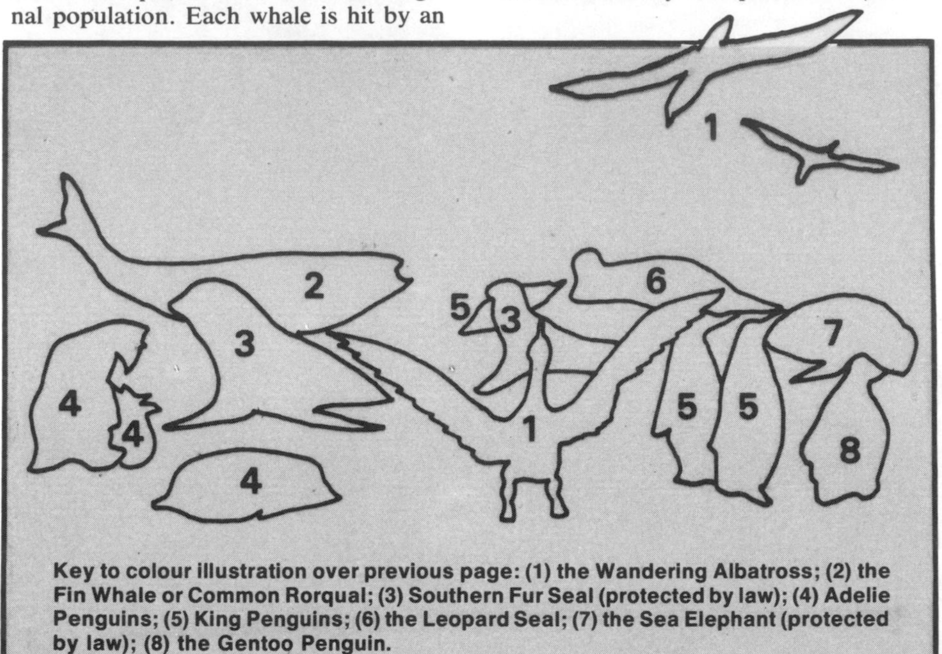


Key to colour illustration over previous page: (1) the Wandering Albatross; (2) the Fin Whale or Common Rorqual; (3) Southern Fur Seal (protected by law); (4) Adelie Penguins; (5) King Penguins; (6) the Leopard Seal; (7) the Sea Elephant (protected by law); (8) the Gentoo Penguin.

Above: Emperor Penguins are the largest of all penguins, reaching well over one metre in height. Their breeding pattern is similar to that of King Penguins with the hatching carried out entirely by males, who gather together in groups to protect the eggs from the fierce cold of the Antarctic winter. Incubation takes about 63 days during which time the male takes no food and loses up to a third of his weight. The female returns after hatching but often, apparently, has difficulty in finding her mate and offspring. Emperor Penguins are thought to be the deepest diving of all birds — down to over 250 m. They are also said to be able to remain underwater for as long as 18 minutes without coming up for air. Their antics often provide amusement for scientists working in this harsh land!

# Why are Worms important to us?

**AN earthworm, lying stranded on the road, or turned up by a garden fork seems a helpless, insignificant enough creature. Yet without him and his kin, human civilisation would not only be poorer, it would be impossible.**

Nothing lush can grow on rock or chalk or gravel. There must be fertile top-soil to produce the abundant vegetation which is vital for Man's existence.

Earthworms are nature's own cultivators of the soil. They transform animal and vegetable waste, particularly dead leaves and plants, into rich humus. They turn natural minerals into soluble plant food. They break up the earth, allowing water to drain through.

In short, they are the first husbandmen, and still the most important.

From the Greek philosopher Aristotle to the English biologist Darwin, and again in the present day, men have appreciated the humble earthworm's place in the scheme of things, but never fully enough.

In a world that is speedily losing its soil fertility through over-cropping, mismanagement and erosion, it is time to take stock again of the worm's true value. Kill off the worms, and the soil will lack constantly renewed fertility. Encourage and preserve them, and the crops will remain satisfactory.

The earthworm is a member of a wide and varied family of primitive creatures called Annelida. The worm can vary in size throughout the world — in fact one collected in the Transvaal of South Africa measured 6.70 m — but the body structure

*continued on next page*

**The earthworm moves its body a bit at a time, anchoring some parts by swelling muscles and stretching or pulling itself forward by thinning others.**

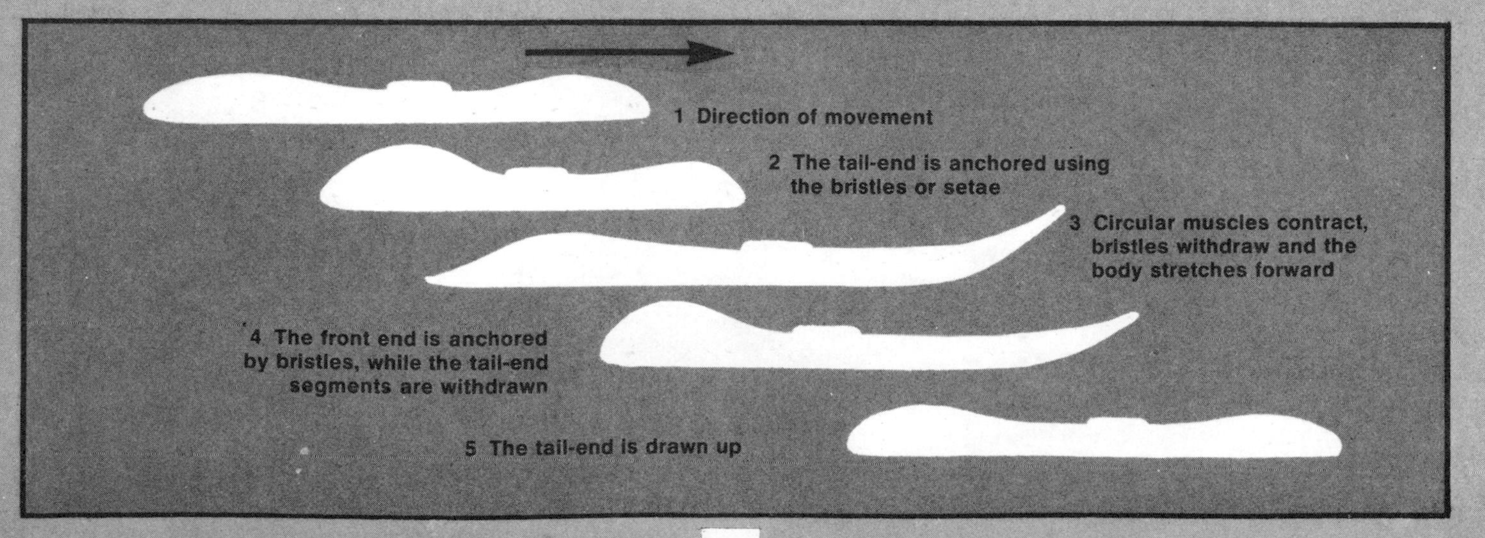

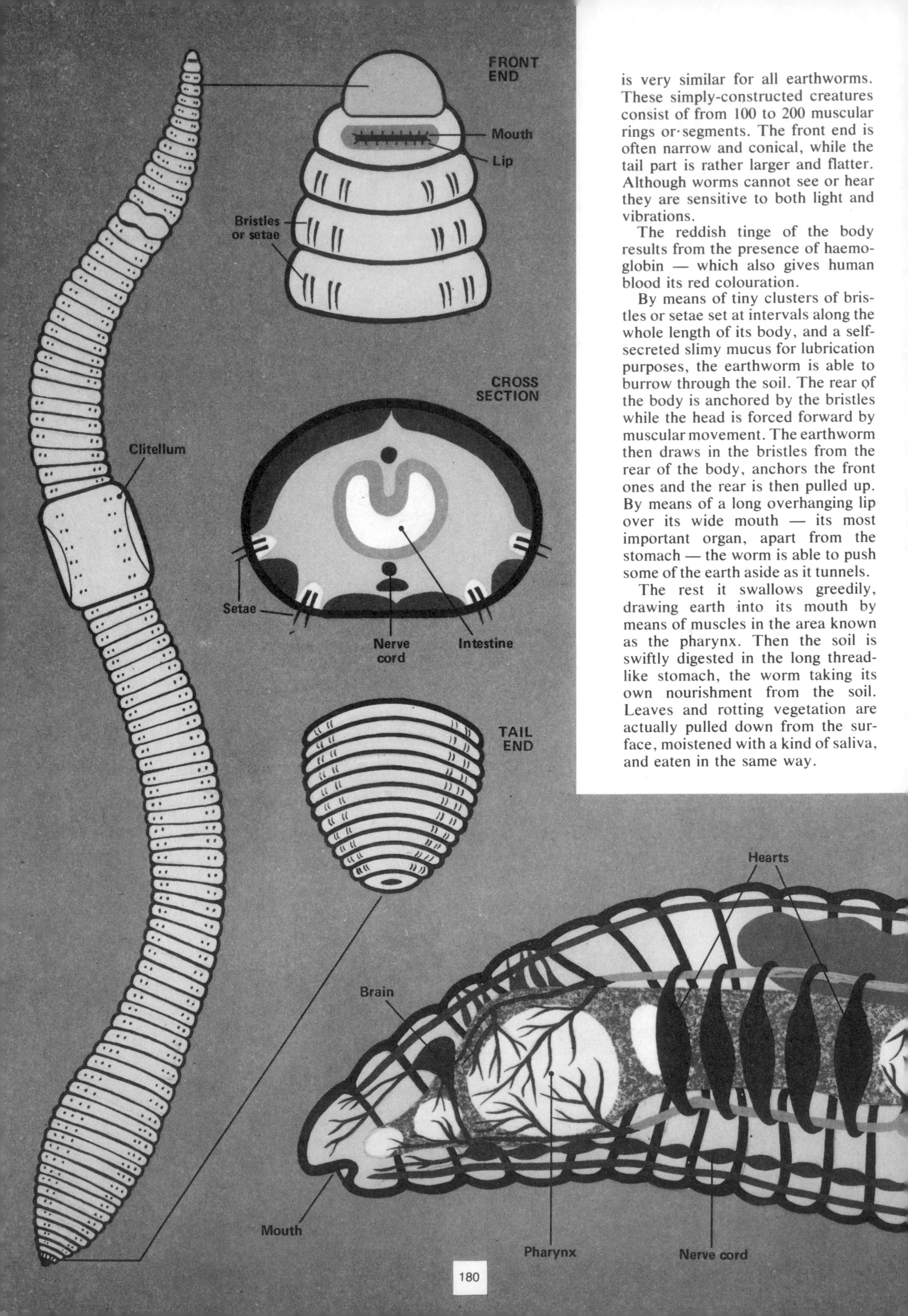


is very similar for all earthworms. These simply-constructed creatures consist of from 100 to 200 muscular rings or segments. The front end is often narrow and conical, while the tail part is rather larger and flatter. Although worms cannot see or hear they are sensitive to both light and vibrations.

The reddish tinge of the body results from the presence of haemoglobin — which also gives human blood its red colouration.

By means of tiny clusters of bristles or setae set at intervals along the whole length of its body, and a self-secreted slimy mucus for lubrication purposes, the earthworm is able to burrow through the soil. The rear of the body is anchored by the bristles while the head is forced forward by muscular movement. The earthworm then draws in the bristles from the rear of the body, anchors the front ones and the rear is then pulled up. By means of a long overhanging lip over its wide mouth — its most important organ, apart from the stomach — the worm is able to push some of the earth aside as it tunnels.

The rest it swallows greedily, drawing earth into its mouth by means of muscles in the area known as the pharynx. Then the soil is swiftly digested in the long thread-like stomach, the worm taking its own nourishment from the soil. Leaves and rotting vegetation are actually pulled down from the surface, moistened with a kind of saliva, and eaten in the same way.

The remaining soil, now very finely ground, is deposited on the surface in the form of the familiar 'worm-casts' which are the bane of tidy gardeners, bowling-green attendants and golfers.

## Rich soil

But these casts consist of pulverised, pre-digested soil which happens to be the richest in the world for growing anything in. Scientific tests show that it contains five times as much nitrate, seven times as much phosphorus, eleven times as much potash, three times the magnesium content and up to 50% more natural humus than ordinary soil. It is worth growing a few seedlings in worm-cast soil just to prove its richness.

And as the myriads of worms in the world, never resting or hibernating, digging deep in dry weather and nearer the top in wet, constantly produce this layer of cast soil, no wonder the earth has been fertile for thousands of years.

The sweetness of the Nile Valley, for so long the home of a civilisation, is owed to the hordes of hungry worms that wait each year for the huge flood of waste vegetable matter the river brings down at flood-time. The same is true of fertile areas all over the globe. Starting long before the advent of man on the earth, the lowly worm still tunnels, burrows and transforms in its primeval but vital way.

It would indeed be remarkable if man finally recognised the earthworm's immense importance by working with him, cultivating him instead of the soil, and relying on nature to do the rest. Remarkable, but by no means impossible.

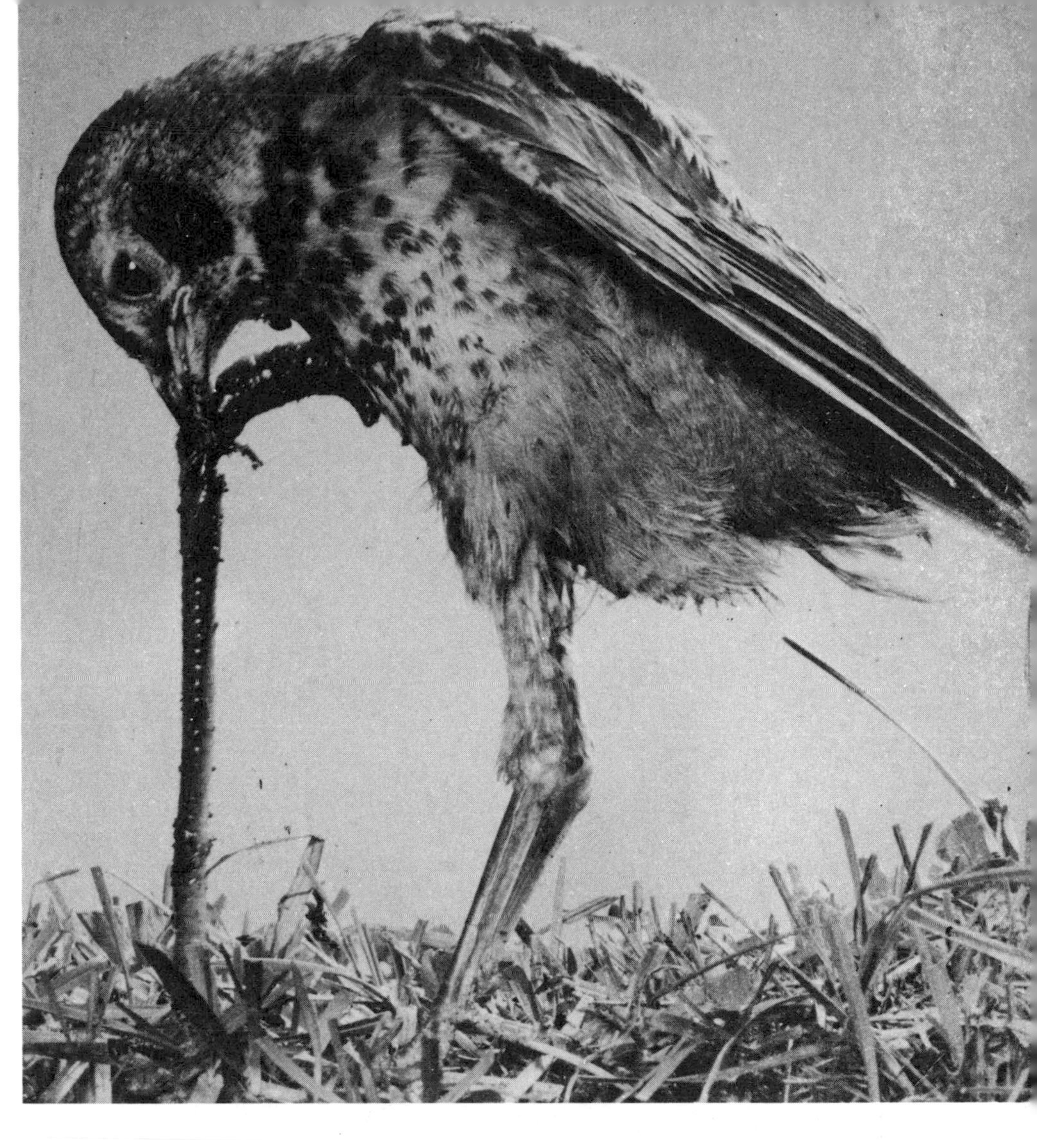

**A bird finds itself a tasty snack. When earthworms appear on the surface they are a prey to ever-ready birds.**

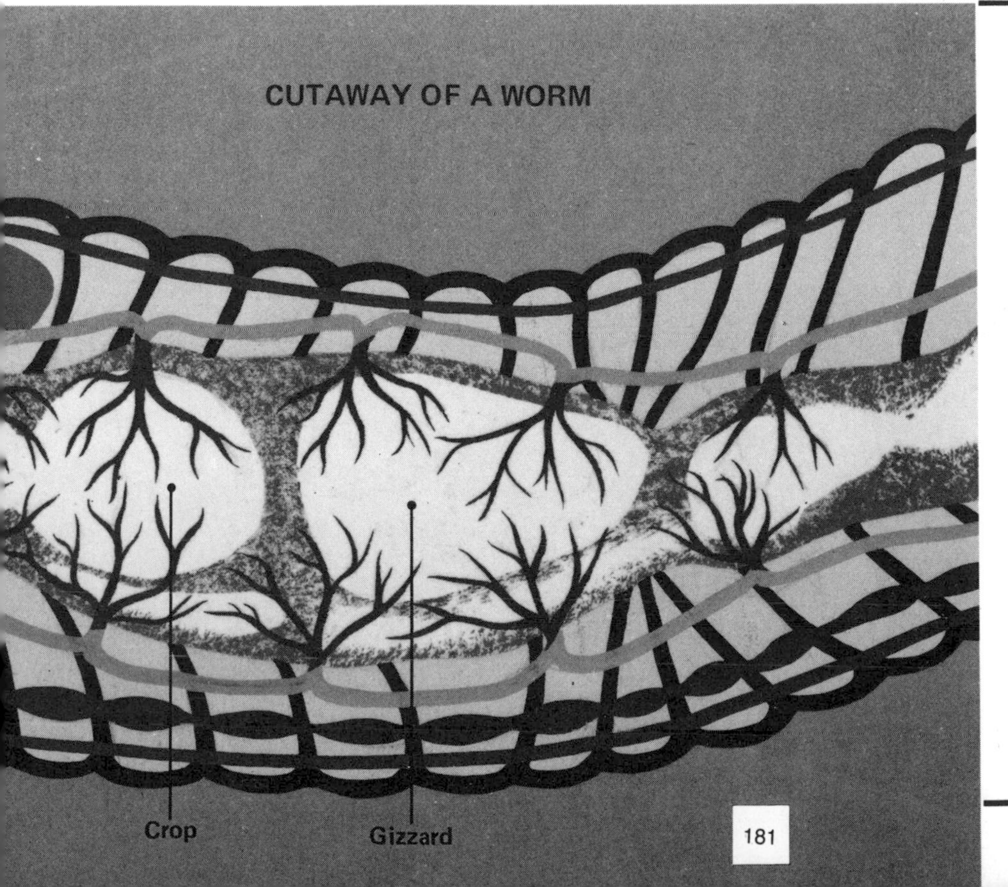


## PROFILE OF A WORM

**The common earthworm reaches a length of 20 cm (8 in) when fully grown. A casual glance shows that the body is made up of segments, which all seem to be the same. However, a closer inspection will reveal that one end, the front, is narrow and conical, and the other, the tail part, is larger and flatter.**

**A saddle-like bulge in the body wall, can be seen in the body of a mature worm. This structure, the clitellum, is connected with reproduction and egg laying and is more easily visible in the summer months.**

**The cutaway picture shows the digestive system. Food is drawn into the mouth by means of a muscular pharynx. From there it moves through a storage cavity, the crop, before arriving in the gizzard where it is broken down. Moving into the intestine the food is fully digested and then absorbed into the blood vessels.**

**Although cold-blooded the worm is by no means heartless. No less than five primitive hearts maintain blood circulation.**

# Who was the Prince of Botanists?

**CAROLUS LINNAEUS was one of the foremost scientists of the 18th century, and perhaps the most important biologist who ever lived. It was Linnaeus who first brought a scientific order to the naming and classification of all living things. His famous books —*Systema Naturae, Genera Plantarum* and *Bibliotheca Botanica* — are historic scientific works.**

Before Linnaeus, it was the practice everywhere to use only the common and local names for plants and animals. This meant chaos in the study of biology since a standard name did not exist for each species so that it could be recognised and identified by scientists everywhere in the world.

Linnaeus was born in Sweden in 1707. His father was a poor church curate living in the country who did not have enough money to give his son a formal education. However, as Carolus grew, his father took him for walks in the countryside he loved, pointing out flowers, their roots and seeds and various species of birds — fixing in the child's memory the Latin name for each.

The young Linnaeus never forgot what his father had taught him about the natural life of the countryside. Before long, he was to astound Swedish men of education with his explanation of the natural order of the world, and at 21 he wrote his first short book on the order of flowers. This made such an impact on the science of botany (the study of plants) that the following years came to be known of as the 'Linnean Age': a whole new understanding of plant life had been given to the world.

One person who recognised the early genius of Linnaeus was the head of the science department at Uppsala University, Professor Rudbeck. He invited Linnaeus to visit him so that they could plan a scientific expedition to the country's northernmost province of Swedish Lapland.

It was in bleak Lapland that Linnaeus saw wild flowers of the tundra that had never been recorded before, and here he watched rare Arctic birds nesting and rearing their young. He also studied the complete life-cycle of the reindeer on which the native Lapps depended for food and much of their way of life. Each night, by the light of flickering campfires, Linnaeus kept a journal of everything he had seen; by the end of the expedition he

had obtained more first-hand knowledge of living nature than any scientist before him.

After returning to Uppsala he methodically arranged all he had written and then lectured extensively on his discoveries. This brilliant work made it clear that Linnaeus was the greatest natural scientist the world had ever known.

Soon he began the monumental task of classifying his discoveries and scientific arguments in a truly logical order. Before Linnaeus, classification had been totally haphazard: plants were put together because they happened to be thorny, or had the same colour flowers or they were merely arranged alphabetically.

Linnaeus called his arrangement the *binomial* (two-name) *system*. The two names it referred to were the *genus* (the general name for related groups) and the *species* (for a specific group). The same basic system is in use today.

Its effectiveness can be measured by the fact that before it was used the number of types of bird listed in the world was over 25,000. The new system established that the true number was about 8,600 species. The same system was used for classifying plants. Latin was used for the system as this was the international language of science and learning. As a result, a scientist in one place could recognise a species referred to by any other scientist by its common Latin name.

Honours were now showered upon Linnaeus. The Queen of Sweden was one of his greatest admirers and he was made president of the Swedish Academy of Sciences. The famous University of Oxford offered him a major professorship.

However, Linnaeus was content with his appointment as Professor of Botany at Uppsala University. Here he organised a unique botanical garden where all the plants were arranged according to his new system as living examples to students. Admirers from all over the world sent rare specimens to stock the garden. The Tsarina of Russia sent him rare flowers from Siberia, and Swedish nobility helped him to obtain special collections of flowers from Asia.

Linnaeus never left Sweden, but devoted his spare time to visiting little-known areas of the country and studying their plant and animal life.

His students at the University were so enthralled by his teaching that at the end of their examinations each year they would march through the city chanting happily "Vivat Scientia! Vivat Linnaeus!" *Long live Science! Long live Linnaeus!*

When he died in 1778 he received the honour of burial at Uppsala Cathedral where his tomb carries the epitaph 'Prince of Botanists'. Today the name of Linnaeus lives on wherever sciences are taught for it was he who first gave a rational order to the enormity of plant and animal kingdoms.

# WORLD OF ADVENTURE

# Who were the Forty-Niners?

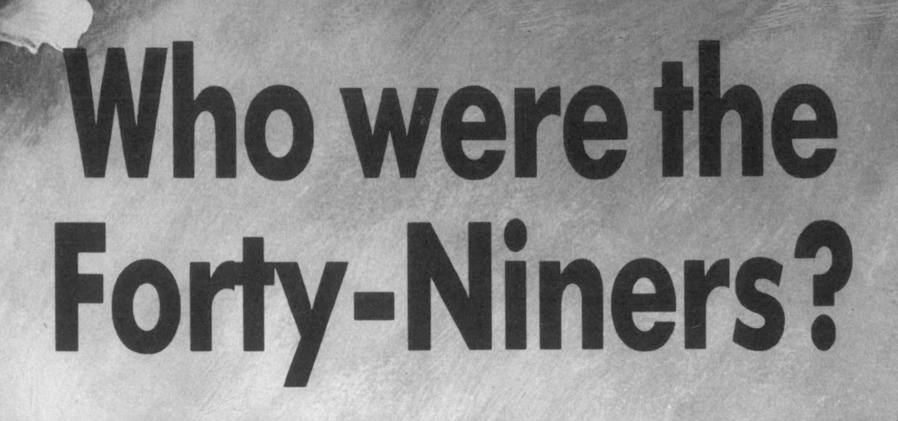

**A WILD-EYED man waving a bottle of gold dust raced down the main street of the tiny town of San Francisco, shouting as he ran: "Gold! Gold! Gold from the American River!"**

It was May 15, 1848, and soon there was madness in the air, madness that grew and grew as gold fever raged. One of those who lived through the insanity later recalled: "All went off to the mines, some on carts, some on horses, and some on crutches, and one went in a litter."

It was the start of the greatest gold rush of all, one that was to set California on its rocket-like rise to fabulous prosperity and to trigger off America's rise to world power. Yet because news — and people — travelled slowly in those days, it was not until 1849 that the world-wide stampede to California began. The Forty-Niners were on their way . . .

There had been a few small gold strikes before 1848, but none to match the historic one on January 24, 1848. It happened while a saw mill was being built on land belonging to a rich businessman, John Sutter, who had come to America from Switzerland. James Marshall, his head carpenter, was in charge of the work, which was taking place on the south fork of the American River, some way from Sutter's Fort, as Sutter's home was grandly called. Marshall made his find in the tail race — the water below the wheel.

"There upon the rock, about six inches beneath the surface of the water, I DISCOVERED THE GOLD. I was entirely alone at the time," he later recalled.

His discovery came at a fateful moment. The USA and Mexico had been at war, and the find came just a week before America officially gained California from Mexico at the peace treaty, the Americans having no conception of their luck.

Sutter swore his employees to secrecy, but it was useless. First rumours circu-

**Below: John Sutter (left) and his head carpenter, James Marshall by the saw mill where Marshall discovered gold on January 24, 1848. Both suffered from the discovery. Sutter was invaded by the gold rush and Marshall lost the pension given to him, due to heavy drinking. Marshall, however, did have a statue erected to him, after his death.**

**The madness of 'gold fever' spread like wild-fire (see above). People came from all over the world in the hope of making a quick fortune. Some did but the vast majority made little or nothing. The nation generally, though, prospered enormously.**

lated, then came the dash down the San Francisco street. The sprinter was a shrewd merchant named Sam Brannan who had stumbled on a talkative Sutter man.

Californians of Spanish descent were not so gold crazy as the local Americans. There were some 14,000 whites in all and only 1,000 took part in the very first rush, nearly all of them Americans. The rush became more and more frantic when lumps of more than 10 kilos were discovered.

Gradually, the news spread round the world. A pattern was set that kept repeating itself for half a century in America, Australia, New Zealand and South Africa. As soon as news of a gold strike broke, entire ships' crews deserted and raced to the goldfields. Office boys and others all over America, Britain and elsewhere left their work and raced for the docks. Everyone from model citizens to killers hit the trail. The vast majority would find little or no gold, but a very few would make huge fortunes.

Getting to California was hard. Some made long sea journeys from Hawaii, Australia, eastern America and Europe — Americans and Europeans having to round Cape Horn as there was then no Panama Canal. Sea voyages were usually safe but slow: other routes were anything but safe.

Thousands headed West across the Plains and the Rockies, many dying from disease, exhaustion, hunger and thirst, while some were killed by Indians. Few had any idea what crossing the American continent involved.

Others risked short cuts across Panama and Nicaragua through dense, steaming, fever-ridden jungles, and many died. The majority of those on every route were woefully ill-equipped, not only for long journeys but for the rugged life of a prospector.

Yet that first gold rush summer of 1848 before the hordes arrived was something of a paradise. There was little crime and a lot of gold. Under a blazing sun men panned for gold beside or in ice-cold streams. Others found it in crevices of rock, in the earth, or lying around.

However, few made real fortunes and some of those that did lost them in gambling sprees.

Sutter suffered from squatters invading his land and died before the Government got around to compensating him, while Marshall, the original finder, was not given a reward — a small pension — until the 1870s. A statue was erected to him by a grateful California *after* his death.

Those who made the most money were traders and businessmen who supplied goods to miners. One of them, an Italian named Ghiradelli, sold sweets and chocolates to miners and ended up a millionaire.

The biggest year of all was 1852 when 81 million dollars' worth of gold was found. San Francisco, whose population was 800 in 1848, was now a boom town, for it was where the money went. Crime was often rampant and had to be put down by vigilante groups. By the end of the century the total amount of gold found in California exceeded the 1,000 million dollars mark.

The losers in all this were the local Indians. There had been 100,000 of them in 1849 in California but, by 1860, there were only some 30,000 left. Few were warlike, unlike the warriors of the plains, and they were killed by violence, disease or overwork. As far as the miners were concerned, they were 'in the way'.

By 1900, mining in California had become very scientific. The easy pickings were gone and much of it happened to be deep underground.

There were always some miners to be seen panning (the pan is still used to this day) but other tools appeared in the 1850s, most of them improvements on the pan: the cradle (or rocker), the long tom and the sluice. Great jets of water were used to blast hillsides into giving up gold-bearing matter. Yet the pan had one unique advantage. It was the only way of preventing the smallest particles of gold from disappearing.

As for the miners, most of them drifted away after their great adventure, but a hard core remained who sought gold all their life, and silver as well. Some of those who went to California in 1849 were to be found heading northwards on the Klondike Stampede in 1898, having taken in a dozen other rushes in between.

They did not think of themselves as having made history, but they had. Not only had gold made California and the nation prosper hugely, it had speeded up the process of westward expansion. In 1848, the United States virtually ended at the Mississippi, despite the few thousand pioneers who had reached Oregon and those who had gone to Texas. After 1848, the nation would soon truly stretch from sea to sea.

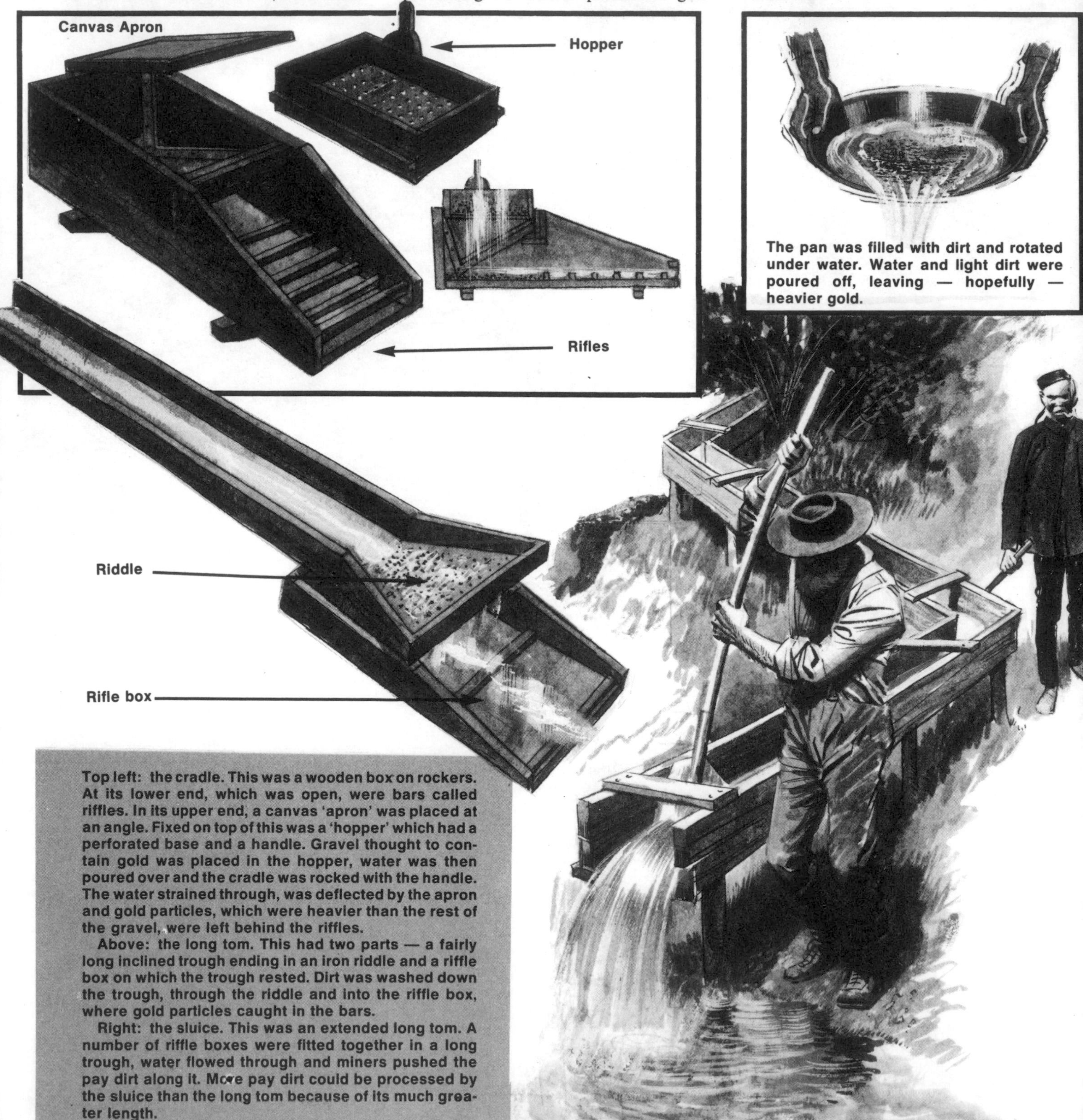


**The pan was filled with dirt and rotated under water. Water and light dirt were poured off, leaving — hopefully — heavier gold.**

**Top left: the cradle. This was a wooden box on rockers. At its lower end, which was open, were bars called riffles. In its upper end, a canvas 'apron' was placed at an angle. Fixed on top of this was a 'hopper' which had a perforated base and a handle. Gravel thought to contain gold was placed in the hopper, water was then poured over and the cradle was rocked with the handle. The water strained through, was deflected by the apron and gold particles, which were heavier than the rest of the gravel, were left behind the riffles.**

**Above: the long tom. This had two parts — a fairly long inclined trough ending in an iron riddle and a riffle box on which the trough rested. Dirt was washed down the trough, through the riddle and into the riffle box, where gold particles caught in the bars.**

**Right: the sluice. This was an extended long tom. A number of riffle boxes were fitted together in a long trough, water flowed through and miners pushed the pay dirt along it. More pay dirt could be processed by the sluice than the long tom because of its much greater length.**

# What was the Nelson Touch?

The memory of England's greatest sea battle after Drake's defeat of the Spanish Armada is kept fresh in all our minds by the continued existence of HMS *Victory,* which is preserved in a dry dock at Portsmouth. Launched in 1765, she was already an old ship by the time of Trafalgar, which makes her survival to this day even more remarkable.

Walking her immaculate gun decks, shown in the picture below, it is difficult to imagine now just how terrible the conditions must have been for her crew, sweating over their belching guns, with the decks slippery with the blood of their dead or wounded comrades.

**IT was the year of 1805, the year when it seemed that at long last Napoleon would invade England, which, for twelve years, had stood in the path of the *Grand Armée's* complete domination of Europe. It was the year when, in the face of all the evidence to the contrary, Napoleon had suddenly convinced himself that his united fleet could annihilate any squadron which the English could put to sea to meet it.**

In August of 1805, he wrote to his admirals: "Come into the Channel. Bring our united fleet and England is ours. If you are only here for 24 hours, all will be over, and six centuries of shame and insult will be avenged."

It was an order, however, which his captains found impossible to obey. Although Napoleon had 2,000 ships and 90,000 men assembled along the coast of France, the British blockade of the French and Spanish harbours had virtually immobilised this gigantic force.

In desperation, Napoleon ordered his fleet at Cadiz to sail out and meet the enemy ships which sat quietly waiting on the green Atlantic swells at Cape Trafalgar, some 80 kilometres east of Cadiz.

"His Majesty counts for nothing the loss of his ships," Napoleon's message ended, "provided they are lost with glory."

In response to this order, a Franco-Spanish fleet of 33, with 2,640 guns, commanded by Admiral Villeneuve, set out from Cadiz to

*Continued on next page*

**Our map, shows where Cape Trafalgar lies between Cadiz and Gibraltar.**

engage the enemy. Massive though this force was compared to the force that awaited them, its destruction was an almost foregone conclusion from the very beginning.

There were several reasons for the inevitable destruction of the Franco-Spanish fleet, not the least being that it was commanded by a man who was haunted by the memory of his humiliating defeat at the hands of a much smaller English force only three months earlier. A man, moreover, that even Napoleon had decided at the last moment was ill-fitted for the task that had been entrusted to him.

As Villeneuve was sailing out of Cadiz, a horseman was hastening down the Spanish Peninsula, carrying a message, informing Villeneuve that he was to hand over his command to Admiral Rosily.

It would be wrong to assume that if the messenger had arrived in time to stop Villeneuve sailing, and the highly capable Admiral Rosily had been in command, the outcome of the Battle of Trafalgar might have been a different one. There were too many other factors weighed in the balance against the Franco-Spanish fleet for this to have happened.

Like Villeneuve, the captains of the French and Spanish fleets were imbued with a sense of impending defeat before they had even encountered the enemy. And with good cause!

Demoralised by a long period of inactivity, and with 1,700 sick men aboard their ships, the French sailed out of Cadiz knowing that only a miracle could give them a victory.

## Press-ganged crews

The Spanish ships, manned mostly by soldiers or by beggars press-ganged from the slums of Cadiz, with gunners who had never fired a gun from a rolling ship, and commanded by Spanish captains who resented being placed under a French admiral, were in an even worse plight.

Most unnerving of all for the captains of the fleet was the knowledge that they were about to pit themselves against the most skilful sea captain of all time — Horatio Viscount Nelson.

Only slightly less awe-inspiring was the British Jack Tar himself, that clay-piped, pig-tailed sailor, who, more often than not, had been recruited by the press gangs from the scourings of the English sea towns. Already an aggressive fighting man by instinct, he had literally been whipped into becoming a magnificent sailor by the iron discipline of autocratic captains for whom the lash was the answer to almost every infringement of the ship's rules.

A seasoned French sailor would have had difficulty in holding his own against such a formidable foe, let alone those pathetic crews sailing out to meet the English fleet.

On the 20th of October, 1805, the Franco-Spanish fleet was sighted, and soon afterwards the area where the British ships waited became bright with patches of gaudy bunting as each ship broke out strings of flags which passed on the message: "The French and Spanish are out at last, they outnumber us in ships and guns and men: we are on the eve of the greatest sea fight in history."

On board the flagship, *HMS Victory*, the message had been delivered to the English commander, a slight, one-armed man, blind in one eye and shabbily dressed in a threadbare frock coat stained with sea salt, its gold lace tarnished to black flattened rags.

## Battle plans

This slatternly-looking admiral was, of course, Lord Nelson, who received the news with the utmost calmness. And why not? His battle plans had already been made and communicated to all his captains. Those plans, he was convinced, would give him a swift victory.

Until the Battle of Trafalgar, the problem of how a fleet could gain an annihilating victory over the enemy was one that had never really been solved, and for want of a better tactic, it had been the custom for the fleets to sail into action in two parallel lines, with each ship taking on a single opponent, firing its guns broadside as it passed.

Inevitably, the enemy would take an opposite tack, and the battle would then become a vastly prolonged affair, with the ships continually sailing on opposite tacks, or engaging on the same tack, until one of the fleets eventually retired.

Nelson had decided to break completely with this tradition. His plan was to divide his fleet into two groups. One group would attack sections of the enemy line and destroy

*Continued on page 192*

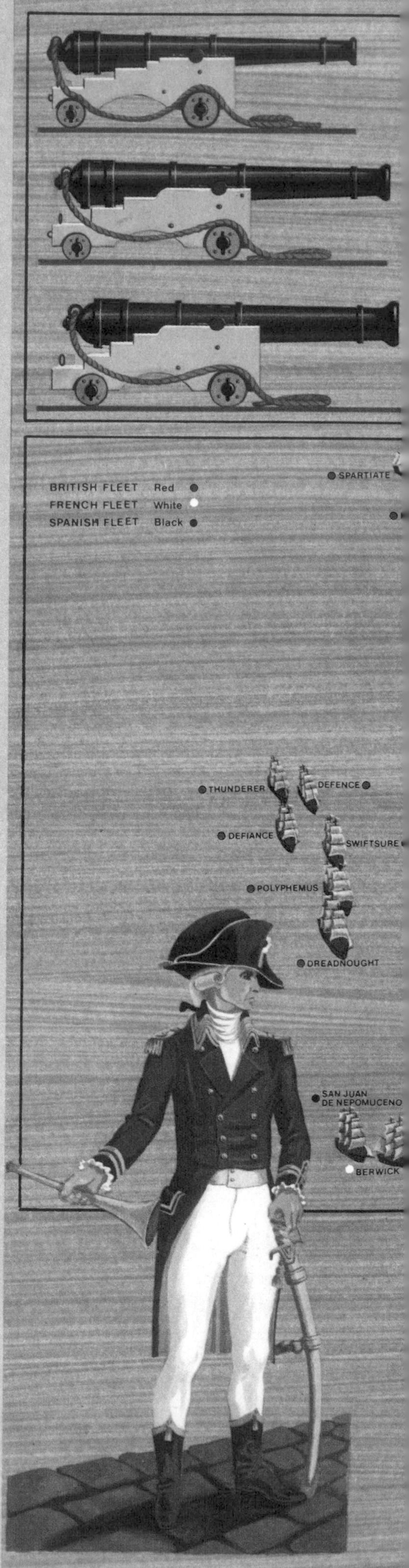


**Shown right is a naval captain of the period. The trumpet he is holding was used for shouting orders up to the mizzen mast. The buttons on the uniform were made of gilt brass with 'roped' edges.**

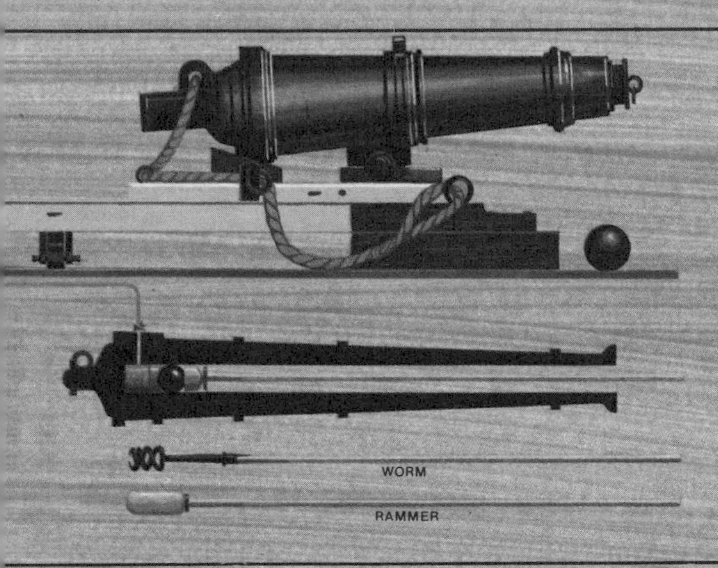


Far left: *The Victory's* main guns were 12 pounders (top) 24 pounders (middle) or 32 pounders. The big gun (left) was called a carronade, named The Smasher. Once the powder hole had been filled, it was fired by a slow match or flintlock. The cartridge and shot were laid by a rammer after the 'worm' had removed cartridge fragments, and the damp sponge had put out any sparks there might be in the barrel.

Right: A carrier for red hot cannon balls carried to the gunners. Below: Various examples of the type of shot hurled at enemy ships.

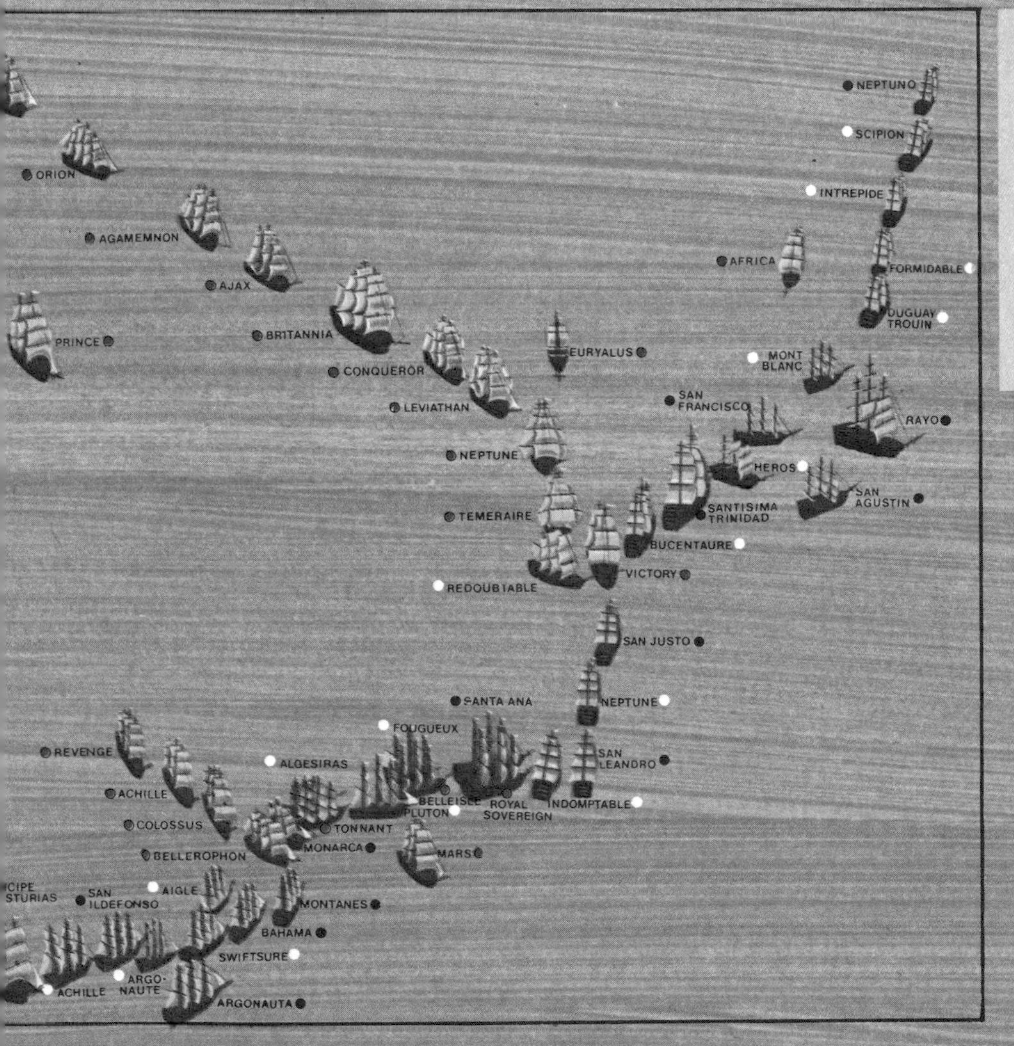


Left: The first stage of the battle, with the *Victory* leading a frontal attack, while the rest of Nelson's fleet attacks at right angles to break through the lines of the enemy ships, and thus cut off their retreat. This tactic was in complete variance with all the accepted rules of naval warfare.

Below: The last stage of the battle, with the French and English ships engaged in a general mêlée. By then 25 French ships were already out of action and trying to make for Cadiz.

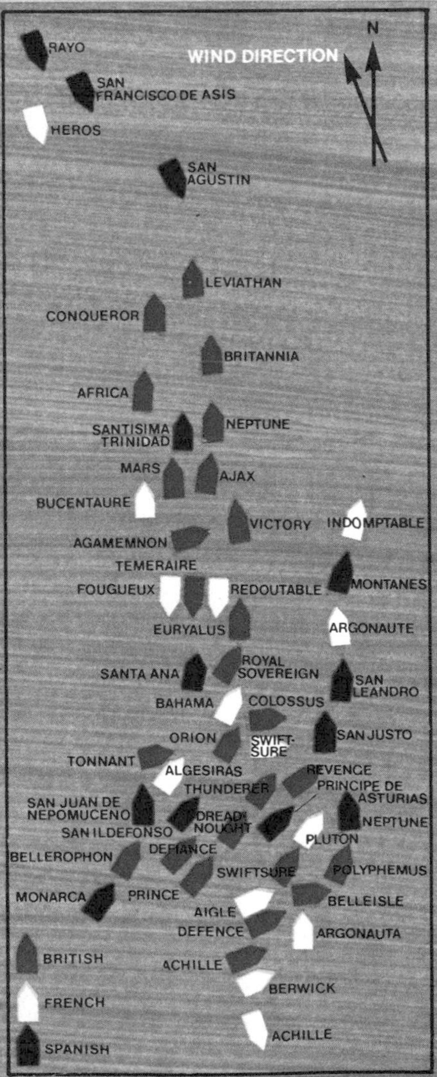


BRITISH ATTACKING SHIP

ENEMY LINE

Left: The raking manoeuvre employed with great success by the British ships. When attacking the enemy line, a British vessel would steer for a gap between enemy vessels. After brilliant seamanship had gained the British ship an advantageous position, a broadside was fired at one enemy vessel before sailing in front of it to unleash yet another broadside into the stern of the next ship in the line. Yet another broadside was then delivered to that crippled vessel from the other side.

them before other ships could come to their aid. The other group would attack the enemy at right angles, break through their lines and then cut off the retreat of the enemy fleet.

This aggressive piece of strategy, which was later referred to as the 'Nelson Touch', was to change the whole course of naval warfare.

The battle did not begin until the following day, by which time the enemy fleet was well in sight, off Cape Trafalgar. Nelson was on deck, now in a freshly laundered uniform and with new ribbons for all the medals on his breast.

### Battle signal

Shortly after, Nelson called for the signal officer. "Make the signal to bear down on the enemy in two lines," he ordered. He then went down to make his will, which was witnessed by Captain Hardy and Captain Blackwood who had come aboard from the *Euryalus*. Afterwards, Nelson went up to the poop and ordered the signal officer to hoist his celebrated signal: ENGLAND EXPECTS THAT EVERY MAN WILL DO HIS DUTY.

It has been said that this famous signal was to have been worded: "Nelson confides that every man will do his duty," and that his name was replaced by that of England at the suggestion of the signal officer, who pointed out that if the words 'confides that' were used, they would have to be spelt out with a long string of flags. The word 'expects' was substituted.

### First blood

The first shot was fired at the English ship *Royal Sovereign* at noon. This salute of iron was received in silence by the *Royal Sovereign,* who waited until she had drawn astern of the Spanish three-decker, *Santa Anna,* then raked her decks with a murderous fire that killed or wounded 400 of her crew.

In the meantime, Nelson's ship was moving on, silent and intent, searching for the French admiral's ship. Eventually, right in front of her, lay the huge Spanish four-decker, *Santissima Trinidad*. Guessing correctly that the French admiral's ship must be nearby, Nelson bore down on her. As he did so, the *Bucentaure,* Villeneuve's ship, and seven or eight other enemy ships, opened fire on the *Victory*. Still she advanced without firing. By the time she had come close enough to rake the *Santissima Trinidad* with her larboard guns, 50 of her men were dead and 30 wounded.

It was at this point that the *Victory* came into collision with the French *Redoubtable*. Locked together, and wrapped in sheets of flame, the two ships drifted slowly through the smoke of battle. Gradually, although the fighting had continued unabated, the smoke cleared a little from the decks of the *Victory,* enough for the marksmen to see the epaulets of the English officers. A marksman kneeling in the mizzen-top aimed his musket at Nelson.

On the quarterdeck of the *Victory,* Captain Hardy had turned to leave Nelson's side to give an order when Nelson fell, mortally wounded. Immediately, Hardy, a sergeant of the marines and two privates, rushed forward to lift him up. Nelson was then carried down to the cockpit, where he ordered that his face should be covered with a handkerchief so that he might not be recognized.

In the meantime, the *Redoubtable's* top marksmen had shot down 40 officers and men, destroying so many that the French, seeing the upper deck clear of all but dead or wounded, tried to board her. It was an enterprise which was to cost them dear. A boatswain's whistle piped, "Boarders; repel Boarders", and the order immediately summoned swarms of smoke-begrimed bluejackets to the deck, where they killed every man who had managed to board the *Victory*.

Below decks, Nelson's life was now ebbing away fast. But he was still alive when Hardy returned from the fighting above to inform him that fourteen enemy vessels had given in. "That's well," Nelson said, "but I had bargained for twenty." He lingered on for a little while longer. After murmuring some inarticulate words, he said distinctly, "I have done my duty. I thank God for it!"

### Ruined dream

Above, beneath the setting sun, his fleet was lying in two groups with the shattered hulks of the enemy ships all around them. The British losses had been heavy; 449 killed and 1,241 wounded. But of the 27 ships of the British fleet, not one had been sunk or captured. Trafalgar was the decisive battle of the Napoleonic Wars.

It had always been essential to Napoleon's master plan to control the world that he should have command of the seas. With his Allied fleet now ruined as a fighting force that dream had been destroyed forever.

Trafalgar, moreover, established England's supremacy at sea for nearly a century and a half, during which time her navy remained the bedrock on which her control of the far-flung British Empire rested through the age of steam and into the 20th century.

THE TIMES
For 7th NOVEMBER. 1805
BATTLE OF
TRAFALGAR
CAPTURE OF
FRENCH AND
SPANISH FLEETS
DEATH OF NELSON
List of Killed and Wounded

**It was not until several days after the battle that The Times newspaper was able to inform its readers of the outcome of the battle. Their joy that England had won a great sea battle was tempered by the knowledge that the country had lost its most beloved naval commander.**

Photo: Mansell Collection

# Why were the Pilgrim Fathers so-called?

**IT was only a tiny ship. Nobody today can be absolutely certain about its size and weight, but it is thought that it was about 27 metres in length — slightly longer than a tennis court — and a modest 183 tonnes. Yet it was destined to become one of the most famous ships in history.**

The *Mayflower* slipped out of Plymouth Ho on September 16, 1620, bound for the east coast of North America. On board it carried 102 men, women and children. The reason for the vessel's fame is that those men, women and children are known today as the Pilgrim Fathers, founders of the modern United States.

The moving spirits behind the voyage were a religious group known as the English Separatists. Their name was inspired by the fact that, following translation of the Bible into English at the start of the 17th century, they insisted on their right to interpret its message themselves rather than having it interpreted for them by the Reformed Church.

For this view they suffered religious persecution. Many fled to Leyden in Holland. Gradually, however, the thoughts of some of the bolder members of the sect turned to the New World where they could live in an even freer religious atmosphere than existed in the Netherlands, and, in addition, bring the word of God to heathen Red Indians.

The trip was financed by a group of businessmen known as the Merchant Adventurers, a voluntary combine of individuals united to do good, plant religion in faraway places — and eventually to reap a profit out of trade with the colony they had helped to create.

**The first colonists arrive in the New World, protected by guns and the word of God.**

Initially, the Pilgrim Fathers embarked in two ships, the *Mayflower* and *Speedwell*, at Southampton on August 15, 1620. But the *Speedwell*, contrary to its name, proved unseaworthy and twice had to seek sanctuary, first in Dartmouth, then in Plymouth, where it was decided that the *Mayflower* should proceed alone.

Of the 102 colonists, only 35 were actually English Separatists. The remainder had been hired by the Merchant Adventurers to protect their investment.

There was scarcely room to move on board. Apart from its 102 passengers, plus a crew estimated at between 20 and 30, the *Mayflower* carried the basic furniture for 19 cottages, household utensils and trading goods. For protection against Red Indians and marauding bands of hostile Frenchmen there were six large guns, four cannon and a variety of personal weapons.

The livestock included pigs, goats, poultry, sheep and rabbits, plus family pets in the form of cats, dogs and cage birds. Then, of course, there was enough food, drink and clothing to see them through what promised to be a harsh winter. One man, William Mullins, obviously pessimistic about the chances of finding anything in North America to protect his feet, took 126 pairs of shoes and 13 pairs of boots.

As Autumn stretches into winter, the North Atlantic becomes a cruel sea. On two days out of three the *Mayflower* encountered gales and storms. It proved a wet, cold and badly-ventilated ship. Yet all but one of the colonists survived the 67-day voyage.



**All utensils had to be taken on the voyage — so did food, furniture and trading goods. Our picture shows some of the primitive household utensils, so different from the modern American's super-modern kitchen equipment.**

Their original destination had been North Virginia, where they had been given a grant of land. Instead they fetched up on November 21 at what is now Cape Cod, Massachusetts, and, hindered by more bad weather from making their way south, decided to make their settlement at a nearby site they named New Plymouth.

The main party landed there on Boxing Day, 1620, with a clear idea of how they would govern themselves. While still at sea they had agreed on 'The Mayflower Compact' for 'the general good of ye Colonie'. This laid down that the 'civill body politick' would be based upon 'just and equall' laws, a theme repeated when the U.S. Constitution was drawn up more than a century and a half later.

That first winter, during which they lived aboard the *Mayflower*, proved even harder than expected. A plague wiped out nearly half of the colonists, leaving only 54 to start the work of building their settlement when the *Mayflower* sailed for England again in the spring.

On a more cheerful note, the colonists had by then reached an understanding with the local Red Indians, who had themselves been smitten by the same plague, leaving only 5,000 of them alive out of 100,000. This understanding was to a considerable extent the work of a remarkable Red Indian named Squanto.

## True friend

As a young man he had been taken to England by an explorer. Having learned the language, he re-crossed the Atlantic as interpreter for another expedition. But he was subsequently hi-jacked and sold in Spain for £20 as a slave.

In Spain he managed to escape, made his way to England and eventually returned to North America as guide-interpreter with yet another expedition.

Squanto showed no rancour over his past experiences with palefaces. He attached himself to the Pilgrims for the rest of his life, teaching them where the best fish were to be caught, where to plant corn, and how to fertilise it with dead herrings.

Little more than a year after they set out from England, the Pilgrims celebrated the gathering of their first harvest with three days of feasting and dancing. Ninety Red Indians joined in and the fare included roast turkey.

This celebration is the origin of the best-known American festival, Thanksgiving. Nowadays it is celebrated on the last Thursday in November, probably a month or more later than the date the Pilgrims chose, but roast turkey is still the main ingredient of the American feast.

Oddly enough, for two centuries after their arrival in Massachusetts the colonists were not known as Pilgrim Fathers but Old Comers or Forefathers. Shortly before the bi-centenary celebrations in 1820, however, an early manuscript was discovered in which they were referred to as 'saints' and 'pilgrims'.

This prompted the American orator Daniel Webster to use the name Pilgrim Fathers in the course of those celebrations — and the name has stuck.

Our artist's impression of the Pilgrims' first Thanksgiving, a little over a year after their historic departure from Plymouth in 1620.

Below are two sorts of dwellings made by the Pilgrim Fathers. Left is a sod or turf hut made, as its name suggests, from turfs. Right is a hut made from bark and poles.

# Who owns Antarctica?

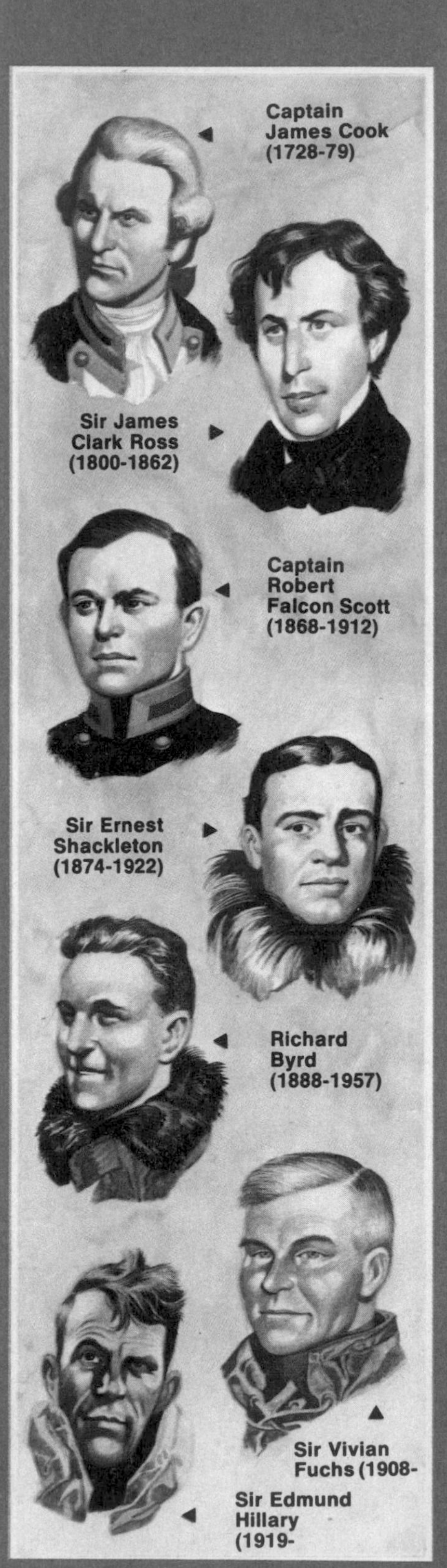


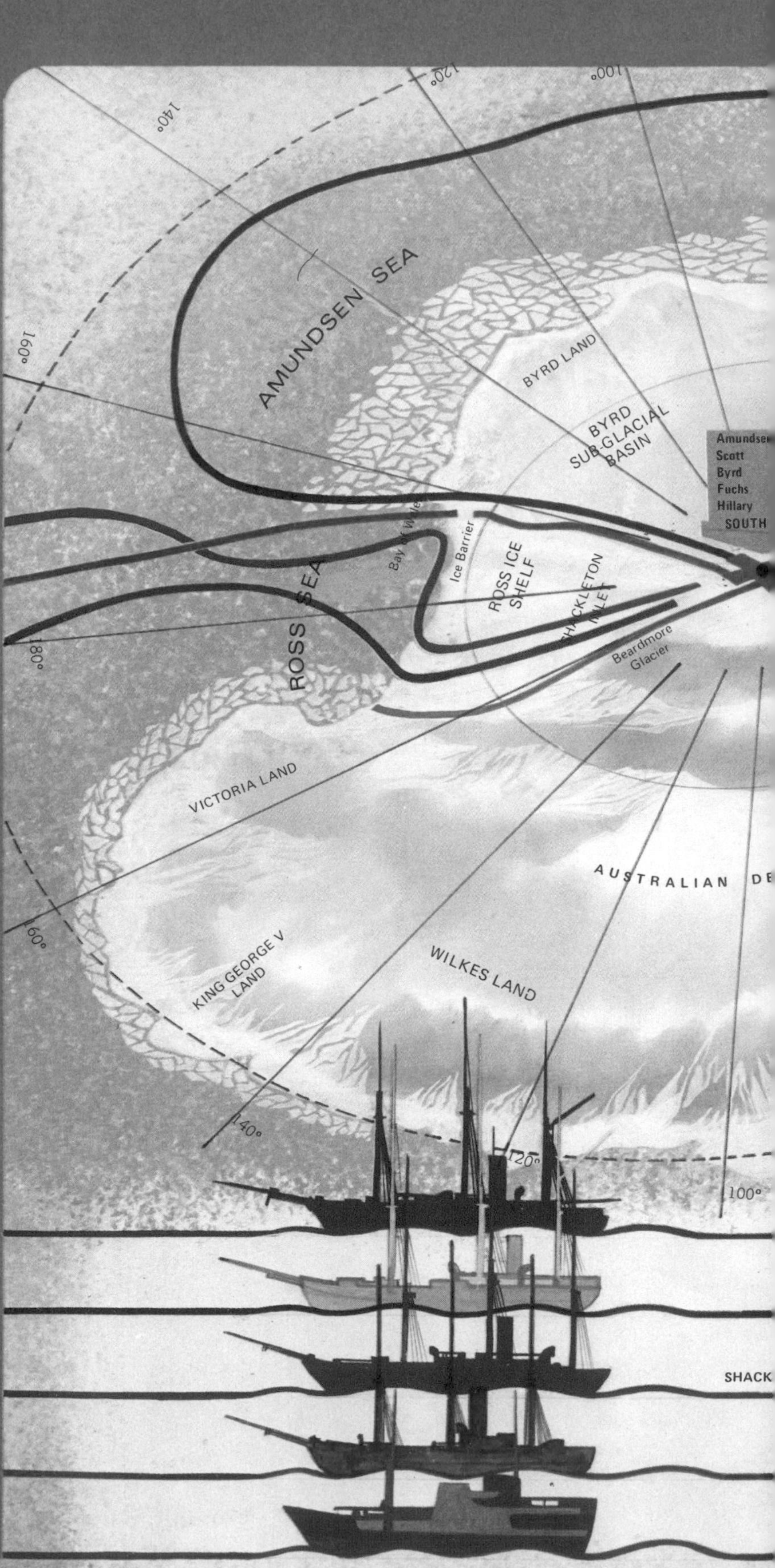

**FOR over 2000 years men had dreamed of a vast southern continent, perhaps one as big as Europe and Asia combined. How else, asked some, could the land masses to the north be balanced?**

**Right down to the 18th century the idea of such a continent was firmly believed, and it was confidently supposed that the mighty land would be fertile and well worth possessing.**

**The truth is very different: a forbidding frozen desert where hills, mountains and valleys are hidden below snow and ice. Just a few rocks and hills can be seen; the rest is a vast ice plateau, the highest and biggest on Earth. And almost in the middle of it is the South Pole. The continent is bigger than the United States.**

The ice cap slowly flows to the sea, producing icebergs. There are enormous glaciers and wide crevasses, which make the going hard and dangerous, and terrible winds make travel even more nightmarish. There is next to no life inland, but on the shores countless penguins abound. The seas contain seals and whales and the skies skua gulls and other birds that can endure the cold. The Antarctic winter is an endless night and in the summer the sun rises only just above the bleak horizon. So much for earlier dreams of a near paradise.

## Beginning

The Antarctic Circle was first crossed in 1773 by that greatest of explorer-navigators, Captain James Cook, commander of the *Resolution*. He sailed past islands until coming up against the pack ice. His first sight of it proved once and for all that the

**First at the South Pole**
**AMUNDSEN Dec. 14th 1911**

longed for great continent of boundless possibilities was a myth.

Cook penetrated even further south the next year and sailing ships, mainly British and American, followed him early in the 19th century, slaughtering seals around the islands he had found. The first sighting of the Antarctic mainland came in 1820. A year earlier a merchant captain, William Smith, had thought he sighted land through the mist, and it was he who, with Lieutenant Edward Bransfield, Royal Navy, made the official sighting of what is Graham Land, the nearest part of the continent to South America. The small South Shetland Islands beside it became part of the British Empire.

The first major exploration of Antarctica took place between 1840-43. It was led by a remarkable navigator, Sir James Clark Ross who, back in 1831, had penetrated the Canadian Arctic and discovered the magnetic North Pole. Now he entered what became the Ross Sea in ships strong enough to push through pack ice. He discovered the great Ross Ice Barrier and named two volcanic peaks, Mount Terror and Mount Erebus after his two ships.

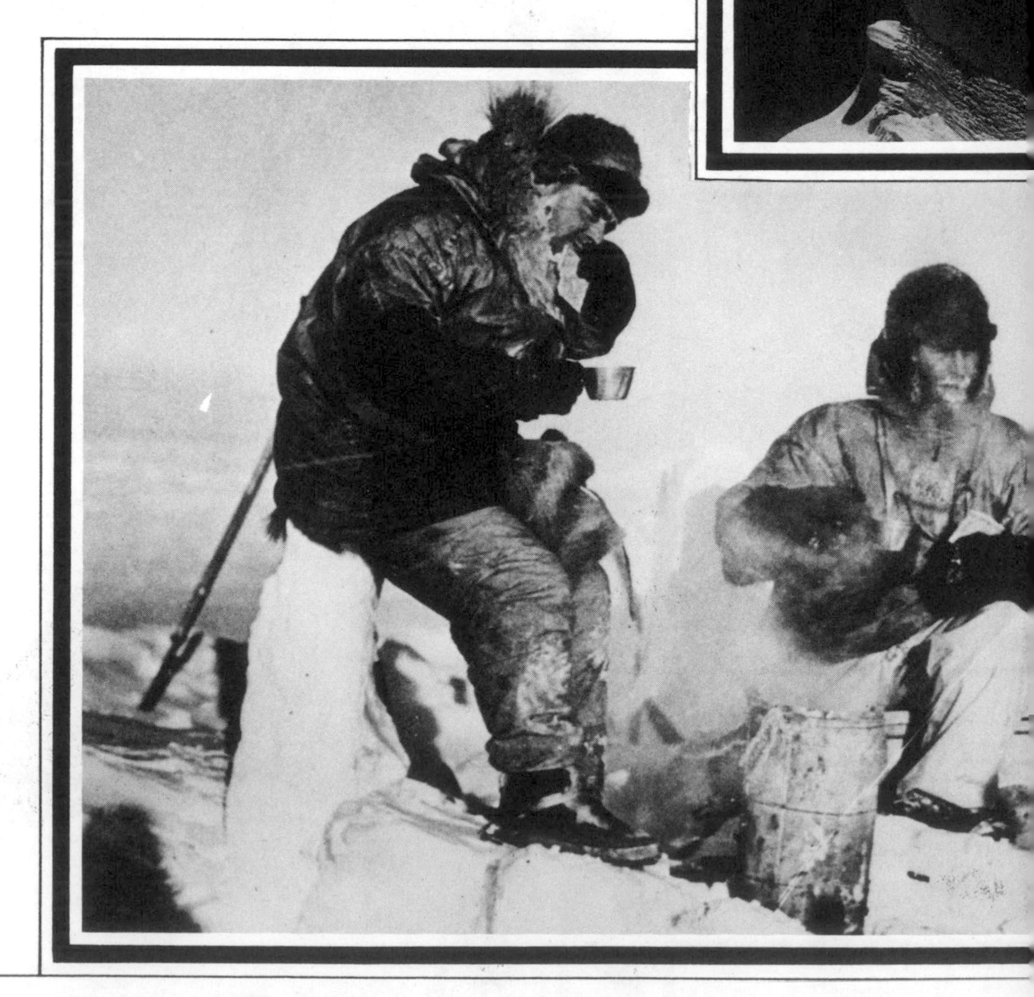

The coastline, white and magnificently mountainous, he named Victoria Land after his queen.

Ross's discovery of the area — a giant gash into Antarctica — was to prove invaluable to later explorers, for it was to become the quickest route to the South Pole. That was many years ahead, however, for public interest was mainly engaged in the search for the North-West Passage. The South Pole and Antarctica were virtually forgotten.

## First Footprints!

In 1872, the steamship HMS *Challenger* made a four-year survey trip in the waters around Antarctica, but it was not until the 1890s that exploration began again in earnest. A Norwegian ship anchored off Victoria Land in 1894 and men first set foot on the mainland. Their names were Borchgrevink and Bull. Four years later, Borchgrevink went back and led a small party which spent the winter in Antarctica — 75 days of almost total darkness and constant cold. They later found that travel on the ice barrier was possible.

Next came the British. An expedition led by Captain Robert Falcon Scott set off in the *Discovery* in 1901 and was away until 1904. Scott penetrated to within 800 km of the Pole by sledge, and later, in 1908, one of Scott's men, Ernest Shackleton, reached the Magnetic South Pole and got within 160 km of the Pole itself before being forced to turn back because supplies were running dangerously low.

The most famous of all Polar expeditions began in 1910. This was led by Captain Scott, who suddenly found himself engaged against his will in a race for the South Pole when the news broke that the great Norwegian explorer, Roald Amundsen, was eager to get there first.

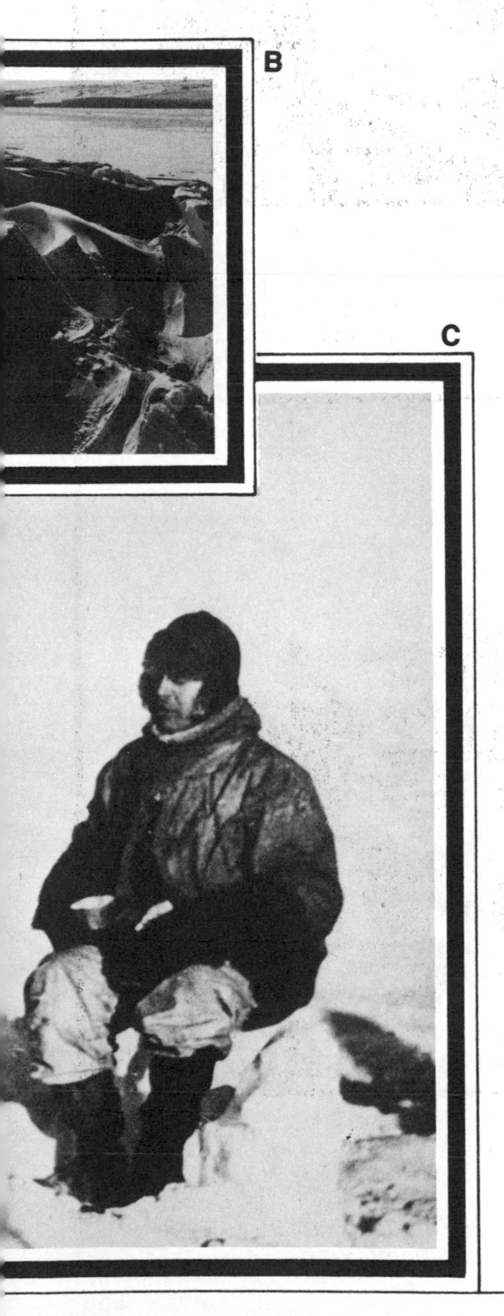

## Great Disappointment!

With four companions, Lieutenant Bowers, Captain Oates, Petty Officer Evans and Dr. Wilson, Scott reached the South Pole on January 18, 1912, a day after they had seen to their intense disappointment a Norwegian flag and dog tracks. Amundsen had reached the longed-for spot five weeks earlier on December 14, 1911.

Heartbroken, the small party set off for their base. But the weather grew worse and worse and their supplies were running low. They became weaker and weaker and finally, within a few kilometres of their destination, they all perished. Evans had been the first to die as the result of a fall, then Oates, whose poor state of health was delaying the survivors, deliberately walked out into a blizzard to die. The bodies of the other three were found — on November 12, 1912.

From then onwards more and more expeditions set out, one led by Shackleton, others by Germans, Norwegians and Australians. The first flight over the South Pole was achieved by Admiral R. E. Byrd, US Navy, in 1929, who had earlier flown over the North Pole and who later explored on land.

Byrd, in fact, had a highly dramatic life. He flew the Atlantic in 1927 in 43 hours but was forced to make a landing in the sea near France. His flight over the South Pole was accomplished in the tri-motored monoplane, *Floyd Bennett* (named after his pilot on the North Pole flight), and with him were just a pilot, a map photographer and a radio operator. It was Byrd who gave the name Little America to a base he established on the Ross Ice Front at the edge of the Ross Sea. He also discovered Marie Byrd Land and named it after his wife,

In the years that followed Byrd's pioneer flight, Antarctica, though still an awesome and challenging place, was mapped and photographed. Weather stations were set up and more and more men began to learn how to live on the icy continent.

In International Geophysical Year (1957-58) mass explorations of Antarctica took place, led by scientists of many nations. A famous feature of the year was the Commonwealth Trans-Atlantic Expedition, a double one which set out from either side of the continent and met at the Pole. The two leaders were Sir Vivian Fuchs and Sir Edmund Hillary, the co-conqueror of Mount Everest back in 1953.

## Useful at Last

Today, the work goes on, for Antarctica becomes steadily more important. It remains a vital area for that controversial industry, whaling, but more happily it plays an ever-growing role in weather forecasting. Though it is owned by Britain, Australia, New Zealand, France and Norway, a large proportion of it is reserved for international scientific research, a fine result of much bravery and endurance in the pursuit of knowledge.

**A**
Sir Edmund Hillary, left, and Dr. Vivian Fuchs greet each other during their Trans-Antarctic expedition in 1958.

**B**
This shows some of the eerie beauty of the pressure ridges of an Antarctic ice crack. There are no land animals normally — but here is one lonely human being!

**C**
A still from the Paramount Pictures film, "With Byrd At The South Pole". Here we see Byrd with two of his companions.

# Who first flew to the North Pole?

1. One of the most famous names in polar exploration is that of the Norwegian, Roald Amundsen. Ever since he had cheered home Nansen, the first man to cross Greenland, he had been fascinated by these mysterious lands. As a young man he joined the navy, ever alert for the chance to travel into the polar regions.

2. It came when he was aged 25. He was chosen as first mate on the Belgian research ship *Belgica*, which left Antwerp in 1897. This was the first ship to spend a winter successfully in the Antarctic. The voyage proved beyond doubt that men with proper food and protection could survive the worst Antarctic conditions.

3. Amundsen now wanted to lead his own expedition and sail through the North-west Passage (an icy sea route north of Canada linking the Atlantic and Pacific Oceans). His ship *Gjöa* left Norway in 1903. The journey took three years and Amundsen learnt the ways of the native Eskimos, especially the use of dog sledges.

4. Amundsen's next target was the North Pole, but in 1909 he heard that the American, Peary, had beaten him to it. So he turned south, and with skilful use of dog teams, he sped across the Antarctic. On December 14, 1911, with his four companions, Amundsen became the first man to reach the South Pole.

5. The North Pole is set on a sea of slowly moving ice, and Amundsen's next scheme was to take a ship into this and allow it to be carried as near to the Pole as possible. In September 1918 he wedged his ship *Maud* into the ice. He docked in Alaska in July 1920 — having sailed from Norway to the Pacific.

6. Amundsen was the first man to sail completely around the world . . . within the Arctic Circle! He was also quick to see the potential of modern inventions in polar explorations. His first attempt to fly over the Pole came in 1925 but his aeroplanes ran out of fuel and had to make emergency landings.

7. But Amundsen did fly over the North Pole using an Italian-built airship, the *Norge.* It arrived over the Pole on May 11, 1926, circled it and dropped the flags of Norway, Italy (for the Italian pilot Nobile) and the United States (for the financial backers). Two years later, Nobile and an Italian crew set out again for the Pole in another airship, the *Italia.* But something went wrong and the airship crashed. Many search parties set out to search for the crew, including Amundsen who took the only aeroplane available to him in the emergency. But although the crew was rescued it was not by Amundsen; he had made his last polar expedition, for the aeroplane disappeared and this extraordinary explorer was never seen again.

# What does

**FOR five long, bitter years of hardship and austerity, the oppressed peoples of Europe had been waiting eagerly for D-Day. By the early summer of 1944 everyone knew it was very near, but no one knew exactly when it would be.**

For D-Day, the day when the Allied armies would set out from southern England to invade and liberate the German-occupied continent of Europe, had to be a total secret. The "D", in fact, stood just for "Day"!

All that Spring, the fields, woods and lanes of Britain's southern counties had been filling up with troops, guns, tanks, lorries — all the paraphernalia of modern war. There were soldiers who had escaped from their occupied homelands, and Americans, Canadians, Britons, Australians, New Zealanders, men from every corner of the free world.

All were waiting for The Day — D-Day.

At their head was the quiet, confident American Supreme Commander, General Dwight D. Eisenhower, who had come to England in 1942 as commanding general of all American forces in European areas. For months, "Ike", as he was called, and "Monty" — Field Marshal Bernard Montgomery, his British second-in-command — had been planning for D-Day.

Strangely, at this most important moment in the story of the war, everything depended upon the weather. Among other things, a later-rising full moon was needed to allow airborne forces to approach the invasion zone on the coast of northern France in darkness, and then to give them moonlight to help identify their dropping zones. And the tides had to be right for the seaborne armada, taking the bulk of the infantry who would storm the beaches.

In May the weather was splendid, but the omens were bad. Depressions and gales were imminent, as Group Captain Stagg of the R.A.F., who was the chief weather expert on the planning staff, warned Eisenhower.

As June dawned over southern England, the generals in their secret headquarters put all the facts together and decided that the invasion of Europe had to be between the fifth and seventh of June. This was not just because of the tides and the moon. It was known that the Germans were about to launch secret weapons on London — the V1 "flying bombs" and V2 rockets — and their bases had to be captured and destroyed. It was vital, too, for the invading army to break out from the invasion zones and set out for Berlin, the German capital, long before the winter came.

On June 4th the weather was terrible. With a heavy heart, Eisenhower decided that the invasion must be postponed for 24 hours, an awful decision to make and a dreadful strain on the waiting troops.

The next correct tides after June 7th were not for a fortnight. So everything now pointed to June 6th as D-Day.

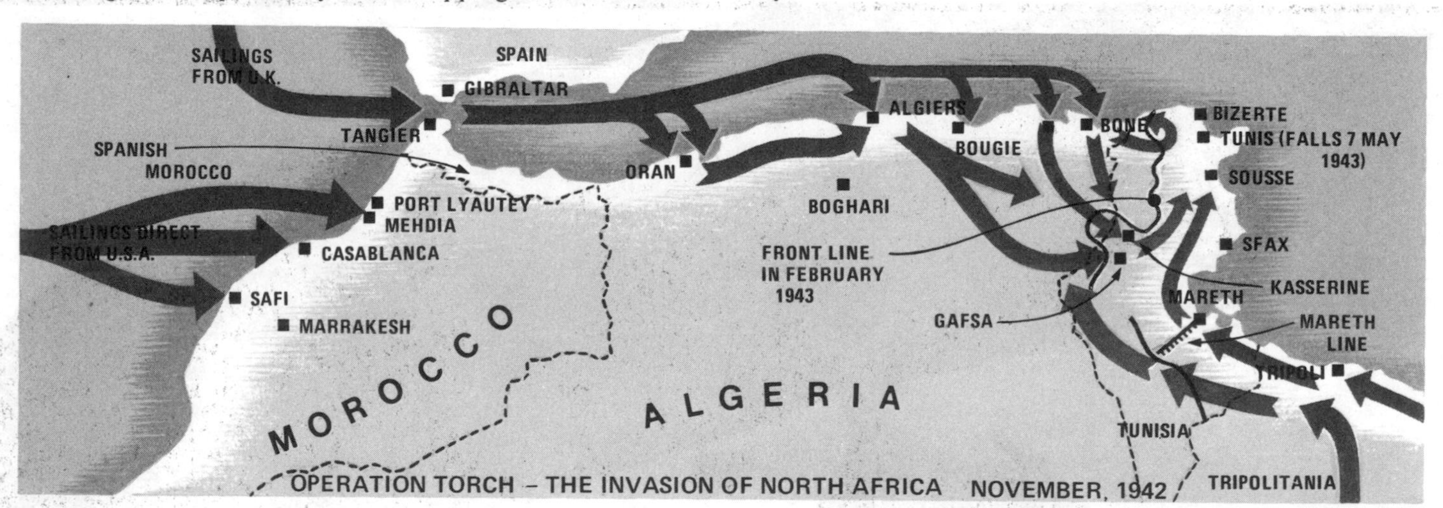

OPERATION TORCH – THE INVASION OF NORTH AFRICA NOVEMBER, 1942

## Learning the art of invasion

Before D-Day had been thought of, the Allies had undertaken several invasions and had learned something from each of them. Operation Torch, or the invasion of North Africa in 1942 was then the greatest invasion the Allies had ever attempted and it took the Germans by surprise. On the 8th November, 1942, over 1,000 aircraft, 200 warships and 350 merchant ships carrying 70,000 troops attacked three north African targets — Algiers, Oran and Casablanca. For the first time, an American, General Dwight Eisenhower, was made Supreme Commander with three British commanders under him. This proved a highly-successful arrangement.

The assault on Siciliy — Operation Husky — in the following year posed different problems. This time, the Germans were prepared for the invasion and were dug in to resist it, so landings had to be accurate, fast and with a rapid build-up of highly-trained troops. Altogether, 160,000 men, 14,000 vehicles, 600 tanks and 1,800 guns were landed. Three thousand aircraft and 3,200 ships lent support and by the end of August, 1943, Sicily had fallen to the Allies.

OPERATION HUSKY – THE INVASION OF SICILY JULY, 1943

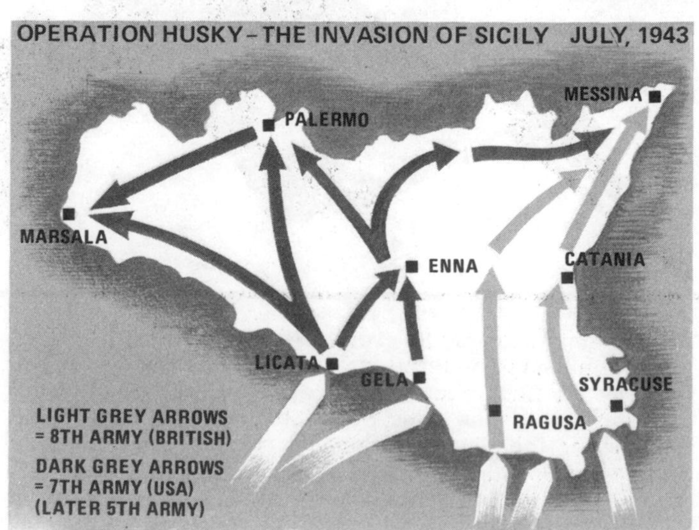

# D-Day mean?

It was raining heavily and a gale was blowing on the fifth when Eisenhower asked Group Captain Stagg for new weather report. The reply brought a great surge of relief and anticipation. There would be a fair period which would last until the afternoon of the sixth.

Now it was up to Eisenhower. He had to be sure of something as uncertain as a weather report to make one of the most dramatic decisions in history. Quietly he spoke the momentous words of the war: "O.K. We'll go."

That Stagg was proved right was later history. Some days afterwards a violent storm hit the beachheads in the invasion zone, but by then it didn't matter.

Shortly before midnight on June 5th, the familiar drone of hundreds of aeroplane engines above the south coast of Britain caused people to lift their black-out curtains (it was still forbidden to show a light, for fear it might be spotted by enemy aircraft) and peer up at the sky. For months the noise of Allied bombers going out and later returning had been heard in the night-sky, but this time it seemed to be much louder.

And indeed it was.

All that Spring the Allied aircraft had been blasting German gun-sites, destroying airfield runways and demolishing bridges all over northern and western France. Some of the attacks had been made hundreds of miles from the intended invasion area, so that the enemy would have no idea where they would be hit on D-Day.

During May alone the Anglo-American air forces unloaded 20,000 tons of bombs on France, systematically destroying communications between the German coastal armies and their bases farther inland. Fifty out of 82 main rail centres were destroyed and 25 more were damaged.

But by June 5th, the invasion count-down had begun. The planes which the southern English could hear extra loudly that night were 1,300 strong, and they were going to blast ten coastal batteries between Le Havre and Cherbourg.

In British airports all the way from Devon to Kent, paratroops, with emergency rations, were already boarding the gliders and transport planes which, within an hour or two, would spill them out all over the Cherbourg peninsula and the country around Caen — the area where the D-Day invasion would strike. (See map on next pages.)

More than a thousand ships of all sizes, from giant liners to dirty tramps and small coastal craft, filled every harbour, packed to the gunwales with machinery and plant for sowing the seeds of freedom on French soil — tanks, guns, ammunition boxes, shells, wagons, medical supplies, food, repair outfits, all loaded according to carefully arranged schedules, so that first things needed might be the first available. Under the hatches, nearly a quarter of a million men sprawled and talked and smoked and slept.

There was nothing more for Eisenhower to do. The whole gigantic war machine had been set in motion. He decided to go and visit some of his men, and he chose an airborne unit.

He stood, hands in pockets, looking up at the sky as, one by one, the 'planes moved off down the runways and climbed slowly into the night. It was midnight when the last 'plane took off, carrying the American 101st. Airborne Division.

**Softening up the enemy**

**Between half past five and eight o'clock on the morning of D-Day, the Allied fleets bombarded the French coast to pave the way for the landings to come on the five main beach-heads — nicknamed Utah, Omaha, Gold, Juno and Sword.**

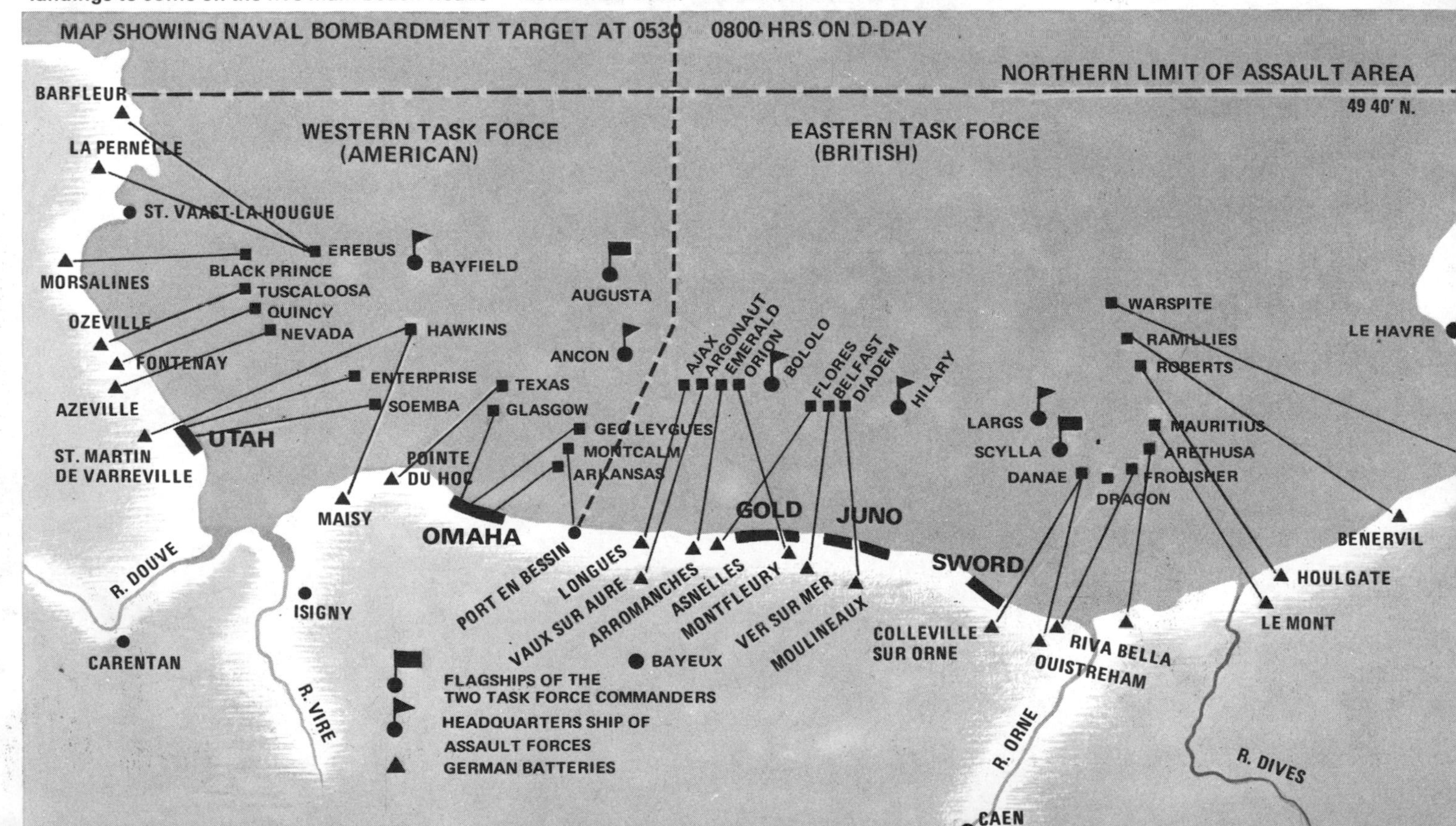

U.S. V CORPS
( 2 DIV)
U.S. VII CORPS
(90 DIV)
Swansea
Cardiff
U.S. V CORPS
(29 DIV)
U.S. VII CORPS
(4 DIV)
U.S. V CORPS
(1 DIV)
U.S. VII
CORPS
( 9 DIV)
BRITISH X
( 50 DI
Falmouth
Fowey
Plymouth
Torbay
Brixham
Dartmouth
Salcombe
Weymouth
Portland
Poole
Southampton
FOLLOW-UP FORCE B
FORCE U
FORCE O
FORCE G
U.S. GLIDER
ROUTE
U.S. 101 ABN DIV
U.S. 82 ABN DIV
Cherbourg
COTENTIN PENINSULA
Valognes
Montebourg
UTAH
Ste. Mere Eglise
Carentan
U.S. VII CORPS
U.S. V CORPS
BRITISH XXX CORPS
BRITISH I CORPS (CDN)
BRITISH I CORPS
Vierville
Isigny
La Madeleine
OMAHA
Formigny
Port-En-
Bessin
Colleville
St. Honorine
Bayeux
GOLD
JUNO
St. Aubin
Creuilly
Arromanches
Le Hamel
La Riviere
SWORD
Ouistreham
Benouville
Caen
St. Lô

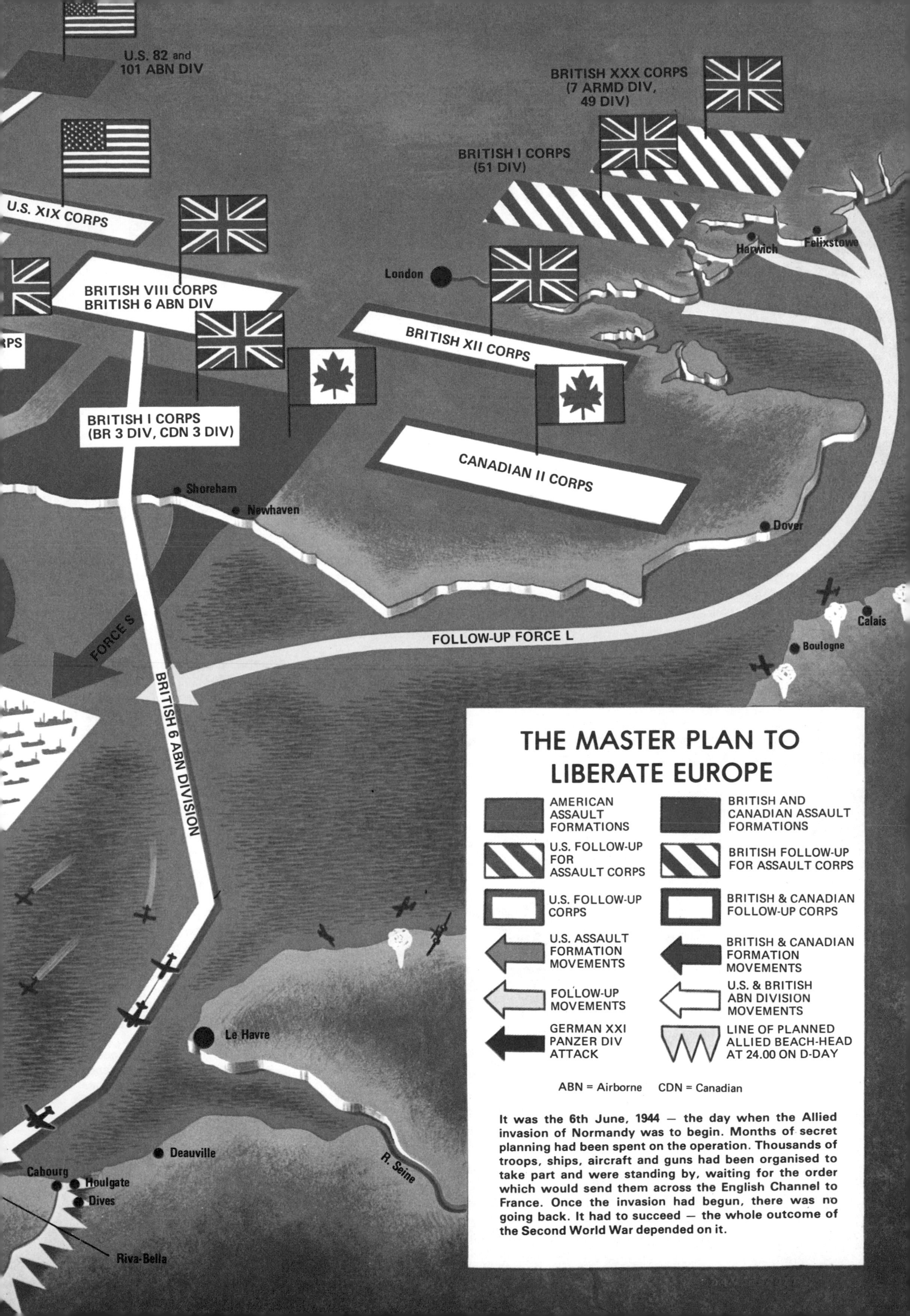


# THE MASTER PLAN TO LIBERATE EUROPE



It was the 6th June, 1944 — the day when the Allied invasion of Normandy was to begin. Months of secret planning had been spent on the operation. Thousands of troops, ships, aircraft and guns had been organised to take part and were standing by, waiting for the order which would send them across the English Channel to France. Once the invasion had begun, there was no going back. It had to succeed — the whole outcome of the Second World War depended on it.

**The planning, the preparations, the waiting — they were all at an end. The greatest invasion in the history of mankind was about to begin.**

# Operation Overlord

**A**S the clock ticked into the first hour of June the sixth, 1944, General Dwight D. Eisenhower, Supreme Commander of the Allied invasion of the German-occupied continent of Europe, stood looking at the night sky. In front of him wave after wave of transport aircraft clawed their way up into the blackness, laden with troops, supplies, guns, and all the paraphernalia of modern war.**

**D-Day had begun. Or, as the military planners had been calling it for the past two years, 'Operation Overlord'.**

## HOW THE BRITISH INFANTRYMAN WAS EQUIPPED ON "D" DAY

Operation Overlord was unique in military history as being the first time that a major seaborne invading force had won against a major defending force. It also changed the possible course of world history for if the advancing Russians, instead of the Anglo-Americans, had liberated western Europe, then France, Belgium, Holland, Scandinavia and West Germany would now undoubtedly be in the position that the satellite countries of the U.S.S.R. are in today.

The key to Overlord was air power. As Eisenhower watched his aircraft disappearing into the night sky, he recalled that with their superior air power, Allied bombers had been striking at the German war machine on a 24 hours-a-day basis for months, in order to 'soften up' the defenders. Part of this effort had been switched later on to the destruction of the railway system of northern France, so that the defenders would be unable to make the swift movement of counter-attacking troops when the blow fell.

The secret of *where* the blow would fall was one of the best kept of the war. The area of Calais was the nearest to the invaders, but it was also the most obvious place, and therefore the most heavily defended by the Germans. Allied strategy lay in making the Germans think, nevertheless, right up to the last moment, that the Pas-de-Calais was the chosen spot.

A much greater weight of bombs was deliberately dropped on this area, and on D-Day itself two squadrons of bombers circled over the Channel off Calais, dropping tons of long, thin aluminium strips called 'window' to fool the enemy

*Continued on page 208*

Our illustration is set forty minutes before the 'estimated landing time' on one of the Normandy beaches. The plan is to destroy the Germans' beach defences so that the lightly protected infantry can land unharmed. To do this, waves of heavy tanks and specialized equipment are sent in first, under cover of the guns of destroyers and rockets fired from tank landing craft.

The destroyers open fire first and continue firing for ten minutes. Then the landing craft carrying large guns commence firing followed by the self-propelled guns on landing craft farther back. Following this bombardment, the landing craft approach the beach as the destroyers provide covering fire, backed up by gunfire from the leading support landing craft and the fire power of the self-propelled guns and rocket-firing landing craft. Landing craft fitted with anti-aircraft guns deal with enemy aircraft not stopped by Allied fighters.

The initial attacking wave is led by tanks specially fitted with buoyancy equipment. These are followed by the assault landing craft with assault troops. Infantry are then brought ashore by landing craft shuttling back and forth from the transport ships standing offshore.

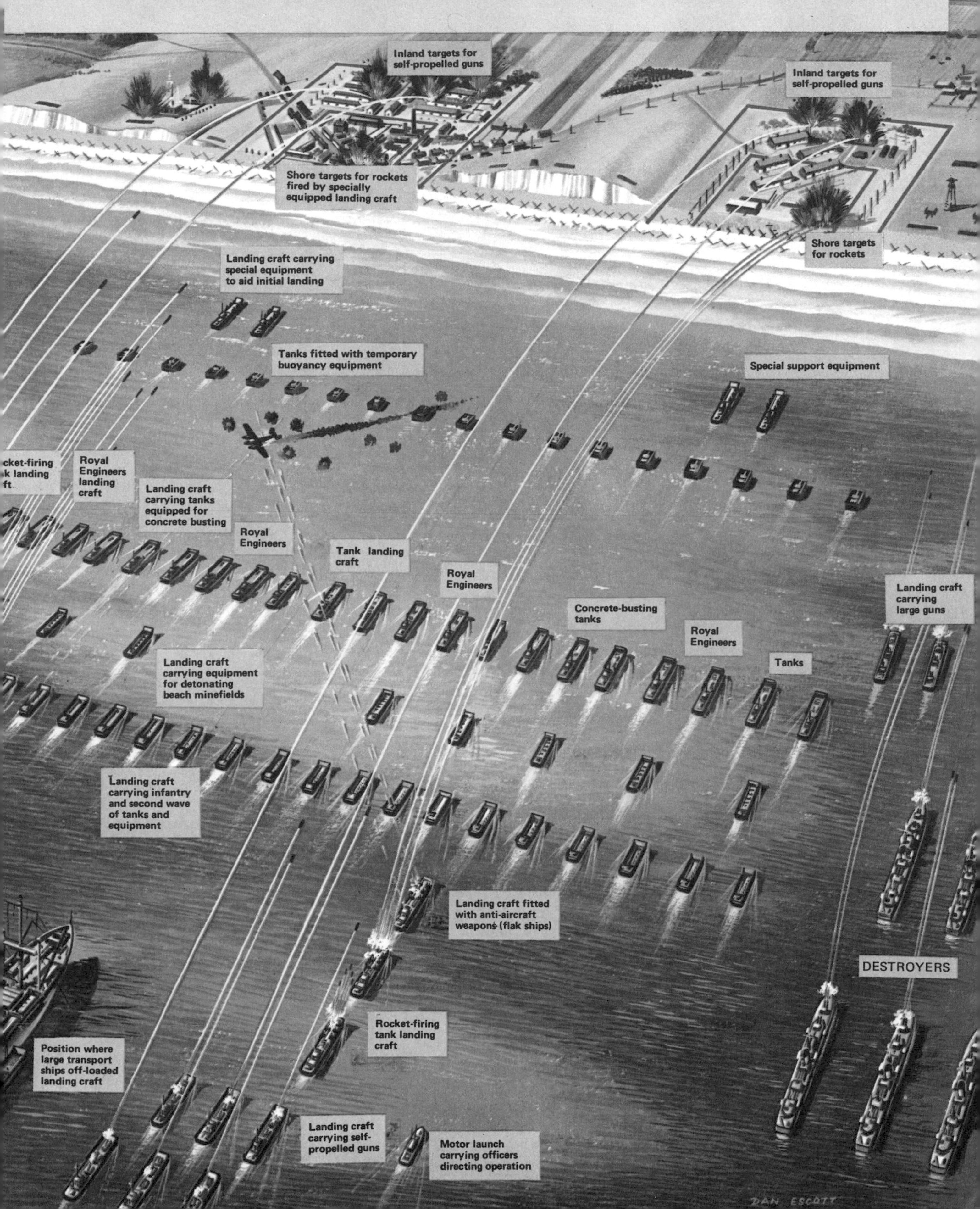

Having landed swiftly, British troops make their way inland on the morning of Tuesday, June 6th.

Digging in and constructing shelters in front of buildings shattered by heavy bombardment during the initial assault on the beaches.
Below: American troops land following anti-tank guns on the Omaha beach-head. The Americans were delayed here by stubborn German resistance and suffered heavy losses of 1,000 dead and 2,000 wounded.

radar that a fleet of ships was approaching the Pas-de-Calais.

The true objective for the assault on occupied Europe was in fact much farther west, at a line of beaches stretching from the Caen area to the east coast of the Cherbourg peninsula in Normandy. Operation Overlord was to be something like the Norman Conquest of 1066 in reverse.

At 1.30 a.m. on D-Day, the British and American parachute troops began to drop into Normandy, beyond the beaches. From then till dawn, Allied bombers dropped 9,000 tons of explosives on the German shore defences.

The first of the seabourne troops — there were to be nearly a quarter of a million soldiers involved in the landings — stormed up the beaches at 6.30 a.m., under the support of massive naval bombardments. The sea was still rough, for the wind had been blowing hard that night, and many of the smaller craft among the 4,000 invasion boats came to grief.

## Wave after wave

Soon, however, the tanks were ashore. Engineers blasted the way through beach defences and wave after wave of assaulting infantry poured through the gaps.

The tanks were waterproofed; when they crawled out of the ocean the waterproofing was blown off. General Sir Bernard Montgomery, Eisenhower's Deputy Commander, had given one comprehensive order: "Don't stop on the beaches, but get inland as far as you can."

German strategy, put forward by their General Erwin Rommel, had been to fight and destroy the invaders on the beaches. This strategy was ruined by surprise — right up to the end the Germans still thought that the main attack was going to be in the Calais area — by the impossibility of moving large counter-attacking forces along the bomb-blasted roads and railways of northern France, and by the sheer ferocity of the assault.

## U-boat screen

Nor could the Germans begin to deal effective blows at the vast armada of Allied ships discharging thousands of troops on the beaches. Twin forces of light warships, British on one side, American on the other, guarded this great argosy.

A special scratch force of small craft acted as a screen against U-boats and E-boats. H.M.S. *Nelson, Warspite and Ramillies* lent the weight of their 15 in and 16 in guns to the bombardment of almost every place along the Seine Bay, as did three American battleships; and, behind this screen, landing ships and landing craft passed to discharge their tanks and men, often in two metres of water.

In some places the landings went badly for the Allies. On the notorious 'Omaha' beach, the U.S. First Division was pinned down for most of the day, suffering 3,000 casualties; although the 4th Division, on their right on 'Utah' beach sustained only a few losses.

A little way inland, paratroops seized a

**AN ARMY FROM THE SEA. Once the beach-heads had been secured, the greatest danger to the reinforcement and supply of the invading troops was the weather. By July 6th, in spite of severe gales in the Channel, 1,000,000 men had been put ashore together with more than 180,000 vehicles and 650,000 tonnes of stores. That achievement would not have been possible without the construction of two artificial harbours, one for the British and the other for the American forces.**
**Some 60 block-ships, forming part of the British harbour, were sunk in position off the beaches at Arromanches on the Normandy coast of France, and huge concrete cassions (floating breakwaters and piers) were towed, in 160 metre lengths, across the Channel and positioned.**
**Then the gales struck, resulting in all the pier sections for the American harbour being lost in mid-Channel. This harbour never was completed. At Arromanches the British harbour stood firm, and by the middle of July the harbour was working to full capacity. Ships large and small unloaded precious supplies on to the huge pier heads connected to the shore by long steel roadways supported by concrete floats.**
**There is no doubt that without the shelter provided by the artificial harbours, neither the large nor shallow-draught supply vessels could have landed the vehicles and equipment so essential for the continuing support of the Allied Armies.**

couple of bridges near Caen and held them despite a violent counter-attack. Some landed in fields, others close to the coast, then, collecting themselves, they rushed for their immediate objectives.

One troop-carrying glider spilled its occupants into the main street of Ste. Mere Eglise. The astonished Germans there surrendered without a fight, but at other places the fighting was both bitter and bloody.

The first shock of the invasion carried the Allied troops several miles inland and they by-passed many German strong-points. But to land an army was one thing; to maintain it there was another.

The enemy began to strike back from the rear, from the hills around Caen, and by flooding the low ground around Carentan. The attackers beat off all these counter-strokes, although only great heroism enabled the 6th Airborne Division to maintain their hold on the two bridges across the River Orne.

Construction gangs with bulldozers feverishly laid out an airstrip even while the beaches were still crowded with men and supplies pouring off the flat-bottomed landing craft as they ran aground. On the first high tide these ships were warped off and drifted at the mercy of the sea. Overhead, thousands of planes maintained the 'air umbrella' throughout the day and into the night, and the thunder of the naval guns from the sea remained non-stop.

Soon Spitfires were able to touch down on emergency landing strips, and forces of up to 1,300 American Liberator and Flying Fortress bombers hammered away at the enemy fortifications. At sea the minefields sown by the Germans were being swept by 2,800 tonnes of mine-sweeping gear.

By June 7th — D-Day plus one in the language of the generals — the airborne troops had linked up with the seaborne tank and infantry formations and a strong German panzer counter-thrust in the neighbourhood of Caen had been repulsed with heavy losses.

There followed a pause for consolidation, while the American forces steadily advanced to seal off the German units holding the vital Contentin Peninsula — the first stage on the way to cutting off enemy formations.

By midnight on D-Day, history's verdict was already assured. Operation Overlord was a complete success. The 'Longest Day', as it has since been called, had been a glorious day, for the bridge-head into occupied Europe was secure. As the flash of the great guns lit up the night sky, a huge army of Allied soldiers had breached Germany's continental fortress, and were poised ready to drive across Europe.

Ahead lay Adolf Hitler's bomb-blasted Germany and Berlin, the Führer's capital and the heart of his evil power.

An impressive list of D-Day statistical information. The figures for ships and aircraft are those amassed for use on D-Day — if not actually used.

| | |
|---|---|
| Allied troops landed by sea | 130,000 |
| Allied airborne troops landed | 22,500 |
| Allied troops killed | 2,500 |
| Allied troops wounded | 8,500 |
| Allied naval ships in combat | 1,213 |
| Allied naval ships in shore bombardment | 137 |
| Lesser allied naval craft | 736 |
| Allied merchant vessels | 846 |
| Allied landing vessels | 4,126 |
| Allied fighter aircraft | 3,830 |
| Allied medium bombers | 930 |
| Allied bombers | 3,440 |
| Allied transport aircraft | 1,360 |
| Allied gliders | 3,500 |
| Allied reconnaissance aircraft | 500 |

# Which American President was known as 'Ike'?

1. Dwight David Eisenhower, who was to become the 34th President of the U.S.A., was born in 1890, at Denison, Texas. His family came from farming stock, although his father tried his hand at a number of jobs to get more money, such as being a store-owner and working on the railway. The family remained poor, and Dwight, along with his five brothers, grew to be self-reliant. Very often there were battles between the brothers and young Dwight learned to look after himself.

2. One of Dwight's friends had entered for the army and persuaded him to do the same. He went to the famous military academy at West Point in 1911 and graduated in 1915. He made no great distinction at West Point, though he excelled at all games and took part in light-hearted pranks with his colleagues.

3. As a young lieutenant in the infantry, he was sent to Fort San Houston, in Texas, and it was there that he met Mamie Doud, who was to become his wife. He saw no active service during the First World War but spent the time as an instructor. After the war, he went to the Staff School and Fort Levenworth and then took on a series of appointments on the Army Staff.

4. In 1935 he served in the Philippines under General MacArthur. He returned to America in 1939 where his promotion became more rapid. By 1941 he held the rank of brigadier-general. With the Japanese attack on Pearl Harbour, when a large portion of the American fleet was destroyed, the United States was brought into the Second World War.

5. Winston Churchill, the British war leader, had met Eisenhower at a conference in America and was so impressed by the qualities of the American General that he asked for him to be in charge of the American forces in Europe. It was in this difficult job that 'Ike's' rare gift for working with men of all nations became valuable. Eisenhower had come to be recognised as an officer who was easy to get on with and who would always listen to others who wanted help. From 1943 to 1945 he commanded the huge Allied Forces brought together in the British Isles for the invasion of Western Europe and he was Supreme Commander of Operation Overlord.

6. Before the war in Europe was over he was asked to stand as President of the United States. He did not like the idea, and after a spell of Chief of Staff to the U.S. Army, he retired and in 1948 became the President of Columbia University. Two years later he was recalled to become the first Supreme Commander of the North Atlantic Treaty Powers. By 1952 he was persuaded to stand as President and was voted into office.

7. The election was a tremendous success and Eisenhower received a record 34 million votes. As President, he spared no effort to promote international understanding and he worked himself unsparingly towards this end. When his four years in office were over, he again stood for President, and was elected once more. The years of tremendous hard work had taken their toll, however, and Eisenhower had a severe heart attack. In 1961 he was succeeded as President by John F. Kennedy, who was later to be so tragically assassinated. Dwight Eisenhower returned to his beloved farm, but was still active and was always available to help those in high places who sought his advice. His heart finally failed him and after a series of attacks, he died on March 29, 1969. In his life Dwight D. Eisenhower had risen from humble background to hold positions of great power. He had risen all the way from farmboy to President.

# When were New Zealand and Australia discovered?

**The ships crew and some of the stores with which Cook set out for the South Seas. He sailed with the secret orders: "You are to proceed to the South Sea in order to make discovery of the continent."**

**List of persons who set out on Captain Cook's first voyage of discovery**

**Key — As employed on voyage — Name and age**

1. Botanist — **Joseph Banks (24)**
   *Knighted, President of Royal Society*
2. Servant — **James Roberts**
   *Servant to Banks, died 1826*
3. Servant — **Peter Briscoe**
   *Servant to Banks, became grocer*
4. Servant — **Thomas Richmond**
   *Servant to Banks, frozen to death 1769*
5. Servant — **George Dorlton**
   *Servant to Banks, frozen to death 1769*
6. Naturalist — **Dr. Daniel Solander (35)**
   *Later keeper of natural history, British Museum*
7. Astronomer — **Charles Green (33)**
   *Died of dysentry 1771*
8. Servant — **John Reynolds**
   *Green's servant, died dysentry 1770*
9. Artist — **Sydney Parkinson (23)**
   *Died 1771*
10. Artist — **Alexander Buchan**
    *Died epilepsy, 1769*
11. Naturalist — **Herman Sporing**
    *Swedish, died 1771*

**OFFICERS AND MEN**

12. Captain — **James Cook (40)**
    *Survived and sailed in two more voyages*
13. Servant — **William Hanson (16)**
    *Cook's servant, survived*
14. 1st Officer — **Zackery Hicks (29)**
    *Died 1771*
15. Servant — **William Harvey (17)**
    *Eventually master's mate, H.M.S. Resolution*

**Rank — Name and age**

16. 2nd Officer — **John Gore**
    *Became Captain, Greenwich Hospital*
17. Servant — **William Harvey**
18. Master — **Robert Molineaux (20)**
    *Died 1771*
19. Servant — **Isaac Morley (12)**
    *Distinguished career, eventually became Admiral*
20. Master's mate — **Francis Wilkinson (22)**
    *Died 1771*
21. Master's mate — **Charles Clerke (25)**
    *Commanded Cook's Resolution on later voyage*
22. Master's mate — **Richard Pickesgill (19)**
    *Commanded other ships*
23. Boatswain — **John Gathrey**
    *Commanded other ships*
24. Servant — **Thomas Jordan**
    *Deserted, Thames, 1771*
25. Bosun's mate — **Thomas Hardman (33)**
    *Sailmaker, 1771*
26. Bosun's mate — **Samuel Evans**
    *Bosun 1771, died 1800*
27. Bosun's mate — **John Reading**
    *Punished for not punishing others, died 1769*
28. Gunner — **Stephen Forwood**
    *Bosun 1771, died 1800*
29. Servant — **Daniel Roberts**
    *Died 1771*
30. Carpenter — **John Satterly**
    *Liked by all, a good man, died 1771*
31. Servant — **Edward Terrell (19)**
    *Sailed in second voyage*
32. Carpenter's mate **George Nowell (25)**
    *Became carpenter on death of Satterly, died 1771*

**Rank — Name and age**

33. Surgeon — **William Monkhouse**
    *First to die of dysentry, 1770*
34. Surgeon's mate — **William Penny (21)**
    *Succeeded Monkhouse*
35. Cook — **John Thompson**
    *Lost right hand but still a good cook!*
36. Servant — **John Mathews**
37. Midshipman — **Jonathan Monkhouse**
    *Best of the Midshipmen, died 1771*
38. Midshipman — **Patrick Saunders**
    *Disrated, deserted Batavia, 1770*
39. Midshipman — **John Bootle**
    *Good journal-keeper, died 1771*
40. Clerk — **Richard Orton**
    *Later promoted to Purser*
41. Quartermaster — **Alexander Wier (35)**
    *Drowned, Madeira, 1768*
42. Armourer — **Robert Taylor**
43. Sailmaker — **John Ravenhill**
    *Comparatively old man – only one not to fall ill at Batavia*
44. Seaman — **Isaac Smith (16)**
    *Cousin of Mrs Cook. Eventually Rear Admiral. Died aged 70*
45. Seaman — **Peter Fowler (18)**
    *Drowned, Rio 1768*
46. Seaman — **Timothy Rearden (25)**
    *Died, Batavia, 1770*
47. Seaman — **William Dawson (19)**
    *Purser on 2nd voyage, died at the Cape*
48. Seaman — **John Ramsey (21)**
    *On all three voyages*
49. Seaman — **Francis Haite (42)**
    *Carpenter's crew, died 1771*
50. Seaman — **Benjamin Jordan (30)**
    *Died 1771*
51. Seaman — **Samuel Jones (22)**

**Rank**

52. Seaman
    *Pur*
53. Seaman
    *Suffe*
54. Seaman
55. Seaman
56. Seaman
    *Carp*
57. Seaman
    *Ca*
58. Seaman
59. Seaman
    *Punishe*
    *(*
60. Seaman
    *Punis*
61. Seaman
62. Seaman
    *Quarte*
63. Seaman
    *Pu*
64. Seaman
    *Punishe*
65. Seaman
    *Puni*
66. Seaman
67. Seaman
68. Seaman
69. Seaman
    *Punishe*
70. Seaman

| ne and age |
|---|
| James Nicholson (21) |
| *or theft, died 1771* |
| Forby Sutherland (29) |
| *sumption, died 1770* |
| Isaac Parker (27) |
| *Bosun's mate* |
| Thomas Simmonds (24) |
| Richard Hughes (22) |
| *n death of Nowell* |
| Samuel Moody (40) |
| *s crew, died 1771* |
| Isaac Johnson (26) |
| Robert Anderson (28) |
| *, attempted desertion.* |
| *on later voyage* |
| Henry Jeffs |
| *assaulting islander* |
| Robert Stainsly (27) |
| *ed at Tahiti* |
| James Grey (24) |
| *1771, later Bosun in* |
| *solution'* |
| William Collett (20) |
| *second voyage* |
| Archibald Wolfe (39) |
| *hiti for stealing nails.* |
| *ed 1771* |
| Mathew Cox (22) |
| *stealing potatoes* |
| Richard Hutchins (27) |
| *sun 1771* |
| Charles Williams (38) |
| Joseph Childs (29) |
| *cook 1771* |
| Alexander Simpson |
| *ealing rum, died 1771* |
| Thomas Knight |

| | Rank | Name and age |
|---|---|---|
| 71. | Seaman | **Henry Stephens (28)** |
| | *Punished for stealing potaotes, 1769* | |
| 72. | Seaman | **Thomas Jones (27)** |
| 73. | Seaman | **Antonio Ponto (24)** |
| 74. | Seaman | **John Dozey (20)** |
| | *Died, Cape, 1771* | |
| 75. | Seaman | **John Tunley (24)** |
| 76. | Seaman | **Michael Littleboy (20)** |
| | *Died, Cape, 1771* | |
| 77. | Seaman | **John Goodjohn** |
| 78. | Seaman | **John Woodworth** |
| | *Died, Batavia, 1770* | |
| 79. | Seaman | **William Peckover (21)** |
| 80. | Seaman | **James Magna** |
| 81. | Seaman | **Richard Littleboy (25)** |
| | *Pûnished for stealing rum, 1769* | |
| | **MARINES** | |
| 82. | Sergeant | **John Edjcumbe** |
| | *eventually Lieutenant* | |
| 83. | Corporal | **John Truscore** |
| 84. | Drummer | **Thomas Rossiter** |
| | *Punished for stealing rum, drunkenness, assault!* | |
| 85. | Private | **William Judge** |
| | *Punished for abuse to officers* | |
| 86. | Private | **Paul Henry** |
| 87. | Private | **Daniel Preston** |
| 88. | Private | **William Wilshire** |
| 89. | Private | **William Greenslade** |
| 90. | Private | **Samuel Gibson** |
| 91. | Private | **Thomas Dunster** |
| | *Punished for refusing fresh beef. Died 1771* | |
| 92. | Private | **Clement Webb** |
| 93. | Private | **John Bowles** |
| 94 | | **Greyhound** |
| 95. | | **Goat** |

**WITH the wind from the wild Yorkshire moorland whipping against his back, a young man stood on the cliffs above the bustling fishing village of Whitby, and gazed down on the scene below.**

The tiny harbour was crowded with sturdy, square-rigged sailing ships — 'Whitby cats' as they were known in nautical circles. It was one of these rugged vessels that James Cook was later to circumnavigate the world, discovering Australia and New Zealand on the way.

But that was not all. More than anyone else, James Cook opened up the Pacific Ocean, that enormous mass of water which covers almost a third of the globe. Singlehandedly, he redrew the map of the world west of the Americas, going where no man had ventured before. He revolutionised our knowledge of the planet we live on.

In a way, it was miraculous that James Cook rose to captain the voyages of discovery that made him famous. Unlike many of the world's great explorers, Cook did not come out of society's top drawer. Those other famous explorers, like Magellan, Da Gama, Tasman, and Bougainville were all able to operate from a position of rank in order to obtain financial backing for their schemes.

Cook, however, was the son of a farm worker. He was born, the eighth of nine children in a tiny cottage in the Yorkshire village of Morton-cum-Cleveland on October 27, 1728.

He was educated at a 'dame' school — where the standards of education were higher than other establishments — and it is said that he never made a mistake at his maths. In later years, this numerical ability was to stand him in good stead; whether he was lost in the midst of a trackless

This model of the Endeavour shows the sturdy lines of the hull and the rigging, simple by the standards of the period, which Cook chose when she was refitted for the voyage.

ocean or drifting helplessly in the Antarctic pack ice James Cook's ability to navigate never let him down.

But at the time, the young man did not know which way his career would lead him, and his father, mindful of his security, apprenticed him to a local haberdasher. Young James soon became restless, however: in July, 1746, aged almost eighteen, he transferred his apprenticeship to a Whitby coal skipper named James Walker.

Walker's business was running coal to London in 'Whitby cats'. It was in these small collier craft that James Cook was to learn the principles of seamanship.

He could not have asked for a better school in which to learn his trade. Along the east coast of England lie some of the most dangerous waters in the world. Swirling currents, shifting currents and submerged rocks made the regular voyage down to London extremely dangerous for the fragile wooden craft of the time. A captain who could ply his trade in those treacherous waters could feel confident virtually anywhere.

By the age of 27, Cook was a good enough seaman to be offered the command of his own collier. But Cook was ambitious. He knew that if he accepted the offer, his prospects in the colliery trade could not extend much further. In 1755, therefore, he enlisted in the Royal Navy as a seaman.

There, his ability was soon recognised, and promotion came quickly. From master's mate on the *Eagle*, a ship of 60 guns, he rose to position of master on the *Pembroke*, a ship of 64 guns.

Soon afterwards, he was sent to Canada to take part in the assault on Quebec, his job being to chart the St. Lawrence River prior to the attack. During those years, Cook provided the Admiralty with charts of an accuracy and clarity never seen before. When he returned to England in 1762, he found himself an acknowledged master of pilotage.

So it was in 1767, when the Royal Astronomical Society proposed a visit to the Pacific island of Tahiti in order to observe the transit of Venus through the southern sky, James Cook was the man they wanted to take them there.

There was, however, another reason for choosing Cook

**Left: a few things Cook brought back from his first voyage of exploration to show Britain how very different life was in the South Seas to anything they had ever encountered before. Below: the attic in Grape Street, Whitby where, as an apprentice, Cook studied mathematics and navigation.**

— and one which even Cook himself did not know until he opened his sealed orders on reaching Tahiti.

For centuries, geographers had speculated on the existence of an enormous southern continent. They called it *Terra Australis Incognita* — the 'unknown southern land' — and estimates of its size varied widely. Some people thought it began off the coast of New Guinea, near the part of Australia which Abel Tasman had bumped into and possibly extended as far south as South America.

But whatever the size of the southern continent, the British Government realised the enormous potential wealth that could be gained from discovering it and claiming it for Britain. When Cook opened his orders in his cabin off Tahiti, he found that he was to sail south, claiming all land that he found in the name of His Britannic Majesty, King George III.

So began Cook's first voyage. It was to ensure his eternal fame, and put his name in the textbooks as the man who first charted Australia and New Zealand.

Entering the Pacific round Cape Horn (the tip of South America), Cook's little collier, converted and renamed *Endeavour*, weighed anchor in Tahiti in September, 1769, almost a year after leaving England. Once the astronomical observations were completed, he set sail for the mysterious southern continent.

After journeying for 2,500 km through bad weather and banks of seaweed, he had found nothing. Turning west, he headed towards New Zealand, the coast of which had been glimpsed by the Dutch explorer Abel Tasman about 120 years previously.

At first, they were prevented from landing by hostile Maori natives; but eventually *Endeavour* beached in what is now called Cook's Bay. Later still, Cook landed in Queen Charlotte's Sound and climbed a hill. From his vantage point, he was able to see that New Zealand was surrounded by sea, and not, as Tasman thought, the tip of a southern continent.

Over the next three months, Cook sailed in and around the two islands that make up New Zealand, drawing up wonderfully accurate charts and maps. Then he set off westwards, sighting Australia on April 18, 1770.

**Fitting out the *Endeavour*. The great advantage of this vessel was that though large enough to carry all the stores Cook required for the voyage she was small enough to maintain and repair.**

A month later he landed in Botany Bay. Continuing up the east coast of Australia, and somehow surviving the 1,500 km wall of coral called the Great Barrier Reef, Cook claimed everything in the name of King George III. He mapped the coastline brilliantly, calling the new territory New South Wales. Then he set off home.

He did not stay long, however. A year later, Cook again set sail for the Pacific in two ships, the *Resolution* and *Adventure*. This time he intended to disprove once and for all the existence of an enormous southern continent.

To this end, Cook decided to sail completely around the world, going as far south as he dared, up to — and sometimes into — the pack ice of the Antarctic. Having circumnavigated the globe as far south as possible, he had

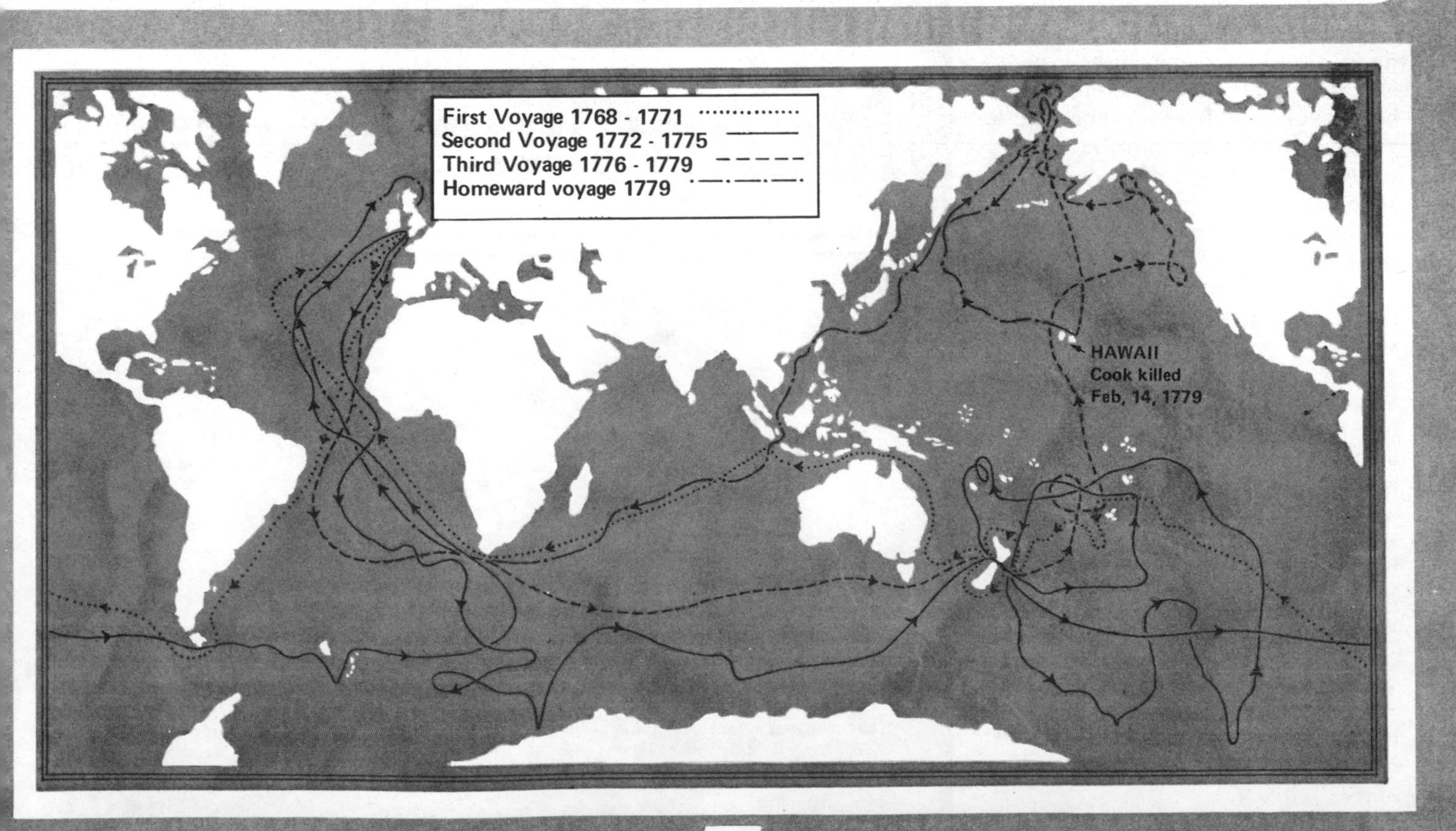

proved conclusively that there was nothing to the south of Australia and the Americas.

Taking time off to perform an astonishing sweep back through the Pacific, Cook discovered a whole series of idyllic islands where the natives wore flowers in their hair and welcomed the explorers as gods.

To the ship's crew, it seemed like Paradise but Cook was careful to respect the natives' customs and way of life. On one occasion, for example, Cook found his quarter deck crowded with grinning Maoris. They had brought him a particularly grisly gift — the head of a Maori.

"The sight of the head . . . struck me with horror and filled my mind with indignation against these Cannibals, but when I considered that any resentment I could shew would avail me but little and being desirous of an eye witness to a fact which many people had their doubts about, I concealed my indignation and ordered a piece of the flesh to be boiled and brought on the quarter deck where one of the Cannibals ate with such relish before the whole ship's company which had such effect on some of them as to cause them to vomit."

By July 1775, Cook was back home. But once again he did not stay long. The call of the sea and the lure of unexplored oceans led him to go in search of that other myth beloved of sailors — the North-west Passage, a strait thought to dissect the Arctic north of America.

On July 13, 1776, Cook put to sea in his old flagship, the *Resolution*.

After two years of searching for the passage, he came to the conclusion that it did not exist, or if it did, to be so packed with ice as to be of little value. Sailing back into the warmer waters of the Pacific, they decided to spend the winter in Hawaii.

The islanders treated the British as old friends, heaping them with flowers and staging lavish banquets in their honour. But then tragedy struck.

On February 14, 1779, Cook went ashore at Kealakukua Beach to sort out a misunderstanding which had arisen between the natives and his men. Tempers flared, and in a scuffle on the beach Cook was repeatedly stabbed and clubbed to death. Only by long and patient negotiations were his officers able to obtain his bones, which they buried at sea.

So perished one of the greatest explorers the world has ever known — a man whose spirit was best summed up in the names of his ships; *Endeavour, Resolution, Adventure* and *Discovery*.

# What was the Mongolian Empire?

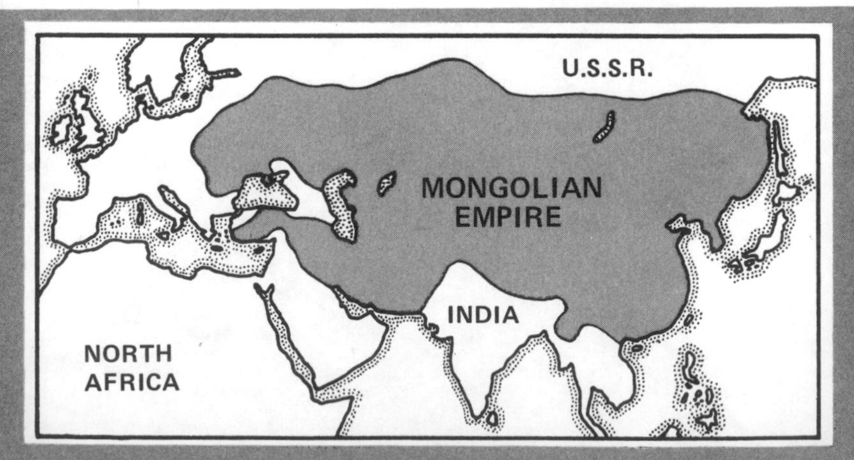


**No empire has ever equalled that of the nomadic Mongols. United for the first time during the 13th century by Genghis Khan, they burst out of their barren heartland around Lake Baikal to conquer nearly half the world. After Genghis, the empire was divided amongst his sons.**

*Continued on next page*

1. The Mongols were a fierce people who lived in central Asia. Always on the move with their herds, they lived in circular huts made of a wicker framework covered with felt. There was never enough pastureland and the many tribes were continually fighting each other to obtain the best land. When the chief of one of the tribes returned from battle with a neighbouring tribe, he found that his wife had given birth to a son. He called the child Temuchin — after the chief of the defeated tribe.

2. When the boy was only 13, the old chief suddenly died. In those troubled times, nobody had much faith in such a young chief, and many left the tribe. But Temuchin's talent for leadership soon became clear to everybody. He reunited his soldiers in compact armies, and launched them against neighbouring tribes. Over 20 years of relentless fighting, he defeated his enemies and united Mongolia under his rule. Temuchin had become the Khan (chief) of all the khans.

3. (Left) At his people's request, he adopted the name Genghis Khan, meaning 'perfect warrior chief'. He knew he must govern strictly with just laws and efficient administration, so he sent ambassadors to neighbouring countries to ask for advice.

4. (Above) As the capital of his empire, Genghis chose Karakorum in the heart of the desolate Mongolian plain. It became a majestic and powerful city, but Genghis chose to live in an enormous tent of white felt, lined with silk.

5. His achievements so far should have been enough, but Genghis Khan yearned to spread his power. He had a proud and compact army, able to overcome any defence. He decided to attack China, seemingly protected by the Great Wall. A horde of 200,000 horsemen led by their invincible chief swept down on the ancient Chinese empire, breaking through the Great Wall at the pass of Wuliang-hai. The avalanche of horsemen now went ruthlessly on, capturing city after city.

6. Although just to his own people, Genghis Khan was a ruthless conqueror. Any city which resisted his armies was sacked and the inhabitants slaughtered. Even some which opened their gates to the advancing armies were similarly treated. The barbaric Mongols had no pity. Soon Genghis had control of all of North China, including the capital Peking.

But still he was not satisfied. Some Mongol ambassadors were murdered by the Shah of what is now eastern Iran and Afghanistan. Genghis led his armies westwards. He and his generals quickly occupied vast areas of Eastern Asia, Asia Minor and southern Russia. In the end, his empire became the most extensive that ever existed, greater than that of Napoleon, Alexander, or Britain in the nineteenth century. Genghis died in 1227 but his successors carried on his terrible tradition.

# Who founded Canterbury Cathedral?

Augustine, sent from Rome to preach Christianity to the Britons, addresses the heathen Ethelbert, King of Kent and his Christian wife Bertha who came from Gaul (now called France).

**Long before the Angles, Saxons and Jutes or English, as we might call them, came to Britain as invaders and settlers, the Britons were Christians. They had learned the faith from their Roman conquerors as the Romans themselves became slowly and steadily converted to Christianity.**

Indeed, after the Roman Emperor Constantine proclaimed himself a Christian and persecution ceased, the new faith flourished in Britain, and in A.D. 314 we find that three British bishops attended a great council of the Church summoned by the Emperor at Arles in France.

All this was soon to change as the Romans withdrew from Britain and the invading English took over. The new immigrants disliked Christianity, which they regarded as a religion of the hated Romans. They seem to have exterminated it completely except in those wild western parts of the islands to which they drove the fugitive Britons.

In place of Christ, the gods Odin and Thor were worshipped. War was now a virtue, and peace a vice. The English chieftains fought each other and when they took prisoners in battle they sold them as slaves to foreign lands.

Thus it happened that some English boys were one day being offered for sale in the slave market at Rome when a priest named Gregory came by.

Noting the fairness of their complexion, which made them look very different from brown-skinned, dark-haired Italian boys, Gregory asked, "Are they Christians or Heathens?"

"Heathens," he was told.

"From which land are they?"

"They are Angles, sir."

"Not **Angles,**" replied Gregory, "but angels, for that is what they would be in the kingdom of heaven."

Some years later Gregory was elected Pope, and, remembering the Angles in the slave market, he despatched a friend of his, a Benedictine Monk named Augustine, to preach Christianity to the English.

With a handful of missionaries to help him, Augustine set out for Britain. But on the journey through Gaul (modern France) the missionaries became panic-stricken about the dangers ahead. Augustine then wrote to Pope Gregory asking if the missionaries could be allowed to go home again.

The letter that Gregory sent back must have been a noble and inspiring one. It urged the missionaries not to give up, but to go forward in faith. And, without further demur, they continued their journey.

Crossing the Channel, they landed at Ebbsfleet, near Ramsgate in Kent, then part of the realm of Ethelbert, the great King of Kent. The choice of landing place was an intelligent one, for although Ethelbert was a heathen, he had married a Christian princess from Gaul, Bertha, and it was thought that he might at least be sympathetic to Augustine and his missionaries.

"We have come from Rome to bring you and your people a joyful message," Augustine wrote to Ethelbert. "All who believe our words will be assured of heaven and happiness."

"Stay where you are for the moment," the King wrote back. "You will be furnished with everything necessary for your comfort while I decide what to do with you."

Some days later Ethelbert visited Augustine and invited him to speak. He took the precaution of sitting in the open air, on the chalky downs within sight of the sea, believing that the magical arts that would be practised by the visitors would be less powerful than inside a building.

## Historic sermon

The missionaries prayed, sang the litany and held up a silver cross and a picture of the Crucifixion painted on a board. Then Augustine preached to the King. Out on the grassy cliff-top, against the sound of the rolling waves, it must rate as the most momentous sermon ever preached in Britain.

At the end of it Ethelbert gave his opinion:

"Your words and promises are very fair, but as they are all new to us, and of uncertain import, I cannot approve of them so far as to forsake that which I have so long followed with the whole English nation.

"But because you have come from afar into my kingdom and wish to impart to us those things which you believe to be true and beneficial, we will not molest you, but give you favourable entertainment . . . Nor do we forbid you to preach and gain as many converts as you can."

The King, who must be given full marks for kindliness and tolerance, then invited his Christian visitors to go and live in Canterbury, the chief town of his kingdom. In that town there was the little church of St. Martin's, built long before by Roman Christians, where Queen Bertha prayed and to where, in due time, came potential converts, attracted by the simple, honest lives of Augustine and his missionaries.

Soon the conversions began to multiply very rapidly. The King himself became a Christian and on one day, in the River Swale, ten thousand of his people were immersed two by two, performing the baptism on each other at the command of Augustine.

Pope Gregory was delighted with the success of his mission. He made Augustine Bishop of Canterbury, and ever since then the Bishop, or Archbishop, of Canterbury, has been the leader of the English Church.

But the Pope wanted the work extended beyond Kent, and Augustine sent missionaries into Essex. One of them, Justus, was consecrated Bishop of Rochester and another, Mellitus, Bishop of London. As a result of their work, the East Saxon King Sabert and many of his people became Christians.

With King Sabert's approval, Ethelbert founded a church, dedicated to St. Paul, in London, and the dome of the great cathedral built in later days still looks down from the same site upon that city.

Gradually, the Christian missionaries made their way right across England. Frequently they met setbacks. Even Kent returned to heathenism for a time after Ethelbert's death. The last part of England to accept Christianity was East Anglia, and within a hundred years of the coming of St. Augustine, the whole country was Christian.

Sometimes the motives for becoming Christian were not always good. Edwin, King of Northumbria, married Ethelbert's daughter, and was sympathetic to his wife's faith. He was inclined to think it might have helped him escape from an assassin's knife and to win an important battle.

But he called his Council together and asked their views.

Coifi, the chief heathen priest, thought it was time for a change, because he had gained little reward from the heathen gods.

Another of the councillors likened the life of a man to the flight of a sparrow through the King's palace. "While he is within he is safe from the wintry storm, but after a short space of fair weather he immediately vanishes out of your sight into the dark winter. So this life of a man appears for a short space, but of what went before, or what is to follow, we are utterly ignorant."

At this King Edwin declared himself a Christian. And to indicate that no one need fear any retribution from the old gods, Coifi hurled his spear at the chief heathen temple.

The watching crowd expected something terrible to happen, but when the heathen idols proved incapable of defending themselves, the people surged forward and temple and idols were burned to the ground.

Left: The common seal of Canterbury Cathedral used on official church documents until the reign of Henry VIII (1509-1547). Then, the Church in England broke away from the Roman Catholic Church and a new seal was made for the cathedral.

## ORIGINS OF THE CATHEDRAL

**When William the Conqueror came from Normandy to England in 1066, the Saxon cathedral in Kent was still intact. It had been built on the site of a chapel founded by St. Augustine in the sixth century. However, the Saxon cathedral and King Canute's crown which was kept there were destroyed by fire in 1067. Rebuilding began under Lanfranc, the first Norman archbishop, conscecrated in 1070, and one of the greatest men ever to sit in the Chair of St. Augustine, the primate's throne. Lanfranc's cathedral was badly damaged by fire in 1174 but parts of it exist within today's building. The present Canterbury Cathedral was begun in 1174 and completed in 1495.**

An Archbishop of Canterbury in his ceremonial robes. His hat is called a 'mitre', his cloak a 'chasuble' and his staff a 'crosier'.

## THE OLDEST ENGLISH CHURCH LIBRARY

**The Cathedral library began as a collection of illuminated manuscripts formed by Augustine monks in 597. It is now the oldest library of religious books in the English-speaking world. Throughout the Cathedral's chequered history, the collection of books has been depleted on occasions by fires or raiders, as in the Civil War period of the 1640s, only to be built up again by kind benefactors such as Archbishop Juxon who built a handsome new library after the restoration of the monarchy in 1660. A later library, created from a Norman dormitory built in Lanfranc's day, was bombed out of existence during the Second World War.**

On December 29, 1170, the Archbishop of Canterbury, Thomas Becket was murdered in the Cathedral by four knights who thought they were carrying out the wishes of Henry II (shown above). The king had passed some laws limiting the powers of the Church and Becket had refused to obey them.

The murder of Becket, depicted on cloister roof.

# CANTERBURY CATHEDRAL

Founded by St. Augustine fourteen centuries ago, Canterbury Cathedral has survived its sometimes turbulent history to become the Church of England's foremost place of worship. Within its walls are the tombs of many famous people: Archbishop Stephen Langton, who joined the nobles in forcing King John to sign the Magna Carta at Runnymede in 1215; Edward, the Black Prince, who led the English army to victory over the French at Crecy in 1346; and King Henry IV who died in 1413, just two years before his more famous son and heir, Henry V, led the English to victory over the French at Agincourt. The place of the Martyrdom and St. Thomas's Shrine are dedicated to the memory of Thomas Becket, the Archbishop murdered in the cathedral in 1170. St Anselm's Chapel commemorates the former archbishop of 1093 while the Warriors' Chapel is the shrine of the East Kent Regiment where its badge, colours and roll of honour are kept.

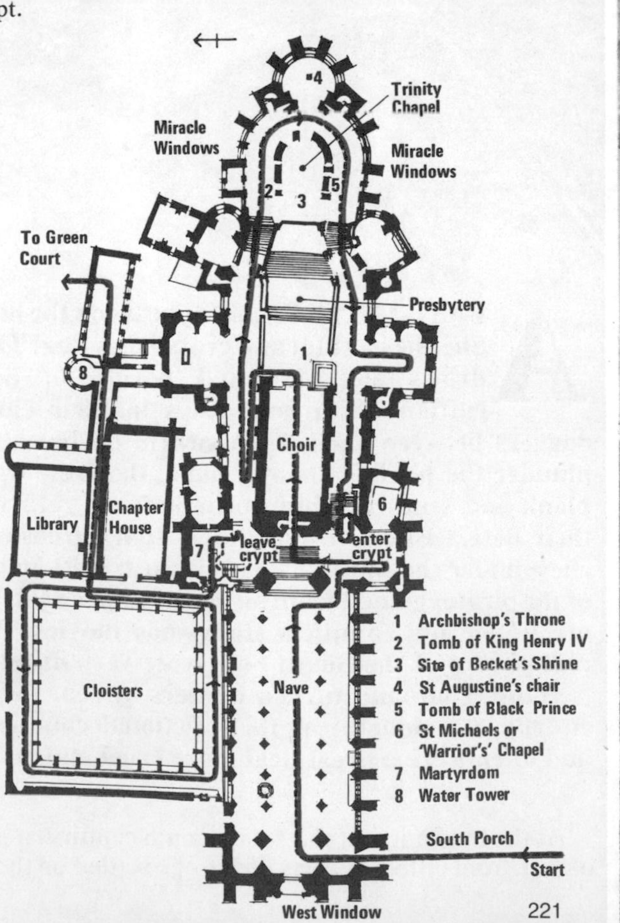


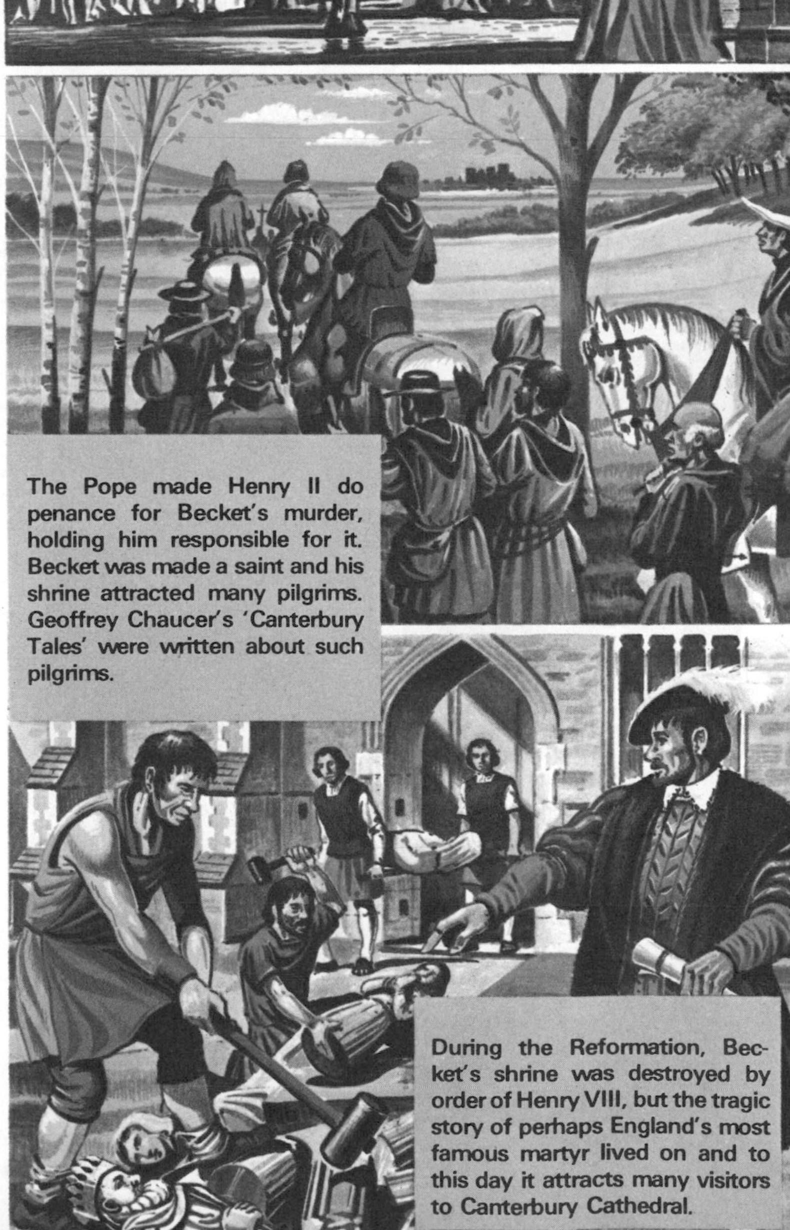

The Pope made Henry II do penance for Becket's murder, holding him responsible for it. Becket was made a saint and his shrine attracted many pilgrims. Geoffrey Chaucer's 'Canterbury Tales' were written about such pilgrims.

During the Reformation, Becket's shrine was destroyed by order of Henry VIII, but the tragic story of perhaps England's most famous martyr lived on and to this day it attracts many visitors to Canterbury Cathedral.

# Who were the Buccaneers?

## The true story of the South Sea Pirates

**A FAST-MOVING ship appears on the horizon. She flies a skull and crossbones flag! The ship draws alongside and hordes of bearded ruffians with gold rings in their ears and daggers between their teeth swarm on board. They plunder the hold for booty, make the crew walk the plank and send the ship to the bottom, returning to their desert island to bury their stolen treasure in a chest under the sand . . . This is the traditional image of the pirate, gained from adventure stories like *Treasure Island* and countless Hollywood movies. But the real pirates of the South Seas were very different.**

**Hunters-on-land turned hunters-by-sea, they were equally as colourful as their fictional counterparts, and often were a great deal more cruel and ruthless.**

At the beginning of the seventeenth century, a number of men from different parts of Europe settled on the island

of Hispaniola (now Haiti and the Dominican Republic). They were sailors who had deserted their ships, religious refugees, runaway slaves — all masterless men who made a living by hunting the vast herds of wild cattle that roamed the island's northern shore.

They were given the nickname 'buccaneers' from the way they preserved the meat that they killed. This was hung in strips over a frame and dried, a process learned from the native Carib Indians. The Indians called the frame a 'boucan', so the white hunters became known as 'boucaniers'. They lived by a strict code of conduct to prevent disputes among themselves. For example, on a hunting-trip, no man was allowed to eat a mouthful of food until as many beasts as there were hunters had been killed. This Code, known as 'The Custom Of The Coast', was strictly enforced and made the buccaneers a strong and united body of men.

Spain was the dominant European power in the Caribbean at this time. The Conquistadores under Cortes had overrun the Aztecs in nearby Mexico and the whole area was part of the great Spanish Empire. Every year, a treasure fleet set sail for Seville, heavily laden with gold plate. They were a tempting prize. And when the Spanish drove the buccaneers from their hunting-grounds in Hispaniola, the outlaws settled on the small, rocky island of Tortuga and, in the 1630s, began attacking the treasure ships that passed them by. At first they put to sea in large, dug-out canoes. Being professional hunters, they were crack shots — it is reported they could hit a coin spinning in the air — and they would attack a huge, cannon-firing galleon, armed with only pistols and long-barrelled muskets. Later, they built one- or two-masted sailing ships with flat-bottomed hulls that enabled them to lurk in the shallow waters along the coast of the Spanish Main. The spoils from each ship were divided up fairly and justly, in accordance with The Custom Of The Coast. But the buccaneers failed to show the same respect to their unfortunate captives who were tortured and killed in a variety of barbaric ways.

The buccaneers were not Spain's only enemy in this



*Continued on next page*

**Kidnapped in Bristol and sold into slavery, Morgan escaped and joined the buccaneers, eventually becoming their leader. He was a brilliant sea captain and soldier. Charles II ignored Spanish complaints against him and in 1674 knighted him, making him lieutenant-governor of Jamaica where he also served as Commander-in-Chief till his death.**

**AN ORIGINAL BUCCANEER (boucanier)**
From the early 1630s the island of Tortuga was occupied by wild adventurers of many European nationalities who lived a simple, sparse existence till they discovered the wealth of Spanish treasure ships.

**THE JOLLY ROGER** is mainly a fiction. It was simpler and cheaper for pirates to fly a simple black flag.

**CUTLASS**
The most favoured weapon of all seamen, whether regular navy or pirate. A heavy, ungainly weapon but still deadly in the right hands.

**CUTTER RIGGED SLOOP.** A fast vessel used by smugglers, pirates, royal navy and customs men alike. They usually carried too much sail for safety and were hard to handle. Buccaneers' sloops were of shallow draught so that they could foil pursuers who could not follow into shallow waters.

**GRAPNELS** were used both for anchoring a vessel and for fixing it to any ship under attack.

**SWIVEL GUN** also known as a raker or murdering piece. It was frequently used to fire small shot such as nuts and bolts, nails and anything else that would maim.

**GOLDEN SPANISH DOUBLOON**

area of the world. The English, French and Dutch were all extending their Empires in the New World and were eager to take from Spain as much as they could. They saw the buccaneers as their allies. Step by step, the pirates were taken over by the various European powers. They were encouraged to leave their hazardous, free-wheeling life for the sake of a safe harbour where they could spend their plundered wealth in the shops and bars. As time went on and the treasure fleets grew fewer, they were then persuaded to mount attacks on neighbouring Spanish cities. Between 1655 and 1671, the buccaneers sacked eighteen cities, four towns and thirty-five villages on the Spanish mainland. This greatly pleased the governments of England, France and Holland, for not only did it weaken their Imperial rival, but also a great deal of the plunder found its way back to the Treasuries of the countries concerned.

The most famous figure during these years — the heyday of the buccaneers — was a Welshman, Henry Morgan. Sent out to the West Indies as a young lad, he was master of his own ship by 1665, doubtless bought from the proceeds of piracy. Morgan was friendly with the Governor of Jamaica, Sir Thomas Modyford, who gave the pirate leader a free hand to mount a series of daring raids which culminated in the capture and burning of Panama City. This Spanish stronghold had always been safe from attack by pirates, being on the western Pacific coast of the Isthmus of Panama. But Morgan's force landed on the eastern shore, marched overland and looted the city which was burned to the ground. The Spanish were outraged and, to pacify them, King Charles II had Morgan arrested and brought back to England. But he was welcomed at Court and, in 1674, he was knighted and sent back to Jamaica as Deputy Governor. But the sack of Panama City heralded the end of the buccaneer era. Morgan failed to divide up the spoils of his piracy in the manner of the old Custom Of The Coast and, now little more than pawns in the hands of their respective governments, the buccaneers were absorbed into their countries' navies.

But their exploits were not forgotten. A Dutchman called Alexander Exquemelin wrote a book about them which was widely read in its day and insured that the buccaneers left their mark on history. Interest in them inspired later voyages of exploration in the Pacific and led to the foundation of the South Sea Company.

# Which English King did not smile for 15 years?

**FOR four-and-a-half years King Henry I had been absent from England. He had achieved much in that time. He had finally quelled the rebellious barons of Normandy; had himself proclaimed duke of that region, thereby linking it to the crown of England; persuaded the King of France to acknowledge his teenage son William as heir to the dukedom as well as the crown of England.**

King Henry, son of William the Conqueror, had every reason to be pleased with himself. On the evening of Thursday, November 25, 1120, he was at Barfleur, ready to return to England.

As he waited on the quayside for the ship that was to take him and his children, he was approached by a man named Thomas Fitz-Stephen.

"Sire," said this Thomas Fitz-Stephen, "my father was the captain who steered the ship in which your father embarked for the conquest of England. I beg you to let me take you back to England in my vessel, *La Blanche Nef* (The White Ship)."

It was too late, Henry replied, his arrangements were already made. But in consideration of Fitz-Stephen's request, he would entrust to him his son William and his daughter Maud and their attendants.

## Tréacherous Reef

As night fell, Henry's ship set sail. It docked in England next morning after a voyage without incident.

Several hours after the King's ship had embarked, The White Ship set sail. She was a new and superb craft of fifty oars, but that night everything on board was far from ship-shape.

The royal children, their attendants, and, worse, the crew, had all been drinking heavily. There was shouting and laughing and, clearly, not much navigating going on. Someone conceived the wild idea of trying to overtake the King's ship, and full sail was crowded on for the gentle south wind.

Suddenly, when the ship was still only a mile and a half out of Barfleur, she was shaken by a great convulsive shudder. At considerable speed she had struck a treacherous reef of rocks called the Raz de Catteville, and her starboard side was smashed in.

A frenzied cry of terror went up from the revellers as The White Ship began to sink at once. Within minutes she slid under the waves.

Some of the cooler sailors had managed to lower a boat and among those in it was Prince William, heir to the throne of England. The boat was being rowed safely away when William recognised the voice of his sister Maud and commanded the boat's crew to return and rescue her.

The rowers obeyed, but before they could find the princess, others began to jump into the boat. The result was that it was swamped and everyone who had been in it was thrown into the water.

Among the struggling mass of drowning people was The White Ship's master, Thomas Fitz-Stephen. He was able to gasp: "Where is the King's son?" and to hear the shouted reply: "We have seen nothing of him." At that, Fitz-Stephen threw up his arms in a gesture of despair and sank beneath the waves.

Indeed, nothing more was ever seen or heard of Prince William or his sister. Only one man survived the sinking of The White Ship — Berthold, a Rouen butcher. He still had his sheepskin coat wrapped around his shoulders and, despite the bitter cold, he managed to support himself until daybreak. Then he was seen by some fishermen, who pulled him into their boat.

It was Berthold who revealed the tragic end of The White Ship. But who was to tell the King in England about the death of the son he idolised?

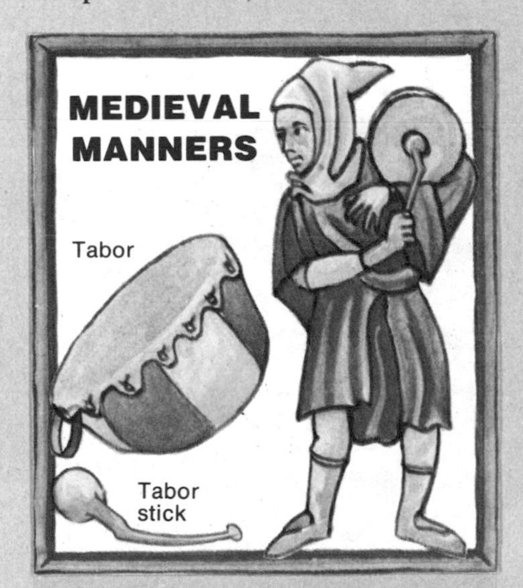


### THE TABOR

**THE Tabor was a small drum held by one hand and beaten by the other. It could be beaten either by the hand itself or by the hand holding a drumstick. Pictures of it appear in very early manuscripts and apparently it remained popular for a long time. Shakespeare mentions it in some of his plays. The size of tabors varied. Some could be held under one arm, others were fitted with a thong which was looped round the arm while being supported on the upper arm or shoulder. Either way left an arm and a hand free to play a three-holed pipe — and this was frequently done, turning the player into a sort of one-man band. The drumstick (if used) was often crooked, since it made beating the tabor at the same time as blowing a pipe slightly easier.**

## Divine Justice?

A nobleman's little boy, told what to say and do, was sent in weeping and, throwing himself at the King's feet, recited the story. The King, it is said, fainted, and when he came to, he was left alone to dwell on the bitterness of his lost hopes.

It was said that the King never smiled again, though he lived for another fifteen years. Henry knew that God was behind everything; that the death of his children was the Creator's way of punishing him for something.

No doubt most Englishmen thought so, too. The loss of The White Ship was clearly divine vengeance in their eyes, for how could such a tragedy have occurred in fine weather on a gentle sea, except by a judgment of God?

They may have felt sorry for the King, but they had always been wary about Prince William. It was said that he had made it clear that when he became King he would govern the English harshly. He was said to have been determined to "yoke the English like oxen to the plough if ever he would reign over them." Whether or not that was simply youth's arrogant boast, the English wept few tears for the loss of their heir to the throne.

Henry's chief aim now was to try to keep the succession in his own family, rather than see England and Normandy split between warring barons and a return to the bad days he had so skilfully ended.

All that was left of that family was a daughter, Matilda, who was married to the Emperor Henry V. The "Emperor" was in fact the ruler of Germany and northern Italy, but as heir to Charlemagne he claimed to rule all Christian Europe, which was called the Holy Roman Empire.

Matilda's marriage was a very grand one for the daughter of an English king. But there seemed little chance of Matilda and the Emperor being involved in the English succession, for the English would never consent to being part of what they regarded as a German Empire.

Desperately, the King married again, in the hope of having another son. His new Queen was Adelisa of Louvain, but they had no children.

Then, in 1125, the Emperor Henry V died, leaving Matilda childless. She came back at once to England, and the King made his barons swear to recognise her as his heir.

England had never before been ruled by a woman, so the barons were doubtful. In any case, this only postponed the evil day, for Matilda had no children.

But the situation changed dramatically in 1127, when Matilda was married to Geoffrey, Count of Anjou in France. The King liked this Geoffrey very much; he was knighted in great splendour and he took for his "device" the leopards which are still the arms of England.

Geoffrey used to wear in his hat a spray of broom, the Latin name of which is *Planta genista*, and because of that Geoffrey and his family came to be known as Plantagenets, or Wearers of the Broom.

Matilda, however, didn't think very highly of Geoffrey. He was much younger than she and not nearly as grand as an Emperor. But presently they had a son, whom they called Henry after his grandfather. One day he was to be the first of the Plantagenet kings of England, all as a result of that trick of fate that sank The White Ship.

The barons of England did not like the Matilda-Geoffrey marriage. Anjou was the ancestral foe of Normandy, and Matilda, who hung on to her title of Empress, despised mere Counts and barons. But there was no one else for them to turn to, so reluctantly they swore once again to obey Matilda.

In December, 1135, King Henry I, now a very old man, ate a large dish of lampreys, a very greasy eel-like fish, which, it is said, brought on his death. He was buried in Reading Abbey, which he himself had founded.

**The first half of the 12th century was around the time when the long Viking type ships that had dominated the northern seas for so long were developing into the 'round' hulk type ships — later to become the Galleons of the Tudor period. Ships of Henry I's reign (1100-1135) were becoming heavier with more beam. Fighting 'castles' were being built at either end (fore and aft) although they had not yet become incorporated in the hull. The ships were more dependent on sails than previously, though oars were still important, as the single square sail used served really only before the wind. Any craft that shipped 50 oars was highly valued. References for these ships, however, (on seaport seals) rarely show oars or give any indication whether they were run through the sides of the hull or were set over the sides in rowlocks.**

DAN ESCOTT

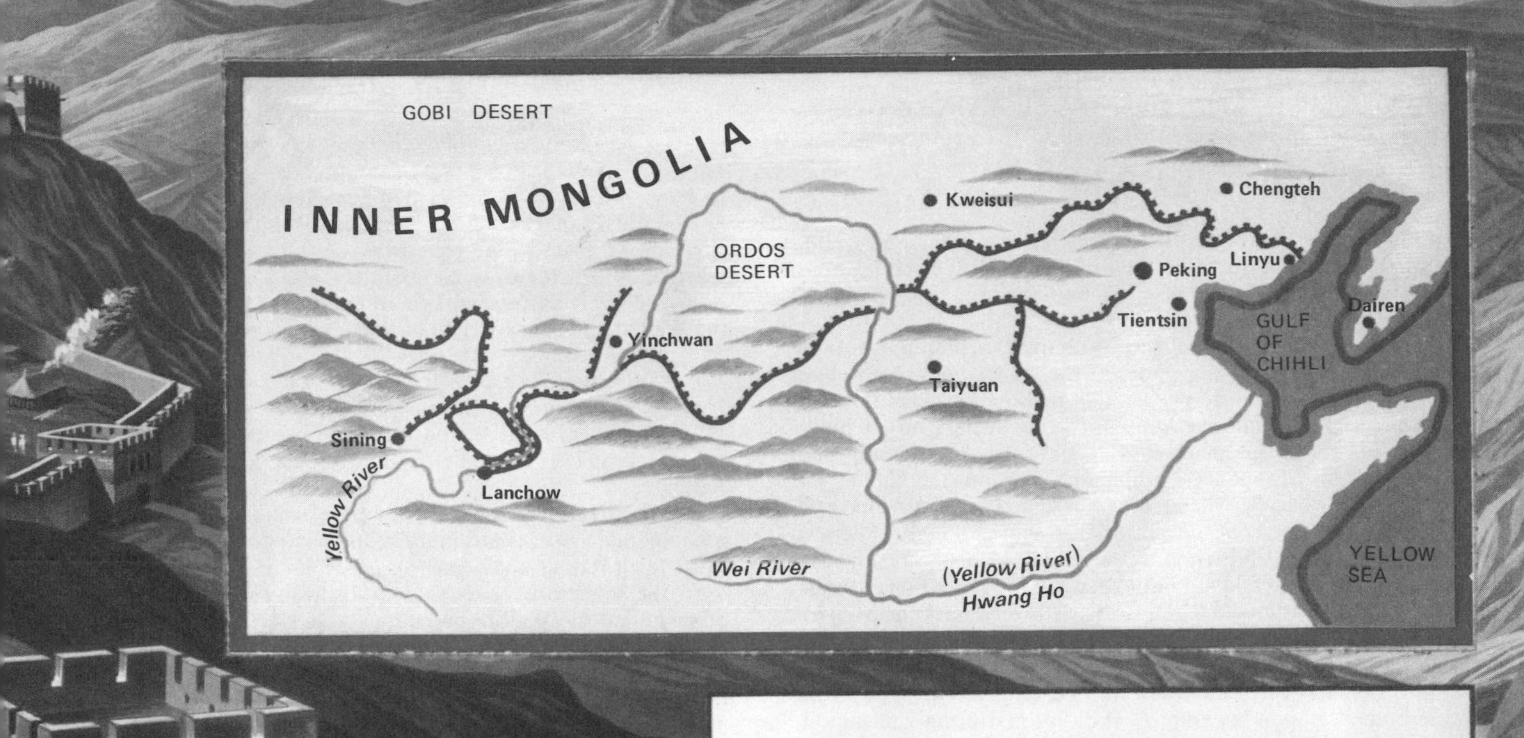


# Why was the Great Wall of China built?

**Visible from the Moon, China's Great Wall is perhaps the most ambitious defence system ever created but it is also a monument to cruelty and grief.**

**EVEN among the awesome band of princes who ruled eastern lands thousands of years ago, Shih-hwang-ti was a most unusual monarch. Every day he was in fear of assassination, and to put off would-be murderers he never slept in the same room for two successive nights.**

The need for plenty of bedrooms was Shih-hwang-ti's least concern. He was a passionate builder, and he had 170 palaces. The largest of them was said to have so many rooms that if he lived in a different one each day it would have taken him thirty-six years to use them all.

---

**This impression of the Great Wall of China shows how it wound up and down over the hilly terrain. The narrow slots of the battlements gave bowmen room to shoot down on attackers, while providing maximum protection. The two guards are infantrymen, they wear helmets of metal or leather, but they have no armour. They are clad in bulky coats made up of loose layers of tightly woven silk. These garments were difficult to cut through with a blade and also resisted arrows. If an arrow did manage to pierce the flesh of the wearer the arrowhead would usually become swathed with a piece of silk. This made it easier to remove the arrow and also protected the wound from further damage caused by the barbs when the arrow was removed. The guards are armed with swords and pole-arms, sharp metal blades mounted on long handles. This type of equipment was in use when the Wall was built and continued to be used for several hundred years.**

Shih-hwang-ti was Prince of the Chinese province of Ch'in when, in 221 B.C., he declared himself the first Emperor of a united China. The vigour and authority of his rule was soon the talk of the East. He broke the power of the feudal families of China and appointed military and civil officials to administer the great areas of land within his power. The type of government which he set up survived in China until this century.

## Enemies

Shih-hwang-ti saw enemies everywhere — outside as well as within his new empire. Soon after he had made himself Emperor he hit on the idea of using his great building urge to keep himself safe from some of these enemies.

In the north of his vast territories, barbarian marauders — the Hsiung-nu, who were ancestors of the warlike Huns who later invaded Europe — were perpetually making inroads from their own bleak country into the well-cultivated, fertile land of China.

Shih-hwang-ti's predecessors in the north had already built some sections of defensive walling to keep out the Hsiung-nu. Now the barbarians made a concerted attack on this half-defended frontier. The new Emperor sent 300,000 soldiers to drive them back, and when the victory was his he resolved to build a wall that would not only keep out the barbarian enemies, but would also keep the Chinese in and firmly mark the frontier.

Shih-hwang-ti never built anything by half-measures. His Wall was going to be one-twentieth of the circumference of the Earth, and to construct it he pressed into service one-third of all the able-bodied men in his empire. It didn't matter how unsuitable they were for the task — writers, clerk, tax officials and common criminals were all forced to toil side by side in order to build the Great Wall of China.

The Emperor had scant regard either for the lives or the welfare of his people. Like ants they were sent north to work in huge flocks on the wall — perhaps a million men and women died in the years of its construction. Prisons disgorged their inhabitants to swell the work-force and prisoners-of-war were sent there to toil — and probably die.

The work went on through all changes of climate — the heat of desert summers, the icy winters. The Wall rolled on, through sand and mud and scaled mountainous heights. It was not allowed to cease.

The immensity of the task, and the savagery of it, staggers the imagination. Where human labour was available in infinite measure, nothing was impossible, no task too great to be undertaken. If the materials for construction were not at hand, then they had to be brought from no matter how far away, at no matter what expense.

The Wall was really a double wall. Hard brick outer walls were filled with clay and built on foundations of stone. About ten metres up, along the top of the Wall, was a roadway wide enough for eight men to march abreast and for horses and chariots to travel along.

## Salvation

Every hundred metres or so there was a watch-tower, standing out from the Wall. From these strongholds signals could be sent to warn soldiers along the Wall of imminent enemy attack. Probably about 25,000 of these towers were built along the Wall.

China is a land that preserves her memories in tales and legends. Within them is a germ of the truth. Stories are told of the men who fell ill as they worked and how they were trampled into the Wall along with the clay; of those who died and were thrown in also.

But, as a Chinese proverb says, "The annihilation of one generation has proved the salvation of others," and for many years the Great Wall served its purpose well, even playing its part as late as 1933 in protecting the Chinese against the attacking Japanese.

For the size of such a feat very little was recorded about this monumental and extraordinary Wall. What now remains of it has often been rebuilt and repaired.

In the ten more years that Shih-hwang-ti reigned after he commanded the Wall to be built, about 1,500 miles of it (about half its total length) were completed. It stretched from the east coast, near the site of China's modern capital of Peking, for hundreds of miles westwards, crossing the great Yellow River. The rest of the Wall was completed under later Emperors.

The height and size of the Wall diminish somewhat as it progresses westwards, but to the end it maintains its high quality of workmanship. Starting from Shan-hai-Kwan, it runs west across the mountains to Kalgan. Then it goes over the plains and lesser ranges of the Hwang-ho basin. From that point the existing boundary between Mongolia and China is faithfully followed to Kiayu Kwan, where the Wall comes to a sudden end.

Modern research has shown that the Great Wall branches off into two distinct loops near Chunwei, and that another loop enclosed a large tract of land west of the capital. Excluding these loops, the Great Wall would stretch from Berlin to Tiflis in the Caucasus.

In the year 210 B.C. Shih-hwang-ti died — and, since he had told everyone that he was immortal, that came as a considerable shock to the court. They believed, therefore, that there must be some mistake, and that the Emperor wasn't really dead. They sat his body in a sedan-chair and carried it all over the vast country, stopping only long enough to allow it to give "audiences". At the end of nine months, no doubt persuaded by the bad smell, they finally decided that Shih-hwang-ti really was dead, and buried him.

**Part of the great wall as it appears today.**

# Who were the Incas?

**UNTIL 1438, the Incas of Peru were a small, not very significant tribe living in and around Cuzco, the city they had founded in about 1200 some 3,475 metres up in the Andes Mountains of South America.**

**Yet only 55 years later, in 1493, they had conquered a vast empire 990,000 km. square, stretching from present-day Ecuador through Peru and down into central Chile. Called Tahuantinsuyu (land of four provinces), this empire was tragically short-lived, for Spanish conquistadors (conquerors), drawn by tales of its fabulous wealth, vanquished and destroyed it after less than fifty years.**

The Spaniards were not, however, dismantling some backward, barbaric empire but a complex, well-organised civilisation in many ways more advanced than their own.

For instance, the way Inca society was organised was unique in its time, and nothing resembling it arose in Europe until our own century. Speaking very generally, Tahuantinsuyu was a "welfare state". The most important components of life — the land, llamas for transport and the gold and silver mines — were 'nationalised' (state-run). No one was very rich or very poor. All were given enough for their needs and were assured of work, food, shelter, llamas, clothing and government aid if natural disasters, such as floods or storms, ruined their crops.

This was not, however, a welfare state in the modern, 20th century sense, where a country is 'owned' by its people. The 'owner' of Tahuantinsuyu was the emperor, the Sapa Inca (Supreme Lord).

The logic behind this was simple. The visible representation of Viracocha, creator of the world, was Inti, the Sun god: everything that lay under the Sun belonged to Inti, and therefore to the Sapa, the direct descendant of Inti. The land was his, the soil was his, the people were his property, the colossal wealth of gold, the 'sweat of the Sun' belonged to him, and so did the silver, 'the tears of the Moon'. This, of course, made the Sapa Inca, Lord of the World, Son of the Sun, more powerful than any monarch in Europe had ever dreamed.

Naturally, the Sapa Inca was regarded with tremendous awe and reverence. His authority was absolute, and obedience to it, unquestioning. Obviously, there was no room here for individuality or personal freedom. Everyone in Tahuantinsuyu lived according to tradition and expected nothing else.

If a man were born to be a farmer, then he was a farmer. His traditional work was producing maize, potatoes, fruits and other foods on the terrace-fields cut into steep Andean moun-

**Left: Inca ruins of Macchu Picchu in the Cuzco department of Peru. They are visited every year by thousands of tourists who marvel at the amazing civilisation and abilities of this by-gone people.**

**Inca children enjoyed games as do modern children. Below is an artist's impression of Incas playing *patolli*, a game probably like modern ludo.**

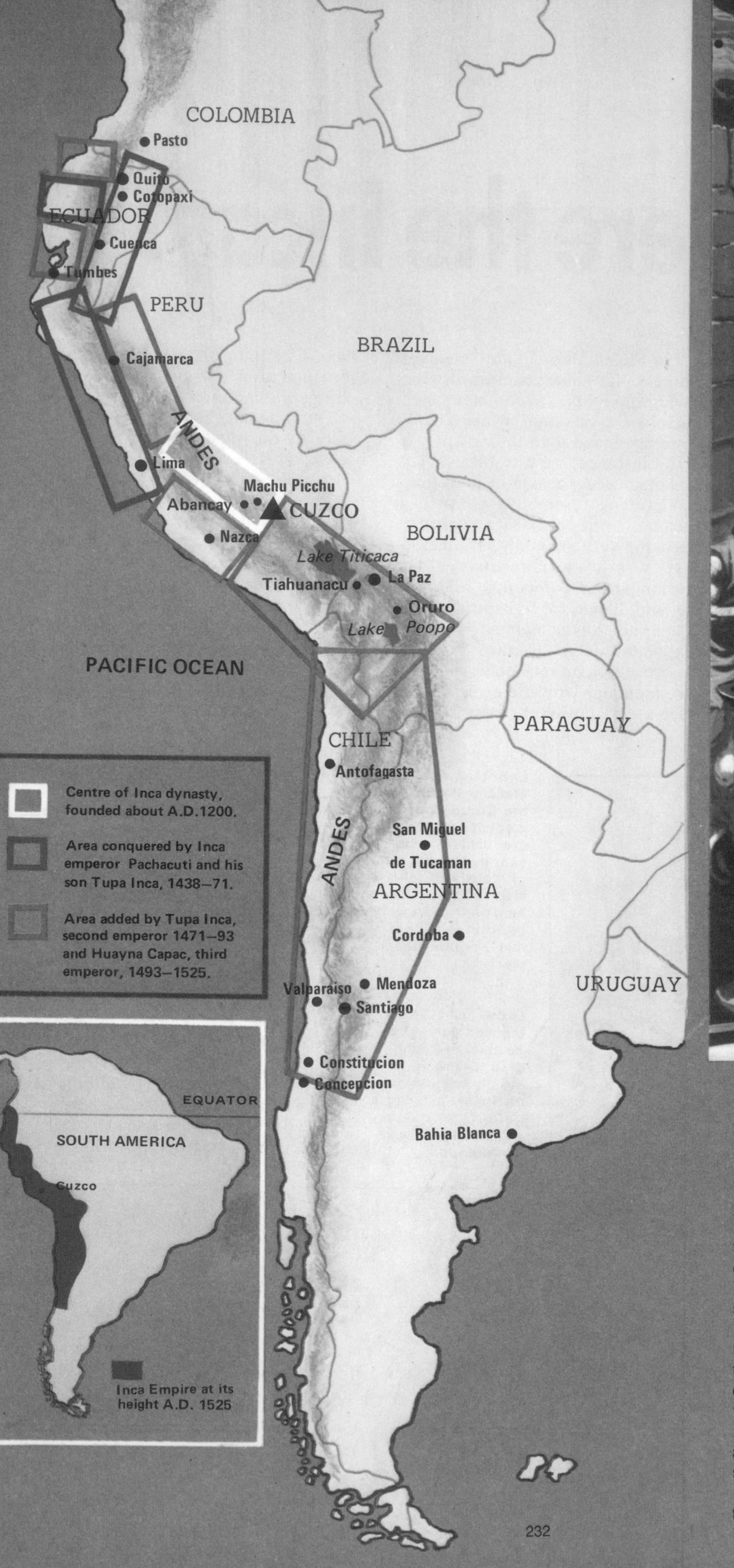

tainsides. The land, which was divided into three parts, had to be worked in the traditional order.

First, came the land cultivated for the Inca gods and their priests. The produce of the second part of the land went to the government, who used it to supply the nobles, government officials, craftsmen and the army. Last came the land whose produce supplied the ordinary people.

This life of unceasing obedience, toil and tradition began at the age of three, when boys and girls were expected to begin their working lives within their 'ayllu' (family group). Here, the rule of life was: "Ama sua, ama llulla, ama shekllu" (Do not steal, do not lie, do not be lazy).

Ways of escaping the dictates of tradition did exist, though only for

Above: an artist's imaginative reconstruction of the everyday life in an Inca community. We see the llama pack animals, the craftsmen and the distinctive round dwellings.

the fortunate few. Girls who were especially beautiful, charming or skilled at weaving and cooking might be picked as "Chosen Women". After training, they became handmaidens to the Sapa or attendants in religious temples. Especially sturdy young boys could be chosen as "Chasquis" (Couriers). Chasquis carried messages between the 'tampu' courier stations, running at 15 km. per hour.

These messages were not in written form, for the Incas had no written language as we know it. They recorded information on knotted strings called 'quipus', which could also be used as calculators.

By European standards, the Incas' lack of a written language denoted a primitive people. So did the fact that the Incas did not use the wheel and, as Sun-worshippers, sometimes sacrificed humans to their gods. However, there was nothing primitive or backward about the work of Inca astronomers. They knew how to predict the times when equinoxes and solstices occurred and how to use observations of the Sun to adjust the yearly calendar to 365 days. They knew far more, in fact, than the astronomers then in Europe.

Inca engineers constructed irrigation systems for the terraces, bringing water from high mountain glaciers up to 804 km. away. They also built underground water reservoirs, drainage systems, and buildings in which huge stones were so perfectly cut and fitted together that they needed no mortar.

Inca bridge-builders were no less skilful. They constructed rope bridges across the mountain ravines which were so strong that the Spaniards found they could ride horses at full gallop across them.

As the Spaniards also discovered, Inca craftsmen were very considerable artists. Their artistry was most dramatically displayed at the Curicancha, the golden temple enclosure in Cuzco, where they created a garden with earth, plants, corncobs, twenty life-sized llamas with shepherds — all of solid gold.

# What was the Richest Ransom in History?

## The Spaniards had only 200 men – but that was all they needed.

**THERE were less than 200 of them, a piratical band of men lured on by dreams of gold, and they conquered an empire of at least five million people. There is nothing to equal their feat in the whole history of mankind, and the fact they were a tough gang of thieves and murderers, led by a rogue, does not lessen their achievement. They were the Spaniards who toppled the Inca Empire of Peru.**

Colossal luck, daring, and the possession of horses and cannons, helped the Spaniards pull off the impossible. For although the Inca Empire was ruled by a king who was a god — that god was doomed to die.

The man who led the Spaniards was a brave, illiterate soldier in his mid-fifties, Francisco Pizarro. When he burst so dramatically on to the world's stage, Spain was already master of Central America.

Pizarro, born in Spain around 1478, heard rumours of the wealth of the Inca Empire and became obsessed with the idea of invading it. In command of a small fleet, he sailed to Spain, where King Charles V showed real interest. On July 26, 1529, Pizarro was ordered to invade and conquer Peru.

He and his men sailed southwards from Panama in December, 1530, but landed too far north and had a grim trek southwards, fighting not only primitive tribes, but fever as well, before reaching the frontiers of the Inca Empire, which then consisted not only of Peru but also of Ecuador, Bolivia and part of Chile.

Though they did not realise it at first, Pizarro and his men had appeared at a fortunate moment for them: the Inca Empire was being torn apart by civil war. In normal times, the Inca ruler, the Sun God, was all powerful. This god-king and a small ruling class were despots, but not particularly cruel ones and, though the people had no freedom and worked for the state, they seem to have been reasonably content. There were fine roads and farms and buildings, many of them earthquake-proof, and in a land without the wheel, runners swiftly carried news all over the empire. With a large and excellent army, the Incas should have been a match for any invaders, but the civil war, a particularly bitter one, had left the nation hopelessly divided.

Pizarro and his men arrived just as Atahualpa, one of the contestants, had gained the upper hand. A bitter fate was to befall him.

Pizarro's men marched wonderingly through the Inca domains. They noted how advanced the people were and nervously considered their own weakness, a mere 180 or so marching perhaps to their doom. The Incas, who were astounded by the Spanish horses, never having seen any, did not molest the intruders, who saw many forts along the way. By sheer good luck, the new ruler Atahualpa was away from his capital, Cuzco, and was actually camped at a mountainous spot called Cajamarca on Pizarro's line of march. An Inca envoy bearing gifts came to invite the newcomers to meet the great Atahualpa and Pizarro agreed, sending on fine presents ahead.

The Spaniards rode down into the valley where the Inca army was encamped outside Cajamarca. Even the boldest Conquistador must have felt uneasy at the sight of it, but the little band marched into the town square and one of Pizarro's officers was sent to Atahualpa to invite him to visit Pizarro. Atahualpa agreed.

What happened next was blackest treachery.

The Spaniards fearfully hid themselves in the buildings that surrounded the town square and waited. Into the

square came some 7,000 or so lightly armed Inca warriors, their ruler being carried on a great litter by 80 lords. A Spanish priest appeared to preach Christianity, which had to be done before blood was shed. Naturally, the Incas were not ready to be instantly converted, and the priest rushed to safety, urging bloodshed.

He got it. A most appalling massacre began with a blast of cannon fire. Cavalry completed the slaughter, Pizarro seeing to it himself that Atahualpa was made captive. After the slaughter and with the Incas beyond the square paralysed by the loss of their king, the Spaniards started looting gold and silver.

Shaken as he was, Atahualpa soon saw that treasure was the object of the Spaniards' bloody exercise and he made the most spectacular ransom offer in history. In return for his freedom, he told Pizarro he would give him a room full of gold, the room to be seven metres by five and the gold to reach a white line on the wall over two metres high. As the gold would be brought in the form of ornaments, not solid, an adjacent room would be filled twice over, the entire ransom being promised within two months.

Even the greedy Spaniards, who could never get enough gold, could hardly believe their luck.

They suspected treachery, of course, being treacherous themselves, but the gold kept coming in, priceless works of art, which the Spaniards were later to melt down. By mid-1533, after Atahualpa had ruled his empire from the Temple of the Sun in Cajamarca for eight months, the incredible treasure trove was complete. By now the Span-

Each year, in modern Peru, there is a celebration of the Inca Sun-worshipping festival of Inti-Raymi.

ish force had received a few reinforcements, but was still hopelessly outnumbered. Atahualpa naturally demanded to be set free. He had been treated fairly well and some friendship had formed between him and Pizarro.

Much good did it do him! With rumours of uprisings in the country, Pizarro's men were getting jittery and it was decided to hold on to Atahualpa. Finally, despite strong objections by those of Pizarro's men who had consciences, Atahualpa was given a farcical trial, condemned to death, and publicly strangled.

Instead of the Spaniards being put to the sword themselves, the rigidly organised Inca world collapsed like a pack of cards, for the Incas's *god* had died. Though fighting went on spasmodically down the years, the Indians of the Inca Empire seemed to lose the will to live. Even today, centuries after the first harsh onset of Spanish rule, many seem to exist in a private, withdrawn world of their own.

As for the conquerors, they later fell out among themselves, many meeting violent deaths. Finally, Pizarro was murdered in 1541 by troops of one of his lieutenants, who had himself been strangled by Pizarro's brother. So ended a saga of bloodshed and treachery; yet for all its nightmare quality, the story of Pizarro and his men remains as exciting as it is appalling. They were some of the most daring adventurers who ever lived, and the toppling of a mighty empire by such a tiny handful remains one of the epics of Mankind.

Above: a modern road zig-zags from the River Urubamba to the ruins of the Inca city of Vilcampampa. In cloud is Machu Picchu.

Left: Part of the ruins of Machu Picchu — the Inca city discovered by Hiram Bingham in 1911. The stone block on the top was a sundial or maybe a ritual object of Inca Sun worship.

# Who was Old Bruin?

A typical ancient samurai — armed, armoured and terrifying to behold.

**LESS than 150 years ago, Japan was still virtually sealed off from the rest of the world. The Japanese were living under a feudal system not unlike that introduced into England by William the Conqueror after his victory at Hastings in 1066. They were in their Middle Ages.**

The Emperor of Japan was regarded as a god, but he had precious little power. That had passed to aristocratic military leaders called shoguns. The title shogun dated back to the 12th century when, after years of civil wars, a warrior family called the Minamoto defeated all their rivals and established themselves as the rulers of Japan, with their own leader Yoritomo as shogun. Other families took over the shogunate down the centuries, and rigid classes were established.

By 1603, the masters of Japan were the Tokugawa shoguns, who were to rule for 250 years. Under them the classes were as follows: the daimyu, who were feudal lords, the samurai, who were warriors, the peasants, the artisans and — least important — the merchants.

Some 60 years before the Tokugawa took control, Europeans had first reached Japan. The very first, in 1542, were Portuguese sailors, seeking trade with the mysterious islanders. Seven years later the first Christian missionaries arrived.

As the years went by, tension gradually mounted between the "barbarians" from the west and the Japanese, and in 1639 the shoguns ordered that all foreigners were to be banned except for a handful of Dutchmen, who were to be allowed a tiny trading post on an island off Nagasaki.

The people of Japan were forbidden to go abroad or even build ships large enough to sail to other countries. As for Christianity, which had begun to flourish, it was ruthlessly suppressed.

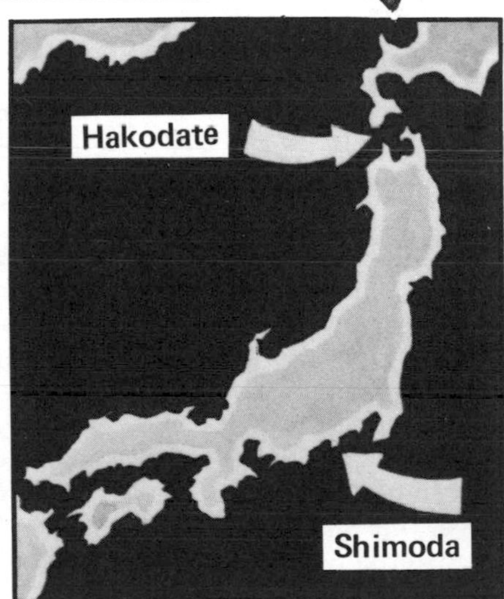


Right: a map of Japan, showing the two ports of Shimoda and Hakodate that the Japanese agreed to open in 1854. Left: Commodore Matthew Perry.

Having bolted her doors to progress, Japan became to the rest of the world a land of mystery. At first, there was little change, but gradually the despised merchants improved their status and resentment began to grow, not only among the fierce samurai, but also among the great families who believed that they should rule in place of the Tokugawas. Yet if change was in the air, nothing much occurred to alter the accepted state of things — until the Americans arrived on the scene.

For many years, a number of nations had been anxious to trade with Japan, notably Britain, Russia and America. The United States was rapidly becoming a world power and, having recently acquired California from Mexico, was looking eagerly across the Pacific.

The US President Fillmore ordered a naval force to sail to Japan in 1853 under the command of Commodore Matthew Perry. Perry was a tough old sea-dog who had seen plenty of action. He was respected rather than loved by his men, and known by them as "Old Bruin". His fleet consisted of four vessels, two being modern steamships, which, of course, startled the Japanese.

The reasons for the expedition were to promote trade, to obtain permission for American ships to use Japanese ports for supplies, and to set up a coaling station (steamships then being powered by coal).

The Americans sailed into Tokyo Bay on July 8th, 1853, and were at once ordered out. Commodore Perry refused to comply and said that if the Government did not send a senior official to receive documents in his

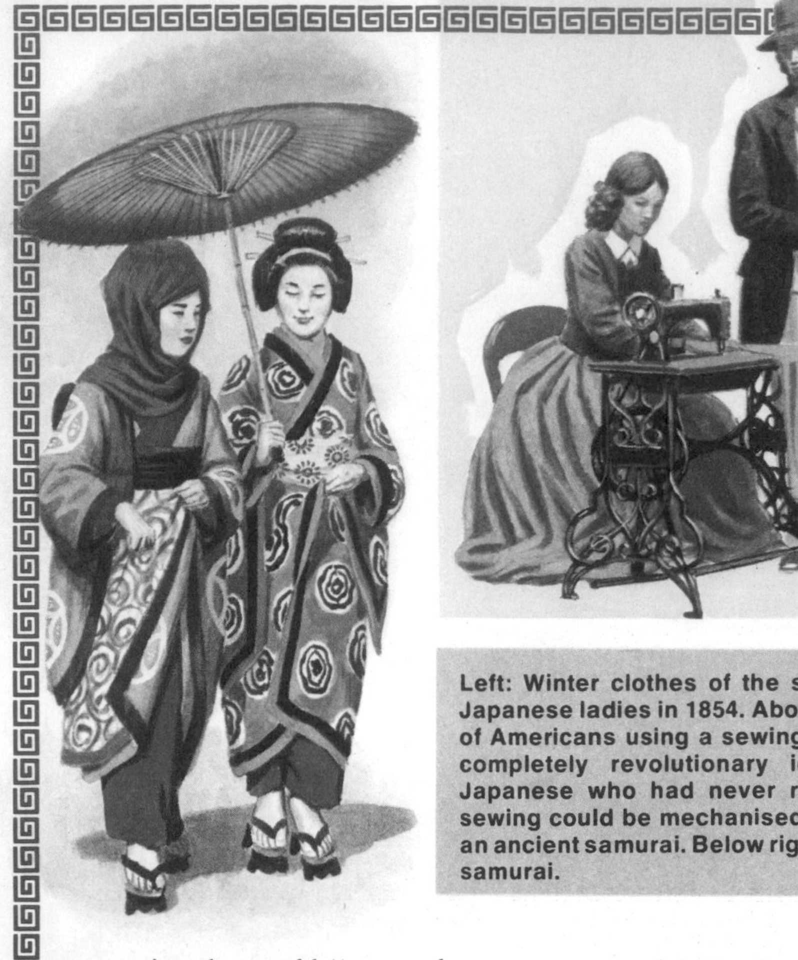

**Left: Winter clothes of the sort worn by Japanese ladies in 1854. Above: a picture of Americans using a sewing machine, a completely revolutionary idea to the Japanese who had never realised that sewing could be mechanised. Below left: an ancient samurai. Below right: a modern samurai.**

**In 1854, having little alternative, the Japanese shogunate gave in to Perry. Ports were opened, traders were admitted and an American consul was accepted. Japan had been freed from her isolation at last.**

possession, he would "go on shore with a suitable force and deliver them personally", whatever the consequences. His ships were made ready for instant action.

It was clear that the newcomers meant business and, at an elaborate ceremony on shore, Perry handed over his documents. They caused consternation among the Tokugawa rulers. Some said that the American demands should be rejected, but others believed it might indeed be time to open Japan to the outside world. However, the outcome was not satisfactory and Perry sailed away, stating that he would be back the following year.

Back he came, this time with eight ships and a flat statement that either the Japanese accept his terms or face a declaration of war. The shogunate gave in. The ports of Shimoda and Hakodate were to be opened up, traders were to be admitted, and an American consul was to be accepted. Perry sailed away in triumph.

There followed 14 uneasy, sometimes dangerous, years as Japan tried to adjust to the new situation. An official treaty was signed in 1858, opening up five ports and allowing

foreigners to live in Tokyo and Osaka, and other nations joined the Americans. The first American consul, Townsend Harris, arrived, only to have his secretary murdered. Three Russian sailors were murdered, and there were other killings, which led to two towns being bombarded from the sea.

Yet there were wise men in Japan who saw the true significance of Perry's visit. They helped overthrow the long rule of the Tokugawa shoguns and, in 1868, the Emperor of Japan, a 16-year-old boy, was "restored" to the power of his distant ancestors. He was surrounded by a brilliant group of advisers, most of them of the samurai class. Thanks to them — and to Perry, who had died ten years before but who had made the all-important breakthrough — Japan had started on the most astonishing transformation of any nation in history.

That is a big claim, but it is the sober truth. Japan leapt from the Middle Ages into the 19th century. Its industrious people rapidly modernised and transformed their country so swiftly that just 50 years after Perry's visit, to the astonishment of the world the Japanese were able to defeat the Russian Empire.

Japan's ambitions were boundless, not least because, though most Japanese were Buddhists, they clung to their ancient faith, Shintoism, which involved ancestor worship and a conviction that Japan was destined to conquer the world.

These ambitions culminated in the air attack on the American base at Pearl Harbour in 1941. In league with Nazi Germany, Japan almost conquered the Pacific, but was finally defeated in 1945. The surrender took place on an American warship in Tokyo Bay 92 years after Perry had entered it.

Japan soon recovered from her disastrous attempt to rule the Pacific. Her hard-working people are now democratically governed and have been a great nation again for many years. But nothing can ever equal her original rocket-like rise to world power in less than two generations.

Commodore "Old Bruin" Perry is hardly a hero of the Japanese, and some would say that change was in the air before his arrival. Yet it might have taken years to come about. As it was, Old Bruin triggered it off.

# Who first climbed Mount Everest?

1. "Chomolungma" (Goddess Mother of the World): this is the name of the highest point on Earth in the language of Tibet. The name "Everest" honours Sir George Everest, the English Surveyor General of India from 1823 to 1843. Mount Everest was named after him in 1858 when measurement by trigonometry in around 1850 had calculated its height as 8,840 metres. Its present accepted height is 8,848 metres, established by another survey between 1952 and 1955.

2. It was not until this century, that man could even try to set foot on the "roof of the world". Permission to go along the northern route through Tibet was granted only in 1920. The first attempt to reach the summit in 1922 was a failure and seven people died. Two years later, in 1924, a survivor of that team, George Mallory and another mountaineer, Andrew Irvine, disappeared during a further attempt. Almost certainly they died before reaching the summit.

3. Other expeditions over the years also failed. Then, after the Second World War, attempts to climb Mount Everest were made again. In 1951 a Swiss party discovered a route which it seemed might make it possible for a later expedition to climb the mountain. This was the southern route through Nepal. With this expedition was a Sherpa guide, called at birth Namgyal Wangdi, later to become famous as Sherpa Tenzing Norgay.

4. In 1953, a British expedition, led by Colonel John Hunt, set off. The preparation of materials and men was arranged down to the smallest detail. Nothing was left to chance. Scientific, modern equipment was used. There were portable stoves for use at great heights; boots capable of withstanding unusual climates and wear; vacuum-packed provisions; waterproof clothes and radio telephones. Hunt was determined to succeed.

5. The expedition also included the man whose name will be for ever linked with Everest, Edmund Hillary, a New Zealand bee-keeper. It included, too, Sherpa Tenzing Norgay. Hillary was 33, tall and thin. Tenzing was 39, small like all Sherpas, but tough and strong with great experience of Himalayan climbing.

6. The base camp was pitched at about 4,875 m. From there, eight further camps were set up at varying heights; the last was over 8,230 m. up and little more than 610 m. from the summit. Some members of the team, including Hillary, Tenzing, Hunt, Evans and Bourdillon, left the seventh camp on 28th May.

7. Hillary and Tenzing were the second pair of Hunt's team to try for the peak. Evans and Bourdillon had already failed. Conditions seemed favourable as they set off on the morning of 29th May but emotionally the two men must have been very tense. Climbing slowly but surely, they moved ever upwards until, at last, they had only a few more metres to go. Finally, at 1.45 p.m., Hillary and Tenzing stood on top of the world's highest mountain, looking down on the snow and rocks beneath them. There, the conquerors of Everest planted the flags of their expedition — at last! For their achievement, Hillary was knighted and Tenzing received the George Cross.

# The Peak of SUCCESS

**Since that first then remarkable achievement, Mount Everest has been climbed over sixty times. And there are some other 'firsts' among them worth mentioning here.**

The first Britons to climb Everest were Douglas Scott and Dougal Haston on 24th September, 1975.

The first successful woman climber was the Japanese mother, Mrs. Junko Tabei on 16th May, 1975.

The first lone climb was made by Austrian Franz Oppurg on 14th May, 1978.

The first European woman climber was the 34-year-old Pole, Wanda Rutkiewicz on 17th October, 1978.

The first to climb Mount Everest without the use of oxygen masks were Reinhold Messner, a 33-year-old from Italy, and Peter Habeler, a 35-year-old Austrian. They did this on 8th May, 1978. Their claim, however, was hotly disputed by a number of Sherpas, including Tenzing Norgay, although today it is usually accepted as true.

*A woman who deserves applause for her great fortitude and courage, although she did not reach the actual summit, is 64-year-old Elizabeth Forster who, in 1973, reached a height of 5,332 m., climbing alone.*

Everest has cost many lives. The snow is very powdery and there is the constant danger of avalanches. Frostbite is another great hazard and as recently as May, 1976, two men, British soldiers, Sergeant John "Brummy" Stokes and Corporal Michael "Bronco" Lane, were so badly frostbitten after their successful climb to the summit, that both had all their toes removed and Lane also lost the fingertips of his right hand.

Between 1965 and 1968, the Nepal government closed the route through their country, so no attempts to reach the "top of the world" were made during that time.

Now the route is open and many climbers of different nationalities have reached the summit, including Britain's Chris Bonnington in 1985.

# Why do Men climb Mountains?

How times have changed! Left: Alpine mountaineers of about 1870. Their survival depended on ability plus nothing more than simple ice-axes and (hopefully) sturdy hemp ropes. Below: The battery of equipment needed by a team for an assault on the North Face of the Eiger in 1968. Such equipment allows climbers to try precipitous routes far too dangerous for their Victorian predecessors.

**LYING back in his warm sleeping bag, Royal Robbins drifted off to sleep with the stars shining high above and the sounds of animals hunting or being hunted in the far off forests ringing in his ears. They presented no danger to him. Anyway, he was tired after a hard day. Tomorrow would be as bad, and the next day and the next . . .**

The ground beneath him was hard and uncomfortable. He started to turn over — and was stopped abruptly by the rope which tethered him.

The ledge on which he was lying was barely a body's width. Above it stretched 450 metres of vertical granite. Below yawned a similar drop. He was halfway up the world's most demanding rock face — the Muir Wall of El Capitan in California's Yosemite Valley.

Three times as high as the Eiffel Tower and with virtually no holds to help the mountaineer, this face represents the ultimate challenge for rock climbers. Royal Robbins, an American, became the first to conquer it solo in 1968. Teams of climbers have tackled it before and since then. In 1970, an American team conquered it over a period of 27 days.

Risking life and limb on a remote mountain for the best part of a month may not be everyone's idea of fun, but to the mountaineer the moment when he clambers at last on to the summit makes it all worthwhile. The sense of achievement is immense. He has used all his skill, courage, strength and endurance to overcome one of Nature's obstacles — and he has conquered fear itself.

He also has the added bonus of the panoramic view of the surrounding countryside. In centuries gone by, before mountaineering came to be regarded as a sport, such a view was of great importance. In the days before Man could fly, it was only by climbing a mountain that he could get an overall view of his surrounding countryside.

Explorers and scientists took mountain climbing very seriously. The first known ascent of a major peak was in 1786 when Dr. Paccard of Chamonix in France and his guide, Balmat, climbed Mont Blanc (Europe's highest mountain at 4,807 m) to carry out scientific observations.

Even further back in time, some mountains came to be regarded as sacred because their peaks seemed to reach up to the heavens. Mounts such as Olympus, Sinai and Fujiyama were climbed in pilgrimage to the gods who were thought to inhabit them.

Mountaineering came to be regarded as a sport around the middle of the 19th century. In 1854, Englishman Sir Alfred Wills and his party scaled the 3,650 m Wetterhorn, and so ushered in the 'Golden Age' of Alpine climbing. In 1857, the Alpine Club was formed and eight years later, the Matterhorn (4,478 m) was climbed for the first time by an Englishman, Edward Whymper, who had gone to the Alps to sketch and instead found himself becoming one of the great mountaineers of the 19th century.

## Tragedy

Sadly, Whymper's Matterhorn expedition met with calamity on the way down. A rope broke and four of the party of seven fell to their deaths. The tragedy caused a great controversy and branded mountaineers as reckless daredevils.

But by 1870, all of Europe's main Alpine peaks had been conquered and by the end of the century, climbers had wearied of trying to find new and more difficult routes up them.

Attention was then focused on the great mountain ranges of other continents. The South American Andes, the North American Rockies, the Caucasus in Southern Russia and the main African peaks were all attempted before climbers eventually moved on to the "roof of the world" — the great mountains of the Himalayas.

In 1950 a French team reached the top of Annapurna I (8,078 m) the highest anyone had yet climbed.

Everest, the world's highest mountain, has been climbed from several different directions. The most favoured route has been southern one which is approached through Nepal. This route was taken by Sir Edmund Hillary and Sherpa Tenzing in 1953.

The most difficult route to the summit of this 8,848 metres high monster is by way of the North East Ridge. This was unsuccessfully attempted by a British team of climbers in 1985.

## Difficult routes

Since then, Everest has been climbed many times as have most of the world's major peaks. Seeking new challenges, mountaineers have started searching for more and more difficult routes to attempt. In recent years many have concentrated on improving their techniques and equipment so that they can clamber up seemingly-impossible rock faces, such as the southeast face of El Capitain, described earlier.

The complete mountaineer must, in fact, be accomplished in three aspects of his sport: hiking, rock climbing, and snow and ice work. Hiking may seem dull and unskilful

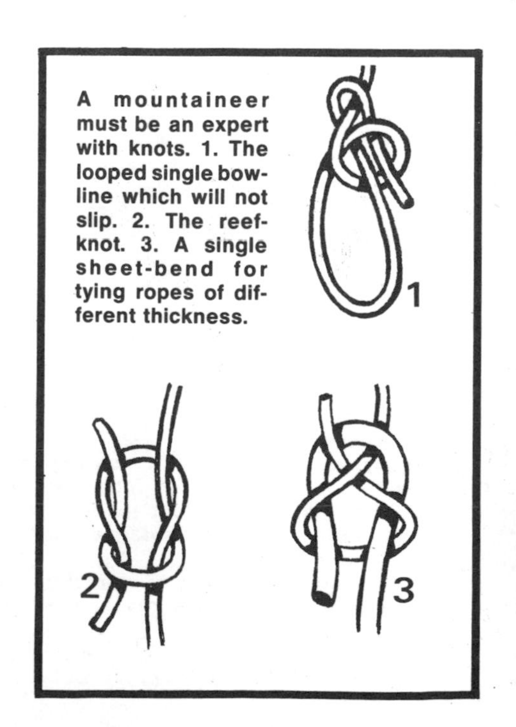

**A mountaineer must be an expert with knots. 1. The looped single bowline which will not slip. 2. The reef-knot. 3. A single sheet-bend for tying ropes of different thickness.**

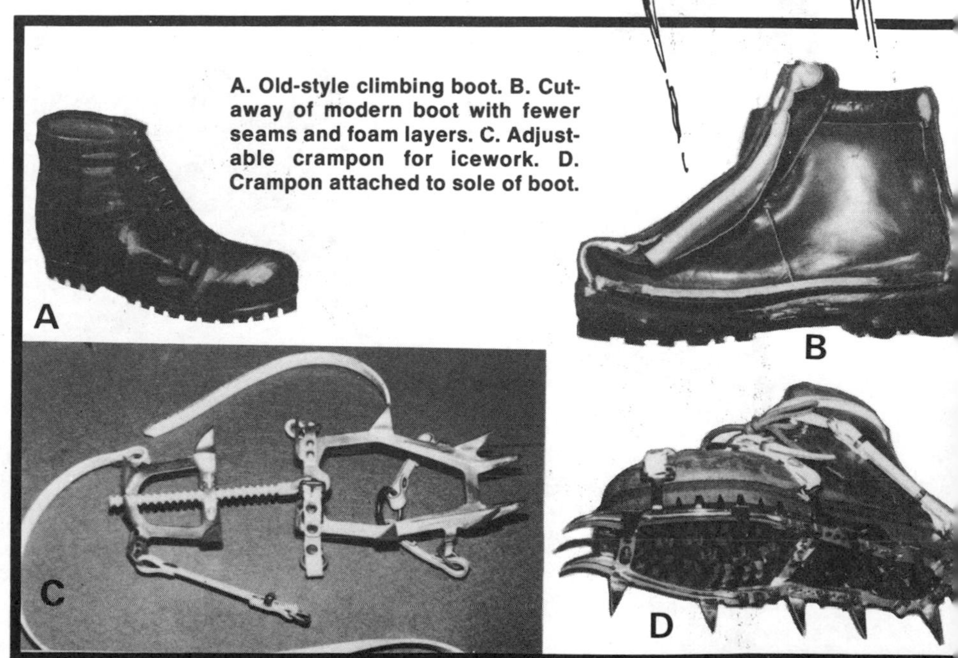

**A. Old-style climbing boot. B. Cutaway of modern boot with fewer seams and foam layers. C. Adjustable crampon for icework. D. Crampon attached to sole of boot.**

On simple overhangs the climber feels for handholds keeping the feet in contact with the rocks. On more difficult overhangs, stirrups or étriers are slung from karabiners fixed to pitons driven into the rock.

compared with the other two, but it is of vital importance. Before a climber reaches a rock face or an ice slope, he often has to hike great distances and must be fit enough to ensure that such treks do not sap the strength which he will require for the vertical climbs ahead. And, of course, he has a long hike back when he comes down!

Like hiking, rock climbing has developed as a sport in its own right. Rock climbing techniques were originally used by mountaineers to conquer rock faces during Alpine ascents. Around the beginning of this century, however, more and more climbers began to find rock climbing a worthwhile end in itself, probably because it was costly and time-consuming for many of them to reach distant mountains where they could practise all their mountaineering skills. Local cliffs provided all the challenge and excitement that they wanted.

To become a rock climber, you have to learn the jargon, or slang of the rock face. For once you set off upwards, you are entering a world of *pitches* (sections of a climb), *stances* (ledges where the leader anchors himself), *kernmantels* (the commonest ropes used), *chimneys* (cracks wide enough to get into) and *pitons* (pegs to which ropes are anchored). More important, you will be learning to act as part of a team with your life being in the hands of others and theirs in yours.

Rock climbs are graded according to their severity, from Easy (E), through Severe (S) to Hard Extremely Severe (HXS). Few people graduate to the latter!

## Vital equipment

Ideally, a rock climber tries to use as little equipment as possible but on very difficult climbs he will need quite a bit. A good pair of boots is as

Top left: *Front-pointing* up a steep ice slope. The climber uses his ice-axe to cut steps up the ice-face, and then as a hand support. The body must be kept straight to avoid strain on the ice. The crampons attached to the boots bite into the ice.
Left: The *layback* method of progressing up the rock face, especially if cracks are present. Holding the near side of the crack firmly, the feet are walked up the opposite wall.

Above centre: A climb is divided into *pitches,* or sections of rock between ledges. The leader scales the first pitch, anchors himself with a belay, and brings up the second man.
Above right: *A chimney* is a crack in the rock wide enough to get into. This is then walked up.
Right: The *cheval* technique of moving along a ridge. Cheval is French for horse.

important as anything, for a climber must have a sound foothold on widely differing surfaces if he is to feel confident. Boots also protect his ankles from injury.

Climbing on ice or snow presents special problems and calls for special equipment. An *ice-axe* is needed for cutting steps in steep ice slopes; boots have to be fitted with *crampons,* spikes which strap on to the soles; and *snow goggles* must be worn at certain times to protect the eyes from snow blindness. On very high mountains, oxygen has to be carried to enable the climber to breathe.

But lack of oxygen is hardly the main danger in this demanding sport. For most climbers, the hazards are more mundane, but nonetheless real.

To the dedicated mountaineer, they are there to be overcome and provided he knows the ropes, so to speak, he feels as safe on a towering rock face as most of us feel cycling along a road.

And if you want to 'learn the ropes', join a climbing group or club where beginners can progress steadily. Watch good climbers if you can, and try and note their mental approach to a difficult climb. Finally, climb as often as you can, for as a famous mountaineer once said, "The best training for climbing is . . . climbing."

***Abseiling*** **(roping-down) is a method of descending at a controlled rate by rope. The ropes are arranged rather like a sling around the body and can be controlled to allow a 'walk' down the rock face. It is better to walk rather than jump or bounce as it is easier to brake the descent.**

**A descendeur is a special climbing device which connects the rope and fastens to the climber to control his rate of descent when abseiling. They usually have a figure-8 shape.**

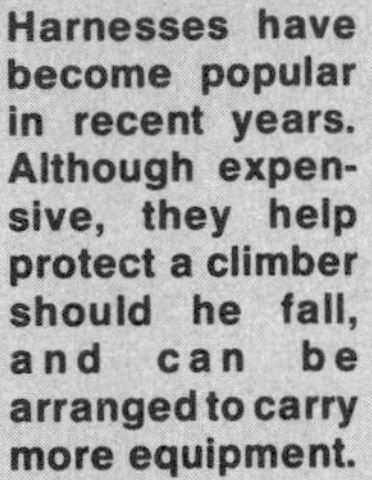

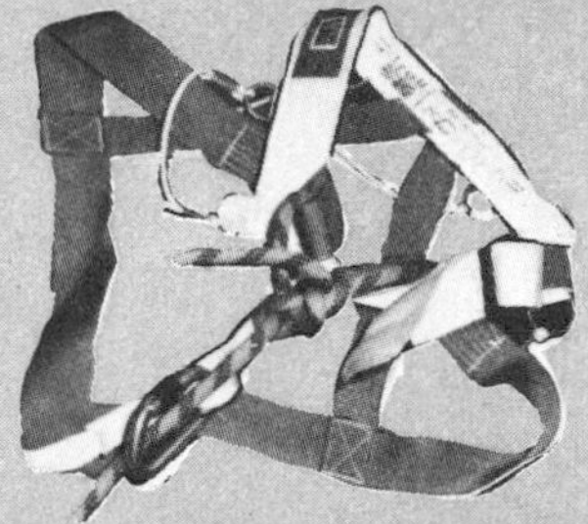

**Harnesses have become popular in recent years. Although expensive, they help protect a climber should he fall, and can be arranged to carry more equipment.**

**The head is very vulnerable, especially in rock climbing. Climbing helmets protect it from the smaller falling stones. They also lessen injury should the head hit rock in a fall.**

**Of specially hardened metals, ice-axes are vital tools in snow and ice.**

**A karabiner is a spring-loaded snap ring that can be attached to a piton hammered in the ice or rock. The rope is then passed through for extra security.**

**Nuts are made of aluminium and have a wire loop attached. They fit very tightly**

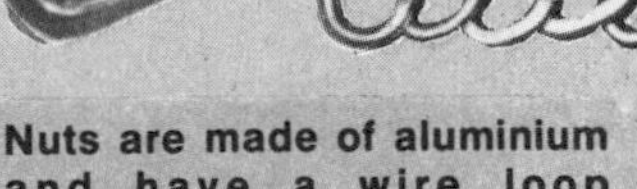

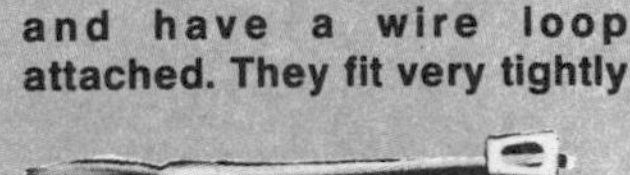

**into rock cracks. Ropes can then be controlled through these loops.**

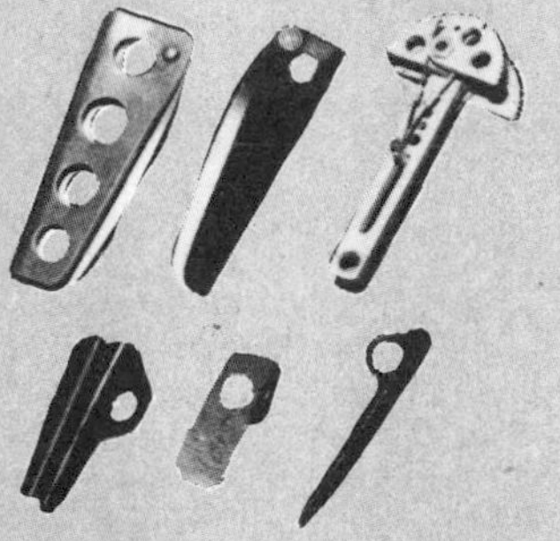

**Pitons are short, tough metal bars or pegs driven firmly into the rock or ice by a peg hammer. They are used to secure ropes or as handholds.**

# Who was the Maid of

1 Joan of Arc, or Jeannette d'Arc, was born in about 1412 in Domremy, a village of France. Her father was a peasant small-holder and it was while tending the family livestock that Joan claimed to hear the voices of St. Catherine, St. Margaret and St. Michael telling her to rescue Orleans from the English, drive them from France and have the Dauphin crowned King of France in Reims. Joan had faith, courage and selflessness, as she went on to prove.

2 In about May, 1428, Joan obeyed her voices and after finally obtaining an introduction to the Dauphin, arrived at Chinon the following February. Joan eventually persuaded the Dauphin to give her an army of between 4,000 and 5,000 men. Wearing a full suit of armour and carrying a white banner she set off for Orleans to raise the siege. After finding a way through the English lines Joan's army arrived in the city in 1429.

3 Her arrival brought great heart to the townsfolk who were on the verge of surrender. She spent several days riding round the city, studying the defences and getting to know the people. Then, on Friday, the 6th May, the Maid led her men from Orleans to attack the English strongpoints set up on the other side of the River Loire, blocking the bridge leading to the main gates. But the English streamed from one of their small forts to attack.

4 They scattered before the Maid, however, and her bravery so inspired her own troops that they followed her and attacked with such force that the English fort was taken and completely in French hands by nightfall. Here her men rested, preparing for the main attack the next day. At first light, Joan's army attacked the English holding the bridge across the Loire. The first French attack broke on the English lines.

# Orleans?

5 Joan was struck by an arrow, and although she was not seriously wounded, her disheartened men started to pull back. Knowing she must renew their confidence, she managed to raise her banner and her troops returned to the fight. Their action proved too much for the English who started to withdraw, but the bridge crashed into the river, drowning hundreds. On the 8th May, 1429, the English marched away. The siege of Orleans was over.

6 Within one week the English had been forced to retreat well beyond the Loire, and the Dauphin, although so reluctant that he had virtually had to be dragged to his coronation, was crowned at Reims. Then Joan was sent on other missions. She was captured at Compiègne and sold to the English. After a mockery of a trial, she was burned as a witch on the 30th May, 1431. She was made a saint in 1920.



# Warrior Saint of France

**Joan was a product of her age, in spite of her orginality and inspiration. She possessed in great measure the two qualities that made life at least bearable in the Europe of the 14th and 15th centuries. They were faith and nationalism.**

**The Hundred Years' War was a territorial dispute between England and France. It was begun in 1337 by Edward III of England claiming 'French' land through his mother, who was a French princess, and was ended in 1453 with the loss of all the land gained during that period, with the exception of Calais. In between were noted victories on both sides —Crécy (1346), Poitiers (1356) and Agincourt (1415) for England — but none was more impressive than Joan's at Orleans for France.**

**That was the only victory gained by a woman. In those days, unlike today, women never wore men's clothes and for them to carry arms or lead troops was unthinkable. Occasionally though, people did see 'visions', did hear voices. And, in any case, war was a noble occupation. Anything worth living for was also worth dying for, so men followed a good leader and fought, where necessary, enthusiastically.**

**Joan appealed to the people because she claimed to have been sent by God in whom they all believed to a greater or lesser extent. She also wished to oust the invader, maintaining foreigners had no place there, an opinion always calculated to arouse anger and patriotism — however misplaced. Joan's life marked the beginning of the end of the Hundred Years' War.**

# Who was the Master of Escape?

1. It was not his real name but the stage-name of Houdini that carried him to world fame. Born Ehrich Weiss in 1873 in Wisconsin, U.S.A., he ran away from home at 12 and found work in a mechanic's workshop. He became fascinated by locks and soon learned to open them with a small piece of wire. This gave him the inspiration for his career as a magician — and he was to be the greatest of his time.

2. At 15 he was performing conjuring tricks in bars under the name of 'Ehrich the Great'. His skill constantly improved: he emerged from double-bottomed cases, untied himself from tightly binding ropes and defeated the most complicated sets of shackles. His speed at freeing himself was amazing and he soon gained the public's attention. At 17 he took the name Houdini.

3. One London newspaper offered him a seemingly impossible challenge. He had to free himself from shackles that an expert had taken five years to make. Before a 4,000 crowd Houdini concentrated intensely, worked out the complex mechanism and was free within minutes. In another challenge he escaped from hundreds of metres of rope that had taken experts nearly an hour to bind him in!

4. His talent was incredible. In two minutes he escaped from a locked jail. He opened safes in a twinkling and invented an instrument that could undo the most intricate locks and devices. However, he destroyed this long before his death to stop it falling into evil hands. Even from tanks of water or milk, tightly bound and shackled, he would emerge unharmed.

5. To stay in the news, Houdini often arranged free but very dangerous exhibitions. Once on the frozen Detroit River, Houdini was shackled and thrown through a hole in the ice. He was supposed to release himself and quickly emerge. But after eight minutes the crowd thought his end had come. Suddenly he popped up smiling: he had managed to breathe in a space between the water and the ice.

6. Houdini could, apparently, even pass through a brick wall! Specially built on a T-shaped steel frame, it was raised slightly off the ground. A seamless carpet was laid under it and screens placed at the sides. With a cry of "I'm off", a trapdoor opened under the wall and the agile Houdini wriggled through. Seconds later he would announce from the other side, "Here I am!", to an astonished audience.

7. Many people tried to explain his skill, and failed. But his suppleness, vitality and willpower were almost superhuman. Houdini imposed exhausting exercises on himself. He could swallow and then regurgitate small tools, use his feet like a second pair of hands and stay under water for four minutes. Above all, this amazing man was capable of dominating fear — he never showed any trace.

8. After the First World War many fake mediums began exploiting relatives of the war dead, claiming to be able to contact them. Although interested in spiritualism, Houdini despised such dishonesty and as a member of the American Scientific Commission exposed many fakers. However, not even the great Houdini could escape death and he died in New York in October, 1926, after a short illness.

Soldiers of the American States

*(The Allies)*

**INFANTRYMAN**

**The musket-armed infantry were the key troops in the open field, where most of the fighting took place. The men fought together as a group. Such a closely formed unit could either fill a field with fire or take a bayonet charge when there was not time to reload the muskets.**

**ARTILLERYMAN**

**Artillerymen were among the most skilful of the soldiers. It took training to produce the required commanders, gunners and bombadiers, and consequently the development of the artillery was a gradual process. Once organised it formed a very competent force.**

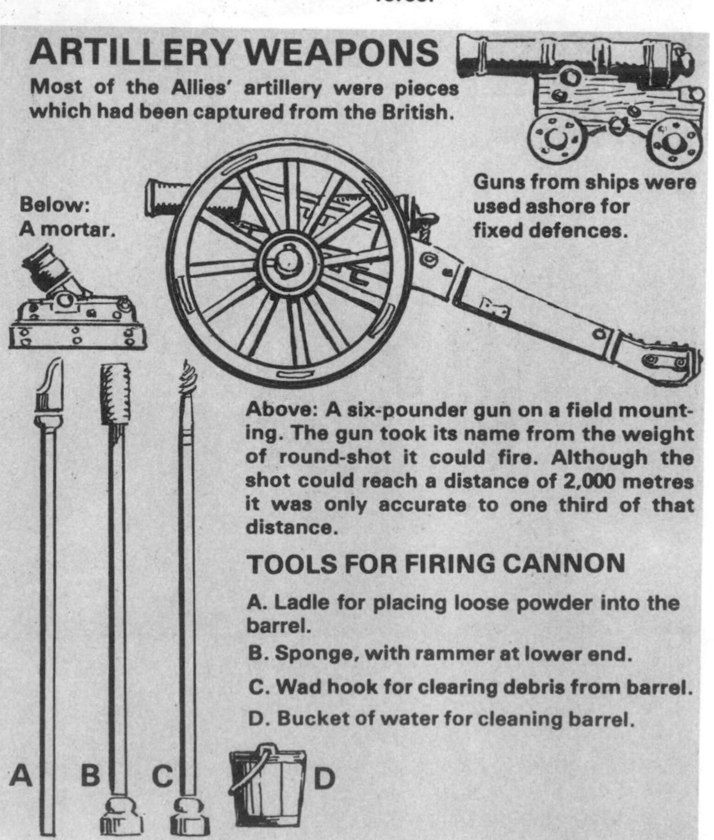


# What battle cost

**One at a time, the English regiments of redcoats marched into the open field, surrounded by their French and American enemies, and stood in a long line. An officer barked an order and, acting as one, the well-disciplined redcoats laid down their muskets and firelocks in the wet grass.**

Then, to the mournful lament of a drum-beat, the regiments marched away from the field, swinging their empty arms.

The scene was Yorktown, a small but prosperous township of some 60 houses which lay near the mouth of the York River, in West Virginia, U.S.A. The day — surely one of the most abject in the story of the British Empire — was October 19, 1781, the day which virtually brought an end to the American War of Independence.

The British, observed the watching Americans, were as unused to offering themselves for surrender as the Americans were then unused to receiving it. An American officer wrote:

"The British officers in general behaved like boys who had been whipped at school. Some bit their lip, some pouted, others cried. Their round, broad-brimmed hats were well adapted to the occasion, hiding those faces they were ashamed to show."

The soldiers, too, were full of emotion. One Highlander embraced his firelock before throwing it to the ground and exclaimed: "May you never get so good a master again!"

## Lost colonies

That day at Yorktown, though, Britain lost a good deal more than a few thousand small arms stacked in a rain-soaked field. For by losing the battle there she had lost her 13 American colonies, and the six-year war she had fought to try to keep them.

The war had begun when the American colonies on the eastern seaboard of the present United States furiously rebelled against the taxes being demanded of them by their British masters.

Fighting began in April, 1775, and Colonel George Washington, later to become the first President of the United States, of America, was put in command of the colonists' army.

Once hostilities started, the Americans were swept along by the tide of their own enthusiasm. They adopted a Declaration of Independence, declared the birth of a new nation, and were joined in their struggle first by France, then by Spain, two nations anxious to get their own back on the English, whose arrogance they hated.

## Key state

For a long time it looked as if the British would win. Five years after the war began they held New York and most of the southern States of Georgia and North and South Carolina. In 1781, Lord Cornwallis, commanding the British forces in the south, pressed on to Virginia, which he thought was a key state.

American morale was then very low. The soldiers were unpaid by the States and they had meagre rations. The result was that many of them deserted, while those who

# Britain her American Colonies?

remained had to obtain their food by force.

At this time an American general wrote: "Instead of having the prospect of a glorious campaign before us, we have a bewildered and gloomy one."

The general reckoned without Cornwallis. For the British commander, who had hitherto distinguished himself in the field, was marching into a self-made trap.

Cornwallis had convinced himself that Yorktown would provide him with an excellent base from which to strike at the rest of Virginia. It could be easily fortified and, as it was a peninsula, easily supplied from the sea. He was expecting reinforcements from the Navy.

He wasn't worried that a small force led by the Marquis de Lafayette had followed him. But he did not know that a strong French fleet was on its way down the coast, to cut him off from the sea.

In the north, George Washington learned of the trap into which Cornwallis had fallen. He hurried south to join the French and together they marched on Yorktown. There were over 16,000 in Washington's force against 7,000 British and their German mercenaries.

## Defensive advantages

From a defensive viewpoint, Yorktown did have certain advantages. To the east and west of it were swamplands which would make the movement of enemy artillery difficult. In front of the town was 800m of open space which could be covered by Cornwallis's own guns.

The British had built earthworks covering the marshy

## THE ARTILLERY IN THE FIELD

When George Washington took command of the army in 1776, he gave the job of training and organizing the artillery to Henry Knox, a 25-year-old student of military arts. Today, Knox's name is known on account of the fort called after him which holds the Federal reserves of gold bullion in the U.S.A., but he played a vital part in the struggle against the British by his insistence on constant training and practice which helped create a well-disciplined force.

## HOW THE GUNS WERE FIRED

Firing a cannon involved good teamwork. The artilleryman in charge had to note the target, estimate its distance, and select the proper ammunition. Each crew member would have a specialist task to perform, which could be one of the following:

Shifting the carriage with a handpike to help the gunner in his aim.

Sponging out the bore and ramming home the shot.

Firing the gun after aimed and primed.

Covering the vent to prevent sparking before the gun was ready to fire.

Inserting the shot into the barrel of the gun.

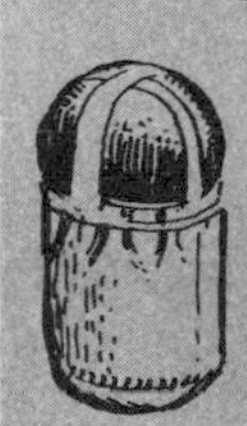

Left: Round shot with its cartridge — a bag of powder.

Left: Grape shot. This was a form of shot which burst scattering fragments over a wide area.

approaches, while their inner system of defence consisted of a stockade, earthworks and entrenchments.

On the night of September 30, Cornwallis withdrew his troops from the outer defences and prepared to fight.

A few days later these abandoned defences, only 600 metres from the centre of the town, were occupied by the Americans and the French. On October 9, having dragged up their heavy artillery, they began their bombardment at close range.

A German mercenary on the British side described it: ". . . It was even more horrible than before. They fired from all their redoubts without stopping. Our detachment could scarcely avoid the enemy's bombs, howitzer shot, and cannon balls any more. We saw nothing but bombs and balls raining on our whole line."

By October 16 Cornwallis knew he was beaten. His food and ammunition were desperately low, he had many sick and wounded men and his defences were now almost non-existent as a result of the incessant bombardment.

## Last gamble

That night the British commander prepared for a last gamble. Under cover of darkness he began moving his troops across the York River to escape as best they could.

A few men did manage to reach the other side, but a sudden storm blew up in the middle of the operation and the attempt was abandoned.

On October 19, their colours cased, the British troops marched out of Yorktown in a sorry condition to the surrender field.

When news of the surrender at Yorktown reached England on November 25, Lord North, the Prime Minister, cried, "Oh, God, it is all over." Even so, his stubborn monarch, King George the Third, who had sometimes been the only man in England who wanted the struggle to continue, insisted that it should go on.

### General Cornwallis

**Charles, Lord Cornwallis (1738-1805) was the general in charge of the British at Yorktown. Despite having his name associated with the military disaster, Cornwallis was undoubtedly one of the most competent of officers to hold an army command during the Revolutionary War. After Yorktown he campaigned with great success in India and won many battles.**

### CORNWALLIS'S MARCH TO YORKTOWN

Allied Forces
British Forces
Westpoint
Williamsburg
Richmond
Jamestown
Gloucester
Yorktown
VIRGINIA
Miles
Suffolk
Portsmouth

May 24, Cornwallis's troops cross the James River.

Aug. 2, Cornwallis's troops start fortifying Yorktown.

Sept 27, Allies complete landings at Jamestown.

Sept. 9 onwards Allies control Chesapeake Bay.

### THE BATTLE OF YORKTOWN 1st-17th October 1781

1. Cornwallis moves into Yorktown.
2. The French take up positions.
3. The American divisions complete encirclement of Yorktown.
4. 1st October: British abandon their outer defence line with the redoubts, which are then occupied by the French.
5. 6th October: French/American forces advance and complete their first siege line.
6. Three days later the Allied artillery is brought up to the line, which commences to bombard British positions.
7. Guns of French artillery fire on British ships at anchor in River York with red-hot shot. Four ships burst into flames but one escapes.
8. 11th October: Allied second siege line is constructed, but is heavily bombarded by two British artillery redoubts.
9. 14th October: In darkness, two storming parties, one French, one American, attack offending redoubts and capture them.
10. 16th October: British situation desperate. Cornwallis decides to ferry remainder of army across York River to Gloucester.
11. However, storm blows up at crucial moment and some boats carried downstream. Project abandoned.
12. 17th October: British offer surrender. 19th October: Conditions of surrender agreed and British army marches out of Yorktown, flags cased, between two flanking rows of allied troops.

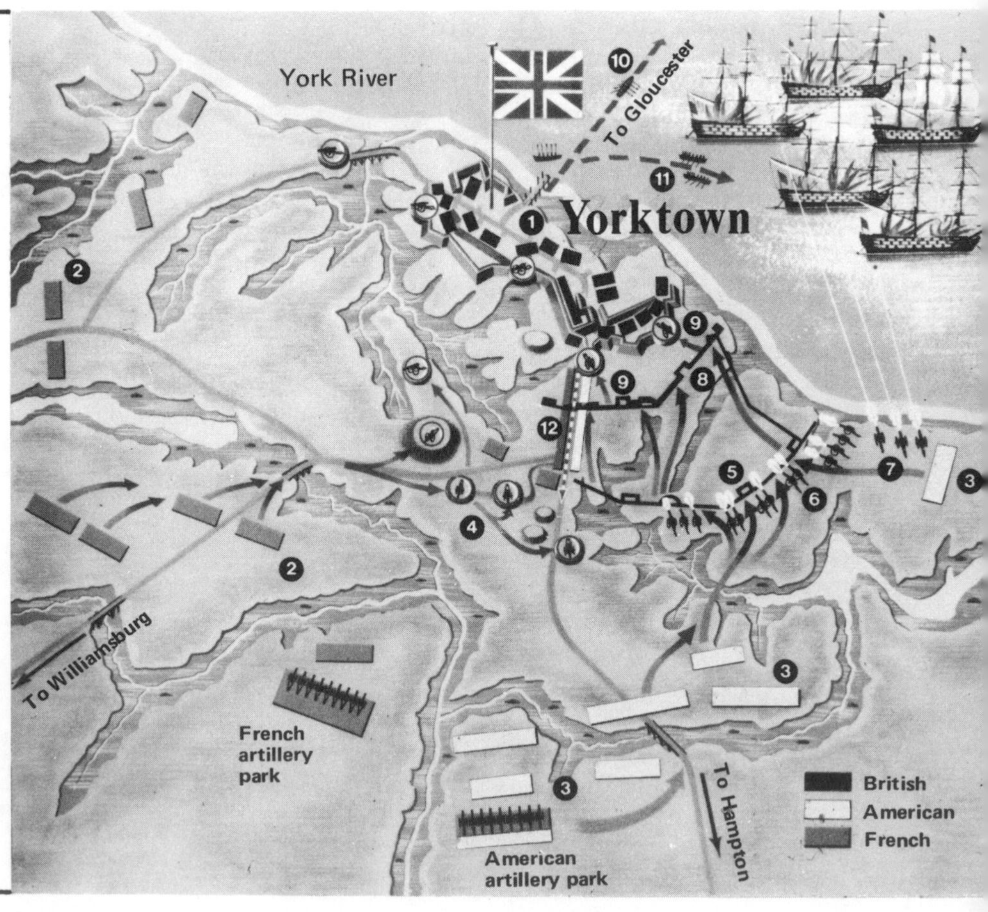

**Surrender of Cornwallis at Yorktown.**
**An engraving after a painting by Arthur Burdett Frost, a famous contemporary American illustrator.**

But the victory at Yorktown had given the Americans a strategic advantage they could not miss. They quickly reconquered the southern States and only New York remained under the British flag. The war was proving costly both in the amount of money to finance unsuccessful campaigns, and in the loss of prestige among other nations.

At last, in March 1782, Lord North resigned the premiership. Soon afterwards the new government opened peace negotiations with the American colonists on the basis of acknowledgement of American independence. A final treaty was signed in September, 1783, and the British left New York, their last stronghold.

## FACTS AND FIGURES

| ALLIED ARMY (Americans + French) | | BRITISH ARMY (British + Mercenaries) | |
|---|---|---|---|
| Total number of men involved | 16,800 | Total number of men involved | 7,973 |
| Total losses: | | Total losses: | |
| Killed | 75 | Killed | 156 |
| Wounded | 1,199 | Wounded | 326 |
| | | Missing | 70 |

## THE SURRENDER OF YORKTOWN

At 9 a.m. on the morning of October 17 a British drummer started to beat the chamade, the signal for a parley. The cannons stopped firing and a British officer, accompanied by the drummer boy, walked towards the American lines waving a white handkerchief. It was the sign that the British had surrendered.

The details and conditions of the surrender had to be worked out, and on the 19th a document was signed.

In outlining his terms Washington specified that, 'The same Honour will be granted to the Surrendering Army as were granted to the Garrison of Charles Town'. The reference was to the British victory in 1780 when Sir Henry Clifton had refused to grant the honours of war to General Benjamin Lincoln's troops. 18thC. confrontations were conducted according to a centuries-old ritual in which every step was catered for by precise rules which both sides generally accepted. The defeated troops were usually accorded honours of war which meant that they would be permitted to march from the town with drums beating and colours flying. Cornwallis had been second-in-command at Charlestown and now he in turn was to suffer the grave indignity of a similar ceremony. Above left, can be seen the British colours which were not allowed to be unfurled. The British wore newly issued uniforms and according to legend the column was led by a band playing the melancholy English tune, 'The World Turned Upside Down'.

**Until the end of the American War of Independence, armies did not appreciate the importance of the improved artillery weapons. No provision was made for transporting guns and local farm wagons and teams of beasts were usually commandeered for that task. Naturally enough, the farmers were not too happy with the arrangements and often they would only agree to transport the weapons to the next village and the next unwilling farmstead.**

# What was the Tragedy of Cooper's Creek?

1. Even today the centre of Australia is barely inhabited and most of the continent's people live along the coast. In the early 1800s virtually nothing was known of the interior. Brave men had ventured inland only to return exhausted with tales of a scorching wilderness. In 1840 two of these, an Englishman, Edward Eyre, and an Aborigine named Wylie, staggered into the town of Albany in Western Australia.

2. They had crossed the corner of Australia from south to west in a nightmare journey that had taken over a year. Slowly the interior was opening up. To speed this up the Philosophical Institute of Victoria decided to sponsor an expedition to cross Australia from south to north. As its leader they chose Robert Burke, a policeman. Seventeen others, including the scientist William Wills, set off with him on August 20, 1860.

3. With them they took along 23 tonnes of stores loaded on to 23 horses and 25 camels, which had been specially imported from India. But before long it became obvious that the mass of provisions was slowing the expedition down. So Burke decided to split the group. The advance party with himself at the head would push on to Cooper's Creek on the River Barro where they would set up a main depot for stores. The others were to follow as quickly as possible with the bulk of the supplies.

4. The advance party reached Cooper's Creek on November 11, but Burke, anxious to move into the interior, decided to set off for the north without waiting for the supplies. He left William Brahe in charge of the depot telling him to wait for three months or until the supplies came up. He then chose three others — Wills, Charles Gray and John King — to go with him. They took six camels and one horse. At first the going was easy. They often passed huge termite hills.

5. But the good luck did not last. Soon rain began to fall heavily and the condition of the ground made the journey so difficult for the camels that they had to be constantly rescued from a morass of mud. All this slowed them down so much that Burke began to worry over the constant delays which were imperilling the expedition. The party were beginning to run out of both time and supplies. Nevertheless, on February 1, 1861 they came to a creek where the water was salty. They were near the sea at last.

Because the camels were making such slow progress, Burke decided to push on ahead with Wills. At last, on February 9, they reached the coast. Their task accomplished they returned to their two comrades and began to retrace their steps to Cooper's Creek. As their provisions were running low it was obvious that they had to get there quickly. But once more the constant rain hampered their progress.

It was a desperate race against time.

6. The continual need to rescue the camels from the mud was now taxing the four men's strength to the utmost. When they ran out of food they killed the horse and all the camels bar two to eat. Then on April 17, Gray died. Burke, Wills and King took a day to bury him. In the end, that day was to cost two of them their lives.

7. William Brahe had now waited one month longer at Cooper's Creek than he had been ordered and still no sign of either Burke or the provisions had been seen. One of his party was seriously ill. He could delay no longer. So burying some food and a message, and carving a brief message on a tree to mark the spot where to dig, he set off back home on April 21. Just nine and a half hours later Burke, Willis and King staggered into the deserted depot. They were starving and bewildered, and gave up all hope of catching Brahe on their worn-out camels. They tried to reach settlements away to the south-west but failed to find a way across the barren country. When all their camels were dead and their supplies used up, they begged food from the Aborigines. But their strength was fading fast. When a rescue party arrived on September 18 they found only King who had been living with the Aborigines. Burke and Wills were both dead.

# Who founded the Red Cross?

**THERE were forty thousand casualties at the bloody Battle of Solferino (June 1859) in Lombardy, Italy, fought between the Austrians, and the French and their allies the Piedmontese. As was customary, many of the wounded were left dying on the battlefield where they had fallen, with no doctor to tend or comfort them. Thousands died where they lay, when they might have survived if only some form of medical service had been there.**

A kind-hearted Swiss, Jean Henry Dunant, was horrified at what he saw and immediately decided to do something about it. He organised local villagers to care for the injured on both sides of the battle.

But he realised that this was not enough. Solferino was not the only battle where lives were needlessly wasted through neglect and lack of care: war had always been like this. Even where medical services existed they were often badly run and quite inadequate, as the English nurse Florence Nightingale had discovered during the Crimean War (1853-1856). Like Florence Nightingale, Henry Dunant realised that the problem of caring for the wounded was an enormous one and needed proper organisation.

## Memory of Solferino

In 1862, Dunant wrote a book *A Memory of Solferino*, in which he suggested that all countries should form special relief societies, and that there should be international agreement regarding the treatment of those injured in war.

Dunant's proposals attracted very wide interest, and in the following year, 1863, a committee was formed which later became the International Committee of the Red Cross. Delegates from sixteen countries met at Geneva, in Dunant's native Switzerland, in 1864.

They agreed in the famous Geneva Convention that wounded soldiers — no matter which side they were fighting on — and the people, buildings and transport used to tend them should be treated as neutrals. To indicate this they were to wear a distinctive red cross on a white background showing that they were not to be harmed.

This, however, was only the start. Later Geneva Conventions laid down rules for protecting victims of warfare at sea (1906), prisoners of war (1929) and civilians in wartime (1949).

At the Geneva meeting of 1864, four national Red Cross Societies were formed — in Belgium, France, Italy and Spain. But within a century more than 100 similar societies were in existence. The American National Red Cross was organised in 1881, and its first president was Clara Barton, a medical worker who had cared for the wounded on the battlefields of the American Civil War (1861-1865). By the time the First World War began in 1914, there were 37 Red Cross Societies throughout the world. Another 26 were founded before 1939, the year in which the Second World War broke out.

The Red Cross symbol was never meant to have any religious significance, but inevitably it became associated

**In June 1859 the armies of France, Italy and Piedmont fought the battle of Solferino. Henry Dunant was in the nearby village of Castiglione. He organised the reluctant villagers to help the wounded soldiers on *both* sides of the battle.**

**After Solferino, Dunant published his experiences in a book called *A Memory of Solferino*. He recommended that those who helped wounded soldiers be considered neutral and should wear an easily recognised distinguishing mark. The Red Cross was born!**

with the red cross crusading Christian knights wore on their surcoats. So when 'Red Cross' societies were formed in Muslim countries they were called Red Crescent after the symbol of Islam. The Iranian society was called the Red Lion and Sun. In Russia, Cross and Crescent were allied in one society, reflecting the mixture of religions which Russians follow.

The terrible sights of war which had so affected Henry Dunant at Solferino in 1859 were, of course, made more and more terrible as time went on and wars were fought with increasingly powerful and destructive weapons. In addition, bigger and bigger numbers of men were involved because war was no longer confined to single battlefields: a 'battlefield' in the Second World War could stretch for many kilometres, and involved not only soldiers, but airmen and civilians as well.

**Henry Dunant was born on May 8, 1828 and died in 1910. In 1901 he was awarded the first ever Nobel Peace Prize for his work in establishing the Red Cross.**

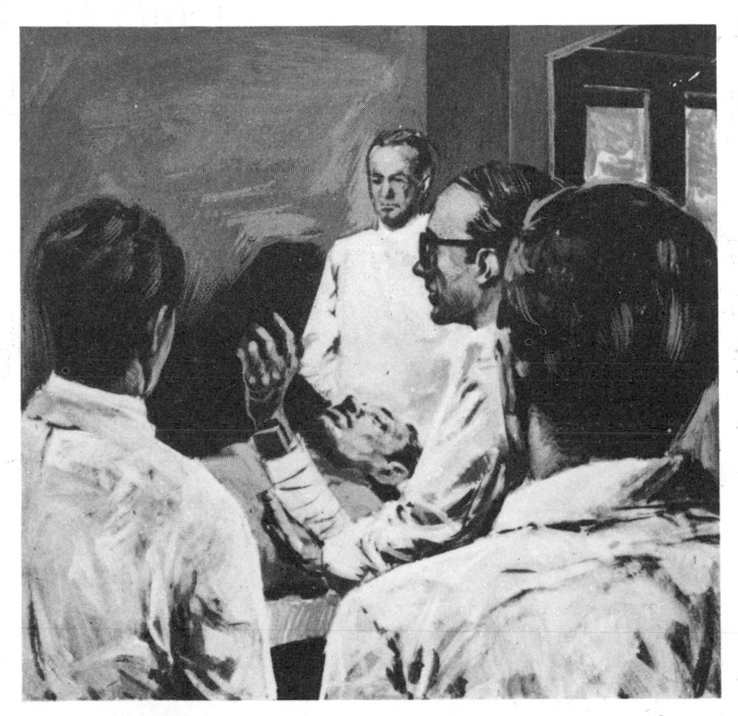

**During both World wars and throughout the many other bitter and bloody smaller wars since, the Red Cross has been on hand to help the wounded. Without it, many thousands would have died and suffered needlessly.**

Because of the greater size of warfare in the 20th century, the work of the Red Cross soon went far beyond simply caring for wounded soldiers. Naturally, the Red Cross still provided ambulances, hospitals, doctors and nurses. However, it also operated canteens for the troops, distributed food to civilians in the battle areas, and when the battle was over, searched for missing relatives and friends who had been driven from their homes by the fighting.

## Help for the needy

Wartime is not the only time when people suffer, for there are millions who in their everyday lives lack proper medicine, education, and also proper food. This was how the Red Cross became involved in large-scale 'relief' operations when thousands of people are made homeless by floods and other natural disasters; and how they came to run a series of 'programmes', including education programmes, accident prevention programmes and other 'campaigns' such as those dealing with safety on holiday beaches and safety for mountain-climbers, potholers and other adventurous folk.

The Red Cross now carries out almost every type of humanitarian work. Yet it is still involved in the results of the Second World War, even though that conflict ended forty years ago: today, the International Red Cross runs the Tracing Centre at Arolsen, near Kassel in Germany, which was set up in 1945 to reunite the families of victims of Nazi concentration camps.

Red Cross societies also run homes for handicapped children, and organise care for the deaf and dumb, the mentally retarded, for old people, orphans, and the blind. The organisation runs hospitals and dispensaries for giving out medicines and drugs in poor countries, such as those in South America, where local services are insufficient. In addition, it provides and maintains blood banks for blood transfusions, and runs a prison visitor service to help people released from prison settle down to ordinary life again. The Red Cross even has a snake farm in Thailand where anti-snakebite serum is produced and is distributed all over the world.

**Nowadays the Red Cross is not only concerned with war. Wherever people may be injured they can often be found offering help and medicine.**

# Who went in search of

1. Poet, scholar, courtier, soldier and explorer — Sir Walter Raleigh was all those things. Born around 1550 in Devon, a county which produced many other notable sea adventurers of the Elizabethan age, young Raleigh grew up amid tales of travel to the New World and attacks on Spanish treasure ships. As soon as he had finished his education at Oxford University, he joined an expedition which was setting off to fight in France.

2. When he returned, the whole country was talking about the exploits another Devon sea dog, Francis Drake. Anxious to become as famous Drake, Raleigh set sail on a voyage of discovery. But his ship was attacked b a squadron of Spanish ships eager to gain revenge for the defeats inflicted o Spain by Drake. Outnumbered, Raleigh's ship was holed and he had to lim home back to England.

3. But Raleigh was undaunted. Still looking for adventure, he went to quell an uprising in Ireland. His success brought him the favour of Queen Elizabeth I, but his sudden rise also produced many jealous enemies. They rejoiced when, in 1592, Raliegh married without the queen's permission. Angry Elizabeth ordered him to be imprisoned in the Tower of London.

4. Elizabeth relented and ordered his release. Anxious to please her, Raleig set off in search of the land of El Dorado, a South American countr rumoured to have the untold riches of Peruvian princes. His journey took hir to the Orinoco River but ended in failure. After much suffering and heav rains, Raleigh turned back.

# Eldorado?

5. For 20 years the mythical treasure of El Dorado haunted Raleigh; in the meantime he again took up the fight against England's old enemy Spain. Joining in an attack on Cadiz he was seriously wounded. Then in 1603 Elizabeth I died and James I, who disliked Raleigh, became king. Raleigh was unjustly accused of treason and imprisoned in the Tower of London for 12 years. There he wrote a *History of the World*.

6. In 1616, he was freed to search again for El Dorado. But he was warned not to fight against the Spaniards with whom England was now at peace. However, once in South America, his son was killed in a skirmish with the Spanish and a Spanish settlement was burned in revenge. On returning to England, he was arrested and beheaded without trial on 29th October, 1618.

# Into the Unknown...

When early navigators ventured across the almost unknown tracts of the Atlantic Ocean, charts and compasses were in their infancy. So they needed an instrument which would enable them to fix their position with some accuracy. The mariner's astrolabe was developed from an Arab device which was used to calculate the positions of the stars.

The marine version of this could be used to sight on the Sun as well as a fixed star by looking along the Alidade (the central, pivoted, vane) and reading off the angle on the graduated 'lim', or face. If the astrolabe were held vertically and the sightings made at the correct time, the mariner's position could be fixed to an accuracy of half a degree.

Knowledge of the astrolabe was carried into Europe when Spain was conquered by the Arabs in the eighth and ninth centuries and adopted by the Portuguese, who produced the first marine version during the late fifteenth and early sixteenth centuries.

The planispheric astrolabe, the forerunner of the marine astrolabe, was probably Greek in origin and was absorbed into the Arab culture where it was fully developed following the Arab conquest of the Near East.

# ...and what could be found there

Although Sir Walter Raleigh is credited with introducing tobacco to England, the first recorded encounter of natives using tobacco was when Christopher Columbus visited the island which is today called Cuba. There he noted 'Indians' smoking a primitive form of cigar, called *tobacos*.

When the first colonies were established in Virginia, local Indians were also seen using the same leaf in long pipes. But it was not until a settler, John Rolfe, discovered a method of curing the leaf to make it palatable to European tastes that smoking became a habit.

# Who were the First

# Americans?

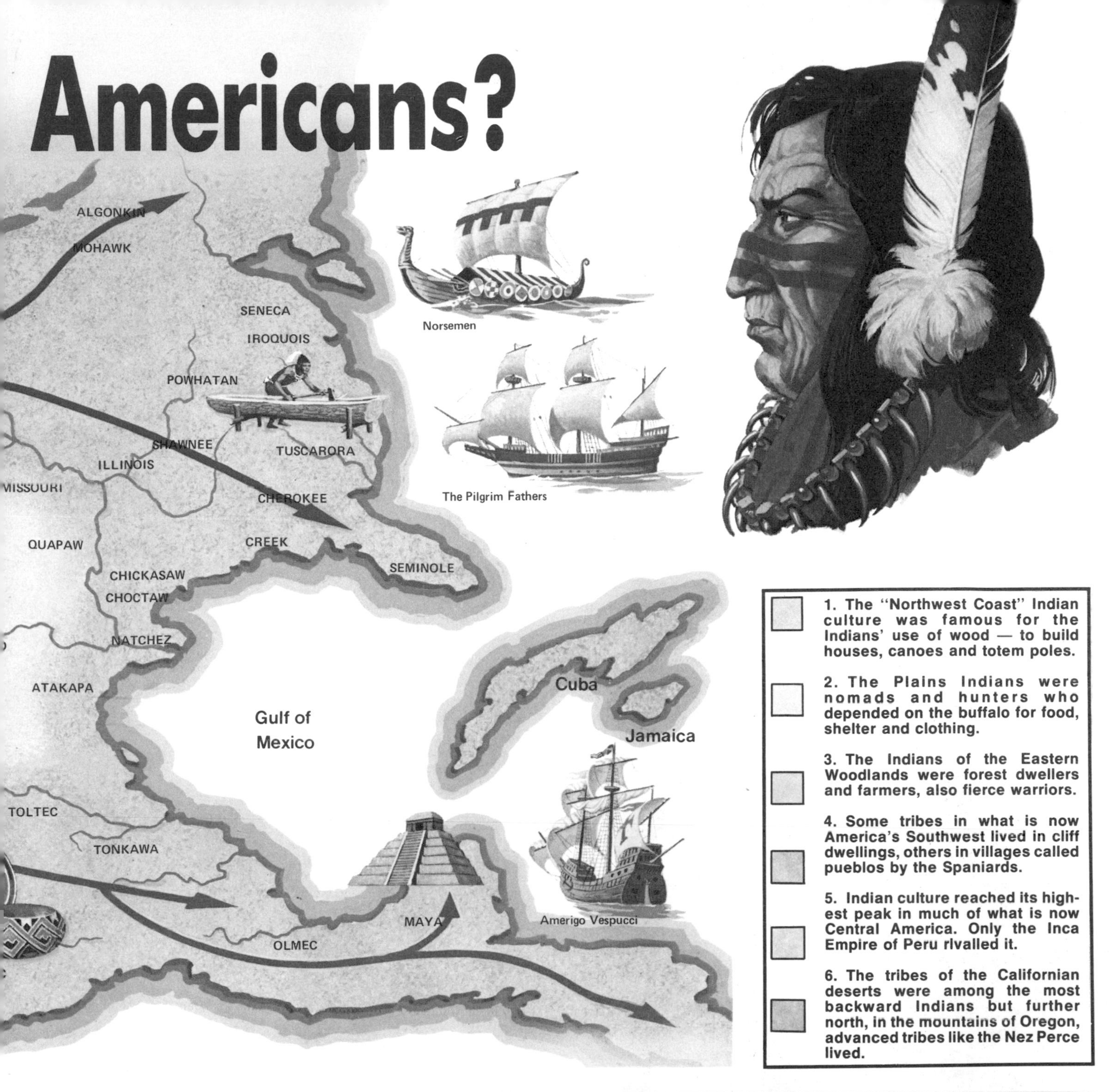


**1. The "Northwest Coast" Indian culture was famous for the Indians' use of wood — to build houses, canoes and totem poles.**

**2. The Plains Indians were nomads and hunters who depended on the buffalo for food, shelter and clothing.**

**3. The Indians of the Eastern Woodlands were forest dwellers and farmers, also fierce warriors.**

**4. Some tribes in what is now America's Southwest lived in cliff dwellings, others in villages called pueblos by the Spaniards.**

**5. Indian culture reached its highest peak in much of what is now Central America. Only the Inca Empire of Peru rivalled it.**

**6. The tribes of the Californian deserts were among the most backward Indians but further north, in the mountains of Oregon, advanced tribes like the Nez Perce lived.**

**THOUSANDS of years before Europeans "discovered" America, the ancestors of today's American Indians truly discovered the New World. Before that moment the Americas, North, Central and South, were empty of any sort of human life.**

No fossils of the apes who preceded Man have ever been found in the New World, nor have remains of our remote half-man ancestors or of off-shoots like the Neanderthalers. The only remains are of Homo sapiens — ourselves.

Carbon 14 dating techniques have fixed the arrival of the first known Americans to around 30,000 years ago and carbon dating is regarded as very sound as long as enough remains are found, which they have been. But this dating goes farther back than the first known boats, so how did the first "Indians", as Columbus mistakenly called their descendants, arrive?

They undoubtedly came across what is now the Bering Strait, dividing Asia and America's far northern state, Alaska. Even today this is a mere 58 kilometres across with islands in between but, in the last ice age, the waters were much lower and, so many believe, at times the

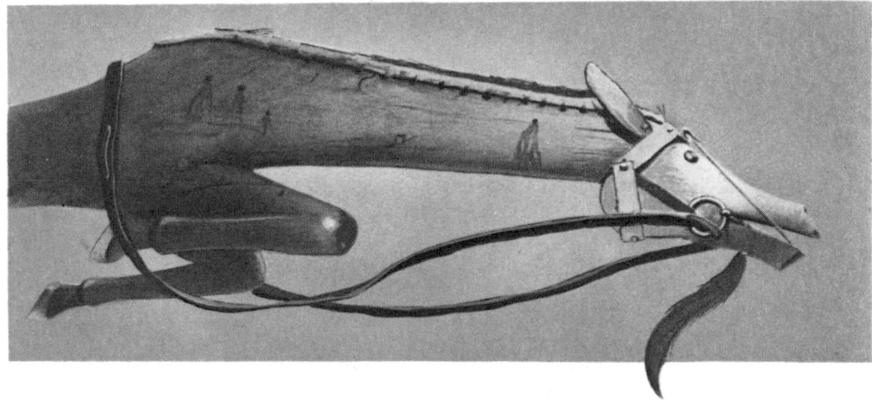

**Above is an example of American Indian sculpture. It is Sioux and is of carved wood. It shows a wounded horse and its leaping figure has remarkable grace and movement. Representations of wounded horses may have been used in a Victory Dance, as they were held to be worthy of battle praise as much as a warrior himself.**

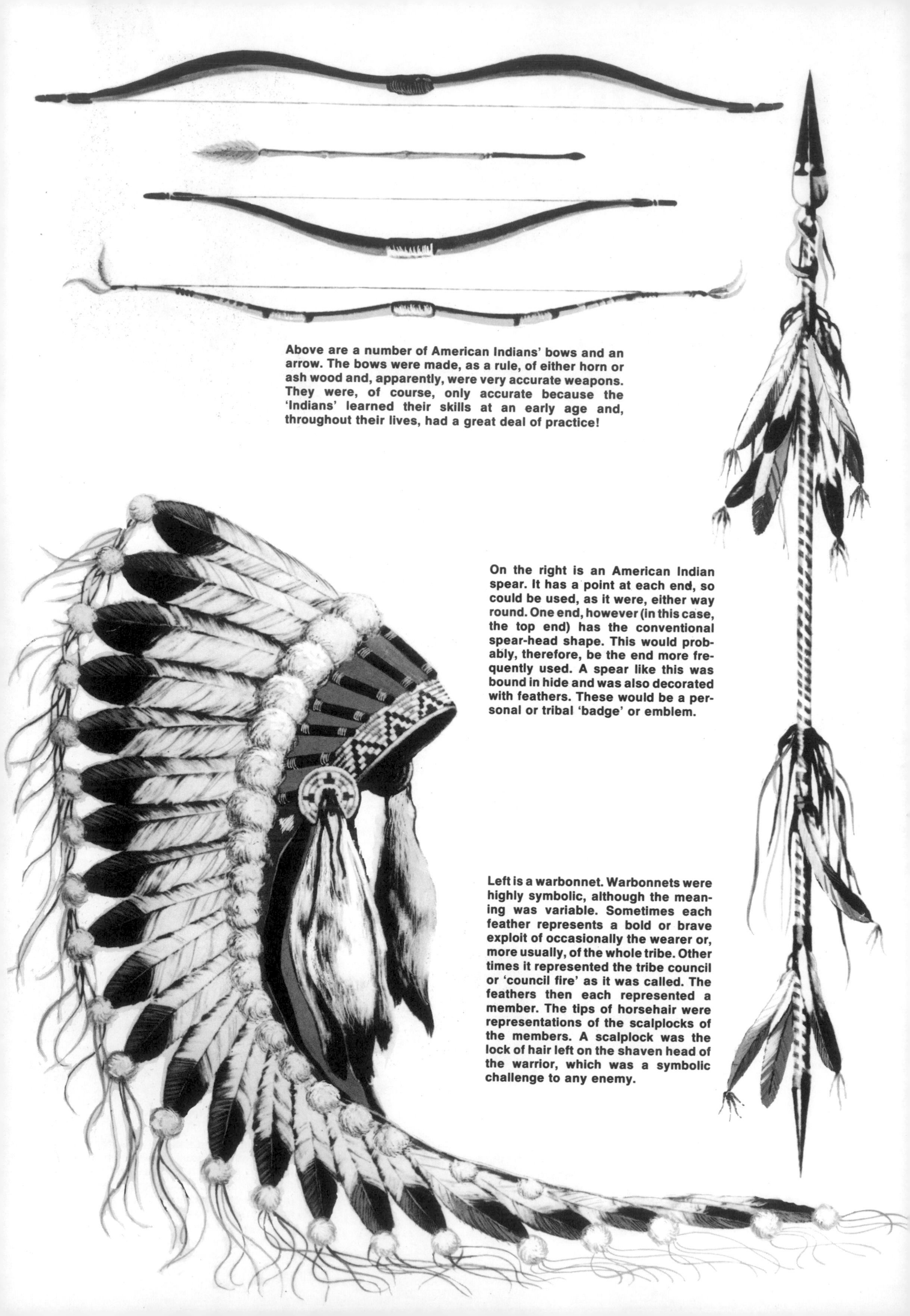

Above are a number of American Indians' bows and an arrow. The bows were made, as a rule, of either horn or ash wood and, apparently, were very accurate weapons. They were, of course, only accurate because the 'Indians' learned their skills at an early age and, throughout their lives, had a great deal of practice!

On the right is an American Indian spear. It has a point at each end, so could be used, as it were, either way round. One end, however (in this case, the top end) has the conventional spear-head shape. This would probably, therefore, be the end more frequently used. A spear like this was bound in hide and was also decorated with feathers. These would be a personal or tribal 'badge' or emblem.

Left is a warbonnet. Warbonnets were highly symbolic, although the meaning was variable. Sometimes each feather represents a bold or brave exploit of occasionally the wearer or, more usually, of the whole tribe. Other times it represented the tribe council or 'council fire' as it was called. The feathers then each represented a member. The tips of horsehair were representations of the scalplocks of the members. A scalplock was the lock of hair left on the shaven head of the warrior, which was a symbolic challenge to any enemy.

"strait" was a grass-covered plain.

Across the plain came men and animals. The fact that some American Indian tribes look distinctly Mongolian only goes to prove the existence of the route still more. Yet why did they come in the first place?

Wanderlust was one reason no doubt, but, more significantly, Siberia was becoming too ice-bound to support life. Whatever the reasons, they came . . .

What are now Canada and the northern United States were experiencing their own last ice age at the time. However, it has been found that for some thousands of years a vast route free of ice existed east of the Rockies. Again, geologists have also found that another great passage appeared as the ice age was drawing to an end. This was further to the West.

Human sites have been discovered which back up this surge southwards, but it must be stressed that if sites are found that prove to be still earlier, it will mean that some humans moved down into the Americas before that last great ice age, which produced the vast icy barrier known to scientists as the Wisconsin Glacier. It was a barrier that linked Greenland to Canada and cut deep into America itself.

How long can it have taken the men, women and children from the north, and their descendants, travelling in bands large and small, to penetrate to the very tip of South America? Many thousands, of course, stopped on the way because they liked an area, or felt safe there. The arrows on the map show some of the routes they chose and where they settled.

## The Great Trek

Probably the great trek continued for some 25,000 years. An unknown number of bands must have stopped for centuries, then moved on, others may have pushed steadily south. It is known for certain that there were cave dwellers not far from the southern tip of the continent around 9,000 years ago. Every few years finds help fill out the still mysterious story, finds like the fossil of a 15-year-old girl discovered in what is now Minnesota, U.S.A. It is reckoned that the clay in which her body lay was deposited on a lake floor 20,000 years ago.

Latecomers, when the Bering Strait had turned into a genuine waterway, used blocks of ice and small boats to make the crossings, over water still used today by the Eskimoes. Though these early Americans were the ancestors of those who fought so valiantly to save their lands from white men, it must be stressed that their own homelands were not static. The Sioux (see Teton Dakota, their proper name, on the map) were driven from their forest homelands by the Great Lakes in historic times by other Indian tribes. They settled on the Great Plains and, like all other Indians, they went on foot until the coming of the horse.

## Wild Horses

Horses were brought to the Americas by the Spaniards early in the 16th century, and some escaped to run wild and be found by the Indians. Most tribes tamed and rode horses, and their life-style changed dramatically. The Plains Indians were all mounted by the late 1700s.

"Indians" is as vague a word as "Europeans", though some scholars can link people together, even those living far apart, not so much by looks but by language similarities. Some tribes advanced far more than others, and nowhere were there more remarkable advances than in Central America. In South America, the Incas of Peru achieved great things until their empire was toppled by the Spaniards in the 1540s, but none of the peoples of North America achieved so much as a number of people in and near what is now Mexico.

## The Aztecs

Among the most famous were the Aztecs (see World of Knowledge 15 and 16) with a capital which was the equal of any European city of the 16th century yet, before them, the Mayas had achieved even greater feats. Sadly, their greatest days were before the coming of the white man, so their past is steeped in mystery. Their buildings, as imposing ruins show, were almost as magnificent as those of ancient Greece. Yet having no local metal, all their tools were of stone. Like all American Indians they failed to invent the wheel, yet they had mathematicians whose calendar was better than Europe's until Pope Gregory's in the late 16th century, and they had fine astronomers.

## The Mayas

They alone of the Indians' developed a system of writing, a form of picture-writing, and developed it perhaps as early as the 4th century AD. They had a numbering system based on 20, which included the first known symbol for zero. They were farmers, their buildings being temples and ceremonial meeting places, and their civilization lasted more than 1,000 years, until just before the Spanish came. Millions still speak their language today, but the Mayas remain mysterious.

Nobody can know what would have happened if the white man had not come when he did to the Americas. The Indians, advanced or backward, were men of the Stone Age. If words like "savage" are used about them, then it must be remembered that their conquerors were very often just as savage.

What is certain is that the Indians of the Americas have fascinated the rest of the world ever since they were first "discovered" by whitemen. Just who the discoverers were is another story, but they were probably Norsemen, which is why they, and not Columbus, appear on the map.

**Right is a collar made of bear claws. Worn around the neck, it proved to an enemy the courage and strength of its owner.**

**Right is a scalp on a frame. American Indians often scalped their enemies and kept the scalps as proof of valour. The scalps were usually stretched like animal skins and were then preserved very carefully.**

**Below is a war-hammer — in this case, one wrapped round with hide.**

# Who was the English heroine

1 Seven miles off the rugged Northumbrian coast of north-east England lie the Farne Islands, a cluster of 25 rocks of various sizes. There, William Darling and his family lived in the Longstone Lighthouse where he was the keeper in the early part of the 19th century. It was a bleak and lonely place and the sea was often frighteningly violent, driving the family into the upper rooms of the tower to seek refuge. In such surroundings, Grace Darling, the seventh of William's nine children, was brought up.

2 Probably taught entirely at home by her parents, Grace is thought to have missed going to the mainland to complete her education, like her brothers. But she was content to work about the lighthouse. Her father was a deeply religious man who loved Nature and he encouraged Grace to learn about birds and animals. On fine days, she would clamber about the rocks, looking for sea-birds' nests or wander on the shore, playing with the baby seals which lumbered from the water with their parents.

3 But William Darling's job was at times one of great danger, and never more so than on the night of 7th September, 1838 — the most celebrated night in the history of Longstone Lighthouse. In a terrifying storm, the steamship *Forfarshire*, sailing from Hull to Dundee with 63 people on board, drifted powerless, because of flooded boilers, on to the jagged Harkers Rock. It was about three o'clock in the morning. Some distance away, at Longstone, were William Darling, his wife and his daughter Grace.

4 While the stricken ship was pounded to pieces, nine people managed to struggle out on to the rocks. They could see the lighthouse in the distance but their desperate cries were carried away on the wind. It was just before dawn when Grace Darling, awakened by the ferocity of the storm, thought she heard voices crying in the distance. She summoned her father who peered through his telescope in the half-light to see the survivors clinging on, wet through, exhausted and with hope fading fast.

# of the Sea?

5 William Darling knew he could not row out to them alone — but he had no man to help him. Seeing this, and determined to save the people on the rocks, Grace insisted on accompanying her father on his perilous trip. Despite Mrs. Darling's pleas, father and daughter set off across a mile of stormy sea. Approaching the rocks, William Darling sprang ashore while Grace kept the coble from being dashed to pieces. On the return trip, they brought back four men and one woman to the lighthouse.

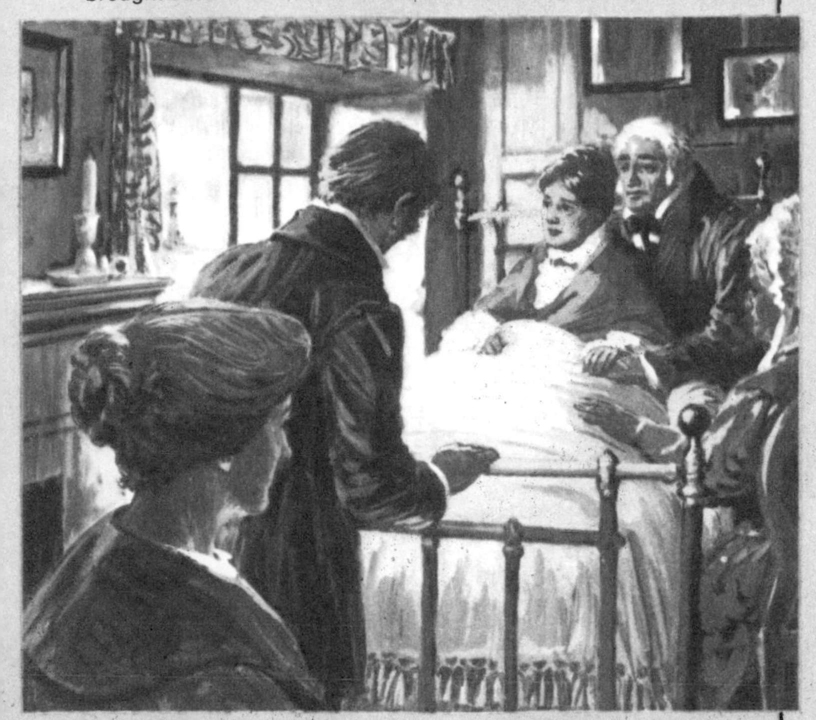

6 Grace was too exhausted to make a second trip for the remaining survivors but her father rescued them, aided by two of the men already saved. Survivors and rescuers stayed in the lighthouse for more than two days until the storm abated and they could reach the mainland. When news of the rescue became public, Grace Darling found herself a heroine and both she and her father received the Gold Medal of the Royal Humane Society. Alas, Grace died only four years later from consumption (tuberculosis).

**Grace's courage quickly made her a national heroine. Mugs and pottery figures were made with her name on them, pictures of her were painted and poems written about her. One such picture, right, was made by a local artist, Henry Perlee Parker. More surprisingly, by 1858, she was also a special heroine to the Japanese, as a booklet in Japanese, now in the Grace Darling Museum, Bamburgh, testifies.**

**Above are drawings of both sides of the gold medal given to Grace in 1838 by the Royal Humane Society. The front (left) shows a boy blowing on a torch, to make the flames (symbols of life) appear again. The back shows a wreath, as given by the ancient Romans in recognition of life-saving. Grace's father, William Darling, also received a similar medal at the same time.**

**Below is Longstone Lighthouse today, still manned but in 1952 much altered and converted to electricity. Right is a radio beacon mast.**

# Which French King united France?

1. In the middle of the 16th century France was a kingdom, but it was not a united realm. The king of France had very little power and the ordinary people were left to suffer from the feuding between various Dukes and noble families. Besieging of castles, looting of towns and the destruction of farmland by rival forces was commonplace.

2. On the death of Henry II in 1559, his three sons ruled in turn, but the most formidable and influential person in France was their mother, Catherine de Medici. In common with most of Europe, France was tormented by religious squabbles, which burst into civil war when the Catholic Catherine and her son, Charles IX, ordered the brutal massacre of Huguenots (Protestants) on St. Bartholomew's Day, August 24, 1572.

3. Amidst this turmoil and unrest, the Huguenots turned for help to King Henry of Navarre. Henry had been born on December 13, 1553, at Pau, in the province of Navarre which was a separate kingdom between the lands of France and Spain. He was heir to the French throne after the sons of Catherine and was a powerful young man who was an inspiring leader in battle. Leading the Huguenot forces against the Catholics, he attacked the strongly defended town of Cahors in 1580 with a small force. Henry, then 26, led his men through the streets fighting for five days and nights almost without rest.

4. In battle Henry's motto was 'To Conquer or to die!' Yet he was merciful in times when it was the custom for the victors to slaughter the vanquished and burn and ravage any town they captured, especially if the citizens held a religious faith different from theirs. Once, when besieging Paris, he saw starving citizens clambering down the walls to escape. Yet Henry had no quarrel with these people so they were allowed to run off.

5. At another time he detected an assassin who had come to kill him and had joined his party. But he cleverly tricked the would-be killer and took his horse and pistols, which he fired into the air before letting the man go. Henry wanted such stories of his mercy to spread through the land. There was no doubt that he was a great soldier, and such was his fame that some cities surrendered to him without a fight, knowing that resistance would be in vain.

6. In 1589 Henry III, the last of Catherine de Medici's sons, was murdered. Thus Henry of Navarre became the rightful King of France. Yet he was a Huguenot and the majority of French people were Catholics, and in fear of what would happen to them if the Huguenots had power, many resisted Henry. He had to fight campaigns to claim his right, and he showed great bravery battling against opponents who were supported by King Philip II of Spain.

7. At Aumale, in Northern France, Henry led a mere hundred horsemen against a Spanish army of 30,000. Overwhelmed, his small force soon had to withdraw, and it was Henry who kept the Spanish host at bay almost single-handed until his men had galloped to safety behind fortifications. Only when he turned did he receive a wound — a bullet in the back. Henry was to fight many battles before he was crowned King in Chartres on February 21, 1594. Because his bravery was respected and he was just to all men he was able to unite all Frenchmen, Catholic and Huguenot alike, loyally to his throne. He said, 'Those who follow their consciences are of my religion, and I am of the religion of those who are brave and good.' As an act of political expediency, however, he became a Catholic himself in 1593. This helped considerably to lessen the religious unrest that was destroying his country. Nonetheless although he brought unity and peace to France, he was to die at the hands of a religious fanatic. As Henry was passing through the streets of Paris on 14 May, 1610, one of the crowd, Francois Ravaillac, forced his way into the royal carriage and attacked Henry with a knife. During his reign Henry of Navarre (Henry IV) had laid the foundations for the Golden Age that France would enjoy in the long, glorious reign of his grandson, Louis XIV.

General James Wolfe

**A thin line of British soldiers stood carved like stone on the Heights of Abraham above Quebec, the capital of French Canada. Towards the red-coated invaders French troops were advancing at a run and, when they were some 37 metres away, the British commander, General James Wolfe, gave the order to fire. The volley that followed, the most decisive single volley in history, destroyed French Canada.**

The battle, fought on September 13, 1759, was part of the Seven Years War (1756-63), known by the Americans as The French and Indian War. It marked the climax of a long power struggle between Britain and France for the mastery of North America. And it was to have an even more historic aftermath for, with the French menace removed, British colonists in America began to be resentful of being ruled by a parliament in London in which they were not represented. Soon they would be breaking away to form the United States of America. That volley was decisive indeed . . .

Between 1700 and 1763, France and England fought three great wars, the last of which, the Seven Years War, was called by Sir Winston Churchill the first World War. It was. Apart from the struggle in North America, war raged across much of Europe and Asia as well. By the end of it, the British were rulers in much of India, along with many sugar-rich Caribbean islands and other gains.

## Growing unrest

Yet the struggle in North America had gone on even between the official wars, a struggle in forests and woods, on lakes and on rivers, as well as in settled country. It was a savage conflict of ambush and destruction, the war whoop and the tomahawk, daring raids and stark terror, as well as the occasional set piece battles.

The French had first settled along the St. Lawrence in the early 1600s. English settlers began colonising at the same time, first at Jamestown in Virginia in 1607, then at New Plymouth in Massachusetts in 1620. The Virginian colony was founded to trade with the Mother Country, the Pilgrim Fathers in Massachusetts to find religious freedom. Thousands followed them and each started other colonies along the coast. The English, later the British, came for many reasons, but basically they wanted land for settlement, farming, etc., which meant there could be no place for the Indians. These first Americans — those that survived — were driven westwards.

Meanwhile, a smaller number of French settled in what is now southern Quebec. They were mostly fur traders and — on the coast — fishermen, and generally they got on well with the Indians, many living like them. The Brit-



*Continued on page 270*

# Who died on the Heights of Abraham?

Louis-Joseph, Marquis de Montcalm Commander of French forces in Canada

A French chasseur. The white uniform seems singularly unsuitable for warfare. It stood out even more that the famous British red coat in the predominantly green surroundings.

A ranger of one of His Majesty's Independent Companies of American Rangers. Recruited from the provincials, these troops were experts in irregular warfare and fought in the woods and across open country against both French troops, and Red Indians.

Major General James Wolfe's uniform was the same red as the tunics of the Redcoats he commanded. However, his was lined and much better tailored.

ish had a fur-trading company, the famous Hudson's Bay Company, founded in 1670, which gave them a foothold in Canada, but the French — soldiers and explorers — were pushing down the Mississippi and the Gulf of Mexico. Fortunately, there were not many of them and, fortunately, the most powerful Indians of the day, the Iroquois, who lived in what is now New York State, and who enjoyed being middlemen in the fur trade, tended to favour the British.

The settlers badly needed British troops to protect them and few at this time dared push westwards into the forests beyond the Appalachian mountains. It was sheer suicide. And regular troops, as events proved, were no match at first for Indians and their French allies who often lived and fought in Indian fashion.

## War begins

The Seven Years War started earlier in America than elsewhere, real warfare, as opposed to endless small raids, erupting in 1754. Would-be settlers from Virginia were claiming the Ohio Valley beyond the mountains and the French had the same idea. The first clash was where Pittsburgh now stands, the British being led by 22-year-old George Washington, destined later to lead the Americans to independence from Britain and, finally, to become the first President of the USA. It was a dramatic start to a long career.

A year later, a British army was annihilated in the same area, the commander Braddock dying because, like his men, he did not understand the realities of war in the forests, worlds away from set piece battles and European parade grounds. Things were not to improve for several years. New France, as Canada was called, had a mere 55,000 people, the British colonies had 20 times as many, but not many who understood what wilderness warfare meant. The French had a great leader in the Marquis de Montcalm, who was only too well aware that time was against him because of the lack of numbers and the refusal of the French Government to support him properly. He needed victory fast.

## New leader

But now Britain found a magnificent war leader in William Pitt, later Earl of Chatham, who from London directed the world war with skill and aggression, choosing the right men, including Wolfe. It was too late to prevent 1757 being another year of humiliation for the British in North America, but 1758 saw the tide begin to turn. Despite one disaster due to inept generalship at Fort Ticonderoga, the British ended the year in triumph, the greatest feat having been the capture of the fortress of Louisburg on Cape Breton Island. Now the way to the heart of French Canada lay open — the way being the St. Lawrence. Britannia ruled the North Atlantic waves. Despite the bravery of Montcalm and his men, the fate of New France was sealed.

James Wolfe, still only in his early 30s, was given the command of the force to take Quebec. He had distinguished himself at Louisburg, but was so junior that his promotion startled many. Not King George II, however. On being informed that young Wolfe was mad, he replied: "Mad is he? Then I hope he will bite some of my other generals!"

The Commander-in-Chief in America, General Amherst, was ordered to launch a four-pronged attack on Canada, but only the assault up river on Quebec was all-important. By June 26th, 1759, Wolfe's army was four miles from Quebec, with Wolfe himself on the Ile d'Orleans. He could see the city and its strong fortifications and fighting soon began, highlights including two attempts by the French to destroy the British fleet with fire-ships. Not until late August, when Wolfe's health had broken down, did a chance of victory suddenly present itself. There was a cove above Quebec called the Anson de Foulon, over which towered near vertical cliffs (though not so vertical now). Yet they were scaleable. On September 12, spies reported to Wolfe that food ships would try to reach Quebec on the next ebb tide, perfect cover for his troops. At 1 am the next morning, 1,700 men set out in 30 landing craft, while war ships made a feint attack elsewhere. More troops would follow later. It was hard rowing, for there was a 6 knot tide, but at 4 am the landing place was reached. There was no guard.

It was a rugged 53 metres climb, but before sun-up Wolfe and 4,500 had scaled the Heights of Abraham and were advancing along the plain. The French commander on the cliff-top had allowed most of his men to go home for the harvest, and the surprise was almost total. There was time for Wolfe to assemble his men in battle order to await Montcalm's Frenchmen regulars, Canadians and Indians, for Montcalm was not told the news of the British arrival until 6.30 am. He was amazed to see the British standing motionless on the Heights.

## Surprise attack

The two battle lines were drawn up by 9.30 and the fighting began at 10. Montcalm thought that the British had dug in at one point before the main action, but they were merely lying down to avoid flanking fire by Canadians and Indians. Then Wolfe's artillery opened fire and the French began to advance. The British regulars stood two deep to await them.

The French fired too soon, having broken their ranks, but still came on, all but the Canadians, who retreated. The British waited, muskets at the ready. They were not accurate weapons, but were deadly in a mass volley by trained soldiers at short range. The result has already been related — that volley which a British historian of the Army later described as the most perfect ever fired on a battlefield. A second volley rang out, then came the order to charge. Wolfe died at the moment of victory, and his valiant adversary Montcalm died from his wounds the next day.

Quebec was besieged and fell on the 18th. Almost a year later, Montreal fell to Amherst, which completed the downfall of New France, the downfall that matchless volley had made certain.

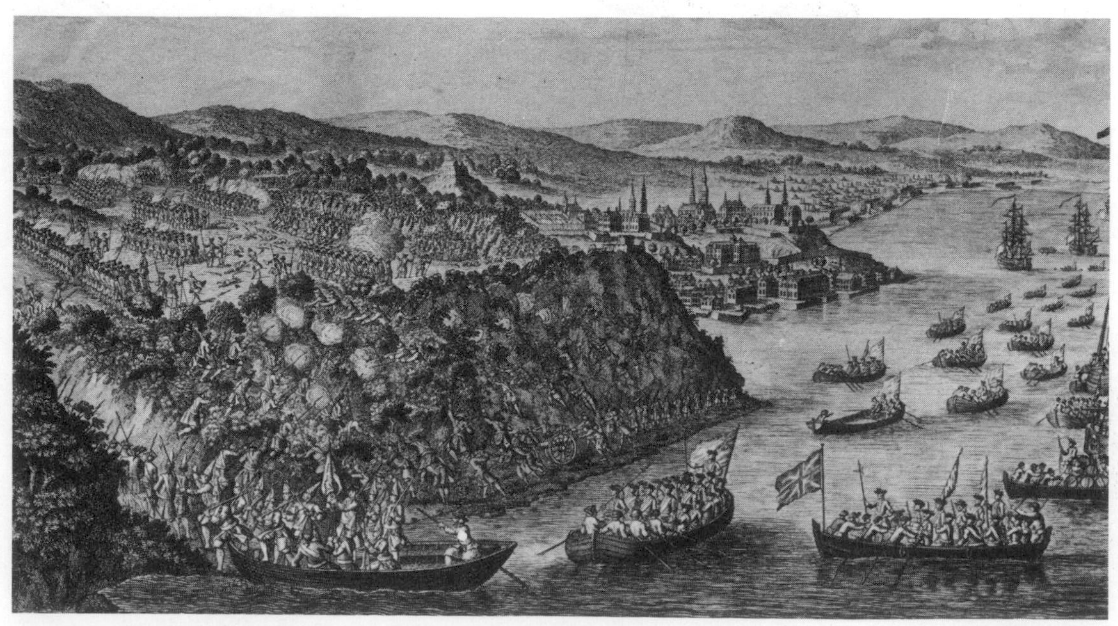

**THE TAKING OF QUEBEC**
**An artist's impression of the storming of Quebec. He has attempted the impossible task of depicting a whole day's action in the same picture (a problem which many artists, before and since, have tried to solve). So he shows the landings from the boats, the scaling of the cliffs and the battle in progress above all at the same time. Long boats are shown ferrying in the assault troops and empty boats returning for more. Artillery men are about to manhandle a field gun up the cliff while British frigates can be seen standing offshore in the background. Quebec appears to have a number of tall churches even then.**

# Who vanquished the English at Bannockburn?

**THEY were no real match. On the one hand was Edward II, king of England who, with his handsome features and tall build, looked soldierly enough; on the other a tattered ill-armed Scottish army.**

Unhappily it was the appearance only that Edward had inherited from his father, the man who had earned himself the nickname of 'The Hammer of the Scots'. It was Edward I who had subdued the fiery and rebellious Scots by force of arms, and who had led his armies into a kingdom that had never entirely acknowledged English rule.

Now his son, who shared little of that lust for battle, faced a redoubtable enemy, Robert Bruce, in a field near Stirling called Bannockburn.

The omens for the Englishmen were not good. On the very eve of the battle, in June 1314, a body of English troops had come upon one of the Scottish outposts and in the ensuing skirmish an English warrior called Sir Henry Bohun had charged through the lines and fallen upon Robert Bruce himself.

Bruce, although taken by surprise and hardly equipped for combat, felled Bohun with his battle-axe. His fellow Scots begged him not to risk his life in personal combat again but Bruce replied dourly: "I have broken my good axe."

Bruce was the claimant to the throne of Scotland. He was brave, shrewd, and as the famous legend about him illustrates, determined. The story of how he saw a spider trying time and again to spin a thread until at last it succeeded — a feat that encouraged him to continue his long struggle against the English — has been handed down over the centuries.

The determined Scotsman, fighting for his own country, was to show himself at Bannockburn a far cleverer general than the soft-living, amusement-seeking English king.

Between Edward's army and the Scots ran the stream called the Bannock Burn, with its banks and treacherous marshes. On such firm ground as there was Bruce told his men to dig pits with spikes in them, and then cover them over with leaves and branches.

Of these preparations Edward was blissfully unaware. His was not a military mind, and his last thought as the day of battle, June 24th, dawned was that the 100,000 strong army he commanded was about to fall into a dreadful and bloody trap.

Edward, at the time of Bannockburn, was still a young man of thirty, who had ruled England for the past seven years since the death of his father.

Unlike Edward I, who had striven to unite both Scotland and Wales under the crown of England and who had made many far-reaching reforms in government, Edward II cared little for such responsibilities of kingship.

One of his first acts upon coming to the throne had been to disband the army assembled by his father which was poised to deliver a crushing blow to the Scots and their leader, Bruce.

Edward preferred the hunting grounds to the battlefield; worse still he surrounded himself by greedy and unscrupulous friends, whose only thought was to enrich themselves at the expense of those less powerful.

Edward virtually handed over the reigns of government to an upstart knight from Gascony called Piers Gaveston but even the notoriously corrupt barons soon began to protest at his excesses and Parliament pressed the king to dismiss his unsavoury protege.

With some reluctance Edward agreed, but within months he reinstated him. This time the barons openly rebelled, captured Gaveston near Scarborough and put him to death.

Meanwhile the Scots had been on the rampage in the north and by 1314, Bruce who had captured many fortresses, was laying siege to Stirling.

It was at this point that Edward decided at last to take some action, and he fondly believed that the huge army he had raised would crush the tiresome Scots.

Edward glanced around him and saw his cavalry drawn up ready for

## ROBERT BRUCE

**DESCENDED from a Norman family who had crossed from Normandy with the Conqueror and were granted lands in Scotland, Bruce for some years fought readily on either side. However, in 1306 he threw in his lot against the English and declared for the cause of Scottish independence. He arranged for his own coronation as King of Scotland. He was, however, defeated in battle by the English and hid for a while in Ireland. In the following year he returned to harry the English forces and it is during those years the fugitive Bruce is supposed to have sheltered in a cave on the brink of abandoning the struggle when he was inspired by the repeated efforts of a spider to climb up to its web however many times it fell. True or not, Bruce continued the struggle and by 1314 only the castle of Stirling remained in English hands north of the border. Edward II's invasion to win back the north was defeated at Bannockburn by a force one third its own number liberating Scotland decisively from English domination, war continuing only on the English side of the River Tweed.**

the charge. The signal was given, and with a mighty thunder of hooves the mounted knights began to gallop forward.

But almost immediately many of the riders fell into the pits that Bruce had dug; others, their heavy armour weighing them down, sank helplessly into the bogs.

As confusion surrounded the charge a hail of spears and arrows from the Scots rained down upon the struggling English advance.

Edward looked on with growing horror and apprehension as a wave of Scotsmen, brandishing their swords and uttering blood-chilling cries, headed toward the English troops and began to cut them to pieces.

The King of England had seen enough. Hurriedly he left the field of battle and fled with his retinue to some safer place.

The outcome of the encounter at Bannockburn was a total victory for Bruce, and the ultimate undoing of all Edward I's campaigns in Scotland.

Edward's standing slumped even further, and a number of the barons, led by Edward's cousin, the Earl of Lancaster, took over the government.

Their rule, however, turned out to be no more judicious than the King's, and it soon became clear that most of them were once again interested in lining their own coffers.

Disenchanted with Lancaster, some of the barons began to desert to Edward, who gathered a force of men together and defeated Lancaster at the battle of Boroughbridge, in York-

shire, in 1322.

The Earl of Lancaster was put to death but this did not signal the end of Edward's troubles. Edward's wife, Isabella, who was the daughter of the King of Spain, was a supporter of the Lancaster party and a sworn enemy of the Dispenser family who now ruled at Edward's behest.

With the help of Roger Mortimer, Earl of March, she had Lord Dispenser and his son, Hugh, executed.

The Queen was not yet done. Having rid herself of Edward's strongest allies she next persuaded Parliament to depose her husband in favour of her son, Prince Edward.

The king was taken to Berkeley Castle in the summer of 1327, a doomed man.

A few weeks later the guards in the castle heard terrible screams coming from the dungeons — the sound of the King of England being put to death by torture with hot irons.

So perished Edward II, one of England's least successful monarchs.

## BANNOCKBURN

**ANCIENT manuscripts and tombstone effigies reveal that Scottish armour and weaponry was always rudimentary and primitive compared with that of England. In fact it was frequently a century behind the times but none of this mattered on the field of Bannockburn. Here it was sheer generalship and strategy, matched with bravery and daring, that won the day against a force superior in armament and numbers.**

# Which Missionary

1 She was quite an ordinary-looking woman — but those who know her story also know that she had the heart of a lion. Her name was Gladys Aylward, and her story really begins on October 18th, 1930. After months of saving to pay for her fare, she was setting off on a journey — a journey which was to take her to a remote mountain town set in the wild and desolate area of north-west China.

2 Gladys Aylward was on her way to become a missionary. But she had chosen a bad time to travel to China, where the civil war was raging over part of her route. It was a dangerous journey. Yet with the help of a Japanese sea captain, who took her from Vladivostock in Russia to Japan in his ship, and then arranged passage from there to China, she reached China safely. But even then her difficulties were far from ended.

3 A long and exhausting ride through the mountains brought her at last to her destination — the ancient walled city of Yang-ch'eng, where she was welcomed into the mission there. Gladys Aylward then set to work on a well-nigh incredible task. This young woman, who had left school at the early age of 13, settled down to study and master five Chinese dialects.

4 The years that followed were full of noble self-sacrifice in which Gladys Aylward spent a great deal of her time caring for the local orphan children. In the spring of 1938, her happy life at Yang-ch'eng was suddenly ruined by the news that the Japanese had invaded Manchuria. It would only be a question of time before they reached the Mission. When the Japanese did come, it was without warning.

# made an Epic Trek?

5 Although the Japanese were everywhere in the area, she would not leave – at least not without her orphaned children. Then comes the most amazing part of her story. Safety lay at the town of Sian, a journey of several weeks through the enemy lines. Calmly, she set off for it, taking some hundred orphaned children and only two men, who carried their food for the journey.

6 Day after day, the children followed her, with hardly a complaint, across the Japanese-infested territory. But the journey was now beginning to have its effect on the tiny bodies of the children who followed her so devotedly. Their food and water had run out, and they were all near to collapse. Fortunately, at this desperate stage they reached a railway line, where they were able to board a train.

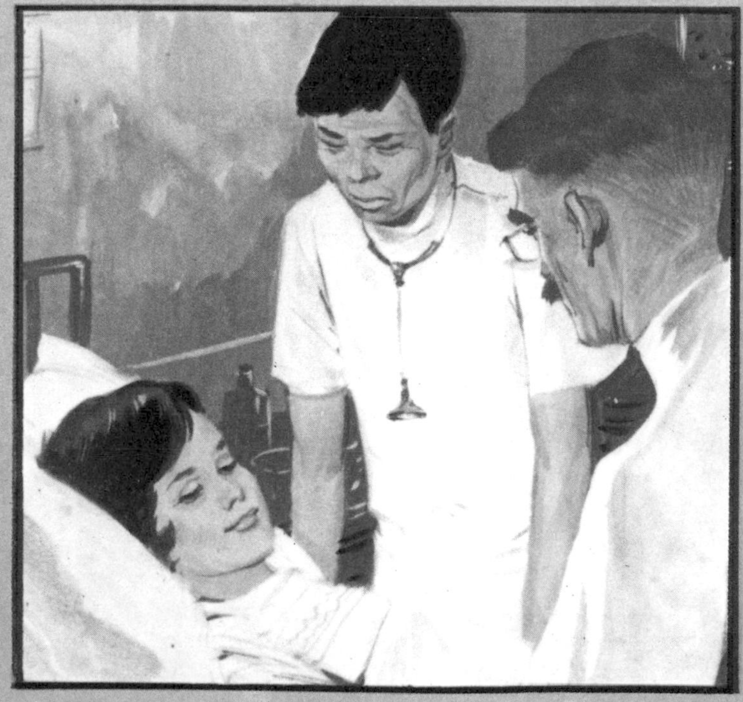

7 Covered with soot, they reached a town called Hua-chou, where they all rested for several days. When they caught another train to Sian, it was only to find that the town had been closed to refugees. Undaunted, Gladys Aylward took them on to the safety of another town, named Fu-ofeng, where she fell seriously ill. But she was happy now — for at last her beloved children were safe.

8 The English doctor there was doubtful that she would survive the fever that racked her body. But she lived — to save more Chinese children from the invading Japanese during World War Two. She stayed in China for another 10 years, helping the poor and the orphaned. Later she founded an orphanage on the island of Formosa (Taiwan) off the mainland of China. She died in Taipei, Taiwan aged 68 in January, 1970.

# What started the American

**The Battle of Bunker Hill goes into the history books as a victory for the British. Yet it was this "victory" that was to destroy the myth of the British army's invincibility**

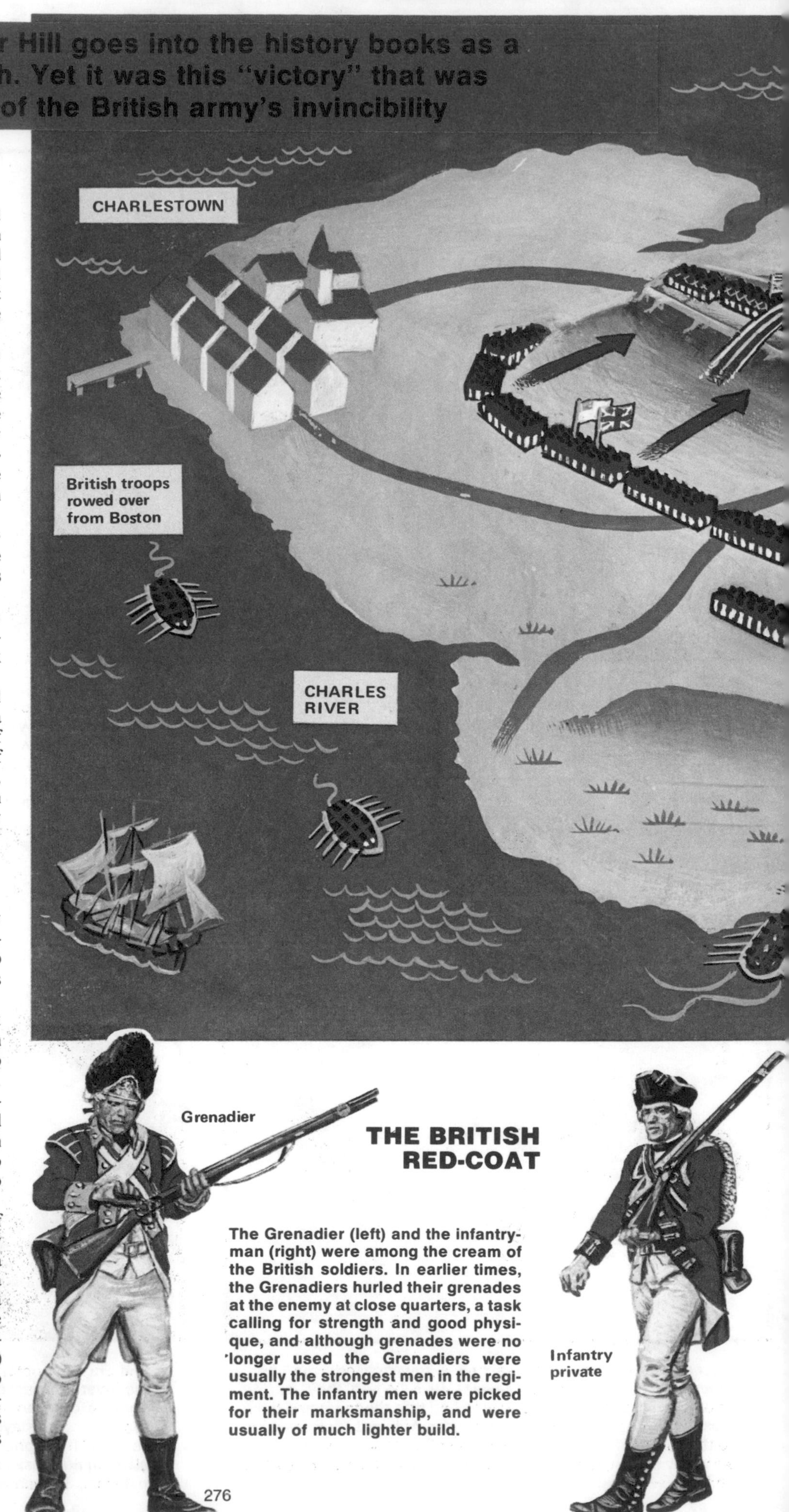


**THE BRITISH RED-COAT**

**The Grenadier (left) and the infantryman (right) were among the cream of the British soldiers. In earlier times, the Grenadiers hurled their grenades at the enemy at close quarters, a task calling for strength and good physique, and although grenades were no longer used the Grenadiers were usually the strongest men in the regiment. The infantry men were picked for their marksmanship, and were usually of much lighter build.**

**COLONEL PRESCOTT marched up and down the parapet which had been hastily built on the hill overlooking the town of Boston. Behind him were the tired troops who had spent most of the night digging the square redoubt.**

**From the British war ships anchored in the nearby Charles River a barrage shook the early morning air. Fortunately the naval guns could not be elevated and so the balls fell harmlessly on the slope below him. But Prescott knew that this bombardment was the forerunner of a massive attack from the British Army garrisoned in Boston.**

**The day was June 17, 1775, and the Battle of Bunker Hill, the first battle in the American War of Independence, was about to begin.**

To understand how the war came about, how Englishmen came to be fighting Englishmen, it is necessary to look back ten years earlier.

In 1765, the British government had decided that the colonists in America should contribute towards the cost of maintaining the army there. One way of raising the money, it was suggested, would be by introducing a tax in the form of a duty on stamps which were necessary to legalise certain documents.

## Protests

The colonists were incensed. Why should they pay taxes to Britain? Feelings ran so high that before this Stamp Act could be put into operation it was repealed.

Two years later the British government introduced another tax — this time on various goods which were imported into the country, goods which included tea. Once again, the colonists raised vehement protests, vowing that they would not buy English goods nor pay English tax. When a new government came into office, one of the first things it did was to remove the duty — except on tea.

The basic problem, the real cause of the American resentment, was not simply a matter of the taxes. The issue of the tea tax was a matter of principle. With a sense of growing independence and a desire to control their own affairs, the colonists refused to admit that a Parliament more than 3,000 miles (4,800 km) away should have unlimited powers to legislate for them. The British government's attitude, on the other hand, was that the colonists were British subjects and therefore subject to British law.

# War of Independence?

The pick and brush were used to clean the pan and touch hole of the musket.

The Continental soldier carried all his possessions on his back, and apart from his musket and ammunition, an essential piece of equipment he always carried was his jacknife.

## THE AMERICAN 'CONTINENTAL' SOLDIER

In the early days of the war the colonists had virtually no uniforms of their own. In the main they wore their own clothes. But in late 1775 this "Continental Army" had adopted brown as its official uniform colour, the various regiments being distinguished by different cuffs, collars and lapels. But a complete uniform was the exception rather than the rule. Later it was decreed that dark blue would be the colour for the infantry.

General Howe

General Clinton

General Burgoyne

With drums beating, and marching as if they were on a parade ground, the British troops begin their advance on the fortification on top of the hill. But there was no sound from the colonists crouched behind their earth parapet. Only when the British were almost on them would they unleash their deadly volleys of musket fire. Twice the British were driven back, and only succeeded when the Americans ran out of ammunition. On the right are the three British generals who were in charge of the attack.

In 1770 a mob in Boston attacked some British soldiers and were driven off with the loss of a number of lives. In 1772 a British warship at nearby Providence was set on fire by local citizens.

And in 1773 the "Boston Tea Party" took place. A group of townspeople, disguised as Indians, stole aboard three British ships in the harbour and hurled the cargo of tea into the sea.

As a punishment the British Parliament closed the port, put the town under the control of a large military force led by General Gage and insisted that the town should pay for the lost tea.

## War begins

War was now near. In the autumn of 1774, colonial delegates gathered at Philadelphia to decide their course of action. A Declaration of Rights was issued protesting against the British treatment. The declaration had no effect on Lord North, the British Premier. Instead, he sent more troops to America.

In April, 1775 General Gage learned of a store of arms and ammunition held by the rebels in the nearby village of Concord and sent a body of troops to capture it. Warned of the British intention, the "Minute-men" (so-called because they were pledged to take to the battle-field at a minute's notice) were ready for the attack.

Halted on the way, at the village of Lexington, the British troops opened fire, killing eight of the Americans before marching on to Concord.

With this skirmish, the war had begun.

Following the battle at Lexington both sides now waited — the British for reinforcements and the Americans, with their untrained and unskilled troops, for ammunition and cannon. So both sides were reluctant to attack.

Although Boston was easily defended from attacks by land or sea, it was dominated by ranges of hills on either side — which meant that if artillery could be got to the top the town and its garrisons could easily be bombarded.

The Americans decided to gain possession of the hills; and on June 16 a thousand men marched silently through the night to occupy Bunker Hill. In fact, at the last minute, it was decided to take their position on Breed's Hill, as this was considered a better position from which to beat off any British attack.

Throughout the night, with Colonel Prescott praying that they would not be seen by British sentries or lookouts on the ships only a quarter of a mile away, the men built their redoubt — a fortification of ditch, parapet and firing platform. At dawn, by which time most of the work had been completed, Prescott's fears were justified.

A sentry on one of the warships spotted the men on the hill, and the big guns opened up. A sleepy Boston garrison stumbled out of bed, at first unable to take in the fact that the Americans had actually built their redoubt during the night.

The British immediately saw the danger. General Gage discussed the situation with the three senior officers who had been sent from England to help him in the campaign — Major Generals Sir William Howe, Henry Clinton and "Gentleman Johnny" Burgoyne — and it was agreed to attack at once.

The plan was to make a direct frontal attack straight up the hill, even though this meant that all the way up they would

be under fire from the American muskets.

Major-General Howe was chosen to lead the attack. He had some 1500 men, with a further 700 in reserve. Crouched behind the redoubt were 1000 Americans, tired, hungry and thirsty.

It was not until mid-day that the small boats and barges needed to ferry the marines and troops across the shallow waters of the peninsula were ready, and not until early afternoon that the British landed on the shore below Breed's Hill. And when General Howe arrived he saw a sight which filled him with dismay — more than a thousand fresh troops coming to support their colleagues on the hill. He quickly sent a message for the reserves to be dispatched.

As soon as they had arrived, Howe prepared to attack, dividing his forces so as to advance from different points. But almost immediately the first set-back befell them. The guns they had brought with them to bombard the fortification before the attack suddenly ceased firing. The artillerymen had brought the wrong-sized shot!

General Putnam

Colonel Prescott

**The two commanders of the American soldiers in the redoubt on top of the hill; and the view, as portrayed by an early artist, of the situation they might have seen as the British troops came storming up the hill towards them.**

## Advance!

Nevertheless, the advance continued, one group under General Pigot attacking from one side and Howe's men attacking from the other. But the Americans had prepared well. Their plans were laid.

The British troops presented a magnificent sight as they advanced up the hill, a glittering array of red and white marching forward in parade-ground-straight lines, their bayonets gleaming.

On and on they came. The Americans waited. Colonel Prescott watched the advancing lines and repeated his command: "Only fire when I give the order." Studying the columns coming up the other side, General Putnam yelled: "Don't fire until you see the whites of their eyes!"

Still the Americans waited. At about 50 metres the British lowered their bayonets to charge — and then the order to fire was given.

Volley after volley thundered into the front ranks, smashing them to pieces. Others pushed forward, but again and again the muskets spat smoke and flame until the British could take no more. They turned and fled.

Pigot's troops fared no better, that withering barrage of fire at short range carving great gaps in the orderly lines. More and more troops were added to the attack but nothing could withstand those thunderous volleys. The red coats turned back.

Within a short time Howe and Pigot had re-organised their men. Once again those precise ranks marched up the hill. And once again they were allowed to get within a cricket-pitch length of the fortification before the American muskets blazed into their faces in a series of devastating volleys. The British retreated, leaving behind a wall of dead and wounded.

Whether or not General Howe realised that the Americans were by now desperately short of ammunition is impossible to say, but with fresh troops arriving from Boston he was determined that he would try a third time. And this time he succeeded. The Americans had run out of powder and ball.

The British troops swarmed over the parapet, their bayonets exacting a bloody revenge for their own lost comrades. Virtually defenceless against the glistening steel wielded by trained and experienced soldiers, the Americans had little choice but to run.

The Battle of Bunker Hill was over. But although it was a British victory, it served little purpose in advancing the cause of the British. The untrained, unco-ordinated, colonists had taken on regular soldiers — and very nearly beaten them. The fight for freedom would continue.

And continue it did until, seven years later at the Battle of Yorktown, the Americans finally won their War of Independence.

**To transport their supplies of powder and shot, the colonist soldiers would frequently seek the loan of a cart from the local farmer. He would take his load to the next farm and transfer it to another cart before returning home. On the right we see some of the powder being taken to Bunker Hill.**

**The British army also needed transport to get them to the foot of Bunker Hill and in this case they used the Navy's longboats. The city of Boston, in which the troops were garrisoned, was on a peninsula, and the only way to get the troops quickly into an attacking position was by ferrying them across the estuary, at that point some 800 metres away.**

# Who was known as

1. As the son of a general, it was almost inevitable that Charles Gordon should choose the army as a career. Born at Woolwich near London on January 28, 1833, he went to preparatory school at Taunton, Somerset, before returning to Woolwich to attend the Royal Military Academy. Although he studied hard, Gordon did not care much for authority and came into conflict with senior officers on several occasions. In fact, disdain for his superiors was one of Gordon's lifelong characteristics and it was to prove his undoing at Khartoum. In 1852 he joined the Royal Engineers, and soon afterwards was sent to fight in the Crimean War. Gordon served with distinction, especially at the siege of Sebastopol where he also showed his talent as an engineer when entrusted with the task of demolishing the dockyard.

2. In 1860 Gordon was sent to China to assist in the suppression of the Taiping Rebellion in which the rebels were attempting to destroy the ruling Mandarin class. He adapted magnificently to the guerilla warfare and showed great personal courage on many occasions. Once he approached an enemy stronghold on foot and calmly sketched the rebels' defences while under heavy fire. In 1864 he led the mopping-up operation on the rebels.

3. While in China, he became interested in the welfare of very poor children, especially their education. Gordon returned to England in 1865. By now he was a popular figure and his achievements in China had won him the nickname 'Chinese Gordon', which stayed with him until his death, when he received the name by which he is more popularly known today. Back home, he began holding classes for poor children at his house in Gravesend.

# "Chinese Gordon"?

4. A man with boundless energy. Gordon tired of home life and in 1874 entered the service of the Khedive Ismail of Egypt. As administrator of the Sudan he had great success in stamping out the slave trade and brought a great measure of peace to this dangerous region. His trim uniformed figure became a symbol of hope for the native population. He resigned in 1880 and returned to England and, seemingly, retirement.

5. But Gordon could not settle and he became secretary to the Viceroy of India but resigned to take up the role of peacemaker in the disputes between China and Russia. A further two years as ministry adviser in South Africa followed but, back in the Sudan, which Gordon knew so well, a crisis was brewing. Led by the Mahdi, the self-styled 'Messiah' of the Mohammedans, the Sudanese natives were in revolt.

6. Gordon was summoned and ordered to make his way to the town of Khartoum and from there supervise the withdrawal of the Egyptian garrisons and evacuate the Sudan. He arrived in February, 1884, and after assessing the situation decided to ignore his direct orders as he felt seasoned British troops could easily defeat the Mahdi. Khartoum was soon under siege, but Gordon insisted on holding out until a British relief force arrived.

7. The progress of the relief force was very slow and the attacks on Khartoum increased. The defences were greatly stretched but Gordon still led by courageous example. Finally the Mahdi, ordered an all-out assault and the defences crumbled. It was January 26, 1885, and Gordon calmly met the attackers on the steps of the Governor's Palace and was speared to death. Perhaps as he would have wished, he passed into legend as 'Gordon of Khartoum'.

# Who used his pen to

1. Thomas Paine was born on January 29, 1737, at Thetford, in the English county of Norfolk. At 13 he went to work in his father's shop but after a few years became a Customs officer for the south coast of England. The job was poorly paid and bribery was rife. After only two years Paine was dismissed for allowing goods to pass through without inspection.

2. After several other jobs, Paine went to London and taught English at an academy. He now had outspoken ideas on politics which impressed Benjamin Franklin, the American politician when they met in 1774. Franklin arranged for him to sail to Philadelphia to meet some influential people. But Paine had to be stretchered ashore after a terrible voyage.

3. He recovered, met Franklin's friends and quickly established himself as a tutor. An essay on the abolition of slavery was published in a Philadelphia newspaper and impressed many people. He became editor of the *Pennsylvania Magazine* publishing more essays. By this time the American colonies were very dissatisfied with British government.

4. In 1776, Paine wrote the pamphlet *Common Sense*. This attacked the British system of ruling the colonies and called for an independent American republic and a constitutional conference. George Washington later said that Paine's words had greatly influenced the colonists. When the war broke out, he saw some action but used his pen even more.

# Fight for Freedom?

5. In recognition of his work, Paine was appointed secretary to the American Congress Committee on Foreign Affairs. His pamphlets urged the colonists to fight on but Paine himself became unpopular and in 1779 lost his job. He returned to London and wrote the famous *Rights of Man* which caused a sensation because of its revolutionary ideas.

6. The outcry forced him to flee to France where there was indeed a revolution. As in America, Paine wrote a document condemning the monarchy and calling for a new republic. This was created, but Paine fell foul of the revolutionary leaders and was thrown into prison. It seemed little could save Paine from the guillotine.

7. Fortunately the French leader Robespierre fell from power and was executed, and Paine was released following a letter from the American minister in Paris, to the Committee of Public Safety. He was now writing his book, *The Age of Reason*, which was a sharp attack on religion of the time. But he had caught fever in prison and needed constant nursing.

Eventually, Paine recovered and in 1802, he returned to America where he owned a small farm. For his last two years he was an invalid and he died in New York in June, 1809, disliked by many and respected by others. Only today, by looking back, can we understand how important and influential were the writings of Thomas Paine.

# When did the First Tank appear?

**THE first people known to have fought in war chariots were the Hyksos (the name means 'Princes of the Lands') who were skilled in rearing horses in the Tigris and Euphrates basin. This warrior race overran Upper Egypt in 1700 B.C. mainly due to the use of war chariots. Later on, the idea of war carts was copied by the Israelites, Assyrians and Persians.**

Cyrus, King of Persia, in the 6th century B.C. had three main types of chariots. The first could carry a wooden tower which operated a field battering ram; the second was drawn by eight yoke of oxen to carry twenty fighting men; and the third type was fast and light with a crew of two. Horses were protected by armour, long axles prevented the chariot from overturning and long scythes protruded from the axles and beneath. It must have been a terrifying sight to opposing foot soldiers.

Alexander the Great used chariots successfully against the Persians in 331 B.C. So did Julius Caesar when he invaded Britain.

In medieval times the chronicler Froissart tells of 'high wheel-barrows reinforced with iron and long pointed spikes in the front', the main armament carried by the occupants being a large siege crossbow. There is a 15th century German engraving showing a war cart or 'ribaudequin' with sword blades in the yokes; it is armed with guns.

In 1482 the famous artist, Leonardo da Vinci, designed an assault car or tank. The bottom half was shaped like a shallow bowl, with slits cut in the bottom to take the lower parts of four wheels. The wheels were operated by gears and cranks from inside, eight men being needed to operate them. A tent-like armoured cover fitted over the base, with loopholes for firearms. Da Vinci even gave a written definition of its tactical use.

In 1596 the mathematician John Napier designed a remarkable assault car. Described as a round chariot of metal, it was fully armoured with a metal twice the thickness required to withstand the musket fire of the time. "The use thereof in moving serveth to break the array of the enemies battle . . . by continual discharge of harquebussiers through small holes, the enemy being abashed and uncertain as to what defence or pursuit to use against a moving mouth of metal."

During the Crimean War, in 1855 a steam engine was used for an assault car, called a 'Locomotive Battery.' In shape it was very much like Leonardo da Vinci's tank but its cover of hardened steel had a serrated surface, intended to shatter the shot instead of throwing it off. It moved on four wheels and carried fourteen-pounder carronades firing through loopholes. For shock action scythes were fixed and hinged, so that they could be folded down when not required.

Lord Palmerston, the British Prime Minister, it is quoted, "refused to have anything to do with this machine as being too brutal for civilised use."

The first armoured car was manufactured in England in 1900. It was named "Pennington' after the inventor and was powered with a 16 h.p. engine. The entire chassis was covered by a quarter inch 'skirt' of steel. The car was manned by a

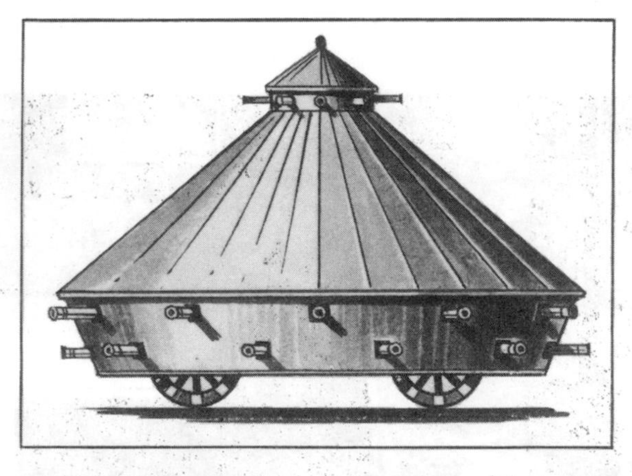

**In 1482 the famous Italian artist and inventor, Leonardo da Vinci, produced this design for a "Secure and Covered Chariot". Slits were cut into the bottom part to take the wheels, which were operated from inside by cranks and gears.**

**'Little Willie', designed by Sir William Tritton and built in September, 1915, was the world's first tank. Its first trials were held at Thetford Heath in Norfolk, but its balance proved defective and it could not surmount obstacles. Further improvements would be necessary before it could be used in action. It weighed 28 tonnes, was eight metres long and had a top speed of 3½ km/h.**

**The first type of tank ever to go into action on a battlefield was 'Big Willie', the British Mark 1. Designed by Major Wilson and Sir William Tritton, it had its first trial in 1916. Its high nose gave a greater capacity for obstacle crossing. The wheels were designed to help in steering, although later these were removed. It was this tank that bore the brunt of tank fighting in the First World War. Incidentally, the name 'tank' was given to these vehicles as a means of preventing any news of their development leaking to the Germans. The ruse was successful, the Germans being taken completely by surprise when they first appeared in France.**

driver and two machine-gunners.

Frederick Simms in 1902 produced a very similar armoured car but further coverage was given to the tyres by a fringe of chain mail attached to the steel skirt. This car also carried two Maxim machine-guns and a pom-pom (an automatic one-pounder cannon.) A year later, Simms exhibited an improved version with two machine guns now mounted on rotating turrets. The driver, however, had to rely on the use of a periscope to enable him to steer.

Following the Battle of the Marne in 1914, the Admiralty Air Department provided armoured cars to protect the air base at Dunkirk and to rescue pilots who had been shot down. They purchased 100 Rolls Royce cars, which were quickly armed and armoured. The cars, however, had no top protection and often crews fell victim to snipers.

Up until this time all the armoured cars had one big drawback: because they were wheeled vehicles they were confined to the roads. They could not cross rough country and they had little value in the sort of battle conditions now being encountered.

From October 1914, the Germans and the Allies faced each other across a No-Man's land zig-zagged with trenches and barbed wire protected by machine guns. They proved impregnable to ordinary attacks, except at an enormous cost of life, and it was apparent that there was no way a wheeled vehicle could operate in such circumstances.

## Experimental work

However, for some time experimental work had been going on with oil-powered, cross country tractors fitted with caterpillar tracks. And in 1915 it was suggested that a combination of reliable combustion engine and a heavily armoured body carried on caterpillar tracks would be the solution.

Nothing came of the first tests, but then Winston Churchill, at that time in charge of the Admiralty, threw all his weight behind the secret development of the new weapon, and rapid progress was made.

In September 1915 'Little Willie' was built, but it narrowly failed to meet the specifications demanded. A few months later 'Big Willie' had its first trials — and the tank as we know it today had been born.

At last a solution was available to end the stalemate position of the No-Man's Land. The first tank attack took place on September 15, 1916, when 50 tanks went into action. They were not the complete answer. Although they had been designed to cover rough ground and obstacles the constant bombardment from the artillery of both sides had filled the terrain with craters which even the tanks found almost impassable.

Nevertheless, the tank had shown that it could provide the answer to trenches and barbed wire barricades. It would continue to be a main weapon of the world's armies.

The first tanks were provided with armour proof only against ordinary bullets, but in 1917 the Mark 1V appeared with armour designed to withstand every form of small arms fire. More than 1,000 of these tanks were produced. The Mark 1V weighed 28 tonnes and was operated by a crew of eight

In order to negotiate the extensive trench system which typified the First World War, it was necessary for the Mark 1V tank to carry a *facine*. This consisted of a large bundle of logs lashed together with chains. When the tank reached a trench needing to be bridged, an explosive charge severed a cable which supported the facine; it then fell forward bridging the trench. The tank then crossed the open gap.

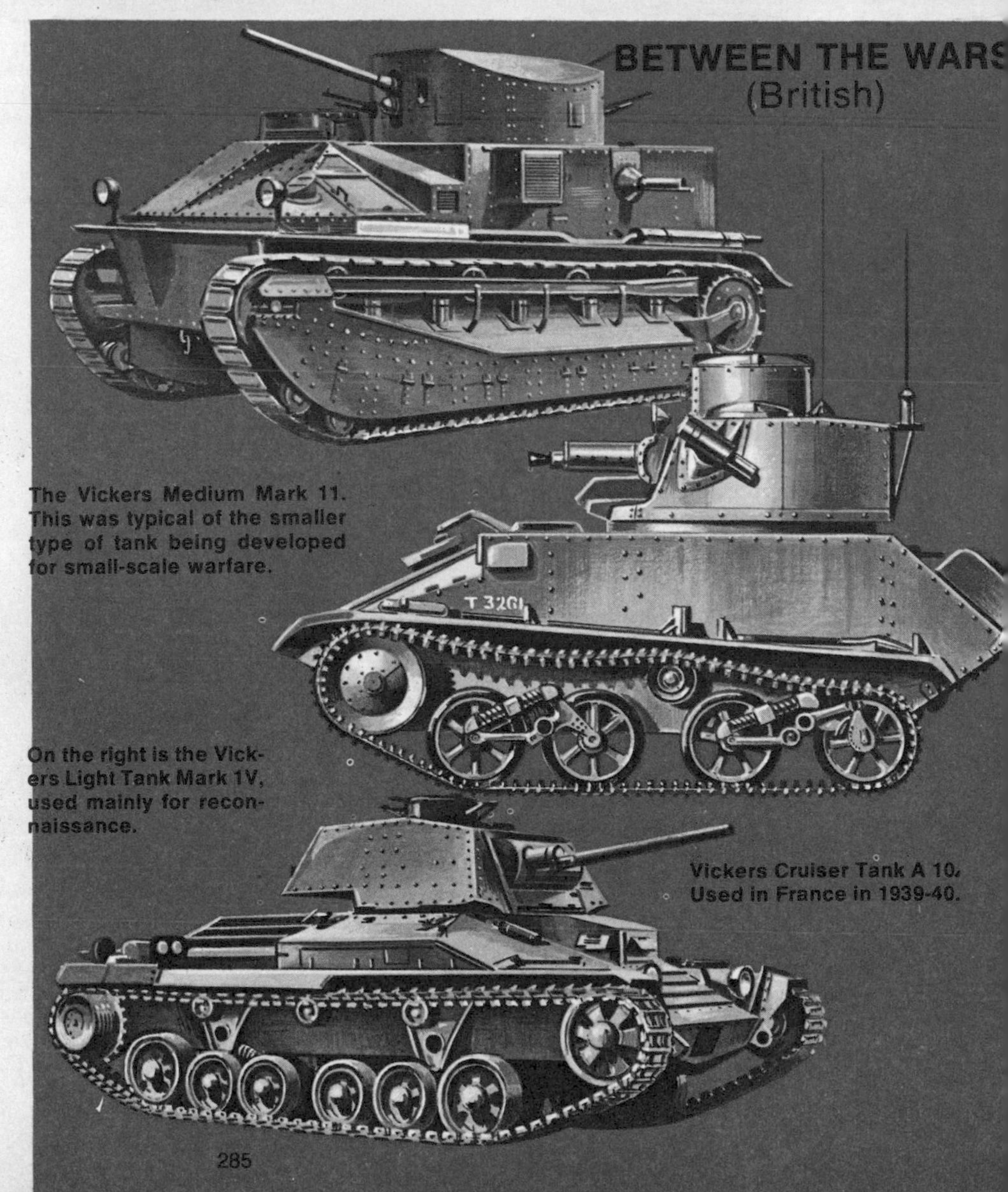


The Vickers Medium Mark 11. This was typical of the smaller type of tank being developed for small-scale warfare.

On the right is the Vickers Light Tank Mark 1V, used mainly for reconnaissance.

Vickers Cruiser Tank A 10. Used in France in 1939-40.

# Who was the Spaghetti Salesman

1. Along the wharfs of Nice, then a part of the Italian state of Piedmont but now part of France, a fair-haired boy could often be seen gazing at the ships. The boy, Guiseppe Garibaldi, couldn't wait to go to sea. Finally in 1823, when he was sixteen, he got his chance, starting as a cabin boy. Ten years later, he had obtained a Master's Certificate allowing him to captain a ship. He was an important sailor at last.

2. But by then he had become interested in politics. A young Italian, Guiseppe Mazzini, had founded a society called 'Young Italy' whose aim was to liberate Italy, which was then split into many small States mostly ruled by Austria. Garibaldi joined the society and they plotted to start a revolt in Piedmont. But the plot failed, and sentenced to death in his absence, Garibaldi fled to South America.

3. Yet he did not settle down to a quiet life in exile. Within a year he volunteered to take command of a ship belonging to the rebel Rio Grande republic which was fighting Argentina. While commanding the ship, he met and eloped with his future wife Anita — then married to another man. Anita joined him on the ship, but soon it was sunk. Garibaldi, Anita and the crew were forced to flee overland to Uruguay.

4. Garibaldi tried being a spaghetti salesman and then a maths teacher, but the quiet life just didn't suit him. When Uruguay rebelled against the rule of Argentina, he formed a brigade of Italian exiles to help fight. By masterminding the heroic defence of Uruguay's capital, Montevideo, he helped the little country to victory. He was then lured back to a hero's welcome in Nice by rumours of revolution in Italy.

# who freed Italy?

5. From then on, Garibaldi led his army of red-shirted volunteers to a number of amazing victories in the cause of one free Italy. In his greatest campaign, he landed with just one thousand men in Sicily, but was able to beat considerably larger forces and go on to invade the mainland of Italy and capture Naples, then Italy's largest city. Sicily, Naples and Piedmont were merged to make the first kingdom of Italy.

6. Garibaldi continued to fight against foreign rule, and eventually Italy became one country ruled by Italians. Because of his service to the country he loved, the Italian government voted him a large gift and an annual pension, which he at first refused but eventually accepted in 1876. From then until his death in 1882 he retired to the Mediterranean island of Caprera to write his memoirs.

## FROM MANY STATES TO ONE

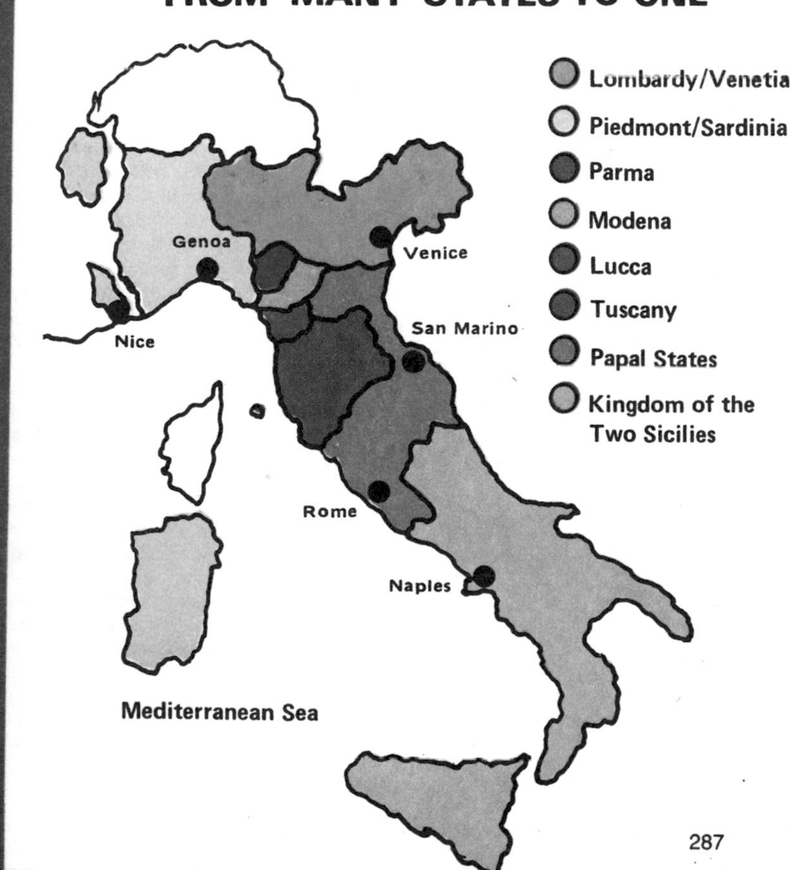


TODAY, all of Italy (bar the tiny republic of San Marino and the Vatican City) is one country. But for much of its history it was divided into many small States, nearly always in a state of war.

The map shows how Italy was divided after the defeat of Napoleon in 1815. The biggest two were the Kingdom of the Two Sicilies and Piedmont/Sardinia which included Savoy and Nice. The Papal States were ruled by the Pope in Rome; Lombardy/Venetia was ruled by Austria; Tuscany, Parma, Modena and Lucca were governed by local dukes and duchesses dependent, to some extent, on Austria.

Piedmont was probably the strongest Italian country, and it was to Piedmont that Garibaldi and Mazzini looked to unite all the States into one country.

It took many years of wars and revolution before this dream came true. With the help of France and then Prussia, Piedmont acquired first Lombardy, then Venetia, from the Austrians, although Piedmont gave Nice and Savoy to France — something for which Garibaldi never forgave the Piedmontese government. The Kingdom of the Two Sicilies was liberated by Garibaldi and his one thousand followers. Revolutions in Tuscany (which had purchased Lucca from its royal 'owner'), Parma and Modena meant that these States too were incorporated into Piedmont.

Only the Papal States remained separate. Despite an abortive revolution and later an attack by Garibaldi and his 'redshirts', they remained so until 1870 — as long as the French were prepared to defend the Pope's kingdom. But on 3rd September 1870, after the battle of Sedan in which the French were decisively beaten by the Prussians and their power destroyed, Rome fell to the Italian armies after token resistance.

Italy was one country, as Garibaldi had dreamt.

# What were the

JUST down the Thames from London, in a dry dock especially constructed by the National Maritime Museum, stands one of the last survivors of a byegone era. Her name means 'short shirt', the garment worn by the witch Nannie in Robert Burns's poem, *Tam - o - Shanter* and she has been described as the most famous clipper of them all.

*Cutty Sark* is the name of this ship, and photographs of it have been used to advertise everything from whisky to fur coats. The reason is obvious at a glance — those smooth lines flowing back from that sharply raked prow, those tall masts covered by acres of snowy white canvas, could only belong to a thoroughbred, a greyhound of the oceans.

**A sketch from an old print showing a tea auction in the great auction room at East India House**

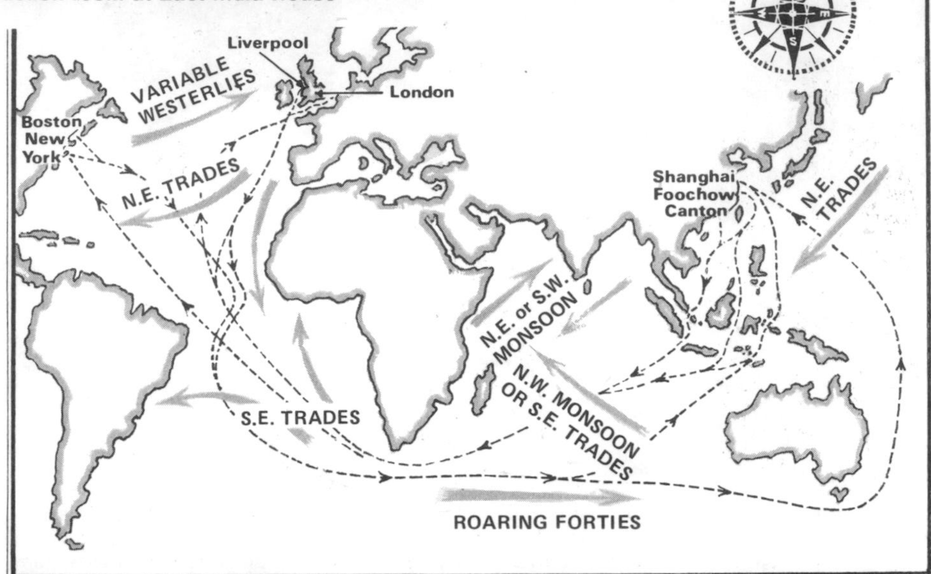


**The map above shows the clipper routes to and from London and New York. There were two seasons for tea, the first, loaded between May and June being the more highly valued. Foochow was the favourite port for the early consignments. Loadings from other ports (Macao, Shanghai and Canton, for example) were between June and August. The clippers depended on the trade winds, also shown in the map above. A clipper sailed best with the wind behind her but great expertise was needed to reach the really fast speeds that all the clipper captains strove to achieve. Sails were not shortened until the last possible moment. The monsoons, of course, were only at certain times of the year so that knowledge of the winds was essential.**

## Record breaking

She has been preserved as a tribute to the era of the clipper ships, those supremely fast, lightweight cargo ships which derived their name from their legendary ability to 'clip' hours off the time taken by more conventional ships. For a short period during the 19th century, the clippers came to dominate the seas, and also the imaginations of a public who thrilled at their record-breaking exploits.

Huge fortunes were made and lost as gamblers staked their savings on the outcome of races between particular ships. Sometimes these races were remarkably close — in 1866, in what came to be known as 'The Great Tea Race', the *Ariel* docked in London just 20 minutes before the *Taeping*, after a journey round the world from China lasting 98 days.

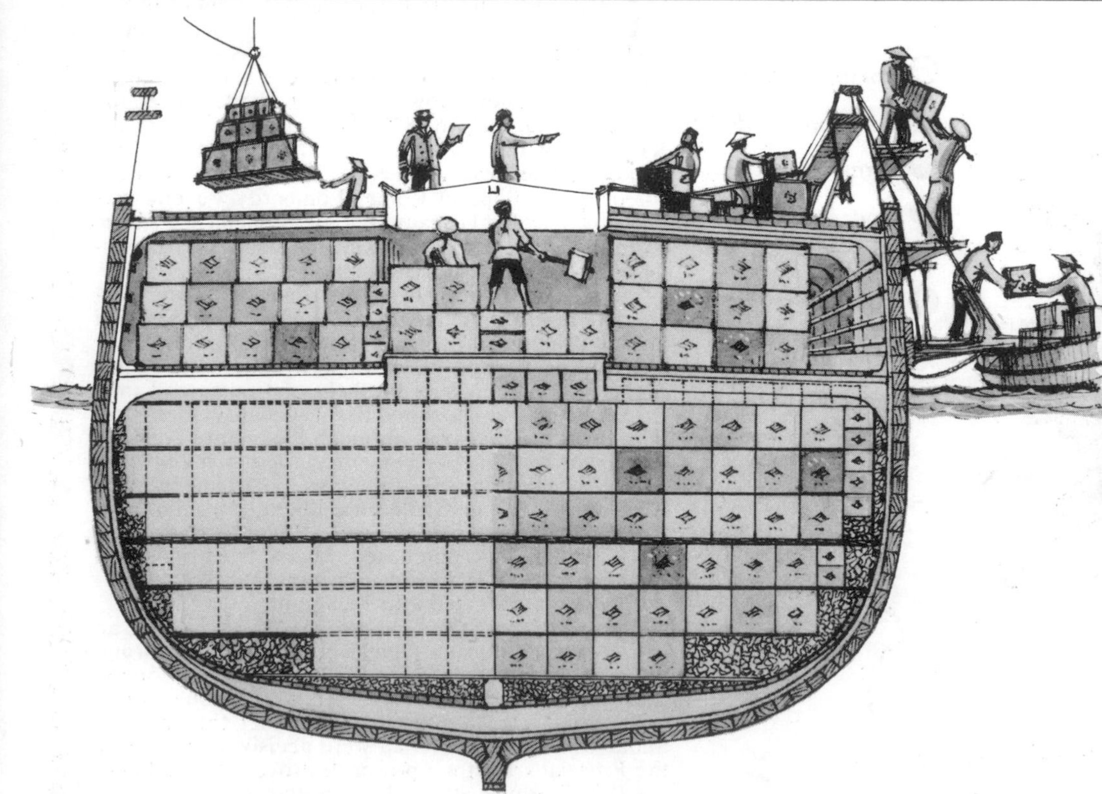


## LOADING TEA

**Loading of the tea was always done with cheap coolie labour. It was essential that the chests were tightly packed to stop damage through sliding about. So they were fitted together like complicated jigsaw puzzles, using chests of different sizes, and were padded with ballast round the lower edges, any gaps being filled with wood shavings. A ship had to be well loaded not only for the safety of the cargo but also for the safety of the ship itself, because if a cargo shifted it could cause listing (making the ship tilt to one side) which could make it capsize. Speed, too, was essential, so loading would go on day and night until it was finished and the journey could begin. Conditions on board the clippers, however, were considerably better than that in other merchant ships and crew members were highly respected by other sailors.**

# Great Tea Races?

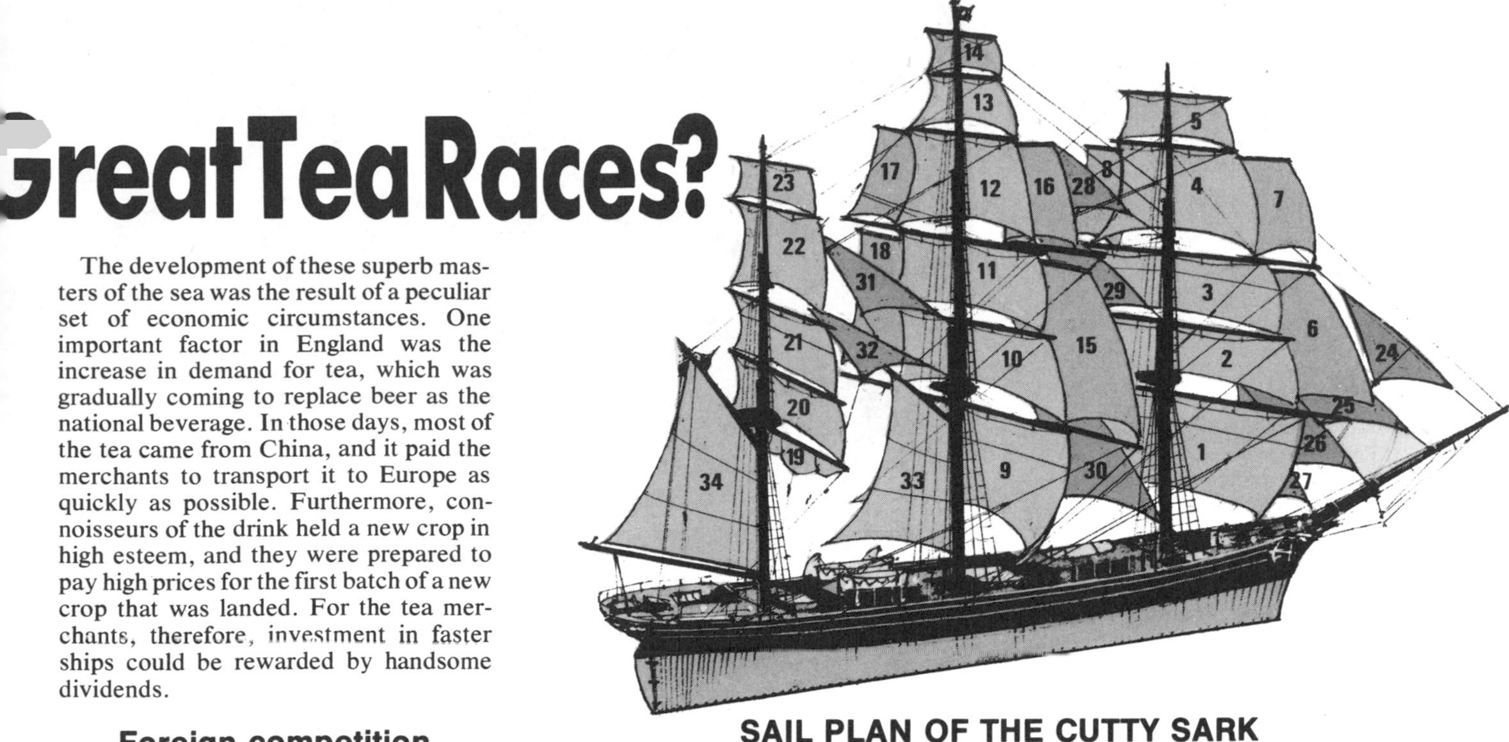


The development of these superb masters of the sea was the result of a peculiar set of economic circumstances. One important factor in England was the increase in demand for tea, which was gradually coming to replace beer as the national beverage. In those days, most of the tea came from China, and it paid the merchants to transport it to Europe as quickly as possible. Furthermore, connoisseurs of the drink held a new crop in high esteem, and they were prepared to pay high prices for the first batch of a new crop that was landed. For the tea merchants, therefore, investment in faster ships could be rewarded by handsome dividends.

## Foreign competition

Then, in 1849, the repeal of the British Navigation Acts opened huge and previously inaccessible tracts of the world to foreign merchants. Until then, they had been barred from the lucrative Far East trade by these laws, which gave British government-licensed companies like the East India Company a virtual monopoly in luxury goods like silks and spices. Now the government forsook its monopoly, and foreign merchants were free to compete on equal terms. They immediately began building faster ships to take advantage of the situation.

Around the same time in America, another economic upheaval was encouraging the development of ships that could cover long distances in the shortest time possible. The California Gold Rush of 1849 led to rumours flying around of gold rocks lying waiting to be picked up, and this in turn led to huge numbers of people wanting to get to California as quickly as possible. The overland route from New York was long and arduous, whereas a clipper could make the journey down the eastern coast of the United States, around South America and up the west coast in a few months.

## Gold fever

Gold had been found in Australia as well, and suddenly it seemed as if the whole world had 'gold fever'. Everyone was affected by it. The Americans, the first to enter the field, began building clippers as fast as they could. Meanwhile, in Britain, shipowners chartered or bought any American clippers they could get. As a result, soon they were building clippers which were as fast as anything the Americans could produce.

Then speed fever began to affect the shipbuilding industry, taking hold of not only the men who owned the ships, but those who sailed them too. Many captains drove their crews mercilessly and sometimes even dangerously in their

### SAIL PLAN OF THE CUTTY SARK

**Many of the crew on the old clippers could neither read nor write but they were not unintelligent or ignorant. They needed to know the names of all the ropes and all the sails. This key is of just the sails of the Cutty Sark shown above. There would have been more than 10 times as many ropes to learn.**

**FOREMAST: 1. Fore course, 2. Fore lower topsail, 3. Fore upper topsail, 4. Fore topgallant (known as the t'gallant), 5. Fore royal, 6. Weather fore topmast stunsail, 7. Weather fore topgallant stunsail, 8. Lee fore topgallant stunsail.**

**MAIN MAST: 9. Main course, 10. Main lower topsail, 11. Main upper topsail, 12. Main topgallant, 13. Main royal, 14. Main skysail, 15. Weather main topmast stunsail, 16. Weather main topgallant stunsail, 17. Lee main topgallant stunsail, 18. Lee main topmast stunsail.**

**MIZZEN MAST: 19. Crossjack, 20. Mizzen lower topsail, 21. Mizzen upper topsail, 22. Mizzen topgallant, 23. Mizzen royal.**

**FORE AND AFT SAILS: 24. Flying jib, 25. Outer jib, 26. Inner jib, 27. Fore topmast staysail, 28. Main royal staysail, 29. Main topgallant staysail, 30. Main topmast staysail, 31. Mizzen topgallant staysail, 32. Mizzen topmast staysail, 33. Main spencer, 34. Spanker.**

### THE CLIPPER 'LINES'

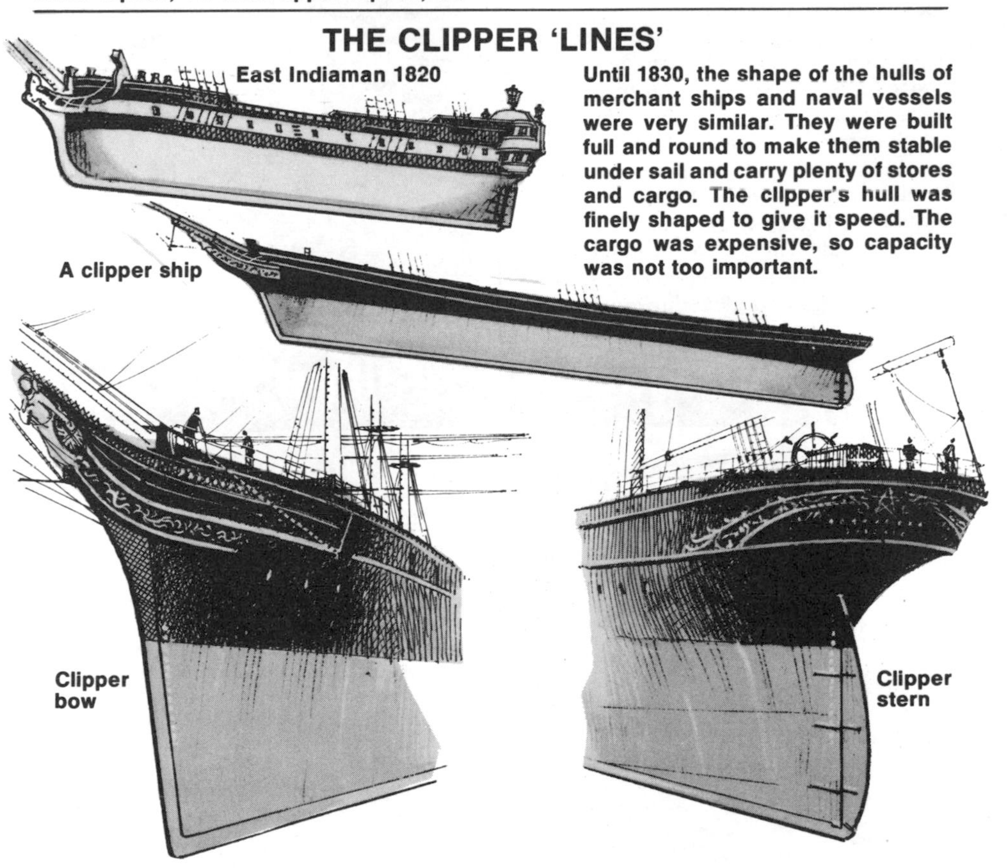


**Until 1830, the shape of the hulls of merchant ships and naval vessels were very similar. They were built full and round to make them stable under sail and carry plenty of stores and cargo. The clipper's hull was finely shaped to give it speed. The cargo was expensive, so capacity was not too important.**

**The graceful bow and fine counter (rounded) stern which characterised the clipper hull.**

attempts to make fast journeys. When passengers protested to Captain Forbes, of the Australia-bound *Marco Polo* that he was carrying far too much sail, he is said to have replied that he would drive his ship to "Hell — or Melbourne"!

A captain with a mania for speed, who could drive his crew to the limits of their endurance, was an essential requirement if records were to be broken. Some of them never left the deck during the entire voyage except to clean up and change their clothes.

On one ship, when a seaman expressed his opinion of the food by throwing a beef bone at the captain, the 'Old Man' promptly winged him with a pistol shot. But captains had to be tough, considering some of the crews they had to handle. On many ships, the carpenter's first job when the hands joined for a voyage was to break off the points of their sheath knives.

### Sharp and narrow

A true clipper had the following characteristics: a prow that was sharp enough to slice through the water rather than ride over the waves; a hull that was at least five times as long as it was wide, and one which was designed for high speed rather than cargo-carrying capacity; and finally, three, sometimes four, masts covered with the maximum amount of sail.

As we have seen, for a short while the American clippers had the edge over their English counterparts, and they easily outstripped the lumbering old craft of the East India Company, which were aptly known as 'tea wagons'. But then Britain joined the race, and the competition became really fierce.

One great feature of the tea trade was the annual race home to Britain with the first of the new season's crop. Most of these races started from the great Chinese tea-exporting port of Foochow, and the scene there in Pagoda anchorage, about 26 km down stream, where big ships then had to dock, was an exciting one. The ships themselves with their glistening hulls, snow-white decks, varnished fittings and gleaming copper and

## THE TEA-CLIPPER'S PRESENT-DAY DESCENDANT – THE SAIL-TRAINING SHIP

**Modern sail-training ships are usua[lly] *windjammers,* the ships which succeede[d] the clippers. Life on board is still har[d]: ropes are hauled by man-powered ca[p]*stans* (left, and above, left). Man-power [is] also used for heaving at the riggin[g] (above, right) and bad weather still has i[ts] dangers. Safety netting prevents men fro[m] being swept overboard in high sea[s] (below). Furling (rolling up) sail needs sk[ill] and confidence as shown in the picture o[n] the right.**

## A clipper's decks were filled with equipment and every piece

**Although the early clippers were all extremely beautiful, there was nothing on them purely for show. The wheel with which the ship was steered invariably needed at least two men to hold it and, in fact, in high winds it was often necessary for the men to be tied with ropes to stop them being swept overboard.**

**As they were timber ships, fire, too, was always a hazard, so fire buckets were essential. Livestock (for example, hens) were often carried in special ventilated chests on deck (see front right).**

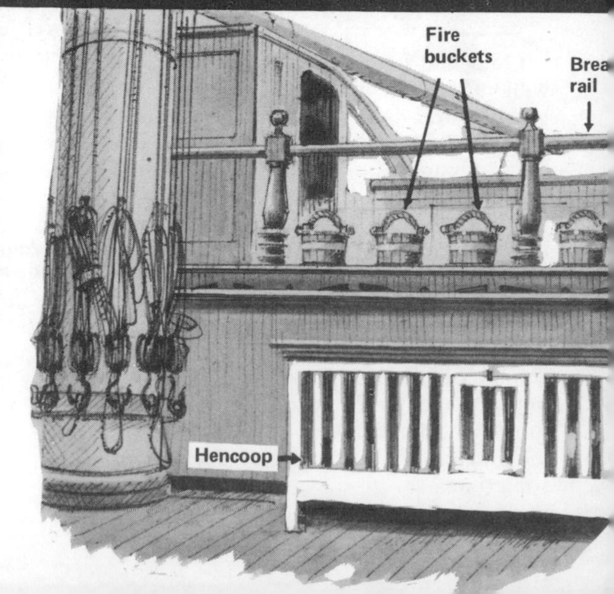

brass, were truly beautiful.

Towards the end of April, the clippers competing in the race would begin to assemble in the harbour. Loading went on day and night, and the excitement and tension reached a climax with a grand regatta just before the start. Then the clippers were away, homeward-bound. It was a race of ship against ship, regardless of nationality, all of them flat out to win.

But sometimes in the Far East, the clippers were put to a more sinister use. It was because of their speed that the clippers became attractive to smugglers engaged in selling the soul-destroying product known as the 'black death' — opium. Millions of people in the East were addicted to the drug, which was usually manufactured in India, and then transported to China.

## Outrunning the pirates

The profits to be made from opium-smuggling were enormous. The smuggler could sell a consignment of the drug for a thousand times what he had paid for it. The only requirement was a ship fast enough to outrun the scores of pirates waiting in the China Seas for just such a ship to pass their way.

However, just as events had conspired to encourage the development of the clippers, so they were fated to enjoy only a short burst of glory. The Opium Wars gave Britain control of Hong Kong, with a consequent crackdown on opium smuggling. Then the Gold Rush lost momentum, and here the clippers were rendered even more unnecessary by the opening of the first trans-American railway in 1869.

In that same year, the Suez Canal was opened, and for the first time steamers could compete with the clippers. Previously they had been limited by the necessity to make regular stops for coal, but the new short cut through Africa reduced the distance between coaling stations by more than 3,000 km. The writing was on the wall for the clippers.

Ten years later, the last of the clippers had vanished from the tea trade. They were the best-manned, best-run and most beautiful sailing vessels the world has ever seen.

**was necessary for the sailing or the safety of the ship!**

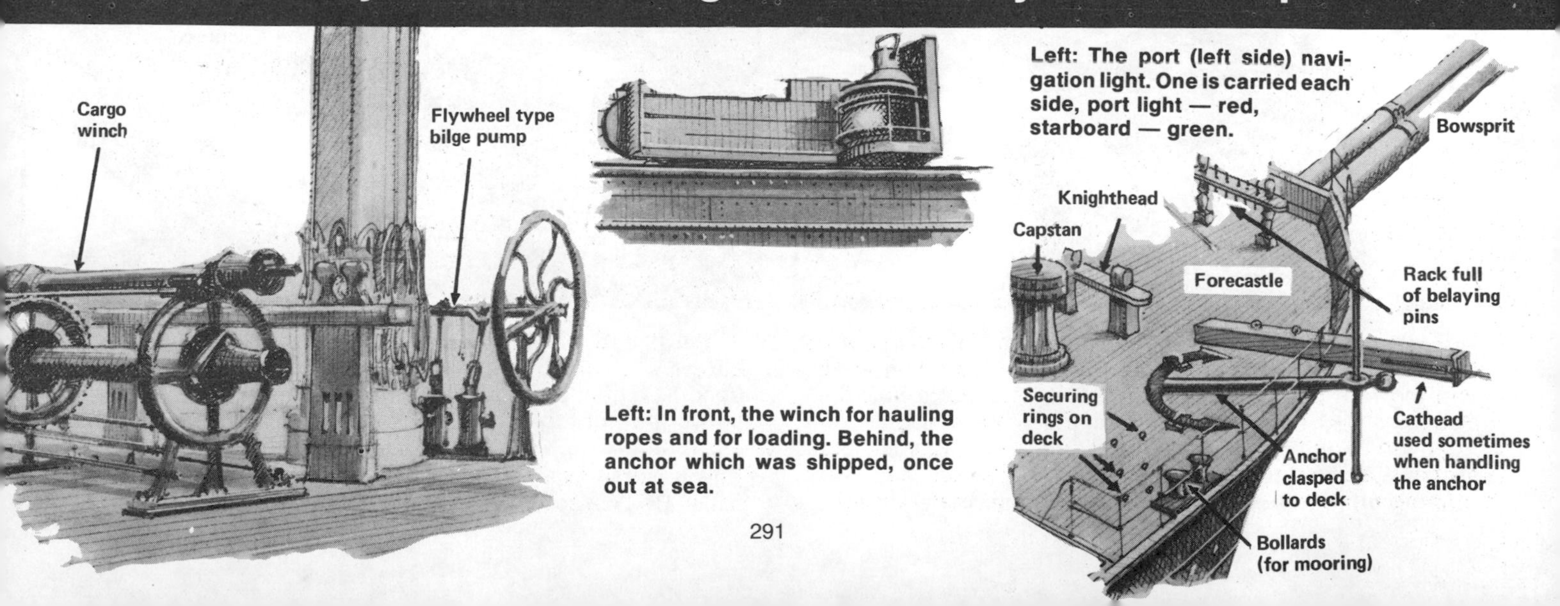


**Left: In front, the winch for hauling ropes and for loading. Behind, the anchor which was shipped, once out at sea.**

**Left: The port (left side) navigation light. One is carried each side, port light — red, starboard — green.**

# Who was Ferdinand de Lesseps?

1. Ferdinand de Lesseps was born on November 19, 1805, in Versailles. His family had been associated with French diplomacy for hundreds of years and in recognition of that faithful service to France, Ferdinand was educated at the State's expense. When he left school at the age of 18 he studied languages for two years in preparation for a career in the diplomatic service. It was a career which began with a posting to Lisbon. Later he was transferred to Tunis and then Algiers. During this period the French government were pursuing an active foreign policy which involved expansion of their interests and conquest in North Africa. Intrigues between local rulers, and negotiations for treaties with them, kept young Ferdinand extremely busy. He distinguished himself by his tact and understanding.

2. From Algiers, de Lesseps moved on to Egypt, where he became deeply interested in plans to link the Mediterranean and the Red Sea by a canal. The idea was not a new one. Schemes had been around from the time of the Ancient Egyptian king Rameses the Second, who actually constructed a canal from the Nile Delta to the Red Sea. Alas, nothing more than plans and schemes had materialised.

3. Ferdinand became Ambassador to Madrid where his career was ruined by political intrigue. He settled down to become a gentleman farmer, and might well have remained so were it not for renewed interest in the canal scheme. In 1854, de Lesseps and an old friend Said Pasha, Viceroy of Egypt, met to examine different projects for the building of the canal. De Lesseps was put in charge of the project.

4. In 1856 the Suez Canal plan was agreed by an international commission of civil engineers. De Lesseps spent all his available capital on surveying the region and was finally forced to seek a loan from Baron de Rothschild, head of the world-famous firm of bankers. On April 25, 1859, de Lesseps turned over the first spadeful of soil (pictured left). It was to be ten years later that the date for opening the canal was announced. Even then on November 17, 1869, an enormous outcrop of rock was discovered at the bottom of the canal bed. The rock was blown up by gunpowder just before the many distinguished visitors arrived for the great opening (see picture above).

5. Twelve years later de Lesseps was asked to work on the making of the Panama Canal, which would join the Atlantic and Pacific Oceans. Work began in February, 1881. Four years later there was an outbreak of yellow fever which halted progress and killed many men, and by 1889 the company de Lesseps formed for the project was liquidated. The French government started an enquiry charging de Lesseps with careless handling of public money put up for the venture. A sentence of five years imprisonment was passed on de Lesseps, but he died on December 7, 1894. The failure of Panama could not diminish the great achievement in opening Suez (picture right).

# Who was the Absent King?

RICHARD I was a handsome, strong and athletic young man, everybody's idea of a dashing and chivalrous knight. Charm he had in plenty, but what he lacked above all — and it was a lack most serious in a king of England — was judgment.

His reign began on a sombre and ominous note. When his father, Henry II died of what many said was a broken heart after Richard and his younger brother had rebelled against him, Richard journeyed to Fontevrault, the French abbey where Henry's body lay.

As Richard approached the corpse of the dead

*Continued on page 296*



# Daily life of

In summer the hearth was set outside

Platter roughly shaped from wood

WHILE King Richard chose to live rough as a soldier from time to time, his poorest subjects back in England had no choice but to live rough all the time. The poorest serfs still lived only the meanest, most basic sort of existence.

They usually lived in the simplest form of dwelling, known as a 'cote'. This was a tent-like construction without any real walls made from poles lashed into a trellis shape, known as wattle with clods of dry turf packed over it in the hope it would keep out the weather. The floor was dug out slightly and smoothed, the soil being daubed over the wattle where it was not covered with turf.

A small circle of stones made a hearth, the smoke from which escaped through a hole in the roof, there being no chimney.

# the Lionheart's loyal poor

The frame of the farmer's house was timber and the walls were wattle and daub. (The wattle here would have been a screen of interwoven twigs — preferably willow withes — supported on stakes covered with clay or mud mixed with straw).

The owner of a few animals might style himself a farmer and live in a house that was just a little grander. At least, it was bigger in size but then it had to be because it was lived in not only by the owner but his animals as well. They frequently used the same entrance, and, once in, only the thinnest partition came between them.

Some timber was used in the construction of this sort of building and the roof was usually thatched. Once again the only chimney was a hole in the roof. There was a very real fire risk with the chance of sparks or embers lodging in the thatch. Unlike the homes of the nobles the stark interiors of these dwellings were quite unrelieved by any kind of furniture. Beds were usually no more than a pile of rushes heaped in a corner, perhaps with a fur or skin to cover them.

Wardrobes and cupboards were unnecessary since poor people owned only one set of clothes. Wooden pegs hammered into walls were enough to hang a few primitive tools on. Jugs and pots were fashioned from the cheapest earthenware and undecorated. Platters and bowls were usually made from wood, as were buckets, since this was the material that was abundant and cheapest. Occasionally drinking vessels might be stitched together from dried cow's hide. There was no room for a kitchen and cooking was done on the open hearth and the washing up in the nearest stream or pond.

Those who lived in these primitive conditions seem not to have resented them or in any way held their king, Richard the Lionheart, to blame. Indeed, he seems to have been extremely popular with these humble people who never could expect to see him but were so loyal in their hearts.

Perhaps the stories of his dashing exploits and conquests brought a little warmth and colour into lives that otherwise were so singularly drab and dull.

monarch, it began to bleed, and people said this proved that Richard had had a hand in his father's death, for it was believed that a corpse always bled in the presence of its murderer.

It was 1189 when Henry died and Richard succeeded him. Henry had done much to improve the laws and administration of England, but Richard had little interest in such matters. Much more to his liking was the thought of leading a crusade to Jerusalem, which had fallen into the hands of the Moslem ruler, Saladin.

Eventually Richard found the money and assembled his troops, but he was reluctant to leave England before he was sure that his rival in Europe, King Philip of France, was also going to join him on the crusade.

However, a year after he came to the throne, Richard set sail and met with Philip in Sicily, as both armies made their way to the Holy land.

Richard had promised to marry Philip's sister — a marriage that would have brought the two nations closer together — but in Sicily he demonstrated his tactlessness by proclaiming instead his engagement to Berengaria, the daughter of the King of Navarre.

The next stop for Richard and his troops was Cyprus, where Berengaria joined him and they were married amid great pomp and ceremony.

At last, in 1191 Richard landed with his army at the Palestinian town of Acre. Such was Richard's reputation as a ruthless general that the garrison promptly surrendered. Richard, in another deliberate snub to Philip, appropriated the Royal Palace for his own quarters, although strictly speaking the French king enjoyed a higher status and should have had the most regal accommodation for himself.

Worse, however, was to follow. Richard also managed to insult another of his allies, the Duke of Austria,when he had the Austrian banner thrown into a drain!

Sadly Richard's capacity for diplomacy was very limited, though there was no denying his military prowess. When Saladin refused to pay a ransom for the Acre garrison Richard had all his prisoners beheaded in full view of the Moslem army.

It was a tactic that made the war increasingly bitter. Nevertheless Richard tried to make peace with Saladin, and sent him gifts, but the Moslem leader refused these advances with disdain.

So Richard pursued his ambition of trying to drive Saladin out of Jerusalem. On the whole the Moslem army was no match for the mercenaries from Europe, and the crusaders drove towards the gates of Jerusalem. There they hesitated. In part the bad blood that existed between the allies and in part the tiredness of the troops explained why Richard did not press the attack.

It was not that he could not have taken Jerusalem. He undoubtedly could, though it might have involved a lengthy siege. What troubled him was the knowledge that his army was far from home, and that his men who had been away for many months, had had enough and wanted to see England and their homes once more.

Richard returned to Acre and was preparing to sail when news came that Saladin had captured Jaffa. Richard sailed south, and using his sailors as infantry, and with only a handful of mounted knights, landed and drove Saladin's army off.

## Richard's return

Such was Richard's haste and perhaps even contempt for his enemies, that he did not even bother to change his soft ship's 'slippers' for boots before going into battle!

But in 1192 he did start on his journey back to England, uneasy in the knowledge that his brother John was claiming the throne for himself in his absence.

Richard's ship was wrecked in the Adriatic, and he tried to make his journey overland in disguise. The English king, thanks to his arrogance and lack of tact, had few friends in Europe. He was caught in Austria and the Duke handed him over to the German emperor.

What a prize! Richard was indeed worth a king's ransom, and the emperor demanded a huge sum for his release. Although the people of England had scarcely seen their king since he came to the throne, they paid up more or less willingly in the form of the heavy taxes that were levied to raise the ransom money.

When Richard at last returned he found his kingdom in disorder. Rebels had captured many of the Royal castles, and some of the barons had joined forces with his brother John.

Richard lost no time in restoring his authority, but he was never able to impose the kind of rule that had been the hallmark of his father. In 1199 Richard was in France when he was struck by an arrow, fired from a cross-bow. The wound in his shoulder became infected and he died on April 6th.

To many of his subjects he was still the popular hero, Richard the Lionheart, the brave and fearless soldier, but as a king of England he was singularly unsuccessful.

**This illustration depicts the Saracen chief Saladin snatching the Holy Cross during a battle near the village of Hattin in 1187, a loss from which the Crusaders never really recovered.**

# Who was the Slave who defied Rome?

Fights between gladiators, usually to the death, were the most popular spectacles in ancient Rome. The best gladiatorial training school was at Capua in southern Italy and it was here, in 73 B.C., that a strong but educated Greek slave named Spartacus arrived to be trained. His wife was also put to work and once, while Spartacus was sleeping, she saw a snake coiled around his head. She took this to be a sign that Spartacus would obtain great power but his life would end in misfortune.

Spartacus was disgusted by the conditions of the school, where the slaves were kept in cramped confines. Eventually 200 slaves, led by Spartacus, planned a breakout but they were betrayed, and only 73 managed to escape, armed with choppers and spits they had taken from the kitchens.

Outside, they found wagons loaded with gladiators' weapons and seizing these they put their pursuers to flight. Spartacus led them to Mount Vesuvius (then believed to be extinct) and the small band hid on the volcano's slopes and in the crater. Soon, Rome despatched an army of 3,000 men to deal with the rebels. Assessing the situation, the Roman commander decided that all the army had to do was block any escape and wait for the rebels to starve and surrender.

But by making strong ladders from thick vines on the mountain, the gladiators descended. Creeping up from behind they surprised and routed the enemy. Thousands of runaway slaves then joined Spartacus.

For the next two years Spartacus trained and organised his followers. They defeated several armies sent against them. Spartacus wanted to reach Sicily and freedom and his rebels even broke through a 70km-long wall built to stop them.

A huge army was then sent against them, and although Spartacus thought it unwise, his overconfident forces wanted a battle. He died bravely fighting overwhelming odds. The Romans took terrible revenge and 6,000 rebels were crucified.

# Who civilised the Saxons?

**WHEN King William Rufus was killed by an arrow while hunting in the New Forest, true-born Englishmen — those who were descended from the Saxons who lived in pre-1066 England — might well have stopped to consider for a moment the path of their fortunes since the coming of the Conqueror.**

They had seen two Norman kings, the Conqueror and his son William Rufus, and unquestionably this new Norman government had made their lives at times very miserable. The Conqueror's introduction of the feudal system, depriving Saxon freemen of even the untilled pasture-land and woodland where they had grazed their animals in common, had reduced them to little better in rank than slaves.

There were now two languages in England, Norman-French, the language of the barons and the upper classes, and the English of the Saxons. Of course this situation could not last, and it is interesting to note that as the two languages blended into one, it remained largely English with an admixture of Norman French words used mostly where there was no clear word in English.

One writer has even suggested that the slave-like condition of the English Saxons after the Conquest can be proved from our modern language. "The names of all animals, so long as they are alive, are Saxon, but when dressed and prepared for food they become Norman, a fact, indeed, which we might have expected beforehand, for the Saxon labourer had the job of tending and feeding the animals, but only that they might appear on the table of his Norman lord.

"Thus ox, steer, cow are Saxon, but beef is Norman; calf is Saxon but veal is Norman; sheep is Saxon but mutton is Norman; and it is the same with swine and pork, deer and venison, fowl and pullet." The only exception appears to be the Saxon word bacon — and that was probably the only meat which, for most of the time, came within reach of the Saxon labourer.

But in the end the fusion of Saxon Englishmen and Norman Frenchmen was good for England. Our islands had fallen behind the other European countries in terms of civilisation, culture and refinement. The Saxon English, strongly influenced by the Danish Vikings, were a greedy, drunken crowd and it was for the Normans to teach them elegant living with their ornate buildings, rich armour, highly-trained falcons, tournaments and delicately set tables for banquets.

If the learning process was a hard one, it was because the English were constantly reminded that they had been conquered. William the Conqueror, for example, protected the lives of his Norman followers by the "murder-fine." If a Norman was found murdered and the murderer wasn't produced, a heavy fine was exacted from the district in which the crime occurred. It thus became highly advantageous to the King's treasury to presume that every murdered man was a Norman until the contrary was proved.

## Trial by ordeal

Most crime was tried at the shire moot, held in the open air by the sheriff, or the hundred moot. The trials were primitive and if judgment was in doubt, the accused man had to face "trial by ordeal".

This might mean being thrown into water (if he drowned he was guilty, if not, he was innocent); or being branded with a red-hot iron (if he blistered after a set period he was guilty, but if his wounds healed he was innocent). The idea behind trial by ordeal was that God could be relied upon to intervene on the side of the innocent.

Trial by combat was another form of trial ordeal; here the accused fought the accuser. Each man was given a club with a piece of sharp horn bound to the end of it, and the battle sometimes went on all day. Thus a man named Ketel, of Suffolk, was accused of theft, lost in a trial by battle and was hanged.

Sometimes the contestants in a trial by battle would pay someone else to fight for them — although they would still have to suffer the sentence themselves if the sub-

**Norman Beds**
**For centuries the bed was considered the most important piece of furniture in any house. Under Norman influence it developed from the simple and uninviting Viking version (top right) to something more comfortable with carved wooden ends and embroidered coverlets and mattresses. Until the twelfth century beds were used for reclining on when eating as well as for sleeping.**

stitute lost. By the middle of the twelfth century paying someone else to do your dirty work was becoming accepted custom. The Scutage tax enabled the barons to pay the King instead of supporting him in war — with the cash so gained the King simply hired bands of European mercenaries to fight for him.

Life for a Saxon Englishman under Norman rule was short, hard, and totally centred on his village and his neighbours. Famine, fever and disease were the commonest enemies. One great famine in the last year of the Conqueror's reign (1086-87) was followed by a typhus epidemic in which, say all the writers of the time, the death rate was enormous.

Leprosy was not uncommon in England: there were three lepers in the city of Gloucester in October, 1273, and the leper-hospital at Ripon, "for all the lepers in Richmondshire", made provision for eighteen.

Unless they were called to war, most of the English labourers would never see anything of the world outside their village boundaries. Some, however, were more fortunate; they might be lucky enough to have received some education at a priest's school and if they lived in a village which had been granted a fair, they would see a colourful cross-section of English and European life at fair-times, which lasted for three or four days once a year.

## Fairs

The fairs were generally laid out in rows of wooden booths, each booth representing a particular trade, whose salesmen might include a German selling silk, a Cornishmen selling tin ware, and there would be cloth from Flanders, wine from France, lead from Derbyshire, all being sold in a bewildering babble of English accents and foreign tongues.

For the local folk the fair was the high-spot of the year — like a summer holiday abroad is today. They would rise early in their mud-brick homes, call at the church for mass (church attendance occurred on many days of the year), then spend the rest of the day at the fair. That exciting day would be broken only by the return home for dinner, cooked over an open fire in the garden to reduce the risk of setting fire to the house. Home-made bread, and some meat if they were lucky, was the usual fare, with home-brewed ale serving as the universal drink. Tea and coffee were still unknown in England and the quickest way to die would be to drink the water, which was filthy.

Because the Englishmen who lived in Norman times did not have much experience of many things, we should not assume that they were all desperately unhappy. The Norman Archdeacon of Huntingdon called the country "Merry England", and with the English, he said, were a free people with a free spirit and a free tongue, and "a still more liberal hand, having abundance of good things for themselves and something to spare for their neighbours across the sea."

Perhaps somewhere between the famine and the fair there was after all a life well worth living.

# Fun and Games in

### FALCONRY

The oppressive side of Norman rule showed itself even in medieval sports.

Only those of the highest rank were allowed to indulge in hawking and falconry though Saxons had long practised the sport and Alfred the Great had been considered expert at it.

A hooded falcon or hawk would be taken into the hunting field and unhooded to fly at and bring down game birds in flight. The hunting birds were either wild, trapped during migration, or eyasses, that is a young bird taken from the nest and reared in confinement. These however

Warlike sports, such as wrestling, were encouraged. There were few rules.

To prepare for the battlefield they practised with the sword and buckler.

# the Middle Ages

were not rated so brave or swift as the wild birds.

Falconry had spread across Europe from Norway where the people became extremely proficient at it and William the Conqueror was a fervent devotee of the sport. It became something of a mania with the nobles and even ladies were keen to try their skills.

Both hawks and falcons were caught, reared and trained by a falconer. The first mention of this trade occurs in 760 A.D. and through all European courts falconers were very highly regarded and often wielded influence outside the hunting field.

Falconry became less exclusive after 1215 when Magna Carta, among its less grand decrees, extended the right to enjoy the sport to 'all true freemen'.

While lords and ladies disported themselves in the hunting field humbler folk contented themselves with the ancient game of bowls. Still played in varying forms all over the world, bowls, after archery, is the world's oldest outdoor pastime.

From rolling balls as far as they would go the game developed into one where the players bowled at a 'jack', at first any immovable object, later a different coloured, different sized ball. The wooden balls with an inbuilt bias that sends the ball on a curving track, seen in the modern game, are a much later development. Nor did the medieval player have the flat surfaced lawns of today. But the hidden mounds and tussocks only served to make the game more exciting.

Bowls was every bit as popular with poor people as falconry was with the nobility. The latter, however, considered it a menace when its popularity threatened the regular practice of archery. Predictably, along with other games, such as football, it was banned.

Young folk amused themselves with simple games like apple-bobbing.

# Who established the

1. Many men have helped to change the course of history. Such a man was Robert Clive who did much to prevent India from becoming a French possession and lay the foundations of the British Empire. Born in 1725 in a little Shropshire village, he displayed reckless courage from an early age. On one occasion he climbed the church steeple, much to the horror of the local inhabitants.

2. Finally, in 1743, his exasperated father sent Clive to Madras in India to work in the offices of the East India Company. India was then a hot-bed of intrigue. While the native princes competed for power, the French Governor, Dupleix, had visions of France as the mistress of India, providing the base for a conquest of a vast empire and was secretly plotting to this end.

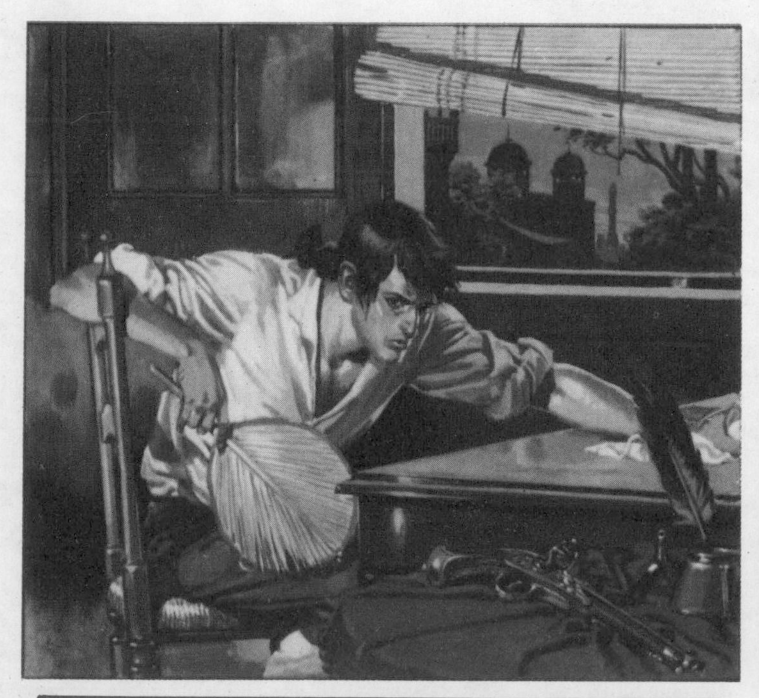

3. Clive was most unhappy in Madràs. His work as a clerk was very dull, he had few friends and earned only £5 a year. In the oppressive heat Clive became deeply depressed and attempted suicide. Twice he put a gun to his head and pulled the trigger — twice nothing happened. Later, the gun was tested and worked perfectly. Clive saw this as a sign that he was to fulfil some great purpose.

4. Soon Clive's dull existence was over. War broke out between England and France and the French marched on Madras. Clive escaped disguised as a native and reached the English settlemnent at Fort St. David. There he joined the military force of the East India Company and fought well in several battles before peace was declared. Sadly he returned to his dreary office job in Madras.

# British in India?

5. A further taste of adventure was not long in coming. A native prince asked the English to help him regain his throne from his rebellious subjects in return for the valuable fort of Devokota. The English agreed and, on hearing this, Clive applied for and received a commission. The expedition was a success, increasing English power and Clive's reputation. However, his health was yet again affected and he went to Bengal to recover. When he returned in 1751, the English and French were again in disagreement, taking sides with different groups of princes who were quarrelling. Clive was made a captain and set out with a small expeditionary force during a fierce monsoon with the task of capturing the important fort of Arcot.

6. Clive captured the fort but then had the problem of defending it. Some 10,000 French and native soldiers attacked time and time again in a siege lasting 50 days. They even used elephants as battering rams. But Clive's military genius won through and the French gave up and fell back. It was the beginning of British supremacy in India. Clive became a rich and honoured man.

7. In 1757 came his greatest hour. At the Battle of Plassey, Clive's 2,000 men defeated a 34,000-strong army of a cruel prince who has massacred English settlers. Clive was a hero everywhere, but enemies he had made accused him of corrupt practices in becoming rich. His name was cleared but he became very depressed and in 1774, he committed suicide.

# When was it no fun to be a Child in England?

**IT was often a risky business and no fun at all being a child in Britain two hundred or more years ago. Out of every 100 children born about 25 would die before the age of one, and another 25 before they got to ten years old.**

As for those who survived, life could still be terribly hard. From the very first moments, new-born babies would be stretched out on a board and then bound tightly to it by broad bands of cloth, known as swaddling clothes. Babies naturally could not move at all in these tightly-bound parcels, and because they were changed so infrequently, their skins often became horribly sore as a result.

At the time, parents believed – quite mistakenly – that this practice of swaddling ensured that their children grew up with straight, strong limbs. It also made it easier for adults to keep toddlers out of trouble, sometimes hanging these little bundles on hooks in the wall for hours at a time.

If babies could live through all this, there was sometimes even worse to come immediately they were old enough to work, not at school – which only became compulsory for all children by 1870 – but at anything that could earn them a little money.

In the countryside, children would be employed as full-time bird-scarers. This would involve long, lonely days in the fields shouting out whenever greedy birds tried to eat the growing crops.

Naturally, children hated this sort of work, but discipline was very tough, with almost all adults believing that beatings were the best and only way to train either an animal or a child. So even if quite tiny children were working for their own parents at various home industries like weaving or lace-making, they could still expect a hefty thump if their concentration ever lapsed.

But it is not fair to put all the blame on the parents for this sort of cruelty. The choice was often between working or starving, and with many mouths to feed it was sometimes essential to make sure that everyone earned what meagre wages

**Left, a baby bound to a board by means of tightly bound broad bands of cloth. It was believed — quite mistakenly — that this practice would ensure the children had strong, straight limbs. Below, a youngster makes as much noise as he can to scare birds away from growing crops.**

were available.

Parents who could no longer cope with their poverty, though, were separated from each other and their children, and then set to hard labour in grim workhouses, which were little better than prisons. Their children, meanwhile, might be forcibly apprenticed to the most dangerous, unpleasant jobs which few others would willingly take on, such as chimney-sweeping or work with the fishing fleets.

In the growing industrial towns children were used as factory workers, since they could squeeze between or underneath close-packed machines more easily than adults.

Once again, parents often depended on the money this brought in to the home, and would sometimes allow their children to work for appallingly long periods, at times up to 17 or 18 hours a day. Some children, therefore, would be forced to walk the equivalent of 20 miles in the course of one day's work on the factory floor.

Not surprisingly, they sometimes had to be carried sleeping to their places of work, and once there, would occasionally nod off, with fatal results if this meant they fell in to the poorly protected machinery around them.

If a still-growing child was expected to do heavy work all day, sometimes in a severely enclosed space, it was not surprising that he or she frequently developed some horrible bodily distortions.

When the great factory reformer, Lord Shaftesbury, was confronted in 1838 by a collection of children crippled or deformed in this way, he reported that, "They stood or squatted before me in all the shapes of the letters of the alphabet."

More fortunate children, meanwhile, may have spent time at voluntary schools instead, but even here the picture remains grim and depressing. Such schools were often badly over-crowded, with teachers who were sometimes poorly trained and ignorant themselves. Lessons might consist of memorising boring material, with control kept by the frequent and brutal application of the rod or the birch.

In boarding schools, merciless bullying by older pupils could go virtually unchecked. One child, for example, lost the use of his right hand after the older boy he 'fagged' for forced him to make toast by holding the bread himself in front of a blazing fire.

Of course, there were always *some* pleasant times for most children in the past, and a few very fortunate families seem to have enjoyed life then as much as they ever could now. But broadly speaking, things only really began to improve quite noticeably for most children towards the end of the last century. By this time, disease began to be conquered, food had become more plentiful, and laws were passed forbidding the employment of all young children.

So if you think that your schoolday has been long and tiring remember the unfortunate children who lived through the bad old days in Britain.

**The working day could be as long as 18 hours in the factories. Not surprisingly, many children fell asleep when they were supposed to be working.**

**A dangerous and unpleasant job was working for the fishing fleets. Even in the roughest weathers the small craft would put to sea to catch fish.**

# Who first conquered the Matterhorn?

**1.** At 4,505 metres, the Matterhorn on the Swiss-Italian frontier is not the highest mountain in Europe (that is Mount Elbrus in the southern U.S.S.R. at 5,642 metres), but just over 100 years ago it was regarded as the steepest and most difficult peak to climb. To a certain 25-year-old Englishman it was a challenge. He tried many times with local guides and once braved the mountain alone.

**2.** This Englishman was Edward Whymper. On his lone attempt, made on the Italian side of the mountain, he climbed higher than anyone had ever done before. Then — he fell, crashing nearly 61 metres in seven or eight breath-taking bounds before pitching into soft snow right on the lip of a sheer precipice, 243 metres above a glacier. Undismayed, Whymper tried again a few days later — but again failed.

**3.** Up till then all serious attempts to climb the Matterhorn had been made on the Italian side, which looked easier. But in 1865, Whymper decided to make an attempt on the Swiss side from Zermatt. His party consisted of Whymper, his friend Lord Francis Douglas, the Reverend Charles Hudson, a beginner, Douglas Hadow and guides, Michael Croz and the Taugwalders — a father and son.

**4.** In many places, the snow was covered with a treacherous sheet of ice but steady progress was made towards the top. Then a long and difficult climb brought them in view of the peak. A slope of about 61 metres was all that stood between them and success. Whymper and Croz hurried on up to the summit and arrived on it in a triumphant dead-heat. The unconquerable Matterhorn had been beaten at last.

5. Then came the descent and, with it, disaster. Croz was leading the way, helping Hadow, when the young man, who was inexperienced and whose boots were unsuitable for mountain climbing it was later claimed, slipped. Croz was dragged with him and then Hudson and Douglas were jerked off their feet. Whymper was roped between the two Taugwalders at the other end of the line. Hearing Croz shout, they immediately flung themselves down in the snow and gripped the rocks as best they could. The rope was dragged tight, as the four men plunged headlong down the almost vertical slope . . . and then the rope snapped.

6. Whymper and the Taugwalders were safe but they could only watch helplessly as their doomed companions fell to the glacier 1,219 metres below — a drop of more than three times the height of the Empire State building in New York. They had absolutely no chance at all. Their glory had been turned, by one false move, to tragedy.

7. The three survivors remained motionless, gazing downwards for half an hour, in a state of shock and fear. Then the trio — all that remained of the seven triumphant men — edged their way slowly down the grim mountain and took the tragic news back to Zermatt. Whymper, however, had faced his challenge and had succeeded.

# Where did 14 against a

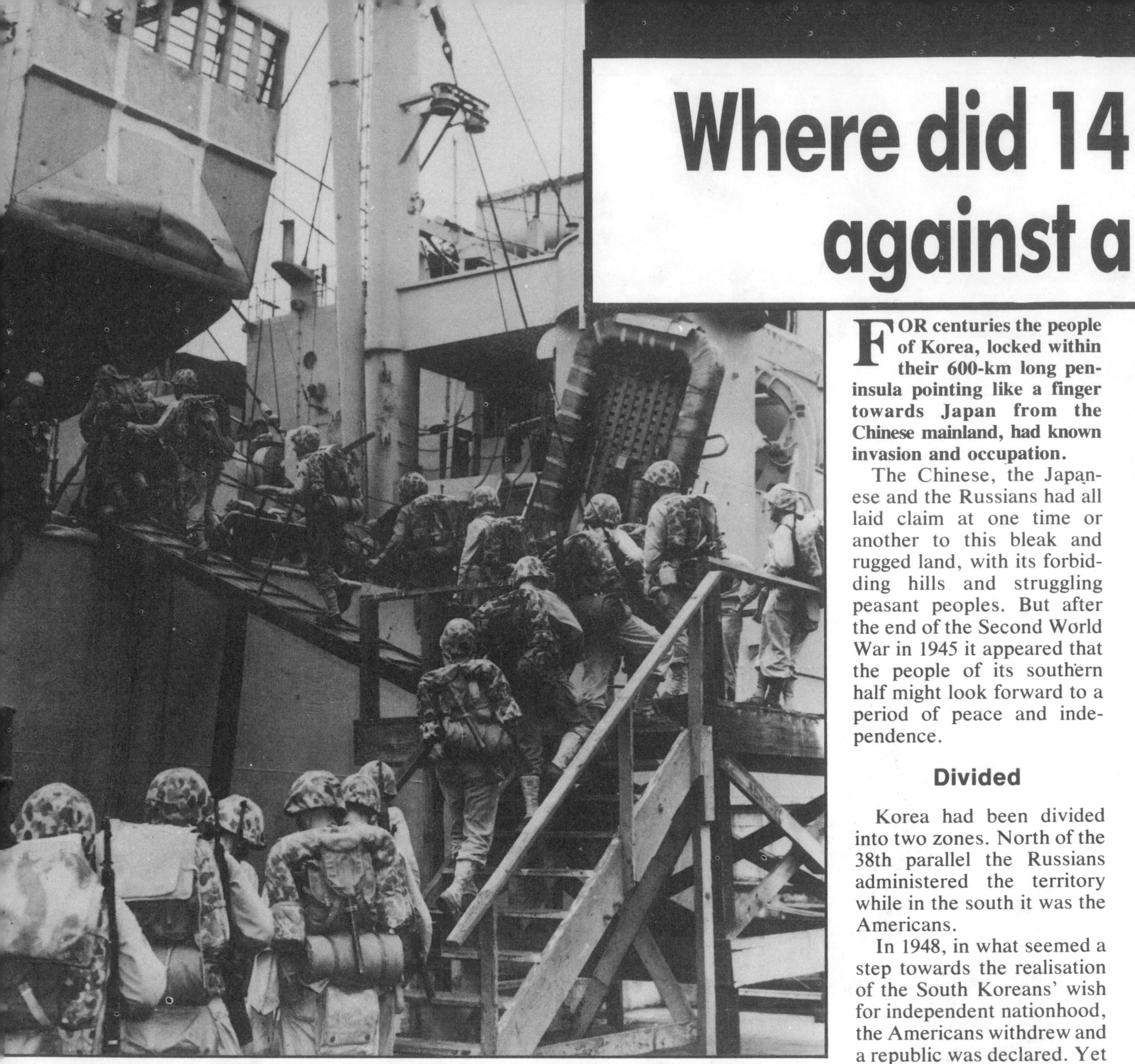

July, 1950. Wearing their tropical combat kit, Infantry troops of U.S. Marine Combat Unit file aboard a ship bound for Korea. The troops had already undergone years of specialised training to be ready for such a mission.

**FOR centuries the people of Korea, locked within their 600-km long peninsula pointing like a finger towards Japan from the Chinese mainland, had known invasion and occupation.**

The Chinese, the Japanese and the Russians had all laid claim at one time or another to this bleak and rugged land, with its forbidding hills and struggling peasant peoples. But after the end of the Second World War in 1945 it appeared that the people of its southern half might look forward to a period of peace and independence.

## Divided

Korea had been divided into two zones. North of the 38th parallel the Russians administered the territory while in the south it was the Americans.

In 1948, in what seemed a step towards the realisation of the South Koreans' wish for independent nationhood, the Americans withdrew and a republic was declared. Yet within two years the sound of guns echoed once again over Korea's rugged terrain.

Early on June 25, 1950, North Korean troops crossed the 38th parallel at eleven points. Russian T-34 tanks rumbled on dusty roads, heading towards the southern capital of Seoul. The North Korean troops were highly trained, and although, within two days of the invasion, President Truman of the United States gave orders for American troops to be landed, these forces and their South Korean allies could do little more than fight a stubborn rearguard action.

September, 1950. The mud-bespattered Americans file along either side of the road as they withdraw from Yongsan.

# Nations fight Single Enemy?

The invasion had taken a world still weary from war by surprise, but the United Nations passed a resolution calling for the North Koreans to withdraw. When this was ignored many of the member nations, including Britain, offered to send troops and other aid to repulse the invaders.

Soon the flags of 14 different nations were flying alongside that of South Korea. The U.N. had gone to war in an endeavour to restore peace to that troubled land.

Meanwhile U.S. troops poured in, and the port of Pusan bulged with troop-carriers and warships of every description. The world's most powerful nation had gathered itself once more to counter an attempt to over-run one of the world's poorest and weakest.

## Early Victory

General MacArthur, the American military leader who had so distinguished himself in the Second World War against the Japanese, once again found himself in a battle. Appointed head of the U.N. forces in South Korea, he quickly staged a daring exploit that turned retreat into a spectacular early victory.

In September he launched an amphibious operation to land troops behind the enemy lines at Inchon. Fraught with risk — for example at some points the Marines had to scale walls that rose directly in front of their landing craft — it nevertheless succeeded brilliantly.

Huge numbers of prisoners were taken, and Seoul was recaptured. The North Koreans retreated and MacArthur ordered his forces in hot pursuit over the 38th parallel. His view, which did not accord with many of the world's politicians, was that if necessary, the war should be taken into China itself.

But MacArthur, in his single-minded aim, had not only alarmed the West, which had no wish to see another world war break out, but had also ignored ominous signs that opposing him was a more powerful force than the North Korean army.

## Chinese

In fierce fighting near the Chinese border a number of Chinese prisoners had been taken, and it was soon apparent that China's involvement was a good deal greater than allowing a few 'volunteers' to fight alongside the North Koreans.

By the end of 1950 it was Chinese troops who were fighting against the U.N. forces, and they swept forward in their thousands, pushing the U.N. troops back towards the 38th parallel. In wave after wave, they pushed on remorselessly, and with little regard for the enormous casualties which they suffered.

MacArthur had misread the intentions of the Chinese, but they, too, seemed to be suffering from a fundamental misunderstanding. They often released American prisoners with the suggestion that they should go back and 'overthrow their capitalist officers.'

As the war settled into a stagnant pattern of attrition, with both sides digging in, MacArthur was relieved of

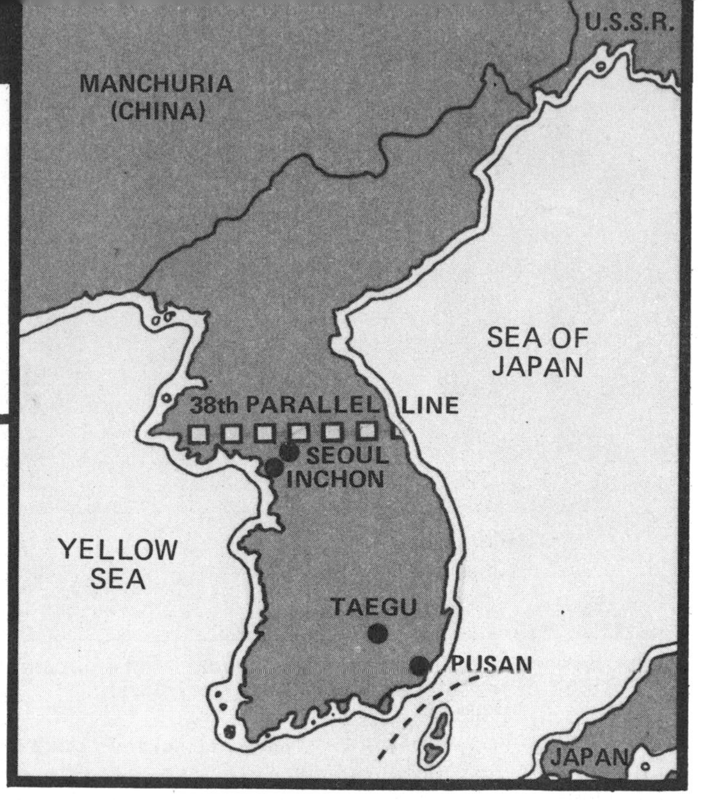


**After 1945, Korea was divided into two zones. The 38th parallel marked the border between North and South Korea.**

**Two American soldiers, as they man a 3.5 bazooka. They wear camouflaged helmets, so that it is hard for the enemy to pick them out against the landscape.**

**South Korean refugees return to Inchon after the city had been secured by the 1st Marine Division.**

American marines assemble their vehicles and equipment after bitter fighting. As can be seen, the conditions were very harsh.

Soldiers of the 1st Division South Korean Army lay an anti-tank mine.

his command. President Truman felt he could not trust the General to carry out *his* orders.

Furthermore Truman felt that MacArthur's aggressive statements would jeopardise the peace talks which had begun between the U.N. forces and the Communists. But these dragged on for months.

While the negotiations went on at Kaesong in a teahouse some of the most bitter engagements of the Korean war took place. Notable was the bloody battle for Hill 1179, in which US marines fought their way inch-by-inch up the rocks over four days of non-stop combat.

The armistice was not signed until 27 July, 1953, just over three years after the Communist invasion. In as much as the sovereignty of South Korea had been restored it was a victory for the U.N. forces. The ceasefire line ran only a few miles north of the 38th parallel, and south of it the Koreans remained outside Communist influence. If it proved anything, it was that a 'limited' war could be fought without the superpowers allowing it to spread into a world conflagration.

But the aim of 'unifying' Korea had failed; the Communists could not win the south; the allies did not impose their will over the north. And both paid a heavy price in casualties.

**Peace has never officially been declared in Korea and the ceasefire has existed since 1953. Consequently, recent troubles in South Korea have provoked fears of a new military threat from the North. There has been massive student unrest in the South against the military-backed government — a situation some observers feel the North could use to their advantage. There has been no evidence of this, but the two adversaries' old allies have been giving rapid advice. The U.S.A. has told South Korea that she must move quickly to a more democratic form of government. The Chinese have said they will never embark on a military intervention in the South. Nonetheless, Korea remains a very tense part of the world.**

Above: A North Korean has been captured. He is forced to lie down while members of the infantry search him for weapons. Below: Korean civilians take to the road as they try to seek safety from the fighting.

# Who first flew the Channel?

1. Probably Man had always dreamed of flying. It is an obvious dream for someone as intelligent and as earth-bound as a human being. But the problem of powered flight had not been overcome until 1903, when Orville Wright made the first flight of over 243 metres in his 12 h.p. petrol motor bi-plane at North Carolina, U.S.A. It must have been both dangerous and very uncomfortable as the pilot had to lie face downwards.

2. Then in 1909, *The Daily Mail* offered £1,000 to the first person to fly across the English Channel. There were three main contenders. The Count de Lambert (French) had to withdraw due to aircraft damage. Hubert Latham (English) set off on July 19 in his Antoinette monoplane but crashed into the sea, being rescued by a French destroyer.

3. That left Louis Bleriot (French). He had made a model aeroplane with flapping wings in 1900 and had made it fly. But the full-size machine would not. So he designed monoplanes. One had a 25 horsepower Anzani engine and was fitted with a lever which would change the direction or raise and lower the 'plane — a joy stick', as it was called. On a trial flight, however, the 'plane crashed.

4. Nonetheless, all was well by July 25. The weather seemed good and, after asking, "Where is Dover?" and being shown the rough direction, Bleriot set off, accompanied by a destroyer, the *Escopette.* He had no compass, as a suitable one would have been too heavy to carry, so he was in danger of getting lost. But Bleriot was a very determined man.

5. Very soon, he left the destroyer behind and very soon, too, he ran into fog. He could not see where he was going. His only hope was that he had started in the right direction and that he could carry on — in a straight line. The wind was fairly strong and, of course, the cockpit was open, so his position could not have been comfortable or safe.

6. His engine then began to get overheated but, luckily, a shower of rain cooled it down and also drove away the fog. At last, he saw the white cliffs of Dover ahead of him. Flying overland at last, he turned west and saw the castle with what looked like a suitable landing space in a field in front of it. He managed to land but rather bumpily, breaking the propeller and causing other damage.

7. He was also hurt himself — but not seriously. In fact, no one actually saw him land. It was not until several minutes later that some policemen appeared on the scene and, after them, the French journalist who had promised to set up the French tricolour on a suitable landing spot. Later a small crowd of people collected to view the great man and his remarkable 'plane. The crossing had taken Bleriot about 40 minutes. Two days later, Latham made another attempt to make the crossing but again was forced down into the sea.

8. Bleriot had won the prize and, when his success was known, he was acclaimed in both London and Paris. Apparently, however, his achievement was soon forgotten. Money from his flight, though, enabled him to open a flying school. He also designed and built many world-famous aeroplanes and is one of the foremost flight pioneers. Nowadays, of course, a cross-channel flight takes only a few minutes and is more comfortable!

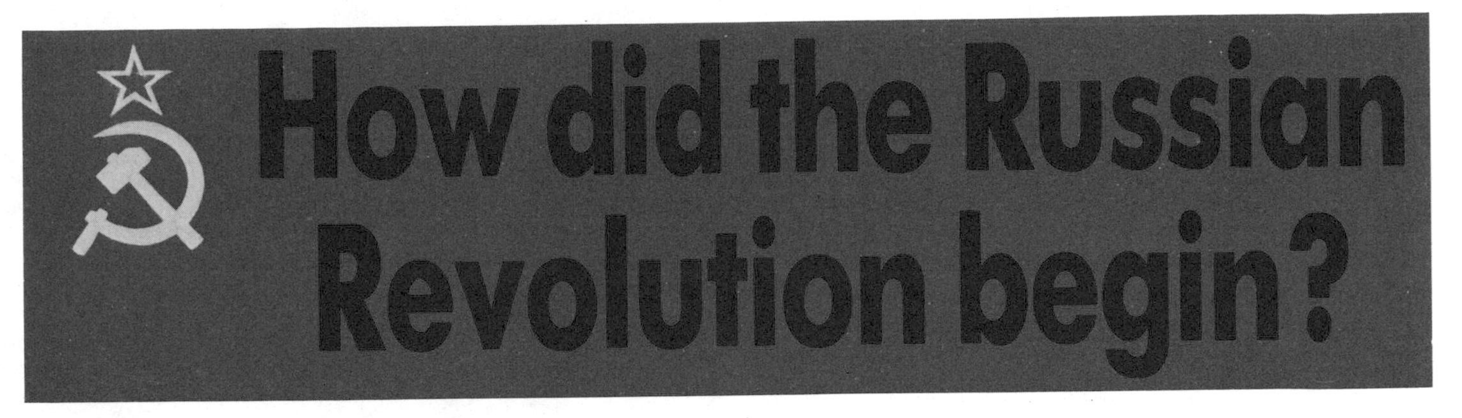

# How did the Russian Revolution begin?

**RUSSIA'S capital was seething with revolt. Weary queues stood for hours at the bread shops and starving workers carried banners through the streets saying, "End the War!"**

The war, the First World War, had been going on for three years and now, in March, 1917, Russia was totally demoralised. When the Cabinet telegraphed the Tsar to come back from his war headquarters, the Tsar simply wired back that the disorders must be suppressed.

But the Russians had had enough of suppression and slavery. As the mob surged towards the Tsar's palace in Petrograd (now Leningrad), the military governor, General Khabalov, ordered his soldiers to shoot. They raised their rifles and fired harmlessly into the air. The revolt was spreading to the army.

Other soldiers, though, fired into the crowd, killing sixty. The rest, far from being intimidated, went beserk. They looted police stations, jails were broken open and the prisoners — criminal as well as political — were freed.

It was then that Tsar Nicholas the Second decided to relinquish the direction of the Russian army in the struggle against Germany and return to Petrograd. His mind was made up for him when two representatives from the Duma (parliament) arrived to persuade him to abdicate.

The Tsar talked to the representatives and to his generals. He would consider proposals for a new government, he said, and would like his son to succeed him. But that, said the royal doctor, was not advisable, because the boy had an incurable illness.

While all this was going on, no one had any idea how successful the revolutionaries were being in the capital. They switched the Tsar's train to a siding and blockaded it there. They had no intention of letting him back.

Nicholas spent the last few hours of his reign in his railway carriage. Now he asked that his crown should go

*Continued on next page*

**Below: Painting showing Lenin addressing revolutionary Congress of Soviets (councils of workers, peasants and soldiers) on November 7, 1917, and declaring that all power had passed into their hands.**

*Photo: Mansell Collection.*

to his brother, the Grand Duke Michael. The Duke, however, at once declined, for he knew the mood of the Russian people.

The revolutionaries wanted more than an abdication. Nicholas and his family were put under arrest and watched all the time by guards. A new government was formed and new hope was born with it. But it soon became clear that this government, headed in due course by Alexander Kerensky, had no intention of withdrawing Russia from the First World War. By staying in the fight they hoped to share the spoils of victory.

## Confused

The Russian people were confused. They wanted bread and they wanted peace. What kind of revolution was this that had brought them neither?

Defiantly, workers, soldiers and peasants banded together all over the country in groups called Soviets. The most powerful of these was the Petrograd Soviet, in which Kerensky himself had once been a prominent figure.

Now the Petrograd Soviet turned against the Kerensky government and began to issue its own orders. The Russian soldiers, it commanded, should only defend while the politicians sought peace.

In faraway Switzerland at this time there was living a Russian exile who was soon to set all these murmurs of discontent boiling again into revolution. His name was Vladimir Ilyich Ulyanov, known to the world as Lenin.

For twenty years, in London, Switzerland and Siberia, Lenin had been planning a Russian revolution. Even so, the events of March, 1917, caught him unawares — he had thought that revolution would not happen in his lifetime.

## German help

Now, seeing his chance, he considered how he might cross a hostile Europe locked in war and return to Russia to assume his leadership of the revolutionaries. In order to take Russia out of the war, he was helped to get back. No decision in history has had greater consequences.

Lenin, a short, stocky, bald-headed man in thread-bare clothes, arrived in Petrograd on April 16 to a tumultuous welcome. But members of his political party — the Bolsheviks — still jubilant about the Tsar's overthrow, were shocked by what he had to say. The revolution was only half a revolution, he told them. The Soviets — the councils of soldiers, workers and peasants — were the key to power, and they must take control of the government.

For six months Lenin drove his Bolsheviks remorselessly, preparing them to seize power. Everywhere he held meetings, captivating huge crowds with his oratory. The message was clear — the people would not have bread until there was peace. Meanwhile, Kerensky ordered a new offensive against Germany.

Sensing the growing strength of the Bolsheviks, Kerensky's government branded Lenin a pro-German traitor and ordered his arrest.

Lenin went into hiding in Finland, determined to stay free so that he could lead a new rising. In Leon Trotsky, president of the Petrograd Soviet, he found a powerful ally. Together they laid their plans.

The rising was fixed for November 7, 1917, and within that day the Soviets had taken power. Kerensky's government melted away, almost without resistance.

**Below: Nicholas (centre) photographed with his son and daughters and a party of Russian officers, just before the Revolution. Anastasia, the Tsar's youngest daughter (second on his right), was rumoured to have survived the slaughter of her family.**

*Photo: Mansell Collection.*

Left: Street fighting in Petrograd (now called Leningrad) during the July demonstration in 1917.

Below: Intent on holding what they had gained, the Bolsheviks patrolled the streets of Petrograd in armoured cars.

Soon Lenin formed a new Bolshevik government. He sent Trotsky to sign a peace treaty with the Germans.

The Russians signed a treaty on the harshest terms. But there was still no internal peace for their racked and tortured country. Now, as armies of counter-revolutionaries invaded Russia, blood began to flow.

It included, tragically, the blood of Tsar Nicholas and his family. In August, 1917, they had been transferred to a village in Siberia. When Lenin took control in November, they were again transferred, this time to a town called Ekaterinburg (now Sverdlovsk). In the following year the Bolsheviks decided that the royals were a danger while they remained alive, and on July 16, 1918, the whole family was shot.

It was the end of the Romanov line, which had occupied the Russian throne for 300 years, and the end of the line altogether for royal rule in Russia.

Although the counter-revolutionary armies soon had the Bolsheviks in full retreat everywhere, the Lenin party fought on. By 1920 Lenin had won — and then he faced a new battle against poverty, famine, illiteracy and disease.

Before he could win it, his life ran out on January 21, 1924.

Winston Churchill said later that had Lenin lived he might well have saved Russia from the savage dictatorship that followed his death. "The Russian people were left floundering in the bog. Their worst misfortune was Lenin's birth . . . their next worst his death."

Certainly the thunder of Lenin's revolution is still echoing loudly around the world.

# Who was the the North

1. To be first at the North Pole had been the ambition of many men before Robert Peary — among them the Englishman, Nares, and the Norwegian, Nansen. Peary, however, was to succeed. Born in Pennsylvania in 1856, he served in the U.S. Navy from 1881 and, from time to time, carried out Arctic exploration. From the beginning, Greenland fascinated him with its grandeur and mystery.

2. During his early trips to the Arctic, he met and made friends with many of the Eskimos, in particular a remote tribe, the 'Arctic Highlanders' from whom he learned how to survive in that wild wilderness. He copied their fishing methods and discovered the value of sledge dogs and the Eskimo snow houses or igloos. All these lessons were to serve him well on later trips.

3. During the expedition of 1891, he established that Greenland was indeed an island. And it was on this trip that he was accompanied by his wife and also by Dr. Frederick Cook, later to challenge Peary's claim as first at the Pole. The early attempts were hampered, too, by lack of a suitable ship for dealing with polar ice. So, at last, Peary had a ship, the *Roosevelt,* built to his own specifications.

4. This was able to crash through pack ice that would have held any other vessel until it was crushed to matchwood. In this ship, he reached Ellesmere Island in 1905. On one occasion it struck a huge iceberg but was undamaged. The 1905 attempt, however, was unsuccessful, as the sledges were stopped by extremely bad weather. So, in 1908, Peary returned to Ellesmere Island and wintered at Cape Columbia.

# first Man at Pole?

5. At Cape Columbia, they were only 665 kilometres from the Pole. Early, the next year, Peary judged they were ready to start what was to prove their final attempt. All equipment and supplies had been checked and double checked down to the last length of rope and tin of dog food. Everything was ready. The expedition left at the beginning of March, 1909, and set out into the white haze.

6. Peary's journey was across the ice-cap that floats on top of the Arctic Ocean. He was also marching at the time of the spring tides, when the great rising and falling of the sea moved and tortured the ice, causing immense cracks to open up across their path. One night, a huge split appeared in the middle of Peary's igloo camp. Fortunately, the gap soon closed and the halves re-united.

7. One by one, the sledges set up supply camps for Peary's return. When 214 kilometres from the Pole, Peary was left to journey on with five sledges, 40 dogs, his negro servant, Matthew Henson, and four Eskimos. The final journey was divided into five marches. At the end of the fifth march, Peary took a reading on his sextant, which gave him the latitude and judged himself five kilometres from the Pole.

8. After a short rest, they journeyed on and, on April 6, 1909, at last stood at the Pole. Peary built a crude igloo and planted in it the U.S. flag. His achievement was somewhat spoiled by the claim of Dr. Frederick Cook to have reached the Pole in 1908. But this claim was later discredited. Nowadays Robert Peary is usually recognised as The First Man at the North Pole.

# WORLD OF ART

# Which Painter started life as a Violinist?

1. The French Revolution (1789-94) and the Napoleonic Wars that followed it, affected the arts as well as politics. The "classical" arts of the 18th century, though not unromantic, obeyed certain rules. "Romantics" regarded these as less important than vivid colours and vitality. The leading French Romantic was Eugène Delacroix, born in 1798. A frail, lonely child, he first showed talent at his Bordeaux school for the violin.

2. In Paris he met an older boy named Géricault, who was also destined to be a major artist. Both were taught by a well-known painter, Baron Guérin. The young Delacroix, his head full of music, poetry and the splendours of architecture, and impressed by his friend's talents, became more and more attracted to painting. Aged 23, he painted "Dante and Virgil crossing the Styx", hoping to have it accepted by the important Paris Salon Exhibition.

3. His teacher was appalled when he saw it. "No one has ever painted like that!" he cried. "All those lurid blues and greens and that hideous flesh colour. You cannot send such a monstrosity to the Salon. You will be the laughing stock of Paris and I shall be mocked for having produced such a pupil." Poor Delacroix had broken the rules! But he sent the picture in, nonetheless, and it caused a sensation. Its vivid colours thrilled viewers and Delacroix was famous.

4. The picture was bought by the French nation and, despite crippling bouts of fever, Delacroix started on other subjects. He loved the colourful stories of the Orient and its landscapes and chose an exciting theme, "The Massacre at Scio". It was a big subject and required many professional models and friends to pose for it. After many months work he was satisfied and sent it to the Paris Salon. It was given a place of honour.

5. Just four days before the opening in 1824, he saw a painting by his friend Géricault, who had tragically died as a result of a fall from a horse. The brilliant colours and the life in the picture, which he saw in the window of a dealer, inspired him. So did a glimpse of the English artist John Constable's great picture "The Hay Wain", which was in the Salon. With just four days to go before the official opening of the Salon, he began repainting his work! It was an astonishing risk to take.

6. The Paris Salon authorities agreed to the startling request by the young artist to remove his painting. Then by day and night he laboured frantically to improve the picture, adding spots of bright colour all over the canvas so that the scene seemed bathed in light. The paint was still fresh and wet when the exhibition opened. It caused a sensation, and was attacked by some critics for its daring. But the French State had no doubts about it and bought it for a record price of 5000 francs.

7. At the suggestion of an English friend and artist, Richard Bonnington, he visited Britain. He loved London and discovered Shakespeare, who with Sir Walter Scott and Lord Byron, was to be the source of many of his inspirations. North Africa, too, was to provide him with many subjects. He had by now become the major painter of the French Romantic Movement and it was greatly to the credit of the authorities that they recognised that they had a genius working in their midst.

8. Revolution was again in the air, and one July day in 1830, when Delacroix was out walking, he saw a crowd marching behind the French flag. In his mind's eye he saw Liberty guiding the people against tyranny. He returned to his studio and painted a masterpiece. Because Revolution was its subject, it was not known for many years, but now it has a place of honour in the Louvre in Paris.

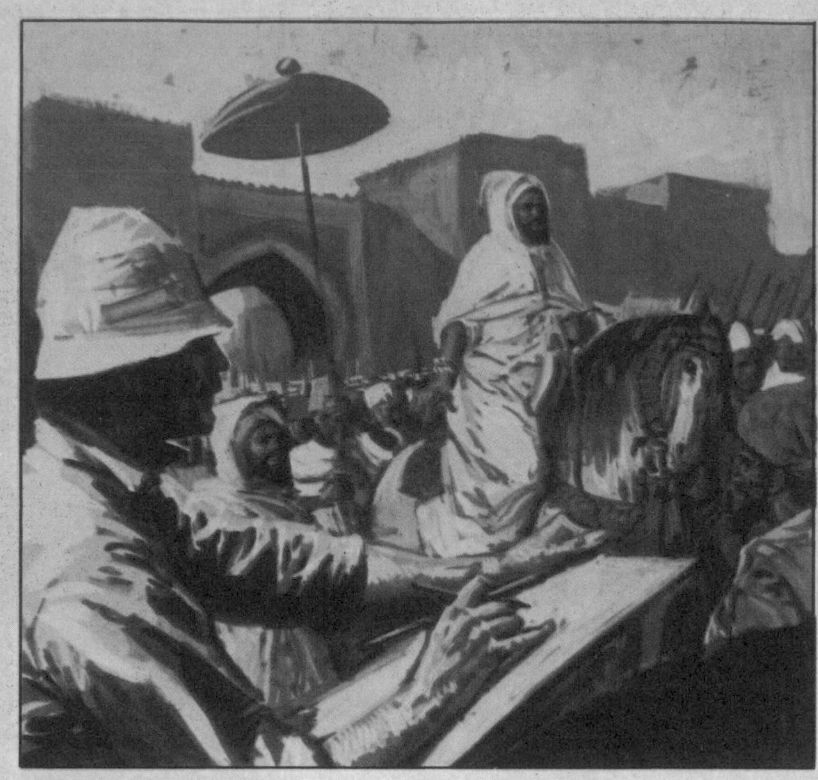

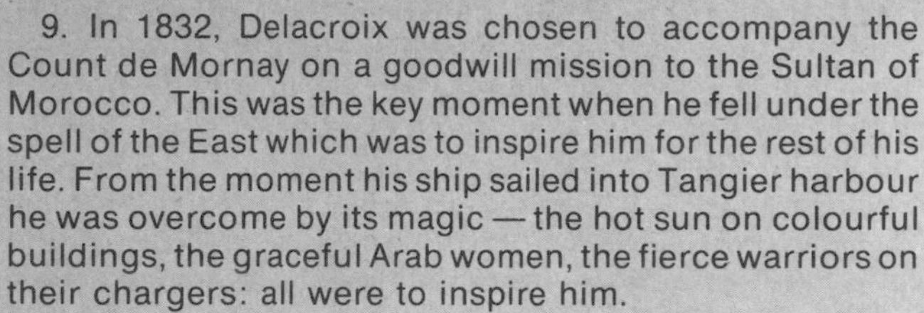

9. In 1832, Delacroix was chosen to accompany the Count de Mornay on a goodwill mission to the Sultan of Morocco. This was the key moment when he fell under the spell of the East which was to inspire him for the rest of his life. From the moment his ship sailed into Tangier harbour he was overcome by its magic — the hot sun on colourful buildings, the graceful Arab women, the fierce warriors on their chargers: all were to inspire him.

10. Everywhere he went to draw, drawings that he would later use as the basis of paintings. He and his party came at last to Meknes and the palace of the Sultan Muley-Abd-El-Rahmann, who rode out of his gate to meet his visitors. Delacroix drew the colourful scene, resting his sketch-book on his pommel. Later, he turned the scene into one of his finest paintings.

11. The Sultan was so impressed by Delacroix that he broke the rules and allowed the artist into his harem to draw his many wives! One day, beyond the city walls, Delacroix watched a fight between wild stallions. Heedless of the fearful risk he was taking, he got as close as possible to sketch the dramatic scene, as unshod hooves lashed the air only a few feet from where he stood. Naturally, this thrilling episode led to his painting another great work of art, which today can be seen in the Louvre.

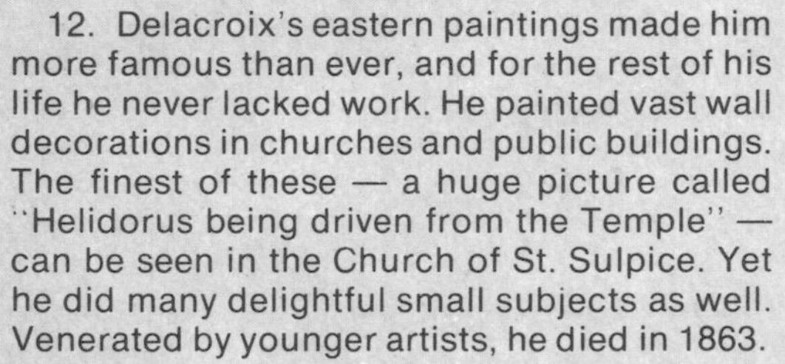

12. Delacroix's eastern paintings made him more famous than ever, and for the rest of his life he never lacked work. He painted vast wall decorations in churches and public buildings. The finest of these — a huge picture called "Helidorus being driven from the Temple" — can be seen in the Church of St. Sulpice. Yet he did many delightful small subjects as well. Venerated by younger artists, he died in 1863.

# What was the Gutenberg Bible?

**EVERY day newspapers, books and magazines — millions and millions of them — carry the printed word and picture to each and every one of us. Printing is a vital part of our lives. Through it we are informed, amused, guided and taught. Through printing, knowledge of all kinds has spread widely. Today it is hard to imagine a time when there was no printing. And yet that time was not so very long ago . . .**

In the relatively short history of printing, one figure stands out — Johann Gutenberg. He was a German who worked at Mainz and Strasbourg in the middle years of the 15th century. Gutenberg was a goldsmith by trade, and it was his knowledge of working with metals that was to lead to the single most important invention of all — moveable type.

Printing — that is making a number of copies from one original by taking an impression on paper or something similar — was not unknown in Gutenberg's time. The Chinese were printing books in the 9th century A.D., and the technique probably spread to Europe from the East after the traveller Marco Polo brought back ideas and techniques he and his companions had seen.

But this early printing was printing by blocks, the same principle as a simple potato print or lino-cut print. A picture and text would be laboriously carved into a block of wood and a number of prints made by inking the 'page' of matter thus formed. One block was for one page and could only be used for that page. If a mistake were made during the carving, the block had to be scrapped and restarted. It was the same with handwritten books — a single mistake and a page was ruined.

Gutenberg changed all this by the brilliant notion of making each letter to be printed — the type — moveable. This meant that any word could be made up, a page printed and then the type dismantled to make up another page.

Gutenberg did this so carefully that each block (or 'body') of metal type was identical in size to the next. When a number of letters were assembled to form a word, and a number of words a line, they all were exactly level with each other giving an even impression.

Type was cast for every letter of the alphabet. A number of copies of each were made and put in order in a special box called a 'case' so the typesetter (or compositor) could select what he needed. Two boxes were used, the one at the top, the 'upper case', for capitals letters, the one at the bottom for 'lower case'. Once the words and lines had been composed these were locked together in pages — several pages at a time — and laid flat facing upwards for inking.

Gutenberg realised that this 'letterpress' process needed a system for pressing the paper to the inked type so he adopted the familiar screw-type machine used by winemakers to press their grapes. Using this method Gutenberg printed his first book, the famous Gutenberg Bible,

**The earliest writing materials — tablets of baked clay. This Assyrian example dates from about 850 B.C.**

**Above: The Chinese were pioneers in printing and paper-making. Our illustration shows a page of the *Diamond Sutra,* the oldest surviving printed book, dating from A.D. 868. Wood blocks were carved back-to-front with a raised image and inked. Paper was then pressed flat onto the picture or writing. But with one block for each page the method was very time-consuming.**
**Right: Despite the introduction of moveable type into Europe, illustrations were still made by block printing. This is a print from one of Caxton's first printed books, *Aesop's Fables.***

Early books (which could only be read by a small number of wealthy people and scholars) were not printed but handwritten. It was a slow and painstaking operation for the scribes and copyists who were often monks.

Top right: Gutenberg made his type by first cutting a steel punch for each letter. This was banged into a matrix of soft bronze, cutting an indented copy of the letter. The matrix was then put in a mould and hot metal poured in. When this hardened it was removed from the matrix, a slim metal block with a raised letter on one end — the type.

which was published in 1455.

But not only did moveable type allow many copies of this and other books to originate from Gutenberg's press, it also allowed the printer to 'proof' each page before he finally printed a number of copies. By inking the type and pressing one sheet down, the machine operator could check to see whether the compositor had done his job properly. Any misspellings or omitted letters could be corrected before the full 'run' was made.

After Gutenberg's astounding invention, Germany became the centre of printing. Very soon though the technique had spread to other countries in Europe.

The man responsible for introducing the new letterpress to England was a merchant, William Caxton, whose first book (printed on a press near Westminster Abbey) was *The Sayings of the Philosophers* in 1477.

Caxton was energetic and industrious, printing in all nearly one hundred works including translations. In particular he tended to concentrate not on Latin texts — as did so many Continental printers — but English ones including great classics such as Chaucer's *Canterbury Tales* and Malory's *Morte d'Arthur*.

Many of the early books were illustrated. Here the technique was the old one of wood blocks, carefully carved and then locked into the frame of type ready for inking. The early printers were also very interested in experimenting with different styles of lettering in type — 'typefaces' — and some of the designs produced hundreds of years ago are still used to this day.

The well stocked printer would carry then, as he does now, different typefaces for different jobs. Each full alphabet of one style is called a 'fount' (pronounced *font*).

Above centre: The compositor or typesetter sets the type correctly in the composing stick. The type case had two parts — the *upper case* for capital letters and the *lower case* for small letters. The lines of type were then laid flat and locked in wooden boxes called *forms.*

Above: A flat-bed screw press of the type used by Caxton and Gutenberg. The sheet of paper was laid flat over the inked type in the form. This was then wound into place under the screw press. Pressure was applied to obtain an even impression. The printed sheet was removed — but only by someone with clean hands!

## But don't forget . . . there could be no printing without paper!

**True paper was invented by the Chinese about 2000 years ago. Their basic method reached Europe around A.D. 1200. Old rags were boiled up, and then beaten and stirred with lots of water to make a *pulp* (above left). A fine wire sieve was then dipped in the pulp and removed horizontally. A layer of pulp was left on the sieve as the water drained through the mesh (above).**

**The matted fibre sheets formed were not ready to be used as paper. To ensure that they were smooth and almost completely moisture-free, the sheets were stacked up and placed under a press (left). This was then slowly turned to apply the correct pressure. The individual sheets were then separated and hung on ceiling wires so that any remaining water would evaporate away.**

Hand in hand with the development of printing went efforts to improve the paper. While books were still being hand written, paper was not always necessary. Parchment made from animal skins that had been rubbed smooth and thin was sometimes used by the monks and copyists. Before that, papyrus made from reeds had been used by the early Egyptians, while the earliest writing material of all was simply tablets of baked clay.

The ingenious Chinese devised a method of chopping up rags, mixing the pieces with water to form pulp, and pouring this onto a bamboo mat through which the water drained leaving a sheet of wet fibres. Once dry this sheet became suitable for writing on. Eventually this pulp process found its way to Europe where hand-made paper, and later machine-made paper, produced using wood pulp were developed. A technique was later devised for making paper not just in small single sheets but long lengths.

### Hungry

The new printing presses were hungry for paper, and each sheet printed could contain two, four or eight pages of the finished book. So paper had to be big enough, plentiful enough and of just the right absorbancy for the inks the ever-experimental printers were trying out.

With the invention of printing with moveable type changes took place that could not have been contemplated earlier. Books were cheaper and more easily obtainable so ideas were able to spread more quickly. The forerunners of today's newspaper began to emerge to spread news and opinions far and wide.

Gutenberg's genius had started a movement that was to grow and grow. And yet – for all the advances in man's knowledge nothing in the history of printing was to surpass in originality his moveable type press.

It was not until hundreds of years later that the next major steps forward were taken.

# How is a Colour picture printed?

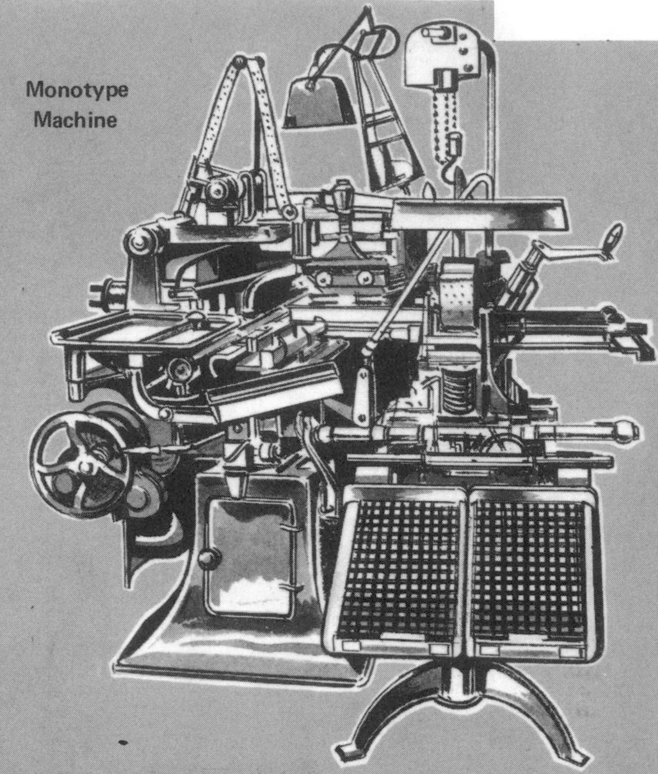


**Above left: The Linotype is a typesetting machine which produces lines of type ('slugs'). The keyboard consists of six rows of 15 keys. As the typesetter reads the copy he presses the keys accordingly. Each of these releases a matrix with a character engraved on it. These are taken to the assembler to form a mould for the line of type. Hot metal is forced into the mould and the slug is cast and trimmed. Monotype machines (above) produce single characters that are made up into lines. The keyboard records information on a paper spool which is fed into the casting machine. Compressed air is passed through a particular hole on the spool to release a character matrix which is held over the mould and the character is cast.**

**WITH the invention of printing using moveable type in the 15th century the stage was set for the new *letterpress* machines to produce thousands of copies of books and broadsheets instead of a few handwritten copies as in the past. But, although the new techniques spread rapidly, the actual methods of printing evolved fairly slowly.**

Indeed if William Caxton's ghost had walked three or even four hundred years after his death he would have seen little difference in the way printers tackled their work. Sheets of paper were still being printed one at a time — in 1800 the London newspaper *The Times* only came off the press at the rate of 250 single sheets an hour. Type was still being composed or 'set' by hand, each character in the alphabet being taken from its wooden case and locked one by one alongside the next. And many presses were still being worked by hand.

Changes came during the early nineteenth century. As in so many industries iron began to replace wood as the material for building machinery. In 1800 Lord Stanhope introduced his iron printing press which applied rapid pressure over the paper laid on the inked type.

Later this presswork became mechanised when steam engines were put to use to drive the presses. Instead of flat pages of type having paper squeezed against them by hand pressure, steam power drove a cylinder that pressed the paper to the type. *The Times* increased its output to 1,000 copies an hour.

But still the most laborious part of the process was in the hands of the compositor or typesetter. How could typesetting be speeded up? Presswork (or 'machining') was getting faster all the time, but the dream of real mechanised printing could not come about until a more rapid method was found of transferring metal type characters into word and page order.

Some machines were invented but they did not prove successful. In particular they did not solve the problem of putting the type back in the type case when it was finished with. In 1886 an American, Otto Mergenthaler, invented a machine that solved the problem. His system was called Linotype.

All the typesetter had to do was type out the characters he needed onto a keyboard arranged like a conventional typewriter. The Linotype machine then set the type by

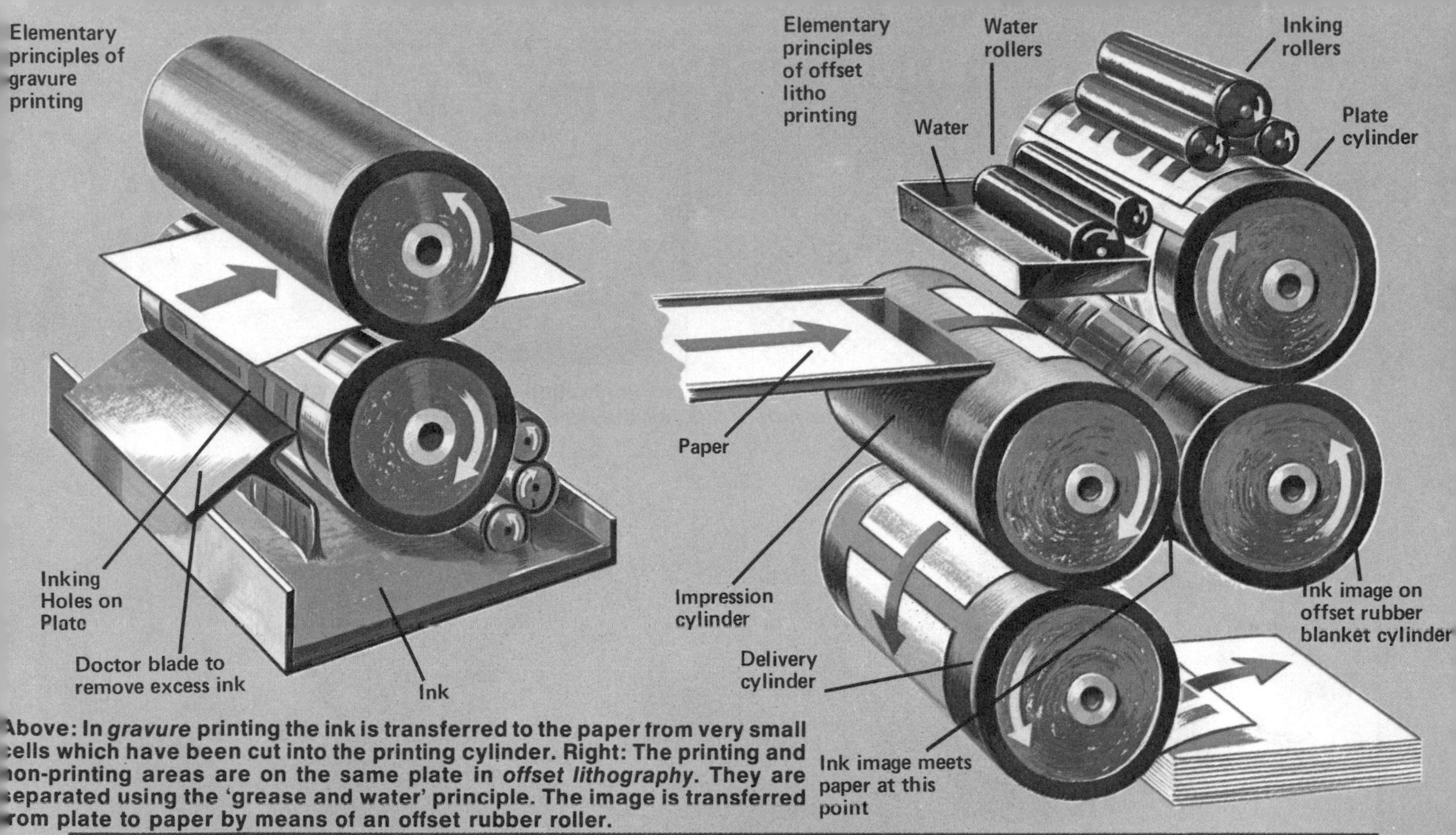


**Above: In *gravure* printing the ink is transferred to the paper from very small cells which have been cut into the printing cylinder. Right: The printing and non-printing areas are on the same plate in *offset lithography*. They are separated using the 'grease and water' principle. The image is transferred from plate to paper by means of an offset rubber roller.**

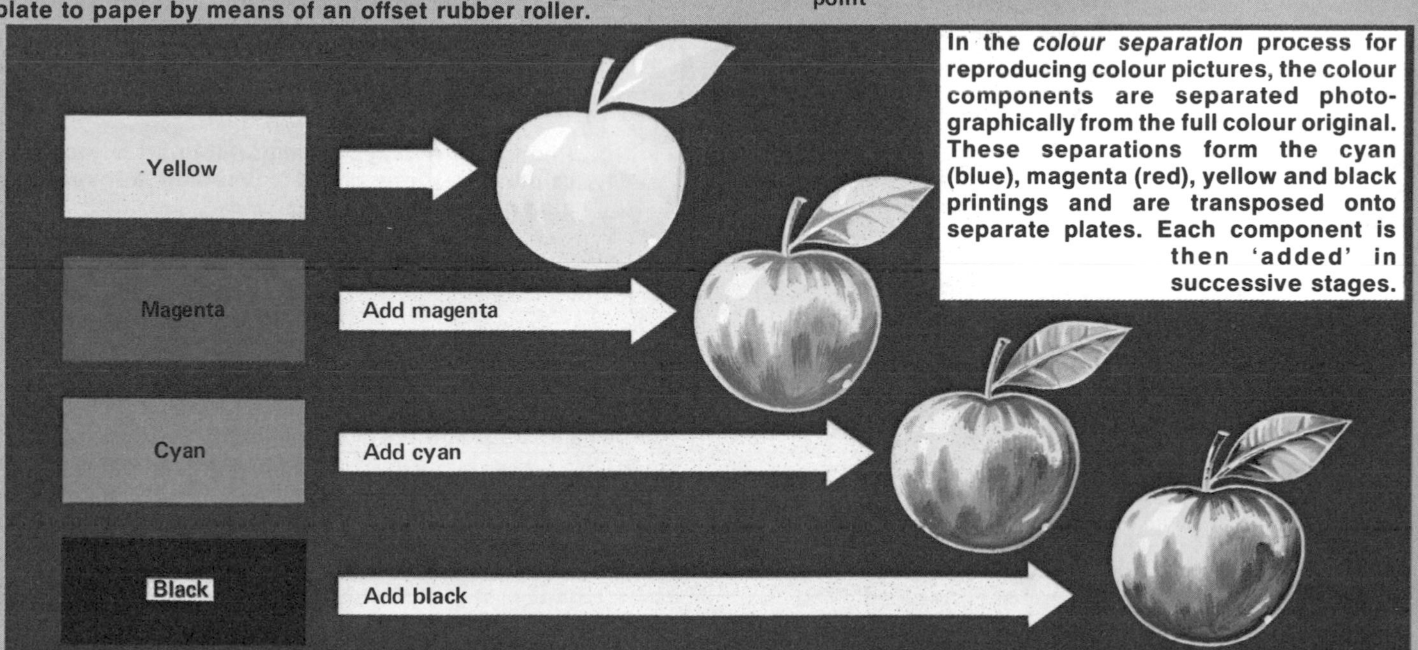


**In the *colour separation* process for reproducing colour pictures, the colour components are separated photographically from the full colour original. These separations form the cyan (blue), magenta (red), yellow and black printings and are transposed onto separate plates. Each component is then 'added' in successive stages.**

Sample of four-colour half-tone printing

casting it from molten metal, a whole line (or *slug*) at a time — hence the name 'Linotype'. Once a page was printed the operators could melt down the type and re-use it.

Just a few years later another American, Tolbert Lanson, developed the *Monotype* system. This gave the compositor the ability to cast not whole lines but single letters as and when he wanted them.

Remember, too, that newly cast type gives a crisp, sharp impression. Using type over and over again can produce worn, broken letters. You can sometimes spot these in books that have gone through many letterpress printings or 'impressions'.

For centuries the only method of printing was letterpress. But in the last century more methods have been added to the printer's skills. One is called *gravure*.

Gravure is in a way the reverse of letterpress. While letterpress uses raised characters, gravure uses characters etched *into* a surface. The letters are etched by acid eating into the surface of metal plates that are curved around rollers. The ink is put into the holes and channels made by these letters. When paper is passed round the roller the ink sticks to it following the shapes of the characters. Gravure is a method often used for printing magazines.

Another more recent printing method is *lithography* — often called simply 'litho' — and based on the elementary principle that grease and water do not mix. You can best understand litho by doing an experiment yourself. Take a flat piece of stone and draw a simple shape on it with a wax candle or greasy crayon. Now gently wet the whole surface of the stone. If you now roll over the stone surface an ink-filled sponge you'll see that the ink tends to stick to the greasy picture.

Specially treated metal plates can be used by printers in much the same way. Often this is done by the *offset* method. A plate is treated to etch in texts or pictures. This plate is wrapped around a roller and inked. The roller turns against another rubber roller and transfers the greasy ink image to it. This 'offset' rubber roller then

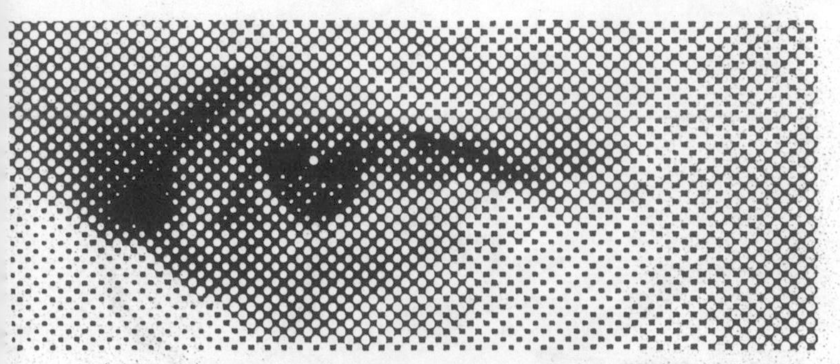

**Some illustrations are reproduced by breaking down the original photo-mechanically into a series of dots or *half-tones*; the larger the dot, the heavier the tone etc.**

**Line illustrations are easier and cheaper to reproduce since they consist of solid lines with no intermediate tones.**

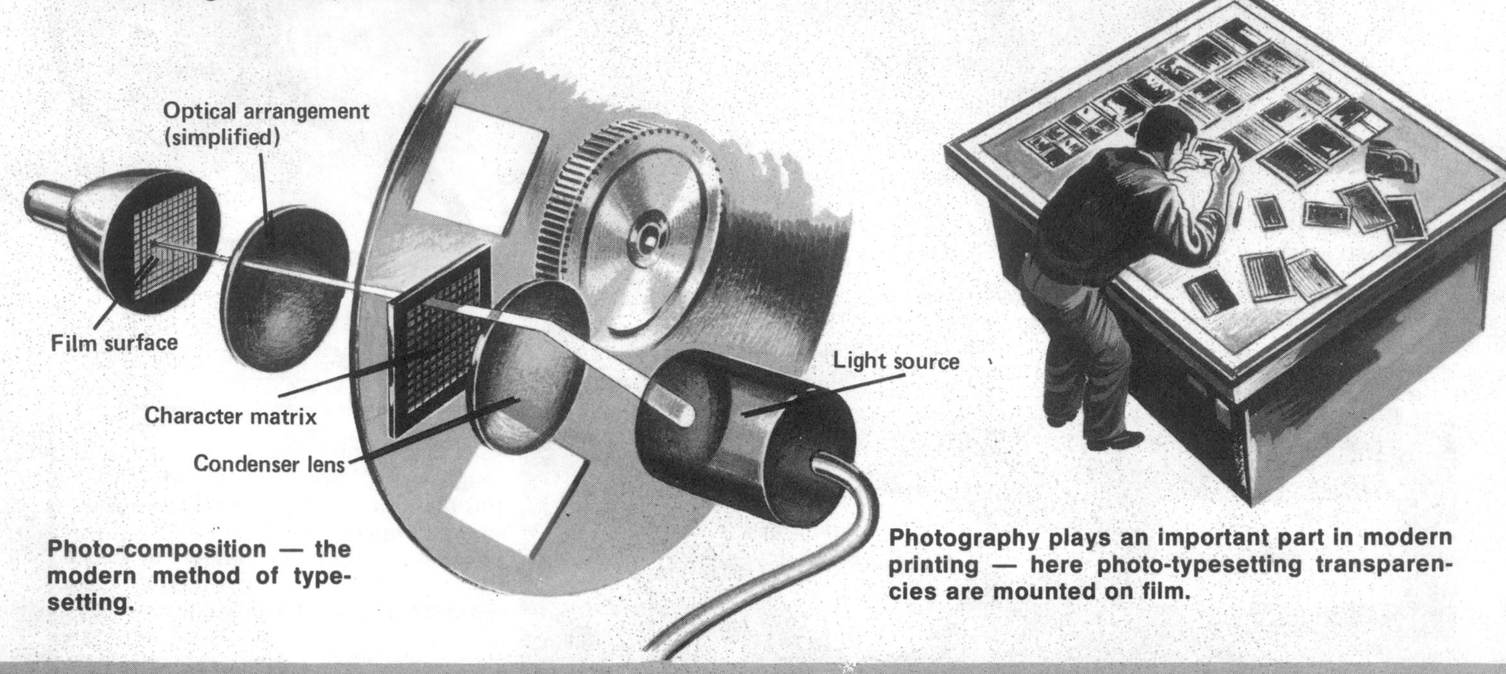


**Photo-composition — the modern method of type-setting.**

**Photography plays an important part in modern printing — here photo-typesetting transparencies are mounted on film.**

transfers this image to an impression cylinder — that is, the cylinder through which paper is fed. The result: an impression on paper identical to that on the original litho plate.

These three methods of printing: letterpress, gravure and litho, enable a vast range of effects to be achieved for different purposes; from producing handsome encyclopedias to strikingly colourful cereal boxes.

All kinds of illustrations can be reproduced. With letterpress, black and white pictures are reproduced using the familiar 'block' system. Drawings and charts have line blocks, that is cut away lines rather like a lino print, while photographs need to be printed with *half-tone* blocks. Here the photograph is rephotographed by a camera that turns the blacks, whites and greys into dots. The parts of the picture that are not to be printed are then cut away.

Lithography gives greater flexibility than letterpress because it enables text, line drawings and photographs to be printed in any arrangement on the same page and on the same paper. A photograph printed letterpress needs a shiny or coated paper for best effect. This is why you will often see a batch of 'plates' on coated paper making up a separate section of a book.

Lithography is also a good way of reprinting a book when the original letterpress type has been taken down and re-used. The book is photographed and this film is then specially treated to turn it into a litho metal plate ready to be put on a roller in the press. This is sometimes called just 'offsetting'.

One of the most fascinating sights in a printing works is when a full colour picture — say for a calendar or a magazine — rolls off the press. Colour pictures are made up from three basic colours — magenta (red), cyan (blue) and yellow — and these can be combined to arrive at any shade you require.

This means printing one colour with another in a colour separation sequence: first printing — yellow only; second printing — magenta with yellow to give oranges and reds; third printing — cyan with blues and greens; fourth and final printing — black to add even greater subtlety and definition. This is a 'four colour' printing, because black to a printer is a 'colour'.

We should not forget that today's printing depends on a number of related technologies: papermaking to ensure that the right texture and grade of paper for the job is available; electronics and mechanical engineering to give us machines that run fast, smooth and true; and photography which is involved in so many aspects of platemaking. It also requires creative people to use these technologies to their best advantage. The age of the hand press is all but past but craftsmen are needed as much now as they ever were.

## PHOTO-COMPOSITION

**Over the last few years photo-composition has taken over much of the work formerly done by the hot metal systems. The basic arrangement is like that shown above (left). The material to be set is fed into the photo-setting system in the form of punched tape. The matrix has characters of the required typeface on it and these are scanned in the correct order by the light source according to the information supplied. The character is projected through the optical arrangement of the photo-setting machine and on to the film. The advantages of photo-composition are that the type is always sharp and films can simply be reduced or enlarged to give the correct type size.**

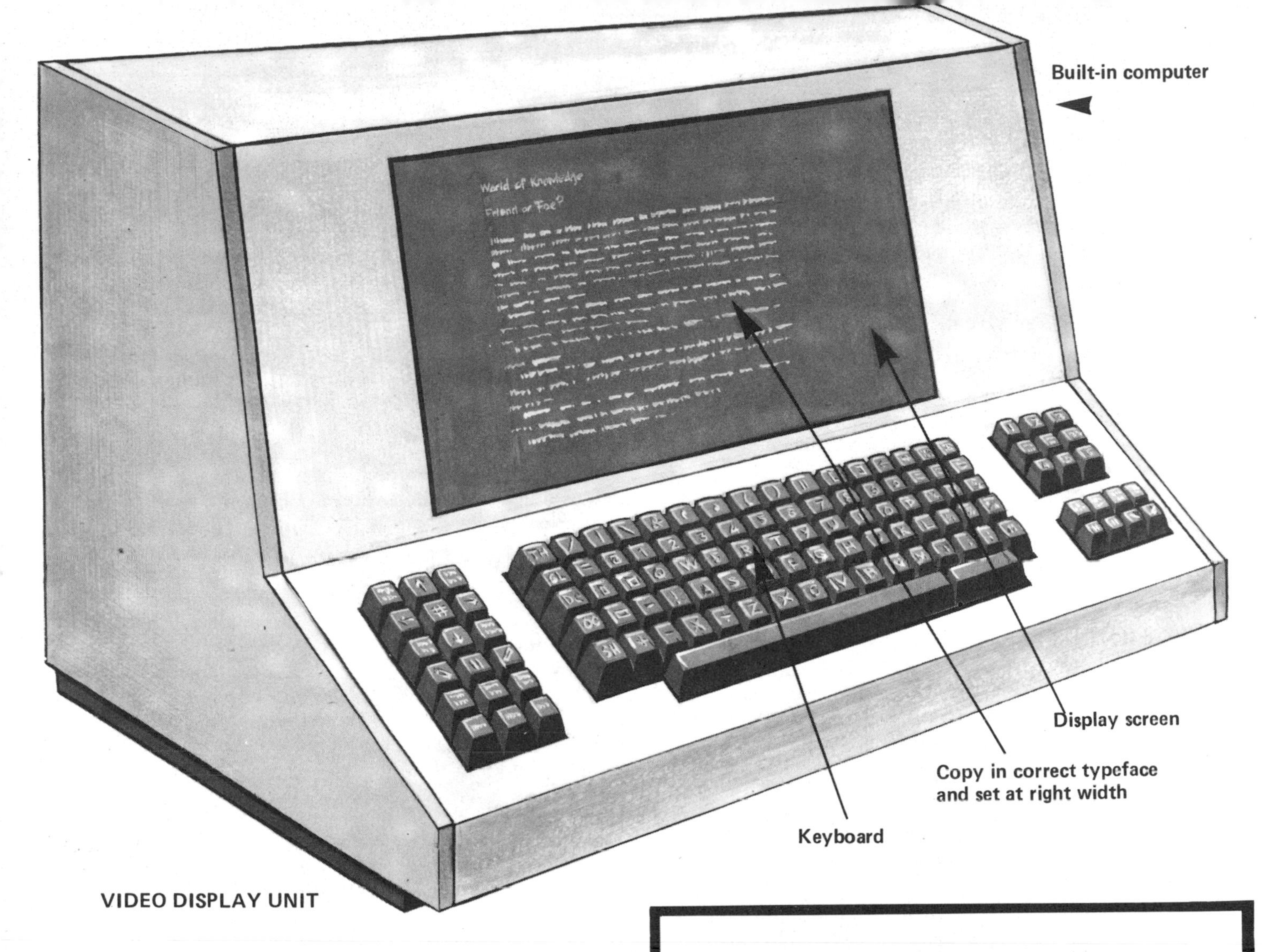

VIDEO DISPLAY UNIT

# Does Printing today need a Computer?

**IT is most probably true to say that if William Caxton's ghost been around 300 years after his death he would not have felt particularly out of place in the printers' works. This would certainly not be the case today. In fact, the past 30 years have seen an incredibly rapid advance in printing techniques compared with the previous 300 years.**

Since 1950 the printing industry has taken full advantage of the progress made in computer and electronic technology. Up until this period all printing processes had been mechanical. This meant that a printing works needed to be of considerable size to accommodate all the machinery needed to produce a range of typefaces. The type itself was heavy and cumbersome to store.

No longer does type have to be set physically by hand because the typefaces are set photographicaly. They are stored on rotating discs and at a signal from an electronic keyboard, the correct letter is photographed on to the film. However, correcting errors on film is a complicated process where the line must be cut out.

The answer to such disadvantages, as in many other industries, was the introduction of computers. Not long ago, computers were thought of as large, expensive and over-complicated. Advances in technology have changed all that — computers are now small, quite cheap and can be built-in to comparatively simple pieces of equipment. They are now being used to speed up many of the processes in printing and they may be linked to almost any printing process.

A first consideration would be to link a computer with hot metal setting. But even this would not match the pace of a computer-controlled phototypesetting system and these are now in use with many printers.

The most modern printing process combines this system with the special piece of equipment pictured on this page — the *video display unit* (V.D.U.). This has a built-in computer which can be programmed to the particular typesetting requirements and is linked

**T.V. transmitter broadcasts Ceefax and Oracle like normal programmes.**

directly with the photo-typesetter. The great advantage is that in one unit the tasks that, at one time, would have been done manually by the editing department and the compositor (typesetter) can now be combined by controlling the display on the screen.

Editing makes sure that the copy to be printed is accurate and reads properly. With the V.D.U., each page of copy can be typed up on to the display screen in the correct typeface. It can then be thoroughly checked for spelling and punctuation mistakes, missing words or lines, and any other errors; the corrections are simply typed in where needed.

Where the compositor was once needed, the V.D.U. takes over. Columns are set to the correct width automatically, lines are correctly spaced and where words overrun a line hyphens can be inserted on the display. The result is a display of copy very like the page you will actually read. This is then filmset on the photo-typesetter and the image transferred photographically on to the printing plate used in lithography or gravure presses.

Such modern techniques have greatly reduced the time needed to prepare copy for the presses. They are particularly useful in setting complicated lists such as telephone directories and timetables where the information can be stored on the computer tape for long periods. And the need for readily-available information may well change the essential nature of printing.

There will always be a need for the printed word in the form of books and magazines which people can enjoy in their spare time. But what of information that can affect people in their daily lives? More than ever before, people want to be kept informed over a great range of subjects — news, weather, prices of stocks and shares and many more — and this is where the changes in printing may come.

For about 200 years printed newspapers have helped provide much of this information. But they still take time to prepare, produce and reach the public. The news is, therefore, not quite up-to-the-minute. In fact, time has often been called a newspaper's greatest 'enemy'. However, since 1970 the Japanese have had a system where whole newspapers are transmitted direct into the home. This system is called *Teleview*. At the press of a button, a receiver about the size of a T.V. prints out an electronically produced copy of the latest edition of the newspaper.

The latest development involves an invention made in Great Britain in 1974 — the *viewdata* system. Using this system, information is available on a whole range of subjects, literally at your fingertips. The basic arrangement is shown in the diagram on this page. Two of the services presently in use — *Ceefax* and *Oracle* — work in only one direction. They are transmitted like normal T.V. programmes supplying constantly updated information which is mostly news.

However a third system *Prestel* — combines T.V. display and the telephone to provide a two-way service. By contacting the *Prestel* computer (which stores over 100,000 pages of information) using a pushbutton keypad about the size of a pocket calculator, you can select the page you require. This is displayed on the T.V. screen in words and simple diagrams. There is the latest news, sports results, food prices, train timetables . . . even T.V. games! One expert has said: "Few people now doubt that information systems like *Prestel* will sweep across the developed world, just as the printed word did after Gutenberg and Caxton."

Computer typesetting, *Teleview* and *Prestel* — printing has come a long way since the marvellous breakthrough of Gutenberg's movable type. But however much techniques change, let us hope that there will still be a place for more traditional methods where quality is important and the highest traditions of craftsmanship are kept.

**Normal T.V. aerial**

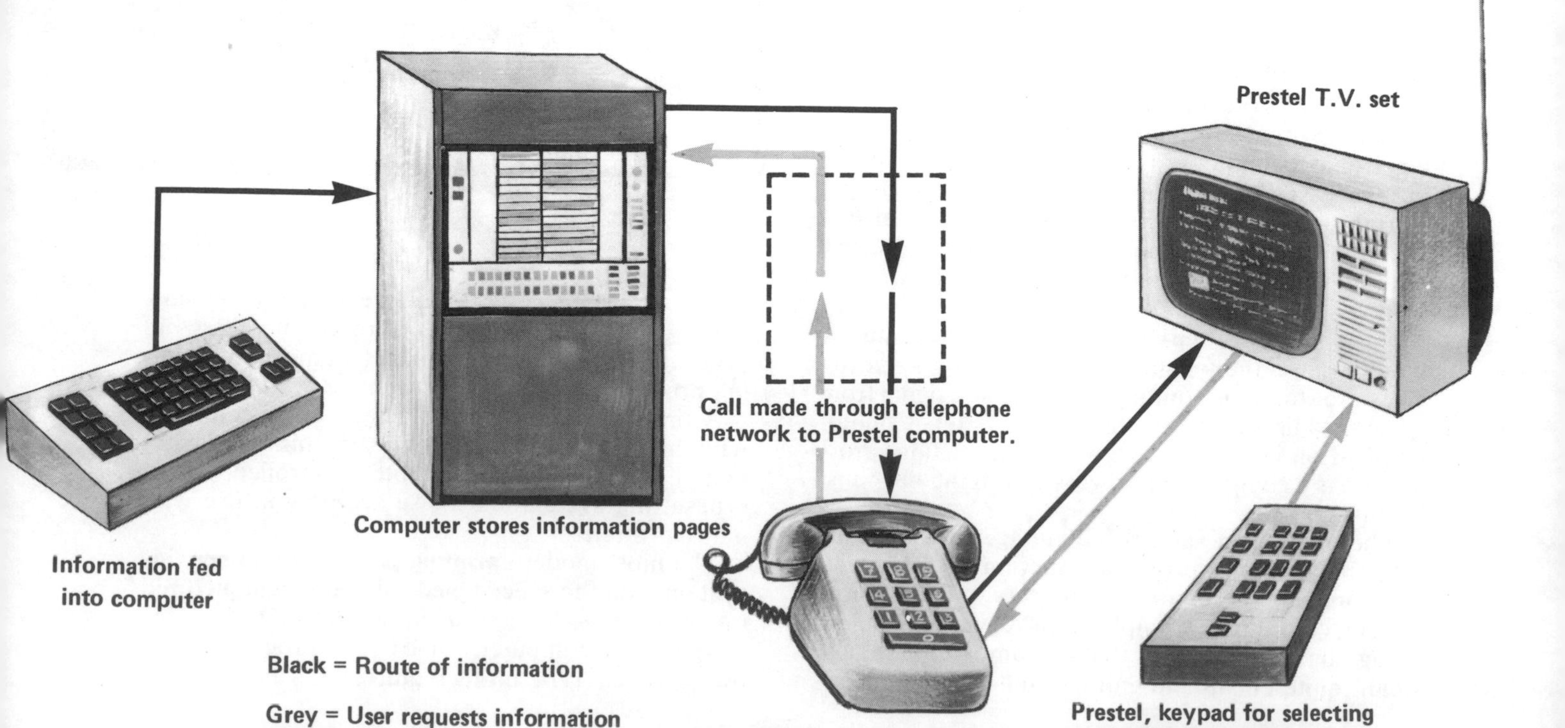

# Who painted 'The Blue Boy'?

1. One of the greatest British painters, Thomas Gainsborough, was born in 1727 at Sudbury, Suffolk. He was the fifth son of a cloth merchant, John Gainsborough, and showed an early interest in painting. He sketched both his mother and father while still a child.

2. In fact, he sketched anything and anyone. Reputedly, he once surprised an intruder to his father's orchard. He made a 'lightning' drawing of the man and the boy's evidence was so good, the intruder was identified and punished. But the local countryside was his favourite subject.

3. When he was 14, in 1741, young Thomas managed to persuade his father to send him to London where he studied for three years, working with the French engraver, Hubert Gravelot and also at the Academy of Arts. He came under the influence, too, of the Flemish school of painters — although in many ways, he remained an individualist.

4. At 18, he returned to Sudbury and, the following year, 1746, married Margaret Burr. The young couple at first lived in Ipswich where Gainsborough managed to earn a modest living by painting portraits. He discovered that people would pay for portraits of themselves but would not so readily pay for unidentified landscapes.

5. Among Gainsborough's friends of this period were Joshua Kirby, an artist and president of the Society of Artists, and Philip Thicknesse who later wrote his first biography. Thomas and Joshua spent many happy hours making sketches of the East Anglian countryside. Gainsborough, in particular, often used these sketches as backgrounds for his later, highly fashionable portraits.

6. Two daughters were born to the Gainsboroughs and these children — Mary, born 1748 and Margaret, born 1752 — were frequently painted by their father. One of these paintings (an impression of which is given above) now hangs in the National Gallery, London. It captures beautifully the charm and innocence of childhood although, in fact, like a number of Gainsborough's pictures, was unfinished. One painting of his daughters was, for many years, in two pieces. A long time after his death, however, it was restored and now can be seen complete.

7. Throughout his life, Gainsborough was inspired by the two art forms of music and painting. Indeed, he learned to play a number of musical instruments tolerably well, including the harp and the violoncello. Reputedly, he hardly ever read a book and, as a child, had little scholastic success. He is supposed to have been particularly fond of painting landscapes, so that his portraits often have quite detailed landscape backgrounds.

Our picture shows a particularly famous Gainsborough portrait/landscape. It is *Mr. and Mrs. Andrews* and depicts the couple in the grounds of their country home. The landscape takes up quite a large part of the picture and is put in with considerable feeling and delicacy. The sky is particularly finely executed. Although Gainsborough's portraits have never been surpassed in beauty, he always thought of himself first and foremost as a landscape painter.

8. In 1759, Gainsborough was persuaded to move to the more fashionable life in the town of Bath, where he became an extremely popular portrait painter, able to command very high prices. To this period, belongs the famous *Blue Boy* (shown above). This portrait of Master Jonathan Buttall was painted as a challenge to his fellow painter, Sir Joshua Reynolds, who maintained that a mass of blue in a picture was artistic death. Gainsborough did not agree with him.

9. He made his point! There is a great deal of blue, too in the portrait of Mrs. Siddons, the actress (above), also one of Gainsborough's most famous portraits. After his move to London in 1774, he painted many portraits of the royal family — including the princesses and Queen Charlotte. George III himself indeed, was painted by Gainsborough as many as eight times.

10. Some while before this (in 1763), Gainsborough had been elected one of the first members of the Royal Academy. He exhibited there on a number of occasions with varying success. In 1784, however, he quarrelled with them, believing that his paintings (particularly one of the princesses) were hung too high up the wall to show their qualities to their best advantage.

11. He never exhibited at the Royal Academy again. And sadly the world was to have the benefit of his genius for only a very few more years. In 1788, he died. He is buried at Kew. But the boy who sat for hours sketching the countryside and people of his own native county of Suffolk is still remembered in his many, superlative works. They are all worth seeing and may be viewed in many famous galleries all over the world.

# How did the Cinema commence?

D. W. Griffith, in the hat, directing one of his silent films. 'Talkies' led to his decline and he died in poverty.

**IT was an unlikely place for a revolution. Down in the basement of a café in Paris, two French brothers, Louis and Auguste Lumière, presented a short film to a select audience. It showed workers leaving the brothers' factory for their dinner hour and it was the first film to be presented publicly on a screen. The date was 1895 and it is a nice coincidence that Lumière is the French for light.**

The Lumières did not 'invent' the motion picture. As with so many other great inventions, a number of people in a number of countries were at work separately on the project. Among them were the American, Thomas Edison, and the Britons, William Friese-Greene and Robert Paul. Edison's contribution was the kinetoscope, designed either by himself or his assistant, William Dickson. It was a box in which just over 15 metres of film revolved on spools. There was a peephole in the box for a viewer.

Though the kinetoscope had some success in America and Europe, Edison did not believe it had a future, so it was left to others to improve it. The Lumières used a Cinematograph, which means moving picture, and which was a combined camera and projector. Their films lasted 45 seconds, and soon they had made the first story film, *Watering the Gardener!*

Edison and others now saw a future in films, and by 1900 films were being shown as extra attractions in music halls and fun fairs. However, once people had got over their surprise — some expected to be soaked by a sea scene — the novelty began to wear off. It had helped that there was no language problem, films being silent, and that everyone was soon using 35mm film, but a new revolution was needed.

It came with the arrival of the story film, something more ambitious than a few seconds of the Lumière's gardener being drenched. By 1901, a brilliant French magician, Georges Méliès, had made an ever-growing number of short science fiction and fairy tale films, directing them as well as writing and acting in them.

But it was the American, Edwin S. Porter, who was the first to make movies for the millions. Not only did he make the first Western, *The Great Train Robbery* in 1903, which lasted 11 minutes, but he pioneered modern techniques.

He saw that it was common sense to shoot films out of sequence. He would shoot every scene that occurred in one setting, then every one that occurred in another, and finally he would edit the separate shots into a clear story. He added to the excitement by switching the action from the escaping train robbers to the forming of the posse, tricks of the trade which are still used.

The film made a fortune, packing every hall where it was shown. More films were rushed into production and "nickel-odeons" were built to house them. These were the first cinemas. Five cents, or a nickel, was the entrance fee, for which the patron saw a number of films, with a pianist playing suitable music.

The silent cinema as a mass attraction had been born.

Hollywood, destined to be the world's film capital, was born soon after. The climate and variety of scenery appealed to film-makers who had been shooting their films in the eastern U.S.A.

## The World's Sweetheart

Here, too was born the star system when an unknown girl named Florence Lawrence was renamed Mary Pickford and became "the World's Sweetheart" as well as the first star to earn a million dollars. She was also a good actress, unlike some silent stars who over-acted abominably.

America's biggest break came in 1914 when Europe's film-making was virtually halted by World War One. Shortly before this, D. W. Griffith, the first great director, had started work. The director is the key figure in filming because he shapes every shot and scene and decides how actors shall interpret their roles.

Griffith made filming an art. He was the first to move the camera about and, though he did not invent close-ups, he showed how important they were. He took a number of shots of the same scene so as to vary close-ups with longer shots and he was an editor of genius.

One result was the first epic film, *The Birth of a Nation,* which was set in and after the American Civil War and remains a masterpiece to this day.

Yet it is for comedy that the silent cinema is best remembered. True, legendany names like the athletic Douglas Fairbanks Senior, William S. Hart, the Western star, and Rudolph Valentino, the "Great Lover", have not been forgotten.

A Cinema film consists of separate pictures showing different movements of the subject concerned (see left).

By presenting to the eye a rapid sequence of pictures, each showing one stage of movement, an impression of movement is obtained. The revolving discs on the right shows an early adaptation of this idea.

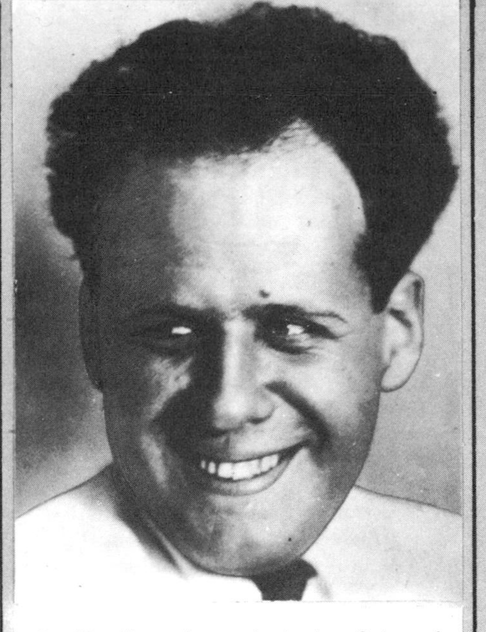

S. M. Eisenstein received the Order of Lenin in 1938 for "Alexander Nevsky", the first of a planned film trilogy. The second, "Ivan the Terrible" was shot in 1944 and 1946.

Louis Lumière, aged 71, in 1935 with his then new stereoscopic film apparatus. The special tinted spectacles helped his illusion.

But Charlie Chaplin, Buster Keaton, the Keystone Kops, Laurel and Hardy and other silent stars — some of whom later "talked" — still delight countless millions all over the world.

The master of many of the revels was Mack Sennett, whose Keystone Studios opened in 1912. Of course, some of his most amazing effects were done by trick photography, but stars like Keaton and Harold Lloyd pulled off many daring and amazing stunts themselves.

American films cheered a war-torn world, and after the war the cinema boomed. Vast studios opened in Hollywood which became big business. With the war over, other nations returned to making movies, most notably the Germans, who made giant strides in the use of the camera. And Soviet Russia produced a genius in Sergei Eisenstein, whose *Battleship Potemkin,* about a mutiny in the old Russian navy, caused a worldwide sensation.

As those who have seen silent films will know, "titles" were inserted into films where they were needed to help tell the story and also some dialogue. Naturally, when the films were shown in non-English speaking areas, translators got to work.

Cinemas became more and more grand, while little cinemas mushroomed everywhere. The money involved was colossal, and so were the profits. Actors whose voices were not so good, but who looked right, could make fortunes in silent movies.

An early hand-operated projector

Suddenly, almost overnight, sound came to the cinema. This tremendous revolution will get a feature to itself, but a single statistic will show just what a revolution it was. In 1927, the year the very first sound film appeared, some 60 million Americans went to the movies. Only two years later, with silent films dead beyond recall, attendance figures reached 110 million.

## The Projectionist

**Nowadays, projecting — that is, showing films — is almost wholly automatic and the projectionist is little more than a machine-minder. This was by no means the case in the early days. When films were first shown, usually in halls normally used for other purposes, film projection was an art. The projector had to be operated by hand (see left), and the action of the film could be slowed down or speeded up, depending on how fast the projectionist turned the handle of the projector. Many of the early films used trick effects to startle or amuse their audiences, and the success on the skill of the projectionist.**

It is possible to make a sort of 'film' by drawing pictures of the different stages of a figure's movement on the pages of a book. By flicking the pages, the figure seems to move. Edison's very early 'optical phonograph', shown on the right, used photographs, not drawings. This projected the pictures by means of a rotating cylinder.

# When did Films begin to speak?

**Experiments to add sound to films had started as early as 1900, when the silent cinema was in its infancy. By 1913, the Frenchman, Eugène Lauste, working in London, had made a sound-on-film projector and a reproducing apparatus. The outbreak of World War One in 1914, however, halted his work.**

Those who followed him could not solve the key problem of how to get good sound. Their efforts were agony on the ears. In the mid-1920s, the firm of Warner Brothers in Hollywood were in a bad way. Only their celebrated dog star, Rin Tin Tin, was bringing in money, and it was feared his popularity might eventually fade. Ruin stared them in the face, but perhaps sound might save them . . .

The brothers made a one-reel film using their 'Vitaphone' process, which was a sound-on-disc system synchronised with a moving picture. The popular entertainer, Al Jolson, was observed — and heard — singing Southern songs on a plantation. He also sang the hit song, *April Showers*.

None of Warner Brothers' rivals was alarmed by the film, for they were convinced the new system was only fit for fairgrounds.

Then a young executive of Warner Brothers, Darryl F. Zannuck, talked his bosses into producing a full-length feature film with sound, not just short efforts. The subject chosen was *The Jazz Singer*, which was already a hit on stage in New York. Al Jolson agreed to make what was to be a mainly silent picture plus a few songs, with snatches of background music. Al, however, began dropping in more and more dialogue: "Wait a minute. You ain't heard nothin' yet. Wait a minute I tell yer . . . You wanna hear 'Toot Toot Tootsie' . . ." and so on.

Warner Brothers saw the light and ordered more dialogue. The result was a sensation. At the Warner Theatre in New York, there were incredible scenes at the premiere, with people sobbing and howling for joy. Warner's rivals had come to scoff, but now raced to send telegrams to their studios ordering sound equipment to be bought — fast.

Some tried to pretend that sound movies were just a fad, but the colossal success of *The Jazz Singer* proved them wrong. Other sound films were soon being made and a new system, called Movietone, improved quality because the sound was recorded along the edge of the film by a method of photography. Soon all talkies were using it.

The only losers were silent stars who were found to have unsuitable voices — ones that were thought to be rather unpleasing.

Many stars made the changeover successfully, however, including Laurel and Hardy, the great comic stars.

Now the golden age of movies began, an age which was to last until the 1950s when television began to keep many peo-

**Above shows the making of an early 'talkie'. Cameramen are enclosed in a booth, for noise from non-insulated cameras ruined the soundtrack.**
**Right, a modern 'talkie' is made. Cameras now are 'blimped'. That is sound is excluded by use of sound-proof covers. The microphone is moved around on a boom and a man listening in through ear-phones operates a sound mixer. This shows filming of a studio shot.**

ple at home. For much of the golden age, folk all over the world were going to the cinema at least once a week and many millions were going twice. Colour, first used as early as 1906, became increasingly common from around 1935.

Westerns, musicals, horror films, gangster movies, comedies and love stories poured off the Hollywood assembly lines. The flood included "B Pictures", for until the 1950s, filmgoers expected — and usually got — two films every time they went to the cinema. The "B pictures" were generally slightly shorter and had lesser stars.

## Star System

The star system probably reached its height during the 1930s and 1940s and, thanks to television, today's young people know many of the stars of those years: for example, Clark Gable, Spencer Tracy, Bette Davis, Gary Cooper, Greta Garbo.

There were many fine directors, one of the best being an Englishman who went to Hollywood — Alfred Hitchcock of thriller fame.

A really remarkable film of the golden age of the talkies was *Citizen Kane,* the very first film directed by Orson Welles, who came to Hollywood in his early twenties from the theatre and radio and made a revolutionary masterpiece.

It was revolutionary because of his marvellous use of sound, music, camera angles, off-screen voices, including an off-screen narrator for some of the time, brilliant lighting and brilliant flash-backs. He even had time to write and produce it and to act the leading role from young manhood to old age. It remains an amazing achievement.

## Foreign Films

In the 1950s, Hollywood got scared. Attendances were falling all around the world because of television and, though new processes like Cinemascope and Cinerama (wide-screen presentations) resulted in occasional huge successes that made fortunes, many more films lost fortunes. Other film industries suffered, too, including Britain's, France's and Italy's. Thousands of cinemas closed and experiments, like films in 3-D, which needed special glasses to see, did not help much. Even the ever-popular Westerns seemed to be losing their touch, though John Wayne plus a good director could usually fill a cinema.

The word went out: fewer but better movies. They have not always been better, but the cinema as mass entertainment flourishes again in a more modest way. It is helped by the fortunes made by hits like *Jaws* 1 and 2, *Star Wars* etc., which make money that can be ploughed back into new ventures. Technically speaking, films are very well made and there are still many good actors though superstars are less frequently created.

The nearest to the old days is, perhaps, India's film industry, which appeals to an enormous local market, though maybe the finest Far Eastern films have come from Japan. Britain's film industry has been crippled for too long by lack of money, yet her technicians and actors are among the best in the world. However, at the time of writing, British money is being used to make a number of Hollywood films, so the omens seem more favourable, especially as more truly British films are at last being produced again.

Meanwhile, millions around the world still go to the movies, and it is hard to believe that there will come a time when they will cease to do so, even if most homes have their own cinema.

Perhaps Al Jolson was right: "You ain't heard (or seen) nothin' yet."

**From the Warner Bros' "Jazz Singer" (above) to the 20th Century Fox "The Empire Strikes Back" (below) — great strides have been made in the technique of adding multiple sound to film.**

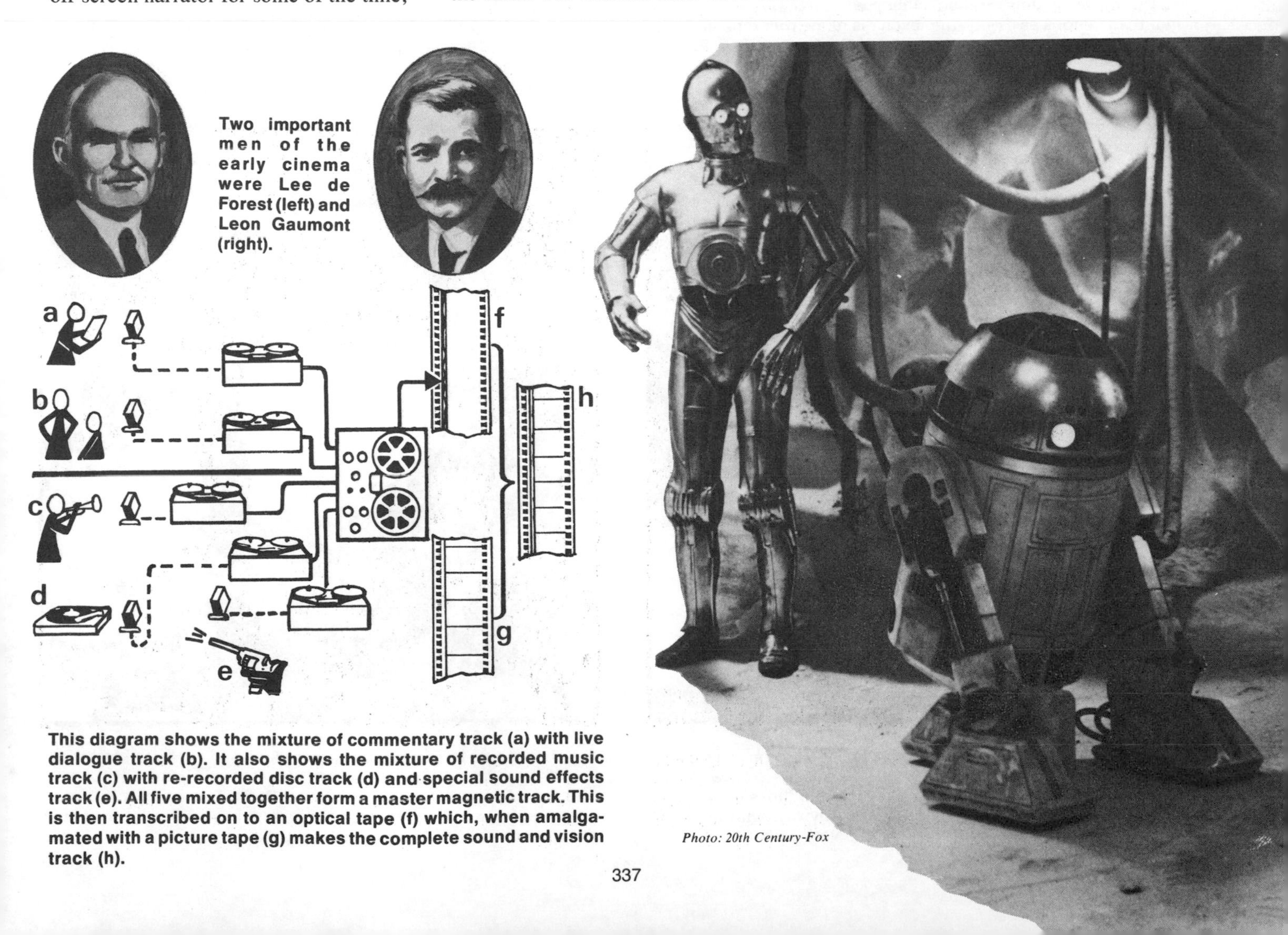


**Two important men of the early cinema were Lee de Forest (left) and Leon Gaumont (right).**

**This diagram shows the mixture of commentary track (a) with live dialogue track (b). It also shows the mixture of recorded music track (c) with re-recorded disc track (d) and special sound effects track (e). All five mixed together form a master magnetic track. This is then transcribed on to an optical tape (f) which, when amalgamated with a picture tape (g) makes the complete sound and vision track (h).**

*Photo: 20th Century-Fox*

# Which famous Poet

1. During his lifetime, Francois Villon was infamous as a criminal rather than famous as a poet, and even his name was variable. Little is known of his birth, except that it probably took place in Paris in 1431, and almost nothing is known of his parents, except that they were very poor. His own surname was either Montcorbier or de Logos and the name Villon he took from his benefactor.

The Paris in which Villon grew up was bleak and often frightening. Robbers were everywhere and famine, plague and wolves were constant companions. Many did not survive. Villon managed to do so but his view of life must have been unhappily coloured.

2. In one respect, however, Villon was lucky. Early on in his life he acquired a benefactor, Guillaume de Villon, a priest — from whom he took his name. He was probably a relative, but in those days, adoption of children by priests was common. Anyway, with his help, Francois became a student of the arts at a very early age.

3. In 1449, he became a Bachelor of Arts, and in 1452 a Master. He was now spending most of his time with students in the city taverns. And, in spite of everything, he loved Paris. The squalor in a way appealed to him. When he was not gambling or drinking, he would spend hours wandering around the streets.

# was a common thief?

4. Then, in 1455, he was involved in a street fight and a priest was killed. Villon fled. He went to a barber-surgeon who dressed his wounds. But he was a wanted man and from that time seems always to have been in trouble with the law.

5. In fact, he was banished. He was lucky again, however, as in 1456, for some reason, he was pardoned. As a result he was allowed to return to Paris. Almost straight away he was in trouble again, being involved in more street fights. Then he began to associate with bands of known thieves. Nonetheless, he also composed poems — particularly the *Petit Testament.*

6. He robbed a chapel and was again banished. Perhaps not wishing to return to Paris this time, he became a wanderer. But in trouble again he was sent to prison and, later, was sentenced to death. He escaped only by an amnesty of Louis XI.

7. Around this time, Villon wrote the work for which he is famous — the *Grand Testament.* His poetry is witty and sensitive and remarkable when his life is considered. For he was again condemned to death and again banished instead. He then fades from history. He is thought to have died about 1485. Today he is still accounted one of the great world poets.

# What is an Etching?

**IN the field of the visual arts, the poor relative to all of them seems to be the art of etching. Oil paintings and water-colours fill room after room in our museums, but etchings generally occupy only a small corner, a rather surprising state of affairs when one considers that most of the world's great painters have produced between them a large body of work in this highly specialized field.**

This is possibly because etchings lack colour, and therefore lack an immediate appeal to the eye. Visually, they look like highly detailed drawings, which, in a sense, they are, though the final result is produced by a printing process.

The word etching comes from an old German word, *etzen,* meaning to eat. An etching, simply put, is made by drawing lines on a piece of metal which is afterwards placed in an acid which eats into the lines made on the metal by the artist. When this process has been completed ink is put on to the lines and a piece of paper is pressed down on it, and in this way a print is produced. This print, however, is something much more than the final end product of a mere mechanical process, which the foregoing might imply.

First, and most important, is the work of the artist, who starts off with nothing more than a polished copper plate, much in the same way an artist starts off with only a blank canvas. This copper plate is coated with a special substance, made chiefly of wax, which will resist acid. This substance is called 'ground'. On the wax, the artist lightly traces his picture. He then goes over it again, using a special needle, until the picture outlined has been freed from the rest of the wax surface. This, in itself, is a highly skilled process. But even so, the artist has only completed the first stage of his work.

In his finished picture, the artist obviously does not want all the lines of his drawing to be of the same thickness, and

**Above: 'Virgin and Child'. Left: 'Four Horsemen of the Apocalypse'. Both fine examples of the skill of Albrecht Durer.**

the only way to stop this happening is by letting the acid work on some lines longer than the others. To achieve this, he has to immerse the plate in the acid for it to make its initial bite in the metal. The plate is then removed, and the lines which the artist wishes to print out more lightly are covered with an acid resistant varnish. The plate is immersed again to allow the acid to continue eating into the remaining exposed lines, making them deeper and heavier, so that they will print heavier lines. This process, known as 'stopping out', is continued until the artist has achieved the range of tones he desires.

The number of satisfactory prints which can be taken off an etched plate varies according to the hardness of the metal and the depth to which the lines have been made on an etching. On the very early engravings, which were made of iron, only fifty or so good prints could be struck off. On a copper plate, the fine lines do not begin to disappear until after 200 to 300 prints have been made.

The oldest known etching to which an approximate date can be given, was made in Germany about 1505. This was a portrait done by Daniel Hopfer, one of a family of armourers who worked in Augsberg. The first actually dated etching was made in 1513, and was the work of a Swiss goldsmith named Urs Graf.

**Right: Rembrandt's 'The Beggars' shows how the artist found the technique of dry-point useful for light and shade effects. Below: A Jacques Callot etching of a gypsy.**

Within two years of that date the great engraver Albrecht Durer of Nuremberg was producing his first etchings, but as these were done on iron, which does not lend itself to delicate work, Durer eventually gave up etching for engraving, an art in which he reigns supreme. Engraving is a process not dissimilar to etching, except that the lines are incised with a tool and not bitten into the metal with acid. The technique of engraving is more suitable for formal designs and draughtsmanship.

The true birth of etching as a completely successful art form began in Holland, first with Anthony Van Dyck, whose work in this field is distinguished by its clear draughtsmanship, and then by that great master of the form, Rembrandt, whose etchings have never been surpassed. Nothing seemed beyond him in the way of subject matter.

Scenes from the Old and New Testaments, portraits, still life and landscapes all reveal his complete mastery of the art of etching. Among his works are a number of revealing self-portraits, which he etched, while studying himself in the mirror.

Rembrandt was also the first one to use the 'dry point' technique, in which the subject is drawn with a dry point, or needle on an untreated copper plate, which, when printed, produces a thin and delicate line. Besides making marks on the plate with a sharp needle, it is possible to make other sorts of marks, either by using a spiky wheel or a wheel with a filed surface across the plate, or by laying a piece of sandpaper on the plate and running it through the press. The resultant roughness on the plate will either print weakly or strongly, according to the amount of ink it holds.

Although there were a number of other well-executed etchings being produced by artists other than Rembrandt during the 17th century, few achieved any stature as an engraver. One of the rare exceptions was Jacques Callot, whose etchings contained hundreds of elegantly drawn tiny figures. A fast and prolific worker, he left behind him more than

1,400 plates when he died in 1635. Besides his etchings of gypsies and beggars, he recorded in vivid detail the horrors of the Thirty Years War.

The work of these pioneers did not go unnoticed by artists in other countries, and by the 18th century, most artists of any importance had turned their hand to this difficult art. In France, Watteau, Boucher and Fragonard, all practised etching. In Italy there was Tiepolo, and his contemporary Canaletto. The third great Italian etcher of that century was Piranesi, whose work dealt mostly with archaeological subjects.

By the 19th century, Spain had its Francisco Goya, but with the exception of his work comparatively little of significance was produced during the first half of that century. The latter half of the century was quite a different matter, seeing, as it did, a tremendous revival of etching in England.

**Two examples of the work of one of Dickens' most successful illustrators, George Cruickshank.**

The previous century had seen in England a number of artists turning to the art of etching with considerable success. The Norwich artists, John Sell Cotman and John Crome, had produced a number of notable etchings, as had Turner and Samuel Palmer, two of our most famous landscape painters. But apart from this handful of artists, and a few other of lesser note, nothing of great importance was produced, and etching seemed to fall somewhat out of favour, both with artists and the public.

Its rebirth during the second half of the 19th century was due mainly to the work of three men, James McNeill Whistler, an American by birth who spent a part of his life in England, Sir Francis Seymour Haden, and the French-born Alphonse Legros, who preferred to spend most of his life in London.

In their wake came more artists who had already made a considerable reputation for themselves as painters, and whose work was to stretch into the 20th century. Among them we must number Walter Richard Sickert, Augustus John, and Frank Brangwyn. Their work helped to popularize etching to such an extent that etchings began to be used for book illustrations. The most famous of these were those done by George Cruikshank, who illustrated the books of Daniel Defoe, Oliver Goldsmith, Sir Walter Scott and Charles Dickens, whose work can be seen at its best in *Oliver Twist*, especially in his haunting etching of Fagin in the Condemned Cell.

**Right: A typical example of the type of etching that was produced by artists in the 1930's.**

**Above: A scene on the banks of the Seine which not only is a fine engraving but also shows the market where many engravings can be purchased quite cheaply.**

# How is a Ballet produced?

Until the middle of the 20th century, ballets tended to be passed on by teacher to student from memory. Dance notation — the ballet equivalent of written music — dates from the 15th century, but not until Joan and Rudolph Benesh devised their system of notation in the 1950s did it become standard practice to record new ballets on paper. The Benesh system, adopted by the Royal Ballet in London in 1955 to record its ballets, employs a five-line stave which represents the human figure. The bottom line represents the floor and the top line the top of the head. The middle line passes through the waist and the remaining two, through the shoulders and knees.

THE lights go down and the conductor enters the orchestra pit to loud applause. The excited hum of conversation from the packed audience dies away and, moments later, the great curtains part. The new ballet has begun . . .

Everything on stage is grace and perfection, which is what the audience expects. But how has this perfection been achieved?

It has been reached by sheer hard work and great skill, above all by the skill of the ballet's "composer", the choreographer. It is he or she who has arranged the steps the dancers are performing and has trained, encouraged, criticised and praised them over many weeks of rehearsals. The choreographer is ballet's equivalent of a playwright, a poet or a composer of music. He is a *creator.*

The choreographer creates a ballet because he wants to put an idea across, or simply because his company needs a new one. He may decide on an 'abstract' ballet, solely concerned with movement and groupings; he may have a basic theme, like love, hate or happiness, and create a ballet without a story but reflecting a mood; he may tell a story in dance.

The choreographer may also create a ballet for a star ballerina for whom he has often created roles.

When the choreographer has decided on his subject, he thinks of the right music for it. If there is time — and there usually isn't! — he may ask a composer to write music specially for the new ballet. But, probably, he will choose music, ancient or modern, that suits his ideas.

## THE SHORTHAND THAT DESCRIBES A BALLET

IN dance notation, the recording is made as seen from behind the dancer's back for ease of reading, with the positions of the hands, feet and body plotted on the stave. A dancer's foot on the floor can be flat, demi-pointe (see pic 3) or full pointe (see photograph) and the foot sign is placed beneath the ground line, through it or above it, respectively. Curved lines indicate movements. Jumps are also shown by curved lines but beneath the stave; and the dancer's position on stage and the direction she faces are indicated by an arrow, the head of which is a dot.

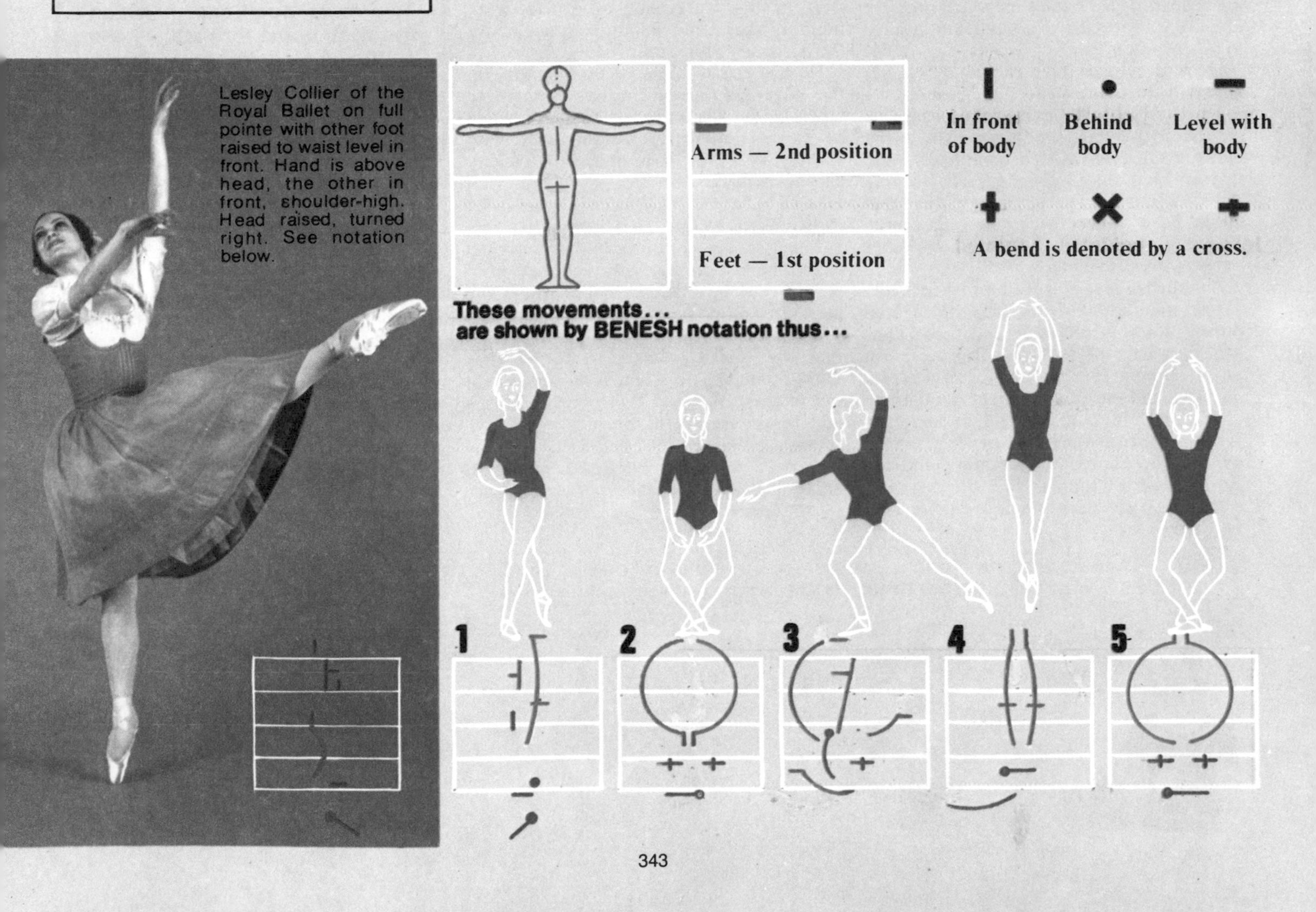


Lesley Collier of the Royal Ballet on full pointe with other foot raised to waist level in front. Hand is above head, the other in front, shoulder-high. Head raised, turned right. See notation below.

## CLASSICAL BALLET

Ballet as we know it was born in France 300 years ago, which is why ballet terms are in French. The art of the ballet dancer demands that every part of the body comes into play so that maximum expression and grace of form is achieved.

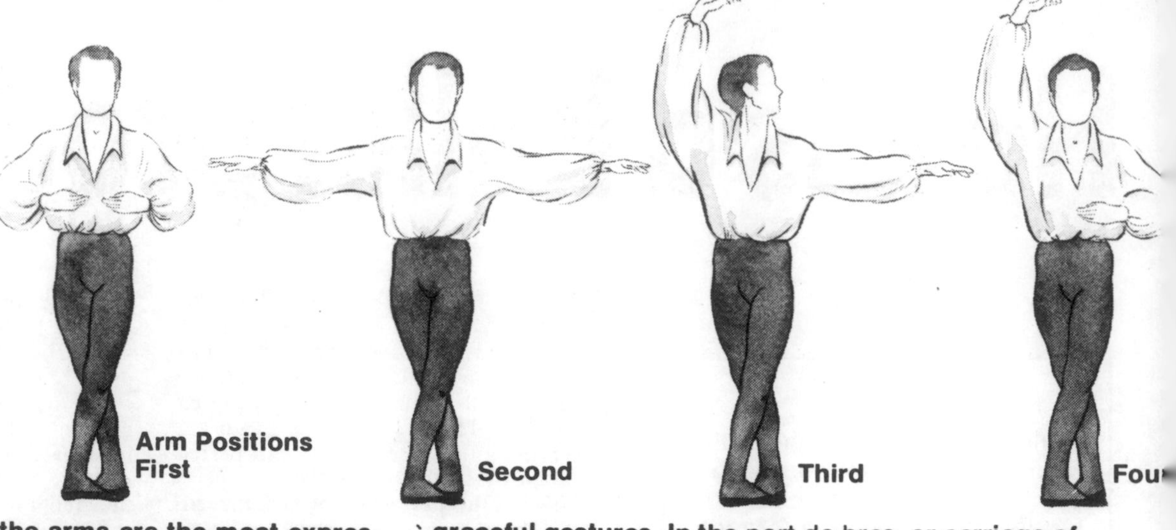


**Apart from the face, the arms are the most expressive part of the body for a ballet dancer and great dancers take years to perfect their arm movements. There are seven positions of the arms which help to express a wide range of emotions by means of graceful gestures. In the** port de bras, **or carriage of the arms, the hands are very important and can be held rather stiffly or loosely depending on which school of ballet one favours.**

Now he can get down to work. But the work must be fitted into his company's already busy schedule. For ballet dancers, whether beginners or super-stars, never stop working. There is always their workout early each morning which begins at the barre, a horizontal wooden pole in a ballet studio. That is followed by other exercises which develop the dancers' athleticism, keeping their bodies tuned to perfection so that any step, however difficult, can be mastered and hours of dancing can be sustained.

Another problem for the choreographer is that many of his dancers will be attending rehearsals for ballets on which they are already working. So exact timetables have to be drawn up.

He will by now have chosen a designer who will create the scenery and costumes.

Now rehearsals have truly begun. A pianist is playing the music which the dancers must all absorb completely, and dancers and choreographer are working hard together. The choreographer will either be a dancer or an ex-dancer and, naturally, must be able to show other dancers what is wanted.

A ballet rehearsal can't be rushed. Only a few minutes of dance may be created during a whole morning, and those minutes may later be scrapped. But there can be no stopping. After all, the weeks are going by and the opening night is looming.

The dancers may find themselves achieving effects they have never managed before; the choreographer may suddenly be inspired by one of his dancers and create a totally new effect; a dancer may suggest a movement or a series of ideas. For ballet is teamwork. During rehearsals, the team, inspired by the choreographer's leadership, strives to achieve a performance which will do justice to its combined talents.

The designer is part of the team and he attends as many rehearsals as he can. It is vital that he does. His job began the moment he was chosen by the choreographer.

He began by building models of the two scenes of the ballet, an outdoors and an indoors one. Once they had been accepted by the choreographer, it was time for the staff in the workshops to get to work building them and painting them, under the designer's close supervision.

He has had to allow plenty of room on the stage for the dancing, as opposed to when he designs a play or an opera, when he can sometimes crowd the stage with scenery. In a play or an opera, the scenery can be realistic, but because of that vital area in ballet for the dancers, it cannot be truly realistic.

Likewise, the costumes he has designed cannot be true to life. Only a suggestion of realism can be made in ballet where the costumes must be suitable for dancing. They must be comfortable but secure as they are under constant strain. So they must be tough and ready for oceans of sweat. Dancers sweat a lot, inevitably. To add to the designer's problems, the costumes must always look perfect!

As you can see, the designer, as well as creating beauty, must be a very practical person indeed.

**Foot Positions**

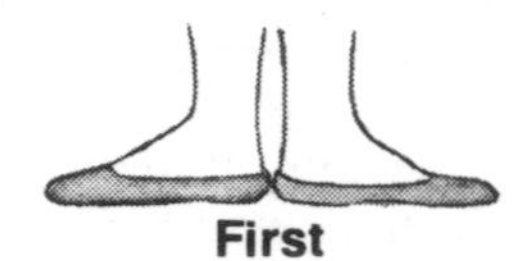


**Sixth and seventh foot positions**

**Two extra positions in which the feet point forward — the sixth and seventh — were created by the famous Russian dancer and choreographer, Serge Lifar, who was ballet master at the Paris Opera in the 1950s and early 1960s. These two positions are not, however, generally used.**

Naturally, the choreographer will be in close touch with the conductor of the work. And the conductor must know the new ballet as well as the dancers do. He must be an expert on ballet for a conductor can make or mar a performance, completely understanding his dancers' needs, or playing too fast for them.

At last, the different components are put together for the first "stage-call", perhaps two days before the dress rehearsal.

**MIME** These are some mime gestures used in classical ballets, such as 'Swan Lake', to tell the story clearly and simply.

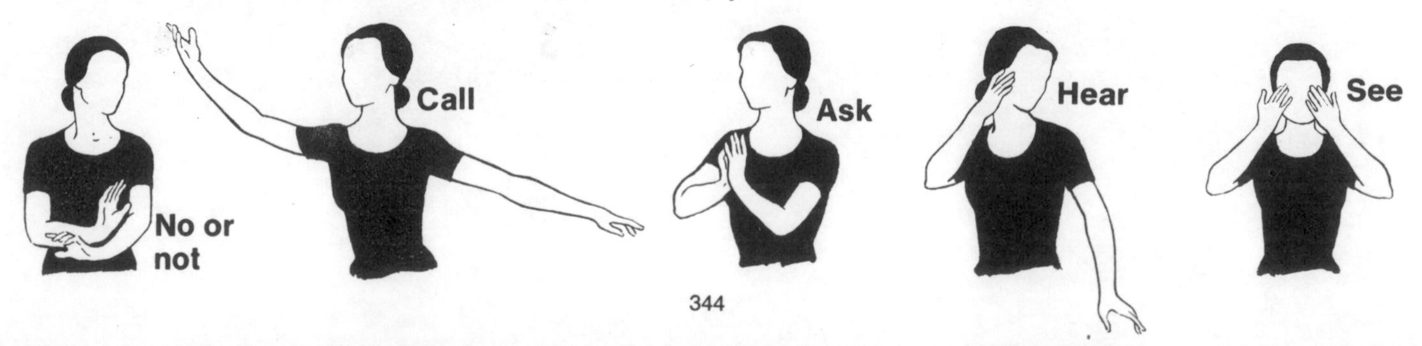

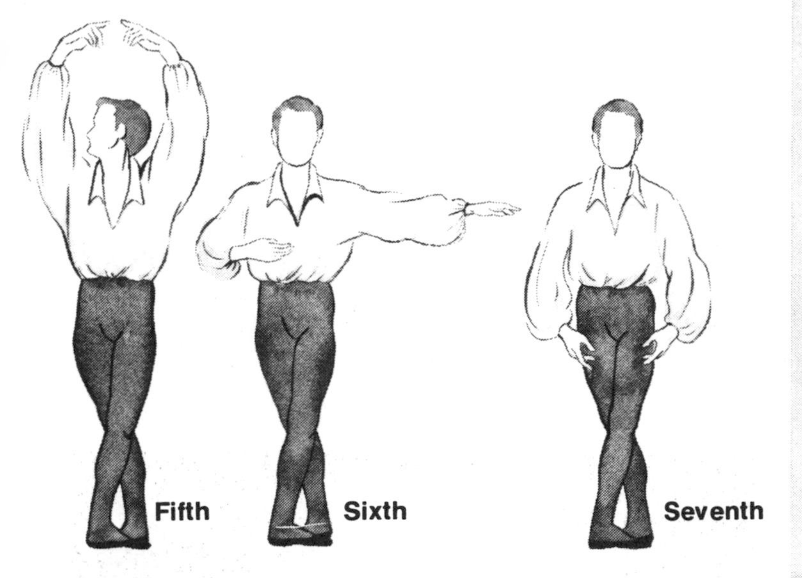


**By 1820, dancing on POINTES had been introduced.**

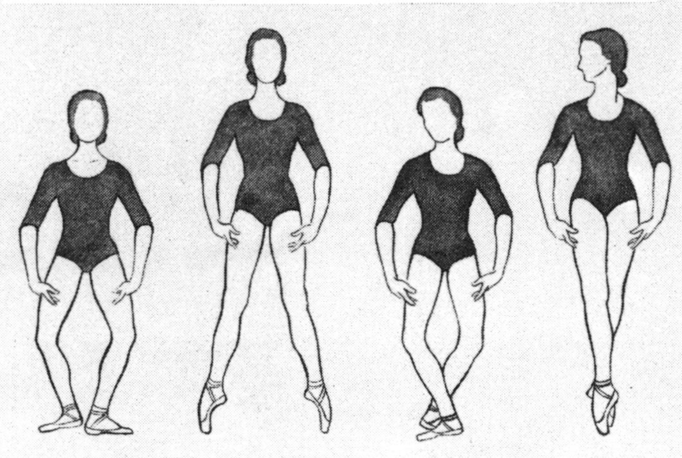

The five positions of the feet (shown below), fundamental to all classical ballet, are the starting and finishing points for all movements such as the *jeté* (a jump in which the weight is transferred from one foot to the other), the *entrechat* (a jump starting and ending in the fifth position during which the feet are rapidly crossed) or the *pirouette* (a turn on one foot). In all five positions, the feet are turned outwards.

In the 1820s, no special pointe shoes existed, so ballerinas padded their shoes with cotton wool and darned the toes to stop them sliding on the floor. But they could not stay up on their pointes for very long. By the 1860s, shoes were blocked and stiffened with glue to give strength and support. Selection of good ballet shoes is important if dancers are not to damage their feet.

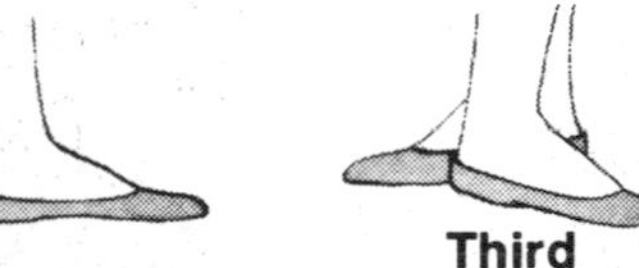

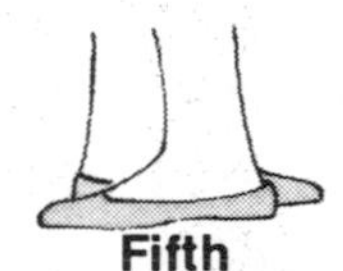

**Second** **Third** **Fourth** **Fifth**

Plenty can go wrong at the stage-call. The cast may be startled by parts of the music heard played by an orchestra for the first time. Several costumes may have to be scrapped. One of the doors on the set may need altering. Someone may be injured and have to be replaced at short notice.

There will also be a lengthy lighting rehearsal. Lighting has always been important in the theatre and now, when so much can be done using modern methods, there is a specialist lighting designer to supervise it.

At the dress rehearsal, the ballet is performed completely or, if it is a short one, it will be run through twice, with the theatre full of experts taking notes.

And now the company awaits the first performance, which gives meaning to all their work. For, only on stage before a live audience can ballet live, and until that great moment comes, no one can be certain if success or failure will be the result.

Right up to the last moment before curtain up, with the audience pouring excitedly into the theatre, there are small things to be done, like adjusting a costume or rearranging something on stage.

The tension is mounting backstage, not the tension of panic, but of highly-professional performers whose reputations are at stake and who are determined to do their very best.

As for the choreographer, his moment of destiny has come. He can only wish his cast luck and await his fate, which is now in their hands.

In the audience are the ballet critics who will be writing about the new work for their newspapers. Right or wrong, they can influence opinion, but so can the regular ballet-goers. If they like the work, they will come again — and again — and they will tell their friends.

Tonight, though, there is no doubt about it. The new ballet is a triumph, with wild cheers at the end and flowers thrown on to the stage by the excited fans. Even the critics are excited, and the choreographer gets a great ovation when he appears with his dancers. Another chapter of ballet history has been made and tomorrow morning the box office will be beseiged. Meanwhile, the dancers will be hard at work, as usual . . .

## Milestones in Ballet

**1661.** The Académie Royale de la Danse founded by King Louis XIV of France — the source of modern ballet.

**1669.** The Paris Opéra founded. It gives its first performance, an opera-ballet, in 1671.

**1738.** The Imperial Ballet School founded in St. Petersburg (now Leningrad). It is the ancestor of the great Kirov Ballet and its famous school.

**1841.** *Giselle,* the greatest Romantic ballet, produced in Paris.

**1877.** *Swan Lake* a failure, but it succeeds in 1895.

**1890.** *The Sleeping Beauty* first produced.

**1909.** The Ballets Russes (Russian Ballet), masterminded by Serge Diaghilev, bursts on Paris, with the dancers Nijinsky, Pavlova and Karsavina and the great choreographer Fokine.

**1931.** Ninette de Valois' Vic-Wells Ballet, ancestor of the Royal Ballet, first performs at Sadler's Wells.

**1935.** American Ballet, later New York City Ballet, founded by George Balanchine. Margot Fonteyn becomes a prima ballerina.

**1961**. Rudolf Nureyev leaves to go to the West from the Kirov Ballet.

**1978.** 80th birthday of Dame Marie Rambert, who founded the Ballet Rambert in 1926.

# Who was Ballet's

1. *Petrouchka* is a highly dramatic, tragic and imaginative ballet about three puppets who are brought to life by the evil genius of their manipulator. One of them, Petrouchka, is also destroyed — his spirit, however, lingering on to shower down curses. It is said to have been the favourite ballet of the great tragic and dramatic Russian dancer, Vaslav Nijinsky and, watching it, one is not surprised.

2. For there are similarities between the 'life' of Petrouchka and the life of Nijinsky. Nijinsky was born in 1890, into a dancing family. From an early age, he travelled with them on their tours throughout Russia and, even as a child, seems always to have been lonely and withdrawn. He had, however, an inborn dancing ability and this soon earned him a place at the Imperial Dancing School, Moscow.

3. Nijinsky did not make friends easily and had difficulty expressing himself except through dancing. When old enough, he joined the Mariinsky Theatre Ballet. His first major performance was in a *pas de huit* incorporated into Mozart's opera, "Don Giovanni". He was a sensation. But, a couple of years later, when still only 18, he was noticed by the great Diaghilev.

4. Diaghilev himself was an extraordinary man. He could not dance, knew nothing at all about dance notation and had no musical talents. But he had enormous enthusiasm, appreciated true artistry when he saw or heard it and could conceive ideas endlessly for later development by others. He saw Nijinsky and at once set about persuading him to leave the Mariinsky Ballet. For he had plans.

# Tragic genius?

5. In 1909, Diaghilev formed a ballet company, the Ballet Russe and, with Nijinsky as its principal male dancer, presented ballets in Paris and later on in other great cities. The productions were superb at all levels but it was Nijinsky whose artistry took Paris by storm. He gave magic to his roles — his gods were divine and his spirits as light and ethereal as air. He made reality and fantasy one.

6. It was Diaghilev, too, who urged Nijinsky to become a choreographer. His first ballet from this point of view was *L'Après-midi d'un Faune,* with music by Debussy. He was assisted by others who had done similar work before. But the resulting originality in style and treatment was pure Nijinsky. He had difficulty, though, in explaining his ideas in words, he had to use the magic of dance.

7. His technique in this ballet created a new style of dancing which, since then, has been much followed. It is unlike true classical ballet, having different movements and less regularity. When Nijinsky danced the role of the faun in the production at the Théâtre du Châtelet, Paris, in May, 1912, it was a huge success. He was persuaded by Diaghilev to write more unusual, exotic ballets.

8. Then, in 1913, Nijinsky married a Hungarian girl, Romola de Pulszky and, in 1914, she gave birth to their first child, a girl, Kyra. In 1920, Tamara, their second daughter was born. Nijinsky was put in charge of an American tour but afterwards — something snapped and he went insane. He never became completely normal again and, in 1950, he died.

# How is an Orchestra arranged?

**ORCHESTRA. In the Ancient Greek amphitheatre, the orchestra (which literally means 'the dancing place') was the space in front of the stage, occupied by the chorus. When opera came into being during the Renaissance, the term was applied to the space in front of the stage occupied by the musicians, and thus subsequently to an assembly of musicians.**

**AN orchestra is a group of musicians, playing instruments of different types and consisting of almost *any* number of people.**

The Ancient Egyptians, of between 5,000 and 4,000 B.C., probably had orchestras of a sort, as they certainly had primitive stringed instruments and drums which were used by musicians playing together. However, they had no means of writing down their music, so it must have been mere improvisation, used as an accompaniment to dancing or story-telling.

The Ancient Greek musicians, though, did have scales and a form of musical notation. They definitely produced tunes, by musicians playing together, and so had a type of orchestra more like the ones we know today.

And in 16th century England there were orchestras even more on a par with modern ones.

The first operas, performed in 17th-century Italy, had singers accompanied by small orchestras of mixed instruments — though probably half were viols, the ancestors of modern stringed instruments.

By the 18th century there were a number of instruments that could be used by a composer in his orchestra. And this growing choice brought about the development of the symphony.

Originally, the word 'symphony' — which actually means 'a sounding together' — was used to describe an overture, or introduction particularly to an opera, or to a part for instruments which introduced or came between verses in a choral work. These somewhat old-fashioned meanings are still occasionally used.

A modern symphony, however, is usually a composition consisting of a number of movements or sections, usually four or three. These sections are often described as 'allegro' (in brisk time — from the Italian word meaning 'lively'), as 'slow', and as 'scherzo' (vigorous and light — from the Italian word meaning 'jest').

The father of the modern symphony was the Austrian composer, Joseph Haydn (1732-1809). During his lifetime he wrote no fewer than 104 symphonies.

There are several types of modern orchestras. 'Symphony' orchestras are large enough to play symphonies (although they do play other types of music, as well); 'chamber' orchestras are small enough for the musicians to be seated in a large chamber or room in a big house (where they were used originally); 'theatre' orchestras, with around 60 players, are used to accompany musical comedies or ballets; 'jazz' orchestras play jazz.

'Band' is the word used sometimes instead of orchestra but, technically, a band is the name for a section of an orchestra — for example the wind section.

There are basically three sections of an orchestra — string, wind and percussion.

Included in the string section are instruments played usually by drawing a bow across strings. These are the violin, the viola, the cello (violoncello) and the double bass. Also in the string section is the harp, which is played by plucking the strings with the fingers.

Included in the wind section are the woodwind instruments. These are the flutes (the smaller, higher-pitched being the piccolo), the oboes (the longer, lower-

Sir Colin Davis, conducting the BBC Symphony Orchestra at the Royal Albert Hall, during a Henry Wood Promenade Concert.

HAYDN

## HAYDN AND THE CLASSICAL ORCHESTRA

The great Austrian composer, Joseph Haydn (1732-1809), has been called the Father of the Symphony. He composed 104 symphonies and was certainly the founder of the symphony orchestra as we know it today. His basic orchestra is pictured below, but during his career he added two timpani (kettle drums) and two trumpets. His young contemporary, Mozart, added clarinets, giving extra 'colour' to the woodwinds, and trombones to highlight a key moment in his opera *The Magic Flute.* Their successor Beethoven inherited their ideas, but in his last symphony, the Ninth, he added cymbals, triangle and bass drum.

MOZART

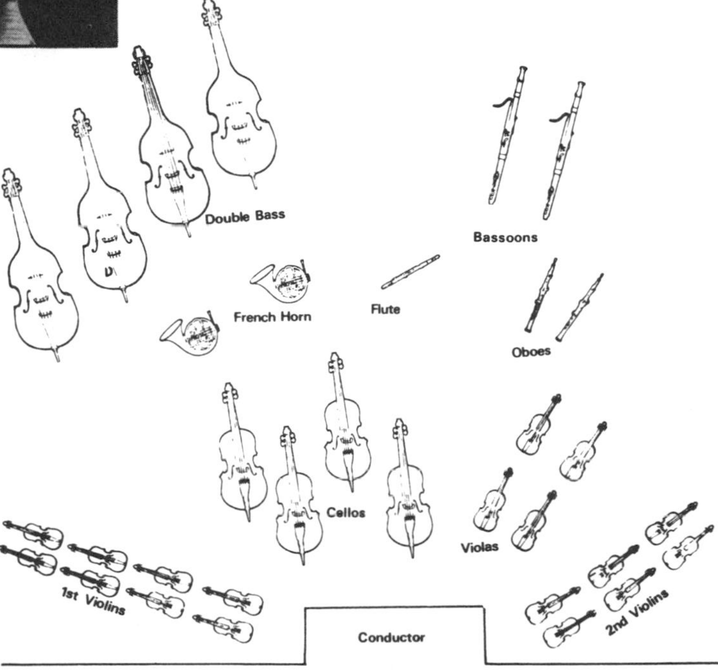

BEETHOVEN

## THE WAGNERIAN ORCHESTRA

WAGNER

Many of the composers who came after Beethoven wanted bigger and bigger effects. It was the Romantic era in the arts and the symphony orchestra had to expand to meet some composers' needs. The French composer Berlioz actually dreamt of having 242 strings and 30 grand pianos! The great orchestral master of the mid-19th century was the German Richard Wagner (1813-83). He sometimes demanded bigger forces than those shown on the right, which is a typical symphony orchestra.

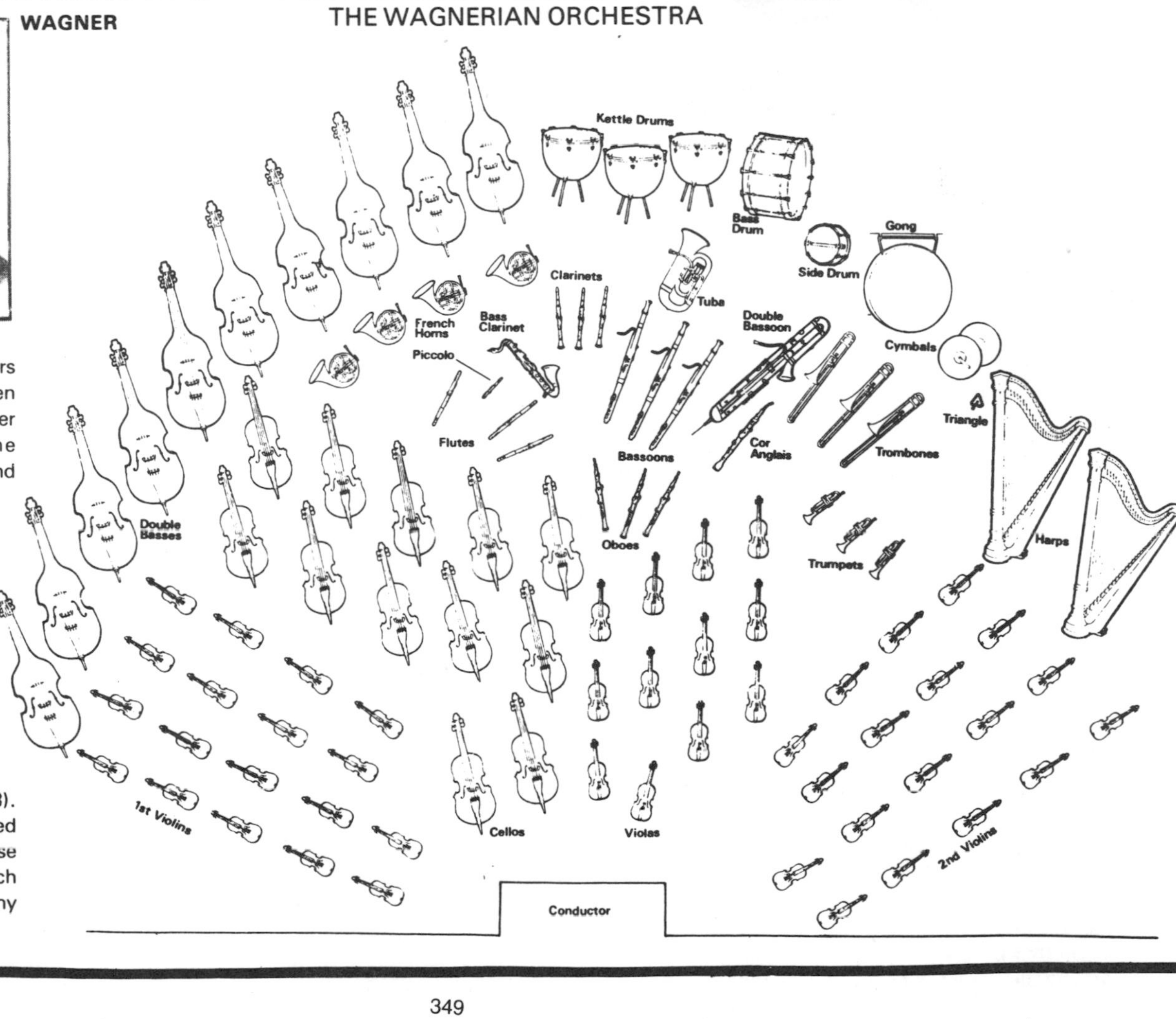

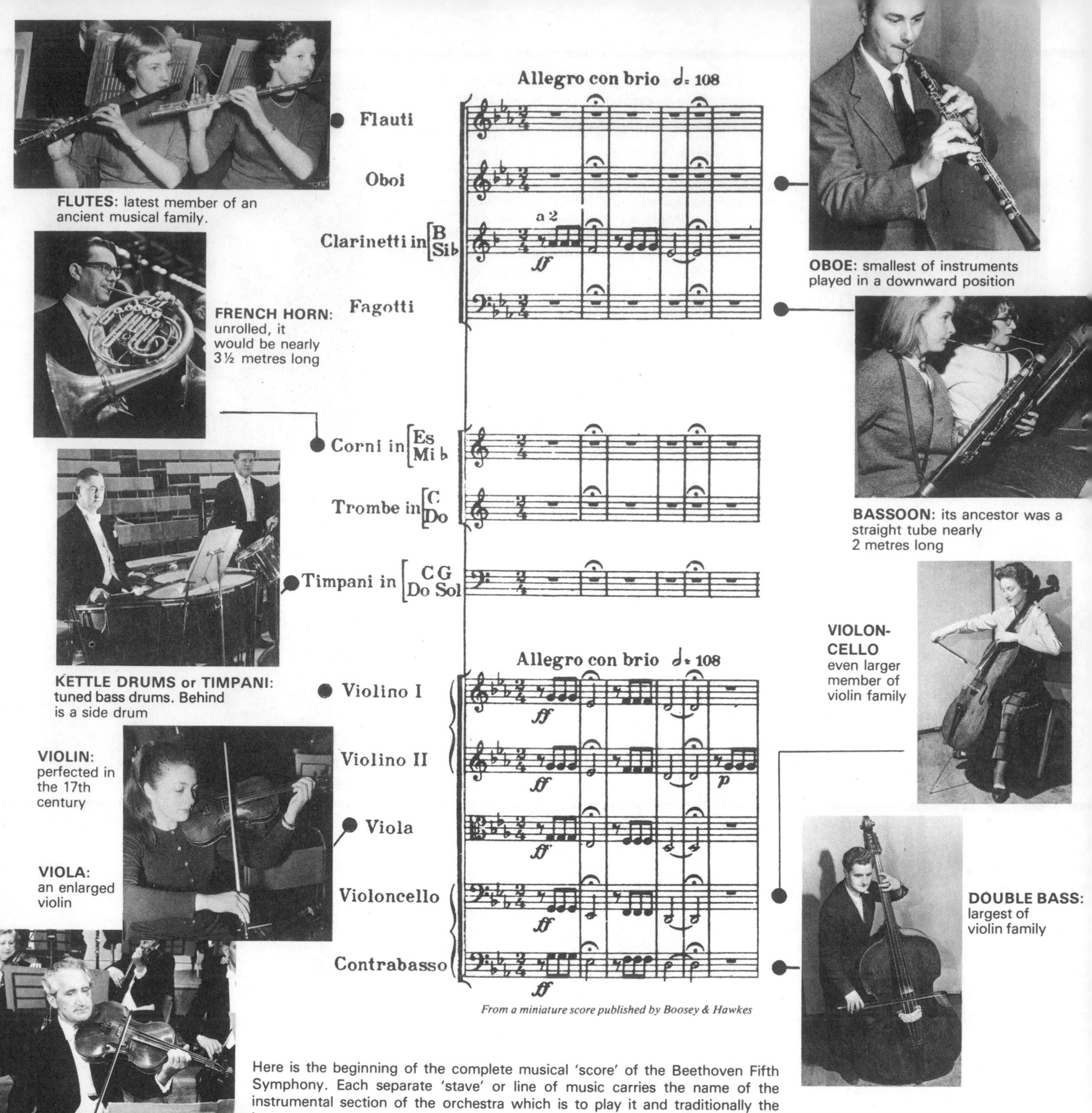


**FLUTES:** latest member of an ancient musical family.

**FRENCH HORN:** unrolled, it would be nearly 3½ metres long

**KETTLE DRUMS or TIMPANI:** tuned bass drums. Behind is a side drum

**VIOLIN:** perfected in the 17th century

**VIOLA:** an enlarged violin

**OBOE:** smallest of instruments played in a downward position

**BASSOON:** its ancestor was a straight tube nearly 2 metres long

**VIOLON-CELLO** even larger member of violin family

**DOUBLE BASS:** largest of violin family

*From a miniature score published by Boosey & Hawkes*

Here is the beginning of the complete musical 'score' of the Beethoven Fifth Symphony. Each separate 'stave' or line of music carries the name of the instrumental section of the orchestra which is to play it and traditionally the instruments are named in Italian — fagotti for bassoons, and so on. The conductor has a complete score; sections of the orchestra are supplied only with their respective parts. But the conductor often works entirely from memory and soloists in a concerto always do.

pitched being the cor anglais), the clarinet and the bassoon (the larger, lower-pitched being the double bassoon). All but the flutes are 'reed' instruments, where the sound is produced by blowing through a reed.

Also in the wind section are the brass instruments. These are the trumpet, the horn, the trombone, the cornet and the tuba. Modern orchestras often have more brass instruments than old orchestras.

Included in the percussion section are instruments that are struck in some way. These are the gong, the cymbals, the triangle, the tambourine, the kettledrum (plural Italian — timpani) and side drum.

Another group is keyboard instruments. Among these are the piano, the xylophone, the glockenspiel, the celeste, the vibraphone and the organ.

Although perhaps the most important of all musical instruments and sometimes used in small orchestras, the piano is rarely used in symphony orchestras.

Orchestras are usually arranged in a large semi-circle, facing the conductor on his podium. The most widely used arrangement is with the strings at the front; behind them, the woodwind; behind them, the brass; and behind them, the percussion. If a conductor so wishes, of course, he can vary this arrangement any way he pleases. Constant use over the years, however, has found it a highly successful arrangement.

In Britain the principal violinist is known as the 'leader' of the Orchestra. He is the players' link with the conductor and it is his job to play any solo violin passages that may occur in a piece. Of course, this does not include those parts which are usually played in a violin concerto by a guest violinist. Additionally, the leader would take over from the conductor in the event of the conductor being taken ill during a performance.

Many people insist that the quality of an orchestra is largely dependent on the leader's ability as a co-ordinator.

In the United States of America, the leader is known as the 'concertmaster' because the word 'leader' in America, also means conductor. In France the name for the leader is 'chef d'attaque' and in Germany, it is 'konzertmeister'.

# Why is a Conductor needed for an Orchestra?

Colin Davis conducts the BBC Symphony Orchestra at a last night of the 'Proms' in the Royal Albert Hall, London.

**TO a storm of applause the conductor comes on to the platform. He mounts the podium, shakes hands with the leader of the orchestra and raises his baton. A second later, the concert begins . . .**

Just how important, though, is this god-like figure, who appears to be welding numerous men and women into one mighty instrument? Is he needed at all? After all, there were no conductors in the modern sense two centuries ago. And a newcomer to the concert hall will note that the players do not seem to be taking all that much notice of the god in front of them.

The same newcomer may know some orchestral musicians who can be very rude about conductors. A well-known drama critic once asked a friend of his who had conducted at that afternoon's concert. The friend, who had played the oboe in it, said: "Sorry! I forgot to notice."

On the other hand there are many, especially those who watch concerts on TV, who believe that the conductor does everything. They gaze in awe at his gymnastics, the sweat on his brow, his facial expressions and forget that it is the players who are actually making the music.

So is the conductor needed?

The answer must be yes. True, the Russians, soon after their revolution in 1917, (in 1922, in fact) tried doing away with the conductor, but went back to one; and the Americans did the same. It proved one thing. Good musicians can play better without a conductor than with a *bad* one.

As in many walks of life, someone has to lead, to make decisions. It helps, of course, if you are a great conductor revered by orchestras and audiences alike: Herbert von Karajan, Sir Georg Solti, Carlo Maria Giulini and others today, and giants like Toscanini and Sir Thomas Beecham in the past. But there are plenty of very fine conductors who are first rate professionals. What are their responsibilities and qualifications?

The conductor must be a true musician who knows everything about every instrument in the orchestra, even though he is not expected to be able to play them all. But he must know how they are played and what their technical problems are. He must be able to learn

Conductors of today use movements of the baton and of the free hand to instruct the orchestra (a) to conclude gently and delicately, (b) to play softly, (c) to play more vigorously and (d) to play with particular feeling. At rehearsal, a good conductor can establish his particular interpretation of a work and this should give his individuality to the performance, when he will appear (top right) to be in complete control.

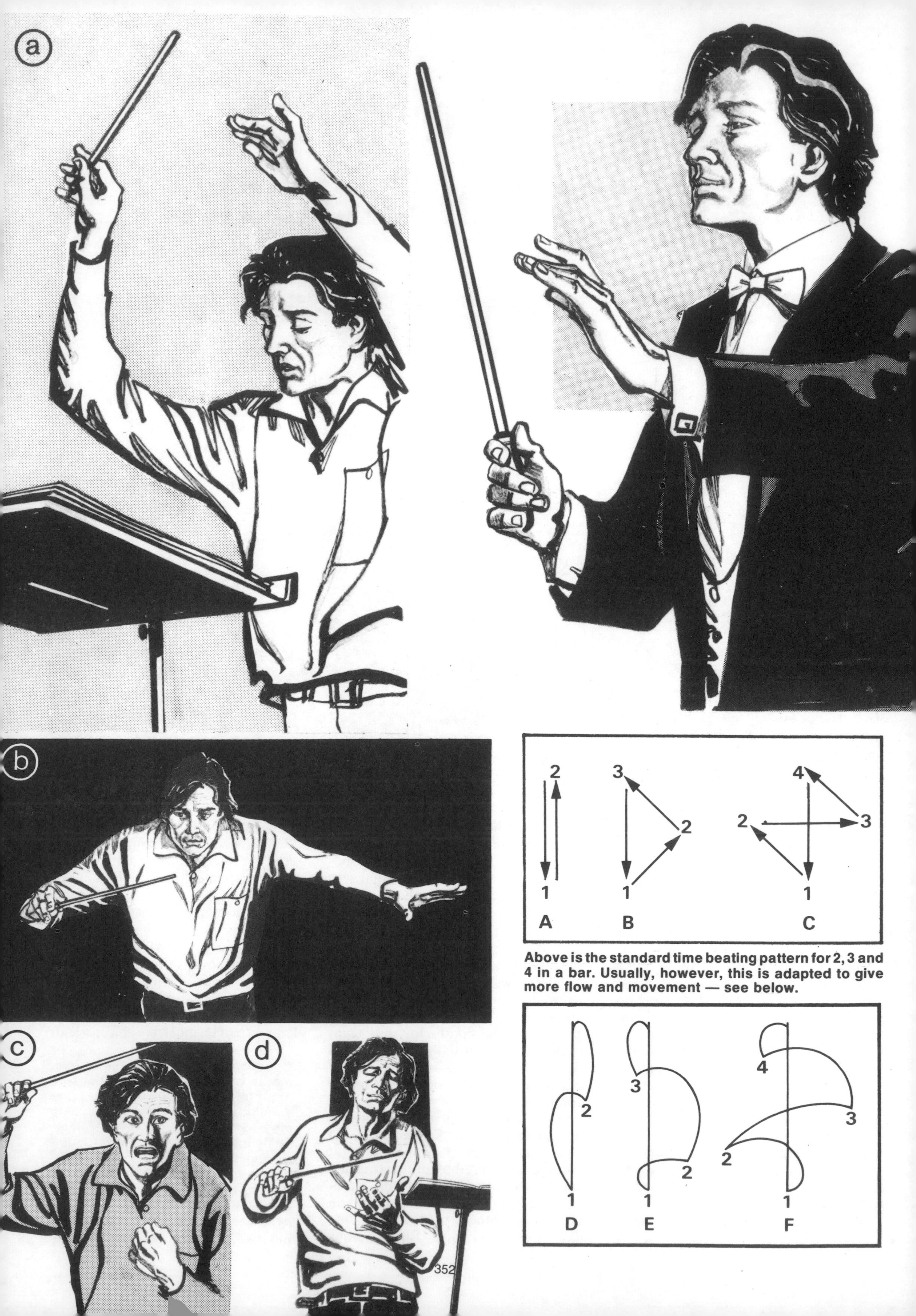


**Above is the standard time beating pattern for 2, 3 and 4 in a bar. Usually, however, this is adapted to give more flow and movement — see below.**

even the most complicated modern score. He must be a leader, a man who can inspire. It is he who decides on the tempo — the speed — of the music to be played: it is not always clear in the score. He beats time, usually but not always, with a baton. Some conductors simply use their hands.

Though the players are looking at their music, they can see the conductor over the top or can look up from time to time — if they want to! The conductor 'cues' his players in at important moments — a key flute solo perhaps — and cues in his singers in the opera house. Conducting opera is much more demanding than the average concert because of the sheer size of the forces involved.

Orchestral musicians will make life a misery for an inefficient conductor, though not at the actual concert. They will play wrong notes — or leave something out — at rehearsals to see if he spots them. Franz Strauss, the horn-playing father of the great composer, Richard Strauss, once vividly summed up the situation:

"You conductors, who are so proud of your power! When a new man faces the orchestra — from the way he walks up the steps to the podium and opens his score — before he even picks up his baton — we know whether he is the master or we!

**Above: the young conductor from America, Michael Tilson Thomas, is seen, conducting the London Symphony Orchestra in 1972. It was his 'Prom' debut and was screened on BBC 1 Television. The opening page of Brahms First Symphony is also shown. This gives an idea of the complexity of a score and the knowledge required by a conductor.**

## The beginning

Tough talk from a notorious conductor baiter! How did this clearly hazardous profession come about?

Conducting, as we know it, began early in the last century. One of the first who definitely wielded a baton in front of an orchestra was the German composer, Ludwig Louis Spohr (1784-1859), who used one as early as 1817. Another was the composer, Carl Weber (1786-1826). At once orchestral performances became better.

The baton was a true revolution, for earlier, composers or others had been in charge of the proceedings from a harpsichord or a piano. Sometimes the first violinist would 'conduct' by sawing away in a lively fashion or by beating time with his bow.

Yet, strangely, batons of a sort had been used in earlier times: short sticks or rolled up paper; while in France some 300 years ago there was a fashion for beating time on the floor with a long stick — or a short one on a table. The great Italian-born French composer, Lully (1639-87), who served Louis XIV, came to a sad end because he beat the floor so hard. One almighty thump with his long cane went through his foot. An abcess, then gangrene, followed, and the chief of the best orchestra in Europe at the time died a wretched death.

Once Spohr and Weber had shown the way, there was no going back, and the conductor as interpreter and as inspirer of his players had arrived to stay. Most of the early giants were also composers, which helped them understand the problems. This was just as well, as scores got more and more complex. Perhaps the first great modern conductor was Hans von Bülow (1830-94), Liszt's son-in-law, who had a prodigious memory. It was he who said: "You must have the score in your head, not your head in the score!" Not that not using a score at all proves that you are a better conductor, but a superb memory is vital.

Today, there are many fine conductors of the younger generation like Claudio Abbado and Riccardo Muti (Italy), James Levine (U.S.A.), Colin Davis (Britain), all following in the steps of senior giants like Karl Böhm (Germany), Sir Adrian Boult (Britain) and others. Britain even had a conductor making a real name for himself in his early 20s, which is very rare — Simon Rattle.

The great Sir Thomas Beecham, adored by players and public alike, was once faced with a very dull audience, who resolutely refused to applaud. He finally swung round on them, stared at them, and said: "Let us pray!"

Musicians and audiences pray that the supply of good and great conductors never dries up.

# Was a Priest the world's

1. Franz Liszt was born on 11th October, 1811 in the village of Raiding, Hungary and, as a child, showed great musical ability. He was taught to play the piano by his father, who worked for Prince Nicolas Esterhazy. Early on, local gypsies forecast fame and fortune for him. They came to this conclusion because his birth coincided with the appearance of 'the great comet'!

2. When only nine, Franz played in public for the first time. He seems to have been a very confident child and to have walked between the gathered businessmen and their wives with no show of nervousness. And his skill impressed them enormously. They agreed to pay for his musical education and he was taken to Vienna. There he was accepted as a pupil by the great musician, Karl Czerny.

3. Czerny is said to have been so moved by the boy's playing of a Beethoven concerto that he wept. He had himself been a pupil of the great Beethoven and admired him immensely. Before long the young Liszt was giving concerts which included works by Beethoven. They were a great success — no one had heard such playing from one so young. But Beethoven had not yet heard him play.

4. What would happen when he did? Eventually, the great master — already, sadly, going deaf — is supposed to have let him perform in front of him. Liszt probably did this in Beethoven's own home. The interpretation reputedly delighted and, perhaps, saddened the mighty composer. He could recognise the boy's greatness and must have wished he could hear him more clearly.

# greatest Pianist?

5. Another story, highly dramatic, if less likely to be true, is that Beethoven was persuaded to attend a concert given by this young prodigy. As the last few notes died away, Beethoven is said to have lumbered on to the stage and to have kissed the boy on the forehead. Whether or not the story is true, there is no doubt that from their first meeting Liszt was a great supporter of Beethoven.

6. While still little more than a child, he toured France, giving concerts in both the provinces and Paris. In 1824, he visited London, and delighted the public with his fiery performances. During the next 20 years he was to spend much of his time travelling across Europe, being greeted with acclaim as the world's greatest pianist. But as well as performing, much of his time was spent composing.

7. Many of his compositions are extremely difficult to play, for Liszt wrote them as an opportunity to display his own dazzling talents. But his religious feelings and his long stay in Rome also led him to write many works for the church, as well as symphonies. In 1856 he became a Franciscan friar, and later he was made an honorary canon of St. Albans in Rome, becoming known as the Abbe Liszt.

8. Liszt lived and worked with many of the greatest musicians of his day, but to the end of his life he was never too proud to hear and encourage youngsters of talent. Perhaps he remembered his own youth. He died in Bayreuth at the age of 75. Even today many people still find it hard to disagree with the claim that he was the greatest pianist of all time.

# Who was the Father of English Literature?

**THE first schools in England were started by monks, followers of the Christian faith brought to the country by Augustine in the year 597. Their pupils were the sons of Anglo-Saxon nobles — a very small privileged minority who thus learned to read and write.**

The monks wrote the first text books themselves. They were Latin grammars and books on science, arithmetic and philosophy. Schoolboys and girls in Anglo-Saxon times had to copy out these text books word for word on their slates. They had no paper, which was expensive, and a slate had an advantage in that it could be wiped clean and used over and over again.

Anglo-Saxon children found it just as easy to learn as most young people do. But if they were bored, the monks would set them problems in the form of stories, so that they would find the sums easier to do. Here is a typical sum: "A swallow once invited a snail to dinner. The snail lived five kilometres away from the place where the swallow had its nest and it travelled along at the rate of only half a metre a day. How long would it take the snail to reach the swallow's nest, where dinner was waiting?"

**Statue of King Alfred the Great (c.848-900) in his home town of Wantage in Berkshire. Alfred is renowned as a man of action, a warrior who fought tirelessly against the Viking invaders, but he also loved to read, according to the monk Asser who wrote his biography in the ninth century.**

The monks, as teachers and book writers, were also the historians of the British Isles and it is from them that we have most of our knowledge of what happened in Britain between the departure of the Romans in A.D. 410 and the arrival of the Normans in 1066.

An unknown monk, or monks, set down in the seventh or eighth century the 6,356 short lines of verse which constitute the epic poem "Beowulf", a story that interweaves fable, legend and history.

In it, Beowulf, the hero, has three great adventures: his slaying first of the monster Grendel, then of Grendel's mother, another monster, and lastly a dragon, when he himself is killed. The poem tells us a great deal about the life and customs of Anglo-Saxon times.

## Literary figure

Undoubtedly the greatest of all the literary monks, and the first great figure in English literature, was the Venerable Bede, a Tynesider who dominated early learning from around 670 to the year 735, when he died. Like all the monks of that time, Bede wrote in Latin, clearly, interestingly and never failing to include the small incidents and lively anecdotes that made his books classics of all time.

Bede's greatest work was "The Ecclesiastical History of the English Nation" in which he tells how the English were converted to Christianity; how, at Whitby in 663, a council met to decide whether the English would follow the customs of the Celtic Church or the Roman Church, and by choosing the Roman Church, ensured that England's history was henceforth linked with Europe's.

Bede entered the monastery at Jarrow in Northumbria when he was seven. He was no traveller, although his learning brought him fame across Europe in his own lifetime. He refused promotion within the church and probably spent most of his life within the grey stone walls at Jarrow. He was, too, a great lover of that northern countryside where, he tells us, salmon leapt in the silver rivers, and seals, dolphins and whales were caught. There were also mussels, "in which were . . . pearls of all colours, red, purple, violet and green, but mostly white."

It was Bede who gave us our system of dating. He called the year in which Christ was born the Year One, and dated all events from it. In fact, Christ was probably born earlier than Year One, but we still use Bede's method today.

On his deathbed the remarkable monk of Jarrow was still hard at work dictating to his pupil monks a translation of St. John's Gospel, urging the monks to write faster so that he could finish before he died. Hours after completing the last sentence, Bede was dead.

We know this, of course, because other monks were writing down the events that were happening in eighth century England. More than a century after Bede, another monk, named Asser, wrote a 'Life of King Alfred', the great monarch who fought stubbornly against England's Viking invaders. Asser's book was certainly added to after his death, so that it can no longer be relied upon to be wholly accurate. Accepting this, it is nonetheless interesting to read what the book says.

Alfred, says Asser, loved reading, but he was never expert at it because "in those days there were no men really skilled in reading in the whole realm of the West Saxons". It is in Asser's book that we read of Alfred's thoughtlessness that led to the incident of the burning cakes when he was in hiding — an episode that shows that the writer-monks had learned from Bede the importance of making a story interesting by including human details.

## Human interest

Perhaps one of the most human of all stories about the birth of English literature, drawn from those centuries of mystery between the Roman withdrawal and the Norman invasion, concerns a peasant named Caedmon, who worked in the stables at Whitby Abbey and who eventually became the first English poet.

In the seventh century, after any bout of eating and drinking, it was the custom of each of the company in turn to sing or make rhymes. Caedmon, it seems, was not much good at either of these things and felt his lack of talent so keenly that when his turn came he would get up and go quietly outside.

On one such occasion he walked out to the stable where it was his job to take care of the horses. Caedmon settled himself into the hay and went to sleep. While he slept, he claimed afterwards, he saw a vision in which a man bade him sing. "Sing of the beginning of all created things," the apparition urged him. Then Caedmon began to sing verses he had never heard before.

When he awoke he remembered all the verses he had sung and enthralled all the company at the next after-the-feasting gathering by repeating them. Caedmon was taken to the Abbess Hilda, who was in charge of Whitby monastery where he worked, and a council of wise men, who listened to his story. All concluded that there was no doubt that in a dream God had put verses into the heart of the ignorant peasant Caedmon.

The Abbess explained a part of the Bible to the stable-hand who then apparently put the story into excellent verse. "Since God has given you this gift," declared the Abbess, "you should become a monk in this monastery."

Caedmon willingly concurred and used his new gift to such good effect that he who was once the monk's servant was now their master, teaching them how to shape Biblical stories into Anglo-Saxon verse. Passed on by travelling minstrels, these verses not only enlivened those dark nights in the Dark Ages, but spread Bible teaching and the message of Christianity through a land where, although few could read or write, many could remember.

So, when Alfred the Great ruled over Southern England in the ninth century, there existed already an embryonic heritage of English literature, confined to the privileged few but already sufficiently well known to provide the basis of much learning.

The Danish invasion, which was temporarily repelled by Alfred, halted the spread of this knowledge for a time, for the marauding Danes destroyed the libraries until "there was not one house of learning left from the Forth to the Humber." But when Alfred had driven the invaders out of southern England and his battles were over, he embraced learning avidly.

It was his great enthusiasm that helped the spread of knowledge and enlightenment in England and caused this inscription to be set many centuries later, on Alfred's statue at Wantage in Berkshire:

"Alfred found learning dead and he restored it. Education neglected and he revived it. The laws powerless and he gave them force. The Church debased and he raised it. The land ravaged by a fearful enemy from which he delivered it. Alfred's name will live as long as mankind shall respect the past."

**Farming in Saxon Times**

**A village depended on its crops and livestock for much of its food and clothing materials, so a great deal of effort was put into farming. These illustrations, taken from an old Saxon manuscript, show how the various activities were carried out.**

**The plough was drawn by oxen (top left); in hoeing and raking the soil, the villeins worked as a team (middle left); sheep had to be guarded against predators (bottom left); haymaking (top right) ensured there was food for the livestock during the winter. At harvest time, after the corn had been reaped (middle right), threshed and winnowed (bottom right) to separate the grain and remove the chaff, each strip owner received his share of the crop.**

All this idyllism began to change distinctly for the worse, however, when the Normans arrived in England. William the Conqueror appointed his abbots not because of their piety or learning but because they were noblemen or warriors, and could keep the countryside in order. Some of them were as cruel and brutal as any battlefield mercenary.

One such infamous churchman was Toustain who, in 1083, arrived from Caen in Normandy to become Abbot of Glastonbury in Somerset. Like other Norman abbots in England, he began by cutting down the rations of his monks, in order, he said, to make them more docile. Then followed a whole series of new rules which, the monks decided, they would not obey.

Enraged, Toustain stormed out of the abbey and returned almost at once with a company of Norman soldiers. The terrified monks fled to the church and locked themselves behind the gate of the choir. But the soldiers burst into the church. Some climbed the beams and shot arrows down on to the crouching monks.

Meanwhile, other soldiers battered down the gate of the choir and charged the monks with swords and lances. They

# The layout of a working monastery

**Our picture shows a reconstruction of a medieval monastery as it would have appeared at a time when it was lived and worked in daily.**

**Though, particularly with a growing emphasis on its contribution to education, the monastery became an integral part of English medieval life, the aim was always for it to be self-contained and self-sufficient.**

**In other words, at its most efficient, it was almost a self-governing village itself as evidenced by the many trades carried on within its walls by the holy brothers.**

defended themselves as best they could with wooden benches and metal candelabra, but several of them were killed and many were wounded.

## Adventurers

It is said that when William the Conqueror heard of this battle in Glastonbury Abbey he removed the abbot. But not long afterwards Toustain was apparently able to buy back his abbacy for five hundred pounds, whereupon he dispersed the monks among other monasteries and had them kept in close confinement.

With such adventurers as Toustain swarming into the monasteries, it is not surprising that in some of them gluttony quickly took the place of fasting. So, we are told, the monks of St. Austine in Canterbury used to have at least seventeen dishes at a meal, and their cook was renowned in Kent for the way he could create a dish to provoke the appetite.

And, says a Norman historian a trifle wistfully, he could mention many similar examples of monastic wickedness in the days of the Conqueror, were the subject not too painful to pursue.

These were the first signs of a slow decline in the standards of the monasteries that was to last over the next few centuries.

# Which Cobbler's Son wrote famous fairy tales?

1. To begin with, Hans Christian Andersen seemed fated to live a life of ill-luck. Born at Odense, on one of the islands of Denmark, he spent the early part of his life living in a single room with his mother and father, a cobbler who had suffered from ill health for most of his life. Hans, however, was a great consolation to the cobbler, who had high hopes for his son, although there were those in the village who thought the lad simple-minded. The only time Hans was really happy was when his father took him for a walk.

2. The cobbler died when Hans was about eleven, leaving his widow to bring up their son alone. Hans was still allowed to go to school, but somehow his mind seemed quite unable to absorb even the simplest subjects. His burning ambition was to become an actor, and whenever a theatrical company came to Odense, he begged the manager to allow him to play some small role in the play. Finally, given his big chance by a kindly manager, he appeared only to be laughed off for his clownish appearance.

3. Undeterred by his disastrous stage debut, Hans spent all his spare time playing with the toy theatre his father had given him, making his puppets act out the plays of Shakespeare. To improve his voice, he read aloud the verses and plays he had written for his theatre. No one in Odense could see that he had gifts that only needed developing, and his life was therefore a lonely one.

In despair, his mother finally decided that her son had spent enough of his life day-dreaming, and she announced that she was going to apprentice him to a tailor. Appalled at the thought of having to spend the rest of his life sewing garments, Hans begged her to allow him to go to Copenhagen instead, where he was sure he would find fame and fortune on the boards of the city's theatres. Reluctantly, she gave her consent, and he set off with only a few coins in his pocket and no friends to turn to when he arrived in the capital. He was only 14.

On his arrival, he made his way directly to the Royal Theatre, where he asked if he might be allowed to see the directors. Ushered into their presence, he announced to them that he wanted to be an actor. The directors looked at the thin, uncouth boy standing humbly in front of them. Then they looked at each other — and burst out laughing. With the sound of their laughter ringing in his ears, Hans left the theatre.

4. As it happened, however, the interview had been overheard by a poet and playwright named Friedrik Guldberg, who had an instinctive feeling that there was much more to Hans than appeared on the surface. He pleaded with the directors to give the boy a chance. Reluctantly they promised to do something for him.

But several weeks passed before 'something was done', for Hans had not told the directors that he was penniless and without a home. Starving and friendless, he wandered the streets of Copenhagen, sleeping in alleyways and parks at night.

At last, the directors redeemed their promise and accepted Hans as a pupil. But their original estimate of him as a potential actor proved only too true. They soon discovered that Hans could not act at all. Furthermore, his voice had broken and he was not even able to sing in the chorus.

Fortunately, one of the directors took pity on him and sent him to school once more. But Hans remained a backward and unwilling pupil, and there followed five of the darkest and bitterest years of his life. His eccentric manner and slow wits made him the butt of his classmates, who tormented him unmercifully. In addition, his habit of quietly sitting in a corner and writing verse when he should have been studying his text books, infuriated his masters, who were not slow to show their displeasure with this impossible pupil who had been foisted on them.

5. But Hans' luck was to change. After trying to write every form of literature without success, one of his plays was put on at the Royal Theatre, where it had a modest success. Four years later, his first book of fairy tales appeared, and very soon afterwards he woke up one morning to find himself famous.

Hans never ceased to be amazed at his success. Originally, he had begun to write down his fairy tales merely to amuse the many little friends he had made in Copenhagen, and it truly astonished him to find that grown-ups enjoyed them just as much as did the children.

He began to travel widely, but he still continued writing, until his fame had grown to such a degree that he was welcome in the houses of people even more famous than himself, including Charles Dickens and Richard Wagner.

Although he was justifiably proud of his international reputation, he remained a modest, easily-hurt man who was always happiest in the company of children, whom he could hold spell-bound with the stories he made up for them on the spot.

6. Hans Christian Andersen had a rare quality. Although he had learned to become a man, he had never lost the innocence of a child. "How beautiful the world is," he remarked just before his death in 1875, "and how happy I am." It was a strange path indeed that Hans had followed to bring him to this contented state of mind, despite all the suffering he had endured as a child.

Authors are not always reliable in judging their own work, and Hans was no exception. He had always dismissed his stories as trifles, but it was these rather than his plays and verse, that gained him immortality. Stories such as *The Tinder Box*, *The Snow Queen* and *The Ugly Duckling* have a timeless charm about them that will continue to enchant countless generations of children to come.

# What was Mercator's Map?

The world is a sphere, and the only really accurate way to represent it is on a globe. Globes were known by the Greeks and Romans and were re-invented in the sixteenth century. But they are clumsy to use — maps are far more convenient.

**WHEN early European explorers began venturing out into the world's oceans in the fifteenth and early sixteenth centuries they discovered an awesome fact. The Atlantic, Pacific and other oceans with their mighty waves, ferocious storms, vast distances, and long, long months at sea were nothing like the waters to which they were accustomed.**

It was a relatively simple matter to sail the tideless, enclosed Mediterranean Sea, or make coast-hugging voyages round Europe. But the oceans presented navigators with colossal problems, and posed questions to which there was no answer.

How wide was the Atlantic Ocean? No one knew until Christopher Columbus crossed it in 1492. How wide was the Pacific? Again, no one knew until the ships of Ferdinand Magellan's fleet traversed it in 1520-2.

But as well as the strange seas and lands, and the unfamiliarity of the tides, those early navigators had another great difficulty. They had no accurate maps. This is not surprising seeing that they were going to unknown lands. But more important, they had no way of making an accurate map.

The maps they had in those days were 'plane' charts — like a modern street-plan. On such a map the area is divided up into small squares by lines (or meridians) running north/south (longitude) and east/west (latitude). Such maps are fairly accurate for mapping small areas, like a town, and moderately accurate even for areas as large as

A map based on the notes of the ancient Greek Ptolemy. He knew the world was round.

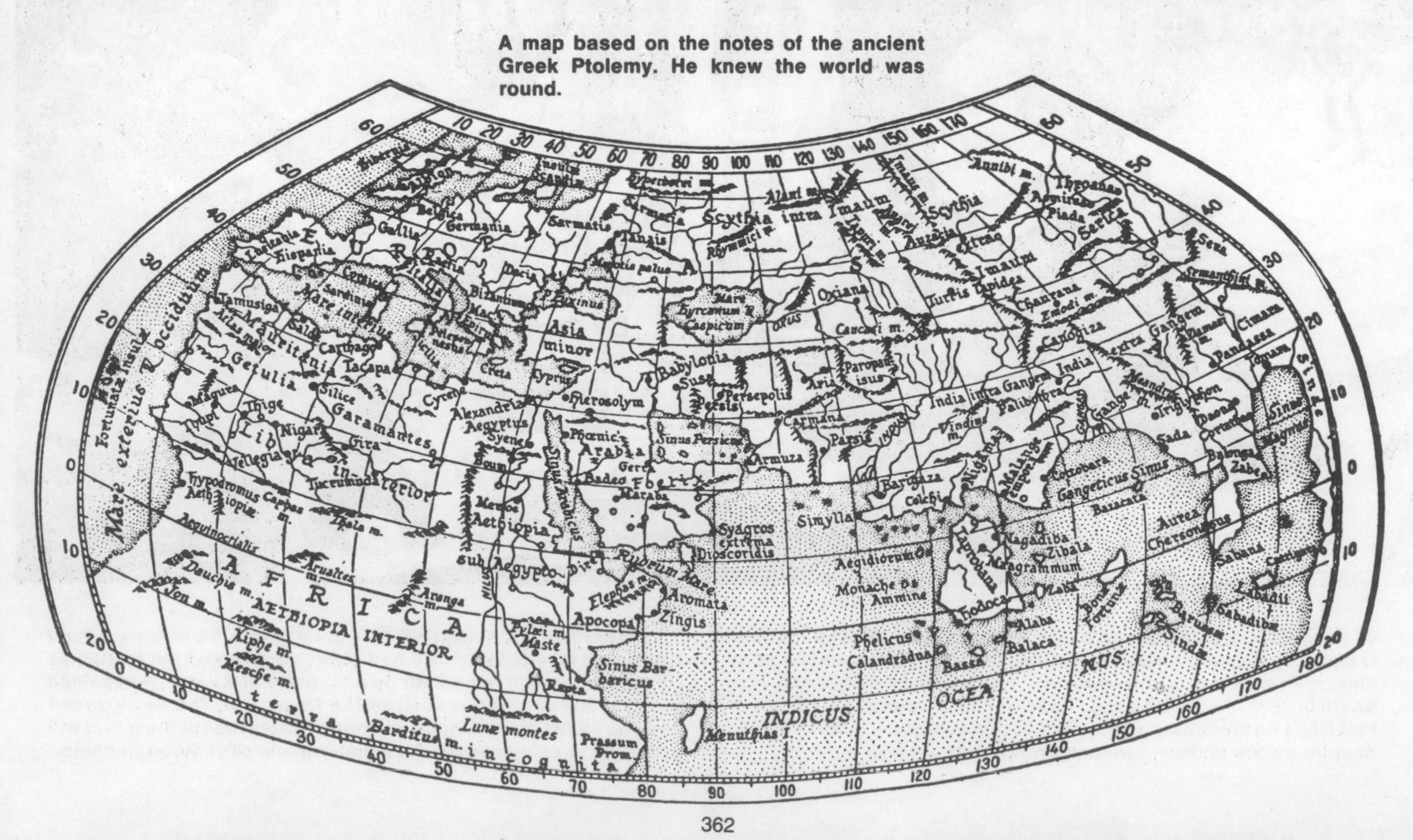

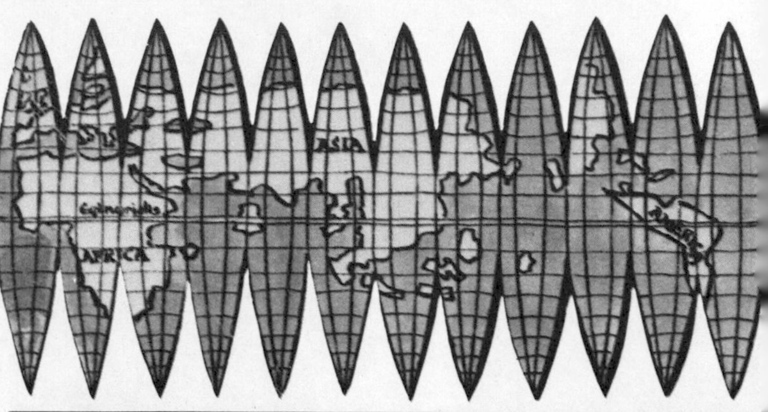


It is impossible to make a flat map of the round Earth without distortion, although many methods have been tried. The map above is printed on strips of paper, called 'gores', which when joined edge-to-edge form a globe. When they are flattened out, oceans and continents are split down the middle, which makes the map difficult to use.

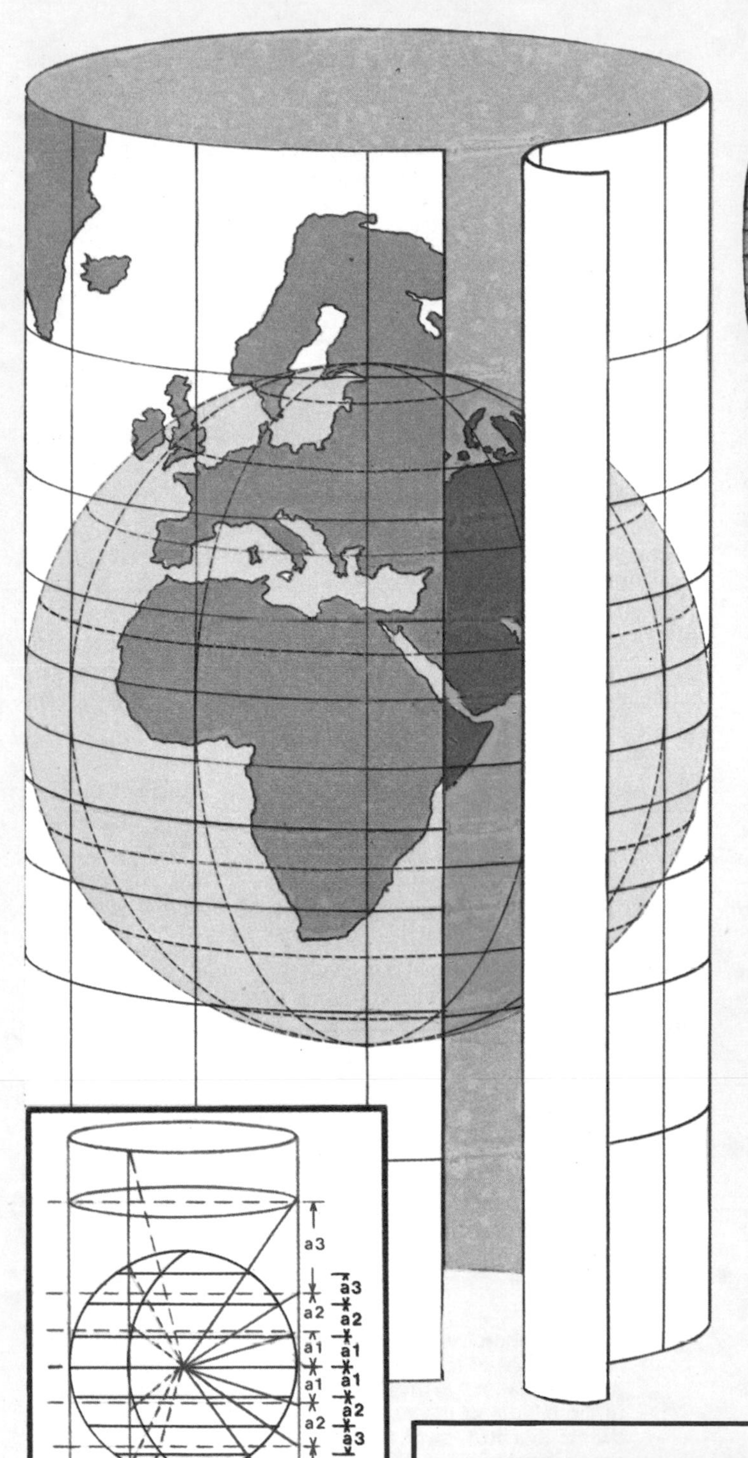


the Mediterranean Sea.

However, when explorers embarked on ocean voyages covering thousands of miles, they were sailing long distances across the curve of the Earths' surface. This was when the plane chart began to prove useless. The Earth is a globe, and a plane chart just doesn't take that into account.

If you look at a globe, you will see that the north/south meridians converge as they near the North or South Pole. And so, if a map is drawn keeping them at the same distance apart, towards the poles distances become increasingly innacurate.

For example, the early plane charts showed the distance between the Lizard, in Cornwall, and the Azores Islands, in the Atlantic Ocean, as 2,736 km — when the real distance is 702 km less. In addition, the longitude of the Azores was 7.5 degrees out from its true position.

But not only were distances wrong but, more importantly, directions too. A straight line plotted on the map did not represent a straight line in the real world. And so if a navigator tried to sail such a line — along a compass bearing for example — he would become hopelessly lost.

*Continued on next page*

Imagine the world as a big spherical light bulb and a cylinder of paper wrapped round it north/south. The shadows of the continents would be thrown up on the paper rather as in the picture above left — the result is a cylindrical projection like Mercator's. On it everything is distorted towards the poles, as is shown by the diagram on the left. On the globe distance a3 is the same as distance a1; on the cylinder a3 is much bigger.

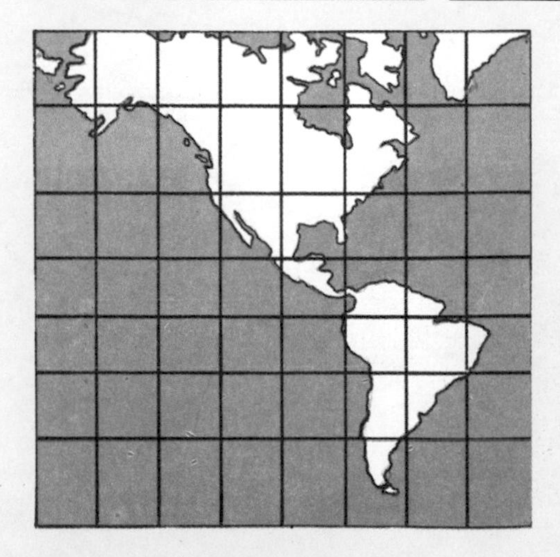

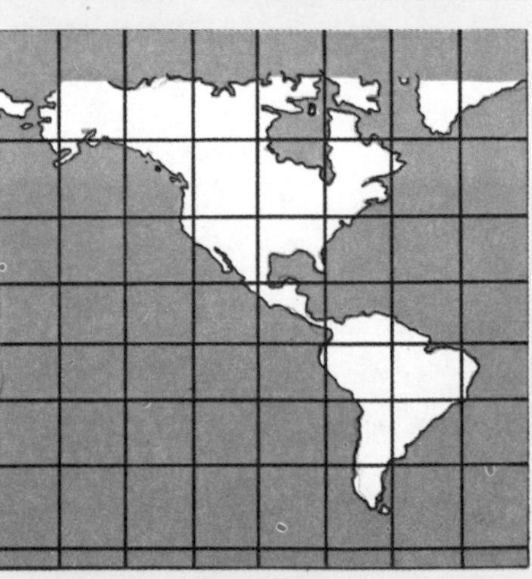

On Mercator's Projection (far left) both longitude and latitude are distorted equally as they reach the poles. This means that although distances towards the poles are grossly exaggerated — and the poles themselves are both everywhere and nowhere along the top and bottom of the map — directions are shown accurately. This is the most important factor in navigation and is why Mercator's map was such a boon to seafarers. To show other things, such as areas, more accurately, modifications like Miller's Projection (left) can be used.

It was this problem that Mercator's famous map projection solved.

Mercator, whose real name was Gerhard Kremer, was born in 1512 in East Flanders, and his first maps, of the Holy Land, were printed in 1537. The following year, Mercator's first world map appeared, and in 1541, his world globe, which was 41 cm in diameter.

The great world chart which Mercator produced in 1569 was the culmination of this and other globes and charts, and though not totally accurate, it was just what ocean-going seamen had been longing for.

In it, Mercator drew the north/south meridians (lines of longitude) parallel to each other just as they were on plane charts. They crossed the east/west meridians (lines of latitude), also shown as parallel, at angles of 90 degrees. However, in order to keep the same ratio or relationship between longitude and latitide as actually existed on the curved surface of the Earth, the distances between the parallels of latitude were gradually increased as they neared the poles. They were 'stretched' just as the distances between lines of longitude were. So, in effect, the Earth *looked* flat on Mercator's Projection, but took into account the fact that it was round — the one vital thing the plane charts had not done.

All a navigator had to do was to draw a line from his starting point to his destination. This line would cut all the parallel meridians on Mercator's map at the same angle, and it showed him the compass course he should follow. Mercator's map had the added advantage of enabling meteorologists to show accurate wind directions on the charts, something very valuable in the days of sailing ships.

Because the polar regions were unavoidably 'flattened out' on Mercator's Projection, it contained some geographical nonsense — for instance, Greenland, an island, looks the same size as Africa, a continent, when it is actually more than twelve times smaller. This inaccuracy, though, is not crucial to navigators at sea. For them, Mercator's map was a splendid gift. It helped bring to an end the years when they had to venture out on to the oceans often not knowing where they were, where they would arrive, or when they would get there.

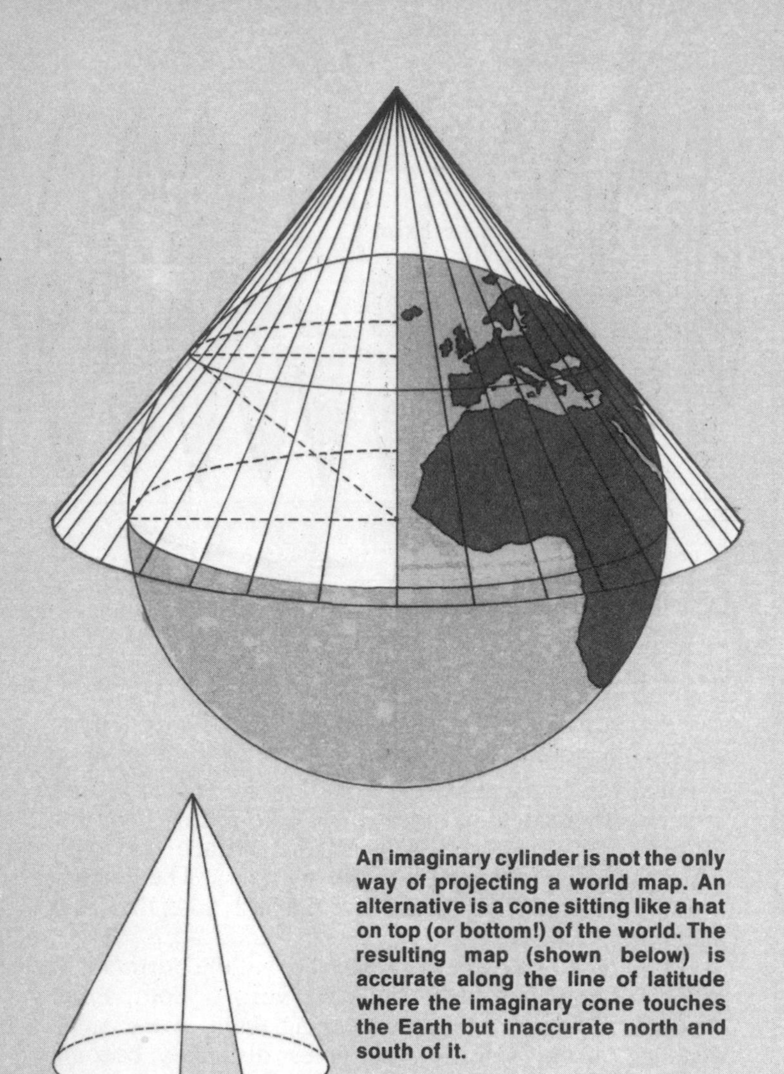

**An imaginary cylinder is not the only way of projecting a world map. An alternative is a cone sitting like a hat on top (or bottom!) of the world. The resulting map (shown below) is accurate along the line of latitude where the imaginary cone touches the Earth but inaccurate north and south of it.**

**A variation on the simple conic projection is shown below left. Instead of the imaginary cone touching the Earth in just one place, it is inserted into the Earth's surface so that in the middle of the map the surface of the cone is below the Earth's surface. A map made from such a projection is accurate along two lines of latitude (where the imaginary cone enters the Earth) and inaccurate along the north and south edges and in the middle.**

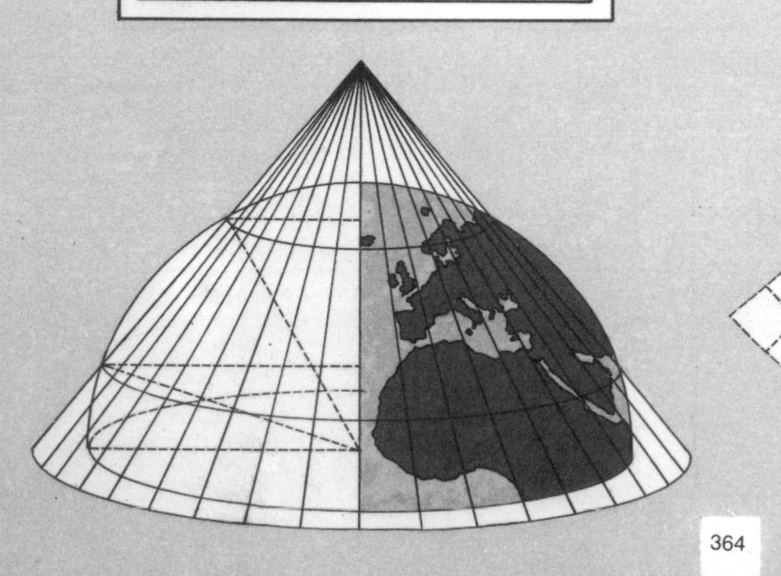

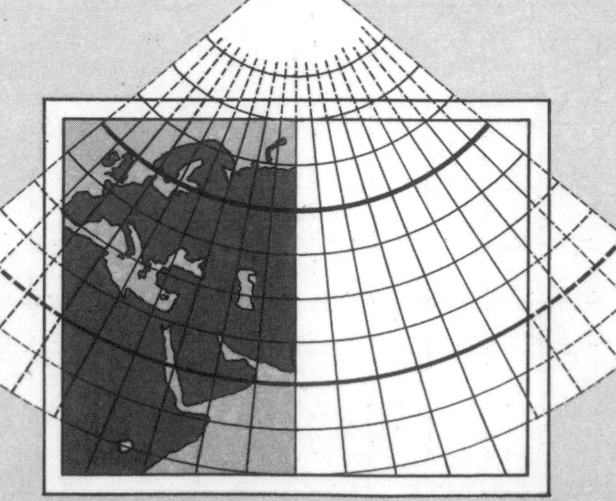

# What is a Lithograph?

**LITHOGRAPHY, a method of printing from a stone, based on the chemical fact that grease and water repel each other, was invented in 1798.**

The process became most popular early in the nineteenth century and many of the great painters of the time made lithographs, including Goya and Daumier as well as several of the Impressionist movement.

The early 1880s saw the sudden flowering of the colour lithograph, inspired by the craze for posters, especially in France where the presiding genius was Henri de Toulouse-Lautrec. Lautrec's famous posters, and prints by Pierre Bonnard and Edouard Vuillard give a vivid and perceptive insight into the Parisian life of the period.

Although the popularity of the lithographic process has fluctuated, the discovery that zinc and aluminium plates could be used as substitutes for the heavy, cumbersome litho limestones, resulted in the process being much used by artists again, the Spanish and French artists, Picasso and Braque in particular.

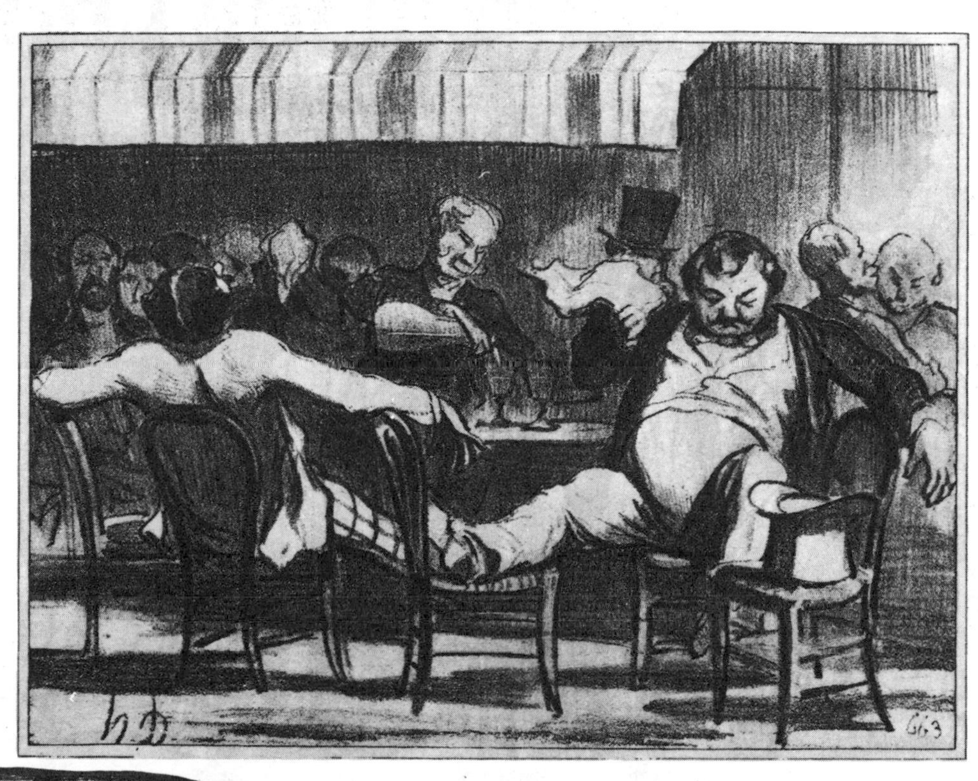

Honore Daumier (1808-1897) Familiar scene on the Boulevards.

Toulouse Lautrec (1864–1892) Mlle. Marcelle Lender. This typical Lautrec Litho was published in a very large edition in the German magazine Pan in 1895.

The principal difference between lithography and the other print making methods is that the impression can be taken from a completely flat surface.

## Inked image

Printing from a flat surface is dependent upon the natural aversion of grease to water. Marks are drawn on the grained surface of the plate or stone with greasy inks or crayons and the whole surface is then dampened with water.

The grained surface holds the water which settles on the unmarked areas, being repelled by the greasy drawing medium. The plate or stone is then rolled over with printing ink which sticks to the greasy marks but not to the wet surface of the untouched zinc or stone.

The inked image is then transferred to paper by running paper and printing surface (plate or stone) through a scraper press.

Such in essence is the principle of lithography. The actual operations are of course much more complicated. Today the stone (whence the term 'lithography' or 'stone-drawing') is rarely used, having been replaced by the more easily handled zinc or aluminium plate.

## Freedom of Expression

In lithography it is not necessary to cut or scratch the surface as in etching, woodcutting or engraving and this is what makes the quality of a lithographic print distinctive. The artist can draw upon the smooth stone or plate naturally and with freedom. This enables him or her to use any graphic means of expression: the drawing can be one of line or in mass – the image soft or strong and of powerful quality.

The process is capable of great refinement and subtlety, of rich exuberance of colour, of delicate drawing and strong contrasts, of a wide and exciting range of textures — the possibilities are virtually unlimited.

# Which famous Composer sung in the Chorus?

**1.** Hector Berlioz had red hair and the fiery disposition that is supposed to go with it. If that is really so, it was a good thing, for he certainly needed a fighting spirit to even make a start as a musician. Born in a village near Grenoble, his musical career started when he found an old flute. The noise he made on it was so terrible that his father reluctantly taught him how to play it properly.

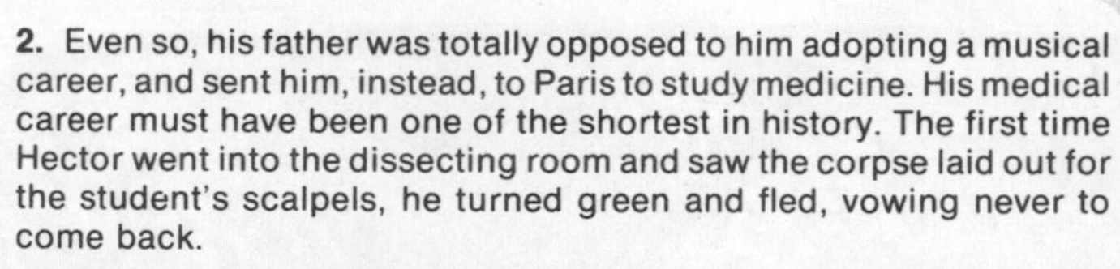

**2.** Even so, his father was totally opposed to him adopting a musical career, and sent him, instead, to Paris to study medicine. His medical career must have been one of the shortest in history. The first time Hector went into the dissecting room and saw the corpse laid out for the student's scalpels, he turned green and fled, vowing never to come back.

**3.** Determined to pursue his musical studies, he began going to the library of the Conservatoire of Music. Typically, the very first time there he made an enemy of the composer, Cherubini, who was also head of the Conservatoire. Entering by the wrong door, he was ordered by Cherubini to go back and come in the right door. Berlioz refused, and was chased out by the doorkeeper.

**4.** Although he made such a bad start at the Conservatoire, Berlioz was determined to get a musical education there. He studied harmony for some time and then enrolled. But from the very beginning, he made it clear that he wished to break away from the traditional methods of writing music — a fact that did not go unnoticed by Cherubini. Not surprisingly, he failed his exam.

**5.** To make matters even worse, his father stopped his allowance, hoping he would go back to Medical School. But that was the last thing that Berlioz intended to do. Instead, he found himself a job singing in the chorus at one of the Parisian theatres, where he earned just about enough to keep him from starving. It was there he met Henrietta Smithson, with whom he fell in love on sight.

In the meantime he had been striving to win the Conservatoire's most coveted prize, the Prix de Rome. He spent three years submitting compositions, and they were all rejected, partially because, one suspects, Cherubini was on the board of examiners. Finally, in 1830, he wrote a piece of music, so perfectly designed to please even Cherubini's conservative tastes, that it could not fail to be accepted.

**6.** Helplessly in love with Henrietta, Berlioz changed his lodgings to be near her. He followed her to and from the theatre, wrote her passionate love letters, and dedicated his music to her — all without even having spoken a single word to her. Under the influence of his overwhelming passion for her, he wrote one of his most famous pieces, *Fantastic Symphony*.

In 1833, Henrietta finally married Berlioz. But the marriage was a failure. For one thing, she met with an accident and had to give up her career on the stage, which meant that she was unable to make any contribution to the household expenses. In addition, Berlioz was an insanely jealous person, who imagined Henrietta was meeting other men. Inevitably, after several years they separated.

**7.** But the years Berlioz had spent with Henrietta could not be called a waste. Through being with Henrietta, he developed an admiration for the works of William Shakespeare, which led him to writing a dramatic symphony called *Romeo and Juliet*, which showed his flair for producing music of great dramatic intensity. This was followed by a funeral march for *Hamlet*.

**8.** Eventually, Berlioz became an international figure. Such had his standing become in the musical world that the great Italian violinist, Nicolo Paganini humbly kissed his hand after playing the viola solo in *Harold in Italy*. His opera, *The Trojans*, however, was a failure, and Berlioz never really recovered from the shock. He died in Paris in 1869 a disappointed man.

# Who was the King of Jazz?

1. George Gershwin was born of Russian-Jewish parents in Brooklyn, U.S.A. on September 26, 1898. He was to become one of the most famous American composers but his early musical life was hard. He was at first badly taught but recovered from this with a good teacher, a Mr. Hambitzer. Then he became a 'song plugger'. That is, he tried to sell tunes to entertainers by playing them a publisher's song

2. Seeing no future in this occupation, he then began to compose his own tunes, at the same time broadening his musical knowledge by studying the works of other writers. An early song, *When You Want 'Em You Can't Get 'Em*, however, was slammed by the critics. People, though, began to notice him. And his song, *Swanee*, sung by Negro Minstrel, Al Jolson, in *Sinbad* was an enormous success.

3. Gershwin's aim became a sort of classical jazz. He hoped to be able to express in music the soul of the America he knew. Undoubtedly, he was helped in this by his meeting with the band leader, Paul Whiteman, a specialist in 'symphonic jazz'. For Whiteman, Gershwin composed his *Rhapsody in Blue*. The blues are a melancholy form of jazz. This piece expresses a mixture of melancholy and turbulence.

4. The original orchestration for *Rhapsody in Blue* was for jazz band and piano but, many times, it was arranged differently by one of Whiteman's own men. It was popular but at first was not liked by everyone. A greater acclamation came later. In 1925, a year after *Rhapsody in Blue*, Gershwin composed his *Piano Concerto in F Major*. He himself performed this at the Carnegie Hall in New York.

5. Gershwin's first great successful musical was the same year as *Rhapsody in Blue.* This was *Lady Be Good.* It was followed by *Tip-Toes* (1925) and *Strike Up The Band* and *Funny Face* (1927). In 1928, however, Gershwin went with other members of his family to Paris. He wished to meet some of his European musical contemporaries. There he talked with the composers, Stravinsky and Milhaud.

6. He was greatly impressed. He realised, though, the complexity of the civilisation of the old world city and, in many ways, felt himself to be just a provincial outsider. This feeling was mixed with admiration for the elegance and vivacity of Paris and he felt he must try to interpret all of it in music. As a result, he composed his now world-renowned symphonic tone poem, *An American in Paris.*

7. On his return to America, Gershwin had many other musical successes. His first film was *Delicious* in 1930. But, for a long time he had dreamed of composing an opera concerned with the Negro life of America, incorporating the melancholy of their songs. So, in 1935, *Porgy and Bess* was born. This was based on a work by Dubose Heyward. Heyward and Ira Gershwin, George's brother, wrote the lyrics.

8. Success for this work came really only after Gershwin's death. (He died of a brain tumour in 1937, aged 38.) It is concerned with the unhappy love affair of the crippled Porgy and his sweetheart, Bess. One of the many marvellous songs is *Summertime,* which today is known by thousands who have never seen a complete performance. Sadly, Gershwin's real fame came too late for him to enjoy.

**You can't just pick precious stones or minerals polished and shining out of the Earth. You have to refine them. Four precious minerals in their 'raw' state are shown below.**

Ruby from Norway

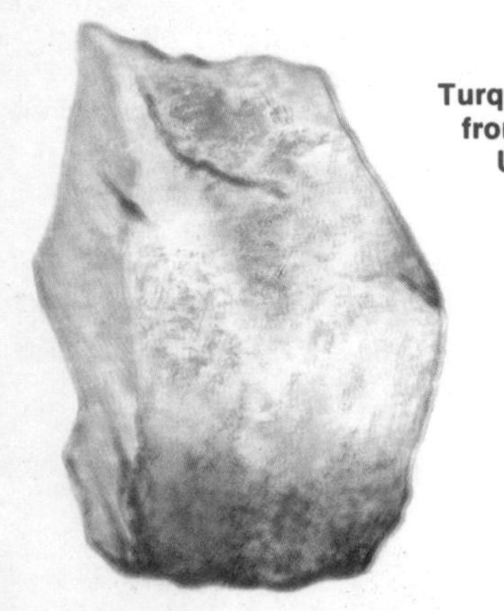

Turquoise from the U.S.A.

Gold from the U.S.A.

Opal from Mexico

# Why is Jewellery

**FROM the earliest times, Man has been fascinated by jewels and precious stones. Often he has attached a mystic significance to them.**

The opal, for instance, is supposed to have the power of luring its possessor into unkown realms; the agate affords its owner protection against violent storms; the topaz makes its wearer fearless and wise; the amethyst preserves its wearer from drunkenness — and so on. Most precious stones, in fact, have been given some mystic property over the centuries, stemming from the assumption that the planets, which are the main influence in astrology, also influence certain stones.

Nor have things changed much. Even in this enlightened age we still speak of lucky and unlucky stones, and readily accept that everyone has a birth sign, with a stone to go with it (see panel).

Although the use of precious stones and metals for ornaments goes back to the earliest times, no one knows exactly when the craft of jewellery making came into existence. Nevertheless, it is generally assumed that it began in the East some time before 3,000 B.C. The armlets, anklets, rings of all kinds, brooches, pendants and ear-rings that were found in the tombs of early Egyptian kings proved how far advanced the Egyptians were in jewellery making even in those ancient times.

## Romans

Jewellery was very popular among the Romans too. They were unrestrainedly lavish in their use of it, to such an extent that they often wore rings on all the fingers of both hands, including the thumbs. In this way, they were able to show off their vast wealth.

Because jewellery can be used to indicate wealth and *status,* governments have sometimes tried to control its use. In 13th century France, for example, ordinary citizens were prevented from competing with their 'betters' by an edict that prohibited them from wearing any precious stones and certain types of gold and

## STONES OF THE ZODIAC

**Medieval people — and many people even today — believed that the planets influenced certain precious stones. Thus each of the twleve birth signs of the zodiac became linked to one or more stones — as we show below.**

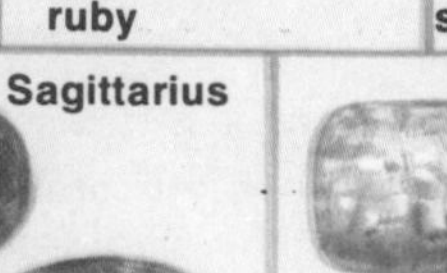

# fascinating?

silver jewellery.

In fact, even as late as 1720, the French Regent, the Duke of Orleans, forbade the wearing of pearls, diamonds, and fine stones, and furthermore ordered jewellers to sell their stocks abroad so that the people at home could not obtain them. Needless to say, the Regent did not penalise himself in a like manner.

In England, too, Edward III laid down a statute which stated that craftsmen and yeomen (small farmers) had no right to possess any gold and silver jewellery, and that only the richer merchants and nobles might own precious stones. Similar laws were also passed in Spain in the 14th century.

### Renaissance

But despite the fact that jewellery was used as a political pawn, jewellery making survived to make its own contribution to that extraordinary period in the 15th and 16th centuries we know as the Renaissance. During this period the way people thought about the world changed greatly, and this was particularly shown in the art of the period.

Renaissance jewellery was marked by its extravagant use of metals, enamels and precious stones. Designs, too, were revolutionised and there were several remarkable partnerships, such as the one in which the painters, Durer and Holbein, made designs for the goldsmith, Benvenuto Cellini.

By the 17th century, jewellery had become more delicate, with jewellers cutting the stones into smaller fragments and setting them in nothing more than a mere claw of silver or gold to hold the stone in place.

About this time, too, jewellery began to be seen more as an accessory to a dress or other article of clothing than as a thing of beauty in its own right. Because of this, the style of jewellery was governed very much by the vagaries of fashion.

More change occurred in the 19th century. Many revivals of old models and attempts at new fashions were made until, in the latter part of the century, the jewellery trade began to

Continued on next page

## GEM STONES — WHERE AND WHAT

**Ruby and Sapphire**
Rubies and sapphires are both forms of the substance corundum, and both come from Sri Lanka and Burma. Rubies are red, sapphires any other colour — usually blue. So-called reconstructed rubies are made by melting useless chips of rubies together in a colouring agent. These synthetic stones can easily be identified under a lens. In genuine rubies, the colour occurs in zones arranged in straight bands; in synthetic stones the zones are curved.

**Emerald**
The finest emeralds come from Columbia, though they are also to be found in southern Africa and near Salzburg in Austria.

**Turquoise**
Turquoises originally came from Persia, but were exported through Turkey, hence their name. When exposed to grease, a turquoise will turn to an ugly cabbage colour, which is why a turquoise ring should always be removed before starting the washing-up.

**Amber**
Amber is the fossil resin of pine trees, and has been used in jewellery since ancient times. Legend has it that amber is the solidified urine of the lynx.

**Opal**
Most opals come from Queensland and New South Wales in Australia. Beautiful though this stone is, it is liable to shrink and crack as it dries out over the years.

**Pearl**
A pearl is formed when a grain of sand or other small particle invades an oyster or mussel shell. The irritation causes the oyster to produce a substance (nacre) which coats the foreign body.

The first artificially cultured pearls did not appear until the 1930s, when over-production made prices collapse, never fully to recover. Cultured pearls are made by inserting a small polished bead of *mother-of-pearl* (the shell lining) of a freshwater mussel surrounded by a piece of living oyster tissue into the shell of another oyster. The oyster then reacts in exactly the same way as when a grain of sand has invaded it.

**Coral**
Coral is the skeleton of a marine animal, and it comes in three shades, white, pink and red. The majority of corals form large colonies, and it is from the accumulated skeletons that the famed coral reefs are formed.

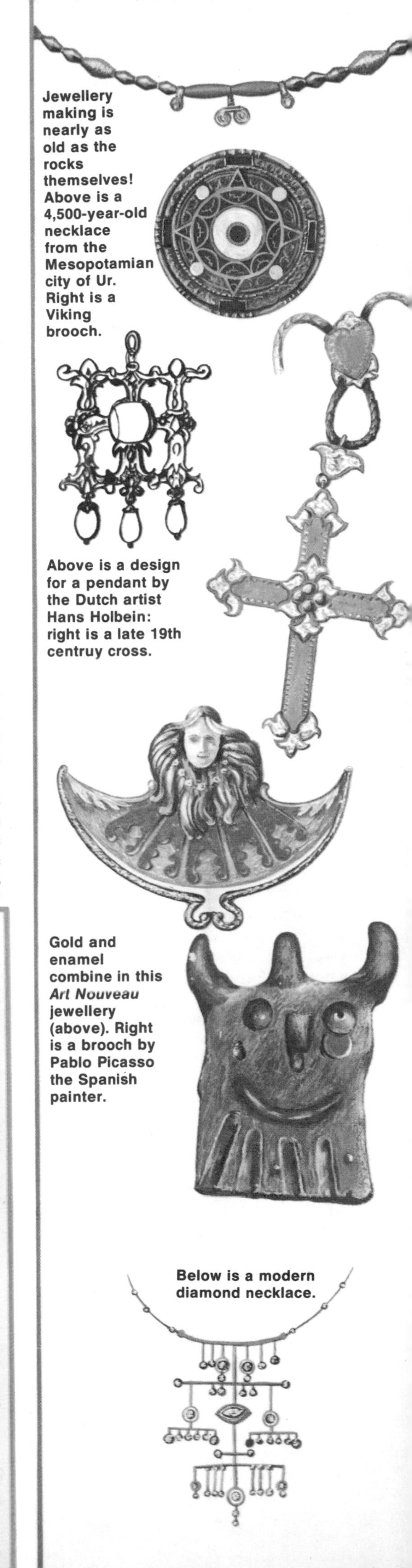

Jewellery making is nearly as old as the rocks themselves! Above is a 4,500-year-old necklace from the Mesopotamian city of Ur. Right is a Viking brooch.

Above is a design for a pendant by the Dutch artist Hans Holbein: right is a late 19th centruy cross.

Gold and enamel combine in this *Art Nouveau* jewellery (above). Right is a brooch by Pablo Picasso the Spanish painter.

Below is a modern diamond necklace.

**The largest diamond ever found was the 'Cullinan'. The biggest gem cut from it — the 'Star of Africa' adorns the British royal sceptre (above).**

### The Queen of all Jewels — The Diamond

The diamond deserves to be considered apart from other precious stones because it has long excelled all the other stones in interest and importance. Nevertheless, it is nothing more than pure carbon which has been changed by great heat and pressure. The heat and pressure turn the carbon from a black and uninviting powder into a pure crystal — the most beautiful stone we have.

For many centuries, the diamond mines of India were the chief source of the world's supply. The Greeks, returning home after their invasion of India in 327 B.C. probably brought back the first knowledge of this precious gem to Europe. They named it *admas,* meaning unconquerable, because of its hardness.

In modern times, most diamonds are found in South Africa, though the finest diamond of them all, the 'Regent' or 'Pit' came from India. This flawless gem is part of the crown jewels of France. The largest diamond ever found is the Cullinan diamond which was discovered in the Transvaal in 1905.

A diamond is so hard that the only thing that will cut it is another diamond.

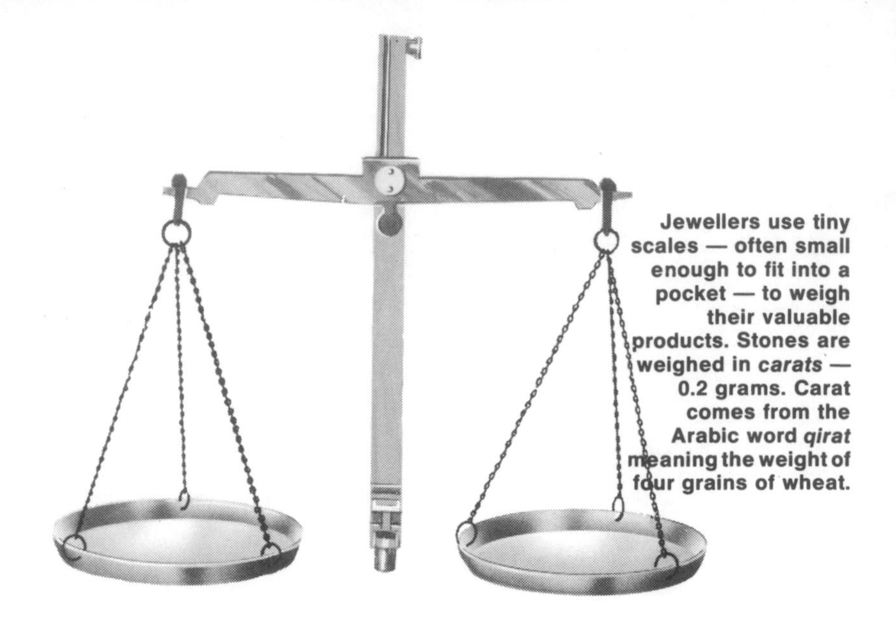

**Jewellers use tiny scales — often small enough to fit into a pocket — to weigh their valuable products. Stones are weighed in *carats* — 0.2 grams. Carat comes from the Arabic word *qirat* meaning the weight of four grains of wheat.**

go into decline. Mechanical techniques led to the mass production of jewellery to such a degree that people became bored with what was being offered them. Something new was needed to rekindle their imagination.

It came with *Art Nouveau,* a movement which began in Paris and was soon flourishing in England. It was a movement which embraced almost all the visual arts and had been influenced by the *pre-Raphaelite* painters, a group dedicated to reducing unrealistic formality in art. Jewellers began using as their motifs such things as dragonflies, roses, nightingales, storks, butterflies and peacocks. They produced jewellery which, almost without exception, is exquisitely designed. But strangely beautiful though these works were, the fashion for Art Nouveau jewellery ended almost as quickly as it had begun.

## Costly

Today, much fine jewellery is still produced by hand, with costly items being turned out in domestic workshops in London and Paris. But the vast bulk of jewellery is now produced in large factories, equipped with ingenious machinery.

As with everything else, the modern craftsman is competing with the factory, with the inevitable result that he belongs to a dying breed, whose continuing existence depends on those with enough money to buy his work.

But then, for the jewellery maker, this has always been the case.

## WHERE TO GO PROSPECTING

**The map below shows the main sources of precious metals (gold, silver and — most valuable of all — platinum) and precious stones (diamonds, emeralds, rubies and sapphires). But smaller deposits are found all over the Earth.**

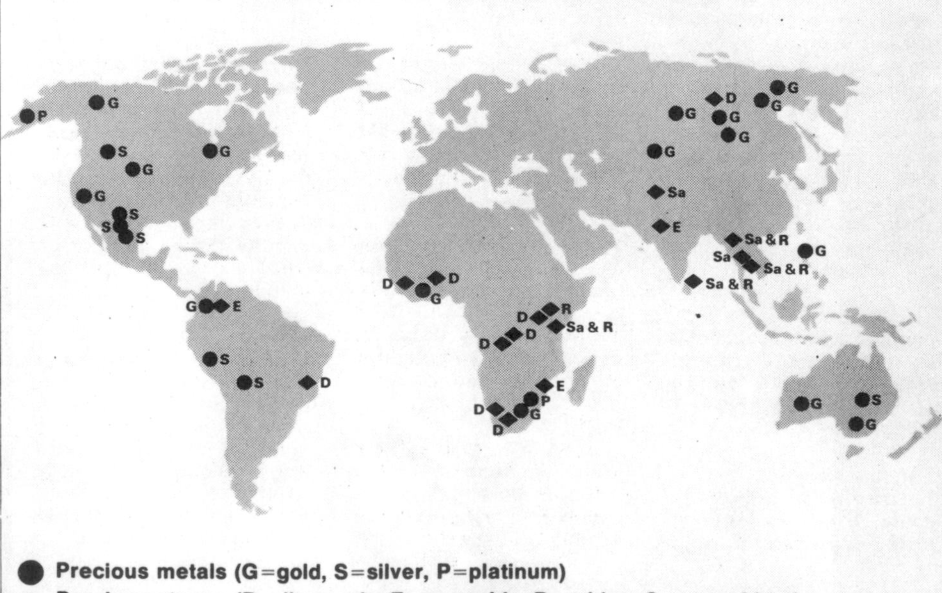

# Who was the Rebel in Paint?

**1.** Francisco José de Goya y Lucientes (known as Goya) was born at Fuendetodos, near Saragossa, Spain in 1746. His father was a master gilder and, early in life, Francisco seems to have been apprenticed to a local artist named José Luzan y Martinez. But to someone of Francisco's nature, helping to paint another man's pictures could not have been very rewarding. Already, there was restlessness within him.

**2.** Probably a lot of the stories concerning his wildness and involvement in brawls and street fights have been exaggerated. But he does seem to have been mixed up in a very serious fight, during which a number of people were killed. As a result of this, he was forced to flee to Madrid where, for a while, he lived fairly peacefully. Then, in more trouble, he was wounded in the back and had to go into hiding until he recovered.

**3.** Later, he decided to go to Rome but did not stay there very long. Instead, rightly judging it safe, he returned to Saragossa where he was given work, painting frescoes in various churches and monasteries. He also painted portraits of local nobility, sometimes finishing in one sitting, although complaining bitterly if any model dropped to sleep from exhaustion. In 1773, he married the sister of the court painter, Francisco Bayeu.

**4.** In 1775, he settled in Madrid, where he joined the team of artists who designed for the royal tapestry-factory, producing a series of cartoons (full-size preparatory sketches) for this purpose. In 1785, he was made court painter to Charles III of Spain and, when Charles IV succeeded to the throne in 1788, was immediately made court painter to him. Apparently, the new king and his queen were both highly impressed by Goya's talents.

**5.** Their patronage led to great prosperity for Goya. He became extremely popular as a portrait painter. A long procession of the powerful, the rich and the beautiful flocked to his studio to be immortalised by the brush of the hot-tempered young genius. Such a painting is the portrait of Dona Isabel Cobos de Porcel — now in the National Gallery, London, which reputedly, he completed in one sitting.

**6.** His style of portrait painting developed considerably over the years. The figures presented became often brutally realistic. That he did not offend his 'customers' says much for the respect in which he was held. But, in 1792, he became seriously ill, probably with the disease known as *labyrinthitis*, inflammation of the bony passages of the internal ear. It left him stone deaf — he lived for the rest of his life in a world of complete silence.

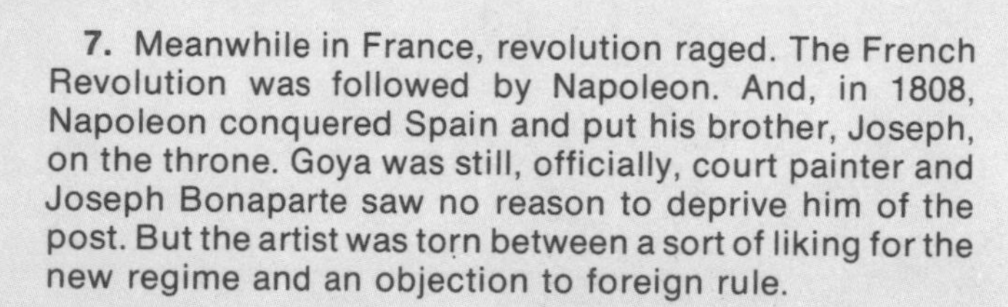

**7.** Meanwhile in France, revolution raged. The French Revolution was followed by Napoleon. And, in 1808, Napoleon conquered Spain and put his brother, Joseph, on the throne. Goya was still, officially, court painter and Joseph Bonaparte saw no reason to deprive him of the post. But the artist was torn between a sort of liking for the new regime and an objection to foreign rule.

**8.** Eventually, he decided to continue, believing that an artist was an artist not a politician. His work during this period of rebellion was truly remarkable. He worked on a series of etchings (not published until 1863), called *Los desastres de la guerra* (The disasters of war). They show with a savage brilliance the horror and futility of war, seen by a man personally involved.

**9.** During this terrible period from the point of view of Spain, however, Goya continued to paint portraits. He painted both Spanish and French generals. And he also, in 1812, met Arthur Wellesley (later the Duke of Wellington). The strong face fascinated Goya. He decided to paint a portrait of this man who was to liberate his country. The picture is now in the National Gallery, London, and was once stolen but returned.

**10.** When the Spanish Royal family was restored in 1814, the son of the former king, Charles IV, became King Ferdinand VII. Perhaps rather surprisingly, since Goya had worked for the French during their occupation, Ferdinand retained him as the court painter. He is reputed to have said, "You are a traitor and deserve to be exiled or even hanged. But you are a great artist, one of the greatest Spain has ever known . . . so you are forgiven."

**11.** Francisco, however, was never really happy working for Ferdinand. His wife had died. He was lonely, deaf and still distressed by memories of the war years. He had, however, bought a country house near Madrid where, between 1820 and 1822, he produced the murals often called the Black Paintings. They were composed mainly in browns, blacks and greys and show Goya's morbid state of mind.

**12.** In 1824, the artist asked Ferdinand for permission to go to France for health reasons and settled in a little villa at Bordeaux. Except for a few brief visits, he never again returned to Spain. But his last years seem to have been happy. He continued painting and adopted a style which in some ways was to be taken up by the Impressionists. He died in 1828, aged 82.

# Who was Grinling Gibbons?

**Wood-carving is one of the oldest crafts known to man. For hundreds of years, splendid works of art have been fashioned and those skills still survive today.**

**OF all the crafts that man has learned not one of them is more ancient than the art of carving, a craft that goes back to the childhood of the world, some 30,000 odd years ago.**

**In the same way that a boy with a jack-knife and a stick of wood will automatically start whittling away, so did our primitive ancestors teach themselves to carve.**

Unhappily, in the case of wood, which can rot, warp, split or crack or be attacked by insects and worms and ants, the wood-carvings of our primitive forebears have long since vanished. It is only when special conditions have prevailed that wood has survived more than a few centuries, such as the wooden carvings taken from the tombs of the Egyptian Pharaoh kings. These survived only because they had been placed in sealed tombs.

These Egyptian wood-carvings provide sufficient evidence in themselves that by then man had already mastered the fundamentals of wood-carving. But although these carvings often show a remarkable understanding of how to achieve quite startling results with fairly primitive tools, it is not until we reach the medieval period that we see the wood-carver as a master craftsman, in complete control of his tools and materials.

By then he had become a highly respected member of the community with his own guild, whose members were constantly being called upon to exercise their craft in the cathedrals and churches of Europe. To this day, many of the marvels they wrought can be seen in the form of pews and screens, altars and ceremonial chairs for visiting bishops — all carved with endless loving labour.

Nor was the wood-carver's work confined to ecclesiastical buildings. As time passed, he was employed by the wealthy to work in their houses, where he made ceiling beams, staircase carvings and wood panelling and ornate mantelpieces. Flower and leaf patterns were often used as decorations, particularly in Tudor times, when the English Wild Rose was widely used.

By the time we reach the 17th century, wood-carving had become an art form as well as being a craft, with Grinling Gibbons, an Englishman, who lived from 1648 to 1721, dominating and influencing the whole European scene.

A personal friend of Sir Christopher Wren, who commis-

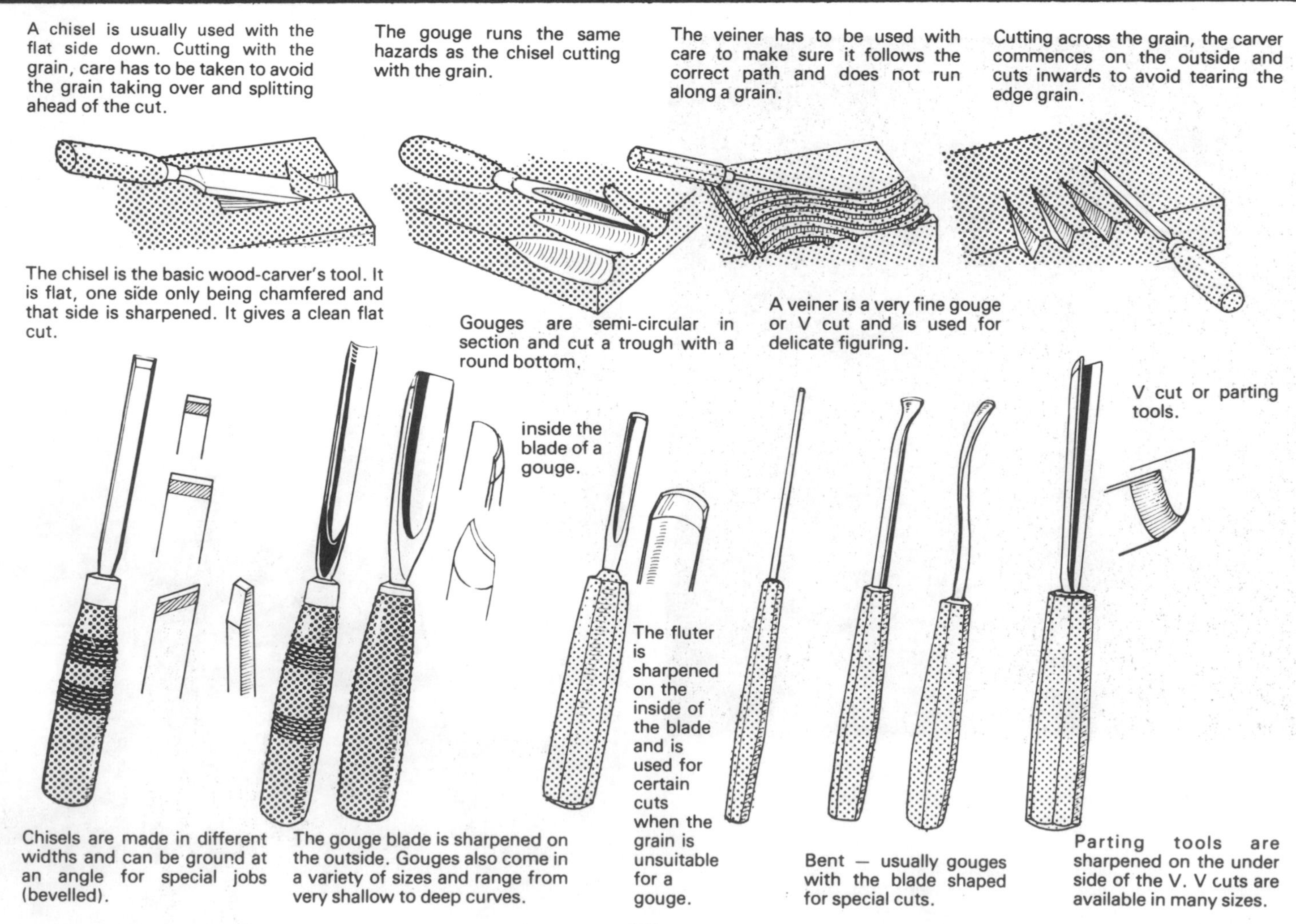

A chisel is usually used with the flat side down. Cutting with the grain, care has to be taken to avoid the grain taking over and splitting ahead of the cut.

The gouge runs the same hazards as the chisel cutting with the grain.

The veiner has to be used with care to make sure it follows the correct path and does not run along a grain.

Cutting across the grain, the carver commences on the outside and cuts inwards to avoid tearing the edge grain.

The chisel is the basic wood-carver's tool. It is flat, one side only being chamfered and that side is sharpened. It gives a clean flat cut.

Gouges are semi-circular in section and cut a trough with a round bottom.

A veiner is a very fine gouge or V cut and is used for delicate figuring.

inside the blade of a gouge.

V cut or parting tools.

The fluter is sharpened on the inside of the blade and is used for certain cuts when the grain is unsuitable for a gouge.

Chisels are made in different widths and can be ground at an angle for special jobs (bevelled).

The gouge blade is sharpened on the outside. Gouges also come in a variety of sizes and range from very shallow to deep curves.

Bent — usually gouges with the blade shaped for special cuts.

Parting tools are sharpened on the under side of the V. V cuts are available in many sizes.

Right: A fine example of the carving skills of Grinling Gibbons. His work is marked by minute detail.

sioned him to carve the choir loft of St. Paul's Cathedral, Gibbons liked to carve bunches of fruit and flowers and occasionally the figures and heads of cherubs.

Although his work is rich and heavy, it is often also marked by particular minuteness of detail, so delicate that he is said to have had in his window a carved pot of flowers that was so finely wrought that the flowers shook with the passing of coaches.

Eventually appointed Master Sculptor and Master Carver to the Crown, he is considered one of the greatest craftsmen in European history. His work can be seen in the Trinity Colleges of York and Cambridge, at Hampton Court Palace and at Windsor Castle.

With the coming of the Industrial Age in the 19th century, the individual craftsman was practically swept out of existence by factories producing cheap furniture on a massive scale. Fortunately, after nearly a century of

Continued on next page

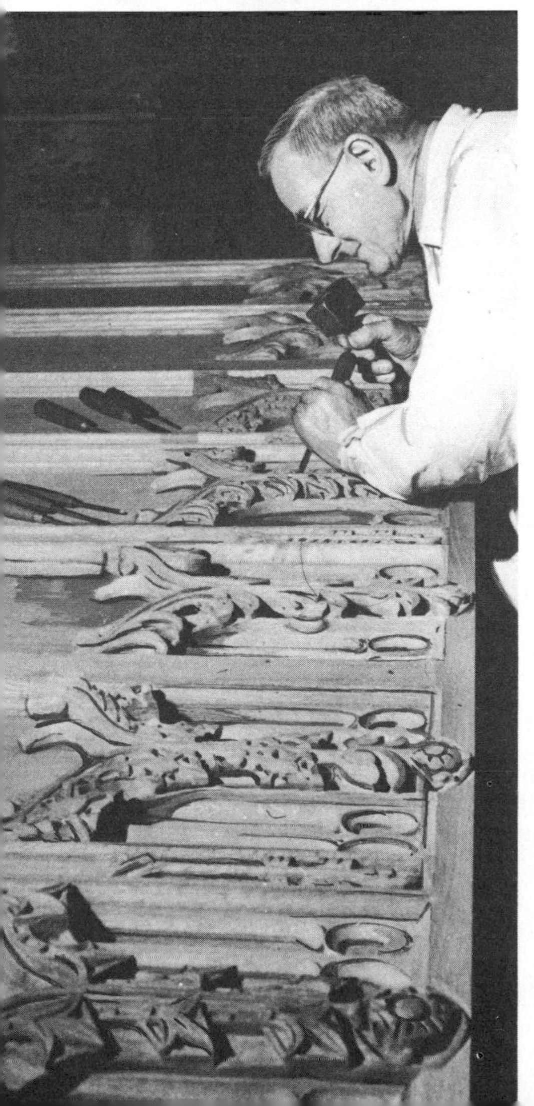

Silence - craftsmen at work! All three pictures show the concentration that is needed to carry out this skilful craft. Top left: Ornamentation for a ceiling is fashioned out of oak. Left: Carving for a screen that will stand in a church. Right: A figure that will appear on the side of a church altar.

having to live with factory furniture, people are now taking a renewed interest in the time-honoured skills and crafts, with the result that the wood-carver is now once more greatly in demand.

His materials and the tools of his trade are still very much the same as they have always been. The wood he uses for carving is often soft wood, such as pine, fir and cedar wood because they are easier to work. On the other hand some of the hard woods such as beech, oak and walnut and mahogany often attract the sculptor with their varied graining, though more difficult to carve on account of the closeness of the grain.

The carver's principal tools are chisels, a gouge and a mallet. A good carver needs very little else beyond some rasps, an oilstone and a tin of machine oil.

The art of the wood-carver lies partially in his appreciation of the particular qualities of his materials and in his ability to allow the material to determine the form. Above all, he must bring to his work an imaginative mind and an appreciation of the potential visual qualities of his materials — something that has always been evident in the work of the master craftsmen of the mid 17th century right up to the age of mass production, when the insensitive use of machine methods so nearly put the wood-carver out of business.

Although the modern craftsman in wood may occasionally use machinery not available to his forbears, he is able to do so without any loss to the individuality of his work because he uses the machinery in an imaginative way. As in all art, it is the personal vision that separates the artist from the journeyman.

**The exquisitely carved 'Angel Of The Annunciation'. Fashioned in oak, it is an example of French work from the 15th century.**

## Maori Legends Carved in Wood

One of the most impressive modern wood-carvings is in New Zealand House, London. It is a Pouihi - a sort of Maori totem pole. This one (15½ metres tall) is the work of the Maori wood-carver, Inia te Wiata, and was carved from one native New Zealand tree - a Totara - brought over to England in three pieces and later divided into six logs. The total weight of the carving is about 11 tonnes and the height in relation to that of an average man is shown in the picture far right. Its representation of New Zealand legends and traditions and its portrayal of her gods and ancient heroes make it unique. But there is tragedy in its story, too. The sculptor, pictured below, was a professional musician and a film and television actor, so the work on the totem pole had to be done in his spare time. Although he began in 1964, when he died in 1971 the sculpture was still unfinished. Luckily, this was done by te Wiata's two sons under the direction of his old teacher, Piri Poutapu. The conception-grand and inspiring as it was — was at last realised and was unveiled by the Queen Mother in June, 1972.

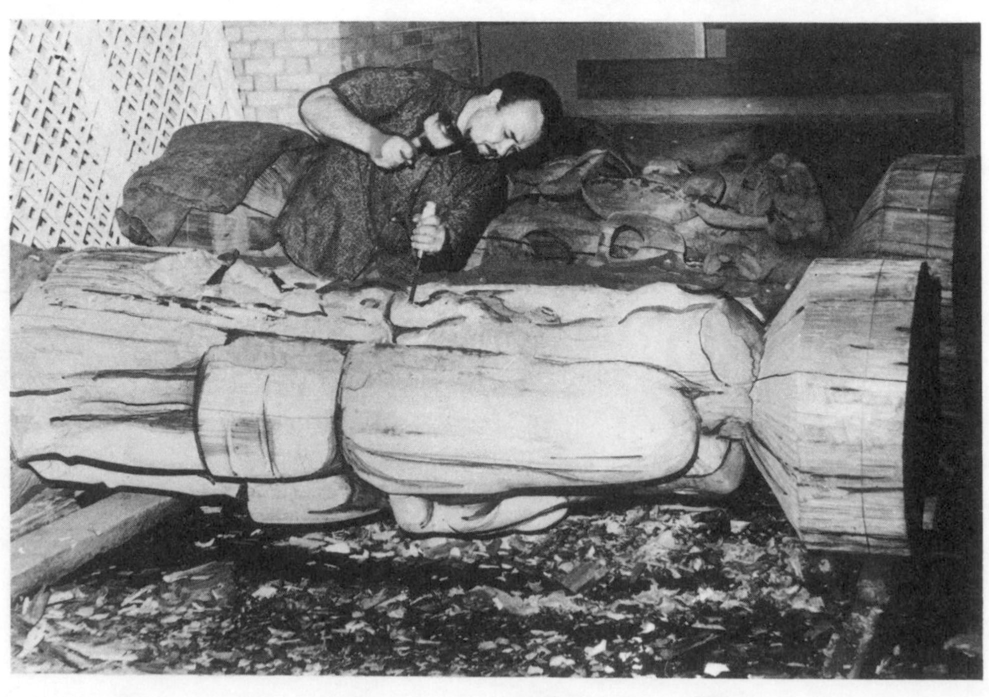

# Who was the Greek from Crete?

1. Dominico Theotocopuli, better known to the world as El Greco (The Greek), was born in Crete in about 1541, the son of a noble family. His first training in art was at a school of religious painting in a monastery. At about the age of 17, he went to Venice, where he copied and learned much from the Venetian painters and became a pupil of Titian, by whom he was influenced a great deal.

2. Though he remained all his life essentially a painter of religious subjects, El Greco's portraits were also outstanding. While he was staying in Rome, a self-portrait of his caused much jealousy among the Roman artists, whom he further annoyed by saying that if Michelangelo's painted ceiling in the Sistine Chapel were pulled down, he – El Greco – would paint a better one in its place.

3. At that time, many of Titian's paintings were being purchased by Philip II, King of Spain, which must have led El Greco's thoughts to the tempting prospect of working in that country. At the age of 35, he went to Spain. On the way, he stopped at Malta and painted a portrait of Vincentio Anastagi, one of the Knights of Malta. This, he thought, was the finest portrait he had done up to that time.

4. On reaching Spain, El Greco went to Toledo, which had been the capital, until Philip II moved his court to nearby Madrid. Toledo in those days was a grave, aristocratic and deeply religious town, which suited El Greco's serious and studious temperament. He loved Toledo dearly and it was to become the lifelong home of the Greek genius from the isle of Crete. Indeed, he was never to leave it again.

5. El Greco's first commission when he arrived in Spain was to design and paint an altar for a church. Before he had finished the task, the news of this brilliant foreign artist had reached the ears of the bishops and nobility of the district. He was asked to paint a picture for Toledo Cathedral. This won him the admiration of the city and a support that he was never to lose. But El Greco had higher ambitions . . .

6. He decided to send Philip II two small drawings of religious subjects, as examples of his work. The king was delighted with them and asked El Greco to paint a large picture based on one of the drawings. He was then so pleased with the result that he ordered El Greco to paint an even larger picture, to hang in the Royal palace. The subject was *The Martyrdom of St. Maurice* and El Greco determined to put every effort into this picture.

7. The painting of *St. Maurice* took him several years. He even made wax figures of all the figures in it. To El Greco, the finished picture was all fire and movement and he was convinced it was the best thing he had ever done. Alas, Philip II had quite different ideas about how the subject should have been treated. He did not like the picture and said so — and he never asked El Greco to paint again.

8. Bitterly disappointed, El Greco returned to painting portraits and religious pictures for people who did appreciate his genius. In the years that followed, masterpieces flowed from his brush. A famous one, indicated above is *The Agony in the Garden,* now in the National Gallery, London. El Greco died at Toledo in 1614. The Greek from Crete is still proudly accepted by Spaniards as one of their greatest artists.

# Who were the First Potters?

**No one knows for sure who made the first piece of pottery. The Chinese, who were once the supreme potters of the world, have claimed that the emperor Hwang Tsi discovered the art somewhere about 2,700 B.C., and as a reward was eventually taken by the gods to their celestial dwelling place. The ancient Egyptians declared that their god, Ptah, showed his skill as a potter by shaping the first man out of Nile mud, before breathing life into him.**

The Greeks, in their turn, claim that Keramos, the grandson of King Minos of Crete, was the world's first potter. It is from his name, incidentally, that we have the word ceramics.

If we dismiss all these unlikely stories, we have only one real fact to go on, and that is that the earliest pottery known was made in Anatolia, Turkey, well before 6,000 B.C. Relics have been found there in the ruins of prehistoric villages. All the rest is surmise, except that almost certainly primitive man did not begin to make pottery until he had abandoned being a hunter/wanderer and had settled down in one place as a farmer.

The problems facing those early potters must have been daunting — leading, no doubt, to the infuriated destruction of countless failures. Making good pottery is not a simple process. The clay has to be freed from impurities, mixed in the right proportions with sand, charcoal and ground-up shells, and then moistened with water. Then it has to be worked by hand into the required shape and baked, either in the sun or by a fire.

Again, there is no telling exactly when and how man learned to purify his clay, or when the potter's wheel, a simple invention which revolutionized the art of pottery-making, came into being. But perhaps none of this is too important.

What *is* important is to realise that the potter's craft has always been, and always will be, a very personal one.

*Continued on next page*

## Coiling

**One of the ways of making pottery is 'coiling'. Starting with a saucer-like base, the potter rolls out a number of coils of clay and with these gradually builds up the vase. The coils are added on the inside of the vase. The potter then thins them to the required thickness.**

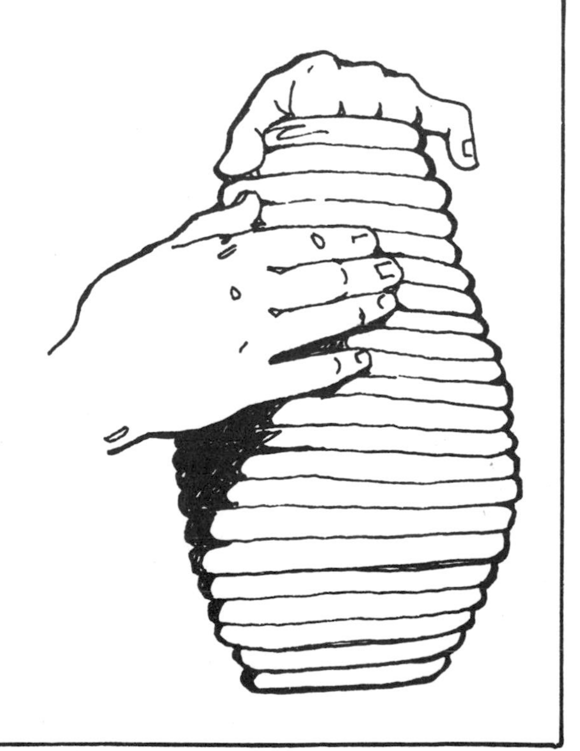

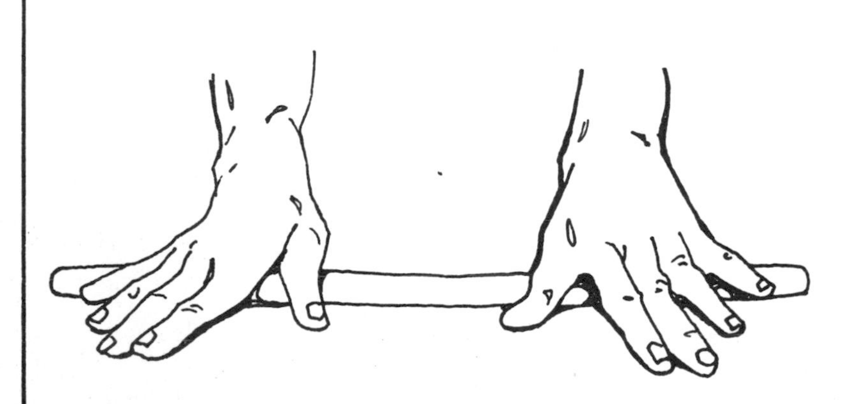

down on the potter's wheel and removing any excess clay with special tools.

However, even though it is dried, the vase or jug is still not ready to contain liquid, for if water is placed inside it the clay will become soft again. The object must therefore be hardened further.

This is done by *firing,* heating in a kiln until the clay is baked permanently hard.

Firing is a very precise operation. Success or failure depends upon a number of factors. The clay must be very dry, and free from air pockets, and the temperature in the kiln must be controlled to rise slowly in order that the clay may dry out completely and expand. Once the necessary temperature has been reached, it must then be allowed to drop slowly. On top of all this, if the kiln door is opened too soon, the rush of cold air will cool the pottery too quickly and it will shrink and crack.

When a piece of pottery comes out of the kiln, it has a rough, dull surface, known as 'biscuit'. Now it has to be glazed, that is given a shiny film or coating.

**Left: The design of the simple 'kick' wheel has hardly changed for thousands of years.**

**Below: This pitcher was made by 'coiling' — a method even older than the potter's wheel.**

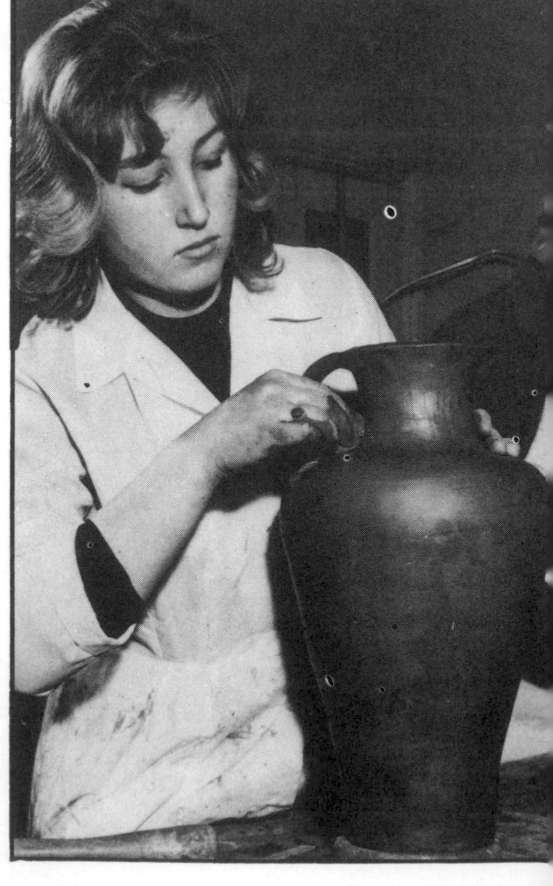

The relationship between any craftsman and his materials is inevitably an intimate one, but never is it more intimate than between the potter and his clay — a material with physical properties that cause it to change constantly.

## Clay

The way clay behaves is unique. It therefore requires a great deal of understanding if the relationship between the potter and the clay is to be successful.

Clay is a special kind of earth which has been made by the decomposition of rock and then carried by water from its source of origin to some other area, often a river bed. However, clay is seldom used in its natural state, and various ingredients such as finely ground flint or stone and other minerals are added to make it stronger and prevent it cracking.

The shaping of pottery can be done in three ways: by modelling the clay by hand, by shaping it in a mould, or by using a potter's wheel. The potter's wheel is simply a small horizontal revolving table. It has scarcely altered during the last 4,000 years beyond the means of supplying power for it.

To make a pot, the potter literally throws his clay on to the centre of the spinning wheel. As he presses the clay with his hands, it rises in a spiral column, between his fingers. It is then pushed down again and again allowed to rise, while all the time the lump of clay is moved towards the centre of the wheel so that the final pot will be properly round.

Then, when the clay is on the centre of the wheel, the potter presses his thumbs into it so that it rapidly forms a cylinder. Next, with one hand inside and the other outside, he adjusts the thickness evenly as he draws up and out the revolving mass, which soon becomes under his hands, a bowl, jug or vase.

The finished object is then allowed to dry naturally. If any further shaping is required it is done at this stage, by placing the object upside

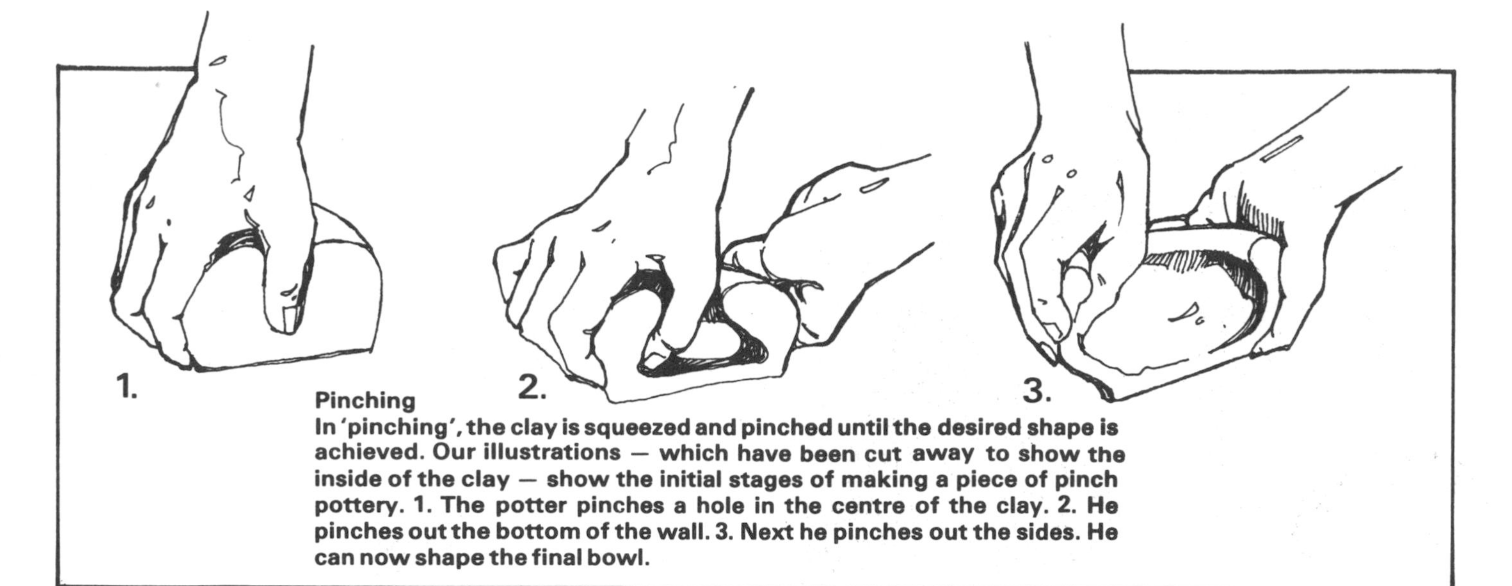


**Pinching**
**In 'pinching', the clay is squeezed and pinched until the desired shape is achieved. Our illustrations — which have been cut away to show the inside of the clay — show the initial stages of making a piece of pinch pottery. 1. The potter pinches a hole in the centre of the clay. 2. He pinches out the bottom of the wall. 3. Next he pinches out the sides. He can now shape the final bowl.**

Each variety of clay requires a glaze especially adapted to suit its particular properties. The recipes of chemicals and minerals which go to make the various colour glazes are too complicated to go into here, and anyway manufacturers supply glazes which have been prepared specifically for the various types of clay. The problem facing the potter, therefore, is not preparing the glazes but their application.

For a glaze to be technically right, the mixture must 'fit' the pot. That is to say, its shrinkage and expansion rates must be very near to those of the pot itself. Although manufacturers know this when they make the glazes, problems arise when the potter is using several glazes on one piece of pottery. Often they are incompatible, and this leads to them running into each other or to bubbling and cracking.

**Below: Placing a pot into a kiln to 'fire' it.**

## Colour problems

Moreover, the glazes, which are usually applied with a brush, have to be put on quickly, as the slower they are applied the thicker the glaze becomes. In addition the potter has to remember thay many colours fade when the pottery is put back into the kiln again to seal or *fix* the glaze on to the clay.

Sometimes the potter will wish to add some form of decoration to his pottery. To do this, he will often apply *slip* — a thin mixture of clay and water — which is applied before the object is put into the kiln. But here again, the potter has to be careful. If the pot becomes too wet it will collapse.

## Hand painting

However, the decoration can also be applied to the object after it has been glazed. This is done by painting either by hand or by using a transfer. The decorated object is then fired again to fix the decoration to the surface.

All in all, the potter must have patience, skill and a steady pair of hands. Not that this seems to act as a deterrent to those wishing to take up pottery themselves. Of all the educational and recreational classes offered at Adult Education centres, pottery-making is one of the most popular — a fact that seems to indicate that, unlike many of the skilled crafts carried out by an ever-decreasing number of craftsmen, pottery-making is likely to endure.

# Who
# Waltz King

**1.** The Vienna of the 19th century was a place where people liked to eat, sing and, above all, dance. It was therefore the ideal place for the talents of the Strauss family to thrive. The story of this family of musicians, whose waltzes occupy an unrivalled place in the annals of Light Music, begins with Johann Strauss, the Elder, who was born in 1804, when people were dancing to a two-step waltz known as the *Landler*.

**2.** Johann's father was drowned when he was young, and from then on the boy was brought up by a stepfather, who had no interest in Johann's love of music. But he did buy the youngster a violin. When Johann announced, at the age of twelve, that he wanted to be a professional musician, his stepfather was so outraged that he promptly took the boy to be apprenticed to a bookbinder.

**3.** Johann loathed his work at the bookbinder's shop, where he spent five unhappy years before he finally fled into the night, taking his beloved violin with him. Reaching the mountains overlooking the Danube, he lay down and fell into an exhausted sleep. As luck would have it, a man named Polischansky found him there, still fast asleep.

**4.** Recognising him, Polischansky gently awakened the boy and took him home, where he managed to persuade Johann's stepfather to allow the boy to take music lessons. In due course, Johann joined a band, and seemed all set to lead the life of a professional but unknown musician. Then one day he happened to take a walk in a park in Vienna, known as the Prater, where his attention was caught by three men playing the violin.

# was the of Vienna?

6. Strauss and Lanner parted, and went their own ways. Later, they were to become good friends again, but before then, much had happened to Johann. He had married and had become a composer, as well as being a conductor. Waltzes and marches flowed from his pen, including the famous Radetzky March. Now known as the Waltz King of Vienna, he still had time to put aside his composing to conduct seven days a week.

5. The leader of the trio was Joseph Lanner, who was the first of the waltz composers. Joseph had met him before, and stopped to talk. As a result of that conversation it was agreed that Johann should join them to make up a quartet. In time the quartet became a large orchestra, under the dual management of Lanner and Joseph. Unfortunately, the two men quarrelled, and finally came to blows on the concert platform.

7. Strauss took his music to most of the capitals of Europe, and they succumbed to those lilting melodies in much the same way as Vienna had done. He arrived in England in 1838, in time for the coronation of Queen Victoria. So popular was his music that he gave 72 public concerts and played at numerous balls.

He overworked himself to such an extent in England that he collapsed with a heart attack. He survived, however, and lived on until 1848, when he died of scarlet fever. He left behind him 250 compositions and three sons, Johann, Joseph and Eduard. One of them was to become the new King of the Waltz.

# Whose Paintings are

1. One of the most famous of Michelangelo's sculptures is, undoubtedly, his statue of *David,* now in the Accademia, Florence. It is an enormous and imposing creation (505 cm high), full of suppressed tension and fire. Placed in front of the Palazzo Vecchio, when unveiled in 1504, its effect was remarkable. Apparently, it aroused such fear, it was actually stoned. Even today, many people do not regard it as beautiful but there is none who denies its power and artistry.

2. Shortly after the *David,* Michelangelo was called upon to produce a painting for a Florentine noble. This is a tondo (round in shape) picture of the Holy Family, known as the *Doni Tondo,* now in the Uffizi Gallery, Florence. The figure of the Virgin here is strangely twisted as she holds the infant Christ on her shoulder. The figures in the background, nude and very much of this world, contrast sharply with the divinity of the central group — painted around 1506.

3. Leonardo da Vinci was a contemporary of Michelangelo but 23 years his senior. By repute, meeting one day in the street, Michelangelo insulted his 'rival' and later a competition was arranged between the two men. Whether this is true or not is unknown but certainly Leonardo produced a battle scene, the *Battle of Anghiari,* at about the time Michelangelo produced the *Battle of Cascina.* But both were cartoons (preliminary drawings) and neither original has been preserved.

4. Earlier, Michelangelo had been asked by the Pope, Julius II, to design and create a tomb for him. Then there were disagreements and various changes in plan. Originally, it was to have had more than 40 statues of which three were completed but only one used. Two were the *Dying Captive* and the *Heroic Captive*, both in the Louvre. The other was the *Moses*. This, sculpted some time between 1513 and 1516, is part of the completed sepulchre in San Pietro in Vincoli, Rome.

# in the Sistine Chapel?

5. At the outset, Michelangelo appears to have been enthusiastic about the monument. He was sent to Carrara to obtain the marble for which the town was and still is famous, to use both on the mausoleum itself and the statues. It has been thought that he may have viewed the work almost as a monument to himself. Certainly he returned to Rome with an enormous number of blocks of marble which he put in St. Peter's Square. But meanwhile, the Pope had changed his mind.

6. He had decided to have built a new church of St. Peter to replace the decidedly derelict one that then existed. He also decided to have his tomb erected in this church. But he did not tell Michelangelo of these plans. Instead, he commissioned a Lombard architect, Bramante, a relative of the artist, Raphael, to make designs for the church. Raphael was also in favour and Michelangelo felt insulted. As a result, the artist left Rome and also his patron — Pope Julius II.

7. Eventually, the Pope and Michelangelo were reconciled but, before the tomb was even begun, two other works were required of the artist. One was a bronze statue of Julius (now lost) and the other a truly colossal task — the painting of the Sistine Chapel ceiling. The chapel was built for and named after Julius's uncle, Pope Sixtus IV, but it was consecrated in 1483 by Julius himself. Michelangelo, unwilling though he was, put all he had — body, mind and skill — into the frescoes.

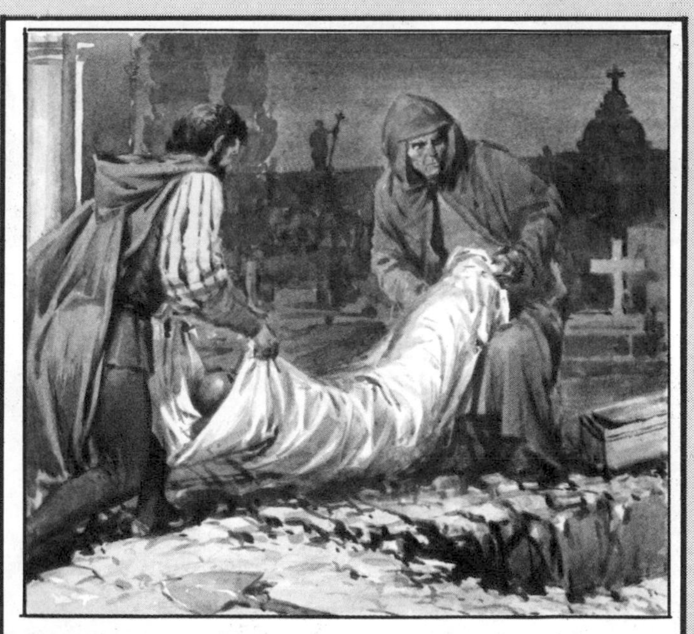

8. It is impossible to do justice to this magnificent work of art by describing it in words. The previous picture is a copy of a small section of it, the *Creation of Adam.* It contains 343 figures — about one for every four days Michelangelo worked — and each figure has a truly superb artistic, spiritual and physical magnificence. It is said that Michelangelo even stole bodies from cemeteries to help him more accurately to portray the human body. But this may be untrue.

# Who was the First of the

He met Zola while a student and often read his highly imaginative poems to his friend.

Paul's father was most unwilling to let him study art but — at last — had to agree.

He often visited the Louvre where he copied works from such old masters as Rubens.

**THE artist, Paul Cézanne, was a founder member of what came to be known as the 'Modern Artists'. He was born at Aix-en-Provence, southern France, in 1839, the son of a hatter who became a wealthy banker.**

His father wanted him to become a businessman, too, but Paul had no interest in any business, including banking. He was interested only in art.

He received a good education and, at college in Paris, became very friendly with another student there, Emile Zola, who was later to become one of the most famous French writers of his day. In fact, Cézanne himself tried writing poetry for a while and some of his poems were greatly admired.

Eventually, however, he decided to devote his life to painting. He received much opposition from his father for this but he did not allow that to stand in his way.

His father accompanied him to Paris where he studied but, on the whole, Paul followed his own inclinations, meeting many Impressionist artists, in particular Manet, and also copying the works of old masters, like Rubens or Titian, in the Louvre.

Like many great artists before him and many after him, he believed he could learn a lot from studying the works of artists he particularly admired.

## Talent

He believed, too, of course, that he had a particular talent and that he must find the best way he could of expressing the feeling and love that lay deep within him.

He knew that this would not be achieved overnight and that he needed time and practice to perfect his technique.

Having decided on his way of life, he never wished to give it up or to change it in any way. He was happiest when he was at work, doing what he felt was right — for him. He could be (and often was) influenced by other people but he would not be governed by them.

For a while, however, the elder Cézanne had his way and Paul returned to Provence to work in the family bank at Aix. Since he was not interested in the work there at all, however, his father at last agreed to let him go back to Paris.

At first, Cézanne's paintings were very much in the style of the Impressionists and he exhibited works at their exhibitions in both 1874 and 1877. The art critics, though, damned him completely. And, being a highly sensitive man, easily hurt and easily disheartened, he gave up and went back to Aix — this time of his own accord!

## Impressed

Reputedly, a young man saw two of Cézanne's paintings in an exhibition at Aix and was immediately so impressed by them that he sought out the artist and enthusiastically expressed his opinion.

Cézanne thought that he was making fun of him and at first was extremely angry, but then the young man's obvious sincerity came over to him and his anger turned to tears.

During his lifetime, Cézanne never made a name for himself and received scant appreciation. He gave some pictures away — giving two to the young man who had so admired him. Many others, he just left lying around.

He always took enormous pains over his work, how-

# 'Moderns'?

For a while Paul worked in his father's bank at Aix. But customers were often neglected.

ever. He was perpetually altering and, in his opinion, improving his pictures. He is said to have repainted parts of some of his works as often as fifty times.

There is, nonetheless, an enormous clarity and freshness about his paintings and a detail which is quite remarkable.

He is famous for his still-lifes and landscapes. Much of the vivid colour of his native Provence is seen in his pictures and his intense love for the warmth and beauty of the countryside is apparent.

Luckily for him and for us, he never needed to work to keep himself alive. He had money left to him by his father. For, in spite of their many and deep disagreements, Cézanne's father left all his money to his son when he died.

Paul Cézanne's life was, in many ways, an uneventful one. Unlike some of his Impressionist friends he did not visit foreign countries. The only exception being a visit to Switzerland for his health.

Most of his time was spent in the place where he had been born, Provence, and he painted there ceaselessly.

Early on he met and was influenced by Impressionist painters, particularly Manet.

## Favourite

He had a gardener, Vallier, who was one of his favourite models. It was on a portrait of Vallier that the artist made his last brush strokes the morning he collapsed. He died a few days later — aged 67. That was in 1906.

Today, although considered by some people to be a Post-Impressionist and by others to be a Cubist, he is usually held to be one of the first of the 'Moderns'.

His works fetch thousands of pounds and most great national collections contain some of his paintings.

It is interesting to remember a story concerning his health visit to Neuchâtel in Switzerland. He is supposed to have left behind there two unfinished canvases. The story says that these canvases were found and painted over at a later date by another artist.

If they could be found now and the other artist's work removed, what price would those Cézanne paintings now fetch? The answer is, quite simply — a price beyond belief!

At the 1877 Impressionist Exhibition, Cézanne showed 16 paintings. But all were scorned.

It is ironic that works of art considered valueless while the artist was alive should be considered priceless after his death.

It is not, however, a situation that is all that unusual. And one day, you yourself may be lucky. There are Cézanne works somewhere about, not recognised as such, maybe painted over by some other artist (as has already been mentioned) just waiting to be found. Someone will find them.

If Cézanne could continue working, hopefully in spite of severe criticism, others can continue looking, and, if that does not appeal to you — there are always the great art collections you can see for yourself the greatness that was — and is — Cézanne!

Some places where Cézanne paintings can be seen today. Stedelijk Museum, Amsterdam; Folkwang Museum, Essen; Gemeente Museum, The Hague; National Gallery, Tate and Courtauld Institute, London; Metropolitan Museum, Brooklyn Museum and Guggenheim Museum, New York; Louvre, Paris.

A young man once tried to tell him how much he admired his work. Angry at first, Paul at last was moved to tears.

# Who gave us 'The

1. A fierce Sun blazed down on the thousands of devout pilgrims flocking into the Muslim holy city of Mecca. Rich and poor united in their desire to honour their religion in its holiest place. But one man, known as Mirza Abdullah el Bushiri, would have been torn to pieces if his true identity had been revealed. For months he had been risking his life. One false move, a single mis-pronunciation, the omission of a tiny religious detail in the life of a devout Muslim — any of these would have meant instant death. For this man was really Richard Francis Burton, the English explorer and the first white man to enter Mecca.

2. To overcome such hazards called for great courage, and Burton was nothing if not courageous. Born at Torquay in the English county of Devon in March 1821, he was an aggressive boy who loved a fight. He also showed no desire to study anything at school except languages, for which he seemed to have a particular flair.

3. Burton spent much of his childhood in France and Italy, but at 19 was sent to the University of Oxford. However, it soon became obvious that lectures bored him. Burton's mind was on adventure.

Shortly after he left Oxford he obtained a commission and sailed for India. But Burton soon tired of army routine and became obsessed with the idea of making an expedition to Mecca. In 1855, with twelve months leave of absence from his regiment and disguised as a Persian, he left for Alexandria. There he latched on to a band of pilgrims bound for Mecca. With them he spent twelve days in an overcrowded boat, under a scorching Sun, before landing and making the dangerous overland journey to Mecca. He had overcome many perils to reach the holy city and when he returned it was to find himself a hero. He now turned his eyes towards Somalia in East Africa, and particularly the town of Harrar where no white man had ever set foot.

# Arabian Knights'?

4. With Captain John Speke (also to become a famous explorer) and two other officers, he set off to pass through 200km of unknown country. The party vanished into the desert and was not heard of for four months. But when it re-emerged they had not only reached Harrar but Burton had spoken with the king and they had stayed for ten days before returning.

5. Not content with this, Burton set off once more across the desert with Speke and the other officers. However, this time they were attacked by Somali tribesmen and one of the officers was killed. Burton and Speke were both wounded but managed to escape. Burton then had to return to England to recover from his wounds.

6. By 1856 Burton had fully recovered and set off on another exploration. Accompanied once more by Speke, he landed on the coast of East Africa and made his way into the jungle in search of the legendary source of the River Nile. After nearly two years of incredible hardship he had still not found it, but he was the first European to set eyes on the great inland sea of Lake Tanganyika. By then both men were seriously ill but while Burton could not go on, Speke continued alone and discovered Lake Victoria which he was convinced was the source of the Nile.

7. However Burton bitterly disputed Speke's claim and the quarrel ended their friendship (*see following page*). It was the end of Burton's major explorations although he still led a busy life. He served in the foreign service as a consul in several countries and found time to write 43 volumes on his journeys and 30 volumes of translations, including the famous *Arabian Nights*. Richard Burton was knighted in 1886 and died in 1890.

# Which Writer sought Adventure?

Ernest Hemingway was one of the most successful writers of the 20th century. His deliberately simple, direct style, influenced many writers of his day. He was born on 21st July, 1899 in a suburb of Chicago, Illinois, the son of a doctor whose great interests were hunting and fishing. As a boy, the young Ernest spent many happy times with his father, learning about and sharing these interests. In most things though, parents and son did not agree.

Ernest disliked and despised them for their prudery and for their conventional way of life. Early on he decided to be as unlike them as possible. After leaving school, he had a job as a sparring partner to a number of not very skilful boxers. Then he decided to try journalism. He went to Kansas City and became a reporter on the *Star*. During the First World War, he was not accepted for military service because of defective eyesight, so volunteered to become an ambulance driver. He was severely wounded but recovered and was decorated for heroism.

He returned to Chicago for a while. Then he married Hadley Richardson and, with her, went to France, working as a foreign correspondent for the *Toronto Star*. Other American writers who met and influenced him there were Scott Fitzgerald, Ezra Pound and — in particular — Gertrude Stein.

On one occasion, he went to the annual fiesta at Pamplona where he watched the young men chasing the bulls for the bullfight through the town streets. This deeply affected him and led to his lifelong love of Spain and interest in bullfighting.

Meanwhile he had begun serious writing. His first important book was a collection of short stories, *In Our Time*, 1925. His first great success was *The Sun Also Rises*, 1926. *A Farewell to Arms* (1929) and *Death in the Afternoon* (1932) followed.

This was a book about bullfighting, in which he saw tragedy, excitement, spectacle and mystery and tried to explain its fascination in words. That he succeeded is proved by its enormous popularity both then and now.

His devotion to Spain survived but his marriage to his first wife, by whom he had one son, did not; neither did that to his second wife, by whom he had two sons.

During the Spanish Civil War, which began in 1936, he visited Spain four times. Not surprisingly he became deeply involved in the war, raising money for those who supported the government. He also acted as a war correspondent. A play came from his experiences of that time, *The Fifth Column*, and a novel — probably one of his most famous — *For Whom the Bell Tolls*. This was made into a highly successful film.

He had married again, this time to a journalist, and with her covered the Japanese/Chinese war. He was to become involved in war again during the Second World War. He had bought an estate in Cuba and from there carried on a considerable amount of counter-espionage. Later, he took part in missions from London across the Channel and was involved in the D-Day landings. He was in the action at the Hurtgen Forest, where the regiment he was with lost 80 per cent of its men.

## Lucky escapes

After the war, Hemingway went back to Cuba. His third marriage having broken down, he married again; this time to Mary Welsh, who had been a war correspondent. He stayed with her, apparently happily, for the rest of his life. They travelled a great deal, and twice while flying in Africa their aeroplane crashed. They were lucky to escape with their lives. Hemingway had started writing again, and in 1953 he was awarded the Pulitzer Prize for his novel, *The Old Man and the Sea*. The following year he was given the Nobel Prize for Literature in 1954.

After the revolution in Cuba in 1960 he soon left that country and he went to live in Idaho. There, although he carried on with his writing, he began to suffer from deep depression. He had electric shock treatment but it was not successful. On 2nd June, 1961, having just left hospital, he shot himself.

Today, Hemingway's popularity has somewhat waned but he was a legend in his own time and to many people he will always be one of the truly great writers of the 20th century.

# Who gave us 'The Laughing Cavalier?

FRANS HALS, it is thought, was born in Antwerp, Belgium in either 1580 or 1581. His parents were both from Haarlem, the Netherlands, but moved to Antwerp a little before Frans was born. They returned to Haarlem, however, around 1600. The artist, as a result, is associated mainly with Haarlem. (A copy of a picture of Haarlem at the time of Hals, painted by the artist, Gerrit Berckheyde is shown in picture 1.)

Nothing at all is known about Hals' life in Antwerp and there are no authenticated pictures dating from that time. He is believed to have trained in the studio of Adam Van Noort where it is known the artist, Rubens, worked for a short time. He is also believed to have been the pupil of the artist, Van Mander.

One of his earliest known paintings is *The Officers of the Civic Guard of St. George,* now in the Hals' Museum at Haarlem.

This is a masterpiece and gives a remarkable presentation of well-fed Dutchmen enjoying a sumptuous banquet. Each of the figures is a detailed portrait — a difficult task for any artist painting a large number of people in a group.

One interesting thing about the painting is that it is dated 1616, when the artist was already 35 years of age. This is the reason some people think his date of birth, established from a statement by one of his pupils, Laurensz Van de Vinne, may be wrong. They believe such a master as Hals must have produced paintings of merit before this age.

He is known, however, to have visited Antwerp around 1616 where he is believed to have met the artist, Rubens (see picture 2, where Rubens is shown on the left). He is also said later to have been visited in Haarlem by the painter, Van Dyck (see picture 3, where Van Dyck is shown on the right). Certainly, he spent the majority of his life in Haarlem and was recognised as a great artist there by other great artists.

In 1610, he married Anneke Hermanszoon and by her had several children. Five years after this marriage, he was at one time believed to have been in trouble with the law for ill-treatment of his wife and also for his drunkenness and resulting violence. His wife, in fact, was said to have died only a few weeks later. Nowadays, however, the story is said to have been due to mistaken identity and unfounded.

Nonetheless, his first wife did die when still fairly young but

Hals married again the next year and had many more children. He lived with his second wife — Lysbeth Reyniers — for almost 50 years.

His large family (see picture 4), unfortunately, brought him serious money problems. And he seems to have suffered from financial difficulties most of his life. Perhaps as a result of this need to make as much money as possible, he altered his style of painting considerably. He devised a technique which needed very little use of actual positive colours. It involved instead a great use of black and white and simple flesh tones (see picture 5).

There are some unfounded stories about his last years, too. Certainly, he was eventually destitute. But there is no reason to believe the story that he lived in the Old Men's Alms House in Haarlem — although he made a painting of it in 1664, only two years before his death.

He was forced to sell all his possessions (see picture 6) and he was sued for debt by both his cobbler and his butcher. For the four years before he died, however, he was awarded a small pension by the municipal authorities.

Surprisingly perhaps, even the number of his paintings that still exist has been questioned. None are signed, so some people claim pictures as his work which other people deny. Totals, as a result, vary from 109 to 250.

Also no preliminary sketches for his pictures have actually been identified, although this may mean that he felt no need to make very many.

Frans Hals died in 1666 and he is buried in the choir of St. Bavon at Haarlem.

Picture 7 shows our artist's impression of two memorable portraits by Hals. They are, left, the *Laughing Cavalier* and, right, *Malle Babbe, The Witch of Haarlem*. The *Laughing Cavalier* is one of the few paintings by Hals in England. It is in the Wallace Collection. It is perhaps the most famous of all his paintings. *Malle Babbe*, the rather frightening portrait of an old woman with an eagle on her shoulder, is not so famous but was much admired by the 19th century French painter, Gustave Courbet. He made a copy of it and he also described it as "the most beautiful painting in the world". No one denies that Courbet was an artist who knew what he was talking about, so perhaps that description is Frans Hals' best epitaph.

**PAINTINGS by Frans Hals are now almost priceless but this has not always been the case.**

*A Music Conversation* was bought by the poet, Lord Byron, for only £28. And in 1786, a portrait, later in the Berlin Museum, sold for only five shillings (25 pence).

Early in this century, however, Hals' true value began to be realised. In 1919, a very small portrait was sold for £25,000. Nowadays such 'low' prices are not even considered.

The *Laughing Cavalier* (shown right), almost certainly is Hals' most well-known painting. Somewhat curiously named, since the figure is not really laughing at all, it depicts a man with a faintly cynical smile on his face.

Most Hals' paintings are in the Frans Hals Museum, Haarlem, in the Netherlands. The building, used as a museum since 1913, was at one time an old people's home, built in 1608. After its purchase by the city and its conversion into a museum, it was largely rebuilt in the original style. Some of the old sections, however, still remain.

Hals' paintings can be seen also in the National Galleries of London and Scotland.

Frans Hals had five sons, all of whom became painters, but only one achieved any lasting success. This was his eldest son Frans, known as the Younger. He died in 1669, only three years after his father.

One brother also made a name for himself as an artist. This was Dirk Hals. He painted pictures of festivals and ballrooms.

Below, **the Frans Hals Museum at Haarlem in the Netherlands.**

# INDEX

Published by The Hamlyn Publishing Group, Bridge House, London Road, Twickenham, Middlesex, England



ISBN 0 600 53193 7
This material was first published in some of The World of Knowledge part-works series, copyright IPC Magazines Ltd.





Printed in Czechoslovakia

52134